438 HAM

WITHDRAWN

KU-225-465

Hammer's
GERMAN
Grammar
and Usage

fifth edition

WITHDRAWN

Hammer's
GERMAN
Grammar
and Usage

fifth edition

Martin Durrell

Routledge
Taylor & Francis Group

LONDON AND NEW YORK

First published 1971

This edition published by Routledge
2 Park Square, Milton Park, Abingdon, Oxon OX14 4RN
711 Third Avenue, New York, NY, 10017, USA

Routledge is an imprint of the Taylor & Francis Group, an informa business

Copyright © 1971 and 1983 the estate of A.E. Hammer
Revisions for the second edition © 1991 Arnold
Revisions for the third edition © 1996 Arnold
Revisions for the fourth edition © 2002 Arnold
Revisions for the fifth edition © 2011 Taylor & Francis

All rights reserved. No part of this book may be reprinted or reproduced or
utilised in any form or by any electronic, mechanical, or other means, now
known or hereafter invented, including photocopying and recording, or in
any information storage or retrieval system, without permission in writing
from the publishers.

The advice and information in this book are believed to be true and
accurate at the date of going to press, but neither the authors nor the publisher
can accept any legal responsibility or liability for any errors or omissions.

British Library Cataloguing in Publication Data
A catalogue record for this book is available from the British Library

ISBN 13: 978 1 444 12016 5 (pbk)

Typeset by Servis Filmsetting Ltd, Stockport, Cheshire

Contents

List of tables

Abbreviations and points for the user

Points

1 Lists of words are in general alphabetical, unless it appeared more helpful to the user to present them in a different order.
2 Where required, the plural of a noun is indicated within brackets after the noun, e.g. *das Lager (-)*, i.e. *die Lager*; *der Hut (¨e)*, i.e. *die Hüte*, etc. *(-en, -en)* or *(-n, -n)* indicate a weak masculine noun, e.g. *der Mensch, des Menschen, die Menschen* (see 1.3.2).
3 If necessary, a stressed syllable in a word is indicated by the mark placed before the stressed syllable, and/or by the use of bold type, e.g. *die **Dok**'toren, unter'schreiben*. Where it is required, a stressed word in context is shown by underlining, e.g. *Wie bist du denn gekommen?*
4 Sentences used for illustration which are ungrammatical in German are indicated by an asterisk, e.g. **Jedoch dann ist er nicht gekommen*.

Abbreviations

In principle, abbreviations have been kept to a minimum. The following have been used where required by considerations of space.

abbrev.	abbreviated	lang.	language
acad.	Academic	lit.	literary
A., acc.	Accusative	masc.	masculine
arch.	archaic	N., nom.	nominative
Austr.	Austrian	neut.	neuter
aux.	auxiliary	N.G.	North German
Bav.	Bavarian	obs.	obsolete
ch.	chapter	occ.	occasionally
cl.	clause	o.s.	oneself
coll.	colloquial	part.	participle
conj.	conjunction	pej.	pejorative
D., dat.	dative	pl.	plural
elev.	elevated	prep.	preposition
esp.	especially	S.G.	South German
etw.	etwas	sb.	somebody
fem.	feminine	sg., sing.	singular
form.	formal	sub. cl.	subordinate clause
G., gen.	genitive	sth.	something
indic.	Indicative	Sw.	Switzerland
inf.	informal	techn.	technical
jd.	jemand	vb.	verb
jdm.	jemandem	vulg.	vulgar
jdn.	jemanden		

Preface to the fifth edition

The fourth edition of *Hammer's German Grammar and Usage* appeared in 2002, and it has become clear from comments and suggestions made by the numerous users, both teachers and learners, who have been kind enough to contact me that a revision would now be timely. However, it was equally clear from these comments that a thoroughgoing revision of the basic structure of the work would not be welcomed. Thus, the relatively traditional layout based on the parts of speech has been retained, since alternative approaches, however theoretically justifiable, would be unfamiliar to many potential users and could detract from the usefulness of the work for everyday reference. Similarly, considerations of the user prevailed again, despite my own reservations, in the decision to retain a separate chapter on expressions of time, although consistency would suggest that the material dealt with there 'really' belongs elsewhere, e.g. in the chapter on adverbs or the chapter on prepositions.

The revision is founded, like all previous revisions, on the basic principle that the work should be a comprehensive descriptive account of modern German for the use of the advanced learner or student of the language whose first language is English – or who can approach German through English, since I am aware that the book has been widely used in other countries. This aim implies that it should cover the whole gamut of variation in usage within modern German, not simply the most prestigious written form which is still, unfortunately, used too exclusively in many teaching manuals, even when they purport to present examples of spoken language. Thus, considerable attention has been paid to giving information on usage in registers other than formal writing or literature, and details given on everyday speech. This also reflects the greater emphasis paid to oral skills, both active and passive, in modern language teaching. The distinction between common spoken usage and the norms of formal writing norms is particularly marked in German, and clear indications are given in this work as to where spoken and written usage diverge, as also in respect of forms which, although they are considered to be grammatically 'correct', are felt to be stilted outside formal writing (and sometimes even there). Similarly, forms which are frequently heard in everyday speech but widely thought of as non-standard or incorrect are included here, as the foreign learner will encounter them every day, but with a clear indication of their status. Important regional variants within standard German are also included and marked accordingly, especially those commonly found in Swiss or Austrian usage, but purely dialectal forms have been ignored.

The major innovations in this edition can be subsumed under a few major headings. The first revision of Mr. Hammer's original work took place some twenty years ago against the background of momentous events in Germany, and many of the new examples were naturally taken from contemporary reports. Although they are not outdated from a linguistic point of view, they now give the work a historical context which is no longer appropriate. Thus, the opportunity has been taken to replace such dated examples by more recent ones. At same time all the information about specific points of grammar and usage has been checked fully against my own database of modern German, the most recent academic research (as reflected – necessarily selectively – in the bibliography) and the extensive corpus of spoken and written German at the Institut für Deutsche Sprache in Mannheim. This invaluable resource has grown exponentially since the preparation of the first revision, and is now available online (at www.ids-mannheim.de). It is naturally complemented now by the material which can be accessed through internet search engines, and these have also been used extensively – although with the appropriate degree of care, since they are not necessarily representative of widespread usage. Nevertheless, these sources can be invaluable in tracing and attesting some of the most recent developments in the language which are unlikely to find their way into conventional print media, notably demonstrating the continued vitality of the language in incorporating recent lexical material – often, although not only, from English. Thus, *der Blog* gives the verb *bloggen*, which is then adapted through the whole range of possible derivations to give *ausbloggen, erbloggen, verbloggen*, and many more. Information about such possibilities is given in Chapter 22.

In common with previous revisions, changes in the numbering and content of individual sections and subsections have been kept to a minimum in order to facilitate cross-reference between editions. Some such changes, however, proved unavoidable. This is naturally the case with Chapter 23, which now contains a section on pronunciation. This is the most important addition in this revision, and was requested by a number of users. Nevertheless, this is not a comprehensive description of German pronunciation, which would require a manual in its own right, but an account of the relationship between sounds and spelling, explaining the main principles of the spelling system and outlining those instances where the spelling does not reflect pronunciation unambiguously. In this chapter, too, details are given on the most recent developments in the controversial reform of German spelling, following the changes in the rules which were implemented in 2006. Naturally, these revisions have been implemented throughout the rest of the book. The other most thoroughgoing revision is in the account of valency in Chapter 18, where it had become apparent that the account of verb complements was overly complex and gave too much prominence to minor complements, such as the genitive object.

Acknowledgements

My debt to others in the preparation of this and previous revisions is immense, and I am immensely grateful, first, to all the native speakers of German, unfortunately too numerous to mention, who have answered questions, given advice and, often unwittingly, provided me with examples and other linguistic data. Many friends, colleagues and acquaintances in Britain, Germany and several other countries – some, sadly, no longer with us – have also assisted me over the years in preparing this and previous editions, and I must express my thanks to all of them, notably to Prof. W. Abraham, Prof. V. Ágel, Prof. J.O. Askedal, Dr. A. Auer, Dr J.S. Barbour, Ms. S. Bayer, Dr C. Beedham, Dr P. Bennett, Prof. D. Brée, Dr W. Brockhaus-Grand, Dr C. Chapman, Mr P.A. Coggle, Dr P. Cook, Prof. M. Dalmas, Mr. T. Despositos, Prof. D. Dobrovolsky, Dr B. Donaldson, Dr D. Duckworth, Prof. L. Eichinger, Prof. P. Eisenberg, Prof. C. Fandrych, Dr. K. Fischer, Prof. J.L. Flood, Prof. A. Gardt, Prof. S. Günthner, Dr P. Gupta, Prof. C. Gutknecht, Prof. C. Hall, Mr W. Hanson, Dr G. Hens, Mr P. Holgate, Mr D.H.R. Jones, Prof. R. Jones, Prof. W.J. Jones, Prof. K.M. Kohl, Ms. A. Krawanja, Prof. E. Lang, Dr. N. Langer, Prof. O. Leirbukt, Prof. E. Leiss, Mrs G. Loftus, Mr D.G. McCulloch, Dr J. Manton, Dr G.D.C. Martin, Dr V. Martin, Prof. U. Meinhof, Dr M. Minden, Prof. H. Ridley, Prof. J. Roche, Prof. D. Rösler, Dr. S. Scheible, Ms M. Schwab, Dr R.W. Sheppard, Prof. H.G. Siefken, Prof. G. Stickel, Dr. P. Storjohann, Ms Susan Tebbutt, Mrs E. Teubert, Prof. J.K.A. Thomaneck, Mrs A. Thompson, Dr B. Thompson, Prof. M.R. Townson, Mr B.A. Watson, Dr S. Watts, Prof. H. Wegener, Dr J. West, Prof. D.N. Yeandle and Prof. G. Zifonun. Thanks are also due to the German Academic Exchange Service, which made a number of visits possible to the Institut für Deutsche Sprache in Mannheim to consult material there and use its library facilities.

Martin Durrell
Manchester, 2011

The phonetic alphabet

On those occasions (especially in Chapter 23) where it is necessary to indicate precise pronunciation the alphabet of the International Phonetic Association (IPA) is used. The following table gives all the IPA symbols used in this book, with examples from German, (British) English or French. Phonetic symbols are conventionally given between square brackets, e.g. *Mann*, pronounced [man]. . Long vowels are indicated by the symbol : placed after the vowel sign.

Vowels

iː	Ger b*ie*ten, Engl b*ea*t		uː	Ger K*u*h, Fr tr*ou*
ɪ	Ger b*i*tten, Engl b*i*t		ʏ	Ger F*ü*lle
eː	Ger b*e*ten, Fr *é*couter		yː	Ger M*ü*hle, Fr m*u*r
ɛ	Ger B*e*tt, Engl b*e*d		œ	Ger H*ö*lle
ɛː	Ger w*ä*re, Fr sc*è*ne		ø	Ger H*ö*hle, Fr p*eu*
a	Ger B*a*nd, Fr p*a*s		aɪ	Ger f*ei*n, Engl f*i*ne
aː	Ger V*a*ter, Engl f*a*ther		aʊ	Ger M*au*s, Engl m*ou*se
ɔ	Ger k*o*mmen, Engl c*augh*t		œʏ	Ger M*äu*se
oː	Ger B*oo*t, Fr *eau*		ə	Ger bitt*e*, Engl chin*a*
ʊ	Ger B*u*tter, Engl b*u*tcher		ɐ	Ger bitt*er*

Consonants

p	Ger *p*assen, Engl *p*ass		ʃ	Ger *sch*ießen, Engl *sh*eet
b	Ger *b*itte, Engl *b*it		x	Ger Bu*ch*, Scots lo*ch*
t	Ger *t*un, Engl *t*on		ç	Ger mi*ch*, Engl. *H*ugh
d	Ger *d*umm, Engl *d*umb		h	Ger *h*olen, Engl *h*ole
k	Ger *k*ommen, Engl *c*ome		m	Ger *m*ich, Engl *m*ine
g	Ger *g*ut, Engl *g*ood		n	Ger *n*eun, Engl *n*ine
f	Ger *f*aul, Engl *f*oul		ŋ	Ger hi*ng*, Engl hu*ng*
v	Ger *w*ann, Engl *v*an		l	Ger *l*aut, Engl *l*oud
s	Ger la*ss*en, Engl *s*at		ʁ	Ger *r*ot
z	Ger sa*ß*, Engl *z*ero		j	Ger *j*a, Engl *y*ear

1 Nouns

NOUNS are words which name living creatures, things, places, ideas or processes. In German they are distinguished by being written with an initial capital letter (see 23.2). A noun is often preceded by an article or other determiner (see Chapters 4 and 5), and often also by one or more adjectives or a longer adjectival phrase (see Chapter 6). Together, these form the NOUN PHRASE:

Determiner	Adjective/adjectival phrase	Noun
die		Gott
ein	ultramodernes	Erde
der	seit vorgestern vermisste	Raumschiff
		Hund

In German there are **three** grammatical categories which relate to nouns, i.e. GENDER (whether the noun is masculine, feminine or neuter), NUMBER (whether the noun is singular or plural) and CASE (how the noun shows its function in the sentence). This chapter gives detailed information about these, i.e.:

- the **gender** of nouns (section 1.1)
- how nouns form their **plural** (section 1.2)
- how the form of nouns changes to show **case** (section 1.3)

1.1 Gender

Every German noun is assigned to one of the three genders: MASCULINE, FEMININE or NEUTER. Grammatical gender is a system for classifying nouns, and it is not the same as 'natural' gender (i.e. 'males', 'females' and 'things', as in English). In this way, the names of the genders in German are misleading and the classification can seem arbitrary, especially as words for 'things' can have any of the three genders:

MASCULINE: **der** Tisch, FEMININE: **die** Wand, NEUTER: **das** Fenster

Gender differences are only relevant in the singular of nouns in German, not the plural:

die Tische, **die** Wände, **die** Fenster

Foreign learners are usually recommended to learn German nouns together with their gender, which is shown by the relevant definite article – **der** Tisch; **die** Wand; **das** Fenster – and this is still the ideal. In practice, though, the meaning or the form (especially the ending) of a noun often gives a useful clue to its gender, as does the way the plural is formed. The gender of 80% of German nouns can be recognised in this way, and a knowledge of these, even if there are some exceptions, is a valuable assistance in learning the gender of nouns. This section shows:

- How gender can relate to the meaning of nouns (sections 1.1.1–1.1.4)
- How gender can be recognised from the form or ending of nouns (sections 1.1.5–1.1.8)
- The gender of compound words and abbreviations (section 1.1.9)
- The gender of loan-words from English (section 1.1.10)
- Nouns with varying or double gender (sections 1.1.11–1.1.12)
- Problems with gender agreement (section 1.1.13)

A: Gender and meaning

Sections 1.1.1–1.1.4 give detail on where the meaning of a noun is relevant for its gender. The most important cases are summarised in Table 1.1.

TABLE 1.1 Gender and meaning

Masculine	Examples
male humans and animals	**der** Arzt, **der** Hahn, **der** Löwe, **der** Bock
seasons, months, days of the week	**der** Sommer, **der** Januar, **der** Montag
winds, weather, points of the compass	**der** Föhn, **der** Nebel, **der** Schnee, **der** Norden
rocks, minerals	**der** Granit, **der** Diamant,
alcoholic and plant-based drinks	**der** Gin, **der** Kakao
makes of car	**der** BMW, **der** Audi, **der** Mercedes
rivers outside Germany	**der** Ganges, **der** Nil, **der** Severn
monetary units	**der** Euro, **der** Dollar, **der** Franken
mountains, mountain ranges	**der** Brocken, **der** Spessart
Feminine	
female humans and animals	**die** Frau, **die** Henne, **die** Löwin, **die** Sau
aeroplanes, motor-bikes, ships	**die** Boeing, **die** BMW, **die** „Bismarck"
rivers inside Germany	**die** Weser, **die** Donau, **die** Maas, **die** Memel
names of numerals	**die** Eins, **die** Vier, **die** Milliarde
Neuter	
young humans and animals	**das** Baby, **das** Kind, **das** Ferkel, **das** Lamm
metals, chemicals, scientific units	**das** Gold, **das** Eisen, **das** Aspirin, **das** Volt
letters of the alphabet, musical notes	**das** A, **das** Ypsilon, ein großes D, **das** hohe C
other parts of speech used as nouns	**das** Stehen, **das** Aber, **das** moderne Deutsch
hotels, cafés, restaurants, cinemas	**das** „Hilton", **das** „Kranzler", **das** „Kapitol"
continents, countries, towns	**das** alte Europa, **das** neue Polen, **das** geteilte Berlin

1.1.1 Nouns with the following meanings are masculine

(a) Male persons and male animals

(see also 1.1.4)

der Arzt, der Ingenieur, der König, der Student, der Vater, der Bock, der Eber, der Hahn

NB: Diminutives in *-chen* and *-lein* are neuter (see 1.1.7), e.g.: *das Büblein, das Karlchen, das Kerlchen.*

(b) Seasons, months and days of the week

der Frühling, der Sommer, der Herbst, der Januar, der Mai, der Mittwoch, der Sonnabend

NB: (i) Compounds, e.g. *das Frühjahr*, *die Jahreszeit*, have the gender of the second element, see 1.1.9.
    (ii) Exceptions: *die Nacht, die Woche, das Jahr.*

(c) Points of the compass and words referring to winds and kinds of weather

der Norden, der Osten, der Süden, der Westen
der Föhn, der Passat, der Taifun, der Wind
der Frost, der Hagel, der Nebel, der Regen, der Schnee, der Sturm, der Tau

NB: Exceptions: *die Brise, das Eis, das Gewitter* (see 1.1.8c), *die Graupel, das Wetter, die Witterung* (see 1.1.6).

(d) Rocks and minerals

der Diamant, der Granit, der Lehm, der Quarz, der Ton

NB: Exceptions: *das Erz, die Kohle, die Kreide, das Mineral.*

(e) Alcoholic drinks and plant-based drinks

der Cocktail, der Gin, der Kirsch, der Schnaps, der Wein, der Wodka
der Kakao, der Kaffee, der Most, der Saft, der Tee

NB: Exception: *das Bier.*

(f) Makes of car

der Audi, der BMW, der Citroën, der Polo, der Rolls-Royce, der Trabant

NB: *der BMW* is a car made by BMW, but *die BMW* is a motor-bike made by BMW (see 1.1.2b).

(g) Rivers outside Germany

(see 1.1.2c for those within Germany)

der Ganges, der Jordan, der Kongo, der Mississippi, der Nil, der Po, der Shannon, der Severn

NB: Those ending in *-a* or *-e* are feminine, e.g.: *die Seine, die Themse* 'the Thames', *die Wolga.* Also: *die Liffey.*

(h) Monetary units

der Cent, der Dollar, der Euro, der Franken, der Pfennig, der Rappen, der Schilling

NB: There are several exceptions, notably: *die Mark, das Pfund.*

(i) Mountains and mountain ranges

der Ätna, der Brocken, der Montblanc, der Mount Everest, der Säntis
der Balkan, der Harz, der Himalaja, der Jura, der Spessart, der Taunus

NB: There are some exceptions, e.g.:
  (i)   compounds: *das Erzgebirge, das Matterhorn, die Zugspitze.*
  (ii) *die Eifel, die Haardt, die Rhön, die Sierra Nevada.*

1.1.2 Nouns with the following meanings are feminine

(a) Female persons and animals

(see also 1.1.4)

die Frau, die Gans, die Henne, die Köchin, die Kuh, die Mutter, die Sau, die Tante

NB: Exceptions: *das Weib, das Fräulein, das Mädchen* (and other diminutives in *-chen* and *-lein*, see 1.1.7).

(b) Aeroplanes, motorbikes and ships

die Boeing, die Cessna, die Tu-154
die BMW (see 1.1.1f), die Honda
die „Bismarck", die „Bremen"

NB: Some names retain the gender of the base word, e.g.: *der Airbus, der Storch; der „Albatros", das „Möwchen".*

(c) Native German names of rivers

This includes many rivers in regions which are no longer in Germany, Austria or Switzerland.

die Donau, die Elbe, die Ems, die Fulda, die Isar, die Lahn, die Maas, die Memel, die Mosel,
die Neiße, die Oder, die Ruhr, die Saale, die Spree, die Weichsel, die Weser

NB: The most important exceptions are: *der Inn, der Lech, der Main, der Neckar, der Rhein.*

(d) Names of numerals

die Eins, die Vier, die Tausend, die Million, die Milliarde

NB: Note, as quantity expressions: *das Dutzend, das Hundert, das Tausend* (see 9.1.5b).

1.1.3 Nouns with the following meanings are neuter

(a) Young persons and animals

(see also 1.1.4)

das Baby, das Ferkel, das Fohlen, das Junge (but see 1.1.12), das Kalb, das Kind, das Lamm

(b) Metals and chemical elements

das Blei, das Eisen, das Gold, das Kobalt, das Kupfer, das Messing, das Uran, das Zinn

NB: Exceptions: *die Bronze, der Phosphor, der Schwefel, der Stahl* (and compounds such as *der Sauerstoff* 'oxygen', see 1.1.9).

(c) Scientific units

das Ampere, das Atom, das Elektron, das Molekül, das Pfund, das Volt, das Watt

NB: *Liter* and *Meter* may be masculine or neuter, see 1.1.11b.

(d) Letters of the alphabet and musical notes

das A, ein großes D, das Ypsilon
das hohe C, das Cis, das Ges

NB: In Swiss usage letters are masculine, e.g.: *der A*.

(e) Other parts of speech used as nouns

This includes verb infinitives, colours, languages and English *ing*-forms, e.g.:

das Ach, das Blau des Himmels, das vertraute Du, das Inkrafttreten, das Jenseits, das Kommen, sein ewiges Nein, das moderne Spanisch, das Doping, das Meeting

(f) Hotels, cafés, restaurants and cinemas

das Hilton, das „Kranzler", das „Roxy"

(g) Names of continents, countries, provinces and towns

For the use of the article with these neuter names, see 4.4.1c.

das gärende Afrika, das viktorianische England, das alte Bayern,
das zerstörte Frankfurt, das historische Neustadt (*despite*: die Stadt)

NB: Exceptions:
   are: *die Arktis, die Antarktis; die Lausitz, die Pfalz, die Schweiz* and all ending in -*a*, -*e*, -*ei* and -*ie* (except *Afrika, China*), e.g.: *die Riviera, die Bretagne, die Türkei, die Normandie.*
   (ii) A few are **masculine**; they are also commonly used with the definite article, see 4.4.1a: *der Irak, der Iran, der Jemen, der Kongo, der Libanon, der Sudan.*

1.1.4 The gender of nouns for humans and animals: special cases

(a) Professions, occupations, nationality, etc.

(i) For many names denoting professions, occupations or nationality the basic designation is masculine, and a feminine may be formed from it with the suffix -*in* (see 22.2.1f):

der Engländer – die Engländer**in**   der Lehrer – die Lehrer**in**
der Koch – die Köch**in**   der Türke – die Türk**in**

or by replacing -*mann* with -*frau*, e.g.:

der Kaufmann – die Kauf**frau**
der Milchmann – die Milch**frau**
der Amtmann – die Amt**frau** (the form *Amtmännin* is obsolete)

(ii) These forms are used where appropriate to refer to female persons:

Sie gilt als die beste **Kundin** von unserem Geschäft	*She is considered our best customer*
Heute Abend habe ich deine **Freundin** Anna gesehen	*I saw your friend Anna this evening*

(iii) Whether the suffix -*in* is used is in practice variable and uncertain nowadays. The use of undifferentiated masculine nouns to refer to women (or men and women) is often considered discriminatory, although it is quite common in practice, even with younger speakers. Indeed, some speakers (male and female) feel that terms like *Professorin* may be derogatory because they suggest that the masculine term is more basic. In general:

- The feminine form is used if it is considered relevant in context:

    Die neue Lehrer**in** scheint sehr beliebt zu sein
    (*Der neue Lehrer* would be odd if a woman is referred to)

- The feminine forms are usual to refer back to a woman (or women) already mentioned:

    Meine beiden Schwestern sind Ärzt**innen** (NOT: Ärzte)
    Hanne Frisch, die Ärzt**in** (NOT: der Arzt), die ihn behandelt hatte
    Sie wurde die erste Professor**in** an einer deutschen Universität

- The masculine form is sometimes used in a general sense to refer to either sex, especially with titles and 'newer' professions (including those which were previously predominantly or exclusively male), or when the profession itself is emphasised, e.g.:

    Sie ist Ingenieur, Autoschlosser, Informatiker
    der damalige Minister für Volksbildung Margot Honecker
    Frau Professor Dr. Hartmann

    This usage is particularly common after the verb *sein*, and it was predominant in the former GDR. However, the use of the feminine suffix is becoming increasingly usual with titles. On the election of Angela Merkel as Federal Chancellor, it was established, after some debate, that the official form of address for her would be *Frau Bundeskanzlerin*.

- The feminine form has always been the norm if *Frau* is omitted, e.g.: *Bundespräsidentin der Schweiz Doris Leuthard; Ute Hartmann ist Professorin für Neuere Deutsche Literatur.*

- In advertisements for jobs, both forms are now usually given:

Wir suchen ab sofort eine(n) Musiklehrer(in)	*We have an immediate vacancy for a music teacher*
Wir brauchen eine/n Mitarbeiter/in für Gemeinde- und Jugendarbeit	*We have a vacancy for a social and youth worker*

- When no feminine form is available, the masculine is used despite the anomaly:

  der Säugling hieß Anna
  der Teenager war schwanger
  unser werter Gast, Frau Dr. Schilling

- Especially in written German, the feminine form is sometimes used to refer to feminine nouns denoting things:

Die ehemalige Sowjetunion war die größte Produzent**in** von Personenwagen im Ostblock	*The former Soviet Union was the largest producer of private cars in the eastern bloc*

In such contexts the masculine form (e.g. *der größte Produzent*) would be equally acceptable.

(iv) In the plural, to refer to both men and women, various possibilities are current. It is not uncommon for the masculine form to be used:

Der Bürgermeister begrüßte **die Besucher** aus der Hauptstadt Wien

However, this may be considered discriminatory, especially where the feminine form is in common usage. Both forms may then be given:

liebe Zuschauer und Zuschauerinnen; die Studenten und Studentinnen

A relatively recent option is to use the feminine form with a capital *I* (sometimes spoken as long [iː]) to indicate both sexes:

die **StudentInnen** der Westfälischen Wilhelmsuniversität Münster

With some words, the problem can be avoided by using a word which is not inherently gender-specific, if one is available, e.g. *die Studierenden der Universität Passau*. However, these tend to be mainly used in official writing and have rarely been adopted in everyday speech.

(b) Animals

The names of species of animals can be masculine, feminine or neuter, e.g.:

der Fisch, **die** Ratte, **das** Pferd, etc.

Many familiar or domesticated animals have different masculine and feminine forms:

der Fuchs – **die** Füchsin
der Gänserich – **die** Gans
der Hahn – **die** Henne
der Kater – **die** Katze

NB: **die** Drohne *drone,* **der** Weisel *queen bee.*

Usually, one of these designates the species (e.g. *der* Fuchs, *die* Gans, *die* Katze) and the other is only used if the sex is known or relevant in context. In the absence of a specific term, male or female animals and birds can be indicated by *das Männchen* or *das Weibchen*, e.g.:

das Zebra**männchen**; das Frosch**weibchen**

(c) Anomalous genders of names of human beings

die Geisel	*hostage*
das Genie	*genius*
das Haupt	*head* (of state, family)
das Individuum	*individual*

das Mannequin	*mannequin*
das Mitglied	*member*
das Mündel	*ward*
(in legal language *der Mündel*)	
die Person	*person*
die Wache	*sentry*
die Waise	*orphan*
das Weib	*woman, wife* (pej. or arch.)

In addition, all nouns in *-chen* and *-lein* are neuter, irrespective of sex, e.g.: *das Bübchen, das Fräulein*, etc. (see 1.1.7).

NB: *zum Waisen machen* 'to orphan'.

Problems of agreement if grammatical and natural gender are in conflict are dealt with in 1.1.13.

B: Gender and form

Sections 1.1.5–1.1.8 give detail on where the form, in particular the ending of nouns, indicates gender. The most frequent cases are summarised in Table 1.2.

TABLE 1.2 Gender and endings

	Masculine endings		
-ant	der Konson**ant**	-ismus	der Sozial**ismus**
-ast	der Kontr**ast**	-ling	der Lieb**ling**
-ich	der Tepp**ich**	-or	der Mot**or**
-ig	der Hon**ig**	-us	der Rhythm**us**
	Feminine endings		
-a	die Pizz**a**	-in	die Freund**in**
-anz/-enz	die Eleg**anz**	-schaft	die Herr**schaft**
-ei	die Bücher**ei**	-sion/-tion	die Explo**sion**
-heit/-keit	die Krank**heit**	-tät	die Universi**tät**
-ie	die Biolog**ie**	-ung	die Bedeut**ung**
-ik	die Pan**ik**	-ur	die Nat**ur**
	Neuter endings		
-chen	das Mäd**chen**	-tel	das Vier**tel**
-lein	das Büch**lein**	-tum	das Eigen**tum**
-ma	das Dra**ma**	-um	das Alb**um**

1.1.5 The form of some nouns shows that they are masculine

(a) Nouns with the following endings are masculine:

-ant	der Konsonant	-ig	der Essig	-or	der Motor
-ast	der Kontrast	-ismus	der Idealismus	-us	der Rhythmus
-ich	der Teppich	-ling	der Feigling		

NB: Common exceptions: *das Labor, das Genus* 'gender', *das Tempus* 'tense'.

(b) Nouns formed from strong verbs without a suffix are masculine

der Betrieb, der Biss, der Fall, der Gang, der Sprung, der Wurf

NB: Common exceptions: *das Band, das Grab, das Leid* 'harm, sorrow', *das Maß* 'measurement', *das Schloss, das Verbot*.

1.1.6 **The form of some nouns shows that they are feminine**

(a) Nouns with the following endings are feminine

-a	die Villa	**-ik**	die Panik	**-tion**	die Revolution
-anz	die Eleganz	**-in**	die Freundin	**-tät**	die Universität
-ei	die Bücherei	**-keit**	die Heiterkeit	**-ung**	die Bedeutung
-enz	die Existenz	**-schaft**	die Botschaft	**-ur**	die Natur
-heit	die Gesundheit	**-sion**	die Explosion		
-ie	die Biologie	**-sis**	die Basis		

NB: Common exceptions are words in *-ma* (see 1.1.7), chemical terms in *-in* (see 1.1.7) and the following: *das Sofa, das Genie, der Atlantik, der Katholik, das Mosaik, der Pazifik, das Abitur, das Futur, das Purpur.*

(b) Most nouns ending in *-t* from verbs are feminine

die Ankunft, die Fahrt, die Flucht, die Macht, die Schlacht, die Sicht

NB: Some common exceptions are: *der Dienst, der Durst, der Frost, das Gift, der Verdienst, der Verlust.*

1.1.7 **Nouns with the following endings are neuter**

-chen	das Mädchen	**-lein**	das Büchlein	**-tel**	das Viertel
-icht	das Dickicht	**-ma**	das Schema	**-tum**	das Eigentum
-il	das Ventil	**-ment**	das Appartement	**-um**	das Album
-it	das Dynamit				

Chemical terms in *-in* are also neuter: *das Benzin, das Protein*

NB: Common exceptions: *der Profit, der Granit, die Firma, der Zement, der Irrtum, der Reichtum, der Konsum.*

1.1.8 **Some other noun endings or prefixes give a clue to gender**

The endings *-el, -er* and *-en; -e; -nis* and *-sal*; and the prefix *Ge-* tend to be associated with particular genders and it is helpful to be aware of this. However, this is a matter of tendency rather than firm rule.

(a) Nouns in *-el, -er* and *-en* are predominantly (60%) masculine

der Flügel, der Schatten, der Fehler

All nouns in *-er* from verbs are masculine: *der Bäcker, der Bohrer, der Lehrer*

The rest fall into three groups:

(i) All nouns from verb infinitives in *-en* are neuter (see 1.1.3e): *das Essen, das Kaffeetrinken*

(ii) About 25% of those in *-el* and *-er* (but none in *-en*) are feminine: *die Butter, die Regel, die Wurzel*

(iii) Remaining nouns in *-el, -en* and *-er* (some 15%) are neuter: *das Fieber, das Segel, das Zeichen*

(b) Nouns in *-e* are mainly (90%) feminine

die Biene, die Blume, die Bühne, die Garage, die Liebe, die Sahne

There are five major groups of exceptions:

(i) Names of male persons and animals (see 1.3.2): *der Affe, der Bote, der Junge, der Löwe*

(ii) Eight irregular masculines (see 1.3.3): *der Buchstabe, der Friede, der Funke, der Gedanke, der Glaube, der Name, der Same, der Wille*

(iii) Two other masculine nouns: *der Charme, der Käse*

(iv) Most nouns with the prefix *Ge-* are neuter (see 1.1.8c), irrespective of whether they end in *-e* or not: *das Gebirge, das Gefälle, das Gemüse*

(v) A few other neuter nouns: *das Auge, das Ende, das Erbe* 'inheritance' (see 1.1.12), *das Finale, das Image, das Interesse, das Prestige, das Regime, das Repertoire*

(c) Most nouns with the prefix *Ge-* [gə] are neuter

das Geäst, das Gebäude, das Gebot, das Gelübde, das Gesetz, das Gespräch

The exceptions fall into three groups:

(i) Names of male or female humans:

der Gehilfe/die Gehilfin	*assistant*
der Gemahl/die Gemahlin (*elev.*)	*spouse*
der Genosse/die Genossin	*comrade*
der Gevatter (*arch.*)	*godfather*

(ii) Eleven other masculines:

der Gebrauch	*use*	der Gehorsam	*obedience*	der Geschmack	*taste*
der Gedanke	*thought*	der Genuss	*enjoyment*	der Gestank	*stink*
der Gefallen	*favour*	der Geruch	*smell*	der Gewinn	*profit*
der Gehalt	*content*	der Gesang	*singing*		

NB: *Gefallen* and *Gehalt* are neuter in other meanings, see 1.1.12.

(iii) Eleven other feminines:

die Gebärde	*gesture*	die Gefahr	*danger*	die Geschwulst	*tumour*
die Gebühr	*fee*	die Gemeinde	*community*	die Gestalt	*figure*
die Geburt	*birth*	die Geschichte	*history; story*	die Gewähr	*guarantee*
die Geduld	*patience*			die Gewalt	*force, violence*

(d) Nouns with the suffixes *-nis* and *-sal* are mainly (about 70%) neuter

das Bedürfnis, das Ereignis, das Erlebnis, das Scheusal, das Schicksal

About 30% are feminine, including:

(i) all those in *-nis* from adjectives: *die Bitternis, die Finsternis*

(ii) all those in *-nis* from verbs denoting a state of mind: *die Besorgnis, die Betrübnis*

(iii) a few other common feminines: *die Erkenntnis, die Erlaubnis, die Kenntnis, die Mühsal*

(e) Nouns with certain endings are most often neuter if they refer to things

These endings are mainly of foreign origin:

-al	das Lineal	**-at**	das Sekretariat	**-iv**	das Adjektiv
-an	das Organ	**-ent**	das Talent	**-o**	das Büro
-ar	das Formular	**-ett**	das Etikett	**-on**	das Mikrophon
-är	das Militär	**-ier**	das Papier		

Nouns with these endings referring to persons are masculine, see 1.1.1.

NB: The most common exceptions are: *der Kanal, die Moral, der Skandal, der Altar, der Kommentar, der Apparat, der Automat, der Salat, der Senat, die Manier, der Kanton, die Person.*

1.1.9 The gender of compound words and abbreviations

(a) Compound nouns usually have the gender of the last component

der Fahr**plan**, die Bushalte**stelle**, das Hallen**bad**

There are a few exceptions to this rule:

(i) Some compounds of *der Mut* are feminine: *die Anmut, die Armut, die Demut, die Großmut, die Langmut, die Sanftmut, die Schwermut, die Wehmut*

(ii) For the compounds of *der/das Teil*, see 1.1.11c.

(iii) Others:

das Gift	BUT die Mitgift *dowry*
der Grat	BUT das Rückgrat
die Scheu	BUT der Abscheu (cf. 1.1.11)
das Wort	BUT die Antwort
die Woche	BUT der Mittwoch

(b) The gender of abbreviations is determined by the base word

der HSV (der Hamburger Sportverein)
die CDU (die Christlich-Demokratische Union)
das BAFöG (das Bundesausbildungsförderungsgesetz)

(c) Shortened words have the gender of the full form

der Akku (Akkumulator)
der Krimi (Kriminalroman)
das Labor (Laboratorium)
die Lok (Lokomotive)
die Uni (Universität)

NB: *das Foto* (despite: *die Fotografie*). In Switzerland, though, *die Foto* is usual.

1.1.10 The gender of English loan-words

Large-scale borrowing of words from English is a feature of modern German. These need to be given a gender, and this tends to be determined by the following principles (which sometimes conflict):

(a) Many English words adopt the gender of the nearest German equivalent

der Airbag (der Sack)	die Band (die Kapelle)
der Airport (der Flughafen)	die Box (die Büchse)
der Bob (der Schlitten)	die Crew (die Mannschaft)
der Lift (der Aufzug)	das Baby (das Kind)
der Shop (der Laden)	das Bike (das Fahrrad)
der Smog (der Nebel)	das Handy (das Telefon)

This principle can result in a word having two genders in different meanings, e.g.: *der Service* 'service' (by analogy with *der Dienst*); *das Service* '(dinner/tea) service' (by analogy with *das Geschirr*).

(b) The ending or the form of some English words can determine the gender

(i) Words with endings similar to German endings often adopt the gender associated with that ending:

> der Broiler, der Container, der Computer, der Folder (*-er* is a masculine ending)
> der Agitator, der Konduktor, der Rotor (*-or* is a masculine ending)
> die Animation, die Supervision (*-sion* and *-tion* are feminine endings)
> die City, die Lobby, die Publicity, die Party, die Story (*-ie* is a feminine ending)
> das Klosett, das Pamphlet, das Ticket (*-ett* is a neuter ending)
> das Advertisement, das Realignment, das Treatment (*-ment* is a neuter ending)

(ii) Monosyllabic nouns from verbs are often masculine (cf. 1.1.5b):

> der Hit, der Hype, der Link, der Look, der Raid, der Rock, der Streik, der Strip, der Talk

(iii) Nouns from phrasal verbs or English *ing*-forms are usually neuter, see 1.1.3e:

> das Blow-up, das Check-up, das Handout, das Teach-in
> das Dumping, das Floating, das Meeting, das Merchandising

NB: There are some exceptions: *der Fallout, die Holding* (company).

(c) If there is no other indication, monosyllabic nouns are most often masculine

> der Chip, der Choke, der Lunch, der Sex, der Spot, der Trend

However, feminines and neuters are not uncommon:

> die Bar, die Couch, die Farm, das Match, das Steak, das Team

(d) No gender has yet become firmly established in a good number of cases

Common examples are:

> der/das Blackout   der/das Deal   der/das Ketchup   der/das Poster
> der/das Break   der/die Forehand   der/das Looping   der/das Radar
> der/das Cartoon   der/die Parka   die/das Soda
> der/das (coll. also: die) Jogurt

Sometimes different German countries settle on different genders. *Blog* is most often *das Blog* in Germany, but *der Blog* in Austria and Switzerland. *Die E-Mail* is used in Germany (presumably because of *die Post*) but *das E-Mail* in Switzerland; whilst in Austria and much of South Germany both genders are found.

1.1.11 Nouns with varying gender

The gender of a few nouns is not fixed, although the variation is often linked to regional or register differences.

(a) Some common examples

Abscheu *abhorrence*	**der** (*occ*. **die**)	Mündel *ward*	**das** (legal **der**)
Aperitif *aperitif*	**der** (*Sw*. **das**)	Puff *brothel*	**der** (*Au*. **das**)
Backbord *port side*	**das** (*Au*. **der**)	(*vulg*.)	
Barock *Baroque*	**der** or **das**	Pyjama *pyjamas*	**der** (*Au*./*Sw*. **das**)
Dotter *yolk*	**der** or **das**	Radio *radio*	**das** (S.G. **der**)

Dschungel *jungle*	**der** (*occ.* **das**, *obs.* **die**)	Sakko *jacket*	**der** (*Au.* **das**)
		Sims (*window-*)*sill*, *mantelpiece*	**der** *or* **das**
Fakt *fact*	**der** *or* **das**		
Filter *filter*	**der** (*techn.* **das**)		
Foto *photo*	**das** (*Sw.* **die**)	Soda *soda*	**die** *or* **das**
Gelee *jelly*	**das** *or* **der**	Spargel *asparagus*	**der** (*Sw.* **die**)
Gischt *spray*	**der** *or* **die**		
Katapult *catapult*	**das** *or* **der**	Steuerbord *starboard*	**das** (*Au.* **der**)
Kehricht *sweepings*	**der** *or* **das**		
Keks *biscuit*	**der** (*Au.* **das**)	Taxi *taxi* (NB: *also common:*	**das** (*Sw.* **der**) **die** *Taxe*)
Knäuel *ball (wool)*	**der** *or* **das**		
Kompromiss *compromise*	**der** (*Au.* **das**)	Tüpfel *dot* (on *i*)	**der** (*Au.* **das**)
Match *match*	**das** (*Au./Sw.* **der**)	Virus *virus*	**der** (*medic.* **das**)
Meteor *meteor*	**der** (*astronom.* **das**)	Zubehör *accessories*	**das** *or* **der**

(b) Liter and Meter

Both these words (and their compounds, e.g. *Zentimeter*) are officially neuter, notably in scientific terminology, i.e. *das Liter, das Meter*. However, they are regularly masculine in colloquial speech, and not infrequently in print, i.e. *der Liter, der Meter*. Written Swiss usage **always** prefers the masculine.

(c) Teil

Teil is most often masculine, *der Teil*, in all meanings:

dieser Teil von Deutschland; er behielt den größten Teil für sich

However, it may be neuter in a few set phrases:

ich für mein (*or* meinen) Teil; das bessere (*or* den besseren) Teil wählen;
sie trug ihr (*or* ihren) Teil dazu bei; er hat sein (*or* seinen) Teil getan

The neuter *das Teil* is also usual in technical language, to refer to a detached part:

jedes einzelne Teil, ein defektes Teil

Compounds of *Teil* are mostly masculine, with the following exceptions:

das Abteil *compartment*	das Gegenteil *opposite*
das (*legal* der) Erbteil *inheritance*	das/der Oberteil *upper part*
das Einzelteil *separate part*	das Urteil *verdict*
das Ersatzteil *replacement part*	

1.1.12 Double genders with different meanings

A number of words have two meanings differentiated by gender:

der Band (¨e) *volume, book*	das Band (¨er) *ribbon, tape*
NB: also: *die Band* (-s) (pron. [bɛnt]) *band, (pop) group.*	das Band (-e) *bond, fetter* (see 1.2.8)
der Bulle (-n, -n) *bull; cop* (coll.)	die Bulle (-n) *(papal) bull*
der Bund (¨e) *union; waistband*	das Bund (-e) *bundle, bunch*
der Ekel (*no pl.*) *disgust*	das Ekel (-) (*coll.*) *nasty person*
der Erbe (-n, -n) *heir*	das Erbe (*no pl.*) *inheritance, heritage*
der Flur (-e) *entrance hall* (N.G.)	die Flur (-en) *meadow* (*elev.*)
der Gefallen (-) *favour*	das Gefallen (*no pl.*) *pleasure*

der Gehalt (-e) *content*
NB: Au. *der Gehalt* also = 'salary'

das Gehalt (¨er) *salary*

der Golf (-e) *gulf*

das Golf (*no pl.*) *golf*

der Gummi (-s) *eraser*

das Gummi (*no pl.*) *rubber (as material)*

der Harz *Harz (mountains)*

das Harz (*no pl.*) *resin*

der Heide (-n) *heathen*

die Heide (-n) *heath*

der Hut (¨e) *hat*

die Hut (*no pl.*) *guard*
  (e.g.: *auf der Hut sein* 'to be on one's guard')

der Junge (-n, -n) *boy*

das Junge (adj.) *young (of animals)*

der Kiefer (-) *jaw*

die Kiefer (-n) *pine*

der Kunde (-n, -n) *customer*

die Kunde (*no pl.*) *knowledge, news (elev.)*

der Lama (-s) *lama*

das Lama (-s) *llama*

der Laster (-) *lorry* (coll.)

das Laster (-) *vice*

der Leiter (-) *leader*

die Leiter (-n) *ladder*

der Mangel (¨) *lack*

die Mangel (-n) *mangle*

die Mark (-) *mark* (coin)

das Mark (*no pl.*) *marrow (bone)*

die Marsch (-en) *fen* (N.G.)

der Marsch (¨e) *march*

der Mensch (-en, -en) *human being*

das Mensch (-er) *slut* (coll., pej.)

der Messer (-) *surveyor; gauge*

das Messer (-) *knife*

der Militär (-s) *military man*

das Militär (*no pl.*) *the military*

der Moment (-e) *moment*

das Moment (-e) *(determining) factor*

der Otter (-) *otter*
  (also: *der Fischotter*)

die Otter (-n) *adder*
  (also: *die Kreuzotter*)

der Pack (-e *or* ¨e) *package*

das Pack (*no pl.*) *mob, rabble*

der Pony (*no pl.*) *fringe (of hair)*

das Pony (-s) *pony*

der Schild (-e) *shield*

das Schild (-er) *sign, plate*

der See (-n) *lake*

die See (*no pl.*) *sea*

die Steuer (-n) *tax*

das Steuer (-) *steering-wheel, helm*

der Stift (-e) *pen, stripling* (coll.)

das Stift (-e) *foundation, home (e.g. for aged)*

der Tau (*no pl.*) *dew*

das Tau (-e) *rope, hawser*

der Tor (-en, -en) *fool* (lit.)

das Tor (-e) *gate*

der Verdienst (*no pl.*) *earnings*

das Verdienst (-e) *merit, achievement*

die Wehr (*no pl.*) *defence*

das Wehr (-e) *weir*

1.1.13 Problems of gender agreement

Difficulty with gender agreement arises most often when grammatical gender and natural gender do not correspond, as in the nouns treated in 1.1.4.

(a) In formal written German, pronouns normally agree with the grammatical gender of the noun, irrespective of natural gender

Wir suchen eine männliche Fachkraft. **Sie** muss im Besitz eines Führerscheins sein
We are looking for a skilled male worker. He must have a clean driving licence

ein**es** der Mitglieder dieses Vereins
one of the members of this club

Ich kann mich jedoch an keine Person erinnern, **die** in dem so benannten Vorort wohnte (*Grass*)
However, I cannot remember any person who lived in the suburb of that name

Es war einmal ein Mädchen aus Alaska, **das** war Sängerin in einem Club in San Diego. Vor drei Jahren, mit 19, nahm **es seine** erste CD auf (*Kurier*)
There was once a girl from Alaska, she was a singer in a club in San Diego. Three years ago, at the age of 19, she recorded her first CD

This rule is rarely adhered to consistently. In practice, the relative pronoun almost always agrees for grammatical gender, but personal pronouns often have the form appropriate to the natural gender of the person referred to (i.e. *sie* or *er*), especially in spoken German:

Das Mädchen da drüben? **Sie** hat doch rotes Haar!	*That girl over there? But she's got red hair!*

Even in writing, natural gender tends to predominate if the pronoun is some distance from the noun it refers to, especially if it is in a different clause or sentence:

Das junge Mädchen ist gestern Abend angekommen. **Sie** ist sehr liebenswürdig	*The young girl arrived last night. She's very kind*
Sie stürzten sich auf das Mädchen, **das** in der Ecke stand, und drohten **ihr** mit Erschießen (*Quick*)	*They rushed upon the girl standing in the corner and threatened to shoot her*

Fräulein (if it is still used) is treated in this way, i.e. as a neuter noun, when it is used on its own, e.g. *das Fräulein, **das** ihn bediente*. But when followed by a name, feminine pronouns are used: *Fräulein Müller, **die** mich gestern bediente*.

(b) Neuter singular pronouns are used to refer to male and female persons

Sie stehen eine Weile schweigend, **jedes** die Hand auf der Schulter des anderen (*Fallada*)	*They stand silent for a while, each with their hand on the other's shoulder*

(c) Adjectives and determiners always agree for grammatical gender

ein jung**es** Mädchen, **das** unartige Bübchen, ein**e** männlich**e** Person

This also applies with *Fräulein* followed by a name, for instance at the start of a letter: *Liebes Fräulein Müller* (although, in practice the address *Fräulein* is very rarely used nowadays).

(d) Personal names in -*chen* and -*lein* are treated as neuter

Unser klein**es** Fritzchen spielt mit seiner Modelleisenbahn
Das Mariechen konnte gestern nicht schlafen. **Es** dachte an **seine** kranke Mutter

In speech the pronouns appropriate to natural gender are often used.

NB: In colloquial South German speech neuter pronouns were often used to refer to a younger girl, whatever her name, and this usage may still be encountered in rural areas. It is considered to be a mark of affection.

1.2 Noun plurals

In English, most nouns simply add *-s* to form their plural. There is no similar general rule in German, and foreign learners are advised to learn the plural of each noun with the noun. This section gives details on all aspects of plural formation and use in German, as follows:

- The formation of noun plurals (section 1.2.1)
- The regular plural of masculine, feminine and neuter nouns (sections 1.2.2–1.2.4)
- Plurals with the ending *-s* (section 1.2.5)
- Unusual plural forms (sections 1.2.6–1.2.7)
- Words with two plurals with different meanings (section 1.2.8)
- Differences between English and German in the use of the plural (sections 1.2.9–1.2.13)
- The use of the plural with nouns of weight, measurement and value (section 1.2.14)

1.2.1 **Seven regular ways of forming noun plurals in German**

These are shown in Table 1.3.

TABLE 1.3 How nouns form their plural in German

Formation of plural	Singular	Plural
no ending (-)	der Lehrer das Segel	die Lehrer die Segel
no ending, with Umlaut (¨)	der Vogel der Bruder	die Vögel die Brüder
add -e (-e)	der Arm das Jahr	die Arme die Jahre
add -e, with Umlaut (¨e)	der Stuhl die Hand	die Stühle die Hände
add -er, with Umlaut if possible (-er)/(¨er)	das Tal das Kind	die Täler die Kinder
add -n or -en (-n)/(-en)	die Frau die Wiese	die Frauen die Wiesen
add -s (-s)	der Streik das Auto	die Streiks die Autos

In practice, the gender of a noun often gives a clue as to how it forms its plural, as shown in Table 1.4.

TABLE 1.4 Plurals and gender

Plural formation	Masculine	Feminine	Neuter
no ending (-)	Those ending in **-el, -en, -er**	**none**	Those ending in **-el, -en, -er, -chen, -lein** Those in **Ge. . .e**
no ending, with Umlaut (¨)	About **20** ending in **-el, -en, -er**	**two**: Mutter, Tochter	**one**: Kloster
add –e (-e)	**most**	Those in **–nis** Kenntnis –nisse	**most**
add -e, with Umlaut (¨e)	Many **monosyllables** that can have Umlaut	about **30**	**one**: Floß
add -er, with Umlaut if poss. (-er)/(¨er)	About **12**	**none**	Many **monosyllables**
add -n or –en (-n)/(-en)	All in **-e**, and a few others	**most**	About **12**

1.2.2 **The plural of masculine nouns**

(a) Most masculine nouns have a plural in (-e) or (¨e)

der Arm – die Arme
der Hund – die Hunde
der Punkt – die Punkte
der Versuch – die Versuche

der Bart – die Bärte
der Bock – die Böcke
der Fuß – die Füße
der Stuhl – die Stühle

Umlaut is found with nearly half the nouns where it would be possible. The following list gives some common masculine nouns which have a plural in (-e) without *Umlaut* even though the vowel could have *Umlaut*:

der Aal	*eel*	der Huf	*hoof*	der Schuh	*shoe*
der Arm	*arm*	der Hund	*dog*	der Star	*starling*
der Beruf	*profession*	der Laut	*sound*	der Stoff	*material*
der Besuch	*visit*	der Monat	*month*	der Tag	*day*
der Dolch	*dagger*	der Mond	*moon*	der Takt	*beat (music)*
der Dom	*cathedral*	der Ort	*place*	der Thron	*throne*
der Druck	*pressure*	der Pfad	*path*	der Verlag	*publishing house*
der Erfolg	*success*	der Punkt	*point*	der Verlust	*loss*
der Grad	*degree*	der Ruf	*call*	der Versuch	*attempt*
der Gurt	*belt*	der Schluck	*gulp*		

Nouns ending in stressed *-al*, *-an*, *-ar*, *-on* and *-or* also usually have the plural ending (-e), without *Umlaut*:

der Bibliothekar – die Bibiothekare
der Major – die Majore

However, the following do have *Umlaut* in the plural:

der Altar – die Altäre	*altar*	der Kardinal – die Kardinäle	*cardinal*
der Kanal – die Kanäle	*canal*	der Tenor – die Tenöre	*tenor*

NB: (i) *der General*, *der Korporal* and *der Kran* have either (¨e) or (-e).
    (ii) *der Erlass* has (-e) in Germany, but (¨e) in Austria and Switzerland.
    (iii) *der Rest* usually has the pl. (-e), but (-er) is frequent in coll. and commercialese, and (-en) in Swiss usage.
    (iv) *der Pastor* (usual pl. (-en)) may have (¨e) in North German usage.
    (v) The plural of *der Saal* is *die Säle*, see 23.5.2.

(b) Most masculine nouns ending in *-el*, *-en* or *-er* form their plural without an ending or *Umlaut*

der Onkel – die Onkel   der Bäcker – die Bäcker
der Haken – die Haken   der Computer – die Computer

NB: Exceptions are the words with *Umlaut* dealt with in section 1.2.2c and the following:
    der Bauer (-n, -n) *farmer, peasant*   der Pantoffel (-n) *slipper*
    der Bayer (-n, -n) *Bavarian*   der Stachel (-n) *thorn; sting*
    der Charakter (-e) *character*   der Vetter (-n) *cousin*
    der Muskel (-n) *muscle*

(c) About twenty masculine nouns ending in *-el*, *-en* or *-er* form their plural solely by umlauting the stressed vowel

der Apfel – die Äpfel   der Bogen – die Bögen

These are:

der Acker	*field*	der Magen	*stomach*
der Apfel	*apple*	der Mangel	*lack*
der Boden	*floor*	der Mantel	*coat*
der Bogen	*arch*	der Nagel	*nail*
der Bruder	*brother*	der Ofen	*stove*
der Faden	*thread*	der Sattel	*saddle*
der Garten	*garden*	der Schaden	*damage*
der Graben	*ditch*	der Schnabel	*beak*
der Hafen	*harbour*	der Schwager	*brother-in-law*

der Hammer	*hammer*	der Vater	*father*
der Kasten	*box*	der Vogel	*bird*
der Laden	*shop; shutter*		

NB: (i) *der Bogen* and *der Kasten* may have the plural (-), without *Umlaut*, in North German. The compound *der Ell(en)bogen* always has (-).
(ii) *der Laden* sometimes has the plural (-), without *Umlaut*, in North German usage in the meaning 'shutter'.
(iii) In spoken South German *der Kragen* and *der Wagen* can have the plural ("). This usage is only fully accepted as standard in Austria.

(d) About a dozen masculines have a plural in (¨er)/(-er)

The vowel takes *Umlaut* if possible. These are:

der Bösewicht	*villain*	der Rand	*edge*
der Geist	*spirit*	der Reichtum	*wealth*
der Gott	*god*	der Ski	*ski*
der Irrtum	*error*	der Strauch	*shrub*
der Leib	*body*	der Wald	*forest*
der Mann	*man*	der Wiking	*viking*
der Mund	*mouth*	der Wurm	*worm*

NB: (i) For the plural of compounds in *-mann*, see 1.2.7.
(ii) *Der Bösewicht* has the plural (-e) in Austrian usage.

(e) Some masculine nouns have the plural (-en)/(-n)

These fall into three groups, depending on the declension of the singular:

(i) The so-called 'weak' masculines which have *-(e)n* in the accusative, genitive and dative singular as well as in the plural. Full details about these are given in 1.3.2.

der Affe – die Affen	der Mensch – die Menschen
der Bär – die Bären	der Student – die Studenten

(ii) Some irregular masculines, see 1.3.3. The following occur in the plural:

der Buchstabe	*letter (of alphabet)*	der Gedanke	*thought*
der Friede	*peace*	der Name	*name*
der Funke	*spark*	der Same	*seed*

(iii) A few other masculines with a regular singular (i.e. the genitive ending *-(e)s*):

der Dorn	*thorn*	der Schmerz	*pain*
der Fasan	*pheasant*	der See	*lake*
der Fleck	*spot*	der Staat	*state*
der Lorbeer	*laurel*	der Stachel	*prickle*
der Mast	*mast*	der Strahl	*ray*
der Muskel	*muscle*	der Typ	*bloke, guy*
der Nerv	*nerve*	der Untertan	*subject*
der Pantoffel	*slipper*	der Vetter	*cousin*
der Pfau	*peacock*	der Zeh	*toe*

Words in unstressed *-on* and *-or* also belong to this group, but shift the stress in the plural, see 23.1.6d:

der 'Dämon – die Dä'monen	der Pro'fessor – die Profes'soren

NB: (i) *der Bau* 'building' and *der Sporn* 'spur' have the irregular plurals *die Bauten* and *die Sporen*.
(ii) *die Seen* is pronounced *See-en* [zeːən], see 23.4.1.
(iii) *der Fleck* has an alternative singular form *der Flecken*.
(iv) *der Zeh* has the alternative (mainly North German) singular *die Zehe*.
(v) *der Typ* may have the 'weak' singular declension in colloquial speech, see 1.3.2c.

1.2.3 **The plural of feminine nouns**

(a) Over 90% of all feminine nouns have the plural (-en)/(-n)

The ending -*n* is used with nouns ending in -*e*, -*el* or -*er*.

die Arbeit – die Arbeiten	die Regel – die Regeln
die Last – die Lasten	die Wiese – die Wiesen

Nouns in -*in* double the consonant in the plural:

die Studentin – die Studentinnen

NB: *die Werkstatt* has an irregular plural with *Umlaut* **and** the suffix -*en*: *die Werkstätten*.

(b) About a quarter of feminine monosyllables have a plural in (¨e)

die Hand – die Hände   die Nuss – die Nüsse

The following are the most common. Note that over half end in -*t*:

die Angst	*fear*	die Haut	*skin*	die Nacht	*night*
die Axt	*axe*	die Kraft	*strength*	die Naht	*seam*
die Bank	*bench*	die Kuh	*cow*	die Not	*need, distress*
die Braut	*fiancée*	die Kunst	*art*	die Nuss	*nut*
die Brust	*breast*	die Laus	*louse*	die Sau	*sow*
die Faust	*fist*	die Luft	*air; breeze*	die Schnur	*string*
die Frucht	*fruit*	die Lust	*desire*	die Stadt	*town, city*
die Gans	*goose*	die Macht	*power*	die Wand	*wall*
die Gruft	*vault, tomb*	die Magd	*maid*	die Wurst	*sausage*
die Hand	*hand*	die Maus	*mouse*	die Zunft	*guild*

Compounds of -*brunst*, -*flucht* and -*kunft* also have a plural in (¨e):

die Feuersbrunst – die Feuersbrünste	die Auskunft – die Auskünfte
die Ausflucht – die Ausflüchte	

NB: *die Sau* and *die Schnur* can have the plural ending (-en) in technical registers.

(c) Feminine nouns in -*nis* and -*sal* have the plural (-e)

In practice few of these nouns have a plural. Those in -*nis* double the consonant in the plural:

die Kenntnis – die Kenntnisse   die Mühsal – die Mühsale

(d) Two feminine nouns have the plural (¨)

die Mutter – die Mütter (see 1.2.8); die Tochter – die Töchter

(e) No feminine nouns have plurals in (-) or (¨er).

1.2.4 **The plural of neuter nouns**

(a) Roughly three quarters of neuter nouns have the plural (-e)

das Bein – die Beine	das Schaf – die Schafe
das Gefäß – die Gefäße	das Ventil – die Ventile
das Jahr – die Jahre	das Verbot – die Verbote

This group includes most neuters of more than one syllable, especially foreign words, with the exceptions listed under other groups.

NB: Nouns ending in *-nis* double the consonant in the plural: *das Zeugnis – die Zeugnisse*
das Knie has the plural *die Knie*, pronounced *Knie-e* [kniːə], see 23.4.1.

(b) About a quarter of neuter nouns have the plural (¨er)/(-er).

Umlaut is used if possible. The majority are monosyllabic, e.g.:

das Blatt – die Blätter	das Kind – die Kinder
das Dorf – die Dörfer	das Tal – die Täler

A few polysyllabic neuters also have this ending. The following are common:

das Gehalt *salary*	das Gesicht *face*
das Gemach *chamber* (elev.)	das Gespenst *ghost*
das Gemüt *mood*	das Regiment *regiment*
das Geschlecht *sex*	das Spital *hospice*

In addition, all nouns in *-tum* take this plural:

das Altertum – die Altertümer

NB: (i) *das Ross* 'steed' (usual pl. *die Rosse*) commonly has the plural (¨er), i.e. *die Rösser*, in Austria and Bavaria, where it is the everyday word for 'horse'.
(ii) A number of words are used colloquially with an (-er/¨er) plural in a derogatory or facetious sense, e.g.: *die Dinger, die Scheusäler.*

(c) Neuter nouns ending in *-el*, *-en*, *-er*, diminutives in *-chen* and *-lein* and words in *Ge...e* have the plural (-)

das Segel – die Segel	das Mädchen – die Mädchen
das Kissen – die Kissen	das Büchlein – die Büchlein
das Messer – die Messer	das Gebäude – die Gebäude

NB: The only exceptions are the two nouns dealt with in 1.2.4d.

(d) Two neuter nouns have plurals in (¨)

das Kloster – die Klöster; das Wasser – die Wässer

das Wasser has the alternative plural *die Wasser* (though neither plural form is often used). Its compounds, e.g. *das Abwasser* 'effluent', always have the plural with *Umlaut*, e.g. *die Abwässer*.

(e) A few neuter nouns have the plural (-en)/(-n)

das Auge – die Augen	das Hemd – die Hemden

The following are the most frequent:

das Auge	*eye*	das Hemd	*shirt*	das Juwel	*jewel*
das Bett	*bed*	das Herz	*heart*	das Ohr	*ear*
das Ende	*end*	das Insekt	*insect*	das Statut	*statute*
das Fakt	*fact*	das Interesse	*interest*	das Verb	*verb*

Scientific terms in *-on* also belong to this group, with a shift of stress in the plural: *das E'lektron – die Elek'tronen.*

NB: (i) *das Herz* has an irregular singular, i.e.: *das Herz, des Herzens, dem Herzen* (see 1.3.4).
(ii) *das Kleinod* 'jewel' has the unusual plural *die Kleinodien*.

(f) One neuter noun has the plural (¨e)

das Floß *raft* – die Flöße

1.2.5 The plural ending (-s)

The plural ending -s occurs with nouns of all three genders, but it is restricted to a few special cases.

(a) (-s) is used with many recent loan-words from English or French

das Atelier – die Ateliers   der Scheck – die Schecks
der Chef – die Chefs   das Sit-in – die Sit-ins
das Detail – die Details   der Streik – die Streiks
das Hotel – die Hotels   das Team – die Teams
das Labor – die Labors   der Waggon – die Waggons
der Park – die Parks

This ending has sometimes been frowned on as 'un-German', and attempts have been made in the past to foster the use of 'native' German plurals with foreign words, recommending forms like *die Parke*, *die Streike*, which many dictionaries and German grammar books still list. However, few such forms are widely used in practice. Only with English words in *-el* and *-er* (e.g.: *der Tunnel* – *die Tunnel*; *der Computer* – *die Computer*), which tend to have the regular endingless plural, is a plural formation other than *-s* common with loan-words from English. However, even for these plural forms with *-s* (e.g.: *die Tunnels*) are frequent.

English loan-words in *-y* have a plural in *-ys*, e.g.: *die Babys*, *die Rowdys*, i.e. not in *-ies* like English *babies*.

(b) (-s) is used with most words ending in a vowel other than unstressed -e

das Auto – die Autos   der Ossi – die Ossis
das Genie – die Genies   der Uhu – die Uhus

(c) (-s) is used with abbreviations and shortened words

der PKW – die PKWs   die Lok – die Loks

NB: This ending is often omitted in speech, especially in South Germany: *die PKW*.

(d) (-s) is used with some north German seafaring words

The most frequent are:

das Deck – die Decks   der Kai – die Kais
das Dock – die Docks   das Wrack – die Wracks

(e) (-s) is used in colloquial speech with some words referring to persons

die Bengels, die Doktors, die Fräuleins, die Jungs (*older*: die Jungens), die Kerls, die Kumpels, die Mädels, die Onkels

This usage is typical of non-standard spoken North German, where some of them are very frequent. The standard plural form (*die Jungen*, *die Kumpel*, *die Mädel*, etc.) is always preferred in writing.

(f) (-s) is used with family and other names

die Müllers, die Buddenbrooks, zwischen den beiden Deutschlands (*Zeit*)

1.2.6 Unusual plural forms

A number of words, particularly those borrowed into German from the classical languages or Italian, have retained unusual plural forms. Some of the more unusual ones are in practice restricted to formal written language.

(a) Most words in -us or -um replace this by -en in the plural

der Genius – die Genien
der Organismus – die Organismen
der Rhythmus – die Rhythmen
der Zyklus – die Zyklen

das Album – die Alben (*coll.*: Albums)
das Museum – die Museen
das Visum – die Visen (*or*: Visa)
das Zentrum – die Zentren

There are a few exceptions, mainly of unusual words, but note *der 'Kaktus – die Kak'teen*, pronounced [kakteːən] (colloquial: *die Kaktusse*); *das Tempus* 'tense' – *die Tempora*; *der Terminus* 'term' – *die Termini*. Some words in *-us* have adopted a native plural:

der Bonus – die Bonusse
der Bus – die Busse
der Globus – die Globusse
  (*rare*: die Globen)

der Krokus – die Krokusse
  (*rare*: die Krokus)
der Zirkus – die Zirkusse

(b) Most words in -ma have a plural in -men

das Aroma – die Aromen (*or*: Aromas)
das Dogma – die Dogmen
das Drama – die Dramen
die Firma – die Firmen

das Paradigma – die Paradigmen
  (*acad.*: Paradigmata)
das Thema – die Themen
  (*acad.*: Themata)

A few have a plural in *-mata*:

das Dilemma – die Dilemmata
  (*now commoner*: Dilemmas)
das Schema – die Schemata
(*also:* Schemen *or* Schemas)

das Komma – die Kommata
  (*in speech usually*: Kommas)

NB: *das Klima* has the common plural *die Klimas*, but in technical usage *die Klimate* is found.

(c) A few words replace -a with -en

die Pizza – die Pizzen
  (*or:* die Pizzas)
die Razzia – die Razzien
  (*or:* die Razzias)

die Regatta – die Regatten
die Skala – die Skalen
die Veranda – die Veranden
die Villa – die Villen

(d) Other frequent words

Many of these have alternatives, with the foreign plural being used chiefly in more formal registers.

das Adverb – die Adverbien
der Atlas – die Atlanten
  (*also coll.*: Atlasse)
die Basis – die Basen
das Cello – die Celli (*or*: Cellos)
das Epos – die Epen
das Examen – die Examina
  (*commoner*: Examen)
der Espresso – die Espressi
  (*or:* Espressos)
das Fossil – die Fossilien
das Fresko – die Fresken
der Index – die Indices
  (*or:* Indexe)

das Mineral – die Mineralien
  (*or:* Minerale)
der Mythos – die Mythen
die Praxis – die Praxen
das Prinzip – die Prinzipien
das Privileg – die Privilegien
das Reptil – die Reptilien
das Risiko – die Risiken
  (*coll.*: Risikos)
der Saldo – die Salden
  (*also:* Saldos *or* Saldi)
das Solo – die Soli
  (*or:* Solos)
das Stadion – die Stadien

das Konto – die Konten
(*also:* Konti *or* Kontos)
das Lexikon – die Lexika
(*also:* Lexiken, Lexikons)
das Material – die Materialien

das Tempo – die Tempi
(*or:* Tempos)
das Textil – die Textilien
das Utensil – die Utensilien

1.2.7 The plural of nouns in -*mann*

Compounds of -*mann* usually replace this by -*leute* in the plural when they refer to the occupation as such or to the group as a whole:

der Fachmann – die Fachleute   der Kaufmann – die Kaufleute

In cases where we think more in terms of individuals than a group, or where we are not dealing with persons, the plural is in -*männer*, e.g.:

die Ehrenmänner, Froschmänner, Schneemänner, Staatsmänner

With some nouns both are used:

die Feuerwehrleute/-männer   die Kameraleute/-männer

There is a slight difference between these in that plurals in -*männer* refer to a set of male individuals, whereas those in -*leute* can be used to refer to a collection of people which possibly includes females. A similar distinction applies with the following, where the forms in -*leute* typically denote groups including females:

die Ehemänner *husbands*, BUT: die Eheleute *married couples* (i.e. *Ehemänner* + *Ehefrauen*)
die Seemänner *seamen* (as individuals), BUT: die Seeleute *seafaring folk* (general)

1.2.8 A few nouns have two plurals with different meanings

The following are the most common:

der Abdruck	die Abdrucke *offprints*
	die Abdrücke *impressions*
das Band	die Bande *bonds* (*elev.*)
	die Bänder *ribbons*
die Bank	die Bänke *benches*
	die Banken *banks*
der Block[i]	die Blöcke *lumps, blocks*
	die Blocks *blocks* (houses, paper)
das Ding	die Dinge *things*
	die Dinger *things* (*coll.*); *girls* (*coll.*)
der Effekt	die Effekte *effects* (*i.e. results*)
	die Effekten *effects* (*i.e. valuables*)
das Gesicht	die Gesichter *faces*
	die Gesichte *visions*
das Land	die Länder *countries, provinces*
	die Lande *regions* (*esp. in historical contexts*)
der Mann	die Männer *men*
	die Mannen *vassals* (*hist.*)
die Mutter	die Mütter *mothers*
	die Muttern *nuts* (*for bolts*)

der Rat	die Räte *councils, officials*
	die Ratschläge *pieces of advice*
der Stock	die Stöcke *sticks*
	die Stockwerke *storeys (sg. also:* das Stockwerk)
der Strauß	die Strauße *ostriches*
	die Sträuße *bunches (of flowers)*
das Wort[ii]	die Wörter *words (in isolation)*
	die Worte *words (connected words, i.e. sayings)*

NB: (i) The plural *die Blöcke* can be used for any meaning of *der Block*, but *die Blocks* can only be used in the meaning 'blocks' of paper, houses, etc. In practice, it is less common.

(ii) The distinction between *die Wörter* and *die Worte* is sometimes ignored in practice, with *Wörter* being widely used in both senses, especially in less formal German. However, there are contexts, especially after *sprechen* and its synonyms, where only *Worte* is possible, e.g. *Am Grabe seines Vorgängers sprach der Bürgermeister einige Worte des Gedenkens.*

1.2.9 In some instances the usual equivalent of a German singular noun is an English plural noun

The following are frequent:

das Archiv	*archives*	die Politik	*politics*
die Asche	*ashes*	das Protokoll	*minutes (of meeting)*
das Aussehen	*looks*	der Pyjama	*pyjamas*
das Benehmen	*manners*	der Reichtum	*riches*
der Besitz	*possessions*	im Rückstand	*in arrears*
der Bodensatz	*dregs*	der Schadenersatz	*damages (legal)*
die Brille	*spectacles*	die Schere	*scissors*
der Dank	*thanks*	das Schilf	*reeds*
das Fernglas	*binoculars*	die Treppe	*(flight of) stairs, steps*
der Hafer	*oats*	die Umgebung	*surroundings*
das Hauptquartier	*headquarters*	die Waage	*scales*
die Hose	*trousers*	die Wahl	*elections*
der Inhalt	*contents*	das Werk	*works (factory)*
die Kaserne	*barracks*	die Zange	*tongs*
der Lohn	*wages*	der Ziegenpeter	*mumps*
das Mittel	*means*	der Zirkel	*(pair of) compasses*
das Mittelalter	*the Middle Ages*		

Many of these German words can be used in the plural in appropriate contexts:

Die meisten Löhne sind erhöht worden	*Most wages have been raised*
Er wohnt zwei Treppen hoch	*He lives on the second floor*

1.2.10 Some German nouns are used only, or predominantly, in the plural

Usually, this corresponds to English usage, e.g.: die Ferien *holidays*, die Leute *people*.

(a) With a few nouns German and English usage differs

die Flitterwochen	*honeymoon*	die Naturalien	*natural produce*
die Geschwister	*brothers and sisters*	die Pocken	*smallpox*
die Immobilien	*property, real estate*	die Ränke	*intrigue (elev.)*
die Kosten	*cost(s)*	die Trümmer	*rubble*

die Kurzwaren	*haberdashery*	die Wirren	*turmoil*
die Lebensmittel	*food*	die Zinsen	*interest* (on a loan)
die Möbel	*furniture*		

Note that *die Eltern* has no commonly used singular corresponding to English 'parent', although *ein Elternteil* is used in formal German.

(b) Usage with the names of festivals

Ostern, *Pfingsten* and *Weihnachten* are generally treated as plurals:

Frohe Weihnachten!   Sie hat uns letzte Ostern besucht

However, *Weihnachten* and *Ostern can* occur as neuter singulars, particularly with an indefinite article, e.g.:

Wir haben ein stilles Weihnachten   *We had a quiet Christmas*
  verbracht
Hast du ein schönes Ostern gehabt?   *Did you have a nice Easter?*

All are followed by a verb in the singular:

Weihnachten steht vor der Tür   *Christmas is almost here*
Pfingsten fällt dieses Jahr spät   *Whitsun is late this year*

1.2.11 Some English nouns have plurals, but their German equivalents do not

In such cases a plural has to be expressed in other ways:

der Atem *breath* – die Atemzüge *breaths*
das Essen *meal* – die Mahlzeiten *meals* (*occ.*: die Essen)
die Furcht *fear* – die Befürchtungen *fears*
der Käse *cheese* – die Käsesorten *cheeses* (*occ.*: die Käse)
der Kohl *cabbage* – die Kohlköpfe *cabbages*
die Liebe *love* – die Liebschaften *loves* (*occ.*: die Lieben)
der Luxus *luxury* – die Luxusartikel *luxuries*
das Obst *fruit* – die Obstsorten *fruits*
der Rasen *lawn* – die Rasenflächen *lawns*
der Raub *robbery* – die Raubüberfälle *robberies*
der Sport *sport* – die Sportarten *sports*
der Tod *death* – die Todesfälle *deaths* (*occ.*: die Tode)
das Unglück *accident* – die Unglücksfälle *accidents*

The following words are used in the singular only in German, and this corresponds to both singular and plural in English:

der Kummer *care(s)*   die Sehnsucht *longing(s)*   der Verdacht *suspicion(s)*

1.2.12 Some German nouns have singular and plural forms but their English equivalents do not

die Auskunft (*piece of*) *information* – die Auskünfte *information*
das Brot *bread, loaf* – die Brote *loaves*

der Blitz *(flash of) lightning* – die Blitze *flashes of lightning*
der Fortschritt *advance* – die Fortschritte *progress*
die Hausaufgabe *(piece of) homework* – die Hausaufgaben *homework*
die Information *(piece of) information* – die Informationen *information*
die Kenntnis *(piece of) knowledge* – die Kenntnisse *knowledge*
die Nachricht *(piece of) news* – die Nachrichten *news*
der Rat *(piece of) advice* – die Ratschläge *(pieces of) advice*
der Schaden *damage* – die Schäden *(instances of) damage*

1.2.13 German normally uses a singular noun for items of clothing and parts of the body if each individual possesses only one of each

Alle hoben **die rechte Hand**   *They all raised their right hands*
Ihnen klopfte **das Herz**   *Their hearts were beating*

To use the plural *die Herzen* in the last example could suggest that each person had more than one heart. Nevertheless, exceptions to this rule are not unknown, especially if the possessive is used rather than the definite article (see 4.6.1), e.g.:

Die Passagiere drehten **ihre Köpfe** (*Frisch*)   *The passengers turned their heads*

1.2.14 Masculine and neuter nouns of weight, measurement or value, preceded by a numeral, have the singular form, not the plural

zwei **Pfund** Kirschen, zwei **Sack** Kartoffeln, drei **Dutzend** Eier, zwei **Paar** Schuhe, zehn **Fass** Wein, zwanzig englische **Pfund**, um ein paar **Dollar** mehr

zwei, drei, mehrere **Glas** Bier   *two, three several glasses of beer*
ein paar **Schluck** (Kaffee)   *a few mouthfuls (of coffee)*
Wir hatten zehn **Grad** Kälte   *We had ten degrees of frost*
zehn **Schritt**   *ten paces*
3 **Schuss** – ein Euro 50   *3 shots for one euro fifty*

The singular is typically used when shopping or ordering in restaurants:

Diese hier sind gerade das Richtige. Geben Sie mir bitte drei **Stück**!
Bringen Sie mir bitte drei **Erdbeereis** und zwei Glas **Bier**!

Masculine and neuter nouns of measurement do have plural endings if they are seen as individual objects:

Auf dem Hof lagen zehn **Fässer**   *There were ten barrels in the yard*

Feminine nouns of measurement do take the plural form:

zehn **Flaschen** Wein   zwei **Ladungen** Holz   vier **Tassen** Kaffee

However, *die Mark* never has a plural ending: *zwanzig Mark*.

NB: For the agreement of the verb with measurement phrases, see **12.1.4f**.

1.3 Noun declension

CASE shows the relationship of a noun or noun phrase to the sentence as a whole (see Chapter 2). It is marked most clearly in German by inflections on the other words in the noun phrase, i.e. the determiner and adjectives, rather than on the noun itself, as shown in Chapters 4–6. However, there are one or two instances where German nouns have inflections for case, and these are explained in this section:

- Case endings for regular nouns (section 1.3.1)
- Case endings for 'weak' masculine and irregular nouns (sections 1.3.2–1.3.4)
- The dative singular ending -*e* (section 1.3.5)
- The genitive singular ending -*(e)s* (sections 1.3.6–1.3.7)
- The declension of names (section 1.3.8)

1.3.1 Case endings with regular nouns in German

The majority of German nouns have only two endings which signal case. These are added to the basic singular or plural forms, giving the regular declension patterns summarised in Table 1.5, where the declension of two typical regular nouns of each gender is given, with the definite article.

TABLE 1.5 Case endings of regular nouns

	Masculine		Feminine		Neuter	
	Singular	**Plural**	**Singular**	**Plural**	**Singular**	**Plural**
Nom.	der Vater	die Väter	die Frau	die Frauen	das Kind	die Kinder
Acc.	den Vater	die Väter	die Frau	die Frauen	das Kind	die Kinder
Gen.	**des Vaters**	der Väter	der Frau	der Frauen	**des Kindes**	der Kinder
Dat.	dem Vater	**den Vätern**	der Frau	den Frauen	dem Kind	**den Kindern**
Nom.	der Park	die Parks	die Hand	die Hände	das Jahr	die Jahre
Acc.	den Park	die Parks	die Hand	die Hände	das Jahr	die Jahre
Gen.	**des Parks**	der Parks	der Hand	der Hände	**des Jahres**	der Jahre
Dat.	dem Park	den Parks	der Hand	**den Händen**	dem Jahr	**den Jahren**

These endings are:

(a) Masculine and neuter nouns add -*s* or -*es* in the genitive singular

des Bahnhof**s**, des Busch**es**, des Fenster**s**, des Mann**(e)s**, des Tal**(e)s**

For the use of -*s* and -*es* see 1.3.6. For the occasional omission of this ending, see 1.3.7.

(b) -*n* is added in the dative plural if possible

den Kinder**n**, den Fenster**n**, den Hunde**n**, den Stühle**n**, den Töchter**n**

If the plural form of the noun ends in -*n* or -*s*, no ending can be added in the dative plural:

den Gärten, den Frauen, den Autos, den Müllers

Other notes on the dative plural of nouns:

(i) Nouns of measurement often drop the -*n* after numerals: *eine Entfernung von zweihundert Kilometer(n)*.

(ii) In colloquial German this dative plural -*n* is sometimes omitted, and one may even see notices such as *Eis mit Früchte*. This is considered incorrect.

(iii) No -*n* is used in the set phrase *aus aller Herren Länder* 'from the four corners of the earth'

1.3.2 'Weak' masculine nouns

A small group of masculine nouns, most of which denote living beings, have the ending *-n* or *-en* throughout the plural and in all singular cases except the nominative. These are called (for no good reason) 'weak' masculine nouns. Table 1.6 shows their declension:

TABLE 1.6 Declension of weak masculine nouns

	Singular	Plural	Singular	Plural	Singular	Plural
Nom.	der Junge	die Jungen	der Student	die Studenten	der Herr	die Herren
Acc.	den Jungen	die Jungen	den Studenten	die Studenten	den Herrn	die Herren
Gen.	des Jungen	der Jungen	des Studenten	der Studenten	des Herrn	der Herren
Dat.	dem Jungen	den Jungen	dem Studenten	den Studenten	dem Herrn	den Herren

In general, nouns ending in *-e* or *-er* have the ending *-n*, like *der Junge*, nouns ending in another consonant have the ending *-en*, like *der Student*. The noun *der Herr*, however, has the ending *-n* in the singular but *-en* in the plural.

(a) Most of these 'weak' masculine nouns refer to male humans and animals

The following nouns belong to this group:

(i) those which end in *-e* in the nominative singular:

der Affe, der Bote, der Chinese, der Franzose, der Schwabe

NB: A few masculine nouns in *-e* follow other declension patterns. *der Käse* and *der Charme* are regular. The eight nouns which decline like *der Name* are irregular and explained in 1.3.3.

(ii) a large number of foreign nouns, in particular those ending in stressed *-and, -ant, -aph, -arch, -at, -ent, -et, -ist, -krat, -log, -nom, -on*:

der Diamant, der Monarch, der Automat, der Student, der Komet, der Komponist, der Demokrat, der Psycholog(e), der Astronom, der Dämon

Also a number with other endings:

der Barbar, der Chirurg, der Kamerad, der Katholik, der Prinz, der Tyrann

(iii) a few native nouns which do not end in *-e* in the nominative singular. The most frequent are:

der Bär	*bear*	der Hirt	*shepherd*
der Bauer	*peasant*	der Mensch	*human being*
der Bayer	*Bavarian*	der Nachbar	*neighbour*
der Bub	*lad* (S.G.)	der Narr	*fool*
der Fink	*finch*	der Oberst	*colonel*
der Fürst	*prince*	der Ochs	*ox*
der Graf	*count*	der Papagei	*parrot*
der Held	*hero*	der Spatz	*sparrow*
der Herr	*gentleman*	der Tor	*fool* (lit.)

(b) Weak masculine nouns have no ending in the singular if they are used without a determiner

This avoids the possibility of ambiguity between singular and plural:

Die Situation war für Arzt und **Patient** kritisch
The situation was critical for doctor and patient alike

Ich schrieb an Christian Schulze, **Präsident** des Gesangvereins
I wrote to Christian Schulze, the president of the choral society

However, the noun *der Herr* always keeps the ending *-n* in the singular even if used without a determiner, e.g. (when addressing an envelope): *Herrn Alfred Bletzer*.

(c) The singular endings of weak masculine nouns are often dropped in colloquial German

i.e. they have the 'regular' forms: *den Bauer, des Bauers, dem Bauer*. For most of these nouns, this usage is not considered to be standard and is avoided in formal writing. However, it has come to be accepted with a few of them which are now in practice found as frequently with the 'regular' endings as with the 'weak' endings. This is the case with the following:

> der Magnet, der Oberst, der Papagei, der Partisan, der Spatz
> (*also, less frequently, with* der Bauer *and* der Nachbar).

On the other hand, *der Typ* 'bloke, chap' (see 1.2.2e) is often heard with the 'weak' singular endings in colloquial speech: *den Typen, des Typen, dem Typen*. 'Weak' endings occasionally occur with other words, even in writing, e.g. *des Autoren, des Zwergen*, but these forms are considered incorrect.

(d) 'Weak' masculine nouns should not be confused with adjectives used as nouns

e.g. *der Beamte, der Vorsitzende*. These seem to have similar endings, but in fact they are the endings of adjectives, see 6.4.

1.3.3 Irregular masculine nouns

Eight masculine nouns are irregular. They have the ending *-n* in the plural and in the accusative and dative singular, but *-ns* in the genitive singular, as shown in Table 1.7.

TABLE 1.7 Declension of irregular nouns

	Masculine		Neuter	
	Singular	**Plural**	**Singular**	**Plural**
Nom.	der Name	die Namen	das Herz	die Herzen
Acc.	den Namen	die Namen	das Herz	die Herzen
Gen.	des Namens	der Namen	des Herzens	der Herzen
Dat.	dem Namen	den Namen	dem Herzen	den Herzen

The following nouns belong to this group:

der Buchstabe	*letter* (of alphabet)	der Glaube	*belief*
der Friede	*peace*	der Name	*name*
der Funke	*spark*	der Same	*seed*
der Gedanke	*thought*	der Wille	*will*

The form of a number of these words is variable: *der Friede, der Funke, der Glaube* and *der Same* are often used with *-n* in the nominative singular, making them quite regular, i.e. *der Frieden, der Funken, der Glauben, der Samen*. Of these *der Frieden, der Funken* and *der Samen* are now commoner in practice than the forms without *-n*, especially in speech, but *der Glaube* is far more frequent than *der Glauben*.

1.3.4 The irregular neuter *das Herz*

The neuter noun *das Herz* has forms which look like those of the irregular masculine nouns, as Table 1.7 shows, with the ending *-ens* in the genitive singular and *-en* in the dative singular.

However, regular singular forms (*des Herzes, dem Herz*) are not uncommon in colloquial speech and medical writing.

1.3.5 Dative singular in -*e*

In older German, regular masculine and neuter nouns, particularly those of one syllable, regularly added -*e* in the dative singular, e.g.:

dem Fluss**e**, dem Mann**e**, dem Tag**e**, dem Tal**e**

This 'dative -*e*' is now uncommon. It is still used occasionally in formal writing, but even there it can sound old-fashioned or facetious. However, it is still current in a few set phrases:

das Kind mit dem Bade ausschütten	*to throw out the baby with the bathwater*
im Falle, dass	*if/in the event that*
bis zu einem gewissen Grade	*to a certain extent*
im Grunde genommen	*basically*
jdm. zum Halse heraushängen	*to be sick of sth.*
jdm. im Halse stecken bleiben	*to stick in sb.'s throat*
nach Hause	*home*
zu Hause	*at home*
im Jahre 2005	*in 2005*
auf dem Lande	*in the country*
im Laufe des Tages	*in the course of the day*
bei Lichte betrachtet/besehen	*seen in the (cold) light of day*
in gewissem Maße	*to a certain extent*
jdn. zu Rate ziehen	*to consult sb.*
in diesem Sinne	*in this sense*
am Tage	*by day*
unter Tage arbeiten	*to work below ground*
(nicht) zum Zuge kommen	*(not) to get a look-in*

Many of these phrases are used equally commonly without the -*e*, e.g. *im Lauf des Tages, am Tag*.

1.3.6 Genitive singular in -*es* or -*s*?

Regular masculine and neuter nouns have the ending -*s* or -*es* in the genitive singular. The choice between these depends on style, rhythm and ease of pronunciation.The ending -*es* can be thought more formal or elevated, and it tends to be preferred with monosyllabic words, words with a stressed final syllable and those ending in more than one consonant. However, there is apparently quite arbitrary variation in frequency between individual words, so that, for example, *des Sturms* is twice as frequent as *des Sturmes*, but *des Lärms* is ten times more frequent than *des Lärmes*. In some cases, though, usage is more fixed:

(a) -*es* MUST be used with nouns ending in -*s*, -*ß*, -*x* or -*z*

des Krebs**es**, des Maß**es**, des Reflex**es**, des Kreuz**es**, etc.

It is also commonly used with nouns in -*sch*, -*st* or -*zt*:

des Tisch**es**, des Dienst**es**, des Arzt**es**, etc.

NB: (i) Neuter nouns in -*nis* have genitive singular -*nisses*, e.g. *des Ereignisses*.
    (ii) Foreign nouns in -*s* and -*x* usually lack the ending (see 1.3.7g).

(b) -s is more usual

(i) with polysyllabic words ending in an unstressed syllable:

des Abends, des Königs, des Lehrers, des Schicksals

(ii) with words ending in a vowel (or vowel + *h*):

des Schnees, des Schuhs, des Uhus

(iii) with names and foreign words:

Schillers Dramen, des Hotels, des Klubs

1.3.7 Lack of inflection in the genitive singular

In some instances (apart from names, see 1.3.8) the ending -(*e*)*s* is omitted in the genitive singular of masculine and neuter nouns:

(a) Frequently with the names of the months and seasons

am Morgen des zehnten Januar(s)
die kräftigste Zyklone des beginnenden Herbst (*NZZ*)

The months in -*er* more often keep the -*s*: *in den ersten Tagen des Oktobers*. The -*s* is also often omitted with the names of the weekdays, e.g. *am Morgen des folgenden Mittwoch*, although this is considered incorrect.

(b) Often with names of artistic styles and epochs

des Barock(s), des Empire(s), des Rokoko(s), etc.

(c) Optionally with abbreviations and other parts of speech used as nouns

ein Stück des eignen Ich(s)   des Lkw(s)
eines gewissen Jemand(s)   die Aussprache des modernen Deutsch(s)
meines Gegenüber(s)

(d) With many foreign nouns (and several native German words)

This is particularly prevalent with words seen as technical terms or specific names:

des Dativ, des Dynamo, des Establishment, des Gulasch, des Holunder, des Interesse, des Islam, des Parlament, des Parterre, des Radar

This usage has increased very noticeably in recent years.

(e) Frequently after prepositions when the noun has no accompanying adjective or determiner

laut Bericht   wegen Schnee geschlossen   trotz Geldmangel

Compare (illustrating the absence and presence of -*s* dependent on the absence or presence of article or adjective):

eine Agrar-Reform, die aber wegen   *an agricultural reform which is proceeding*
  Geldmangel und **gebremsten Eifers**   *only slowly because of a lack of money*
  nur langsam vorankommt (*Zeit*)   *and moderated zeal*

However, usage is variable on this point, and the genitive ending is still by no means unusual in written German:

eine Strafuntersuchung gegen mehrere
 Stadtpolizisten wegen **schwerer**
 Körperverletzung und **Amtsmissbrauchs**
 (NZZ)

a criminal investigation against several
 city police officers for grievous bodily
 harm and abuse of office

(f) Foreign nouns ending in -s and -x usually have no ending in the genitive:

des Atlas, des Chaos, des Index, des Globus, des Sozialismus, des Zirkus

However, several foreign words such as *der Bus* and *der Kongress* have been fully assimilated and are treated as German words, e.g. *des Busses, des Kongresses.*

1.3.8 Declension of proper names and titles

(a) Proper names without titles and geographical names add -s in the genitive singular

Helmut Kohls Politik
die Werke Johann Sebastian Bachs
die Straßen Deutschlands

Elisabeths Bücher
der Tod Friedrichs des Großen
Deutschlands Straßen

Personal names ending in -s, -ß, -x, -z do not add -s in the genitive. In writing an apostrophe may be used:

Fritz' Schwester, Agnes' Hut, Perikles' Tod, Marx' Einfluss

In speech, a construction with *von* is usual and may be used in writing as an alternative to the apostrophe, see also 2.4.:

der Hut von Agnes, der Tod von Perikles, der Einfluss von Marx

With geographical names in -s, -ß, -x, -z, only a phrase with *von* is possible:

die Straßen von Paris

die Geschichte von Florenz

NB: In colloquial speech, the generic names of members of the family are treated as names, e.g.: *Tantes Haus, Mutters Kleid, Vaters Anzug.*

(b) Proper names rarely have the ending -s in the genitive singular if they are used with an article

die Rolle des Egmont
die Werke eines Johann Sebastian Bach

die Gedichte des alten Goethe
die Briefe dieses Thomas Schmidt

(c) Geographical names used with an article

(i) With German names, the ending -(*e*)s is optional:

eines vereinigten Europa(s)

die Einwohner des geteilten Berlin(s)

However, if the article is part of the name (e.g. with rivers), the ending *is* normally used, e.g. *an den Ufern des Rheins* (less frequent: *des Rhein*).

(ii) Foreign geographical names usually lack the ending -s:

an den Ufern des Nil

die Berge des High Peak

(d) Proper names with titles in the genitive singular

(i) If there is no article, only the name is declined:

König Heinrichs Politik
Onkel Roberts Haus

die Politik König Heinrichs
Bundeskanzler Schröders Amtsantritt

(ii) If there is an article, only the title is declined:

die Siege des Kaisers Karl   die Hauptstadt des Landes Niedersachsen

(iii) If the title is a weak masculine noun, the ending *-n* is optional:

Wir bedauern Genosse(n) Schmidts Versetzung nach Bautzen

However, *Herr* is always declined (see 1.3.2b), and a following title may then lack the ending *-s*: *der Vortrag des Herrn Generaldirektor(s) Kramer*.

(iv) *Doktor* and *Fräulein*, used as titles, are never declined:

die Erfolge unseres Doktor Meyer   die Mutter dieses Fräulein Sauer

(e) Titles and names of books, plays, newspapers, hotels, companies

(i) These are normally fully declined:

ein Lied aus Schillers „Räubern", aus Brechts „kaukasischem Kreidekreis"
Sie las es in der „Süddeutschen Zeitung", im „Spiegel"
Ich wohne im „Goldenen Apostel"

(ii) After a word which describes what kind of thing it is, a full title in quotation marks remains in the nominative:

in Brechts Drama „Der kaukasische Kreidekreis"
im Hotel „Goldener Apostel"
in der Wochenzeitschrift „Der Spiegel"

(iii) A short title in the genitive with an article may drop the *-(e)s*:

in der letzten Strophe des Erlkönig(s)

(iv) Names of companies should always be declined in full (although they are sometimes not declined in practice):

der Überschuss bei der Süddeutschen Zucker-AG
die Verwaltung der ehemaligen Deutschen Reichsbahn

2 Case

The grammatical category of CASE relates to the inflection of a NOUN, PRONOUN or NOUN PHRASE which indicates its role in the sentence or clause. German has four cases: NOMINATIVE, ACCUSATIVE, GENITIVE and DATIVE.

English only has case forms for the possessive in -s and in some pronouns like *I – me, he – him*, etc.. Relationships between elements in the sentence are shown in other ways, chiefly through word order (e.g. *My brother* [subject] *gave his friend* [indirect object] *the book* [direct object]) or by using prepositions (e.g. *My brother gave the book **to** his friend*).

Inflection for case plays an essential part in showing the structure of a German sentence. This is particularly apparent in relation to verb valency (see Chapter 18) and word order (see Chapter 21). All the German cases have a variety of uses, as summarised in Table 2.1. Details are given in the remainder of this chapter, as follows:

- the uses of the **nominative** case (section 2.1)
- the uses of the **accusative** case (section 2.2)
- the uses of the **genitive** case and its replacement by a phrase with *von* (sections 2.3–2.4)
- the uses of the **dative** case (section 2.5)
- case use in **apposition** and **measurement phrases** (sections 2.6–2.7)

2.1 The nominative case

2.1.1 The nominative is the neutral case and is used with nouns or pronouns in isolation

Ein schöner Tag heute, nicht?
Und **dein Onkel**, wann siehst du ihn wieder?

  Und **du**, was meinst du dazu?

Similarly for persons and things addressed and in exclamations:

Was beunruhigt dich, **mein Lieber**?	**Herr Müller**, Telefon für Sie!
Ach **du liebe Zeit**!	**Der unverschämte Kerl**!

It is also used in so-called 'absolute' phrases, where the noun phrase is placed outside the main framework of the clause:

als er an den Mann dachte, zu dem er jetzt gehen musste, **dieser Mann aus Röders Abteilung** (*Seghers*)	*when he thought of the man he now had to go to, that man from Röder's company*
Er saß am Feuer, **der Hund zu seinen Füßen**	*He sat by the fire, (with) the dog at his feet*

The type of absolute phrase seen in the last example is found mainly in formal, especially literary German; other registers generally prefer a construction with *mit*, e.g. *mit dem Hund zu seinen Füßen*.

TABLE 2.1 Chief uses of the cases in German

Nominative	
marks the subject of the verb	**Der Fußballspieler** schoss ein Tor. *The football player shot a goal.*
marks the complement of copular verbs like *sein* used with the noun in isolation	Brecht ist **ein großer Dichter**. *Brecht is a great writer.* **Dein Freund**, wann siehst du ihn wieder? *Your friend, when will you see him again?*
Accusative	
marks the direct object of the verb	Ich kaufe **einen kleinen Fernseher**. *I'm buying a small television.*
used after some prepositions	Sie tat es für **ihren Bruder**. *She did it for her brother.*
used in many adverbials (e.g. to mark length of time)	Anita blieb **den ganzen Tag** zu Hause. *Anita stayed at home the whole day.*
used in conventional greetings and wishes	**Guten Tag! Herzlichen Glückwunsch!** *Good morning/afternoon! Congratulations!*
Genitive	
links nouns (especially to show possession)	Der Ton **des Radios** ist furchtbar. *The sound of the radio is awful.*
used after a few prepositions	Sie lief trotz **ihres hohen Alters** schnell. *She ran fast despite her advanced age.*
Dative	
marks the indirect object of the verb	Ich gebe **dem Hamster** sein Futter. *I'm giving the hamster its food.*
marks the sole (dative) object of some verbs	Sie will **ihrem Freund** helfen. *She wants to help her friend.*
can show possession, esp. with clothing and parts of the body	Sie zogen **dem Verletzten** die Hose aus. *They took the injured man's trousers off.*
used after some prepositions	Wir suchten überall nach **dem Geld**. *We looked everywhere for the money.*
used with many adjectives	Dieses Gespräch war **mir** sehr nützlich. *This conversation was very useful for me.*

2.1.2 The main function of the nominative case is to mark the SUBJECT of the FINITE VERB

Der Zug war nicht pünktlich
Heute war **der Zug** nicht pünktlich

Heute war ausnahmsweise **der Mittagszug**
nicht pünktlich

For further details see 18.2. As the subject is shown through case marking it does not have to precede the verb, as it does in English, cf. 21.2.3.

2.1.3 The nominative is used in the PREDICATE COMPLEMENT of COPULAR VERBS

i.e. with the verbs *sein, werden, bleiben, heißen, scheinen* and with the passive of *nennen*

Karl ist, wird, bleibt **mein Freund**
Er scheint **ein großartiger Turner**

Ich will **ein Schuft** heißen
Er wurde **der Weise** genannt

Further details about these verbs is given in 18.6.

2.2 The accusative case

2.2.1 The main function of the accusative case is to mark the DIRECT OBJECT of TRANSITIVE VERBS

Ich habe **einen Salat** gegessen   Die Putzfrau hat **den Fußboden** gebohnert
Sie hat mir **den Inhalt** erklärt   Er hat **die Tauben** im Park vergiftet

Full details are given in 18.3. A very few verbs, e.g. *kosten* and *lehren*, take two objects in the accusative, see 18.3.3.

2.2.2 Some intransitive verbs can be used with a 'cognate' accusative noun

This is a noun whose meaning is related to that of the verb and which thus repeats or explains more fully the idea expressed by the verb:

Er starb **einen schweren Tod**   Sie schlief **den Schlaf** der Gerechten

2.2.3 Most conventional greetings and wishes are in the accusative case

Guten Morgen, Tag, Abend   Gute Nacht   Guten Rutsch (ins neue Jahr)
Schönen Sonntag   Besten Dank   Herzlichen Glückwunsch
Viel Vergnügen   Gute Besserung   Angenehme Reise.

In effect this is an elliptical construction, with a verb such as *wünschen* being understood.

2.2.4 A few adjectives are used with the accusative case

e.g. *etwas gewohnt sein*. Details are given in 6.5.2.

2.2.5 The accusative case occurs in some adverbial phrases

(a) To denote length of time or a point in time

Es hat **den ganzen Tag** geschneit   Ich war **einen Monat** in Stuttgart
Ich sah ihn **letzten Freitag**   Er kommt noch **diesen Monat** zurück

For further detail on usage, see 11.4.1. The accusative is also used in dates in letters: *Essen, den 4. August*.

(b) To express a measurement or value

This is frequent with adjectives of measurement:

Das ist **keinen Pfennig** wert   Der Tisch ist **ein(en) Meter** breit
Das Kind ist **vier Jahre** alt   Der Sack wiegt **einen Zentner**

(c) To express the distance covered with verbs and adverbs denoting motion

Ich bin **den ganzen Weg** zu Fuß gegangen   Sie kam **den Berg** herauf
Wir sind **die Straße** heruntergekommen   Sie kam **die Treppe** herunter

This **adverbial accusative** is particularly common with the direction adverbs formed with *hin-* and *her-* (see 7.2.4).

2.2.6 The accusative case is sometimes used in 'absolute' phrases

This usage without a verb is mainly restricted to formal literary German:

Wilhelmine, **den Kopf geneigt**, erlaubt   *Wilhelmine, her head bowed, allows*
ihm, ihr Haar zu lösen (*Wolf*)   *him to untie her hair*
Den Bauch voller Fracht, fliegt der Jet   *Its belly full of freight, the jet flies to*
nach Fernost (*Spiegel*)   *the Far East*

This construction is uncommon even in literary German, and a construction with *mit* is often used, as is usual in other registers, e.g.: *mit dem Bauch voller Fracht.*

2.2.7 The accusative case is used with certain prepositions

(a) Some prepositions are <u>always</u> followed by the accusative case (see section 20.1)

e.g. *bis, durch, für, gegen, ohne, um.*

(b) Ten prepositions are followed by the accusative case if they express movement in a particular direction

These are: *an, auf, entlang, hinter, in, neben, über, unter, vor, zwischen* (see section 20.3).

2.3 The genitive case

In modern German the genitive case is mainly restricted to more formal, especially written registers. This section outlines its current uses with this general proviso. In some contexts a phrase with *von* may be preferred, especially in colloquial speech (see 2.4). For the genitive forms of personal pronouns see 3.1.2; for the genitive of the relative pronoun, see 5.4.1c.

2.3.1 The main function of the genitive case is to link nouns or noun phrases

For this, English typically uses the preposition *of*. We often think of the genitive as the 'possessive' case, but its range is wider, since it can be used:

(a)   **to express possession:**   das Haus meines Bruders
(b)   **as a partitive:**   die Hälfte des Kuchens
(c)   **for the subject of a verbal noun:**   die Abfahrt des Zuges
(d)   **for the object of a verbal noun:**   der Umbau des Hauses
(e)   **to qualify a noun:**   ein Strahl der Hoffnung
(f)   **to define a noun:**   die Pflicht der Dankbarkeit

For the use of the genitive case in measurement phrases, see 2.7.

2.3.2 A noun phrase in the genitive case usually follows the noun phrase on which it depends

die Gefahr **eines Erdbebens**   das Rauschen **der Bäume**

The main exception to this rule is that proper names in the genitive usually come first:

Karls Freund   **Annas** Stereoanlage   **Frau Benders** Haus
Heinrich Bölls Werke **Figaros** Hochzeit   **Deutschlands** Grenzen

However, in written German, personal names without a title, and geographical names may also follow:

ein Freund **Karls**   die Werke **Heinrich Bölls**   die Grenzen **Deutschlands**

Otherwise, the genitive comes first only in old-fashioned literary style or set phrases:

seiner Vorfahren großes altes Haus   *the large old house of his ancestors*
  (*Th. Mann*)
Undank ist **der Welt** Lohn   *Never expect thanks for anything*

In other contexts this order sounds facetious:

da wir **des Postministers** Kabelpläne   *as we reject the post minister's plans for*
  verwerfen (*Zeit*)   *cable television*

2.3.3 A few verbs take an object in the genitive case

e.g. *bedürfen, gedenken, sich ermächtigen*. For details see 18.7.

2.3.4 A noun phrase in the genitive case occurs as the predicate complement of the verb *sein* in a few set expressions

The following are still commonly used:
Wir sind gleichen Alters   *We are of the same age*
Ich bin der Ansicht, dass . . .   *I am of the view that . . .*
Ich bin der Auffassung, dass . . .   *I am of the opinion that . . .*
Hier ist meines Bleibens nicht (literary)   *I cannot remain here*
Er ist guter Dinge   *He is in good spirits*
Wir waren guter Laune   *We were in a good mood*
Sie ist der Meinung, dass . . .   *She is of the opinion that . . .*
Er wurde anderen Sinnes (literary)   *He changed his mind*
Dann sind wir des Todes   *Then we are doomed*
Sie sind der festen Überzeugung, dass . . . *They are firmly convinced that . . .*
Das Wort ist griechischen Ursprungs   *The word is of Greek origin*

2.3.5 The genitive case occurs in a few adverbial phrases which are mainly fixed expresssions

(a) **A noun or noun phrase in the genitive case can denote habitual or indefinite time**
e.g.

eines Tages, eines schönen Sommers, eines Sonntagabends, dieser Tage
montags, wochentags, werktags

See 11.4.2 for further details.

(b) other adverbial genitives

unverrichteter Dinge	*without achieving anything*
letzten Endes	*after all*
meines Erachtens (*abbrev.*: m.E.)	*in my view*
allen Ernstes	*in all seriousness*
stehenden Fußes (*literary*)	*immediately*
gesenkten/erhobenen Hauptes	*with one's head bowed/raised*
leichten/schweren Herzens	*with a light/heavy heart*
Sie fährt erster Klasse	*She is travelling first class*
seines Weges gehen (*literary*)	*to go on one's way*
meines Wissens (*abbrev*: m.W.)	*to my knowledge*

2.3.6 A few adjectives are used with the genitive case

A frequent English equivalent is a construction with *of*. For details see 6.5.3.

Er ist **einer solchen Tat** nicht fähig   *He is not capable of such a deed*

2.3.7 The genitive case is used with certain prepositions

e.g. *innerhalb, statt, trotz, während, wegen*. Full details of these are given in 20.4.

2.4 Genitive case or *von*?

A prepositional phrase with *von* is often used rather than a genitive. The genitive is widely used in writing, especially in technical registers, but it tends to be avoided entirely in colloquial speech except with names (e.g. *Ruths Buch, Peters Fahrrad*), and a paraphrase with *von* is usually preferred, e.g.:

colloquial speech:	das Dach **vom Haus**, der Ring **von seiner Frau**
usual written German:	das Dach **des Hauses**, der Ring **seiner Frau**

However, even in written German there are contexts where the genitive is not possible and where the paraphrase with *von* <u>must</u> be used. There are other written contexts where this paraphrase is considered to be an acceptable alternative to the genitive. This section explains those contexts where the paraphrase with *von* rather than the genitive must or can be used in written German. In other contexts a prepositional phrase with *von* is normally used in colloquial speech only.

2.4.1 In some contexts a phrase with von rather than the genitive is commonly used in written German

(a) if a noun stands by itself or is used with a word which does not decline

der Bau **von Kraftwerken**	*the building of power stations*
die Wirkung **von wenig Wein**	*the effect of a little wine*
der Preis **von fünf Fahrrädern**	*the price of five bicycles*
ein Strahl **von Hoffnung**	*a ray of hope*

(b) with a descriptive phrase

eine Frau **von bezaubernder Höflichkeit**	*a woman of enchanting politeness*
ein Ereignis **von weltgeschichtlicher Bedeutung**	*an event of global historical significance*

(c) with personal pronouns

The genitive forms of personal pronouns are rarely used, see 3.1.2:

fünf **von euch**	*five of you*
ein Freund **von ihr**	*a friend of hers*

(d) in partitive constructions with *viel*, *wenig* and indefinite pronouns

viel/wenig **von dem**, was sie sagte	*much/little of what she said*
etwas **von ihrem Charme**	*something of her charm*
welches **von diesen Büchern**?	*which of those books?*
nichts **von diesem Zauber**	*nothing of this magic*

2.4.2 In some contexts it is equally acceptable to use a phrase with *von* or the genitive case in written German

(a) to avoid consecutive genitive noun phrases in -(e)s

der Turm **von dem Palast** des Königs der Turm **des Palastes** des Königs ⎱	*the tower of the king's palace*

Consecutive genitive noun phrases are considered inelegant, but they are not unknown, e.g. *die Existenz **eines Verdachts eines Verstoßes** gegen den Atomsperrvertrag* (SZ).

(b) if a noun is just qualified by an adjective with no article

der Bau **von modernen Kraftwerken** der Bau **moderner Kraftwerke** ⎱	*the building of modern power stations*

There is also a clear preference for a phrase with *von* in these contexts if the first noun is qualified by an indefinite article, e.g. *ein fader Geruch **von aufgewärmten Speisen*** (*Zweig*).

(c) with nouns qualified by indefinite pronouns

die Ansicht **von vielen Politikern** die Ansicht **vieler Politiker** ⎱	*the view of many politicians*

(d) in most partitive constructions

i.e. following number words (except those listed at 2.4.1d above):

eines **von den wenigen alten Häusern** eines **der wenigen alten Häuser** ⎱	*one of the few old houses*
viele **von meinen Freunden** viele **meiner Freunde** ⎱	*many of my friends*
zwei **von seinen Kindern** zwei **seiner Kinder** ⎱	*two of his children*

(e) With geographical names which have no article:

die Zerstörung **von Dresden** die Zerstörung **Dresdens** ⎱	*the destruction of Dresden*
die Hauptstadt **von Deutschland** die Hauptstadt **Deutschlands** ⎱	*the capital of Germany*

2.5 The dative case

The dative case has the widest range of all the German cases, with many idiomatic uses. It is used

- as the indirect or sole object of a verb (sections 2.5.1–2.5.2)
- as a 'free' dative with other verbs where it is not a grammatical requirement (section 2.5.3)
- to indicate possession (section 2.5.4)
- with many adjectives (section 2.5.5)

In all these contexts it typically marks a person (rather than a thing) in some way concerned or affected, if not necessarily very directly, by the action or the event expressed through the verb.

2.5.1 The dative case marks the indirect object of transitive verbs

For details see 18.4.2. It is used typically with verbs of giving and receiving, etc., and it often corresponds to an English indirect object indicated by the word order or a phrase introduced by *to* or *for*:

Ich zeigte **dem Polizisten** meinen Führerschein	*I showed the policeman my driving-licence/ I showed my driving-licence to the policeman*
Ich habe **meinem Freund** ein Buch gebracht	*I brought my friend a book/I brought a book to/ for my friend*

2.5.2 Many verbs take a sole object in the dative case

e.g.: *danken, dienen, folgen, gratulieren, helfen, schmeicheln.*
Details are given in 18.4.1.

2.5.3 The dative case often marks a person affected in some way by the action or event expressed by the verb

In these uses the dative case is not necessarily a grammatical requirement of the verb and it is often referred to as a **'free' dative**. They are often idiomatic and lack a clear English equivalent.

Various types of 'free' datives have been identified, but there are similarities between them all (and between them and the possessive dative, see 2.5.4). 'Free' datives are most common with verbs which express an activity, especially moving and making things, or which indicate a change of state.

(a) The dative case can indicate a person on whose behalf the action is done

(i) This is sometimes referred to as the **'dative of advantage'** or **'benefactive' dative** and often corresponds to an English phrase with 'for':

Sie schrieb **mir** seine Adresse auf	*She wrote his address down for me*
Ich habe **ihr** die Tür geöffnet	*I opened the door for her*
Er füllte **meinem Vater** das Glas	*He filled the glass for my father/my father's glass*

(ii) It is sometimes used with things, especially things being altered, repaired or improved:

Sie setzt **dem Auto** einen neuen Motor ein	*She's putting a new engine in the car*

(iii) In this 'benefactive' sense a dative reflexive pronoun is common in idiomatic colloquial speech if a physical action is involved:

Ich will **mir** das Buch anschauen	*I want to go and look at that book*

(iv) A phrase with *für* **is a frequent alternative to the dative case in this sense, especially in spoken German:**

Er will **mir/für mich** Blumen kaufen	*He's going to buy some flowers for me*
Ich habe **ihr die Tür/die Tür für sie** geöffnet	*I opened the door for her*

The construction with *für* may be preferred if the dative is ambiguous. For instance, *Er hat seinem Vater einen Brief geschrieben* could mean 'to his father' or 'for his father', whereas *Er hat **für seinen Vater** einen Brief geschrieben* is quite clear.

(b) The dative case can indicate a person who is disadvantaged by the action

This **'dative of disadvantage'** characteristically indicates a person who is affected by something undesirable happening to the person or thing which is the subject or direct object of the verb:

Mir ist Großmutters Vase kaputtgegangen	*Grandmother's vase broke on me*

(c) The dative case can mark a person from whose standpoint an action or event is judged or in respect of whom the statement holds good

This usage typically involves an adjective qualified by *zu* or *genug*:

Mir verging die Zeit zu schnell	*I felt that the time passed too quickly*
Fährt sie **dir** schnell genug?	*Is she going fast enough for you?*

A similar dative of the person concerned is frequent with the verb *sein* and a noun. In such cases, English uses a phrase with 'to' or 'for':

Das Wiedersehen mit dir war **mir** ein Vergnügen	*It was a pleasure for me to see you again*
Dem Schüler war diese Zensur ein Trost	*This mark was a consolation to/for the schoolboy*

(d) The 'ethic dative' shows the speaker's emotional involvement

It is only found with the first person, in commands or exclamations:

Dann soll **mir** mal so einer vorbeikommen!	*Just let me catch one like that coming past!*
Seid **mir** doch nett!	*Be nice, for my sake!*

2.5.4 **The dative of possession**

(a) The dative case often indicates possession

This is especially frequent with parts of the body or articles of clothing, but it is also found with close relatives and prized possessions (like vehicles or houses). The definite article is used rather than a possessive determiner (see 4.6), and the dative usually precedes the item possessed:

Einem Mann ist das Bein gebrochen worden (*FR*)	*One man's leg was broken*
Mir muss der Mund offen geblieben sein (*Borst*)	*My mouth must have hung open*
Dem Alten ist gerade die Frau gestorben	*The old man's wife has just died*
Das Kind ist **mir** vors Auto gelaufen	*The child ran in front of my car*

If the possessor is the subject of the sentence, a reflexive pronoun in the dative case is used. This may be optional if no ambiguity is involved:

Er wischte **sich** den Schweiß von der Stirn   *He wiped the sweat from his brow*
Willst du (**dir**) den grünen Pullover   *Are you going to put your green*
  anziehen?   *pullover on?*

There is some variation in the use of the possessive dative, but, as a rule, the following guidelines apply:

(i) It is not used if no-one else could possibly do it to one or for one:

Er machte die Augen auf   *He opened his eyes*
Sie hob den Arm   *She raised her arm*
Er nickte mit dem Kopf   *He nodded his head*

(ii) It must be used if the body part or article of clothing is used with a preposition (other than *mit***):**

Ich habe **mir** in den Finger geschnitten   *I've cut my finger*
Die Mütze fiel **mir** vom Kopf   *The cap fell off my head*
Regen tropfte **mir** auf den Hut   *Rain was falling on my hat*

(iii) It must be used where reference is not to the subject of the sentence:

Die Mutter wäscht **ihm** die Hände   *His mother is washing his hands*
Wir zogen **dem Verletzten** die Hose aus   *We took the injured man's trousers off*

(b) If the dative is used rather than a possessive construction, the person is seen as affected by the action as well

Possession can also be indicated by using a genitive phrase or a possessive like *sein* or *mein*. However, using these often has a different meaning to that of the possessive dative. Compare:

Regen tropfte **ihm auf den Hut**   (he was wearing it and getting wet)
Regen tropfte **auf seinen Hut**   (he wasn't necessarily wearing it)
Sie strich **dem Jungen übers Gesicht** (normal for: 'she ran her hand over the
                                          boy's face')
Sie strich **über das Gesicht des Jungen** (only possible if the boy is dead or
                                          unconscious)
Er zog **ihr die** Jacke an   *He helped her on with her jacket*
Er zog **sich ihre** Jacke an   *He put her jacket on*

(c) With some verbs the accusative case is an alternative to the dative case to indicate possession of parts of the body

If the accusative is used, the whole person is seen as more directly affected:

Der Hund biss **ihm/ihn** ins Bein   Ich klopfte **ihm/ihn** auf die Schulter
Alle Glieder schmerzten **ihm/ihn**

In practice, accusative and dative are equally common and usual with the following verbs:

beißen   küssen   schmerzen   stechen   stoßen   zwicken

With some verbs, the accusative occurs, but the dative is more common:

hauen   klopfen   schießen   schlagen   schneiden   treten

(d) In colloquial speech a phrase in the dative case rather than a genitive is often used to indicate possession

This construction is very widespread, but it is universally regarded as a non-standard colloquialism:

Das ist **meiner Mutter** ihr Hut	*That's my mother's hat*
Meinem Onkel sein Garten ist ganz groß	*My uncle's garden is quite big*
Dem Huck Finn sein Vater (*Andersch*)	*Huck Finn's father*

The use of the dative case with *sein* to indicate possession is a non-standard regionalism, mainly heard in the West and South-West:

Ist der Hut **dir**? *Is that your hat?*

Standard German would use: *Gehört der Hut dir?*

2.5.5 The dative case with adjectives

(a) The dative is the most common case governed by adjectives

e.g.: *Er ist **seinem Bruder** sehr ähnlich.* Full details are given in section 6.5.1.

(b) Adjectives with *zu* or *genug* may govern a dative case or a phrase with *für*

A phrase with *für* can come before **or** after the adjective, whereas the dative always precedes it:

Diese Uhr ist **mir** zu teuer/**für mich** zu teuer/zu teuer **für mich**	*That watch is too expensive for me*
Dieser Mantel ist **mir** nicht warm genug/**für mich** nicht warm genug/nicht warm genug **für mich**	*That coat is not warm enough for me*

(c) The dative case is used in impersonal constructions with *sein* and *werden* with certain adjectives expressing sensations

The person in the dative is experiencing the sensation; it corresponds to a simple subject in English:

Es ist **mir** kalt/**Mir** ist kalt *I am cold*

For the omission of *es*, see 18.2.4e. This construction occurs with the following adjectives:

bange	heiß	schlecht	übel	(un)wohl
gut	kalt	schwindlig	warm	

English learners need to be aware that *Ich bin kalt* or *Ich bin warm*, etc. are **never** used in the meaning 'I am cold', 'I am warm', etc.

2.6 Apposition

A noun phrase is said to be **'in apposition'** to another noun phrase if it immediately follows and expands it by giving some additional information about it, e.g.

Wilhelm, der letzte deutsche Kaiser
Berlin, die Hauptstadt der Bundesrepublik Deutschland

Comparative phrases introduced by *als* and *wie* are also normally 'in apposition' to the noun they qualify, e.g. *ein Tag wie jeder andere*, *er gilt als großer Staatsmann*, *Jürgen ist größer als du*, and the rules given below apply to them as well.

Apposition in measurement phrases is dealt with in section 2.7.

2.6.1 A noun phrase in apposition usually has the same case as the noun which it follows

Es spricht Herbert Werner, **der Vorsitzende des Vereins**	*The speaker is Herbert Werner, the chairman of the society*
6,8 Prozent der Frauen empfinden die Arbeitslosigkeit als **einen Makel** (*LV*)	*6.8% of women feel that being unemployed is a stigma*
der „Mythos der Schweiz" als **eines Landes mit vier Landessprachen** (NZZ)	*The 'myth of Switzerland' as a country with four national languages*
in Michelstadt, **einem kleinen Städtchen im Odenwald**	*in Michelstadt, a little town in the Odenwald*
für Heinrich Böll als **gläubigen Katholiken**	*for Heinrich Böll as a devout Catholic*
nach einem Tag wie **diesem**	*after a day like this*

2.6.2 There are some exceptions to the general rule for case use in apposition

The rule given in 2.6.1 is followed in the vast majority of cases in both spoken and written German. However, a few exceptions are found:

(a) Exceptions are particularly common in two contexts

(i) After a genitive, an unqualified noun in apposition is usually in the nominative:

nach dem Tod meines Onkels, **Bürgermeister** der Stadt Krefeld	*after the death of my uncle, the mayor of the city of Krefeld*

(ii) In dates a weekday introduced by *am* may be followed by the date in the dative or the accusative:

am Montag, **dem** 2. Juli 2011   *or:*   am Montag, **den** 2. Juli 2011

(b) Other exceptions to the general rule are occasionally encountered

These are in practice much less common alternatives, i.e.:

(i) the nominative or dative case is sometimes used after a noun phrase in the genitive case:

nach dem Tod meines Onkels, **der/dem früheren Bürgermeister dieser Stadt**
die Wirtslaute des „Birnbaumes", **einem kleinen Dorfhaus** (BZ)

(ii) the genitive case is sometimes used after a phrase with *von*:

Sacramento ist die Hauptstadt von Kalifornien, **des reichsten Bundesstaates**

Despite what is sometimes claimed, these and similar exceptions are neither common nor becoming more frequent.

2.6.3 **German often uses appositional constructions with geographical names**

die Insel Rügen   die Universität Hamburg   die Stadt Bremen

In most such constructions English has 'of': 'the University **of** Hamburg', etc.

NB: German uses *bei* with battles, e.g. *die Schlacht bei Lützen* 'the battle of Lützen'.

2.7 **Measurement phrases: genitive, *von* or apposition?**

There is much variation and uncertainty in respect of case usage in measurement phrases. The most widely accepted current usage is given in this section.

NB: For the use of singular nouns in measurement phrases, e.g. *zwei Pfund Kirschen*, see 1.2.14.

2.7.1 **Nouns and noun phrases after a noun of measurement are most commonly in the same case as the noun of measurement**

In effect, this means that the two nouns or noun phrases are in apposition (see 2.6):

eine Flasche **Wein**	*a bottle of wine*
eine Flasche **deutscher Wein**	*a bottle of German wine*
er kauft zwei Flaschen **deutschen Wein**	*he is buying two bottles of German wine*
mit einer Tasse **heißem Tee**	*with a cup of hot tea*
von vier Kilo **grünen Erbsen**	*of four kilograms of green peas*

NB: In spoken German it is not uncommon to hear datives for accusatives and vice versa, e.g. *Er kauft zwei Flaschen deutschem Wein*, *mit einer Tasse heißen Tee*. This is considered incorrect in writing.

2.7.2 **The genitive case is sometimes used in measurement phrases**

eine Flasche sommerabendlichen Dufts (*Süßkind*)	*a bottle of the perfume of a summer evening*
zehn Jahre treuer Mitarbeit	*ten years' faithful service*

This alternative **only** occurs in the sequence: noun of measurement + adjective + noun. In the masculine and neuter singular it is restricted to formal writing, but it is not uncommon in speech in the plural (see also 2.7.3a below).

2.7.3 **Usage with words of rather vague quantity**

e.g.: *die Anzahl, die Gruppe, der Haufen, die Schar, die Reihe, die Sorte*. Usage with these varies according to whether the following noun has an adjective with it:

(a) If the following noun has an adjective with it (or is an adjective used as a noun)

In these contexts the following noun is most often in the genitive case in written German, but it can be in a phrase with *von* (as it almost always is in speech):

zwei Gruppen **junger Arbeiter**	*or* zwei Gruppen **von jungen Arbeitern**
große Mengen **neuer Autos**	*or* große Mengen **von neuen Autos**
eine Reihe **ernsthafter Probleme**	*or* eine Reihe **von ernsthaften Problemen**
die wachsende Anzahl **Asylsuchender**	*or* die wachsende Anzahl **von Asylsuchenden**

(b) If these words are followed by a single noun

Normal usage is a phrase with *von*, although simple apposition (see 2.7.1) is also possible:

eine Art **(von) Museum**   eine große Menge **(von) Schallplatten**
eine Anzahl **(von) Touristen**

2.7.4 **Usage with nouns of number**

i.e.: *das Dutzend, das Hundert, das Tausend, die Million, die Milliarde*. If these are used in the plural without a preceding numeral, they are followed by a phrase with *von*:

Dutzende **von Anfragen**   Tausende **von Briten**   Millionen **von Menschen**

If the following noun has an adjective with it, they are followed by a phrase with *von*, or by a phrase in the genitive case, or by a phrase in apposition.

Tausende/tausende **von jungen Arbeitern** *or* Tausende/tausende **junger Arbeiter**
or Tausende/tausende **junge Arbeiter**

NB: In such contexts, *Dutzend, Hundert* and *Tausend* can be spelled with an initial capital **or** small letter, see 9.1.5.

If they are used in the singular **or** the plural with a numeral, the following noun is usually in apposition, less commonly in the genitive:

zwei Millionen **hungernde(r) Menschen**	*two million starving people*
ein Dutzend **Eier**	*a dozen eggs*
Allein im Bahnhof kam es im Februar zu	*In the station alone there were more*
mehr als einem Dutzend	*than a dozen pickpocket thefts*
Taschendiebstählen (*MM*)	*in February*

2.7.5 **Usage when the noun of measurement is in the dative case**

In such contexts usage is particularly uncertain and variable. The following alternatives are current and equally acceptable:

(a) with nouns of measurement in -*er*

e.g.: *Zentner* 'hundredweight', *Liter*, *Meter*, etc. The dative plural ending -*n* can be attached to these rather than to the following noun:

mit zwei Zentner**n** Äpfel *or* mit zwei Zentner Äpfel**n**

(b) If the following noun is plural, it can be in the dative or the nominative

i.e. it may lack the usual -*n* of the dative plural:

mit einem Haufen **Butterbrote(n)**   *with a pile of sandwiches*
mit einem Dutzend **Kühe(n)**   *with a dozen cows*

(c) If the following noun has an adjective with it there is a range of acceptable possibilities

(i) If the following noun is singular, it can have the 'weak' adjective ending -*en* **or** the expected 'strong' ending -*em*:

von einem Pfund **gekochten** Schinken   *of a pound of cooked ham*
von einem Pfund **gekochtem** Schinken

(ii) If the following noun is plural, it can be in the genitive

This means that all three of the following alternatives are current and acceptable:

mit einem Strauß rote Rosen (*nominative*)
mit einem Strauß roten Rosen (*dative*)
mit einem Strauß roter Rosen (*genitive*)

2.7.6 Usage in contexts where the noun of measurement is in the genitive case

In such contexts a phrase with *von* is <u>always</u> used, e.g. *der Preis von einem Pfund gekochtem/ gekochten Schinken* to avoid a stilted construction like *der Preis eines Pfundes gekochten Schinkens*.

3 Personal pronouns

Pronouns are a limited ('closed') set of small words which stand in place of NOUNS or NOUN PHRASES.

In particular they stand for nouns or noun phrases which have already been mentioned or which are so well known to the speaker and the listener that they do not need to be repeated in full. Pronouns are used in the same grammatical contexts as nouns or noun phrases and thus, in German, they change their form to indicate the same grammatical categories as nouns, i.e. CASE, PLURAL and GENDER.

There are a number of different classes of pronouns, most of which are treated in Chapter 5. In this chapter we explain the forms and uses of the PERSONAL PRONOUNS, i.e. those which refer to:

- the speaker(s) (the FIRST person)
- the person(s) addressed (the SECOND person)
- other person(s) or thing(s) mentioned (the THIRD person)

In particular, this chapter deals with

- the forms of the **personal pronouns** (section 3.1)
- **reflexive** and **reciprocal pronouns** (section 3.2)
- the use of the **second person pronouns** *du*, *ihr* and *Sie* (section 3.3)
- the uses of the **third person pronouns** (sections 3.4–3.5)
- special uses of the **pronoun** *es* (section 3.6)

3.1 The forms of the personal pronouns

The personal pronouns have distinct forms to indicate PLURAL, CASE and, in the third person, GENDER. These forms are given in Table 3.1.

3.1.1 The declension of the personal pronouns

TABLE 3.1 Forms of the personal pronoun

	Person	Nominative		Accusative	Genitive	Dative
Singular	1st	ich	*I*	mich	meiner	mir
	2nd	du	*you*	dich	deiner	dir
	3rd masculine	er	*he/it*	ihn	seiner	ihm
	feminine	sie	*she/it*	sie	ihrer	ihr
	neuter	es	*it*	es	seiner	ihm
Plural	1st	wir	*we*	uns	unser	uns
	2nd familiar	ihr	*you*	euch	euer	euch
	polite (sg/pl)	Sie	*you*	Sie	Ihrer	Ihnen
	3rd	sie	*they*	sie	ihrer	ihnen

Some notes on the forms of the personal pronouns given in Table 3.1

(a) In everyday speech, personal pronouns are reduced and weakly stressed

'ch soll**'s 'm** geben   *for*:   **Ich** soll **es ihm** geben
Jetzt kannst**e'n** sehen   *for*:   Jetzt kannst **du ihn** sehen

These reductions are seldom used in written German, with the exception of *'s* for *es*, which is quite common in written dialogue and poetry.

(b) In rapid colloquial speech, the subject pronouns *ich*, *du* and *es* are often omitted entirely

Such omissions are never found in written German, except to represent colloquial speech.

(Ich) weiß es nicht   Kannst (du) morgen kommen?   (Es) scheint zu klappen

(c) In South Germany *mir* is commonly heard for *wir*

This usage is almost universal in everyday colloquial speech in the South, but it is non-standard and unacceptable in all more formal registers.

Mir gehen jetzt ins Kino   *for*:   **Wir** gehen jetzt ins Kino

3.1.2 **The genitive of the personal pronouns**

(a) The genitive forms of the personal pronouns are only used in very formal registers

mittels einer Passbildaufnahme **seiner** selbst (*Grass*)	*by means of a passport photograph of himself*
Ist die Politik erst einmal auf die Straße verlegt, dann wird sich die Straße **ihrer** annehmen (*OH*)	*If politics is moved onto the streets, the streets will take it over*

Even in writing, these phrases can sound rather stilted and awkward, and alternative constructions are often preferred, i.e.:

(i) With verbs, an alternative construction or a different verb can be used (for further information, see 18.5):

Erinnern Sie sich **an mich** (*rarely:* meiner)
Er braucht **mich** nicht (*rarely:* Er bedarf meiner nicht).

(ii) After prepositions the dative case is used in speech and is now generally acceptable in writing:

wegen **uns**, trotz **ihnen**, statt **ihm** (*or:* an seiner Stelle)

To refer to things, the adverbs *stattdessen*, *trotzdem*, *währenddessen* and *deswegen* are used rather than the preposition with a pronoun.

(iii) After the prepositions which have alternative constructions with *von* (see 20.4.2b) the prepositional adverb *davon* (see 3.5) is used rather than a pronoun in the genitive, e.g.: *innerhalb davon*, *unweit davon*. Alternatively, the prepositions may be used on their own, as adverbs: *außerhalb* 'outside (it)', *jenseits* 'on the other side (of it)'.

(iv) In other contexts, *von* is used (see 2.4.1c):

sechs **von ihnen**, drei **von euch**, ein Freund **von mir**

(b) The genitive personal pronouns usually only refer to persons or animals

Ich bedarf **seiner** nicht   *I don't need him*

The demonstratives *dessen* or *deren* are used to refer to things:

Ich bedarf **dessen** nicht   *I don't need it*

Nevertheless, this usage is not absolutely fixed, and personal pronouns are sometimes used to refer to things:

Er lässt seinen Autoschlüssel im   *He leaves his car key in the kitchen*
    Küchenschrank, so dass andere   *cupboard so that other members of*
    Familienmitglieder sich **seiner**   *the family can use it*
    bedienen können (*MM*)

(c) Special forms of the genitive pronouns are used with the prepositions *wegen*, *um … willen* and *-halben*

(see also 20.4). They are compounded with the preposition with an intervening *t*:

meinetwegen, **deinet**wegen, um **ihret**willen, um **unsert**willen, **seinet**halben

(d) The genitive forms *mein*, *dein* and *sein* are archaic

These forms have been replaced in modern German by *meiner*, *deiner* and *seiner*, but they are occasionally still used for stylistic effect:

Man gedachte **sein** (*for*: seiner) nicht mehr

3.2 Reflexive and reciprocal pronouns

3.2.1 Forms of the reflexive pronoun

The REFLEXIVE PRONOUN is a personal pronoun which refers back to the subject of the sentence or clause, e.g. *Ich wasche **mich*** 'I wash myself', *Sie wäscht **sich*** 'She washes herself'. In German it has a special form *sich* which is used for the third person (singular and plural) and for the 'polite' second person, in the accusative and dative cases. In the first and second persons, the personal pronouns given in Table 3.1 are used as reflexive pronouns.

The German reflexive pronoun is used much more widely than English forms in *-self*, in particular with certain verbs which are occur exclusively or predominantly with a reflexive pronoun – the so-called REFLEXIVE VERBS (see 18.3.6 and 18.4.3). Table 3.2 shows the forms of the reflexive pronoun in the accusative and dative cases, as used in the present tense and imperative of the reflexive verbs *sich setzen* 'sit down' and *sich (das) einbilden* 'imagine (that)'.

TABLE 3.2 Forms of the reflexive pronoun

Accusative		Dative		
ich setze	**mich**	ich bilde	**mir**	das ein
du setzt	**dich**	du bildest	**dir**	das ein
er/sie/es setzt	**sich**	er/sie/es bildet	**sich**	das ein
wir setzen	**uns**	wir bilden	**uns**	das ein
ihr setzt	**euch**	ihr bildet	**euch**	das ein
Sie setzen	**sich**	Sie bilden	**sich**	das ein
sie setzen	**sich**	sie bilden	**sich**	das ein
setz	**dich!**	bilde	**dir**	das ein!
setzt	**euch!**	bildet	**euch**	das ein!
setzen Sie	**sich!**	bilden Sie	**sich**	das ein!

3.2.2 **The genitive pronoun is sometimes used reflexively in formal written German**

It mainly occurs in conjunction with certain adjectives (see 6.5.3). To avoid ambiguity, it always occurs with *selbst*:

Er ist **seiner selbst** sicher	*He is sure of himself*
Sie war **ihrer selbst** nicht mehr mächtig	*She had lost control of herself*

3.2.3 **The reflexive pronoun is used after a preposition to refer back to the subject of the sentence**

Er hatte kein Geld bei **sich**	*He had no money on him*
Sie schlossen die Tür hinter **sich**	*They closed the door behind them*

3.2.4 **Usage in infinitive constructions without *zu***

It is not always clear in these constructions who the reflexive pronoun refers to. Normal usage is as follows:

(a) A reflexive pronoun is normally taken as referring back to the OBJECT **of the finite verb**

Er hörte seinen Freund **sich** tadeln	*He heard his friend blaming himself*
Er ließ den Gefangenen **sich** ausziehen	*He made the prisoner get undressed*

(b) A non-reflexive pronoun refers back to the SUBJECT **of the finite verb**

Er hörte seinen Freund **ihn** tadeln	*He heard his friend blaming him*
Er ließ den Gefangenen **ihn** ausziehen	*He made the prisoner undress him*

(c) A reflexive pronoun after a preposition refers back to the subject of the finite verb

Peter sah eine dunkle Gestalt **vor sich** auftauchen	*Peter saw a dark shape appear in front of him*
Eva ließ mich **bei sich** wohnen	*Eva let me live at her place*

3.2.5 **In infinitive clauses with *zu*, the choice of pronoun depends on who is understood to be the subject of the infinitive**

(see also 13.2.4b):

Karl versprach Peter, **sich** zu entschuldigen	(Karl is to apologise)
Karl versprach Peter, **ihn** zu entschuldigen	(Karl is excusing Peter)
Karl bat Peter, **sich** zu entschuldigen	(Peter should apologise)
Karl bat Peter, **ihn** zu entschuldigen	(Peter is asked to excuse Karl)

3.2.6 *selbst* or *selber* **is used together with a pronoun as the equivalent of emphatic 'myself', 'yourself', etc.**

The distinction is stylistic, in that *selber* tends to be used primarily in less formal registers. They are always stressed:

Ich habe **selbst/selber** mit dem Minister darüber gesprochen	*I spoke to the minister about it myself*
Er hat **selbst/selber** den Brief gelesen	*He's read the letter himself*

NB: Unstressed *selbst* has the meaning 'even' and always precedes the pronoun (or noun) which it qualifies, e.g.: **Selbst er** hat den Brief gelesen.

3.2.7 **Reciprocal pronouns**

These are the equivalent of English 'each other'. For these, German uses either the reflexive pronoun or *einander*. The latter is less common in speech than in writing, but it is the only possible alternative after prepositions, when it is written together with the preposition (*durcheinander*, *miteinander*, etc.):

Sie sahen **sich** (*or* **einander**) oft	*They often saw each other*
Wir gehen **uns** (*or* **einander**) aus dem Wege	*We avoid each other*
Wir verlassen **uns** aufeinander	*We rely on each other*
Sie sprachen **voneinander**	*They were talking about each other*
NB: Sie sprachen von **sich**	*They were talking about themselves*

If the reflexive pronoun could be ambiguous, *selbst* can be added to confirm that the sense is reflexive or *gegenseitig* to show that it is reciprocal:

Sie widersprachen **sich selbst**	*They contradicted themselves*
Sie widersprachen **sich gegenseitig**	*They contradicted each other*
(*or*: Sie widersprachen **einander**)	

3.3 **Pronouns of address**

For English 'you', German distinguishes between the FAMILIAR pronouns *du* and *ihr*, and the POLITE pronoun *Sie*.

Since the loss of the old form *thou*, English has lacked any distinction of this kind, and English-speaking learners of German need to establish which is appropriate in context. The use of these pronouns is anchored in social convention, and it is important for English learners to realise that these conventions can be very different from those in the English-speaking world. Since the late 1960s the use of *du* and *Sie* (commonly referred to as *duzen* and *siezen*) has shifted with changing social attitudes. The use of *du* has become more widespread, particularly among younger people, and Germans nowadays sometimes feel insecure about which one to use in unfamiliar surroundings. However, consciousness of the need to use the 'right' one is still very strong.

Essentially, *du* signals intimacy, affection and solidarity. People who use *du* to one another are conscious of belonging to the same group or standing together, whereas *Sie* signals a degree of social distance and, perhaps above all, respect (rather than simply 'politeness'). Thus, in the 'wrong' situation *du* sounds disrespectful, intrusive of personal privacy and even offensive. (In extreme cases it can be such a gross insult that people have been prosecuted for using it.) On the other hand, *Sie* in the 'wrong' situation sounds stand-offish or pompous.

Outside school or university, when talking to fellow pupils or fellow students (where the use of *du* is universal), non-native speakers are advised to let native speakers take the initiative in proposing the use of *du*. It is very important for English speakers to be aware that the use of *du* (and first names) is still much less frequent or acceptable between adults than is the use of first names in the English-speaking countries, especially between colleagues at work and casual acquaintances. It has a quite different social meaning to the use of first names in English and can be interpreted as indicating a lack of respect rather than friendliness.

As a general rule, the use of *du* is more widespread in Austria than in Germany, and even more so in Switzerland.

3.3.1 The uses of *du*, *ihr*, and *Sie*

(a) *du* is used

(i) when speaking to children (up to about the age of fourteen – in schools to the 10th class), to animals and inanimate objects, to oneself and to God.

(ii) between relatives and close friends, between schoolchildren and students, predominantly between blue-collar workmates, between non-commissioned soldiers and between members of clubs, interest groups and (especially left-wing) political parties.

The use of *du* to persons regarded as of lower social status – with the expectation that they should use *Sie* back – is now obsolete. When it resurfaces it is offensive, often deliberately so; it is particularly reprehensible (and racist) when used indiscriminately to non-Europeans.

(b) *ihr* **is used to address two or more people whom the speaker would individually address with** *du*

As *ihr* is unambiguously plural, whereas *Sie* can be singular or plural, it is sometimes used to address a group, even if one would not use *du* with every single one of them, e.g. (at work):

    Ich wollte **euch** doch alle zum Kaffee einladen

Occasionally, *ihr* may be used to address any group to stress plurality, even if all would normally be addressed individually as *Sie*. In this way, *ihr* can sometimes function as a kind of neutral compromise to mask the speaker's uncertainty about whether to use *du* or *Sie*.

(c) *Sie* **is used in all other cases**

It is used especially to adult strangers and generally in middle-class professions (e.g. to colleagues in an office, a shop, or a bank).

Usually, the use of *du* is linked to that of first names, that of *Sie* to formal titles (*Herr Engel*, *Frau Kallmeyer*, etc.). However, the use of *Sie* and first names (so-called 'Hamburger Siezen') is not uncommon from adults to older teenagers and in 'trendy' circles (in the latter case possibly in imitation of the American use of first names).

3.3.2 *du* and *ihr* and their forms (*dich, dein, euch,* etc.) may be spelled with initial capitals in letter-writing

    Ich danke **dir/Dir** recht herzlich für deinen Brief

The first spelling reform of 1996 prescribed that capitals should no longer be used. However, this ruling was almost universally ignored and subsequent revisions have permitted the use of capitals again, as an alternative, see 23.2.3..

3.3.3 Other forms of address

(a) **Titles are often used in shops, restaurants, etc. to address customers**

    Was wünscht **der Herr**?   Was möchten **die Herrschaften** zu Mittag essen?

NB: The use of singular titles of rank with a plural verb (e.g. *Was wünschen gnädige Frau, Herr Major?*) is now archaic or facetious.

(b) **In older German the singular pronouns** *Er* **and** *Sie* **(spelled with capitals) were used to address people of a lower social standing**

This usage is now obsolete (except facetiously), but it persisted into the early twentieth century, especially in Austria.

3.4 Third person pronouns

3.4.1 The third person singular pronouns agree in gender with the noun to which they refer

In this way, *er*, *sie* or *es* can thus all correspond to English *it* when referring to things.

Dein Bleistift? Ach, **er** lag vorhin auf dem Tisch, aber ich muss **ihn** jetzt verloren haben	*Your pencil? Oh, **it** was lying on the table a little while ago, but I must have lost **it** now*
Er hörte meine Meinung und stimmte **ihr** bei	*He heard my opinion and agreed with **it***
Darf ich Ihr Buch noch eine Woche behalten? Ich habe **es** noch nicht gelesen	*May I keep your book another week? I haven't read **it** yet*

NB: Possible conflicts between grammatical and natural gender in the agreement of the pronoun are explained in 1.1.13.

3.4.2 In informal colloquial speech, the demonstrative pronouns *der*, *die*, *das* are often used rather than a third person personal pronoun

Der kommt wohl nicht mehr	*for*:	**Er** kommt wohl nicht mehr
Ich hätt' **die** nicht wieder erkannt	*for*:	Ich hätte **sie** nicht wieder erkannt

Although extremely common in spoken German, this usage is only regarded as (just) acceptable in standard German to refer to things. It is usually avoided in writing to refer to people, and in speech it is considered rude if the person referred to is present. However, it can occur if there is a possible ambiguity or a need for emphasis:

Sie hatte die Fernsehanstalten massiv unter Druck gesetzt, als **die** sich in Gibraltar umtaten (*Zeit*)	*She had put massive pressure on the television companies when they were nosing around in Gibraltar*

diese, see 5.1.2, would be a possible alternative to *die* in this context.

3.4.3 Third person pronouns are used in comparative clauses with *wie*

This makes it absolutely clear what is being compared:

Das waren Reichtümer, wie **sie** Fürsten nicht besaßen (*Süßkind*)	*These were riches such as princes did not possess*
Ein Kuchen, wie **ihn** deine Mutter backt, ist was Besonderes	*A cake like your mother makes is something special*

3.5 Third person pronoun or prepositional adverb?

The prepositional adverb (sometimes also called the 'pronominal adverb') is formed by prefixing *da(r)* to a preposition, e.g. *damit*, *daran*, *darüber*.

3.5.1 **The prepositional adverb is often used rather than a preposition followed by a third person pronoun**

The general rule is that the personal pronoun is used when referring to people (e.g. *Ich spiele **mit ihr***, i.e. *mit meiner Schwester*) whereas the prepositional adverb is used when referring to things (e.g. *Ich spiele **damit***, i.e. *mit der Puppe*). There are variations, however, and modern usage is broadly as follows.

(a) The pronoun *es* is not normally used after prepositions

Here the prepositional adverb is the norm, although occasional exceptions may be encountered.

Da steht mein neues Auto. Ich habe lange **darauf** (NOT: auf es) warten müssen — *There's my new car. I had to wait a long time for it*

(b) Preposition plus personal pronoun is always used to refer to individual persons

(but **not** groups of people, see (d) below):

Du darfst nicht **mit ihr** spielen — *You mustn't play with her*
Ich kann mich nicht **an ihn** erinnern — *I can't remember him*

(c) When reference is to a specific thing (or things), either preposition plus pronoun or the prepositional adverb may be used

Ich habe diese Geschirrspülmaschine seit drei Wochen und bin sehr zufrieden **damit/mit ihr** — *I've had this dishwasher for three weeks and am very satisfied with it*

In practice, the prepositional adverb is more frequent. If the combination preposition plus pronoun is used, it emphasises the thing referred to more strongly.

(d) The prepositional adverb is used to refer to abstracts and to groups of people

darunter and *davon* (i.e. 'among whom' or 'of whom') are particularly frequent to refer to groups of people.

Wie findest du den Vorschlag? Bist du **damit** einverstanden? — *What do you think of the suggestion? Do you agree with it?*
Ich erwarte zehn Gäste, **darunter** einige sehr alte Bekannte — *I am expecting ten guests, among them some very old acquaintances*
Die meisten davon wollten keinen Ärger machen — *Most of them didn't want to cause trouble*

(e) The prepositional adverb is always used to refer to whole sentences

Ihr Mann hat eine neue Stelle gekriegt. **Darüber** freut sie sich sehr — *Her husband has got a new job. She's very pleased about it*

(f) If motion is involved, a separable prefix with *hin-* or *her-* is used

The prepositional adverb is not used in such contexts, (see also 7.2.4):

Wir fanden eine Hütte und gingen **hinein** — *We found a hut and went into it*
Sie kam an einen langen Gang und eilte **hindurch** — *She came to a long passage and hurried through it*

3.5.2 **Four common prepositions do not form a prepositional adverb**

i.e.: *außer, gegenüber, ohne, seit*
These are used with pronouns with reference to people *or* things:

Außer ihm ist keiner gekommen	*Nobody came apart from him*
Vor uns ist das Rathaus, und **ihm**	*In front of us is the town hall and*
gegenüber liegt der Dom	*opposite it is the cathedral*
Ohne es wäre unser Erfolg nicht	*Without it our success wouldn't have*
möglich gewesen	*been possible*

With reference to things, the pronoun is usually omitted after *gegenüber* and *ohne*, e.g.: *(ihm) gegenüber liegt der Dom; ohne (es) wäre es nicht möglich gewesen. außer* and *seit* are never used with a pronoun, the adverbs *außerdem* 'besides (that)' and *seither* 'since (then)' being used instead.

NB: The prepositions which govern the genitive do not form prepositional adverbs. For the use of pronouns with them, see 3.1.2.

3.5.3 **Further notes on the use of the prepositional adverb**

(a) In colloquial speech the prepositional adverb is often split

Da weiß ich nichts **von**	**Da** kann ich nichts **mit** anfangen

This usage was originally typical of North Germany, but it has recently become more widespread.

(b) When the prepositional adverb replaces preposition plus pronoun, the second syllable is usually stressed

da'durch, da'mit, dar'an

In spoken German the first syllable may be reduced, e.g.: *dran, drauf, drin, drunter*. However, if the prepositional adverb replaces a preposition plus a demonstrative, (i.e. = 'with **that**', 'in **that**', etc., see 5.1.1i), then the **first** syllable is stressed, e.g.: '*dadurch*, '*damit*, '*daran*.

'Damit war alles unter	*With that everything was sorted*
Dach und Fach	

(c) The prepositional adverb is often used to anticipate a following *dass*-clause or infinitive clause

Ich verlasse mich **darauf**, dass sie rechtzeitig kommt

Details are given in 6.6.2, 18.6.14 and 19.2.5b.

3.6 **Special uses of the pronoun *es***

The pronoun *es* has an extended range of uses beyond simply referring back to a neuter noun. In many constructions it functions as a grammatical particle (sometimes called a 'clitic').

es cannot be stressed. If emphasis is needed *es* is replaced by *das* for most uses explained in this section, e.g.:

Sind **das** Ihre Handschuhe?	**Das** bist du.	Ich mache **das** schon.

3.6.1 *es* **can refer to elements other than neuter nouns**

(a) *es* **can refer to a whole phrase, sentence or situation**

Willst du die Brötchen holen? Angela macht **es** schon	*Will you get the rolls? Angela is already doing it*
Ich weiß, dass sie gestorben ist, aber Uwe weiß **es** noch nicht	*I know that she is dead, but Uwe doesn't know (it) yet*

(b) *es* **can refer back to the predicate complement of** *sein* **or** *werden*

In English nothing equivalent or a different equivalent is required:

Er soll zuverlässig sein, und ich bin sicher, dass er **es** ist	*He is said to be reliable and I am sure he is*
Ist Jürgen ein guter Schwimmer? Ja, er ist **es**	*Is Jürgen a good swimmer? Yes, he is (one)*
Sein Vater ist Arzt, und er wird **es** auch	*His father is a doctor and he's going to be one, too*

3.6.2 Impersonal and other uses of *es* as the subject of a verb or as the predicate of *sein*

(a) *es* **is used as a formal subject in many impersonal constructions**

(i) With all kinds of impersonal verbs or verbs used in impersonal constructions:

es regnet   **es** klingelt   **es** fehlt mir an Geld   **es** bedarf noch einiger Mühe

Details on the use of *es* as an impersonal subject are given in 18.2.4.

(ii) As an indefinite subject, communicating the idea of a vague, impersonal agent:

Erst wurde es dunkel, dann gewitterte **es**	*First it got dark, then there was thunder and lightning*
Ihn trieb **es** in die schottischen Hochlande (*Zeit*)	*He felt a desire to go the Highlands of Scotland*

(iii) In impersonal reflexive constructions, often with the force of a passive, see 15.4.3b:

Es schreibt sich so leicht mit diesem Filzstift	*It's so easy to write with this felt-tip pen*

(iv) In impersonal passive constructions and in passive constructions with verbs which do not govern the accusative (see 15.1.3–4):

Es wurde in dieser Zeit viel gearbeitet	*A lot of work was done at this time*
Es wurde im Nebenzimmer geredet	*There was talking in the next room*
Es kann ihm doch nicht geholfen werden	*He can't be helped, though*

es is always omitted in this construction if it is not in first position in a main clause, e.g.: *In dieser Zeit wurde viel gearbeitet. Wir wissen doch, dass in dieser Zeit viel gearbeitet wurde*

(b) *es* **can be used as an indeterminate subject with the verbs** *sein* **and** *werden* **followed by a noun or an adjective**

(i) This corresponds to the English use of *it*:

Es ist der Briefträger, ein Polizist	*It's the postman, a policeman*
Es wurde spät	*It got late*
Es ist Mittag	*It's midday*
Es ist Sonntag heute	*It's Sunday today*

es can be omitted in non-initial position in time phrases, e.g.: *Jetzt ist (es) Mittag. Er weiß, dass (es) heute Sonntag ist.*

(ii) *es* can be used with a plural verb, corresponding to English 'they':

Es sind Ausländer	*They're foreigners*
Sind **es** Ihre Handschuhe?	*Are they your gloves?*
Was sind **es**?	*What are they?*

(iii) In this indeterminate function, *es* can refer back to a non-neuter or plural noun, as an alternative to the expected masculine, feminine or plural pronoun:

Seine Mutter lebt noch. **Es/Sie** ist eine alte Frau	*His mother is still alive. She's an old woman*
Siehst du die Kinder dort? **Es/Sie** sind meine	*Do you see the children there? They're mine*

(c) *es* **with** *sein* **and a personal pronoun (= English 'It's me', etc.)**

(i) The German construction differs from the English one, with *es* following the verb:

Du bist **es**. Ich bin **es**	*It's you. It's me*
Seid ihr **es** gewesen?	*Was it you?*
Sie werden **es** wohl sein	*It will probably be them*

(ii) 'Cleft sentence' constructions with relative clauses (like English 'It was you who rang the bell') are based on this construction in German:

Er war **es**, der es mir sagte	*It was him who told me*
Du warst **es** also, der geklingelt hat	*So it was you who rang the bell*

Other cleft sentence constructions, especially those corresponding to the English type 'It was this morning that I saw her', are used much less frequently in German than in English (see 21.2.3a).

(d) *es* **is often used as a 'dummy subject' in initial position in order to permit the 'real' subject to occur later in the sentence**

(i) This construction is particularly frequent if the 'real' subject is a noun phrase with an indefinite article or an indefinite quantifier. It gives more emphasis to the 'real' subject, see 21.2.2d. With *sein*, this *es* corresponds to 'there' in 'there is/are', see 18.2.5b:

Es ist ein Brief für Sie da	*There's a letter for you*
Es waren viele Wolken am Himmel	*There were a lot of clouds in the sky*

This *es* is omitted if it is not in first position in a main clause, e.g.: *Viele Wolken waren am Himmel. Ich weiß, dass ein Brief für mich da ist.*

NB: For *es ist/sind* and *es gibt* for English 'there is/are', see 18.2.5.

(ii) *es* may be used in this construction with any verb in German. The verb agrees with the 'real' subject, not with the *es*:

Es saß eine alte Frau am Fenster	*There was an old woman sitting at the window*
Es hatte sich auch ihr Verhältnis zu den Nachbarn verändert	*Their relationship to their neighbours had changed, too*
Es liegen zwei Briefe für Sie auf dem Schreibtisch	*There are two letters for you lying on the table*

This construction is particularly frequent with verbs of happening:

Es ist gestern ein schwerer Unfall **passiert**	*A serious accident happened yesterday*

In spoken German *da* is a common alternative to *es* in this function: ***Da** hat eine alte Frau am Fenster gesessen*.

(e) *es* **can be used to anticipate a following subordinate or infinitive clause which is the real subject of the verb**

Es freut mich, **dass** du dein Examen bestanden hast	*I am pleased that you have passed your examination*
Es fällt mir ein, **dass** ich ihn schon gesehen haben muss	*It occurs to me that I must already have seen him*
Es war mir nicht möglich, früher **zu** kommen	*It wasn't possible for me to come earlier*
Es liegt mir fern, Schwierigkeiten **zu** machen	*The last thing I want is to make difficulties*

If the clause precedes the verb there is no need for the *es*, e.g.: *Dass du dein Examen bestanden hast, freut mich*.

This 'anticipatory' *es* is sometimes omitted if it is not in first position in a main clause:

Dann fiel **(es)** auf, **dass** er kein weißes Hemd trug	*Then it was noticed that he wasn't wearing a white shirt*
Ihm steht **(es)** nicht zu, ein Urteil **zu** fällen	*It's not up to him to pass judgement*

Usage is variable as to when *es* is omitted; the following general tendencies reflect current usage:

(i) The omission of *es* is especially frequent (but not obligatory) with the following verbs:

auffallen	sich erweisen	gelten *to be valid*	hinzukommen
aufgehen	sich ergeben aus	sich herausstellen	vorschweben
dazukommen	feststehen	hervorgehen	sich zeigen
einfallen	folgen aus		

(ii) With many verbs, especially those expressing feelings and emotions, *es* can be omitted before a following *dass*-clause if the main clause begins with a pronoun:

Ihn interessiert (es) nur, dass ihr Vater viel Geld hat	*The only thing that interests him is that her father's got a lot of money*
Damit hängt (es) natürlich zusammen, dass er im Gefängnis sitzt	*Of course, that's connected with the fact that he's in prison*

(iii) *es* can be omitted with the verb *sein* if the main clause begins with the noun or adjective complement of *sein*:

Wichtig ist (es), dass er es weiß	*It's important for him to know it*
Wichtig ist (es), diesen Satz richtig zu verstehen	*It is important to understand this sentence correctly*
Ein Glück ist (es), dass du kommst	*It's fortunate you're coming*

With *klar*, *leicht*, *möglich*, *schwer* and *wichtig*, *es* can be omitted in these constructions if the main clause begins with a pronoun:

Ihm war (es) völlig klar, dass er jetzt springen musste	*It was quite clear to him that he had to jump now*

NB: *es* is not omitted before *wenn*-clauses: *Mir ist es recht, wenn sie jetzt kommt.*

3.6.3 *es* as the object of a verb

(a) An accusative *es* is often used to anticipate a following infinitive or *dass*-clause which is the object of the verb

Ich konnte **es** kaum ertragen, ihn so leiden zu sehen	*I could hardly endure to see him suffer like that*
Ich habe **es** erlebt, dass Riemann die beste Rede gehalten hat	*I have known Riemann to give the best speech*

(i) This 'anticipatory' *es* is variable, and there are no hard and fast rules as to when it is used and when not. However, it is especially frequent with the following verbs, so that the advice to the foreign learner is to use it with them:

ablehnen	erleben	leiden	verantworten
angewöhnen	ermöglichen	leisten	verdienen
aufgeben	ertragen	leugnen	vergessen
aushalten	fertig bringen	lieben	vermeiden
bedauern	genießen	merken	versäumen
begrüßen	gönnen	mögen	vertragen
bemerken	halten für	schaffen	verzeihen
bereuen	hassen	schätzen	wagen
betrachten als	hindern	übel nehmen	zulassen
dulden	hinnehmen	überlassen	
erfahren	lassen	unterlassen	

The phrases *nicht erwarten können* and *nicht wahrhaben wollen* are also most often found with an anticipatory *es*, as is *finden* followed by an adjective, e.g.: *Ich finde es schön, dass du da bist.*

(ii) Verbs of saying, thinking and knowing, e.g.: *ahnen, denken, erzählen, fühlen, glauben, hören, sagen, wissen* are also often used with an anticipatory *es* in conjunction with certain adverbs and particles, in particular *bereits, deutlich, doch, genug, ja, oft* and *schon*, or when there is an appeal to the listener's prior knowledge, e.g.:

Ich habe (es) ihm deutlich gesagt, dass er schreiben muss	*I've told him clearly enough that he's got to write*
Ich ahnte (es) schon, dass sie schwanger ist	*I already suspected she was pregnant*
Ich weiß (es) ja selber, dass die Ampel rot war	*I know myself that the lights were red*

(b) *es* corresponds to English 'so' as the object of a few verbs, especially *sagen* 'say' and *tun* 'do'

Er hat **es** gesagt	*He said so*
Warum hast du **es** getan?	*Why did you do so?*

es can also be used with *glauben* and *hoffen*, but it is not obligatory:

Kommt sie? – Ich glaube/hoffe (es)	*Is she coming? – I think/hope so*

(c) *es* **is used as an object in a number of idiomatic verbal phrases**

A selection of the most frequent:

es auf etwas absehen	*to be after sth.*
es auf etwas ankommen lassen	*to take a chance on sth.*
es jdm. antun	*to appeal to sb.*
sie hat es ihm angetan	*he fancies her*
es mit jdm./etwas aufnehmen können	*to be a match for sb./sth.*
es bei etwas belassen	*to leave it at sth.*
es weit bringen	*to go far*
es zu etwas bringen	*to attain sth. (esp. a position)*
er hat es zum Oberst gebracht	*he got to be a colonel*
es an etwas fehlen lassen	*to be lacking in sth.*
es eilig haben	*to be in a hurry*
es gut/schlecht haben	*to be (un)fortunate*
es in sich haben	*to be a tough nut to crack*
es sich leicht/schwer machen	*to make it easy/difficult for oneself*
es gut mit jdm. meinen	*to mean well with sb.*
es mit etwas genau nehmen	*to be punctilious with sth.*
es mit jdm. zu tun haben	*to have to deal with sb.*
es sich mit jdm. verdorben haben	*to have fallen out with sb.*
es mit etwas (*dat.*) versuchen	*to try (one's hand at) sth.*

3.6.4 *es* is used with a few adjectives in constructions with the verb(s) *sein* and/or *werden*

in particular with adjectives which govern the genitive of nouns (see 6.5.3), e.g.: *Ich bin es nun überdrüssig.* The following adjectives occur in this construction:

los   müde   satt   teilhaftig   überdrüssig   wert   würdig   zufrieden

Also:

Ich bin **es** gewohnt	*I am used to it*
Ich wurde **es** gewahr (lit.)	*I became aware of it*

NB: When *gewohnt sein* and *wert sein* are used with a following *dass*-clause, the *es* may optionally be used to anticipate the subordinate clause, e.g.: *Ich bin (es) nicht mehr gewohnt, am frühen Morgen aufzustehen.*

4 The articles

German, like English, has a definite and an indefinite article.

The ARTICLES belong to a closed set of small words known as DETERMINERS. They are used with NOUNS to link them to a particular context or situation. Besides the articles, the determiners include all those words, like the DEMONSTRATIVES (*dieser, jener*, etc.), the POSSESSIVES (*mein, sein*, etc.) and INDEFINITES (*einige, etliche*, etc.), which are used to determine nouns and typically have first position in a NOUN PHRASE, before any adjectives, as the chart below shows.

Determiner	Adjective/adjectival phrase	Noun
der	runde	Tisch
ein	schnelles	Auto
eine	sehr langweilige	Stunde
das	in der bayrischen Hauptstadt gebraute	Bier

Only the form and use of the articles are explained in this chapter; the other determiners are dealt with in chapter 5.

The definite and indefinite articles change their form ('decline') to indicate the grammatical categories of the nouns they are used with, i.e. CASE, PLURAL and GENDER. In practice the forms of the article are the main way these categories of the noun are shown in German, and mastering them is an essential stage in being able to use German competently.

In most instances (85%) German and English agree on whether the definite, indefinite or no ('zero') article is used with a noun in a particular context. However, as the articles are very frequent words, the instances where the two languages do not correspond are significant, in particular where German uses a definite article when English has none.

This chapter deals with the **forms** and **uses** of the **articles** as follows:

- The **declension** of the definite and indefinite articles (section 4.1)
- The use of the articles with **abstract nouns**, **generalisations** and **names** (sections 4.2–4.4)
- The use of the articles in **time expressions** (section 4.5)
- The use of the definite article to indicate **possession** (section 4.6)
- Other contexts where **German and English differ** in the use of the articles (sections 4.7–4.8)
- The use of the articles with **p**repositions (section 4.9)

4.1 The declension of the articles

4.1.1 The forms of the DEFINITE ARTICLE

The declension of the definite article *der/die/das* is given in Table 4.1, with further information on these forms given in the remainder of this section.

(a) In spoken German the definite article is relatively unstressed and reduced forms are usual

der: [dɐ]   *die*: [dɪ]   *das*: [d(ə)s] or [s]
den: [d(ə)n] or [n]   *dem*: [d(ə)m] or [m]   *des*: [d(ə)s]

TABLE 4.1 Declension of the definite article

	Masculine	Feminine	Neuter	Plural
Nominative	der	die	das	die
Accusative	den	die	das	die
Genitive	des	der	des	der
Dative	dem	der	dem	den

These reductions are rarely reflected in writing, but they are the norm in unaffected speech, since the full forms, e.g. [deːm], have the force of a demonstrative (i.e. = 'this' or 'that', see 5.1.1). Compare:

Ich habe **'n** Tisch gekauft   *I bought the table*
Ich habe **den** [deːn] Tisch gekauft   *I bought that table*

(b) The definite article cannot be omitted in pairs of words if a different gender or number is involved

In English we can say 'the house and garden(s)' or 'the son(s) and daughter(s)', with the definite article being understood to refer to the second noun as well. This is only possible in German if the two nouns have the same gender or number. In other contexts the second article with its different form **must** be included:

das Haus und **der** Garten/**die** Gärten   **der** Sohn und **die** Tochter/**die** Töchter

On the other hand, *die Söhne und Töchter* is correct, since both nouns are plural and would have the same article.

NB: This rule naturally applies to all the other determiners, and to adjectives used with nouns, e.g.: *sein Sohn und seine Töchter* but *seine Söhne und Töchter*; *guter Wein und gutes Bier* but *alte Männer und Frauen*, see 6.2.6.

(c) Contracted forms of the definite article are used with some prepositions

We can distinguish:

(i) Contractions which are usual in both speech and writing, i.e.:

ans = an + das   **am** = an + dem   **beim** = bei + dem   **ins** = in + das
im = in + dem   **vom** = von + dem   **zum** = zu + dem   **zur** = zu + der

The uncontracted forms are only used if the article is relatively stressed. This often depends on style and sentence rhythm, although many Germans consider the uncontracted forms to be 'better style' in formal writing. Uncontracted forms are also particularly frequent to refer back to something recently mentioned in order to make it clear that it is the one meant. Note the difference between:

Er ging **zu der** Hütte (i.e. the one we were just talking about)
Er ging **zur** Hütte (i.e. the one we all know about).

Where the force of *der* is demonstrative (i.e. = 'that', see 5.1.1), only the uncontracted form is possible:

Einer der Affen war besonders lebhaft.   *One of the monkeys was particularly*
  Klaus wollte unbedingt eine Aufnahme   *active. Klaus really wanted to take*
  von dem Affen machen   *a picture of that monkey*

Similarly, where the noun is particularised, e.g. by a following relative clause, the uncontracted form is usual:

an dem Nachmittag, an dem sie anrief	*on the afternoon when she called*
Er geht **zu der** Schule, wo sein Vater früher war	*He goes to the school where his father used to be*

On the other hand, only the contracted forms are used in set phrases and expressions, e.g.:

am Dienstag	**am** 10. Mai	**am** einfachsten
im Frühling	**im** Freien	**im** Gang
zum Frühstück	**zur** Zeit	**im** Vertrauen
Ich nahm ihn **beim** Wort	Sie war **beim** Kochen	

Compare:

Am Dienstag kam er spät zur Arbeit	*On Tuesday he came to work late*
An dem Dienstag kam er spät zur Arbeit	*That Tuesday he came to work late*

(ii) Contractions which are common in speech and sometimes used in writing. These are:

aufs = auf + das	**durchs** = durch + das	**fürs** = für + das
übers = über + das	**ums** = um + das	**unters** = unter + das

Written German usually prefers the uncontracted forms of these, using the contracted ones chiefly in set phrases, e.g.:

aufs Land fahren	**übers** Herz bringen
fürs Leben gern	**ums** Leben kommen

(iii) Contractions which are usual in spoken German, but only very occasionally found in writing, usually in set phrases or in imitation of casual speech. These are:

außerm	hinterm	hintern	hinters	überm
übern	unterm	untern	vorm	vors

(iv) Other contractions are regular in everyday colloquial speech but not normally used in writing, e.g.:

an'n	bei'n	durch'n	in'n	mit'm	nach'm	seit'm

4.1.2 **The forms of the** INDEFINITE ARTICLE

The declension of the indefinite article *ein* and its negative counterpart *kein* is given in Table 4.2, with further information provided in the remainder of this section.

TABLE 4.2 Declension of the indefinite article *ein* and negative *kein*

	Masculine	Feminine	Neuter	Masculine	Feminine	Neuter	Plural
Nominative	ein	eine	ein	kein	keine	kein	keine
Accusative	einen	eine	ein	keinen	keine	kein	keine
Genitive	eines	einer	eines	keines	keiner	keines	keiner
Dative	einem	einer	einem	keinem	keiner	keinem	keinen

(a) The indefinite article has no plural

Indefinite plural nouns are used without an article, as in English:

Hier gibt es gute Weine   *There are good wines here*

(b) In spoken German the indefinite article is relatively unstressed and reduced forms are frequent

ein: [n]   *eine*: [nə]   *einen*: [nən]
einem: [nəm]   *einer*: [nɐ]   *eines*: [nəs]

These reductions are rare in writing (except to render the flavour of colloquial dialogue) but they are the norm in unaffected speech, where the full forms, e.g. [aɪn], [aɪnən], etc., would be interpreted as the numeral *ein* 'one'. Compare:

Ich habe **'n** Buch gekauft   *I bought a book*
Ich habe **ein** [aɪn] Buch gekauft   *I bought **one** book*

(c) The indefinite article *ein* has a negative form *kein*

Unlike *ein*, *kein* has a plural form, and its declension is given in Table 4.2. It is used chiefly where a corresponding positive sentence would have an indefinite article or no article, and it is thus usually the equivalent of English *not . . . a*, *not . . . any* or *no*. Further details on its use are given in 5.5.16:

Es war ein angenehmer Anblick   Es war **kein** angenehmer Anblick
Kennst du einen Arzt?   Kennst du **keinen** Arzt?
Hier gibt es gute Weine   Hier gibt es **keine** guten Weine
Ich habe Geld   Ich habe **kein** Geld

4.2 Articles with abstract nouns

4.2.1 German often uses the definite article with abstract nouns where English typically has no article

This is particularly the case where the reference is to a specific and definite whole, known and familiar to the speaker and listener, e.g.:

(a) abstract nouns

Er fürchtet **das Alter**   *He is afraid of old age*
Er liebte **die Demokratie**   *He loved democracy*
Wir hängen von **der Industrie** ab   *We depend on industry*
Die Zeit vergeht   *Time passes*
Das Volk lebt **im Elend** (*Spiegel*)   *The people are living in misery*
Die Menschheit braucht nichts nötiger   *Humanity needs nothing more*
   als **den Frieden**   *urgently than peace*

(b) infinitives used as nouns

Er hat **das Schwimmen** verlernt   *He has forgotten how to swim*
Das Kaffeetrinken kam im 17.   *Coffee-drinking came to Europe in*
   Jahrhundert nach Europa   *the 17th century*

4.2.2 **In certain contexts abstract nouns are used with no article**

Clear rules are difficult to formulate precisely, but the following generalisations are broadly valid:

(a) No article is used in contexts where the idea is referred to not as a whole, but in a vaguely general, indefinite and partial sense, which comes as a new idea in the context

Typically in such contexts *some* or *any* can often be inserted in the corresponding English sentence without changing its essential meaning:

Zu dieser Aufgabe gehört **Mut**	*This task demands (some) courage*
Es war nicht das erste Mal, dass **Verrat** seinen Lebensweg gekreuzt hatte (*Hermlin*)	*It was not the first time that (some) treachery had crossed his path*
Unentschlossenheit wäre jetzt verhängnisvoll	*(Any) indecision now would be fatal*
Bewegung ist gesund	*(Any) exercise is healthy*

Compare the following sentences:

Unter seinen Anhängern entstand **Misstrauen**	*(Some) distrust arose among his followers*
Das Misstrauen wächst unter seinen Anhängern	*Distrust is growing among his followers*

In the first sentence 'distrust' is a new concept of a rather **v**ague, general and indefinite nature. In the second it is a specific and familiar notion.

In practice such a partial or indefinite sense is often present when an abstract noun, particularly one denoting a human quality or emotion, is used with an adjective. In such contexts no article is used in German:

Ich verachte **kleinliche Eifersucht**	*I despise (any) petty jealousy*
Im Heer wuchs **neuer Mut**	*In the army new courage was growing*
Er neigt zu **unnötiger Verschwendung**	*He tends to unnecessary extravagance*

(b) In proverbs, sayings and set phrases:

Alter schützt vor **Torheit** nicht	*There's no fool like an old fool*
Not kennt kein Gebot	*Necessity knows no law*
Stolz ist keine Tugend	*Pride is not a virtue*

(c) In a few other contexts

- in general statements, see 4.3.1.
- in pairs of words and enumerations, see 4.8.1.
- in some constructions with the verbs *sein* and *werden*, see 4.8.2.
- in many phrasal verbs, see 4.2.3.

4.2.3 **The use of the article with abstract nouns in phrasal verbs**

e.g.: *Abschied nehmen, in Druck geben, in Erfahrung bringen*

The use of a definite or no article with these is often a matter of individual idiom, e.g.: *zum Abschluss bringen* but *zu Ende bringen*, and a dictionary should be consulted. However, the following general rules usually apply:

(a) Infinitives used as nouns have a definite article in phrasal verbs with prepositions

ins Rollen kommen, **zum** Kochen bringen

(b) Feminine nouns in phrasal verbs with *zu* have a definite article

zur Kenntnis bringen, **zur** Verfügung stehen

(c) Phrasal verbs with *außer* and *unter*, and most of those with *in* have no article

außer Gefahr sein, jdn. **unter** Druck setzen, jdn. **in** Verlegenheit bringen

NB: Those with *in* followed by an infinitive used as a noun **do** have an article, see (a) above.

(d) Most phrasal verbs with *gehen*, *halten* and *setzen* have no article with the noun

in Erfüllung gehen, **in** Gang halten, **in** Brand setzen

(e) Abstract nouns used with *haben* have no article

Aufenthalt haben, Angst haben, Durst haben, Geduld haben, Mut haben

(f) Most phrasal verbs consisting of a verb and an object noun with no preposition have no article

Anspruch erheben, Antwort geben, Abschied nehmen, Rücksicht üben, Krieg führen, Not leiden, Zeit sparen

(g) An article is used with phrasal verbs if the noun is qualified by an adjective

This applies even if the phrasal verb normally lacks an article:

jdn. in Gefahr bringen	*lead sb. into danger*
jdn. in (eine) große Gefahr bringen	*lead sb. into great danger*
jdn. in die größte Gefahr bringen	*lead sb. into the greatest danger*

4.2.4 The use of the article with some other groups of nouns is similar to that with abstract nouns

(a) Names of substances

These have a definite article if they are understood as general concepts, but no article if they are used in an indefinite or partial sense:

Die Butter kostete 3 Euro das Pfund	*Butter cost 3 euros a pound*
Faraday hat **die Elektrizität** erforscht	*Faraday investigated electricity*
Die Bauern bauen hier **Roggen** an	*The farmers grow rye here*
Wir importieren **Kaffee** aus Afrika	*We import coffee from Africa*

NB: (i) The definite article occurs in some set phrases, e.g.: *beim Bier sitzen; Das steht nur auf dem Papier; Man kann nicht von der Luft leben.*
   (ii) Usage is optional in generalisations, see 4.3, e.g.: *(Die) Elektrizität ist eine wichtige Energiequelle.*

(b) Names of meals

A definite article is used if they are referred to as known quantities, but the article is optional if the reference is indefinite or partial:

Das Mittagessen wird um 13 Uhr eingenommen	*Lunch is taken at 1 p.m.*
Wir sollen uns vor **dem Frühstück** treffen	*We are to meet before breakfast*
Ich habe **(das) Mittagessen** bestellt	*I have ordered lunch*
Wann bekommen wir **(das) Frühstück**?	*When are we getting breakfast?*

(c) Names of sicknesses and diseases

These have a definite article when they are referred to in general as known quantities, but there is no article when they are referred to in an indefinite or partial sense, or as a new idea in the context, particularly after *haben*:

Er ist an **der Schwindsucht** gestorben	*He died of consumption*
Sie ist an **den Masern** erkrankt	*She fell ill with measles*
Die Grippe hat Tausende weggerafft	*Influenza carried off thousands*
Ich habe **Kopfschmerzen**, **Gelbsucht**	*I've got a headache, jaundice*

Singular names of specific illnesses are used with the indefinite article to refer to a bout of that disease. This is in particular the case when the noun is modified by an adjective:

Er ist an **einer Lungenentzündung** gestorben	*He died of (a bout of) pneumonia*
Er hat **einen Schnupfen**, **eine Erkältung**	*He's got a cold*

(d) Names of languages

These nouns from adjectives have two forms, see 6.4.6a:

(i) an inflected one, always used with the definite article, which refers to the language in a general sense:

Das Spanische ist **dem Portugiesischen** sehr nahe verwandt	*Spanish is very closely related to Portuguese*
eine Übersetzung aus **dem Russischen** **ins Deutsche**	*a translation from Russian into German*

(ii) an uninflected form, which refers to the language in a specific context. With this, article use is similar to that in English:

das **Deutsch** der Auswanderer	*the German of the emigrants*
Luthers **Deutsch**	*Luther's German*
Sie kann, versteht, lernt **Deutsch**	*She knows, understands, is learning German*
Sie kann **kein Deutsch**	*She doesn't know any German*
eine Zusammenfassung **in Deutsch**	*a summary in German*

4.2.5 A definite article is usual in German with some other nouns which often lack an article in English

(a) historical periods, literary and philosophical movements, religions

der deutsche Expressionismus	*German Expressionism*
Diese Auffassung ist charakteristisch für **den Islam**	*This view is characteristic of Islam*
Marx begreift **den Feudalismus** als notwendige Stufe der historischen Entwicklung (*Knaur*)	*Marx considers feudalism to be a necessary stage in the process of history*

(b) arts and sciences

Ich erwarte von **der Literatur** mehr Anregung als **vom Leben** (*Grass*)	*I expect more stimulus from literature than from life*
Darüber schweigt **die Geschichte**	*History is silent about that*
ein Lehrbuch **der Astronomie**	*a textbook of astronomy*
Sie liebt **die Musik**	*She loves music*

NB: No article is used for school or university subjects, e.g.: *Sie hat eine Zwei in* **Geschichte** *aber eine Vier in* **Mathe**. *Else studiert* **Astronomie** *in Göttingen.*

(c) institutions, company titles and buildings

Sie geht in **die Schule**	*She goes to school*
Er wurde **ins Parlament** gewählt	*He was elected to parliament*
Die Bundesrepublik gehört **der NATO** an	*The Federal Republic belongs to NATO*
Er arbeitet bei **der BASF**	*He works for BASF*
im Kölner **Dom, das** Ulmer **Rathaus**	*in Cologne cathedral, Ulm town hall*

NB: No article is used with names of buildings with a proper name in apposition, e.g.: *Schloss Sanssouci, Burg Gibichstein, Kloster Beuron.*

4.3 The use of articles in generalizations

4.3.1 Generalisations about people and things can be expressed in different ways

Compare the following possibilities in German and English:

(a)	Die Tanne ist ein Nadelbaum	*The fir is a conifer*
(b)	Die Tannen sind Nadelbäume	[no direct English equivalent]
(c)	Eine Tanne ist ein Nadelbaum	*A fir is a conifer*
(d)	Tannen sind Nadelbäume	*Firs are conifers*

German tends to use constructions like (a) above, especially in writing, whereas English has a clear preference for sentences like (d), so that the following example illustrates a characteristic type of equivalence:

Das Auto ist der Fluch der modernen Stadt (*Zeit*)	*Cars are the curse of modern cities*

Construction (b), with a definite article and a plural noun, is quite common in German, but it is only used in English with a limited number of nouns (especially nouns of nationality). Compare:

Die Beschwerden vermehren sich	*Complaints are increasing*
Die Steuern waren drückend (*Brecht*)	*Taxes were oppressive*
Die Italiener lieben die Musik	*The Italians love music*

English 'man'; in the sense 'human being' is usually found with no article, while *der Mensch*, with a definite article, is regular in German in general statements of type (a) above, e.g.:

Der Mensch ist ein seltsames Geschöpf	*Man is a strange animal*

4.3.2 Nouns which have no plural can be used either with the definite article or with no article in general statements

This applies in particular to abstract nouns and names of substances:

(Der) Frieden ist das höchste Gut der Menschen	*Peace is man's greatest good*
(Das) Rauchen schadet der Gesundheit	*Smoking is injurious to health*
(Das) Eisen ist ein Metall	*Iron is a metal*

4.4 **The use of articles with geographical and other proper names**

4.4.1 **Usage with geographical and astronomical names**

(a) Masculine names of countries

With these, the definite article is usual, but optional:

(der) Libanon **(der)** Iran **in/im** Sudan

With masculine names of regions or provinces the use of the definite article is the norm, e.g.: *der Balkan, der Bosporus.*

(b) Feminine and plural names of countries and regions

These are **always** used with a definite article:

die Schweiz	**die** Türkei	**die** Ukraine
die Lausitz	**die** Normandie	**die** Steiermark
die USA	**die** Niederlande	

(c) Neuter names of countries and cities

No article is used with most of these:

Deutschland Norwegen Spanien Leipzig London Ulm

However, some neuter names of regions and provinces are normally used with the article:

das Elsass	**das** Engadin	**das** Ries	**das** Wallis *Valais*
das Rheinland	**das** Vogtland (and all others in *-land*)		

Traditional German regions are sometimes designated by an adjectival noun, e.g.: *Jetzt kommen wir **ins Bayrische**; Das Dorf liegt **im Thüringischen**.* The definite article is always used with these.

NB: Use of the article is optional with *Tirol: in/im Tirol.*

(d) Other geographical and astronomical names always have a definite article

This is so even where English has no article:

der Mont Blanc	**der** Genfer See	**der** Bodensee *Lake Constance*
der Mars	**die** Venus	**der** Jupiter

(e) The definite article is commonly used to refer to street names

Ich wohne in **der** Goethestraße
Wir treffen uns auf **dem** Schlossplatz
Der Alexanderweg ist die zweite Querstraße **zur** Humboldtstraße

However, no article is used in addresses: *Frau Gerlinde Haarmann, Weserstraße 247, 34125 Kassel.*

4.4.2 **In standard German there is usually no article with personal names**

There are some exceptions to this rule:

(a) In colloquial speech a definite article is frequent with names

Ich sehe **die** Monika   Gestern war ich bei **der** Frau Schmidt

This usage is particularly characteristic of South German speech, but it has spread into North Germany in recent years.

(b) To clarify case or gender

(see also 4.7.1):

der Vortrag **des** Klaus Müller   Das hat Klaus **dem** Wolfgang Pedersen gesagt
Ich habe eben mit **der** Rupp (i.e. **Frau** Rupp, NOT **Herr** Rupp) gesprochen

(c) To individualise the person concerned more strongly

Der Lehmann hat einen ausgezeichneten Vortrag gehalten
die Briefe Leopold Mozarts an **das** Nannerl (*Hildesheimer*)

(d) to refer to characters in plays

Er hat in der vorigen Saison **den** Hamlet gespielt

4.4.3 All geographical and proper names are used with a definite article when qualified by an adjective

das heutige Deutschland
das viktorianische England
das zerstörte Dresden
das kalte Moskau
der junge Heinrich
der alte Doktor Schulze

This applies also to saints' names: *der heilige Franziskus* 'Saint Francis'.

4.5 The use of articles in time expressions

4.5.1 Names of months and seasons usually have the definite article

Der April war verregnet
Wir fahren **im August** nach Italien
Der Frühling war dieses Jahr spät
Im Winter friert der Bach zu

The names of the months have no article after prepositions other than *an*, *bis zu* and *in*, see 4.5.3, or after *Anfang*, *Mitte*, *Ende*:

Es war kalt für April
Der Fahrplan gilt von Mai bis Oktober
Ende Februar hat es geschneit
Er kommt erst Anfang Mai

No article is used with these words after *sein* and *werden*, see 4.8.2c, e.g.: *Es ist, wird Sommer; Es ist Januar*, or when the name is qualified by *nächsten, letzten, vorigen, vergangenen*: *nächsten Oktober, letzten Herbst*.

4.5.2 **The major festivals have no article**

Weihnachten   Silvester   Neujahr   Pfingsten   Ostern

Note though: *der Heilige Abend* 'Christmas Eve', *der Karfreitag* 'Good Friday'

4.5.3 **All time nouns are used with the definite article after the prepositions *an*, *bis zu* and *in***

am Mittwoch	**am** 27. Januar	**bis zum** Montag
am Tag *by day*	**in der** Nacht *at night*	**in der** vorigen Woche
in der Gegenwart *at present*	**im** Jahre 1945	

After other prepositions in time expressions there is normally no article, see 11.5.

4.6 **Definite article or possessive?**

4.6.1 **The definite article is used to refer to parts of the body and articles of clothing**

(a) This is usual in German, whereas in English a possessive determiner is used

Hast du **die** Zähne geputzt?	*Have you cleaned your teeth?*
Sie hat **das** Bein gebrochen	*She has broken her leg*
Sie strich **den** Rock glatt	*She smoothed her skirt*

Das Mädchen zog **den** rötlichen Kamm aus **dem** Haar, nahm ihn in **den** Mund und fing an, mit **den** Fingern **die** Frisur zurechtzuzupfen (*Böll*)

A possessive dative is frequent in such constructions, and it is essential when the relevant person is not the subject of the verb, see 2.5.4, e.g.:

Sie nahm es **(sich)** in den Mund	*She put it in her mouth*
Die Mütze fiel **mir** vom Kopf	*My cap fell off my head*
Wir zogen **dem Verletzten** die Hose aus	*We took the injured man's trousers off*

(b) However, a possessive determiner is used rather than the definite article in a few contexts

(i) when the owner has been named in a previous sentence, or when the part of the body or article of clothing is the first element in the sentence:

Ein Fremder erschien. **Seine** Stirn glänzte.	*A stranger appeared. His forehead glistened.*
Sein Anzug war altmodisch	*His suit was old-fashioned*
Meine Beine sind nicht krumm (*Brecht*)	*My legs aren't crooked*

(ii) when the owner must be specified, but the verb does not permit the use of a possessive dative:

Ich erblickte eine Wespe auf **meinem** Ärmel	*I caught sight of a wasp on my sleeve*
Sie legte **ihre** Hand auf **seine** Hand (*Wendt*)	*She put her hand on his hand*

(iii) to emphasise the owner or avoid ambiguity:

Langsam hob sie **ihre** rechte Hand	*Slowly, she raised her right hand*
Hast du **deine** Zähne geputzt?	*Have you cleaned your teeth?*
Zieh (dir) lieber **deinen** Mantel an!	*Put your coat on (i.e. not mine!)*
Ich zog mir **seine** Hose an	*I put his trousers on*

4.6.2 **The definite article is used rather than a possessive with some abstract nouns**

This is particularly frequent with nouns denoting human attributes and emotions, which are thus seen as 'part' of the person concerned. A possessive dative may occur under the same conditions as with body parts:

Du musst versuchen, **die/deine** Angst zu überwinden	*You must try to overcome your fear*
Ich werde ihm **die Faulheit** austreiben	*I shall rid him of his laziness*
Der Appetit ist mir vergangen	*I've lost my appetite*

4.6.3 **The definite or indefinite article is commonly used with the adjective *eigen***

The appropriate one of these can be an alternative to using a possessive determiner.

Er hat **den/seinen** eigenen Sohn erschlagen	*He has killed his own son*
Jetzt haben wir **eine/unsere** eigene Wohnung	*We've got our own flat/a flat of our own now*

Note, as a set phrase with no article: *Das haben wir **mit eigenen Augen** gesehen.*

4.7 **Miscellaneous uses of the definite article**

4.7.1 **The definite article is sometimes used to make the case of a noun clear**

i.e. even in contexts where an article would not usually be expected. This applies in particular in the genitive and dative cases.

(a) Examples of the definite article used to mark genitive case

der Geruch **des** Seetangs	*the smell of seaweed*
ein Ausdruck **des** Erstaunens	*an expression of surprise*

In practice no noun (other than a proper name) can be used in the genitive without a determiner or an adjective which shows the case. In this way, the article is essential in the first of the sentences below to show that the noun is in the genitive case:

Sie bedarf **der** Ruhe	
Sie braucht Ruhe	*She needs rest*

If ambiguity could arise from the use of a definite article, then a phrase with *von* must be used (see 2.4). Thus 'the smell of wild boar' has to be given with *der Geruch von Eber* if *der Geruch des Ebers* could be understood in the context to mean 'the smell of the wild boar'.

(b) Examples of the definite article used to mark dative case

Ich ziehe Kaffee **dem** Tee vor	*I prefer coffee to tea*
Dieses Metall gleicht **dem** Gold	*This metal resembles gold*
Er hat sich **der** Physik gewidmet	*He devoted himself to physics*

4.7.2 **The definite article can be used in a distributive sense**

In such contexts English commonly uses the indefinite article or 'per':

Die Butter kostete 3 Euro **das** Pfund	*The butter cost 3 euros a/per pound*
Sie kommt zweimal **die** Woche zu uns (*or*: zweimal in der Woche)	*She comes to us twice a week*
Wir fuhren 80 Kilometer **die** Stunde	*We were doing 80 kilometres per hour*

pro (see 20.1.7d) and (with measurements) *je*, both without an article, are common alternatives to the definite article:

Wir zahlten 2 Euro **pro/je** Meter	*We paid 2 euros a/per metre*
Es kostet 20 Euro **pro** Stunde	*It costs 20 euros an hour*

4.7.3 **The definite article is always used with *meist***

Er hat **das meiste** Geld	*He has (the) most money*
die meisten Jungen	*most of the boys*
die meisten meiner Freunde	*most of my friends*

4.8 **Miscellaneous uses of the zero article**

In a number of contexts no article is used in German where the usual English equivalent construction has a definite or indefinite article.

4.8.1 **Nouns used in pairs or enumerations often lack the definite article**

This can even be the case when a single noun in the same construction would require an article. In many cases these are conventional or set phrases:

Form und Inhalt	*(in) form and content*
Tag und Nacht	*day and night*
mit Müh und Not	*with great difficulty*
Es geht um Leben und Tod	*It's a matter of life and death*
in Hülle und Fülle	*in plenty*
Rhein, Main und Donau sind schiffbare Flüsse	*The Rhine, the Main and the Danube are navigable rivers*
In Industrie und Handwerk bleiben Tausende von Arbeitsplätzen unbesetzt (*Spiegel*)	*In industry and trade thousands of job vacancies remain unfilled*

4.8.2 **No article is used in some constructions in the predicate of the verbs *sein, werden, bleiben***

(a) With nouns denoting professions, nationality, origins or classes of people in general

Er ist **Arzt, Bäcker, Installateur**	*He is a doctor, a baker, a plumber*
Ich bin **Deutscher, Engländer, Schwede**	*I am a German, an Englishman, a Swede*
Franz ist **gläubiger Katholik**	*Franz is a devout catholic*
Helmut blieb **Junggeselle**	*Helmut remained a batchelor*
Danach wurde er **Marxist**	*After that he became a Marxist*

But the indefinite article **is** used if the noun refers to a specific individual, not to a class of person:

Sie ist **eine bekannte Anwältin**	*She is a well-known lawyer*
Er ist **ein richtiger Schauspieler**	*He's a real actor*

The indefinite article is also used in descriptive constructions with professions and positions, e.g.:

Er hatte den Titel **eines Professors**, die Stelle **eines Untersuchungsrichters**
He had the title of professor, the position of examining magistrate

(b) With certain nouns, mainly in formal writing

i.e. *Bedingung, Fakt, Gegenstand, Grundlage, Sache, Schwerpunkt, Tatsache, Voraussetzung, Ziel*. These usually precede the verb *sein*:

Tatsache ist, dass . . .	*It is a fact that . . .*
Bedingung dafür ist, dass er den Vertrag unterschreibt	*The condition for this is that he signs the contract*
Auch Anfang Januar brauchen Autofahrer wieder Geduld. **Grund** sind einige Baustellen, Straßensperrungen und Verkehrsänderungen (*MM*)	*At the beginning of January, too, drivers will need to be patient again. This is because of some road works, road closures and diversions*

(c) With the names of the months and the seasons, and abstract nouns used in a general sense

This goes against the usual rule with these, see 4.2 and 4.5:

Es war schon **April**	*It was already April*
Jetzt ist **Sommer**	*It's summer now*
Heute Abend ist **Tanz**	*There's a dance on tonight*
Das ist **Geschmackssache**	*That is a matter of taste*

4.8.3 No article is used in phrases introduced by *als* 'as'

Ich kannte ihn **als Junge**	*I knew him when I was a boy*
Er sprach **als Franzose**	*He spoke as a Frenchman*
die Bedeutung des Passes **als wichtige(r) Handelstraße**	*the significance of the pass as an important trade route*
Als überzeugter Demokrat kann ich das nicht gutheißen	*As a convinced democrat, I cannot approve of that*
Er gilt **als bester Tenor** der Neuzeit	*He is reckoned to be the best tenor of modern times*

NB: (i) An article can be used with verbs which are usually followed by *als*, e.g. *ansehen, betrachten, fühlen, gelten: Er gilt als* **(der)** *beste Tenor der Neuzeit.*
   (ii) The article can be used in the genitive case, e.g.: *mit der Verhaftung des Generals als* **(des)** *eigentlichen Putschführers.*

4.8.4 The article can be omitted in appositional phrases in formal written registers

Zunächst kamen wir nach Florenz, **(der) Hauptstadt der Toskana**	*First we arrived in Florence, the capital of Tuscany*
dieses Zürich, **(der) Treffpunkt der Kaufleute** (*Frisch*)	*this Zurich, the meeting place of businessmen*
Neil Armstrong, **(der) amerikanischer Astronaut**, betrat als erster Mensch den Mond (*Zeit*)	*Neil Armstrong, the American astronaut, was the first man to set foot on the moon*

4.8.5 **No article is used in some formulaic expressions referring to people**

This usage is restricted to formal, especially official registers, e.g.:

Angeklagter hat gestanden, dass . . .	*The accused confessed that . . .*
Unterzeichneter bittet um rasche Entscheidung seiner Angelegenheit	*The undersigned requests a speedy decision in the matter concerning him*
Verfasser behauptet, das Problem gelöst zu haben	*The author claims to have solved the problem*

4.8.6 **Articles are often omitted for stylistic effect in headlines and advertisements**

Verbrechen gestanden. Münchner Kaufmann vom Geschäftspartner erschlagen (*HA*)	*Crime admitted. Munich businessman killed by partner*
Wohnung mit Bad gesucht möglichst nahe Stadtzentrum	*Flat with bathroom required as close as possible to city centre*

4.8.7 **The most usual equivalent in German for the English indefinite determiners 'some' or 'any' is to use the noun without an article**

Ich möchte **Suppe**	*I should like some soup*
Brauchen Sie **Marken**?	*Do you need any stamps?*
Ich habe **(rote) Äpfel** gekauft	*I bought some (red) apples*
wenn du noch **Schwierigkeiten** hast	*if you have any more difficulties*
Hast du **Geld** bei dir?	*Have you got any money on you?*

For further information on German equivalents for *some* and *any*, see 5.5.9b.

4.8.8 **No article is used with adverbial genitives**

e.g.: *schweren Herzens* 'with a heavy heart', see 2.3.5b.

4.9 **Article use with prepositions**

Article use with prepositions can be quite idiomatic. Usage in phrasal verbs and time phrases is dealt with in sections 4.2.3 and 4.5.3. More detail, in particular concerning differences between English and German use of articles in set phrases with prepositions, can be found in Chapter 20 under the individual prepositions. In this section we deal with some cases where general rules can be stated.

4.9.1 **The indefinite article is often omitted in adverbial or adjectival phrases consisting of preposition, adjective plus noun**

This is common where a set phrase is extended by an adjective and is characteristic of formal registers:

ein fahrender Virtuose **mit italienischem Namen** (*Th. Mann*)	*a travelling virtuoso with an Italian name*
ein Mann, der **solchem Rat** nicht folgte und **zu schrecklichem Ende** kam (*Hildesheimer*)	*a man who failed to follow such advice and met a terrible end*

Wir erhielten den Betrag **in frei**   *We received the sum in a freely convertible currency*
konvertierbarer Währung

This usage is also the norm in phrases with *mit* which are alternatives to adverbial genitives (see 2.3.5b):

Sie ging **mit schnellem Schritt** (= schnellen   *She crossed the road at a fast pace*
Schrittes) über die Straße

4.9.2 The definite article can be omitted in prepositional phrases if the following noun is qualified by a genitive or another prepositional phrase

auf Anraten des Arztes	*on the advice of a doctor*
in Gegenwart von zwei Kollegen	*in the presence of two colleagues*
die Studie, die Smith noch **in Diensten** der Bank verfasste, . . . (*Spiegel*)	*the study which Smith wrote in the service of the bank . . .*
unter Ausnutzung aller Möglichkeiten	*by exploiting all possibilities*

4.9.3 A few prepositions are used with no article in some or all of their uses

The most noteworthy (because of the differences to English) are:

(a) *mit* **is often used with no article when a part-whole relationship is involved**

ein Zimmer **mit Bad**	ein Opel **mit Schiebedach**
ein Hut **mit breitem Rand**	eine Suppe **mit Wursteinlage**

(b) *ohne* **is used with no article in German in cases where English has an indefinite article**

Er geht gern **ohne Hut**
Ich übersetzte den Text **ohne Wörterbuch, ohne Mühe**
Sie trat **ohne Brille** auf
Wie hast du die Tür **ohne Schlüssel** aufgemacht?

(c) A few other prepositions are used without a following article

Most of these belong to formal written registers. More information is given under the individual prepositions in Chapter 20:

ab: ab ersten/erstem Mai; ab Bahnhof; Preise ab Fabrik *ex works*
gemäß: Die Angelegenheit wurde gemäß Verordnung entschieden

NB: An article is normally used if *gemäß* follows the noun, e.g.: *den geltenden Verordnungen gemäß*.

infolge:	Die Straße ist infolge schlechten Wetters gesperrt
kraft:	Er handelte kraft Gesetzes
laut:	Der Fahrer wurde laut Gesetz verurteilt
mangels:	Der Angeklagte wurde mangels Beweises freigesprochen
per:	per Einschreiben *by registered mail*; per Anhalter fahren *to hitch-hike*
pro:	pro Stück; der Preis pro Tag *per day*, pro männlichen Angestellten
von . . . wegen:	Diese Angelegenheit muss von Amts wegen geklärt werden
zwecks:	Junge Dame möchte netten, gebildeten Herrn zwecks Heirat kennen lernen (*FAZ*)

5 Other determiners and pronouns

DETERMINERS are a limited set of small words used with NOUNS to relate them to a particular context or situation.

They typically occupy the first position in a NOUN PHRASE, before any adjectives.

Determiner	Adjective/adjectival phrase	Noun
dieser	heidnische	Gott
einige	fleißige	Studenten
sein	ultramodernes	Raumschiff
jedes	vom Kultbuchautor Adams erfundene	Computerspiel

The determiners include the DEFINITE and INDEFINITE ARTICLES, which are dealt with in Chapter 4, and all other words used to determine nouns, like the DEMONSTRATIVES (*dieser, jener*, etc.), the POSSESSIVES (*mein, sein*, etc.), the INTERROGATIVES (e.g. *welcher*) and indefinites (*einige, etliche*, etc.).

PRONOUNS are a limited set of small words which stand in place of NOUNS or NOUN PHRASES.
In particular they stand for nouns or noun phrases which have already been mentioned or which do not need to be repeated in full. They include the PERSONAL PRONOUNS, which are dealt with in Chapter 3, DEMONSTRATIVE PRONOUNS, POSSESSIVE PRONOUNS, INTERROGATIVE PRONOUNS, the RELATIVE PRONOUNS (the 'who' and 'which' words) and INDEFINITE PRONOUNS.

Determiners and pronouns qualify or stand in place of nouns. Thus, in German, they typically change their form ('decline') to indicate the same grammatical categories as nouns, i.e. CASE, PLURAL and GENDER. In German, many of the same basic forms can be used either as determiners or pronouns, e.g.:

   Mein Auto fährt sehr schnell (determiner) – **Meines** fährt aber schneller (pronoun)

A few of them (like *mein/meines* in the example) have different sets of endings depending on whether they are being used as determiners or pronouns, which is why it is important to distinguish between these.

This chapter deals with the following sets of determiners and pronouns:

- **demonstratives** (section 5.1)
- **possessives** (section 5.2)
- **interrogatives** (section 5.3)
- the **relative pronouns** (section 5.4)
- **indefinites**, **quantifiers** and other determiners and pronouns (section 5.5)

5.1 Demonstratives

5.1.1 *der* 'that'

der is the most frequent demonstrative in spoken German. It can be used to point in a general way to something distant or something near at hand and thus it can be the equivalent of both 'this' and 'that'.

(a) *der*, when used as a determiner, has exactly the same written forms as the definite article

i.e. as given in Table 4.1. However, it differs from the definite article in speech because it is always stressed, e.g. *den* [deːn], *der* [deːɐ], etc. It is thus quite distinct from the definite article, whose spoken forms are typically always unstressed and reduced, e.g. *'n, d'n* or *d'r*, etc., see 4.1.1. Compare:

Ich möchte ein Stück von **d'r** Wurst	*I would like a piece of the sausage*
Ich möchte ein Stück von **der** [deːɐ] Wurst	*I would like a piece of this/that sausage*

In written German the demonstrative force of *der* may sometimes be clear from the context, especially when a relative clause follows, e.g.:

Ich kann dir **die** Hefte der Zeitschrift schicken, die dir noch fehlen	*I can send you those issues of the journal which you haven't got yet*
Bei **der** Lehrerin würde ich auch nichts lernen	*I wouldn't learn anything from that teacher either*

In many cases, though, it would be difficult to tell the demonstrative *der* apart from the definite article in writing, and *dieser* or *derjenige* is preferred. In colloquial speech the demonstrative force of *der* can be strengthened by adding *da* or *hier* after the noun, depending on whether 'this' or 'that' is meant, e.g. *der* Mann da 'that man', **der** Mann hier 'this man'. These forms are not used in writing.

NB: In spoken German, especially in the South, *denen* is sometimes used rather than *den* in the dative plural, e.g. Mit **denen** Sachen *kann ich eh nichts anfangen*. This is not generally regarded as standard.

(b) The declension of demonstrative *der* used as a pronoun

This is identical to the declension of the determiner, except in the **genitive**, and in the **dative plural**. The forms are given in Table 5.1.

TABLE 5.1 Declension of *der* used as a pronoun

	Masculine	Feminine	Neuter	Plural
Nominative	der	die	das	die
Accusative	den	die	das	die
Genitive	dessen	deren	dessen	deren/derer
Dative	dem	der	dem	denen

NB: The genitive forms *dessen* and *deren* are compounded with a following *-halben*, *-wegen* or *-willen*, with *-t-* inserted, e.g. *dessentwegen, um derentwillen*, etc., see 20.4.1and 20.4.3

(c) The use of *der* as a pronoun

When it is being used as a pronoun, *der* cannot be confused with the definite article, as there is no noun following, and it is used freely in writing. It usually corresponds to English 'the one'/'this one'/'that one':

mein Wagen und **der** meines Bruders	*my car and my brother's*
Die Sache ist nämlich **die**: Er ist schon verheiratet	*It's like this: he's already married*
Diese Seife ist besser als **die**, die ich gebrauche	*This soap is better than the one I use*
Wir können **dem** nicht so viel Bedeutung beimessen	*We cannot attach so much importance to that*
Die sind mir zu teuer	*Those (ones) are too expensive for me*
Das Buch liegt auf dem Tisch. Ja, auf **dem** da drüben	*The book's lying on the table. Yes, on that one over there*

(d) Pronominal *der* is often used instead of a third person pronoun

This usage is frequent in writing to refer to things, but to refer to persons it is more typical of colloquial speech, , see 3.4.2:

Ist der Teller kaputt? Ja, **den** hat Astrid fallen lassen	*Is the plate broken? Yes, Astrid dropped it*
Keine Möwen. **Die** waren weiter draußen (*Grass*)	*No gulls. They were further offshore*
Hast du Peter gesehen? Ja, **der ist** gerade reingekommen	*Have you seen Peter? Yes, he's just come in.*

(e) *der* can be strengthened by the addition of *da* or *hier*

This makes it more clear whether '**this** one (here)' or '**that** one (there)' is being referred to, e.g. *das da* 'that one', *das hier* 'this one'. This usage is limited to informal colloquial speech.

(f) The genitive of the pronoun *der* can be used for a possessive pronoun to avoid ambiguity

i.e. where it might not be completely clear what *sein* or *ihr* could refer to

Sie war die Tochter des Schriftstellers Thomas Mann und **dessen** viertes Kind (*Spiegel*)	*She was the daughter of the writer Thomas Mann and his fourth child*
Dennoch wurden sie alle geprägt von ihrer Stadt und **deren** geistiger Tradition	*Nevertheless they were all moulded by their city and its intellectual tradition*
Erboste Bauern nahmen britische LKW-Fahrer gefangen und plünderten **deren** Konvois (*Zeit*)	*Angry farmers held some British lorry-drivers captive and plundered their (i.e. the lorry-drivers', not the farmers') convoys*

In colloquial speech, the genitive of *der* is sometimes used instead of a possessive for emphasis, e.g.: *Ich kann **deren** Mann nicht leiden.*

(g) In the genitive plural *derer* is sometimes used rather than *deren*

It is most frequently used to refer forwards with a following relative clause, as in the first example below (see also 5.4.1c). The traditional rule that it can **only** be used in this way is no longer adhered to strictly, as in the second example below:

| eine Beleidigung der Intelligenz all **derer**, die ihre Stimme abgegeben haben (*HMP*) | *an insult to the intelligence of all those who cast their votes* |
| Wie soll man **derer** habhaft werden, wenn sie jemanden umgefahren haben? (*FR*) | *How can they be got hold of when they have knocked somebody down?* |

(h) The pronoun *das* **is used as an emphatic form of** *es*

Like *es* (see 3.6), it can be used with either singular or plural forms of the verb *sein*. In the corresponding English constructions we distinguish between 'that' and 'those':

Das sind meine Bücher	*Those are my books*
Das ist mein Arm, meine Hand, mein Knie	*That is my arm, my hand, my knee*

(i) A form of the prepositional adverb is normally used rather than a preposition followed by the demonstrative pronoun

e.g. *damit* 'with that', *darin* 'in that'. The stress is on the first syllable (see 3.5.3b):

'Damit kann man die Büchse doch nicht aufmachen, oder?	*You can't open the can with that, can you?*

To refer to something near or something just mentioned, a prepositional adverb with *hier-* can be used, e.g. *hiermit* 'with this', *hierin* 'in this'

'Hierüber lässt sich nichts mehr sagen	*There is nothing more to be said about this*

NB: Forms in *hie-*, e.g. *hiemit, hienach* are generally old-fashioned, but still frequent in Swiss and Austrian usage.

However, when a relative clause follows, a preposition followed by the demonstrative pronoun is used in written German (although the prepositional adverb may sometimes be heard in speech). See also 5.4.3c:

Ich richtete meine ganze Aufmerksamkeit **auf das** (NOT darauf), was er erklärte	*I focused my whole attention on what he was saying*

5.1.2 *dieser* 'this'

The declension of *dieser* is given in Table 5.2. It is the same whether *dieser* is used as a pronoun or as a determiner. Many other determiners and pronouns have the same set of endings.

TABLE 5.2 Declension of *dieser*

	Masculine	Feminine	Neuter	Plural
Nominative	dieser	diese	dieses	diese
Accusative	diesen	diese	dieses	diese
Genitive	dieses	dieser	dieses	dieser
Dative	diesem	dieser	diesem	diesen

There is an increasing tendency to use the form *diesen* in the genitive singular masculine and neuter of the determiner rather than *dieses* if the noun has the ending -(e)s, e.g. *im Februar diesen Jahres* (MM) (for: *dieses Jahres*). However, this usage is not (yet?) generally accepted as standard.

(a) As a determiner and a pronoun *dieser* **refers to something near at hand, corresponding to English 'this'**

As a determiner, *dieser* occurs in both spoken and written German, but as a pronoun it is mainly used in writing:

Diese Erklärung ist unbefriedigend	*This explanation is unsatisfactory*
Dieser Junge arbeitet aber gut	*That boy really does work well*
Er hat den kleinen Wagen nicht gekauft, weil ihm **dieser** (spoken: der hier) viel besser gefallen hat	*He didn't buy the small car, because he liked this one much better*

dieser is often used simply to point to an object or person in contexts where the difference between near and distant is not crucial. In such contexts it often corresponds to English 'that', e.g. *Warum hast du dieses Top gekauft?* 'Why did you buy this/that top?'

(b) The short pronoun form *dies* is commonly used for *dieses*

It refers to something close by or recent and its use corresponds closely to that of English 'this':

Dies geschieht nicht oft
Gerade **dies** hatte ich vergessen

dies, like *das*, can be used irrespective of gender or number, with a plural verb where appropriate: *Dies sind meine Schwestern; Dies ist meine Frau.*

NB: In formal writing, *dies* is occasionally used as a determiner for *dieses*, i.e. in the nominative or accusative singular neuter, e.g. **Dies** *Werk malte Konrad Witz aus Basel* (Borst).

5.1.3 *jener* 'that'

jener declines like *dieser*, see Table 5.2. Whether as a determiner or a pronoun, it is nowadays largely restricted to formal written German, especially in the following contexts:

(a) to contrast with *dieser*

Herr Schröder wollte nicht dieses Bild verkaufen, sondern **jenes**	*Mr Schröder did not want to sell this picture, but that one*
Wir sprachen über dieses und **jenes** (*less formal*: über dies und das)	*We talked about this and that*

(b) to refer to something distant, but well-known

Werfen wir einen kurzen Blick über den Eisernen Vorhang **jener** Zeit (*Sonnenberg*)	*Let us cast a short glance at the Iron Curtain of those times*

(c) with a following relative clause

Deshalb hat er auch eine Menge Anhänger unter **jenen**, die Comedy mögen (*HMP*)	*That is why he has a lot of fans among those who like comedy*

5.1.4 *derjenige* 'that'

Both parts of *derjenige* decline, as shown in Table 5.3. It is an emphatic demonstrative determiner or pronoun and is typically used with a following restrictive relative clause, corresponding to English 'that (one), which/who'. Although it was originally more typical of formal and official registers, it is now quite frequent in speech as well as in writing.

Wir wollen **diejenigen** Schüler herausfinden, die musikalisch begabt sind	*We want to find those pupils who are musically gifted*
Beihilfen sollen nur **demjenigen** zufließen, der unter der Armutsgrenze lebt. (*FR*)	*Assistance should only go to those who are living below the poverty line*

5.1.5 *derselbe* 'the same'

Both parts of *derselbe* decline, like *derjenige* (see Table 5.3). However, unlike *derjenige*, it can be used with a contracted preposition, e.g. *am selben Tag, zur selben Zeit.* It corresponds to English 'the same':

TABLE 5.3 Declension of *derjenige* and *derselbe*

	Masculine	**Feminine**	**Neuter**	**Plural**
Nominative	derjenige	diejenige	dasjenige	diejenigen
Accusative	denjenigen	diejenige	dasjenige	diejenigen
Genitive	desjenigen	derjenigen	desjenigen	derjenigen
Dative	demjenigen	derjenigen	demjenigen	denjenigen
Nominative	derselbe	dieselbe	dasselbe	dieselben
Accusative	denselben	dieselbe	dasselbe	dieselben
Genitive	desselben	derselben	desselben	derselben
Dative	demselben	derselben	demselben	denselben

Er besucht **dieselbe** Schule wie dein Bruder	*He goes to the same school as your brother*
Sind das **dieselben**?	*Are those the same?*
Sie wohnt **im selben** Haus	*She lives in the same house*
Es läuft auf (ein und) **dasselbe** hinaus	*It all comes to the same thing*

The difference between *derselbe*, i.e. 'the very same', and *der gleiche*, i.e. 'one which is similar' (cf. *Er trägt den gleichen Hut* 'He is wearing the same (i.e. a similar) hat'), is often ignored in spoken German, either being used in both senses. It is widely felt, though, that this distinction <u>should</u> be upheld, at least in writing.

5.1.6 *solch* and other equivalents of 'such'

solch- occurs in a number of forms, i.e.:

- **inflected** *solcher*, which declines like *dieser* (Table 5.2), except that in the genitive singular masculine and neuter it usually has the ending *-en* if the noun has the ending *-(e)s*, e.g. *Der Vorzug solchen Spieles* (Th. Mann).
- **endingless** *solch*, used with an indefinite article: *solch ein Unsinn*
- *solch-* used after the indefinite article *ein* or another determiner, with the endings of an adjective: *ein solches Buch, jeder solche Gedanke, alle solchen Frauen*

The use of these forms is as follows:

(a) The commonest variants for the determiner are *ein solcher* in the singular and inflected *solche* in the plural

This applies to both written and spoken German:

Eine solche Auflockerung könnte dem politischen Diskurs gut bekommen (*Zeit*)	*Such a relaxation of tension could benefit the political debate*
Einen solchen Wagen würde ich nie kaufen	*I would never buy a car like that*
Solchen Leuten kann man alles erzählen	*You can tell people like that anything*
solche großen Häuser	*such big houses*

NB: In informal colloquial speech, *so ein* is also current in the singular for 'such a', e.g. *in so einer Stadt, so ein Geschenk*. In the plural, simple *so* may be used, e.g. *Das sind so Sachen*. These forms are not used in formal registers, and certainly not in writing.

(b) Inflected *solcher* as a determiner in the singular is found principally in formal registers

It has a rather old-fashioned or literary ring:

bei **solchem** Wetter	*in such weather*
ein Mann, der **solchem** Rat nicht folgte (*Hildesheimer*)	*a man who failed to follow such advice*

(c) Usage as a determiner with a following adjective

(i) the most usual equivalent with singular count nouns for English 'such a' followed by an adjective is *ein so* (more colloquial *so ein*):

ein so großes Haus ⎫
so ein großes Haus ⎭   *such a big house*

(ii) In spoken German *so* is also used with plural count nouns and singular mass nouns, but the written language prefers inflected *solcher*:

so große Häuser (spoken) ⎫
solche großen Häuser (written) ⎭   *such big houses*
bei so gutem Wetter (spoken) ⎫
bei solchem guten Wetter (written) ⎭   *in such good weather*

(iii) In formal registers uninflected *solch* is not uncommon if an adjective follows. It also occurs in a few set phrases:

Das ist häufig die Gefahr nach **solch** guten Leistungen (*NUZ*)	*That is often the danger after such good results*
mit **solch** unermüdlichem Eifer	*with such tireless enthusiasm*
Solch dummes Gerede!	*Such stupid gossip!*

(d) In formal registers uninflected *solch* can be used as a determiner with a following indefinite article

This is more emphatic than if the article comes first:

Geprobt haben sie **solch** eine Situation allerdings nicht (*NUZ*).	*However, they haven't tested a situation like that*

NB: Uninflected *solch* is sometimes used <u>without</u> *ein* before a singular neuter noun, e.g.: *solch Wetter*. This has a very old-fashioned sound.

(e) Pronoun usage

(i) The most usual variants are *solche* (plural) and *so einer* (singular):

Ich habe **solche** oft gesehen	*I've often seen ones like that*
So eines kann ich mir nicht leisten	*I can't afford one like that*

(ii) Singular *solcher* is used after *als*:

Der Fall als **solcher** interessiert mich	*The case as such interests me*

(iii) Singular (*k*)*ein solcher* is restricted to literary registers. In the singular it sounds rather stilted:

Sie hatte auch **einen solchen**	*She had one like that, too*
Leider haben wir **keine solchen** mehr	*I'm afraid we haven't got any more like that*

(f) The adjective *derartig* is a common, more emphatic alternative to *solch-*

It is used with *ein* in the singular, or with no article in either singular or plural:

Er fuhr mit **einer derartigen** Geschwindigkeit gegen die Mauer, dass . . .	*He drove into the wall at such a speed, that . . .*

Erfahrung im Umgang mit **derartiger** Kälte hat niemand (*Bednarz*)	*Nobody has experience in dealing with that degree of cold*
Derartige Gerüchte hören wir oft	*We often hear rumours like those*

NB: If another adjective follows, *derartig* may be uninflected, e.g.: *Er fuhr mit einer derartig(en) hohen Geschwindigkeit gegen die Mauer, dass . . .* In some contexts, though, there can be a difference in meaning. Compare *ein derartig dummes Geschwätz* (i.e. 'gossip which is stupid to such an extent') and *ein derartiges dummes Geschwätz* (i.e. 'such gossip which is stupid').

(g) *dergleichen* and *derlei*

dergleichen and *derlei* do not decline. They are used as determiners or pronouns meaning 'such-like', 'that kind/sort of':

Dergleichen Behauptungen stören mich	*Assertions like that bother me*
nichts **dergleichen**	*nothing of the kind*
und **dergleichen** mehr (*abbrev.*: u.dgl.m.).	*and so forth*
Er hatte ein langes Messer oder **dergleichen** in der Tasche	*He had a long knife or something of the kind in his pocket*
Die rotblonde Miss Leclerc hatte **derlei** Tricks nicht nötig (*BILD*)	*The strawberry blond Miss Leclerc didn't need tricks like that*
Sie sah **derlei** nicht ungern (*Jacob*)	*She wasn't averse to that kind of thing*

5.2 **Possessives**

5.2.1 **The possessives have distinct base forms for each grammatical person**

These are given in Table 5.4 together with the personal pronoun to which they relate.

TABLE 5.4 Base forms of the possessive pronouns and determiners

Singular			Plural		
ich	**mein**	*my*	wir	**unser**	*our*
du	**dein**	*your*	ihr	**euer**	*your*
er	**sein**	*his/its*	Sie	**Ihr**	*your (polite)*
sie	**ihr**	*her/its*	sie	**ihr**	*their*
es	**sein**	*its*			

NB: (i) To refer back to indefinites, the masculine form *sein* is used: *Wer hat **seine** Zahnbürste vergessen? Niemand hatte **sein** Heft mit.*
(ii) A demonstrative is sometimes used instead of a third person possessive to avoid ambiguity, see 5.1.1f.

5.2.2 **When used as determiners the possessives have the same endings as the indefinite article**

Table 5.5 gives the forms of *mein* 'my' and *unser* 'our'.

The following is to be noted in relation to these declensions:

(a) The -*er* of *unser* and *euer* is part of the root and <u>not</u> an ending

As Table 5.5 shows, the endings are attached to this root.

(b) When *unser* and *euer* have an ending, the -*e*- of the root is often dropped

e.g. *unsrer, unsren, eurer, euren.* Alternatively, the -*e*- of the endings -*en* or -*em* may be dropped, e.g. *unsern, unserm, euern, euerm.*

TABLE 5.5 Declension of the possessive determiners

	Masculine	Feminine	Neuter	Plural
Nominative	mein	meine	mein	meine
Accusative	meinen	meine	mein	meine
Genitive	meines	meiner	meines	meiner
Dative	meinem	meiner	meinem	meinen
Nominative	unser	unsere	unser	unsere
Accusative	unseren	unsere	unser	unsere
Genitive	unseres	unserer	unseres	unserer
Dative	unserem	unserer	unserem	unseren

With *unser*, the full forms, as given in the table, are the more usual ones in written German, although the reduced forms, which are the norm in speech, are quite permissible.

With *euer*, the forms with no *-e-* in the root, i.e. *euren, eurer, eures, eurem*, are by far the most common in both spoken and written German.

NB: In the genitive singular masculine and neuter the ending *-en* is now sometimes found if the noun has the ending *-(e)s*, e.g. *die Launen meinen Bruders*. This usage is increasingly common but it is generally considered to be incorrect.

5.2.3 When used as pronouns, the possessives have the endings of *dieser*

Table 5.6 gives the full forms of *meiner* 'mine' and *unserer* 'ours'.

TABLE 5.6 Declension of the possessive pronouns

	Masculine	Feminine	Neuter	Plural
Nominative	**meiner**	meine	**meines**	meine
Accusative	meinen	meine	**meines**	meine
Genitive	meines	meiner	meines	meiner
Dative	meinem	meiner	meinem	meinen
Nominative	unserer	unsere	unseres	unsere
Accusative	unseren	unsere	unseres	unsere
Genitive	unseres	unserer	unseres	unserer
Dative	unserem	unserer	unserem	unseren

(a) The forms of the possessive pronouns

(i) Note in particular that, unlike the possessive determiners, the possessive pronouns have endings in the nominative singular masculine and the nominative/accusative singular neuter (i.e *meiner, meines*). Compare:

Das ist nicht **mein** Hut, sondern **deiner**
Hast du **dein** Fahrrad? Ich sehe **mein(e)s** nicht
Seine Sammlung ist größer als **meine**
Ihr Garten ist größer als **uns(e)rer**
Er sprach mit **meinen** Eltern, ich mit **seinen**
Ich nehme **uns(e)ren** Wagen. In **seinem** habe ich immer Angst

(ii) The *-e-* of the nominative/accusative neuter ending *-es* is often dropped in writing, and almost always in speech, i.e. *meins, deins*. With *unseres* and *eueres* the *-e-* of the ending is dropped, i.e. *unsers*, *euers*. Otherwise, *unserer* and *euerer* can drop the *-e-* of the root or the ending as with the possessive determiner, see 5.2.2 above.

(iii) Endingless forms of the possessive are occasionally found in set phrases, archaic expressions or poetic language:

Dein ist mein Herz!   Die Welt ist **unser**
Die Rache ist **mein**

(b) Alternative forms of the possessive pronoun

The following types of phrase are sometimes used instead of *meiner*, *deiner*, *unserer*, etc. The possessive forms are used as adjectives after a definite article, and they have the endings of adjectives. They can be spelled with a small or a capital initial letter (see 23.2.1g):

(i) *der meinige/Meinige* 'mine', *der deinige/Deinige* 'yours', *der uns(e)rige/Uns(e)rige* 'ours', etc.

(ii) *der meine/Meine* 'mine', *der deine/Deine* 'yours', *der uns(e)re/Uns(e)re* 'ours', etc.

Seine Sammlung ist größer als **die meine/die meinige**

These forms are much less common than *meiner*, etc., and are found mainly in formal written German. Type (ii) is rather more emphatic than *meiner*, etc., while type (i) is current mainly in set phrases, e.g.: *die Deinigen* 'your people' (i.e. your family); *Ich habe das Meinige getan* 'I've done my bit'.

5.2.4 Differences between German and English in the use of the possessives

(a) A definite article is often used rather than a possessive to refer to parts of the body and articles of clothing

e.g.: *Sie hat sich **den** Arm gebrochen* 'She has broken her arm'. Details are given in 4.6.

(b) Some idiomatic equivalents

Das gehört mir. Gehört das dir?	*That's mine. Is that yours?*
ein Freund von mir / einer meiner Freunde	*a friend of mine*
Freunde von mir	*friends of mine*
Das ist eins von meinen Büchern	*That's a book of mine*
mein Vater und meine Mutter (*see* 4.1.1b)	*my father and mother*

5.3 Interrogatives

INTERROGATIVES are words used to ask a question. In English they typically begin with *wh-*, like *which* or *who*.

5.3.1 *welcher* 'which'

(a) *welcher* **can be used as a determiner or a pronoun**

It has the same endings as *dieser*, see Table 5.2. The forms are the same whether it is used as a determiner or a pronoun.

Welches Bier willst du trinken?	*Which beer do you want to drink?*
Welchen Zug nehmen wir denn?	*Which train shall we take?*

Aus **welchem** Land kommt sie denn?	*Which country does she come from?*
Welcher berühmte Schriftsteller hat diesen Roman geschrieben?	*Which famous author wrote this novel?*
Hier sind zwei gute Weine. **Welchen** möchtest du zuerst probieren?	*Here are two good wines. Which one would you like to try first?*
Er fragte mich, **welchen** (Wein) ich zuerst probieren wollte	*He asked me which (wine) I wanted to try first*

(b) Some special uses of *welcher*

(i) In formal written German the endingless form *welch* is sometimes used before an adjective, as an alternative to the declined form:

Welch berühmter Schriftsteller hat diesen Roman geschrieben?
Die Künstler zeigten, **welch** reiches Kulturgut sie mitbrachten (*MM*)

(ii) In the genitive singular masculine and neuter the determiner can have the ending *-en* rather than *-es* if the following noun has the ending *-(e)s*:

Welch**en**/Welch**es** Kindes Buch ist das?
Innerhalb welch**en** Zeitraumes müssen nicht bestandene Prüfungen wiederholt werden? (*Uni Innsbruck*)

In practice, the genitive tends to be avoided if possible.

(iii) *welcher* can have the neuter singular form *welches* when it is used as a pronoun in an indefinite sense with the verb *sein*, irrespective of the gender and number of the noun it refers to:

Welches ist die jüngere Schwester?	**Welches** sind die besten Zeitungen?
Welches ist der längste Fluss in Amerika?	

Using endings in agreement with the following noun would be equally possible in these examples: *Welche ist die jüngere Schwester?* etc.

(c) *welcher* **is used in exclamations (= 'What (a) . . .!')**

Welcher Unterschied!	**Welcher** schöne Tag!
Welche Überraschung!	**Welchen** unglaublichen Unsinn hat er geredet!

Endingless *welch* can be used instead of declined *welcher* in exclamations if *ein* or an adjective follows:

Welch ein Unterschied!	**Welch (ein)** schöner Tag!
Welch eine Überraschung!	**Welch unglaublichen** Unsinn hat er geredet!

Der Smogalarm machte erneut deutlich, in **welch hohem** Maße die Luft mit Giftstoffen verseucht ist (*MM*)
  The smog alarm made it clear once again to what high degree the air is polluted with poisonous substances

This exclamatory use of *welch(er)* is mainly found in formal German. *was für (ein)* (see 5.3.2), is more current in speech.

NB: The form *welcher* has a number of other uses, i.e.
   (i)   as a relative pronoun (= 'who', 'which'), see 5.4.2.
   (ii) as an indefinite (= 'some', 'any'), see 5.5.26.

5.3.2 *was für (ein[er])* 'what kind of (a)'

(a) *was für (ein[er])* **can be used as a determiner or a pronoun**

(i) Used as a determiner, *ein* in *was für ein* declines like the indefinite article, see Table 4.2. Simple *was für*, without *ein*, is used in the plural and before mass nouns in the singular:

Aus **was für einer** Familie stammt er?	*From what kind of a family does he come?*
Sie können sich denken, in **was für einer** schwierigen Lage ich mich befand	*You can imagine in what an awkward situation I found myself*
Was für ausländische Marken haben Sie?	*What kinds of foreign stamps do you have?*
Was für Käse soll ich kaufen?	*What kind of cheese shall I buy?*

The case of *ein* depends on the role of the noun phrase in the sentence, i.e. it does not depend on *für* and is not automatically in the accusative.

(ii) When used as a pronoun, *was für einer* 'what kind (of a one)' has the endings of the pronoun *einer* given in Table 5.10. In the plural *was für welche* is used:

Er hat sich ein neues Auto gekauft. **Was für ein(e)s?**	*He has bought a new car. What kind?*
Ich habe Blumen gebracht. **Was für welche?**	*I have brought some flowers. What kind?*

NB: (i) *was für welcher* is used in place of *was für einer* in the singular in colloquial north German speech, e.g.: *Er hat einen neuen Wagen gekauft. Was für welchen?*
(ii) *was für (ein)* is also used in concessive clauses, see 19.6.2c.

(b) *was* **is often separated from** *für (ein[er])*

This is especially frequent in speech, but the construction is used in writing, too:

Was hast du denn **für ein** Auto gekauft?
Was sind das **für** Vögel?

(c) *was für (ein[er])* **is used in exclamations (= 'What (a) . . .!')**

It is in practice commoner than *welcher*, see 5.3.1 (c), especially in less formal registers. In this usage the separated form is more frequent:

Was für eine Chance!	*What a chance!*
Was für herrliche Blumen!	*What lovely flowers!*
Er ist ein Schauspieler – und **was für einer**!	*He's an actor – and what an actor!*
Was sind das **für** wunderschöne Häuser!	*What lovely houses these are!*

NB: If there is a verb in these exclamations, it may, alternatively, go to the end, like in a subordinate clause: *Was für wunderschöne Häuser das **sind**!*

(d) In colloquial speech *was für (ein[er])* **is often used for** *welcher* **'which'**

see 5.3.1. This usage is not generally considered acceptable in standard German:

Was für ein Kleid ziehst du an?	*Which dress are you going to wear?*

5.3.3 *wer, was* 'who, what'

(a) *wer* **and** *was* **are used only as pronouns**

(i) *wer*, like English 'who', only refers to persons. It does not distinguish gender and it has the case forms given in Table 5.7:

TABLE 5.7 Declension of *wer*

Nominative	wer
Accusative	wen
Genitive	wessen
Dative	wem

Examples of use:

Wer hat diesen Brief geschrieben?	*Who wrote this letter?*
Wen hast du heute gesprochen?	*Who(m) did you speak to today?*
Wem wollten sie vorhin helfen?	*Who(m) did they want to help just now?*
Mit **wem** hast du gespielt?	*Who(m) did you play with?*
Wessen Bücher sind das?	*Whose books are those?*
Ich kann Ihnen sagen, **wer** spielte	*I can tell you who was playing*

(ii) *was*, like English 'what', refers only to things. Its only case form is the genitive *wessen*:

Was bewegt sich dort im Gebüsch?	*What is moving there in the bushes?*
Was hat sie dir zum Geburtstag geschenkt?	*What did she give you for your birthday?*
Wessen schämst du dich?	*What are you ashamed of?*
Weißt du, **was** er getan hat?	*Do you know what he did?*

The genitive form *wessen*, whether referring to people or things, is felt to be clumsy and tends to be avoided nowadays, even in written German. Thus *Wem gehören diese Bücher?* is used rather than *Wessen Bücher sind das?* and *Warum schämst du dich?* rather than *Wessen schämst du dich?*

As *was* has no dative, a paraphrase has to be used in contexts where it would be needed, e.g.:

Welcher Ursache kann man seinen Erfolg zuschreiben?	*To what can one ascribe his success?* (Literally: 'To what cause . . .?')

(b) Nominative *wer* and *was* are usually followed by a singular verb

(i) Compare the examples in (a) above and the following:

Wer **kommt** denn morgen?	*Who's coming tomorrow?*
Was **liegt** dort in der Ecke?	*What's that lying there in the corner?*

(ii) However, with *sein* the appropriate singular or plural form of the verb is used, as in English:

Wer **ist** das an der Tür?	*Who's that at the door?*
Wer **sind** diese Leute?	*Who are those people?*
Was **ist** der Vogel da?	*What's that bird there?*
Was **sind** die längsten Flüsse der Welt?	*What are the longest rivers in the world?*

(iii) To emphasise quantity, *alles* is often added to sentences with *wer* and *was*. This usage is typical of colloquial speech:

Wen kennen Sie hier **alles**?	*What people do you know here?*
Was hat er denn alles **gefragt**?	*What were the things he asked?*

(c) *was* is not used in combination with most prepositions

The compound forms *wo(r)*+preposition, e.g. *woran, womit, wozu*, etc., are used instead.

(i) These forms are like those of the prepositional adverb with *da(r)-*, see 3.5:

Womit schreibst du?	*What are you writing with?*
Worüber sprechen Sie?	*What are you talking about?*
Weißt du, **worauf** wir warten?	*Do you know what we are waiting for?*

NB: Some prepositions are not used in the form with *wo(r)-*, i.e.: *außer, gegenüber, hinter, neben, ohne, seit, zwischen*.

(ii) The forms *wodurch, wonach, wovon* and *wozu* can only be used if there is no idea of movement involved, e.g.:

Wodurch weiß er das?	*How is it that he knows that?*
Wonach soll man sich denn richten?	*By what is one to be guided?*
Wovon sollen wir leben?	*What are we to live on?*
Wozu gebraucht man das?	*What is that used for?*

Compare: *durch was?* 'through what?', *von wo?* or *woher?* 'where . . . from?', *wohin?* 'where . . . to?'.

(iii) In colloquial German *was* (irrespective of case) is often used with a preposition instead of *wo(r)*+preposition, e.g.: *Von was sollen wir leben?* This usage is very widespread in speech, but it is not regarded as acceptable in standard German, and avoided in writing.

(d) *wer* **and** *was* **are commonly used in exclamations**

Wer hätte so was erwartet!	*Who would have expected such a thing!*
Wem hat er nicht alles geholfen!	*Who(m) hasn't he helped!*
Was haben wir gelacht!	*How we laughed!*
Was er nicht alles tut!	*The things he does!*

(e) *was* **can be followed by an adjective used as a noun, with the neuter ending** *-es*

See 6.4 for further details on these forms. The adjective is separated from *was* and placed later in the sentence:

Was haben sie **Wichtiges** besprochen?	*What important matters did they discuss?*
Was ist **Komisches** dran?	*What's funny about it?*
Was könnt ihr hier **anderes** erwarten?	*What else can you expect here?*
(*Fallada*)	

(f) *was* **can be used in the sense of 'why?' or 'what for?'**

This usage is typical of informal spoken registers:

Was sitzt ihr da rum?	*What are you doing just sitting around?*

was in this usage often carries a tone of reproach.

(g) Idiomatic differences between German and English

In a few contexts German has *wie* where English uses 'what'.

Wie ist Ihr Name, bitte?	*What is your name, please?*
Wie heißt Ihr Bruder?	*What's your brother called?*
Wie ist das Buch?	*What's the book like?*

(h) Other uses of *wer* **and** *was*

(i) *wer* and *was* are used as relative pronouns (= 'who', 'which', 'that') in some contexts, see 5.4.3 and 5.4.5.

(ii) *wer* and *was* are used in some concessive clauses (i.e. = 'whoever', 'whatever'), see 19.6.2.

(iii) For the colloquial use of *wer* as an indefinite (i.e. = 'someone'), see 5.5.27.

5.4 **Relative pronouns**

RELATIVE PRONOUNS introduce subordinate clauses (called '**relative clauses**') which describe or qualify nouns, e.g. *die Frau, die heute kommt* 'the woman **who** is coming today'; *das Buch, das ich gerade lese* 'the book **which** I am just reading'. In this way relative clauses have the same function as adjectives.

In English, we often drop a relative pronoun, especially in speech (*The book (which) I am just reading*), but in German it can **never** be left out in this way.

5.4.1 *der* 'who', 'which', 'that'

(a) *der* **is the most commonly used relative pronoun in German**

der declines for the categories of gender, plural and case. Its forms, which are almost identical to that of the demonstrative pronoun *der*, are given in Table 5.8.

TABLE 5.8 Declension of the relative pronoun *der*

	Masculine	**Feminine**	**Neuter**	**Plural**
Nominative	der	die	das	die
Accusative	den	die	das	die
Genitive	dessen	deren	dessen	deren
Dative	dem	der	dem	denen

der takes its **gender** and **number** from the noun it refers to, e.g.

der Mann, **der** heute zu uns kommt (**masculine**)
die Frau, **die** heute zu uns kommt (**feminine**)
das Kind, **das** heute zu uns kommt (**neuter**)
die Leute, **die** heute zu uns kommen (**plural**)

Its **case** is determined by the role it plays in the relative clause:

der Mann, **der** zu uns kommt (**subject** of *kommt*)
den Mann, **den** ich kenne (**accusative object** of *kenne*)
der Mann, **dem** ich helfen musste (**dative object** of *helfen*)
der Mann, mit **dem** sie gekommen ist (after **preposition** *mit* governing the **dative** case)

(b) **Relative clauses are less frequent in spoken German than in writing**

In speech, a construction with a main clause (and the verb in second place) and the demonstrative pronoun *der* is often used rather than a subordinate relative clause (with the verb at the end). This is usually considered to be poor style in writing, unless colloquial speech is being imitated, as in the following examples:

Er trug ein Heft bei sich, **in dem** standen die Namen der fünfzig Verräter (*E.W. Heine*)

He had a little book with him in which the names of the fifty traitors were written down

Es gibt Leute, **die** freuen sich über die Fahrt (*Bichsel*)

There are people who are pleased about the trip

(c) The genitive of *der*

(i) The genitive forms of *der* correspond to English 'whose' or 'of which':

die Frau, **deren** Namen ich immer vergesse	*the woman whose name I always forget*
Sie blickten auf das Mietshaus gegenüber, in **dessen** Erdgeschoss sich eine Schreibwarenhandlung befand	*They looked out on the apartment house opposite, on the ground floor of which there was a stationer's*
ein Mann, von **dessen** Erfolg ich hörte	*a man of whose success I heard*

NB: It is incorrect (though a common mistake by Germans) to decline *dessen* and *deren*, i.e.: *ein Mann, von dessem* (correct: *dessen*) *Erfolg ich hörte.*

(ii) In the genitive plural and the genitive singular feminine *derer* is sometimes used rather than *deren*:

Geoforscher verweisen auf gewaltige Klimasprünge in der Erdgeschichte, angesichts **derer** die heutige Erwärmung keineswegs beispiellos ist (*HAZ*)	*Geologists point to violent variations in the climate in the history of the earth, in the light of which the present warming is in no way exceptional*
die ungewöhnliche Autorität, **derer** sich die katholischen Bischöfe in Polen erfreuen (*Spiegel*)	*the extraordinary authority which is enjoyed by the Catholic bishops in Poland*

This usage has traditionally been considered incorrect, but *derer* is in practice more frequent than *deren*, especially in the genitive plural. However, *deren* is usually preferred if a noun follows: *die Frau, deren Tochter du kennst.*

(iii) After prepositions, the shorter form *der* also occurs for *deren*:

eine lange Übergangszeit von sechs Jahren, innerhalb **der** die Länder die Juristenausbildung umstellen können (*Zeit*)	*a long transitional period of six years, within which the Länder can reorganise the training of lawyers*

(iv) Constructions of the type 'one of whom', 'most of which', 'some of which' correspond to constructions with *von denen* in German:

die Studenten, **von denen** ich **einen** nicht kenne	*the students, one of whom I don't know*
eine Anzahl Jungen, **von denen** ich **die meisten** kenne	*a number of boys, most of whom I know*
viele Bilder, **von denen einige** ganz gut sind	*a lot of pictures, some of which are quite good*

(v) *dessen* and *deren* are compounded with *-halben*, *-wegen* and *-willen* with the insertion of a *-t-*, e.g. *derentwegen, um dessentwillen*:

ein charismatischer, weltberühmter Darsteller, **dessentwegen** die Frauen in Ohnmacht fallen (*Presse*)	*a charismatic, world-famous actor on whose account women faint*

(d) Relative pronouns with first and second person personal pronouns

Normal usage is for the pronoun to be repeated in the relative clause, e.g.:

du, **der/die du** ja nicht alles wissen kannst	*you, who cannot know everything*
für mich, **die ich** noch gar nicht ordentlich lesen konnte (*Dönhoff*)	*for me, who couldn't read properly yet*
ich, **der ich** seit 20 Jahren seinem Volke diene	*I, who have been serving my people for 20 years*

The alternative construction with a third person verb, e.g.: *ich, **der** seit 20 Jahren seinem Volke **dient*** (*FAZ*), is possible, but less frequent in practice. It is most common when the relative pronoun is separated from the personal pronoun by other words, e.g. *Was kannst du tun, der nicht alles wissen kann.*

5.4.2 *welcher* 'who, which, that'

(a) *welcher* **is chiefly used as a stylistic variant of** *der*

It has the same endings as *dieser*, see Table 5.2, but it is not normally used in the genitive. It is restricted to formal written German, and even there it can be considered clumsy and is much less frequent than *der*.

die Gerüchte, **welche** über die wirtschaftliche Lage meines Vaters am Orte umgelaufen waren (*Th. Mann*)	*the rumours which had been circulating in the town about my father's financial situation*
Der Herr tat doch immer so, als umgäbe ihn eine vielköpfige Familie, **welcher** er Anweisungen zu geben hätte (*Grass*)	*The gentleman always acted as if he was surrounded by a large family to which he had to give instructions*

It is frequent (although never necessary) to avoid repeating forms of *der*, e.g.: *Die, **welche** zuletzt kamen, waren erschöpft*. But compare, as perfectly acceptable (see 5.4.5b): *Die, **die** gingen, haben in der DDR mehr verändert, als die, **die** geblieben sind* (*FR*).

(b) *welcher* **is used in formal German before a noun which refers back to part or whole of the preceding clause**

This use corresponds to that of English 'which'. In this construction *welcher* agrees with the following noun for case, number and gender:

Er wurde zum Stadtdirektor ernannt, **welches Amt** er gewissenhaft verwaltete	*He was appointed town clerk, which office he administered conscientiously*
Er sagte ihr, sie müsse den Betrag sofort zurückzahlen, **welcher Forderung** sie dann auch nachging	*He told her she had to repay the amount immediately, which request she then complied with*

5.4.3 *was* is used as a relative pronoun in some contexts

The only case form of *was* in this usage is the genitive *wessen* (although this tends to be avoided). *was* is used:

(a) After neuter indefinites

i.e. *alles, einiges, etwas, folgendes, manches, nichts, vieles, weniges*:

Nichts/Etwas/Alles, **was** er sagte, war mir neu	*Nothing/Something/Everything (that) he said was new to me*
Sie mieden alles, **was** ihre Unabhängigkeit einschränken könnte (*Walser*)	*They avoided anything which could restrict their independence*

After *etwas*, *das* may be used as an alternative to *was* if something specific is referred to:

Gerade in diesem Moment fiel ihr etwas ein, **das** sie erstarren ließ: Die Gasrechnung (*Baum*)	*Just then she remembered something that made her go rigid: the gas bill*
Ich erinnere mich an etwas Merkwürdiges, **das** er sagte	*I remember something strange that he said*

das is occasionally found after other indefinites, but this usage is considered incorrect.

NB: (i) After prepositions, forms of *was* are replaced by the prepositional adverb in *wo(r)-*, see 5.4.4b.
(ii) *was* is often heard for *das* to refer to a neuter noun, e.g.: *das Buch,* **was** *er mir geliehen hat*. This usage is non-standard.

(b) After a neuter adjective used as a noun referring to something indefinite

Das Richtige, **was** man sich ansehen müsste, finden wir nie (*Fallada*)	*The right things* [in museums] *that one ought to look at, we never find*
Das Erste, **was** Evelyn sah, waren Mariannes Augen (*Baum*)	*The first thing Evelyn saw was Marianne's eyes*

If the adjective refers to something specific, *das* can be used: *Das Gute,* **das** *er getan hat, wird ihn überdauern*, although the difference in meaning can be very slight. However, *was* is <u>always</u> used after superlatives.

(c) After the indefinite demonstrative *das*

Eben **das**, **was** uns fehlte, hat er uns verweigert	*He denied us just what we were lacking*

If *das* is in the genitive or dative, or after a preposition, it cannot be omitted. This differs from English, where often only 'what' is needed. Compare:

Ich hörte nichts von **dem**, **was** er mir sagte	*I didn't hear anything of what he said to me*
eine Antwort auf **das**, **was** er gerade dachte (*Walser*)	*an answer to what he was just thinking*
ein eifriger Leser **dessen**, **was** neu auf den Markt kommt (*Zeit*)	*a keen reader of what is new on the market*

(d) To refer back to a whole clause

Er hat sein Examen bestanden, **was** mich sehr erstaunt	*He has passed his examination, which surprises me very much*
Er sagte, er hätte mich damals gesehen, **was** ich nicht glauben konnte	*He said he had seen me then, which I couldn't believe*

5.4.4 Relative pronouns after prepositions

(a) Standard usage, especially in writing, is the appropriate form of *der* after the preposition

The construction corresponds more closely to that of written English than to that with a 'stranded' preposition at the end of the clause which is typical of spoken English (compare the alternative translations of the first example):

die Frau, **auf die** Sie warten	*the woman for whom you are waiting* / *the woman (who) you are waiting for*
der Stuhl, **auf den** du dich setzen wolltest	*the chair you wanted to sit down on*
der Stuhl, **auf dem** du sitzt	*the chair you are sitting on*
der Bleistift, **mit dem** sie schreibt	*the pencil she is writing with*
die Stadt, **in der** ich wohne	*the town I live in*

(b) The form *wo(r)*+preposition as a relative pronoun

The forms of the prepositional adverb in *wo(r)*- (e.g. *worauf, woran, wovon*, etc., see 5.3.3c) are used as relative pronouns in some constructions.

(i) *wo(r)*+preposition is used in all contexts where *was* is used as a relative pronoun (see 5.4.3), since *was* is not used after a preposition:

Das, **woran** du denkst, errate ich nie	*I'll never guess what you're thinking of*
Es kam etwas, **womit** kein Mensch auf der Welt hätte rechnen können (*Süßkind*)	*Something came which nobody on earth could have reckoned with*
Er hat sein Examen bestanden, **worüber** ich mich freue	*He has passed his examination, which I am very pleased about*

If *etwas* refers to something specific, preposition + *das* can be used instead of *wo(r)* + preposition:

Ich spürte, dass noch etwas geschehen war . . . etwas, **für das** sich nur ein Anlass ergeben hatte (*Lenz*)

(ii) *wo(r)*+preposition used to be a common alternative to the preposition followed by *der* to refer to things, e.g.: *das Heim, worin ich geboren wurde* (*Th. Mann*). This usage is now uncommon even in formal registers.

NB: The use of prepositional adverb with *da(r)*- (e.g. *darauf, daran*, cf. 3.5) as a relative pronoun to refer to things, e.g.: *das Heim, **darin** ich geboren wurde*, is now wholly obsolete.

(iii) Especially in North Germany, *wo(r)*+preposition is sometimes split (in a similar way to *da(r)*+preposition, see 3.5.3), e.g.:

Das ist etwas, **wo** ich mich nicht **mit** abfinden kann (*standard:* womit ich mich nicht abfinden kann)	*That is something I can't get used to*

This usage is widespread, but not generally accepted as standard.

(c) In spoken German *wo* is often combined with a prepositional adverb later in the clause

e.g.:

Da in der Ecke ist das Sofa, **wo** du **d(a)rauf** schlafen kannst (*standard:* auf dem du schlafen kannst)	*There in the corner is the sofa you can sleep on*

This is probably the most frequent alternative in informal colloquial speech, but it is considered unacceptable in formal, especially written registers.

NB: The variation on this construction with a simple preposition, e.g. *der Ball, wo der Junge mit gespielt hat* is if anything even less acceptable, although it, too, is very frequent in speech.

5.4.5 'the one who', 'he/she who', 'that which'

There are a number of German equivalents for these English constructions.

(a) *wer* and *was* can be used in generalisations

Wer viele Freunde hat, ist glücklich	*He who has many friends is happy*
Wer wagt, gewinnt	*Who dares wins*
Und **was** noch schlimmer ist, er merkt es selber nicht	*And what is worse, he doesn't realise it himself*
Was du sagst, stimmt nicht	*What you say is not right*

If there is a difference in case or construction between the two clauses, an appropriate demonstrative pronoun can be added to begin the main clause:

Wen es zum Lehrerberuf hinzieht, **der** bevorzugt eher die philosophischen Fächer	*Those who are attracted to the teaching profession favour Arts subjects*
Was wir getan haben, **darüber** müssen wir auch Rechenschaft ablegen	*What we have done we shall also have to answer for*

Often, though, no such clarifying demonstrative pronoun is used:

Wen es zum Lehrerberuf hinzieht, bevorzugt eher die philosophischen Fächer (*Zeit*)

(b) Relative pronouns following demonstrative pronouns
The following alternatives are found:

(i) demonstrative *der* followed by relative *der*. Despite the repetition, this is the commonest alternative:

Die, **die** gingen, haben in der DDR mehr verändert, als **die**, **die** blieben (*FR*)	*Those who left changed more in the GDR than those who stayed*

(ii) in more elevated styles, demonstrative *der* followed by relative *welcher*:

Die, **welche** ich kaufen wollte, waren mir zu teuer	*The ones I wanted to buy were too expensive for me*

(iii) demonstrative *derjenige* followed by relative *der* (or, in elevated style, *welcher*). This is frequent in both speech and writing:

Diejenigen, **die** (welche) in den hinteren Reihen saßen, konnten nichts sehen	*Those who were sitting in the back rows couldn't see anything*

(iv) demonstrative *jener* followed by relative *der* (or *welcher*). This is not uncommon in formal writing:

bei jenen, die es sich zur Aufgabe gemacht haben, Schüler zu fördern (*MM*)	*with those who have made it their business to support schoolchildren*

(v) *der* can be used as a compound relative (e.g. 'he who'). This is common in speech:

Die hier sitzen, sind Verfluchte (*Wolf*)	*Those who are sitting here are cursed*
Der ihm Brötchen und Bockwurst verkaufte, kam aus Winsen an der Luhe (*Surminski*)	*The man who sold him rolls and sausage came from Winsen an der Luhe*

5.4.6 **Other forms of the relative pronoun**

(a) To refer to a place, *wo* can be used as a relative pronoun as an alternative to *der* with a preposition

die Stadt, **wo** (*or:* in der) ich wohne	*the town where I live*

If motion to or from a place is involved, *wohin* or *woher* are used:

die Stadt, **wohin** (*or:* in die) ich ging	*the town to which I went*
das Dorf, **woher** (*or:* aus dem) er kam	*the village from which he came*

NB: The use of *wo* as a general relative pronoun (e.g.: *die Frau, **wo** jetzt kommt*) is a widespread non-standard regionalism.

(b) Usage with time words

In such contexts English often uses 'when' as a relative. A number of alternatives exist in German, depending on register:

(i) Preposition with *der* is the most widely accepted form for writing:

Den Tag, **an dem** er ankam, werde ich nie vergessen	*I shall never forget the day when he arrived*
in einer Zeit, **in der** die Jugend immer unabhängiger wird	*at a time when young people are becoming more and more independent*

(ii) *als* (for past time) or *wenn* (for present or future time) are possible alternatives. *da* is sometimes used in formal (especially literary) German:

In dem Augenblick, **als** der Hund aufsprang, schrie er (*Valentin*)	*At the moment when the dog jumped up, he cried out*
an seinem nächsten Geburtstag, **wenn** er volljährig wird	*on his next birthday, when he comes of age*
Ach, wo sind die Zeiten, **da** Pinneberg sich für einen guten Verkäufer hielt? (*Fallada*)	*Alas, where are the days when Pinneberg considered himself a good salesman?*

(iii) The use of *wo* as a relative indicating time is common, especially in speech, and it is not uncommon in writing. However, many Germans do not accept it as standard and prefer other alternatives in formal, especially written registers:

im Augenblick, **wo** er die Tür aufmachte	*at the moment when he opened the door*
Wir leben in einer Zeit, **wo** Verkaufen arm macht (*Remarque*)	*We live in a time when selling makes one poor*
jetzt, **wo** ich das weiß	*now that I know that*

(c) *wie* **is used to indicate manner, principally after** *die Art*

die Art, **wie** er zu mir sprach	*the manner in which he spoke to me*
so, **wie** ich es gewohnt bin	*just as I am used to*

(d) *warum* **is used to indicate cause, chiefly after** *der Grund*

weshalb is an alternative in formal registers:

der Grund, **warum** (weshalb) ich nach Aachen ging	*the reason why I went to Aachen*

5.5 Indefinites, quantifiers and other determiners and pronouns

This section deals with the meaning and use of the remaining determiners and pronouns, in alphabetical order. A list of them, with their most frequent English equivalents, is given in Table 5.9. The declension of adjectives after these determiners is explained in 6.2.3.

5.5.1 *aller, alle* 'all (the)'

(a) *all-* **'all (the)', used as a** DETERMINER, **has various alternative forms**

(i) Inflected *aller*, with the endings of *dieser* (see Table 5.2), used on its own:

Alle Kinder spielen gern	*All children like playing*
Alle Schüler waren gekommen	*All the pupils had come*
mit **allen** denkbaren Mitteln	*with all conceivable means*
alles Glück dieser Erde	*all the happiness of this world*

This is the commonest alternative in the plural, especially in the nominative and accusative, but in the singular it is largely restricted to formal registers and set phrases. Plural *alle* may correspond to English 'all the' or 'all (of) the', e.g. *alle Schüler* 'all the pupils'/'all of the pupils'. *alle* is **never** followed by a genitive.

An adjective following *alle* in the plural has **weak** endings, e.g. *alle guten Kinder*, see 6.2.3b.

NB: In the genitive singular masculine and neuter, the ending *-en* is used rather than *-es* if the noun has the ending *-(e)s*, e.g.: *solch verfehlte Ablehnung all**en** (less frequent: alles) Verhandelns (Zeit)*.

TABLE 5.9 Indefinites, quantifiers and determiners

aller, alle	*all (the)*	**folgende(r)**	*the following*	**manch(er)**	*some*
ander	*(the) other*	**irgend(-)**	*some-*	**mehrere**	*several*
beide(s)	*both*	**jeder**	*each, every*	**meinesgleichen**	*people like me*
einer	*one*	**jedermann**	*everyone*	**nichts**	*nothing*
ein bisschen	*a little*	**jedweder**	*each, every*	**sämtlich(e)**	*all (the)*
ein paar	*a few*	**jeglicher**	*each, every*	**unsereiner**	*someone like me*
ein wenig	*a little*	**jemand, niemand**	*someone, no-one*	**viel, viele**	*much, many*
einige(r)	*some*	**kein(er)**	*no, none*	**wenig, wenige**	*a little, a few*
etliche	*some*	**lauter**	*nothing but*	**welcher**	*some*
etwas	*something*	**man**	*one*	**wer**	*someone*

(ii) Inflected *aller* followed by the definite article:

alle die Bücher	*all the books*
alle die Mühe	*all the trouble*

This is quite common in the plural, especially in colloquial speech, and with feminine nouns in the nominative and accusative singular.

(iii) Uninflected *all* followed by the definite article:

all das schlechte Wetter	*all the bad weather*
all die Schüler	*all the pupils*
mit **all dem** Geld	*with all the money*

This is the most frequent alternative in the singular, and it is quite frequent in the plural. Attempts to establish a consistent difference of meaning between inflected and uninflected forms are unconvincing.

NB: The most idiomatic equivalent of English *all* with a singular noun is often a phrase with *ganz*, see (g) below.

(b) *all-* is often used in conjunction with another determiner

In the plural both inflected and uninflected forms are found, in the singular only uninflected *all*:

all mein Geld
von **all diesem** Brot
all/alle meine Brüder
nach **all ihrer** Mühe
mit **all/allen diesen** Schwierigkeiten

NB: Only the inflected form is used before *solch*, which then has the endings of an adjective, e.g.: *alle solchen Frauen*.

(c) *all-* used as a PRONOUN **declines like** *dieser*

(see Table 5.2), but it has no genitive singular forms. The neuter singular *alles* is used for 'everything', the plural *alle* for 'everyone':

Alles ist bereit	*Everything is ready*
Ich bin mit **allem** einverstanden	*I agree to everything*
Alle waren anwesend	*Everybody was present*
Sind das **alle**?	*Is that all (of them)?*

(d) Plural *alle* **'all' is often used with a personal pronoun**

Sie hat uns **alle** beleidigt	*She insulted us all*
Ich habe mit ihnen **allen** gesprochen	*I have spoken to all of them*
Das ist unser **aller** Hoffnung	*That is the hope of all of us*

alle usually follows the pronoun, but in the nominative it can be separated from it. In this case it has slightly less emphasis. Compare:

Sie **alle** sind gekommen
Sie sind **alle** gekommen   } *They have all come*

(e) Uninflected *all* **and inflected** *alles* **are commonly used with the demonstratives** *das* **and** *dieses*

This corresponds to English 'all that' or 'all this'. Uninflected *all* always precedes the demonstrative, but inflected *alles* may precede or follow the demonstrative, or, with less emphasis, be separated from it:

Ich habe **all das/alles das/das alles** schon
    gesehen   } *I've already seen all that*
Das habe ich **alles** schon gesehen

Ich bin mit **all dem/dem allen/allem** dem   *I agree to all that*
    einverstanden

Mit all diesem werde ich nicht fertig   *I can't cope with all this*

NB: In the dative singular, when *all-* follows the demonstrative, it can have the ending *-en* as an alternative to *-em*, e.g.: *dem/diesem allen* or *dem allem*.

(f) A noun can be qualified by a following inflected *all-*

all- follows the verb if the noun comes before the verb. This usage is most common in the plural:

Die Kinder spielen **alle** im Garten
Die Semmeln sind **alle** trocken

In the singular this construction is colloquial and restricted to the nominative and accusative singular feminine and neuter:

Das Brot ist **alles** trocken
Ich habe **die Milch alle** verschüttet

Singular *alles* is often used with a plural noun after the verb *sein* in the sense 'nothing but': *Das sind alles Lügen*.

(g) The use of *ganz* **for English 'all'**

In practice, the adjective *ganz* is often the most idiomatic equivalent of English 'all', particularly with singular nouns. Thus, English 'all my money' may correspond in German to *mein ganzes Geld* or *all mein Geld*, with the former being rather more frequent. Compare also:

Der **ganze** Wein war schlecht	*All the wine was bad*
diese **ganze** Unsicherheit	*all this uncertainty*
mit seiner **ganzen** jugendlichen Energie	*with all his youthful energy*

With collective nouns, time expressions and geographical names *ganz* is often the only possible equivalent for English 'all':

Die **ganze** Familie kommt	*all of the family is/are coming*
den **ganzen** Tag (lang)	*all day (long)*
der **ganze** Januar war kalt	*all January it was cold*
ganz Europa, **ganz** Schweden, **ganz** München	*all (of) Europe, all (of) Sweden, all (of) Munich*
in der **ganzen** Schweiz	*in all of Switzerland*

The use of *ganz* with a plural noun is colloquial, e.g.: *Nach dem Sturm waren die ganzen Fenster kaputt*. In such cases *sämtliche* (see 5.5.23) is a common alternative in formal registers, e.g.: *Nach dem Sturm waren sämtliche Fenster* ('all the windows') *kaputt*.

(h) Other uses of *all-*

(i) *alles* can be used to emphasise a large number of people or things with the interrogatives *wer* and *was*, cf. 5.3.3b, e.g.: *Wer kommt denn alles? Was hast du dort alles gekauft?*

(ii) In regional colloquial speech in the South and West, *all(e)s* (often spelled *als*) is used to emphasise the continuous nature of an action (= English 'to keep on doing sth.'), e.g.: *Er hat als geflucht* 'He kept on cursing'.

(iii) In colloquial North German *alle* is used in the sense of 'all gone': *Die Butter ist jetzt alle. Meine Geduld ist alle.*

(iv) *alle* is compounded with the demonstrative pronoun in the phrases *bei alledem* 'for all that', *trotz alledem* 'in spite of all that'.

(v) *alles* occurs frequently with an adjective used as a noun, see 6.4.5, e.g.: *alles Wichtige* 'all (the) important things'.

5.5.2 *ander* 'other'

(a) In most contexts *ander* **is used simply as an adjective**

However, it has a few special forms and uses which resemble those of a determiner or pronoun. The following examples illustrate the range of its most common uses:

der **and(e)re** Student	*the other student*
mein **anderes** Auto	*my other car*
der **and(e)re**	*the other one*
irgendein **and(e)rer**	*some/any other one*
die drei **anderen**	*the three others*
alle **anderen**	*all the others*
alles **and(e)re**	*everything else*

(b) Notes on the spelling and forms of *ander*

(i) The first *-e-* is often dropped in writing, e.g. *andre, andrer, andres*. With the endings *-en* and *-em*, though, it is more usual to drop the second *-e-*, e.g. *ander(e)m, ander(e)n* (less common: *andrem, andren*).

(ii) When used with a preceding determiner and no following noun, it differs from other adjectives in not normally being spelled with a capital letter: *der and(e)re, alles and(e)re*, etc. However, an initial small or capital letter can be used after *etwas* and *nichts*: *etwas and(e)res/And(e)res, nichts and(e)res/And(e)res*, see also 23.2.1c.

(iii) When *ander* is used without a preceding article or other determiner, a following adjective has the same ('strong') endings as those of *ander*, <u>except</u> that *-en* is the norm in the dative singular masculine and neuter:

anderes dumm**es** Gerede
andere italienisch**e** Maler
mit ander**er** modern**er** Musik
aus ander**em** wertvoll**en** Material

NB: (i) 'another cup of tea' = *noch eine Tasse Tee*.
　　(ii) For the adverb *anders* 'else', see 7.3.5.

5.5.3 *beide* 'both'

(a) *beide* **'both' can be used as a determiner or a pronoun**
It has the same endings as the plural of *dieser* (see Table 5.2), and a following adjective has **weak** endings:

Ich habe **beide** Bücher gekauft	*I bought both books*
Beide Brüder sind gekommen	*Both brothers came*
beide jungen Mädchen	*both young girls*
Seine Brüder sind **beide** gekommen	*His brothers both came*
Beide sind gekommen	*Both came*

When used as a pronoun, *beide* can be strengthened by *alle*:

Alle beide sind gekommen	*The two of them came*

(b) *beide* **can be used as a simple adjective after a definite article or another determiner. It then has the endings of an adjective ('weak' declension) and often corresponds to English 'two':**

Seine **beiden** Brüder sind gekommen	*His two brothers came*
Die **beiden** Brüder sind gekommen	*The two brothers came*

(c) **Used with a personal pronoun,** *beide* **usually has the endings of plural** *dieser*
wir **beide**, sie **beide**, von euch **beiden**, unser **beider**

There is some variation in usage with *wir* and *ihr*:

(i) In isolation *wir beiden* can be used rather than *wir beide*. It is generally less common, but it is usual if a noun follows, e.g.: *wir beiden Freunde*.

(ii) *ihr beiden* is more usual than *ihr beide* in isolation, e.g.: *Ihr* **beiden***, wollt ihr mitkommen?* Within a clause either is current, e.g.: *Wollt ihr* **beide(n)** *schon mitkommen?*

(iii) If *beide* is separated from the pronoun, only the ending *-e* is usual:

Wir wollen **beide** schon mitkommen.	Ihr wolltet **beide** mitkommen, oder?

Beide halten sie ein Wahlergebnis für möglich, das eine große Koalition erzwänge (*Zeit*)
They **both** *consider an election result possible which would force a grand coalition*

(d) The neuter singular *beides* is used collectively to refer to two things

In this usage it can be the equivalent of English 'either'

Sie hatte einen Hut und einen Regenschirm mit und ließ **beides** im Zug liegen	*She had a hat and an umbrella with her and left both on the train*
Sprechen Sie Deutsch oder Englisch? – **Beides**	*Do you speak German or English? Both.*
Beides ist möglich	*Either is possible*

If *beides* is the subject of *sein*, the verb can be singular or plural:

Das Hotel und die Landschaft: **beides ist/sind** schön	*The hotel and the scenery: both are lovely*

NB: The use of *beides* to refer to people is purely colloquial, e.g.: *Ich habe mit den Brüdern Schmid zu Mittag gegessen.* **Beides** *ist/sind* (in writing: *Beide sind*) *Vegetarier.*

(e) Other uses of *beide* and other equivalents of English 'both'

Einer von beiden könnte uns helfen	*One/Either of the two could help us*
An beiden Enden des Ganges hängt ein Bild	*At either end of the corridor there is a picture*
in beiden Fällen	*in either case*
Keiner von beiden ist gekommen	*Neither of them came*
Sowohl seine Frau **als (auch)** seine Tochter sind krank	*Both his wife and his daughter are sick*

5.5.4 *einer* 'one'

(a) The pronoun *einer* declines like the possessive pronoun *meiner*

The forms are given in Table 5.10. The pronoun *einer* has different endings from those of the indefinite article *ein* in the nominative singular masculine (*einer*) and the nominative/accusative singular neuter (*eines*).

TABLE 5.10 Declension of the pronoun *einer*

	Masculine	Feminine	Neuter
Nominative	einer	eine	eines
Accusative	einen	eine	eines
Genitive	eines	einer	eines
Dative	einem	einer	einem

The genitive forms of *einer* are not in common use. A paraphrase with *von* (see 2.4) is usually preferred, e.g.: *die Empfehlung von einem ihrer Freunde*, rather than: *die Empfehlung eines ihrer Freunde* 'the recommendation of one of her friends'.

NB: (i) *eines* is often written *eins*, reflecting its usual pronunciation.
(ii) For the use of *eins* as a numeral 'one', see **9.1.2**.

(b) *einer* corresponds to English pronoun 'one'

einer der Männer, **eine** der Frauen, **ein(e)s** der Kinder	*one of the men, one of the women, one of the children*
Ein Fenster war offen und **ein(e)s** war zu	*One window was open and one was shut*
Ich sprach mit **einer** der Damen	*I spoke to one of the ladies*
eines der Themen, die der slowenische Außenminister angesprochen hat (*Presse*)	*one of the topics which the Slovenian foreign minister touched on*

Unstressed *einer* has the negative *keiner*, see 5.5.16, stressed *einer* has the negative *nicht einer*. Compare: *Ich habe **keinen** gesehen* 'I haven't seen one' and: *Ich habe **nicht einen** gesehen* 'I haven't seen a single one'.

(c) *einer* **often has the sense of 'someone', 'anyone'**

Einer muss es getan haben	*Someone must have done it*
einer, der ihn kannte	*a person/someone who knew him*
Mit so **einem** will ich nichts zu tun haben	*I don't want anything to do with anyone like that*
Da kam **einer** durch die Glastür	*Someone came through the glass door*

This is common in spoken German. It is often equivalent to *jemand*, see **5.5.15**, although this more clearly refers to an indefinite 'somebody' whose identity is quite unknown. *jemand* is also generally more polite, whereas *einer* can sound offensive, particularly in the feminine, e.g.: *Da war gerade **eine** mit sechs Kindern.*

The case forms of *einer* are used for those which *man* lacks (principally the accusative and dative, see **5.5.18**), but using *einer* for *man* in the nominative (e.g.: *Und das soll **einer** wissen!* for: *Und das soll man wissen!*) is restricted to colloquial speech.

(d) *ein-* **can be used as an adjective with the definite article, the demonstratives or the possessives**

It then has the 'weak' adjective endings (see Table 6.3), but it never has an initial capital letter, even when there is no noun following:

Der **eine** deutsche Tourist beschwerte sich	*One German tourist complained*
das **eine**, das ich brauche	*the one thing I need*
Mein **einer** Sohn ist gestorben (coll.)	*One of my sons has died*
Dieser **eine** Schnaps wird dich nicht gleich umwerfen	*This one schnapps won't knock you out*

der eine linked to a following *der andere* corresponds to English '(the) one . . . the other', etc. In German, though, the definite article is usually present, whereas it can be lacking in English, and the plural *die einen* can occur in the meaning 'some':

Das eine Buch habe ich gelesen, **das andere** aber noch nicht	*I've read one of the books, but not the other one yet*
Die einen sangen, **die anderen** spielten	*Some were singing, others were playing*

(e) Some idiomatic uses of *einer*

Das ist aber **einer**!	*He's quite a lad*
Du bist mir **einer**! (see 2.5.3c)	*You're a nice one!*
Eins wollte ich noch sagen	*There's one more thing I wanted to say*
Trinken wir noch **eins**?	*Shall we have another (drink)?*
Es ist mir alles **eins**	*It's all the same to me*
Er redet **in einem** fort	*He talks without stopping*

5.5.5 *ein wenig, ein bisschen* 'a little'

(a) *ein wenig* **corresponds to English 'a little'**

The *ein* does not decline. A phrase with *von* (see 2.4) is used rather than a genitive:

Ich hatte noch **ein wenig** britisches Geld	*I still had a little British money*
Der Zug hatte sich **ein wenig** verspätet	*The train had got a little late*

Der Saal war **ein wenig** ruhiger geworden	*The room had become a little more quiet*
mit **ein wenig** männlicher Eitelkeit	*with a little male vanity*

(b) *ein bisschen* **can replace** *ein wenig* **in most contexts**

It could be used in all the examples in (a) without any difference in meaning, but it can sound more colloquial. Unlike *ein wenig*, it can, optionally, be declined in the dative singular, e.g. *mit ein(em) bisschen Geld*. This is normal when it is used as a pronoun, e.g. *Mit einem bisschen wäre ich schon zufrieden*. It also differs from *ein wenig* in that it can occur with a preceding adjective:

ein winziges **bisschen** Käse	*a tiny little bit of cheese*
mit einem ganz kleinen **bisschen** gesundem Verstand	*with a very little bit of common sense*

NB: In spoken South German usage the form *ein bisse(r)l* is a frequent variant for northern *ein bisschen*.

(c) *bisschen* **may also be used with a demonstrative, a possessive or** *kein*

mit **dem bisschen** Verstand, den er hat	*with the little sense that he has*
mit **ihrem bisschen** Talent	*with her bit of talent*
Er hat **kein bisschen** Humor	*He hasn't got the least sense of humour*

5.5.6 *ein paar* 'a few'

The *ein* of *ein paar* does not decline. A phrase with *von* (see 2.4) is used rather than a following genitive. The phrase *ein paar* is close in meaning to *einige*, see 5.5.7, but it sounds more colloquial:

Ein paar Flaschen Wein haben wir noch im Keller	*We've still got a few bottles of wine in the cellar*
Willst du **ein paar** haben?	*Do you want a few?*
mit der Hilfe von **ein paar** alten Freunden	*with the help of a few old friends*

The *ein* can be replaced by another determiner, which <u>is</u> declined. Such combinations can sound disparaging or pejorative:

Was soll ich mit den **paar** Mark anfangen?	*What am I supposed to do with these lousy few marks?*
der Wert meiner **paar** Möbel	*the value of my few bits of furniture*
Die Straßenbahn kommt alle **paar** Minuten	*The tram comes every few minutes*

NB: *ein paar* should not be confused with *ein Paar* 'a pair'. Compare *ein paar Schuhe* 'a few shoes' but *ein Paar Schuhe* 'a pair of shoes'.

5.5.7 *einiger, einige* 'some'

einig- refers to a limited amount or number. It corresponds to English unstressed 'some', (or 'a few', as it is close in meaning to *ein paar*, see 5.5.6). It declines like *dieser* (see Table 5.2) except that the genitive singular masculine and neuter form (which is little used) is *einigen*, and a following adjective in the plural usually has **strong** endings, see 6.2.3b.

(a) The use of *einiger* **in the singular is limited**

The usual German equivalents of English unstressed *some* in the singular are *etwas* (see 5.5.9), or, most commonly, simply no article or determiner at all (see 4.8.7), e.g.: *Ich habe heute (etwas) Fleisch gekauft* 'I bought some meat today'.

When *einig-* is used in the singular it implies a rather unusual or unexpected quantity and often comes close to English 'no little'. It is most frequent with mass and abstract nouns (especially *Entfernung* and *Zeit*), adjectives used as nouns and collectives:

mit **einigem** Glück	*with some degree of luck*
bei **einigem** guten Willen	*with a certain degree of good will*
vor ihm in **einiger** Entfernung	*some distance in front of him*
vor **einiger** Zeit schon	*some time ago now*
nach **einigem** Überlegen	*after some consideration*
Diese Schlangen, die ihr Gift spucken, zielen bis drei Meter weit noch mit **einiger** Treffsicherheit (*Grzimek*)	*These snakes, which spit their venom, can aim up to three metres with no little accuracy*

In the singular *einig-* is mainly used as a determiner rather than as a pronoun, but the neuter singular *einiges* does occur as a collective indefinite pronoun:

einiges davon	*some of it*
Ich habe noch **einiges** zu tun	*I've still got a few things to do*

(b) *einige* **is widely used both as a determiner and a pronoun in the plural**

Sie wollte **einige** Ansichtskarten von Rothenburg kaufen	*She wanted to buy some postcards of Rothenburg*
In der Stadt gibt es **einige** Friseure	*There are a few hairdressers in the town*
unter Verwendung **einiger** technischer Mittel	*by using some technical methods*
Einige mussten stehen	*Some/A few had to stand*
Sie hat schon **einige** mitgebracht	*She's already brought some/a few*

German often uses no determiner in contexts where English uses unstressed 'some' to refer to a number of things. Thus, a common alternative to the first example above would be: *Sie wollte Ansichtskarten von Rothenburg kaufen.*

NB: *einige* is often used with numerals to mean 'a few', e.g. *einige tausend Bücher* 'a few thousand books'.

5.5.8 *etliche* 'some'

etliche is similar in meaning to *einige*. However, it typically implies 'more than the expected number' and it is quite widely used in this sense in both spoken and written German. In this way, it approaches English 'several' or 'a fair number of'. It declines like *dieser* (see Table 5.2) and it is almost only used in the plural, as a determiner (much less commonly as a pronoun). A following adjective usually has **strong** endings, see 6.2.3b.

Warum ist die Bahn so unpünktlich geworden? Da gibt es **etliche** Ursachen (*Spiegel*)	*Why have the railways become so unpunctual? There are several/a (good) number of reasons for this*
Etliche dieser Stücke sind auch für Anfänger relativ leicht zu bewältigen (*SWF*)	*Some/A number of these pieces are relatively easy to manage, even for a beginner*

NB: In Switzerland *etwelche* is used with much the same meaning as *etliche*, e.g. *Den FC Flawil plagen vor dem morgigen Spiel zwar etwelche Personalsorgen* (*SGT*).

5.5.9 *etwas* 'something', 'anything'

etwas is used as an **indefinite pronoun**, to **qualify nouns**, and as an **adverb**. It has no case forms and is not used in genitive constructions, a phrase with *von* (see 2.4) being used if necessary.

(a) As an indefinite pronoun, *etwas* **corresponds to English 'something' or 'anything'**

Etwas störte mich	*Something bothered me*
Ich habe **etwas** für Sie	*I've got something for you*
Hast du **etwas** gesagt?	*Did you say anything?*

In this use, *etwas* is commonly reduced to *was* in colloquial speech unless it occupies first position in the sentence, e.g. *Ich habe **was** für Sie; Hast du **was** gesagt?*
etwas is often used with *von* in a partitive sense, i.e. 'some (of)':

Ich möchte **etwas** von diesem Kuchen	*I would like some of this cake*

In contexts like this, *etwas* can be omitted: *Ich möchte von diesem Kuchen.*

(b) Qualifying a noun, *etwas* has the sense of 'some', 'any' or 'a little'

It is used chiefly with mass and abstract nouns in the singular. However, as an equivalent to unstressed English 'some' or 'any', German very commonly does not use any determiner at all (see 4.2.2a, 4.8.7 and 5.5.7b), and *etwas* could be omitted in all the examples below:

Ich brauche **etwas** frisches Fleisch	*I need some fresh meat*
Er hat kaum **etwas** Geld	*He has hardly any money*
Bringen Sie mir bitte **etwas** Brot	*Please bring me some bread*
Sie muss **etwas** Geduld haben	*She needs a little patience*
Etwas mehr Aufmerksamkeit wäre nützlich gewesen	*A little more attention would have been useful*

etwas is commonly used with a following adjective used as a noun, (see 6.4.5). The adjective has the 'strong' adjective endings:

etwas ganz Neu**es**	*something quite new*
Er hat von **etwas** ganz Neu**em** gesprochen	*He spoke of something quite new*

(c) As an adverb, *etwas* means 'somewhat', 'a bit'

Er ist **etwas** nervös	*He is somewhat/rather/a bit nervous*
Es geht ihm **etwas** besser	*He is somewhat/a bit better*
Er zögerte **etwas**	*He hesitated somewhat/a bit*

5.5.10 *folgend* '(the) following'

folgend can be used as a simple adjective, but it has some special forms and uses which resemble those of a determiner or pronoun. Unlike English 'following', it is often used without a preceding article or other determiner. In these contexts a following adjective usually has 'weak' endings in the singular and 'strong' endings in the plural, see 6.2.3:

alle **folgenden** Bemerkungen	*all the following remarks*
Sie machte **folgende** Bemerkungen	*She made the following remarks*
Sie machte **folgende** treffende Bemerkungen	*She made the following apposite remarks*
folgender interessante Gedanke	*the following interesting thought*
mit **folgender** nachdrücklichen Warnung	*with the following firm warning*
Sie sagte mir **Folgendes**: . . .	*She said the following to me: . . .*
Im **Folgenden** wird diese Frage näher erläutert	*In the following this question will be clarified more precisely*
Aus **Folgendem** lässt sich schließen, dass . . .	*From the following it may be deduced that . . .*

When *folgend* is used as a pronoun meaning 'the following', as in the last three examples, it has an initial capital letter.

5.5.11 *irgend* 'some . . . or other'

(a) The principal use of *irgend* is to emphasise indefiniteness

It occurs in combination with many indefinite pronouns, adverbs and determiners, giving them the sense of 'some . . . or other' or 'any . . . at all'. All these compounds of *irgend* are nowadays written as single words, e.g. *irgendetwas, irgendjemand, irgendwo*.

(b) *irgend* can be compounded with most interrogative adverbs to form indefinite adverbs

(see 7.5 for the basic forms of these interrogative adverbs), i.e.:

irgendwann 'sometime or other, any time'; *irgendwie* 'somehow, anyhow'; *irgendwo* 'somewhere, anywhere'; *irgendwohin* '(to) somewhere, anywhere'; *irgendwoher* 'from somewhere, anywhere':

Du musst es **irgendwie** machen	*You'll have to do it somehow*
Er fährt heute Nachmittag **irgendwohin**	*He's going somewhere this afternoon*
Gehst du heute Abend **irgendwohin**?	*Are you going anywhere tonight?*

(c) With *einer*, *(et)was*, *jemand* and *wer*, *irgend* stresses indefiniteness

irgendeiner, irgendjemand and *irgendwer* correspond to English 'somebody, anybody', *irgendetwas* to 'something, anything'. In practice, *irgendeiner* and *irgendwer* are commoner than simple *einer* and *wer* (see 5.5.4 and 5.5.27) to mean 'somebody, anybody':

Irgendwann wurden von **irgendwem** diese Briefe aus dem Kasten genommen (*Böll*)	*At some time or other someone (or other) took these letters out of the letter-box*
Versteht er **irgendetwas** vom Wein?	*Does he know anything (at all) about wine?*
Irgendeiner soll es gesagt haben	*Someone (or other) is supposed to have said it*
Hat denn **irgendjemand** angerufen?	*Did anybody phone?*

Note that only *irgendjemand* and *irgendetwas*, <u>not</u> simple *jemand* or *etwas*, are possible in response to a question:

Wer hat eben geklopft? **Irgendjemand**	*Who just knocked? Someone or other*
Was willst du denn kaufen? **Irgendetwas**	*What are you going to buy, then? Something or other*

In colloquial North German, *irgend* can be compounded with the prepositional adverb with *wo(r)-* (see **5.3.3c**), in place of *irgendetwas* with a preposition:

Ich habe mich **irgendworan** gestoßen (written: *an irgendetwas*)	*I knocked against something or other*

(d) irgendein(er) and irgendwelcher

These correspond to 'some (or other), any (whatsoever)', often with the sense of 'no matter which/who'. They are used as determiners or pronouns.

(i) The determiner *irgendein* has the endings of the indefinite article *ein*, see Table 4.2. It is used in the singular with countable nouns:

Er zeigte mir **irgendeine** Broschüre	*He showed me some brochure or other*
Hat er **irgendeine** Bemerkung gemacht?	*Did he make any remark (at all)?*
Die Selbstmordquote soll höher sein als in	*The suicide rate is supposed to be higher than in any*

irgendeinem anderen Ort der Welt   *other place in the world*
(*Bednarz*)

(ii) The pronoun *irgendeiner*, which declines like *einer* (see Table 5.10) has only singular forms and can only refer to countable nouns. The masculine and feminine forms are used in the sense of 'somebody, anybody':

Irgendeiner muss dich gesehen haben   *Someone or other must have seen you*
Wenn du wirklich einen neuen Tisch suchst,   *If you're really looking for a new table, you must*
  musst du hier im Geschäft **irgendeinen**   *have seen one here in the shop which you like*
  gesehen haben, der dir gefällt
Ich habe ein paar Bücher über Israel. Sie   *I've got a few books about Israel. You can borrow*
  können sich **irgendeins** ausleihen   *any one you like*

(iii) *irgendwelcher*, which declines like *dieser* (see Table 5.2), is used as a determiner in the singular with mass and abstract nouns, and in the plural. A following adjective in the plural most often has weak endings, see 6.2.3. The genitive is rarely used in the singular:

Wenn irgendwelche anderen Idioten auf   *If any other idiots want to get married on RTL ...*
  RTL heiraten wollen, . . . (*HMP*)
Er hat **irgendwelches** dumme(s) Zeug   *He was talking some stupid rubbish or other*
  geredet
Wenn Sie **irgendwelche** Probleme haben,   *If you have any problems (at all), turn to us*
  wenden Sie sich an uns (*Bednarz*)

NB: Colloquially, *irgendwelcher* is often used for *irgendein*, e.g. *Er zeigte mir **irgendwelche** Broschüre.*

(e) *irgend so ein* **(plural: *irgend solche*) corresponds to English 'one/some of those', 'any/some such'**
It often has a pejorative tone:

Wer war es? Es war **irgend so ein**   *Who was it? It was one of those men who sell*
  Vertreter für Doppelfenster   *double glazing*
Er machte **irgend solche** komische   *He made some such odd remarks*
  Bemerkungen

(f) *irgend* **is used as an independent adverb with the sense of** *irgendwie*
i.e. 'somehow, anyhow, in some way':

wenn **irgend** möglich   *if at all possible*
Ich würde mich freuen, wenn es **irgend** geht *I would be pleased if it's possible somehow*

5.5.12 *jeder* 'each', 'every'

(a) *jeder* **is only used in the singular, as a determiner or a pronoun**
When used as a determiner, *jeder* corresponds to English 'each', 'every', when used as a pronoun to English 'everyone', 'everybody'. It declines like *dieser* (see Table 5.2), except that *jeden* (rather than *jedes*) is frequent in the genitive singular masculine and neuter if the following noun has the ending -(e)s, e.g. *am Ende jeden/jedes Abschnitts*. It is not used in the genitive as a pronoun.:

Sie hat **jedem** Kind einen Apfel gegeben   *She gave each child an apple*
nach **jedem** solchen Versuch   *after each such attempt*
Er kam **jeden** Tag zur selben Zeit   *He came every day at the same time*
In diesem kleinen Ort kennt **jeder jeden**   *In this little place everyone knows everybody else*

jeder often has an individualising sense (i.e. 'no matter which/who'), in which case it can be the equivalent of English 'any':

Das weiß doch **jeder** gebildete Bürger	*Any/Every educated citizen knows that, though*
Die industrielle Revolution verwandelte die Lebensbedingungen der Menschen radikaler als **jeder** andere Ereigniszusammenhang der neueren Geschichte (*Jaeger*)	*The Industrial Revolution changed people's living conditions more radically than any other set of events in recent history*

NB: The neuter *jedes* can refer back to both sexes: *Seine Eltern waren sehr tüchtig, jedes auf seine Weise.*

(b) The combination *ein jeder* is more emphatic than *jeder*

It is used chiefly as a pronoun and is particularly frequent in the individualising sense of stressed 'any', i.e. 'no matter which/who'. In this combination, *jeder* has the same endings as a simple adjective:

Ein jeder wollte was sagen	*Everyone wanted to say something*
Das könnte doch **ein jeder** machen	*But everybody/anybody (at all) could do that*
Das kannst du doch nicht **einem jeden** erzählen	*But you can't tell that to just anybody*
Die Wünsche **eines jeden** werden berücksichtigt	*The wishes of every individual are taken into account*

5.5.13 *jedermann* 'everybody', 'everyone'

jedermann is only used, as a pronoun, in elevated, formal registers and set phrases. Its meaning is the same as that of *jeder*, which is much more commonly used. Its only case form is the genitive *jedermanns*.

Jedermann wusste, dass Michael den Wehrdienst verweigert hatte	*Everyone knew that Michael had refused to do military service*
Das ist nicht **jedermanns** Sache	*That's not everyone's cup of tea*

5.5.14 *jedweder, jeglicher* 'each', 'every'

jedweder and *jeglicher* decline like *dieser* (see Table 5.2). They are used as determiners or pronouns as alternatives to *jeder*, but both are largely restricted to written registers.

(a) *jedweder* is rather more emphatic than *jeder*

It has a rather old-fashioned ring and is used sparingly, even in formal registers:

Auch sonst bleiben den Insassen jedwede Motorgeräusche verborgen (*HMP*)	*Otherwise, too, the occupants are cut off from any sort of noise from the motor*

(b) *jeglicher* stresses the individuality of the items in question

It is most often used in the sense of stressed 'any' (i.e. 'no matter who/what'). It is most frequent nowadays with abstract nouns and in negative contexts. Unlike *jeder*, it can also be used in the plural. Adjectives following *jeglicher* have the strong declension; on, see 6.2.3a:

Das entbehrt **jeglicher** Grundlage	*That is completely unfounded*
Gorbatschow lehnte **jegliche** Änderung der Grenzziehungen in der Sowjetunion ab (*FR*)	*Gorbachov turned down any alteration of the frontiers in the Soviet Union*

die vollkommen unbefangene Ablehnung	*the completely natural rejection of all kinds of*
jeglicher demagogischer Attraktionen	*attractive demagogery*
(*Pörtner*)	

5.5.15 *jemand* 'somebody', 'someone', *niemand* 'nobody', 'no-one'

(a) Declension and use of *jemand* and *niemand*

jemand 'somebody', 'someone' and *niemand* 'nobody', 'no-one' have the case forms shown in Table 5.11.

TABLE 5.11 Declension of *jemand, niemand*

Nominative	jemand	niemand
Accusative	jemanden	niemanden
Genitive	jemandes	niemandes
Dative	jemandem	niemandem

In the accusative and dative, forms without endings are at least as common as the forms with endings in both speech and writing:

> Ich habe **niemand/niemanden** gesehen
> Ich habe **jemand/jemandem** das Paket gegeben

The genitive forms tend to be avoided by paraphrasing, i.e. *Hat jemand diese Aktentasche liegen lassen?* rather than: *Ist das jemands Aktentasche?*

Pronouns and determiners referring back to *jemand* and *niemand* have the masculine singular form: *Niemand, **der** es weiß; Jemand hat **seine** Tasche vergessen*

NB: (i) In colloquial speech, *einer* and *wer* are common alternatives to *jemand*, see 5.5.4 and 5.5.27, as is *keiner* for *niemand*, see 5.5.16.
  (ii) The indefiniteness of *jemand* may be emphasised by combining it with *irgend*, see 5.5.11c.

(b) *jemand* and *niemand* with a following adjective

When followed by an adjective, *jemand* and *niemand* are usually endingless in the accusative and dative. The adjective is treated as a noun (see 6.4), and it can have the ending *-es* in all cases, or, alternatively, the endings *-en* in the accusative and *-em* in the dative cases.

> Jemand Fremd**es** ist gekommen
> Ich habe jemand Fremd**es/en** gesehen
> Ich habe mit jemand Fremd**es/em** gesprochen

jemand and *niemand* can be used in a similar way with *ander*, which, unlike other adjectives, always has a small initial letter in all these forms:

> Jemand ander**s** ist gekommen
> Ich habe jemand ander**s/anderen** gesehen
> Ich habe mit jemand ander**s/anderem** gesprochen

NB: The endings *-en* and *-em* are more typical of South German usage. Here, too, the ending *-er* is used in the nominative case, e.g. *jemand anderer, jemand Bekannter*. However, this is considered to be a non-standard regionalism.

5.5.16 *kein, keiner* 'no', 'not . . . any', 'none'

(a) *kein* **is the negative form of the indefinite article**

See 4.1.2. It declines exactly like *ein*, with the forms given in Table 4.2. It is used typically where a corresponding positive sentence would have an indefinite or no article, and it thus usually corresponds to English 'not a', 'not . . . any ' or 'no':

Sie hat ein Auto	Sie hat **kein** Auto
Wir haben frische Brötchen	Wir haben **keine** frischen Brötchen
Ich habe Zeit	Ich habe **keine** Zeit

(b) *kein* or *nicht* **in negation?**

It sometimes seems difficult to know whether to use *kein* or *nicht* in negation. In general, *kein* is used to negate an indefinite noun (i.e. one with an indefinite article or no article), as in the examples given under (a) above. *nicht* is used in other cases, notably to negate a whole sentence, e.g. *Sie will heute mitkommen – Sie will heute **nicht** mitkommen*. However, there are contexts where the choice is not completely obvious, i.e.:

(i) German phrases with an indefinite noun (and thus negated with *kein*) which have rather different English equivalents:

Ich bin Deutscher
Ich spreche Deutsch
ein Problem von großer Bedeutung

Ich bin **kein** Deutscher
Ich spreche **kein** Deutsch
ein Problem von **keiner** großen Bedeutung

(ii) Phrasal verbs with nouns, e.g. *Atem holen*, *sich Mühe geben*, *Freude empfinden* and all those with *haben*, e.g. *Angst*, *Durst*, *Hunger haben*, etc. are generally negated with *kein*:

Er hat sich **keine** Mühe gegeben
Dabei hat er **keine** Freude empfunden
Ich habe **keinen** Durst, Hunger
Sie hatten **keine** Angst

Phrasal verbs with *nehmen* have *kein* **or** *nicht*:

Er hat **keine/nicht** Rücksicht auf mich genommen
Sie wollen **keine/nicht** Rache nehmen
Sie hat **keinen/nicht** Abschied von ihm genommen

nicht occurs with phrasal verbs where the noun is so closely linked to the verb that it is felt to be the equivalent of a separable prefix:

Er spielt **nicht** Klavier
Sie läuft **nicht** Schi
Sie haben in Berlin **nicht** Wurzel gefasst
Er hat **nicht** Wort gehalten
Er kann **nicht** Auto fahren

(c) *kein* and *nicht ein*

kein is the usual equivalent of English 'not a' (and using *nicht ein* for *kein* is typical of English learners' German). Nevertheless, there are a few contexts where *nicht ein* is used:

(i) if *ein* is stressed, i.e. 'not one/a (single)':

Die TAP besitzt **nicht ein** Flugzeug, denn alle 38 Maschinen sind geleast (*NZZ*)
TAP doesn't own a single aeroplane, as all 38 planes are leased

(ii) for direct contrasts:

Das ist eine Ulme, **nicht eine** Eiche   *That's an elm, not an oak*

(iii) *nicht ein* is more usual than *kein* after *wenn* 'if': *Man hätte ihn kaum bemerkt, wenn ihm **nicht ein** Schnurrbart etwas Distinguiertes verliehen hätte.*

(d) Some idiomatic uses of *kein* as a determiner

Sie ist noch **keine** zehn Jahre alt   *She's not yet ten years old*
keine zwei Stunden vor meiner Abreise   *within two hours of my departure*
Es ist noch **keine** fünf Minuten her   *It is less than five minutes ago*
Sie ist schließlich **kein** Kind mehr   *After all, she's no longer a child*

(e) The form *keiner* is used as a pronoun

It has endings like those of *einer*, see Table 5.10. It is rarely used in the genitive:

Keiner von uns hat es gewusst
Zum Schluss hat sie **kein(e)s** der Bücher gekauft
Haben Sie einen HD-fähigen Fernseher? Nein, wir haben **keinen**
In **keinem** dieser neuen Häuser möchte ich wohnen
kein(e)s von beiden *neither of them*

NB: (i)   The neuter form *kein(e)s* is used to refer to people of different sex: *Ich fragte meine Eltern, aber **keins** (von beiden) wusste es.*
  (ii) The use of *keiner* for *niemand* to mean 'no-one', 'nobody' (see 5.5.15a) is frequent in speech but generally avoided in writing as non-standard.

5.5.17 *lauter* 'only', 'nothing but'

lauter is indeclinable. It is used only as a determiner, i.e. before nouns:

Dort lag **lauter** Eis und Schnee   *Nothing but ice and snow lay there*
Es kamen **lauter** junge Leute   *Only young people came*
Er hat **lauter** solchen Unsinn geredet   *He only talked rubbish like that*

5.5.18 *man* 'one'

(a) The indefinite pronoun *man* corresponds to English 'one'

However, unlike 'one', it is not restricted to elevated registers. Rather, it corresponds to the general use of 'you' in spoken English, or, frequently, to 'we', 'they' or 'people' (and overusing *Leute* in contexts where *man* would be appropriate is typical of English learners' German). It is also often used in contexts where English would most naturally use a passive construction, e.g. *Man sagt* 'It is said', see 15.4.1. The corresponding pronouns are possessive *sein* and reflexive *sich*:

Als **man** sich zum Abendessen setzte,   *When they/we sat down to dinner the old gentleman*
  fehlte der alte Herr   *was missing*
Man hat sich nach dir erkundigt   *People were asking after you*
Man sollte seinen Freunden helfen   *One ought to help one's friends*
Hier spricht **man** meistens unter sich noch   *Here people mainly still speak Low German amongst*
  Plattdeutsch   *themselves*

man is sometimes used, for reasons of politeness, to refer to the speaker, e.g.: *Darf **man** fragen, wohin Sie fahren?* In certain situations this can acquire a note of sarcasm. This is always so when it is used to refer to the listener, e.g.: *Hat **man** schon wieder zu tief ins Glas geguckt?*

NB: *man* should **never** be referred back to with *er*, e.g.: *Wenn man müde ist, muss **man** (not: er) sich setzen.*

(b) *man* only has a nominative case form
In the accusative and dative *einen* and *einem* (see 5.5.4) are used:

Man weiß nie, ob er **einen** erkannt hat | *You never know whether he has recognised you*
So Leid es **einem** tut, man muss manchmal hart sein | *However much you regret it, you have to be hard sometimes*

NB: The use of the nominative form *einer* for *man* (see 5.5.4) is frequent in colloquial speech, but generally avoided in writing as non-standard.

5.5.19 *manch* 'some', 'many a'

manch always has the rather special sense of stressed 'some', i.e. 'a fair number, but by no means all'. This may be equivalent to English by 'many a' and in certain contexts comes close to the sense of English 'several'. *manch* has a number of alternative forms.

(a) As a determiner, *manch* is most often used in the inflected form *mancher*
i.e. with the endings of *dieser*, see Table 5.2.

In the genitive singular masculine and neuter, the form *manchen* is occasionally found besides the more frequent *manches* if the following noun has the ending -(e)s, (e.g. *manches Mannes* or *manchen Mannes*).

mancher can be used in the singular or the plural. The singular form (like English 'many a') may put more emphasis on the individual items, whereas the plural (like English stressed 'some') stresses the collectivity. In practice, however, the difference between, for example, *mancher schöne Tag* and *manche schöne Tage* is slight. A following adjective usually has **strong** endings, see 6.2.3.

An **manchen** Tagen blieb er lange im Bett | *Some days he stayed in bed a long time*
Von der Abzocke **mancher** Skiregionen ist hier keine Spur (*HMP*) | *Here there is no sign of the rip-off you get in a good number of skiing areas*
ein überhöhter Preis, wie er in **manchen** Reparaturwerkstätten seit Jahren üblich ist (*BILD*) | *an exorbitant price, such as has been usual in some garages for years*

(b) Uninflected *manch* is commonly used as a determiner in the following constructions
(i) before the indefinite article *ein*. This is a less common alternative to inflected *manch*, and it is mainly used in formal writing. The individual items are emphasised rather more strongly:

Da gibt es mancherlei Grund zum Zweifeln – **manch ein** Zeitgenosse wird sagen: zum Verzweifeln (*Zeit*) | *There are many kinds of reasons for doubt – many contemporaries will say: for despair*

(ii) before an adjective, where the uninflected form is a widespread and frequent alternative to the inflected one, especially in the singular:

Sie konnten dem Kanzler **manch** guten Tipp geben (*MM*) | *They were able to give the Chancellor many a good tip*

. . . um neben **manch** Komischem auch etliches Entlarvende bieten zu können (*MM*)	*. . . to be able to present quite a few revealing things besides much that is comical*

(iii) before neuter nouns. This alternative sounds rather old-fashioned, but it has become fashionable again recently:

Und so ist manch Dachstubentalent ins Scheinwerferlicht geraten (*NUZ*)	*In this way many a hidden talent has emerged into the limelight*

(c) As a pronoun *mancher* **declines like** *dieser*

See Table 5.2. It is not used in the genitive:

Mancher hat es nicht geglaubt	*Not many believed it*
Das ist schon **manchem** passiert	*That has happened to quite a few people*
Manche trinken Tee, andere lieber Kaffee	*Some people drink tea, others prefer coffee*
manche meiner Bekannten	*a fair number of my acquaintances*

manch einer is a fairly frequent alternative to inflected *mancher*:

Manch einer musste auf die Mittagspause verzichten (*MM*)	*Some had to give up their lunch hour*

5.5.20 *mehrere* 'several'

mehrere is used, as a determiner or a pronoun, in the plural only. It has the same endings as *dieser*(see Table 5.2). A following adjective usually has strong endings, see 6.2.3.

Ich habe **mehrere** Bücher darüber gelesen	*I have read several books about it*
Mehrere standen draußen und warteten	*Several people were standing outside waiting*
Es ist doch viel spannender, mit **mehreren** Jungen auszugehen, als immer an einem zu kleben (*BILD*)	*But it's much more exciting to go out with several boys than always to stick with one*

5.5.21 *meinesgleichen* 'people like me'

meinesgleichen is indeclinable. Parallel forms can be formed for the other persons, i.e. *deinesgleichen, seinesgleichen, ihresgleichen, unsresgleichen, euresgleichen*. If they are used as the subject of a verb, it has the endings of the third person singular. They can now sound rather old-fashioned:

Ich und **meinesgleichen** interessieren uns für so etwas nicht	*I and people like me aren't interested in things like that*
Euresgleichen hat es wirklich leicht	*People like you really have it easy*
Dieser Wagen hat nicht **seinesgleichen**	*This car has no equal*

5.5.22 *nichts* 'nothing', 'not . . . anything'

nichts does not decline:

Aus **nichts** wird **nichts** (Proverb)	*Nothing comes of nothing*
Nichts gefiel ihr dort	*She didn't like anything there*
nichts als Schwierigkeiten	*nothing but difficulties*

nichts is often used with a following adjective used as a noun, which has the strong endings, see 6.4.5:

nichts Neues	*nothing new*
Er hat von **nichts Neuem** gesprochen	*He didn't speak of anything new*

It is also common with *von* in partitive constructions, i.e. 'nothing (of)':

Ich möchte **nichts von** dem Essen	*I don't want any of the food*
nichts von alledem	*nothing of all that*

NB: In colloquial speech *nichts* is almost invariably pronounced *nix*.

5.5.23 *sämtlich* 'all (the)'

sämtliche inflects like *dieser*, see Table 5.2. It is used, as a determiner or a pronoun, in the plural only, as an emphatic alternative to *alle*. A following adjective has weak endings, see 6.2.3.

Sämtliche gezeigten Tiere wurden am Freitag von Experten bewertet (*SGT*)	*All the exhibited animals were judged on Friday by experts*
die Anschriften **sämtlicher** neuen Mitglieder	*the addresses of all the new members*

sämtliche is rather more limited in meaning than *alle*, since it can refer to all the members of a subgroup of persons or things, but not to all those which are in existence. Thus, one can say *Sämtliche* (OR: *Alle*) *Bäume in dem Wald wurden gefällt*, but only: *Alle* (NOT: *Sämtliche*) *Menschen sind sterblich*.

sämtliche can also be used with a preceding definite article or other determiner, in which case it has the endings of an adjective:

Meine **sämtlichen** Verwandten haben mir geschrieben	*All my relatives wrote to me*

As an adverb, *sämtlich* is used in the meaning 'without exception':

Sämtlich waren sie dem Staat eigen (*Johnson*)	*They all belonged to the state*

5.5.24 *unsereiner* 'someone like me', 'one of us'

unsereiner declines like *dieser*, see Table 5.2. There are parallel forms for the other persons, i.e. *eurereiner*, *ihrereiner*, although these are less frequent in practice:

Unsereiner kann das nicht wissen	*Someone like me can't know that*
Mit **unsereinem** spricht sie nie	*She doesn't talk to the likes of us*

NB: In the nominative and accusative, the neuter form *unsereins* is a common alternative to the masculine, especially in colloquial speech.

5.5.25 *viel* 'much', *viele* 'many', *wenig* 'a little', *wenige* 'a few'

The various forms and uses of *viel* 'much', 'many', 'a lot of' and *wenig* '(a) little', '(a) few', 'not many' are broadly similar. Both occur as a determiner, a pronoun, or an adverb. Both have alternative uninflected and inflected forms, in the latter case with the endings of *dieser* (see Table 5.2). In certain constructions and uses the uninflected forms are more usual, in others the inflected, without any identifiable difference in meaning. Adjectives following inflected *viele* and *wenige* in the plural usually have strong endings, see 6.2.3.

NB: (i) *ein wenig* 'a little' is invariable, see 5.5.5.
    (ii) For the comparatives of *viel* and *wenig*, see 8.2.4.

(a) Used as pronouns, *viel* and *wenig* most often have no endings in the singular, but they do have an ending in the plural

They are not used in the genitive singular:

Sie hat **viel**/**wenig** versucht
Er will **viel**/**wenig** haben
Viel/**Wenig** von dem Kuchen
Sie hat **viel**/**wenig** verraten
Ich bin mit **viel**/**wenig** von dem einverstanden, was du sagst
Viele/**Wenige** von diesen Büchern
Ich habe **viele**/**wenige** gesehen

The inflected neuter singular forms nominative/accusative **vieles**, dative **vielem** are occasionally used, chiefly in formal writing:

Sie hat **vieles** versucht   *She has tried a lot of things*
Mit **vielem** bin ich nicht einverstanden   *There's much I don't agree with*

Inflected forms of *wenig* (i.e. *weniges*, *wenigem*) are rare.

(b) Used as determiners, *viel* and *wenig* usually have no endings in the singular, but they do have endings in the plural

The genitive singular is scarcely ever used, a phrase with *von* being preferred:

Dazu ist **viel** Mut nötig   *Much courage is needed for that*
Ich trinke **wenig** Milch   *I don't drink much milk*
Er handelte mit **viel** Geschick   *He acted with a lot of skill*
Sie ist mit **wenig** Geld ausgekommen   *She managed with little money*
die Wirkung von **wenig** Wein   *the effect of not much wine*
der Genuss von **viel** Obst   *eating a lot of fruit*
Viele Probleme wurden besprochen   *Many problems were discussed*
Gestern waren **wenige** Zuschauer im   *There weren't many spectators at the ground*
   Stadion   *yesterday*
Er hat **viele**/**wenige** Freunde   *He has a lot of/few friends*
die Reden **vieler** Politiker   *the speeches of a lot of politicians*
mit **vielen**/**wenigen** Ausnahmen   *with a lot of/few exceptions*

There are some common exceptions to this usage:

(i) Inflected singular forms are sometimes used in formal registers with a following adjective used as a noun (see 6.4.5), e.g.: *Er hat **vieles**/**weniges** Interessante gesagt* (for less formal *Er hat **viel**/ **wenig** Interessantes gesagt*).

(ii) Inflected forms are quite common in the dative singular masculine and neuter, e.g.: *Mit **viel**/ **vielem** Zureden konnten wir einiges erreichen.*

(iii) Uninflected plural forms are occasionally found, mainly in colloquial speech: *Im Grunde interessieren mich furchtbar **wenig** Dinge außer meiner eigenen Arbeit (Langgässer).*

(iv) Inflected singular forms are found in a few set phrases, notably *vielen Dank*.

(c) *viel* **and** *wenig* **can be used with a preceding definite article or other determiner**
They then have the usual adjective endings:

Ich staunte über das **viele** Geld, das er ausgab	*I was amazed at the large amount of money that he spent*
der Mut dieser **vielen**/**wenigen** Frauen	*the courage of these many/few women*
Sie hat ihr **weniges** Geld verloren	*She lost her little bit of money*
die **wenigen**, die ihn erkannten	*the few who recognised him*

(d) *wenig* **in constructions like** *wenig gutes Fleisch* **can be ambiguous**
It could mean 'not much good meat' or 'not very good meat'. If the context does not resolve the ambiguity, the first meaning can be made clear by replacing *wenig* by *nicht viel*, i.e. *nicht viel gutes Fleisch*, the second by using *nicht sehr*, i.e. *nicht sehr gutes Fleisch*.

Similarly, *weniger gutes Fleisch* could mean 'meat which was less good' or 'a smaller amount of good meat' (English 'less good meat' is similarly ambiguous). This ambiguity can also be resolved if necessary by paraphrasing, i.e. *nicht so gutes Fleisch* or *nicht so viel gutes Fleisch*.

(e) **The spelling of** *so viel*, *wie viel*, *zu viel*, **etc.**
These combinations with *viel* and *wenig* are spelled as separate words: *so viel*, *wie viel*, *zu viel*, *zu wenig*, see 23.3.3.

5.5.26 *welcher* 'some', 'any'

When used as an indefinite pronoun *welcher* has the endings of *dieser*, see Table 5.2. It is typical of colloquial speech, other alternatives (i.e. *einige*, *manche*, *etwas*) usually being preferred in formal registers.

It is used without restriction in the plural, but in the singular it can only refer to a mass noun. It refers back to a noun which has just been mentioned or to 'some people' identified by a following relative clause:

Hast du Käse? Ja, ich habe **welchen**	*Have you got any cheese? Yes, I've got some*
Wenn kein Wein da ist, hole ich uns **welchen**	*If there's no wine left, I'll get us some*
Ich brauche Marken. Kannst du mir **welche** geben?	*I need some stamps. Can you give me some/any?*
Hier sind **welche** vom Westfernsehen (*Bednarz*)	*Here are some people from Western television*

NB: For the use of *welcher* as an interrogative, see 5.3.1, as a relative pronoun, see 5.4.2.

5.5.27 *wer* 'someone', 'somebody'

wer is used as a pronoun in colloquial speech, where formal registers prefer *jemand* (see 5.5.15):

Dich hat wieder **wer** angerufen	*Someone's been on the phone for you again*
Die hat wohl wieder **wen** angelächelt	*It looks as if she's picked some bloke up again*
Hast du wenigstens **wem** Bescheid gesagt?	*Have you at least told someone about it?*

NB: For the use of *wer* as an interrogative pronoun, see 5.3.3.

6 Adjectives

ADJECTIVES are words which describe, modify, or qualify nouns and pronouns. They do this in two main ways:

- either on their own or as part of a longer adjectival phrase. They then form part of a NOUN PHRASE, and they come immediately before the noun, after any determiners. This is called the **attributive** use of the adjective:

Determiner	Adjective/adjectival phrase	Noun
eine	**kaltes**	Wasser
das	**hohe**	Wand
die	**ultramoderne**	Raumschiff
	jetzt über das Internet erhältlichen	Games

- or by being used as a COMPLEMENT to a noun which is the subject or object of a verb, see also 18.6. This is called the **predicative** use of the adjective:

Helga ist aber **klein**   Das Mädchen lag **krank** im Bett
Er isst die Würstchen **warm**   Sie strich die Wand **gelb**

In German, **attributive adjectives** (and <u>only</u> attributive adjectives) have endings which indicate the same grammatical categories as nouns, i.e. CASE, PLURAL and GENDER. They are said to decline in AGREEMENT with the noun. There are two main sets of adjective endings in German, the so-called STRONG and WEAK declensions. Which one is used depends on whether or not there is also a determiner in the noun phrase, and what kind of ending it has (if any).
Predicative adjectives have no endings.

This chapter deals with the forms and uses of adjectives in German:

- the **strong** and **weak declension** of adjectives (sections 6.1–6.3)
- adjectives used as **nouns** (section 6.4)
- the use of **cases** with adjectives (section 6.5)
- the use of **prepositions** with adjectives (section 6.6)

We can compare the extent to which a particular person or thing possesses the quality expressed by an adjective by using special endings, e.g. *schön – schöner – schönst*. This is called the COMPARISON of adjectives, and it is dealt with in detail in Chapter 8.

6.1 Declension of adjectives

6.1.1 In German, adjectives are only declined when they are used attributively

ein gut**er** Mensch   diese schön**en** Tage   frisch**es** Brot

When used **predicatively**, or in phrases separated from the noun, they have **no endings**:

Der Mensch war **gut**   Er trat **ungeduldig** in das Zimmer
Er fühlte sich **gesund**   Wir essen die Möhren **roh**

Mein Vater, in Hamburg **tätig**, . . .   Das Klima machte ihn **krank**
Sie hielt ihn für **dumm**   Das gilt als **sicher**

Optimistisch wie immer, sie ließ sich von ihrem Vorhaben nicht abhalten
ein erstklassiger Kellner, **rasch**, nicht **schwerhörig** (*Wohmann*)
Das Gewehr gehörte zu ihm wie eine Frau zu einem Mann, **schweigsam**, **schön** und **zuver-
lässig** (*E.W. Heine*)

The use of an endingless adjective after the noun is typically poetic: *O Täler **weit**, o Höhen!*
(*Eichendorff*), but it is quite frequent as a stylistic device in advertising and technical language:

Henkel **trocken**   Schrankwand in Eiche **rustikal** oder Kiefer **natur**
Whisky **pur**   700 Nadelfeilen **rund** nach DIN 8342

6.1.2 **There are two basic declensions of adjectives in German**

These are usually called the STRONG and WEAK declensions. The endings of these declensions are
shown in Table 6.1, and they are illustrated in full noun phrases in Tables 6.2, 6.3 and 6.4. These
tables are all arranged with the neuters next to the masculines to show the overlap between the
endings more clearly.

TABLE 6.1 The endings of adjectives in the strong and weak declensions

	Strong					Weak			
	Masc.	**Neut.**	**Fem.**	**Plural**		**Masc.**	**Neut.**	**Fem.**	**Plural**
Nom.	-er	-es			**Nom.**	-e			
Acc.	-en		-e		**Acc.**				
Gen.			-er		**Gen.**	-en			
Dat.	-em			-en	**Dat.**				

(a) The strong declension has relatively more distinctive endings

They are identical to those of *dieser* (see Table 5.2), except that the genitive singular masculine
and neuter ends in *-en*:

ein Stück international**en** Gewässers (*Presse*)
die Perfektion rein**en** Klanges (*hifi ad*)

However, with **weak masculine nouns** which have the ending *-en* in the genitive singular (see
1.3.2), the strong adjective has the ending *-es*, e.g. *das **Gesuch** obiges Adressaten*. However, such
forms are infrequent.

(b) The weak declension has only two endings, *-e* and *-en*

-e is used in the **nominative singular** of all genders and the **accusative singular feminine and
neuter**. *-en* is used in all other combinations of case, plural and gender.

6.2 **The use of the strong and weak declensions**

The underlying principle governing the use of the strong and weak declensions is as follows:

The **strong** endings (which are more distinct) are used if there is no determiner in the noun phrase
with an ending which indicates the case, gender and number of the noun as clearly as possible.

The **weak** endings are used if there is a determiner with an ending in the noun phrase.

TABLE 6.2 Strong adjective declension, with no determiner

	Masculine		Neuter		Feminine		Plural	
Nom.	guter	Wein	gutes	Brot	gute	Suppe	gute	Weine
Acc.	guten	Wein	gutes	Brot	gute	Suppe	gute	Weine
Gen.	guten	Weins	guten	Brotes	guter	Suppe	guter	Weine
Dat.	gutem	Wein	gutem	Brot	guter	Suppe	guten	Weinen

TABLE 6.3 Weak adjective declension, with the definite article

	Masculine			Neuter			Feminine			Plural		
Nom.	der	gute	Wein	das	gute	Brot	die	gute	Suppe	die	guten	Weine
Acc.	den	guten	Wein	das	gute	Brot	die	gute	Suppe	die	guten	Weine
Gen.	des	guten	Weins	des	guten	Brotes	der	guten	Suppe	der	guten	Weine
Dat.	dem	guten	Wein	dem	guten	Brot	der	guten	Suppe	den	guten	Weinen

6.2.1 The STRONG declension is used in the following contexts in accordance with this principle

(a) When there is no determiner in the noun phrase

frische Milch	frisches Obst	durch genaue Beobachtung
mit neuem Mut	aus deutschen Landen	das Niveau französischer Filme

This also applies to adjectives used after **numerals** (including the genitives *zweier* and *dreier*, see 9.1.3a), after preceding **genitives**, and after the **genitive** of the **relative pronoun**:

zwei schöne Pfirsiche	*two fine peaches*
Karls unermüdlicher Eifer	*Karl's tireless zeal*
in Astrids kleinem Arbeitszimmer	*in Astrid's little study*
mein Freund, dessen ältester Sohn krank war	*my friend, whose eldest son was ill*

(b) When the determiner in the noun phrase has no ending

ein älterer Herr	unser kleines Kind	kein schöner Tag
mein neues Kleid	viel indischer Tee	ein paar grüne Äpfel
manch reiches Land	welch herrliches Wetter!	mit was für englischen Büchern
lauter faule Äpfel	bei solch herrlichem Wetter	

An important effect of this rule is that strong endings are used after the endingless forms of the indefinite articles *ein* and *kein* and of the possessives (i.e. *mein, dein, unser*, etc.). The declension of adjectives after these determiners, which seems to mix strong and weak endings, is sometimes called the mixed declension. For reference, it is illustrated in full in Table 6.4.

TABLE 6.4 Mixed adjective declension, with the indefinite article

	Masculine			Neuter			Feminine		
Nom.	ein	guter	Wein	ein	gutes	Brot	eine	gute	Suppe
Acc.	einen	guten	Wein	ein	gutes	Brot	eine	gute	Suppe
Gen.	eines	guten	Weines	eines	guten	Brotes	einer	guten	Suppe
Dat.	einem	guten	Wein	einem	guten	Brot	einer	guten	Suppe

6.2.2 The WEAK declension is used after most determiners with endings indicating the case, number and gender of the noun

This rule follows the principle given above and applies, in particular:

(a) After the definite article and demonstrative *der*

der weiße Wein   den weißen Wein   des weißen Weines   die weißen Weine

(b) After the indefinite articles *ein* and *kein* and the possessives, IF they have an ending

i.e. except in the nominative singular masculine and the nominative/accusative singular neuter, where the strong endings are used (see 6.2.1b). This is illustrated in Table 6.4:

einen weißen Wein   seinem weißen Wein   ihrer weißen Weine

(c) After *dieser, jener, jeder* and *welcher*

dieser weiße Wein   diesen weißen Wein   diesen weißen Weinen
jenes weißen Weines   jedem weißen Wein   von welchem weißen Wein?

6.2.3 There is some variation in the use of the strong and weak endings after certain determiners

In general, following the principle given above, the adjective has **weak** endings following any determiner which itself has an ending showing the case, number and gender of the noun. However, usage is not fixed after some of the indefinites and quantifiers given in section 5.5. The following summarises general current practice:

(a) Weak endings are always used in the SINGULAR

mancher brave Mann   mit folgender nachdrücklichen Warnung
durch irgendwelchen puren Unsinn   mit einigem bühnentechnischen Aufwand
mit allem möglichen Fleiß   (*Zeit*)
von vielem kalten Wasser   aus wenigem schlechten Wein
solches dumme Gerede

NB: As a solitary exception, *jeglicher* is most often followed by strong endings, e.g. *jegliches **organisches** Leben* (Grzimek).

(b) Usage in the PLURAL varies for different determiners

(i) After *alle, beide* and *sämtliche* the weak endings are usual:

alle fremden Truppen   sämtliche schönen Bücher
beide bekannten Politiker   aller interessierten Zuschauer

NB: Strong endings are occasionally found, especially with *beide*, e.g. *beide bekannte Politiker*.

(ii) After *irgendwelche* and *solche* either weak or strong endings are used. The weak endings are more frequent:

solche schönen (*less common*: schöne) Tage
irgendwelcher interessierten (*less common*: interessierter) Zuschauer

(iii) After *manche* either weak or strong endings are used. The strong endings are more frequent:

manche schöne (*less common*: schönen) Aussichten

(iv) After *einige, etliche, folgende, mehrere, viele, wenige* the strong endings are the general rule:

einige neue ICE-Verbindungen
folgende bezeichnende Beispiele
vieler nichtbeamteter Österreicher (*Kurier*)

etliche fremde Besucher
mehrere große Städte
weniger günstiger Zeiten

NB: Weak endings are occasionally found, most often in the genitive plural, e.g. *einiger großen ausländischen Firmen* for (much more frequent) *einiger großer ausländischer Firmen*.

(v) For adjective endings after *ander*, see 5.5.2.

(c) Some indefinites and quantifiers may themselves be preceded by another determiner

i.e. by a definite or indefinite article, by one of the demonstratives *dieser* or *jener*, or by one of the possessives *mein, dein*, etc. They are then treated like adjectives and have a weak or strong adjective ending as appropriate, as does any further following adjective:

eine **solche** interessante Nachricht
mit der **folgenden** krassen Behauptung
mit seinem **wenigen** deutschen Geld

aller **solchen** guten Wünsche
diese **vielen** alten Dörfer
mein **sämtliches** kleines Vermögen

(d) Some indefinites and quantifiers have alternative endingless forms

The conditions under which these occur are explained under the relevant determiner in section 5.5. These endingless forms are followed by adjectives with strong endings, following the general principle explained above:

viel deutsches Geld   manch schöner Tag   solch dummes Gerede

6.2.4 Two or more adjectives qualifying the same noun all have the same ending

dieser schöne, große Garten
gutes bayrisches Bier

mein lieber alter Vater
die Lösung wichtiger politischer Probleme

An occasional deviation from this rule is that in the dative singular masculine or neuter, a second (or subsequent) adjective may, optionally, have the weak ending *-en* rather than the strong ending *-em*:

mit dunklem bayrischem/bayrischen Bier
nach langem beunruhigendem/beunruhigenden Schweigen
nach wochenlangem politischen Tauziehen (*Presse*)

Using the weak ending *-en* in such contexts is not accepted as standard by some authorities. However, although it is less frequent than the strong ending *-em*, it is by no means unusual in all kinds of written German, and it is the norm with adjectives used as nouns, see 6.4.2b.

6.2.5 The adjective is still declined if a noun is understood

'one' often has to be supplied in the equivalent English construction:

Welches Kleid hast du gewählt?
  Das **rote**
Ich habe mein Taschenmesser verloren.
  Ich muss mir ein **neues** kaufen

Which dress did you choose?
  The red one
I've lost my penknife. I'll have
  to buy myself a new one

Deutsche Weißweine sind süßer als **französische**	*German white wines are sweeter than French ones*

NB: Adjectives used in this way with a noun understood are spelled with a <u>small</u> initial letter, not a capital, since they are not adjectives being used as nouns, see 6.4 and 23.2.1.b.

6.2.6 Adjectives governing more than one noun with a different gender cannot be understood

In English an adjective (with or without a determiner) can be understood in a series of linked noun phrases, e.g. *my old aunt and uncle, dear Ruth and Martin, the new table and chairs*. This is <u>not</u> possible in German if the nouns involved are of a different gender or number. The adjective (and determiner) <u>must</u> be repeated, with different endings as appropriate:

mein alt**er** Onkel und meine alt**e** Tante	lieb**e** Ruth, lieb**er** Martin
der neu**e** Tisch und die neu**en** Stühle	

6.2.7 In a few special cases an attributive adjective has no ending

(a) In older German, adjectives sometimes lacked the strong ending *-es* before a neuter singular noun in the nominative or accusative

This usage is retained in a few idioms and set phrases, e.g.:

etwas auf gut Glück tun	*to take a chance*
sich lieb Kind machen	*to ingratiate oneself*
Gut Ding will Weile haben	*Nothing good is done in a hurry*
Ruhig Blut bewahren!	*Keep calm!*
Kölnisch Wasser	*eau de Cologne*
ein gehörig/gut Stück	*a substantial/good piece*
ein gut Teil	*a large proportion*

(b) Some foreign adjectives ending in a full vowel do not take endings

Many of these are colour terms, i.e.: *lila, rosa*:

eine **klasse** Idee	ein **lila** Mantel	die **orange** Farbe
ein **rosa** Kleid	eine **prima** Ware	eine **super** Schau

In writing, a suffix such as *-farben* or *-farbig* is an acceptable alternative for the colour terms, e.g. *ein rosafarbenes Kleid*. In colloquial speech, an *-n-* is sometimes inserted as a base for the usual endings, e.g. *ein rosanes Kleid*. This is widespread but considered incorrect in written German.

(c) An adjective used as an adverb to qualify a following adjective has no ending

See also 7.3.1c. Compare the difference between the following:

ein unheilbar**er**, fauler Junge	*an incurable, lazy boy*
ein unheilbar fauler Junge	*an incurably lazy boy*

However, this distinction is not always clear-cut, and the first of a pair of adjectives is sometimes left uninflected even if it is not being used as an adverb. This is a common stylistic device in writing:

ein reingebürtiger Pole von **traurig** edler Gestalt (*Grass*)	*a pure-bred Pole with a sad, noble figure*
seine **hochrot** abstehenden Ohren (*Grass*)	*his deep red, protuberant ears*

einzig regularly has no ending if it can be considered as qualifying a following adjective e.g. *die einzig(e) mögliche Lösung*. For similar usage with *derartig*, see 5.1.6f.

(d) Adjectives in -*er* from town names do not add endings

die Leipziger Messe, die Lüneburger Heide, der Kölner Dom

(e) Adjectives in -*er* from numerals do not add endings

die neunziger Jahre *the nineties*

(f) Endingless adjectives are used with names of letters and numerals

groß *A*, klein *z*, römisch *IV*, arabisch *4*

(g) *halb* and *ganz* have no endings before geographical names used without an article

halb Berlin, ganz Deutschland, ganz Europa

NB: See 9.3.2 for details on the use of *halb*.

6.2.8 Adjectives used after a personal pronoun usually have strong endings

ich arm**er** Deutscher
Wer hat dich dumm**en** Kerl gesehen?
Wer konnte euch treulos**en** Verrätern helfen?
Wer kümmert sich um uns früh**ere** Kollegen?

However, weak endings are found in a few contexts:

(i) In the (rarely used) dative singular, weak or strong endings can be used in the masculine and neuter, e.g.: *mir mittellos**em**/mittellos**en** Mann*, but the feminine almost always has weak endings, e.g.: *Er hat mir alt**en** (rarely: alt**er**) Frau geschmeichelt*.

(ii) Weak endings are more usual in the nominative plural: *wir jung**en** Kollegen; ihr hilflos**en** Kerle*. However, for 'we Germans' *wir Deutsche* and *wir Deutschen* are equally common.

6.3 Irregularities in the spelling of some adjectives

6.3.1 The spelling of inflected adjectives in -*el*, -*en*, -*er*

(a) Adjectives in -*el* drop the -*e*- when an ending is added

ein **dunkler** Wald, eine **respektable** Leistung

NB: When used as a noun, *dunkel* drops the -*e*- of the ending, e.g. *im Dunkeln* 'in the dark'.

(b) Adjectives in -*en* can drop the -*e*- when an ending is added

This is usual in everyday speech, but uncommon in writing: *eine **metallene** (rarely written: metallne) Stimme, ein **seltener** (rarely written: seltner) Vogel*.

(c) Adjectives in -*er*

Foreign adjectives and those with -*au*- or -*eu*- before the -*er* always drop the -*e*-:

eine **makabre** Geschichte, mit **teuren** Weinen, durch **saure** Milch

Other adjectives in *-er* usually keep the *-e-* in written German, although it is usually dropped in speech: *eine **muntere*** (rarely written: *muntre*) *Frau*.

NB: (i) The *-e-* of the comparative ending *-er* (see 8.1) is rarely omitted in writing, e.g.: *eine **bessere*** (rarely in writing: *bessre*) *Lösung*.
(ii) For the spelling of declined *ander*, see 5.5.2.

(d) The *-e-* is quite often left out in *-el-* or *-er-* in the middle of an adjective which has endings
neb(e)lige Tage, eine **wäss(e)rige** Suppe, etc.

6.3.2 *hoch* 'high'

hoch has the special form *hoh-* to which the usual endings are added: *der Berg ist **hoch***, but *ein* **hoher** *Berg*.

6.3.3 A few adjectives have alternative base forms with or without final *-e*

e.g.: *Er ist feig* or *feige* 'He is cowardly'. They are:

blöd(e)	bös(e)	fad(e)	irr(e)	leis(e)	mild(e)
müd(e)	öd(e)	träg(e)	trüb(e)	vag(e)	zäh(e)

With all except *blöd(e)*, *mild(e)* and *zäh(e)*, the alternative with *-e* tends to be preferred in written German. In speech the form without *-e* is more frequent unless the adjective is stressed.

6.4 Adjectives used as nouns

6.4.1 All adjectives and participles can be used as nouns in German

They are written with a capital letter:

der **Alte** *the old man*	die **Alte** *the old woman*
das **Alte** *old things*	die **Alten** *the old people*

English cannot turn adjectives into nouns as easily, except in a few restricted cases ('the young', 'the old', 'the Dutch', 'the good, the bad and the ugly', etc.). and we usually have to supply a dummy noun like 'man', 'woman', 'thing(s)', 'people' to be used with the adjective. The overuse of the corresponding German words like *Ding* or *Leute* is a characteristic feature of the German of English learners.

Idiomatic German exploits fully the possibilities of concise expression offered by the fact that adjectives can be used as nouns in this way. In particular, they are often used where full clauses would be needed in English:

Die Farbe dieser Vögel war das für mich **Interessante**	*The colour of these birds was what interested me*
Er hat sich über das **Gesagte** aufgeregt	*He got annoyed about what had been said*
Das **Erschreckende** an diesem Vorfall war seine scheinbare Unabwendbarkeit	*What was terrifying about this occurrence was its apparent inevitability*
Die gerade **Eingestiegenen** waren ein älterer Herr und eine elegante Dame	*The people who had just got in were an elderly man and an elegant lady*

ein Ort, wo das irgendwie zu	*a point where concrete reality,*
denkende **Konkrete** unwiederbringlich	*however it may be imagined, becomes*
in **Abstraktes** umschlägt	*irrevocably abstract*

NB: Adjectives used as nouns in this way are different from adjectives being used with a preceding noun understood. These are spelled with a **small** initial letter, see 6.2.5. Compare *Kennst du den Alten?* 'Do you know the old man?' with *Hast du einen neuen Wagen gekauft? Nein, einen alten (Wagen* understood). 'Did you buy a new car? No, an old one.'

6.4.2 The declension of adjectives used as nouns

(a) Adjectives used as nouns decline like attributive adjectives

They have weak or strong endings according to the rules given in 6.2. They thus have the same endings as any preceding adjective, e.g.: *ein zuverlässiger Angestellter, von einer unbekannten Fremden*. The declension with the definite and indefinite articles of a typical masculine adjective used as a noun, *der Angestellte* 'employee', is shown in Table 6.5.

TABLE 6.5 Declension of adjectives used as nouns

		Definite article		Indefinite article	
Singular	**Nominative**	der	Angestellte	ein	Angestellter
	Accusative	den	Angestellten	einen	Angestellten
	Genitive	des	Angestellten	eines	Angestellten
	Dative	dem	Angestellten	einem	Angestellten
Plural	**Nominative**	die	Angestellten		Angestellte
	Accusative	die	Angestellten		Angestellte
	Genitive	der	Angestellten		Angestellter
	Dative	den	Angestellten		Angestellten

NB: *der Angestellte* is naturally only used of a <u>male</u> employee. A female employee will be *die Angestellte, eine Angestellte,* with the appropriate endings, see 6.4.3.

Adjectives used as nouns in this way should not be confused with 'weak' masculine nouns, whose declension looks quite similar, see Table 1.6. Note the difference between the endings of adjectives used as nouns and 'weak' masculine (or other regular) nouns:

Adjective used as noun	**'Weak' masculine (or other) noun**
der Deutsche, des Deutschen *German*	der Franzose, des Franzosen *Frenchman*
NB: ein Deutsch**er**	NB: ein Franzose
das Junge *young of an animal*	der Junge, des Jungen *boy*
NB: ein Jung**es**	NB: ein Junge
die Fremde *female stranger*	die Fremde *foreign parts*
NB: mit der Fremd**en**	NB: in der Fremd**e** *abroad*

(b) In a few contexts adjectives used as nouns decline in a different way from other adjectives

(i) In the dative singular and the genitive plural the adjective used as a noun can have the weak ending *-en* if preceded by an adjective with the strong endings *-em* or *-er*. This is a general rule with the masculine nouns, but less regular with feminines or in the genitive plural:

Ich sprach mit Karls alt**em** Bekannt**en**, mit Helmuts englisch**er** Bekannt**en**/Bekannt**er**
die Freistellung zahlreich**er** Angestellt**er**/Angestellt**en**

(ii) In apposition (see 2.6), the weak ending is used in the dative singular even if there is no determiner:

Er sprach mit Karl Friedrichsen, Angestellt**en** (*rarely*: Angestellt**em**) der BASF in Ludwigshafen
Er sprach mit Heike König, Angestellt**en** (*never*: Angestellt**er**) der BASF in Ludwigshafen

In practice, such constructions are avoided. The nominative case is used: *mit Karl Friedrichsen, Angestellter der BASF,* or an article is added: *mit Karl Friedrichsen, dem/einem Angestellten der BASF.*

(iii) The neuters *das Äußere, das Ganze* and *das Innere* can have the weak or the strong endings in the nominative/accusative singular after the indefinite article or the possessives if another adjective comes first:

sein schlichtes Äußer**e(s)**   ein einheitliches Ganz**e(s)**   mein eigenes Inner**e(s)**

6.4.3 Masculine and feminine adjectival nouns usually refer to people

(a) The gender is indicated by using the appropriate article

e.g. *der* Fremde 'the (male) stranger', *die* Fremde 'the (female) stranger'. Many common ones correspond to simple nouns in English:

der Abgeordnete *representative*	der Gesandte *emissary*
der Adlige *aristocrat*	der Heilige *saint*
der Angestellte *employee*	der Industrielle *industrialist*
der Asylsuchende *asylum-seeker*	der Jugendliche *young person*
der Beamte *civil servant*	der Obdachlose *homeless person*
der Bekannte *acquaintance*	der Reisende *traveller*
der Deutsche *German*	der Staatsangehörige *citizen*
der Erwachsene *adult*	der Überlebende *survivor*
der Freiwillige *volunteer*	der Verlobte *fiancé*
der Fremde *stranger*	der Verwandte *relative*
der Gefangene *prisoner*	der Vorgesetzte *superior*
der Geistliche *clergyman*	der Vorsitzende *chairman*

(b) A few feminine adjectival nouns represent special cases

(i) A few referring to things are always feminine, i.e.:

die Elektrische *tram* (old South German)	die Gerade *straight line*
die Rechte, Linke *right, left (hand);*	die Variable (*mathematical*) *variable*
(*political*) *right, left*	

e.g.: *überdrüssig des Terrors einer revolutionären Linken* (SZ)

(ii) Some feminines which were originally adjectival nouns are now most often treated as regular feminine nouns:

die Brünette *the brunette*	die Variable *the variable*
die Gerade *the straight line*	die Vertikale *the vertical*
die Parallele *the parallel (line)*	die Horizontale *the horizontal* (e.g.: *aus der*
	Horizontale (*no longer*: Horizontalen)

The older forms with adjectival endings are still found, and especially after a numeral *drei Parallele* is quite frequent besides the more usual *drei Parallelen.*

(iii) *die Illustrierte* 'the magazine' is still most often treated as an adjectival noun, e.g.: *in dieser Illustrierten* rather than *in dieser Illustrierte.* In the plural, though, adjective endings and noun endings are equally common, e.g.: *Wir haben zwei Illustrierte/Illustrierten gekauft.*

(iv) Exceptionally, the feminine form corresponding to *der Beamte* is *die Beamtin.* This is as a regular feminine noun, with the plural *die Beamtinnen.*

6.4.4 **Neuter adjectival nouns usually denote abstract or collective ideas**

Es ist schon **Schlimmes** passiert   *Bad things have already happened*
Er hat **Hervorragendes** geleistet   *He has achieved outstanding things*
der Schauer des **Verbotenen** und   *the frightening fascination of what*
   Versagten (*Zweig*)   *is forbidden or denied*
... zugleich immer aufbauend auf   *... at the same time always building*
   das **Erreichte** (*Mercedes advert*)   *on what has been achieved*

NB: *das Junge* 'the young' (of an animal), see 1.1.12.

Especially in spoken German, the names of regions within the German-speaking countries often take the form of neuter adjectival nouns, e.g.:

Jetzt kommen wir ins **Hessische**   Hier sind wir im **Thüringischen**
Der Baron von Münchhausen kam im **Braunschweigischen** zur Welt (*Kästner*)

6.4.5 **Neuter adjectival nouns are frequently used after indefinites**

especially after *alles, nichts, viel(es), wenig*, see 5.5. These have weak or strong endings depending on whether the indefinite itself has an ending, e.g.:

alle**s** Gute   nichts Neue**s**
von alle**m** Gute**n**   von nichts Neue**m**
weitere**s** Interessante   lauter Neue**s**
folgende**s** Neue   viel/wenig Interessante**s**
viele**s** Interessante   von viel Interessante**m**
von viele**m** Interessante**n**

6.4.6 **Words denoting languages and colours have the form of neuter adjectival nouns**

(a) Names of languages
For the use of the article with these nouns, see 4.2.4d.

(i) The most common form, used to refer to the language in a specific context, or when an adjective precedes, is a neuter adjective. It has no endings, except that, optionally, -*s* can be added in the genitive (see 1.3.7c):

Wir lernen **Spanisch, Französisch, Russisch, Englisch**
Die Aussprache des modernen **Deutsch(s)**
eine Übersetzung aus **dem amerikanischen Englisch**

(ii) To refer to the language in a general sense, a declined adjectival neuter noun is used. It always has the definite article.

Das Englische ist **dem Deutschen** verwandt
eine Übersetzung aus **dem Tschechischen**

This form cannot be used with a preceding adjective; if an adjective is present, then the endingless form is used.

Mit meinem schlechten Deutsch komme ich nicht weit

(b) Names of colours

These usually have the form of an endingless neuter adjectival noun which has no endings, except that -s is usually added in the genitive singular. The plural is endingless in written German, though -s is sometimes used in speech:

das **Grün** der Wiesen	dieses hässlichen **Gelbs**
von einem glänzenden **Rot**	die beiden **Blau** (*spoken*: Blaus)
in **Schwarz** gekleidet	

In a few set phrases with the definite article this noun is declined:

ins **Grüne** fahren	Es ist das **Gelbe** vom Ei
ins **Schwarze** treffen	das **Blaue** vom Himmel herunter versprechen

6.5 Cases with adjectives

Many adjectives can be used with a noun dependent on them, which then takes a particular case (we say that the adjective 'governs' a noun in that case). The case varies depending on the individual adjective, e.g.:

- dative: *Sie ist ihrem Bruder sehr ähnlich* (section 6.5.1)
- accusative: *Ich bin den Lärm nicht gewohnt* (section 6.5.2)
- genitive: *Sie ist der deutschen Sprache mächtig* (section 6.5.3)

6.5.1 Adjectives which govern the DATIVE

(a) The dative is the most common case used with adjectives

Sie waren **ihrem Freund** beim Umzug behilflich	*They helped their friend when he moved house*
Dieses Gespräch war **mir** sehr nützlich	*This conversation was very useful for me*
Er war **seinem Gegner** überlegen	*He surpassed his opponent*
Ein **ihr** unbekannter Mann trat herein	*A man she didn't know walked in*

The following list gives a selection of frequent adjectives which govern the dative.

ähnlich* *like, similar*	günstig *favourable*
angenehm[†] *agreeable*	heilig *holy, sacred*
begreiflich *comprehensible*	hinderlich *awkward*
behilflich *helpful*	klar *obvious*
bekannt *known, familiar*	lästig[†] *troublesome*
bequem *comfortable*	leicht[†] *easy*
bewusst *known*	möglich[†] *possible*
beschwerlich[†] *arduous*	nahe* *near, close*
böse *angry*	nötig *necessary*
dankbar *grateful*	nützlich[†] *useful*
eigen *peculiar*	peinlich[†] *embarrassing*
entbehrlich[†] *unnecessary*	schädlich[†] *injurious, harmful*
ergeben *devoted, attached*	schuldig *owing*
erwünscht *desirable*	schwer *difficult*
fern *distant*	teuer *expensive*
fremd *strange*	treu* *faithful*

gefährlich[†] *dangerous*
gefällig *obliging*
nicht geheuer *scary*
gehorsam *obedient*
geläufig *familiar*
gemeinsam *common*
gerecht *just*
gesinnt *inclined*
gewogen (lit.) *well-disposed*

überlegen *superior*
verhasst *hateful*
verständlich[†] *comprehensible*
wichtig[†] *important*
widerlich *repugnant*
willkommen *welcome*
zugänglich[†] *accessible*
zuträglich *beneficial*

The adjective usually **follows** the noun (or pronoun) dependent on it, but those marked with * in the list above may come first. Those marked with † may alternatively be used with *für* (before or after the adjective), e.g.: *Das war **für mich** unangenehm/unangenehm **für mich*** (see also 6.6). *böse* can also be used with *auf* or *mit* (see 6.6).

(b) Some adjectives which govern the dative are only used predicatively

Sie ist **mir** zuwider   *She is repugnant to me*

These are:

abhold (arch., lit.) *ill-disposed*
feind (arch., lit.) *hostile*
freund (lit.) *friendly*
gram (lit.) *angry (with)*

hold (arch., lit.) *favourably disposed*
untertan *subordinate*
zugetan *well-disposed*
zuwider *repugnant*

This group also contains all the adjectives meaning 'all the same', e.g.: *Das ist **mir** gleich* 'That's all the same to me', i.e.: *einerlei, egal* (coll.), *gleich, piepe* (coll.), *schnuppe, wurs(ch)t* (coll.). *zugetan* is occasionally used predicatively: *Die mir sonst sehr zugetane Oberschwester*.

(c) Some adjectives expressing sensations are used in the predicate of *sein* with a dative of the person experiencing the sensation

e.g.: *Es ist mir heiß, kalt, schlecht, übel, warm*. More detail on these is given in 2.5.5c.

6.5.2 **Adjectives which govern the** ACCUSATIVE

These occur mainly in verbal constructions with *sein* or *werden*, although some can be used with a following *dass*-clause or an infinitive clause with *zu*.

jdn./etwas ***gewahr** werden (*lit.*)
    Wir wurden unseren Irrtum gewahr
etwas **gewohnt** sein
    Ich bin den Lärm nicht gewohnt
etwas ***leid** sein
    Ich bin das schlechte Essen leid
etwas/jdn. **los** sein/werden
    Endlich bin ich den Schnupfen los
etwas/jdn.* **satt** sein/haben
    Er ist/hat es gründlich satt
jdm. etwas **schuldig** sein
    Sie ist ihm eine Erklärung schuldig
etwas ***wert** sein
    Es ist das Papier nicht wert, auf
    dem es steht (*MM*)

to become aware of sth./sb.
    We realised our mistake
to be used to sth.
    I'm not used to the noise
to be tired of /fed up with
    I'm fed up with the bad food
to be/get rid of sth/sb.
    At last I've got rid of the cold
to be sick of sb./sth.
    He's thoroughly sick of it
to owe sb. sth.
    She owes him an explanation
to be worth sth.
    It's not worth the paper it's
    printed on

NB: (i) The adjectives asterisked can be used with a genitive in formal registers, see 6.5.3; in the case of *satt* this is only possible in conjunction with *sein*, not with *haben*.

    (ii) *schuldig* is used with a genitive in the sense of 'guilty', e.g.: *Er ist des Verbrechens schuldig* 'He is guilty of the crime'.

6.5.3 **Adjectives which govern the** GENITIVE

(a) The genitive with adjectives is mainly restricted to formal German

A number of the adjectives concerned have alternative constructions in less formal registers, as indicated below, while a few adjectives most often used with a following accusative (see 6.5.2) can alternatively be used with a genitive in more formal registers. With the exception of *bar*, they follow the noun:

bar *devoid of*	Seine Handlungsweise war bar **aller Vernunft**
	His action was devoid of all reason
bewusst *conscious of*	Ich war mir **meines Irrtums** bewusst
	I was conscious of my mistake
fähig *capable of*	Er ist **einer solchen Tat** nicht fähig
(or with zu + *noun*)	*He is not capable of such a deed*
froh *pleased at*	Sie war **seines Erfolges** froh
(usually: über)	*She was pleased about his success*
gewahr *aware of*	Wir wurden **unseres Irrtums** gewahr
(more often with acc.)	*We became aware of our mistake*
gewiss *certain of*	Sie können **meiner Unterstützung** gewiss sein
	You can be certain of my support
mächtig *master of*	Sie ist **des Deutschen** absolut mächtig
	She has a complete command of German
müde *tired of*	Wer des Schauens und Kaufens müde war (*SGT*)
	Whoever was tired of looking and buying
schuldig *guilty of*	Der Angeklagte ist **des Hochverrats** schuldig
(see 6.5.2)	*The accused is guilty of high treason*
sicher *sure of*	Er ist sich **seiner Sache** noch nicht sicher (*Zeit*)
	He is not quite sure of his ground
überdrüssig *tired of*	Er sagte, er sei des Lebens überdrüssig (*HMP*)
(or, rarely, with acc.)	*He said he was tired of life*
wert *worthy of*	der Wille, erhalten zu wollen, was des Erhaltens wert ist (*SGT*)
(often with acc.)	*the desire to keep what is worth keeping*
würdig *worthy of*	Er ist **dieser Ehre** nicht würdig
	He is not worthy of this honour

NB: A reflexive pronoun is always inserted when *bewusst* and *sicher* are used with a genitive.

(b) *voll* and *voller* are used in a number of alternative constructions

(i) In formal written language *voll* and *voller* are used with the genitive: *Das Theater war voll aufmerksamer Zuschauer*, *ein Korb voller grüner Äpfel*. Alternatively, *voll* and *voller* are used with the dative singular *ein Korb voll grünem Obst*, *mit einer Schüssel voller warmem Wasser* (*Grass*).

(ii) With a noun standing alone, *voll* or *voller* can be used with a nominative: *ein Korb voll Obst*, *voll(er) Äpfel*.

(iii) With a noun qualified by an adjective, *voll von* can be used: *ein Korb voll von herrlichem Obst*, *roten Äpfeln*

(iv) *voll mit* is also frequent, particularly in spoken registers: *ein Korb voll mit herrlichem Obst, roten Äpfeln*

(c) A few adjectives governing the genitive are largely restricted to predicate use after *sein*, *bleiben* and/or *werden*

These are used only in formal (particularly legal or official) written German:

ansichtig	bedürftig	eingedenk	geständig	gewärtig	habhaft
(un)kundig	ledig	teilhaftig	verdächtig	verlustig	

An example from official legal language:

Er ist **der Bürgerrechte** für verlustig erklärt worden
He has been deprived of his civic rights

6.6 Adjectives with prepositions

6.6.1 Many adjectives can be linked to a noun by means of a preposition

We speak of the adjective governing a particular preposition:

Das ist **von** dem Wetter **abhängig**   die **um** ihre Kinder **besorgte** Mutter
Er war **mit** meinem Entschluss **einverstanden**

Which preposition is used depends on the individual adjective, and the preposition often retains little of its full meaning. A selection of adjectives governing prepositions is given below, especially those which are frequent or which have a construction different from their usual English equivalents.

The prepositional phrase may precede or follow the adjective. If it contains a noun it commonly comes before the verb, but it may follow; if it contains a pronoun it almost invariably follows the verb, e.g.:

either:	Er ist **über den neuen Lehrling** verärgert
or (less usual):	Er ist verärgert **über den neuen Lehrling**
but always:	Er ist verärgert **über ihn**

NB: *arm* and *reich* usually precede a phrase with *an*, even if it has a noun, e.g. *Das Land ist arm/reich an Bodenschätzen*.

(a) Frequently used adjectives governing a preposition

abhängig von	*dependent on*
angewiesen auf etwas/jdn. sein	*to have to rely on sth./sb.*
Wir waren **auf uns selber** angewiesen	
ärgerlich auf/über	*annoyed with*
arm an	*poor in*
aufmerksam auf	*aware of*
Sie machte mich **auf meinen Irrtum** aufmerksam	
begeistert von/über	*enthusiastic about*
berechtigt zu	*justified in*
Sie sind **zu diesem Vorwurf** berechtigt	
bereit zu	*ready for*
Die Truppen waren **zum Einsatz** bereit	

besorgt um	*anxious about*
bezeichnend für	*characteristic of*
blass, bleich vor	*pale with*
Er war völlig blass/bleich **vor Entsetzen**	
böse auf/mit	*cross with*
Bist du böse **auf mich/mit mir**? (*or*: Bist du **mir** böse, *see* 6.5.1)	
charakteristisch für	*characteristic of*
dankbar für	*grateful for*
Ich war ihm **für seine gütige Hilfe** dankbar	
durstig nach	*thirsty for*
eifersüchtig auf	*jealous of*
einverstanden mit	*in agreement with*
Bist du **mit diesem Vorschlag** einverstanden?	
empfänglich für	*susceptible, receptive to*
Sie ist sehr empfänglich **für Schmeichelei**	
empfindlich gegen	*sensitive to*
Sie ist sehr empfindlich **gegen Kälte**	
ersichtlich aus	*obvious, clear from*
Das ist **aus seiner letzten Bemerkung** ersichtlich	
fähig zu	*capable of*
Sie ist **zu einer solchen Tat** nicht fähig (*or genitive, see* 6.5.3a)	
fertig mit etwas sein	*to have finished sth.*
Bist du **mit dem Essen** schon fertig?	
geeignet für/zu	*suitable for*
Er ist **für diese/zu dieser Arbeit** nicht geeignet	
gefasst auf	*ready, prepared for*
Mach dich gefasst **auf seine Reaktion**!	
geil auf (*coll.*)	*keen on*
Ich bin so geil auf Tennis, sagte er (*MM*)	*I am so keen on tennis, he said*
gespannt auf	*extremely curious about*
Ich bin **auf diesen Film** sehr gespannt	*I am dying to see that film*
gewöhnt an	*accustomed/used to*
Ich bin jetzt **an diesen Kaffee** gewöhnt	
gierig nach	*greedy for*
gleichgültig gegen/gegenüber	*indifferent to(wards)*
höflich zu/gegenüber	*polite to(wards)*
hungrig nach	*hungry for*
interessiert an	*interested in*
müde von	*tired from*
Er war müde **von der schweren Arbeit** (see also 6.5.3a)	
neidisch auf	*envious of*
neugierig auf	*curious about*
reich an	*rich in*
scharf auf (*coll.*)	*keen on*
Er ist scharf **auf seine Rechte**	
schuld an etwas sein/haben	*to be blamed for sth.*
Wer war/hatte **an dem Streit** schuld?	
sicher vor	*safe from*
stolz auf	*proud of*
stumm vor	*dumb with*
typisch für	*typical of*

überzeugt von	*convinced of*
unabhängig von	*independent of*
verheiratet mit	*married to*
verliebt in	*in love with*

Sie ist **in den Bruder** ihrer Freundin verliebt

verschieden von	*different to/from*
versessen auf	*(very, mad) keen on*

Er ist versessen **auf alte Sportwagen**

verwandt mit	*related to*
vorbereitet auf	*prepared for*
wütend auf	*mad at, furious with*

Er war wütend **auf seine Chefin**

zornig auf	*angry with*
zuständig für	*responsible for*

NB: If they are governed by an adjective, *auf* and *über* are always followed by the accusative case, and *vor* is always followed by the dative.

(b) *über* **(with the accusative) is used with many adjectives to mean 'about'**

Sie war erfreut, erstaunt, froh, verwundert über seinen Erfolg

Frequent adjectives which govern *über* (see also 20.3.12e):

aufgebracht *outraged*	erfreut *delighted*
beschämt *ashamed*	erstaunt *amazed*
bestürzt, betroffen *full of consternation*	froh *glad* (see 6.5.3a)
empört, entrüstet *indignant*	glücklich *happy*
entzückt *delighted*	traurig *sad*
erbittert *bitter*	verwundert *astonished*
erbost *infuriated*	

6.6.2 Many adjectives governing prepositions can be used with a following *dass*-clause or an infinitive clause with *zu*

These clauses are often anticipated by the prepositional adverb, i.e. *da(r)* + preposition, e.g. *daran*, *damit*, see 3.5:

Er ist **davon** abhängig, dass ihm sein Bruder hilft	*He is dependent on his brother helping him*
Er ist **davon** abhängig, das Geld zu erhalten	*He is dependent on receiving the money*
Wir sind **dazu** bereit, Ihnen darüber Auskünfte zu geben	*We are prepared to give you some information about this*
Sie war **darüber** froh, dass sie ihn noch sehen würde	*She was pleased that she would still see him*

There are no hard and fast rules for when the prepositional adverb is used in these constructions and when it is not. With a number of the adjectives given in section 6.6.1 it is quite optional and pairs of sentences like the following are equally acceptable and grammatical:

Ich bin gewöhnt, jeden Tag eine Stunde zu üben
Ich bin daran gewöhnt, jeden Tag eine Stunde zu üben

Using the prepositional adverb seems to focus emphasis on the content of the dependent clause or infinitive phrase. In practice it is more commonly used than left out, even where it is optional, especially in written German.

6.6.3 **Extended phrases with adjectives can be used attributively**

In German extended adjectival phrases can be used attributively, i.e. before the noun, in a way quite unknown in English. Such phrases include a noun phrase (in the case governed by the adjective) or a prepositional phrase (with the preposition governed by the particular adjective), and they can sometimes be very long. This **extended attribute** construction is very common in formal German, especially in technical and official registers:

dieses **seinem Vorgesetzten äußerst nützliche** Gespräch	*this conversation which was very useful to his superior*
zum Einsatz bereite Truppen	*troops ready to be deployed*
eine **von rhetorischen Effekten freie** Rede	*a speech free of rhetorical devices*
eine **für sie ganz typische** Haltung	*an attitude quite typical of her*

This construction is also very common with participles, see 13.5.3.

7 Adverbs

The traditional term ADVERB covers a range of words with a variety of uses. Typically, adverbs are words which do not decline and which express relations like time, place, manner and degree. They can be used:

- to qualify verbs: *Sie hat ihm **höflich** geantwortet*
- to qualify adjectives: *ein **natürlich** eleganter Stil*
- they often relate to the sentence as a whole, e.g. *Er hat ihr **sicher** geholfen*

In practice all authorities differ, sometimes quite radically, on what are to be considered as adverbs in German and how they are to be classified in terms of their function. In this chapter we use a simplified classification for practical purposes, and this is summarised in Table 7.1.

TABLE 7.1 Main types of adverb

Adverbs	Use	Examples
time	answering the question **when**	damals, lange, oft, gestern, heute
place	answering the question **where**	hier, dort, oben, draußen, überall
direction	answering the question **where to/from**	dahin, daher, hinüber, herein
attitude/viewpoint	commenting on what is said, or answering a **yes/no** question	hoffentlich, leider, wahrscheinlich, natürlich, psychologisch
reason/cause	answering the question **why**	dadurch, daher, deshalb, folglich, trotzdem
manner	answering the question **how**	irgendwie, anders, telefonisch
degree	answering the question **how much/ small** . . . (often with adjectives)	sehr, außerordentlich, relativ, etwas, ziemlich
interrogative	w-words introducing questions	wann?, weshalb?, wieso?

Phrases, often with a preposition, can have the same function as an adverb in a sentence. Compare:

Sie hat **heute** gearbeitet – Sie hat **den ganzen Tag** gearbeitet
Sie ist **trotzdem** gekommen – Sie ist **trotz des Regens** gekommen
Sie blieb **dort** – Sie blieb **in der alten Stadt am Rhein**

The term ADVERBIAL is commonly used to refer to both single words (i.e. adverbs) and phrases like the above (traditionally called **adverbial phrases**) which function adverbially. This chapter only deals with adverbs proper (i.e. single words) and concentrates on those adverbs of German and their uses which present significant differences to their most usual English equivalents, in particular:

- adverbs of **place** (section 7.1)
- adverbs of **direction** (section 7.2)
- adverbs of **manner, viewpoint, attitude** and **reason** (section 7.3)
- adverbs of **degree** (section 7.4)
- interrogative **adverbs** (section 7.5)

Adverbs of **time** are dealt with in Chapter 11 with other time expressions (specifically in section 11.6). **Modal particles** like *doch*, *schon* and *wohl* are treated in Chapter 10. The **comparative** and **superlative** forms of adverbs (e.g. *Sie fährt schneller, am schnellsten*) are explained in Chapter 8.

7.1 Adverbs of place

This section deals with those adverbs which indicate position.

7.1.1 *hier, dort, da*

(a) *hier* **refers to a place close to the speaker (= English 'here')**

Ich habe deine Tasche **hier** im Schrank gefunden

(b) *dort* **refers to a place away from the speaker (= English 'there')**

Ich sah deine Schwester **dort** an der Ecke stehen

(c) *da* **is a less emphatic alternative to** *dort*

It is used more frequently than *dort* and usually refers to a place away from the speaker:

Ich sah ihn **da** an der Ecke stehen

da is sometimes used to point in a general, unemphatic way when the difference between 'here' and 'there' is not crucial. In such contexts it can sometimes correspond to English 'here':

Herr Meyer ist momentan nicht **da**   *Mr Meyer is not here at the moment*

This usage is particularly common in the South, and universal in Austria.

7.1.2 *oben, unten*

German lacks noun equivalents for 'top 'and 'bottom 'and often uses phrases with *oben* and *unten* in contexts where these would be used in English:

oben auf dem Turm	*at the top of the tower*
Sie stand ganz **oben** auf der Treppe	*She was standing right at the top of the stairs*
unten auf dem Bild	*at the bottom of the picture*
Bis unten sind es noch zwei Stunden zu Fuß	*It's another two hours' walk to the bottom*
Die Säule wird **nach unten hin** breiter	*The column broadens out towards the bottom*
Sein Name steht **unten** auf der Liste	*His name is at the bottom of the list*
ganz **unten** im Kasten	*right at the bottom of the chest*
auf Seite 90 **unten**	*at the bottom of page 90*
von **oben** bis **unten**	*from top to bottom*

7.1.3 The adverb *mitten* is the most usual equivalent for the English noun 'middle'

It is usually followed by a preposition. In some contexts *mitten* has other English equivalents:

Mitten im Garten ist ein Teich	*In the middle of the garden there is a pond*
Sie stellte die Vase **mitten** auf den Tisch	*She put the vase in the middle of the table*
mitten in der Nacht	*in the middle of the night*
mitten in der Aufregung	*in the midst of the excitement*
Ich war **mitten** unter den Leuten auf der Straße	*I was in the midst of the people in the street*
Er bahnte sich **mitten** durch die Menge einen Weg	*He forced his way through the middle of the crowd*
mitten auf der Leiter	*halfway up/down the ladder*

7.1.4 *außen, draußen, innen, drinnen*

außen and *innen* mean '**on** the outside', '**on** the inside', i.e. they refer to the outer or inner surface of the object. *draußen* and *drinnen*, on the other hand, mean 'outside' and 'inside', i.e. away from the object or contained within it:

Die Tasse ist **außen** schmutzig	*The cup is dirty on the outside*
Ich musste **draußen** warten	*I had to wait outside*
Die Äpfel sind **innen** faul	*The apples are rotten inside*
Drinnen ist es aber schön warm	*Indoors it's nice and warm, though*
Dieses Fenster geht **nach innen** auf	*This window opens inwards*
Wir kommen **von draußen**	*We are coming from outside*
Er schloss die Tür **von außen** zu	*He shut the door from the outside*
von außen/innen gesehen	*seen from the outside/inside*

NB: The use of *außen* and *innen* to mean 'outside' and 'inside' is now archaic or regional (especially Austrian).

7.1.5 Indefinite place adverbs

i.e. the equivalents of English 'somewhere', 'anywhere', 'everywhere', 'nowhere'.

(a) *irgendwo* **corresponds to 'somewhere' or, in questions, 'anywhere'**

Ich habe es **irgendwo** liegen gelassen	*I've left it somewhere*
Hast du Paula **irgendwo** gesehen?	*Have you seen Paula anywhere?*

In spoken German simple *wo* is commonly used for *irgendwo* if unstressed: *Ich habe es wohl **wo** liegen gelassen.*

(b) *überall* **corresponds to 'everywhere', or to 'anywhere' in the sense of 'no matter where'**

Erika hat dich **überall** gesucht	*Erika was looking for you everywhere*
Sie dürfen hier **überall** parken	*You can park anywhere here*

(c) *nirgendwo, nirgends* **correspond to 'nowhere', 'not . . . anywhere'**

Er war **nirgendwo/nirgends** zu sehen	*He was nowhere to be seen*
Ich habe dich gestern **nirgends** gesehen	*I didn't see you anywhere yesterday*

(d) *anderswo, woanders* **correspond to 'somewhere else', 'elsewhere'**
(in questions also = *anywhere else*):

Sie müssen ihn **anderswo/woanders** suchen	*You'll have to look for him somewhere else*
Hast du ihn **anderswo/woanders** gesehen?	*Have you seen him somewhere/anywhere else?*

7.2 Adverbs of direction: *hin* and *her*

By using the adverbs *hin* and *her*, German can express direction away from or towards the speaker more consistently than is possible in English. These adverbs have a wide range of uses and can occur alone or linked with another word. In general, *hin* denotes **motion away from** the speaker (or the person concerned), while *her* denotes **motion towards** the speaker (or another point of reference).

7.2.1 *hin* and *her* are compounded with position adverbs to form direction adverbs

By using these compound forms, German differentiates between **position, movement away from the speaker** and **movement towards the speaker**. This can be illustrated by the interrogative adverbs:

Wo wohnen Sie?	*Where do you live?*
Wohin gehen Sie?	*Where are you going (to)?*
Woher kommen Sie?	*Where are you coming from?*

The other adverbs of position given in section 7.1.1 and 7.1.5 compound in a similar way with -*hin* and -*her* to indicate direction to/from:

Sie wohnt **hier**	*She lives here*
Sie kommt **hierher**	*She's coming here*
Leg das Paket **hierhin**!	*Put the parcel down here*
Sie wohnt doch **da/dort**	*She lives there*
In den Ferien fahren wir **dorthin/dahin**, wo wir voriges Jahr waren	*In the holidays we're going where we were last year*
Sie kommt **dorther**	*That's where she comes from*
Er stand **dort** an der Ecke	*He was standing there on the corner*
Wie wollen wir **dorthin** kommen?	*How are we going to get there?*
Er geht heute Nachmittag **irgendwohin**	*He's going somewhere this afternoon*
Sie geht **überallhin**	*She goes everywhere*
Morgen fahren wir **anderswohin**	*We're going somewhere else tomorrow*

wohin, woher, dahin and *daher* are often split, especially in spoken German, with *hin* and *her* being placed at the end of the clause (and written together with the verb):

Wo kommt deine Mutter **her**?	**Wo** gehört dieses Buch **hin**?
Da gehe ich praktisch nie **hin**	**Da** kommt er doch nicht **her**, oder?
ein kleines, gutes Restaurant, **wo** keine Amerikaner **hin**kamen (*Baum*)	

NB: (i) *von wo* and *von da/dort* are common alternatives in spoken German to *woher, daher/dorther*: ***Von wo** kommt er? Er kommt **von da/dort**.*
  (ii) *dahin* is used with *sein* in the meaning 'finished, lost', e.g.: *Sein Leben ist **dahin**; Mein ganzes Geld war **dahin**.*
  (iii) If these words are used in an extended sense they cannot be split, e.g. *woher* in: ***Woher** weißt du das?* 'How do you know that?' and *daher* in the meaning 'that is why', e.g.: ***Daher** hat sie sich aufgeregt.*

7.2.2 *hin* and *her* combine with many verbs as a separable prefix

(a) With most verbs they indicate the direction of movement

In such contexts they do not need a specific 'here' or 'there' element. The English equivalents (if any) can be idiomatic, especially if the verb does not primarily denote movement:

Heute ist eine Wahlversammlung, und ich gehe **hin**	*There's an election meeting today and I'm going there/to it*
Ich hielt ihm die Zeitung **hin**	*I held out the newspaper to him*
Ich hörte einen Ruf und sah **hin**	*I heard a cry and looked over in that direction*
Komm mal **her**!	*Come here*
Gib den Schlüssel **her**!	*Give me the key*
Er hat mich mit dem Auto **her**gefahren	*He drove me here*
Halt den Teller **her**!	*Hold out your plate*
Setz dich **her** zu mir!	*Come and sit down over here by me*

(b) Some verbs compounded with *hin*- and *her*- have a derived, abstract or figurative meaning

sein Leben für etwas **hingeben**	*to sacrifice one's life for sth.*
Das wird schon **hinhauen** (*coll.*)	*It'll be OK in the end*
Nach dem Interview **war** ich völlig **hin**	*After the interview I was shattered*
Die Burschen **fielen** über ihn **her**	*The youths attacked him*
Das Thema **gibt** doch nicht viel **her**	*There's not a lot to this topic*
Es **ging** recht lustig **her**	*It was good fun*
Sie hat ein Zimmer für ihn **hergerichtet**	*She got a room ready for him*
Mit der Qualität der Abiturienten **ist** es nicht mehr weit **her** (*Spiegel*)	*The quality of school-leavers isn't up to much any more*

7.2.3 *hin* and *her* can emphasise direction with a preceding prepositional phrase

(a) In such contexts they are usually optional

Wir wanderten bis zu den Bergen (**hin**)	Er blickte zur Decke (**hin**)
Wir fuhren nach Süden (**hin**)	Er ging zum Fenster (**hin**)
Wir wanderten durch das Tal (**hin**)	Sie flogen über den Berg (**hin**)
Eine Stimme kam von oben (**her**)	Rings um ihn (**her**) tobte der Sturm

NB: (i) The combination *an . . . hin* (see 20.3.2a) means 'alongside'. The noun is in the dative case: *Der Weg führt an der Wiese* **hin** 'along the meadow'.

(ii) *von . . . her* is commonly used to mean 'in respect of': *Das war schon verfehlt von der Zielsetzung her* (see 20.2.8a).

(b) With *hinter, neben, vor* and *zwischen, her* is used to indicate relation of movement to another person or thing moving in the same direction.

The noun in this construction is always in the dative case, see 20.3:

Er ging **hinter** ihr **her**	*He was walking behind her*
Der Hund lief **neben** mir **her**	*The dog was running beside me*
Ein deutscher Wagen fuhr **vor** ihm **her**	*A German car was driving in front of him*
Sie ging **zwischen** uns **her**	*She was walking between us*

The adverbs *hinterher* and *nebenher* are used in a similar sense, e.g.: *Er lief hinterher, nebenher* 'He was running behind, alongside'.

(c) Phrases with *auf* giving reasons or causes can be strengthened by *hin*

See also 20.3.5d:

Das tat er **auf** meinen Vorschlag **hin**	*He did it at my suggestion*
auf die Gefahr **hin**, erkannt zu werden	*at the risk of being recognised*

7.2.4 *hin*- and *her*- combine with prepositions to form directional adverbs

e.g. *hinab, herab, hinauf, herbei*, etc. These occur mainly as separable verb prefixes. In general they link the direction indicated by the preposition with the notion **away from** or **towards** the speaker.

(a) Six prepositions form pairs of compounds with *hin*- and *her*-:

hinab, herab *down*	hinein, herein *in*
hinauf, herauf *up*	hinüber, herüber *over*
hinaus, heraus *out*	hinunter, herunter *down*

They are characteristically used in conjunction with a preceding prepositional phrase or a noun phrase in the accusative case (see 2.2.5c):

Wir stiegen die Treppe **hinauf**	*We climbed up the stairs*
Wir kamen die Treppe **herab/herunter**	*We came down the stairs*
Er ging in das Haus **hinein**	*He went into the house*
Er kam in das Zimmer **herein**	*He came into the room*

hinaus and *heraus* are used with a preceding phrase with *zu* to indicate movement or vision out of or through doors, windows etc., e.g.: *Er blickte **zur** Tür **hinaus** '* She looked out the door'; *Sie warf es **zum** Fenster **heraus** '*She threw it (out of) the window'.

NB: *hin/herab* and *hin/herunter* have identical meanings. Those with *-unter* are more usual in spoken registers.

(b) Other prepositions or adverbs combine with only one of *hin-* or *her-*:

With *hin-*: **hindurch** *through*   **hinweg** *away*   **hinzu** *in addition*
With *her-*: **heran** *along; up (to)*   **herbei** *along*   **herum** *round*   **hervor** *forth, out*

Er drang durch die Menge **hindurch**	*He pushed through the crowd*
Die Rollbahn sauste unter uns **hinweg**	*The runway sped away beneath us*
Sie legte einige Papiere **hinzu**	*She put down some papers in addition*
Sie trat an den Tisch **heran**	*She stepped up to the table*
Einige Polizisten kamen **herbei**	*A few policemen came along*
Er kam um die Ecke **herum**	*He came round the corner*
Die Bücher lagen auf dem Tisch **herum**	*The books were lying around on the table*
Er zog einen Revolver unter dem Tisch **hervor**	*He pulled a revolver out from under the table*

NB: Formal German used to make a distinction between *herum* 'round in a circle' and *umher* 'criss-crossing; higgledy-piggledy'. Nowadays, though, *herum* is commonly used in both senses in both speech and writing.

(c) The adverb with *hin-* or *her-* often repeats the direction given by a previous preposition

Der Vogel flog **in** das Zimmer **hinein**	Er kam **um** die Ecke **herum**
Wir kamen **aus** dem Wald **heraus**	Sie gingen **durch** das Tal **hindurch**

These constructions can seem tautologous, but if the adverb is omitted, the effect is usually that the verb is emphasised rather than the direction and the adverb should thus be used **unless** the verb is to be stressed. Compare:

Der Vogel ist in das Zimmer **geflogen** (i.e. it flew rather than hopped)
Der Vogel ist in das Zimmer **hinein**geflogen (i.e. it didn't fly **out**)
Wir wollen die Truhe in dein Zimmer **tragen** (i.e. carry, not push)
Wir wollen die Truhe in dein Zimmer **hinüber**tragen (i.e. take it **across** – not up or down)

If another word in the sentence bears the main stress, the adverb is optional:

Der **Vogel** ist in das Zimmer (hinein)geflogen
Wir wollen die **Truhe** in dein Zimmer (hinüber)tragen

(d) Verbs with the simple prefixes, e.g. *ab-, an-, auf-*, etc. usually have a derived, extended or other non-literal sense

(see also 22.5.1) This is because direction as such is indicated by using the forms in *hin-* or *her-*. Compare:

Er ist (in das Zimmer) **hineingegangen**	*He went in(to the room)*
Die Zeitung ist **eingegangen**	*The newspaper went bust*

Er hat den Koffer **hereingebracht**	*He brought the suitcase in*
Das **bringt** nichts **ein**	*That's not worth it*
Er **kam** (aus dem Haus) **heraus**	*He came out (of the house)*
Mit 100 Euro **kommen** wir nicht **aus**	*We won't manage on 100 euros*
Ich **ging** zu ihm **hinüber**	*I went over to him*
Er ist zur SPD **übergegangen**	*He went over to the SPD*

(e) Some verbs with *hin*- and *her*- compounds have figurative meanings

sich zu etwas **herablassen**	*to condescend to (do) sth.*
Er **gibt** eine Zeitschrift **heraus**	*He edits a journal*
Es **kommt** auf dasselbe **heraus**	*It all comes to the same thing*
Er **leierte** die Predigt **herunter**	*He reeled off the sermon*
Die Verhandlungen **zogen sich hinaus**	*The negotiations dragged on*

(f) In colloquial German, both *hin*- and *her*- are often reduced to *r*- in compound forms

(irrespective of the direction involved). This is especially frequent in North German usage:

Wollen wir jetzt **raus**gehen (written: *hinausgehen*)
Wollen wir die Jalousien **runter**lassen? (written: *herunterlassen*)

These forms are often used in writing to give the impression of informal colloquial speech, e.g.:
*Ich ging morgens Bahnhofstreppen **rauf** und **runter** und nachmittags Bahnhofstreppen **runter** und **rauf*** (Böll)

7.2.5 Some special meanings and uses of *hin*- and *her*-

(a) *hin*- **often has the sense 'down':**

Sie legte sich **hin**   Der Junge fiel **hin**   Er setzte den Stuhl **hin**

(b) *vor sich hin* **means 'to oneself' (see 20.3.16b):**

Das murmelte er so **vor sich hin**   Sie las **vor sich hin**

(c) *hin und her* **means 'to and fro', 'back and forth':**

Er ging auf der Straße **hin und her**

(d) *hin und wieder* **means 'now and again':**

Hin und wieder sehe ich ihn in der Stadt

(e) *her* **is used in the sense of 'ago' in time phrases (see 11.5.13):**

Das ist schon lange **her**

7.3 Adverbs of manner, viewpoint, attitude and reason

A large number of adverbs fall into these categories, or into related subgroups which are not dealt with specifically. It is convenient to deal with them all together here.

7.3.1 Adverbs of manner and viewpoint

(a) Adverbs of manner typically answer the question *Wie?*

Wie ist sie gefahren?	Sie ist **schnell** gefahren
Wie hat sie gesungen?	Sie hat **gut** gesungen
Wie hat er es gemacht?	Er hat es **anders** gemacht

When they occur in a sentence with *nicht*, the *nicht* always refers specifically to the manner adverb:

> Sie hat **nicht deutlich** gesprochen (she did speak, but not clearly)
> Werder Bremen hat gestern Abend in Leverkusen **nicht gut** gespielt (they played, but not well)

(b) Adverbs of viewpoint indicate a context in which the statement is to be understood

They can be paraphrased by 'seen from a . . . point of view' or ' . . .-ly speaking', e.g.:

> Die Stadt liegt **verkehrsmäßig** ungünstig
> (i.e. in terms of road and rail communications)
> **Finanziell** war diese Entscheidung eine Katastrophe
> (i.e. financially speaking)
> Deutschland ist **wirtschaftlich** stärker geworden
> (i.e. from an economic point of view)

(c) Most adjectives (and participles) can be used as adverbs

Most of these are in practice adverbs of manner or viewpoint. In English such adverbs are typically marked by the suffix '-ly', but German has no such ending, and these words have exactly the same form whether they are being used as adjectives or adverbs. Compare:

Er hat die Sache **überraschend schnell** erledigt	*He settled the matter surprisingly quickly*
Ein Dokument zeigt doch, dass er **mäßigend** und **bremsend** zu wirken versuchte (*Zeit*)	*A document nevertheless shows that he tried to exercise a moderating and calming influence*

An adverb qualifying an adjective before a noun is marked as such by having no ending. Compare:

ein **schön** geschnitzter Schrank	*a beautifully carved cupboard*
ein **schöner**, geschnitzter Schrank	*a beautiful carved cupboard*

NB: This distinction is not always maintained in practice, see 6.2.7c.

These adjective-adverbs can be very widely and flexibly used in German, often with compounding, in a way which lacks a direct English equivalent:

Er hat mir **brieflich** mitgeteilt, dass er anderer Meinung sei	*He informed me by letter that he was of a different opinion*
Widerrechtlich geparkte Fahrzeuge werden **kostenpflichtig** abgeschleppt	*Illegally parked vehicles will be removed at the owner's expense*
Das Mitbringen von Hunden ist **lebensmittelpolizeilich** verboten	*Bringing dogs (into the shop) is forbidden by order of the food inspectorate*

7.3.2 Adverbs of attitude

Adverbs of attitude express the speaker's comment on the content of the statement, i.e. whether he or she thinks it is probable, likely, welcome, well-known or the like. In many ways their function overlaps with that of the modal particles (see Chapter 10). Because they relate to the sentence as a whole they are sometimes called *Satzadverbien* in German.

> **Anscheinend** ist sie erst um sieben gekommen
> (i.e. it appears to the speaker that she only arrived then)
> Er fährt **leider** schon heute ab
> (i.e. the speaker thinks it is unfortunate that he's going)

Natürlich/Selbstverständlich darfst du das machen
  (i.e. the speaker's opinion is that it goes without saying)
Sie wird uns **sicher(lich)** helfen
  (i.e. the speaker thinks that it is certain)

These adverbs of attitude have a number of characteristic features. In particular, although they can occur in a negative sentence, they cannot themselves be negated:

Sie kommen **hoffentlich** noch heute
  (one can't say *nicht hoffentlich*)
Er fährt **leider** nicht weg
  (*nicht leider* is not possible)
Sie ist **wahrscheinlich** nicht gekommen
  (*nicht wahrscheinlich* . . . does not make sense)

Unlike adverbs of manner, they cannot answer the question *Wie?*, but they **can** be used to answer a yes/no question:

Singt sie heute? Ja, **bestimmt/leider/vielleicht/zweifellos**, etc.
  (None of these words can answer the question *Wie singt sie?*)

7.3.3 Adverbs of reason

A large group of adverbs indicate cause, circumstance, condition, purpose or reason. The most frequent members of this group are:

allenfalls *at most*	deswegen *therefore*
andernfalls *otherwise*	folglich *consequently*
dabei *at the same time*	gegebenenfalls *if necessary*
dadurch *thereby*	gleichwohl (formal) *nevertheless*
daher *therefore*	infolgedessen *consequently*
dann *in that case*	jedenfalls *in any case*
darum *therefore*	mithin (formal) *consequently*
dazu *to that end*	nichtsdestoweniger *nevertheless*
demnach *therefore*	somit *consequently*
demzufolge (formal) *therefore*	sonst *otherwise* (see 7.3.5b)
dennoch *nevertheless*	trotzdem *nevertheless*
deshalb *therefore*	

7.3.4 Many German adverbs have a verb or a subordinate clause construction as their only or most natural idiomatic English equivalent

The most frequent equivalent of English 'to like', for example, is to use the German adverb *gern* with *haben* or another verb, e.g.: *Ich esse **gern** Käsekuchen* 'I like cheesecake'; *Sie hat Ihren Lehrer ganz **gern*** 'She quite likes her teacher'. A number of the most useful of these adverbs are given below. In some cases a construction with a verb is also possible in German, so that 'It must be admitted that it isn't easy' could correspond to *Man muss zugeben, dass es nicht einfach ist* or to *Es ist freilich nicht einfach*. In general, the equivalents with adverbs sound more idiomatic and concise:

Das Problem ist **allerdings** schwierig	*I must admit that the problem is difficult*
Er wurde **allmählich** rot im Gesicht	*He began to get red in the face*
Er hat **andauernd** gespielt	*He kept on playing*
Er ist **angeblich** arbeitslos	*He claims to be unemployed*
Er ist **anscheinend** nicht gekommen	*He seems not to have come*
Wir können Ihnen **bedauerlicherweise** nicht weiter behilflich sein	*We regret that we can be of no further assistance to you*
Er ist **bekanntlich** ein hervorragender Linguist	*Everyone knows that he is an outstanding linguist*
Hier können Sie **beliebig** lange bleiben	*You can stay here as long as you wish*
Am besten behalten Sie das für sich	*You'd better keep that to yourself*
Thomas kommt **bestimmt** mit	*I'm sure Thomas is coming with us / Thomas is sure to be coming with us*
Wir haben **erfreulicherweise** das Spiel gewonnen	*I'm glad to say that we won the game*
Es ist **freilich** nicht einfach	*It must be admitted that it isn't easy*
Gegebenenfalls kann man auch eine andere Taste wählen	*If the need should arise, another key may be selected*
Im Sommer spielt er **gern** Tennis	*He likes playing tennis in summer*
Dienstags hat er **gewöhnlich** Tennis gespielt	*He used to play tennis on Tuesdays*
Hoffentlich erreichen wir die Hütte vor Sonnenuntergang	*I hope we shall reach the cabin before sunset*
Sie kann **leider** nicht kommen	*I'm afraid she can't come*
Im Winter spielt er **lieber** Fußball	*He prefers playing football in the winter*
Ich habe Reiten **lieber** als Radfahren	*I prefer riding to cycling*
Er kommt **möglicherweise** noch vor dem Abendessen	*It is possible that he will be coming before dinner*
Sie erschien **nicht**	*She failed to appear*
Die Firma stellt diese Ersatzteile **nicht mehr** her	*The company has ceased/stopped making these spare parts*
Nimm dir **ruhig** noch etwas zu trinken	*Don't be afraid to help yourself to another drink*
Alle Insassen sind **vermutlich** ums Leben gekommen	*It is presumed that all the passengers lost their lives*
Er las **weiter**	*He continued to read/went on reading*
Ich habe sie **zufällig** in der Stadt gesehen	*I happened/chanced to see her in town*
Zweifellos wird auch dieses Jahr sehr wenig Schnee im Allgäu fallen	*There is no doubt that very little snow will fall in the Allgäu this year either*

7.3.5 *anders* and *sonst*

These two adverbs are very similar in meaning and both can be equivalents of English *else*. However, they are not always interchangeable.

(a) *anders* **means 'else' or 'differently'**

In origin, *anders* is the genitive of the adjective *ander*, see 5.5.2. It usually has the written form *anders* (very occasionally *anderes*), which differentiates it from the nominative/accusative singular neuter of *ander*, which is normally written *andres* or *anderes*. It is used as follows:

(i) In the meaning 'else' with *jemand* and *niemand*:

Es ist jemand **anders** gekommen	*Somebody else came*
Der Schirm gehört jemand **anders**	*The umbrella belongs to somebody else*

Ich habe mit niemand **anders** gesprochen	*I didn't talk to anybody else*
Sie hat niemand **anders** als dich gesucht	*She wasn't looking for anyone else but you*

NB: In standard German, *jemand, niemand* do not inflect in combination with *anders*, see 5.5.15b. In South German usage, inflected forms of *ander* sometimes occur rather than invariable *anders*, most commonly in the accusative and dative, e.g. *jemand/niemand anderer* (rare), *jemand/niemand anderen, jemand/niemand anderem*.

(ii) *anders* is used in the meaning 'else' with *wo, wohin, woher, (n)irgendwo*. Note the various alternative combinations:

woanders/anderswo/irgendwo anders	*somewhere else/elsewhere*
Ich gehe irgendwo anders hin/ woandershin/anderswohin	*I'm going somewhere else*
Er kommt anderswoher, nicht aus Hamburg	*He comes from somewhere else, not from Hamburg*
nirgendwo anders	*nowhere else*
Ich gehe nirgendwo anders hin	*I'm not going anywhere else*

(iii) *anders* also means 'different(ly)', 'in a different way':

Er ist ganz **anders** als sein Bruder	*He is quite different to his brother*
Du musst es irgendwie **anders** anpacken	*You'll have to tackle it differently*
Es ist etwas **anders**	*It is rather different*
Compare:	
Es ist etwas and(e)res	*It is something else*
Das klingt jetzt anders	*That sounds different now*

(b) *sonst* **means 'else' or 'otherwise'**

(i) In some contexts *sonst* can overlap with the meaning of *anders* 'else' or *ander* 'other', 'different' (see (a) above). Compare the following possible alternatives:

Kannst du **etwas anderes/sonst (noch) etwas** vorschlagen?	*Can you suggest anything else?*
War **noch jemand anders/sonst noch jemand** da?	*Was anyone else here?*
Niemand anders/Niemand sonst hat mir geholfen	*Nobody else helped me*
sonst wo/sonst irgendwo/irgendwo sonst/anderswo, etc. (see (ii) above)	*somewhere/anywhere else*
Ich muss **noch sonst wohin/ anderswohin**	*I've got to go somewhere else*
Wenn **noch andere Probleme/sonst noch** Probleme auftauchen . . .	*If any other problems arise, . . .*
Wer anders kann es gesagt haben?/ (more common: **Wer** kann es **sonst** gesagt haben?)	*Who else can have said it?*

(ii) However, if the sense is clearly 'different' or 'other', only *ander* or, where appropriate, *anders*, can be used. Compare:

Da ist Professor Niebaum und **niemand anders**	*That's Professor Niebaum and nobody else* (i.e. not a different person)
Da ist Professor Niebaum und **sonst niemand**	*That's Professor Niebaum and nobody else* (i.e. he's the only one there)

(iii) If the meaning is clearly 'in addition', 'apart from that', 'otherwise', then only *sonst* is possible:

Wer kommt **sonst** noch?	*Who else is coming?*
Mit wem haben Sie **sonst** noch gesprochen?	*Who else did you talk to?*
Was hat sie **sonst** noch gesagt?	*What else did she say?*
sonst irgendwann	*some/any other time*
Sonst geht alles gut	*Otherwise all is well*
Wir müssen uns beeilen, **sonst** verpassen wir den Zug	*We'll have to hurry, otherwise we'll miss the train*
länger als **sonst**	*longer than usual*

7.3.6 **Adverbs in -*weise***

The suffix *-weise* is very productive for the formation of adverbs of manner or attitude. It is most often added to nouns or adjectives.

(a) Adverbs formed from a noun or a verb + *weise* are in the main manner adverbs with the meaning 'by way of', 'in the form of'

andeutungsweise *by way of a hint*	pfundweise *by the pound*
ausnahmsweise *by way of exception*	probeweise *on approval*
beispielsweise *by way of example*	ruckweise *by jerks*
beziehungsweise *or, as the case may be* (see 19.1.3b)	schrittweise *step by step*
bruchstückweise *in the form of fragments*	stückweise *piecemeal*
dutzendweise *by the dozen*	stundenweise *by the hour*
familienweise *in families*	teilweise *partly*
gruppenweise *in groups*	versuchsweise *tentatively*
massenweise *on a massive scale*	zeitweise *temporarily*
paarweise *in pairs*	zwangsweise *compulsorily*

Die Flüchtlinge strömten **massenweise** über die Grenze	*The refugees were flooding in hordes across the border*
Sein neues Buch ist **stellenweise** ganz gut	*His new book is quite good in places*
Er wird **stundenweise** bezahlt	*He is paid by the hour*

These forms, which were originally only adverbs, are increasingly used as adjectives as well:

eine **probeweise** Anstellung	die **teilweisen** Verbesserungen
eine **ruckweise** Bewegung	eine **stundenweise** Bezahlung
der **stückweise** Verkauf	die **stufenweisen** Fortschritte
eine **schrittweise** Anhebung des Rentenalters auf 70 Jahre (*HMP*)	

Predominantly, though, they are used with nouns which denote a process, chiefly those which are derived from verbs, as in the examples above. Combinations like *der stückweise Preis* or *eine auszugsweise Urkunde* are not (yet?) generally regarded as acceptable.

(b) Many adverbs of attitude are formed from adjectives or participles with the suffix *-weise* and the linking element *-er-*

e.g. *möglicherweise* from *möglich, bezeichnenderweise* from *bezeichnend*. Similarly:

bedauerlicherweise *regrettably*	liebenswürdigerweise *obligingly*
begreiflicherweise *understandably*	möglicherweise *possibly, perhaps*

dummerweise *foolishly*	natürlicherweise *of course*
erstaunlicherweise *astonishingly*	normalerweise *normally*
fälschlicherweise *erroneously*	überflüssigerweise *superfluously*
glücklicherweise *fortunately*	unglücklicherweise *unfortunately*
interessanterweise *interestingly*	unnötigerweise *unnecessarily*
komischerweise *funnily*	unvermuteterweise *unexpectedly*

As these are adverbs of **attitude**, indicating a comment by the speaker on the statement, their meaning is different from that of the adjective-adverb of **manner** from which they are derived, and from that of the corresponding phrase with *Weise*, as the following examples show:

Er war **merkwürdig** müde	*He was strangely tired*
Er war **merkwürdigerweise** müde	*Strange to say, he was tired*
Er war **in merkwürdiger Weise** müde	*He was tired in an unusual way*
Er hat **vernünftig** geantwortet	*He replied sensibly*
Er hat **vernünftigerweise** geantwortet	*Sensibly enough, he replied*
Er hat **auf vernünftige Weise** geantwortet	*He replied in a sensible way*

NB: These adverbs in -*erweise* are <u>never</u> used as adjectives.

7.4 **Adverbs of degree**

7.4.1 **Adverbs of degree (or 'intensifiers') are used to emphasise, amplify or tone down another part of speech**

Their main use is to modify adjectives or other adverbs.

(a) A selection of the most frequent adverbs of degree in German

außerordentlich *extraordinarily*	mäßig *moderately*
äußerst *extremely*	nahezu *virtually*
beinahe *almost, nearly*	recht *really*
besonders *especially*	relativ *relatively*
durchaus *absolutely, thoroughly*	sehr (see 7.4.3) *very*
etwas *a little*	überaus *extremely*
fast *almost, nearly*	verhältnismäßig *relatively*
ganz *quite*	völlig *completely*
genug *enough*	vollkommen *completely*
geradezu *virtually*	wenig *little*
höchst *extremely, highly*	ziemlich *fairly*
kaum *hardly, scarcely*	zu *too*

This list is not exhaustive; many more occur, particularly in colloquial speech, e.g. *echt, enorm, irrsinnig, ungeheuer, unheimlich, verdammt*.

eine **durchaus** selbstkritische Einsicht	*a thoroughly self-critical understanding*
Der Kaffee ist **etwas** süß	*The coffee is a little sweet*
Er fährt schnell **genug**	*He's driving fast enough*
Das ist **geradezu** lächerlich	*That is little short of ridiculous*
Die Suppe war nur **mäßig** warm	*The soup was (only) moderately warm*
eine **nahezu** optimale Lösung des Problems	*a virtually optimal solution to the problem*
Er arbeitet **recht** gut	*He works really well*
ein **überaus** ehrliches Geschäft	*a thoroughly honest transaction*
Dieser Schriftsteller ist **wenig** bekannt	*This author is little known*

(b) *hoch* 'highly' is used with a small number of abstract adjectives

It is usually compounded with them: *hochempfindlich, hochfrequent, hochinteressant, hochgeschätzt, hochqualifiziert, hochwahrscheinlich.* The superlative form *höchst* is used in the same way in a few cases, e.g. *höchstwahrscheinlich.*

(c) *lange* and *längst* are used before a negative to indicate a considerable difference in degree

lange is often preceded by *noch*:

Das ist **noch lange nicht** gut genug   *That is not nearly good enough*
Dieses Buch ist **lange/längst nicht** so gut   *This book isn't nearly as good as his last one*
    wie sein letztes

7.4.2 Some adverbs of degree are used only or principally with adjectives in the comparative or superlative

bedeutend *significantly*:
    Die Donau ist **bedeutend** länger als der Rhein
beträchtlich *considerably*:
    Die Zugspitze ist **beträchtlich** höher als die anderen Gipfel in den
    bayrischen Alpen
denkbar *possible*:
    Sie hat den **denkbar** schlechtesten Eindruck gemacht
entschieden *decidedly*:
    Er hat **entschieden** schlechter gespielt als vor einem Jahr
viel *much*:
    Diese Schule ist **viel** größer als meine
weit *far*:
    Der Wagen ist **weit** schneller, als ich dachte
bei weitem (*by*) *far*:
    Er ist **bei weitem** besser als Jochen
    Er ist **bei weitem** der Beste in der Klasse
weitaus (*by*) *far*:
    Isabella ist **weitaus** reifer, als man ihrem Alter nach schließen dürfte
    Der neueren Geschichte ist das **weitaus** größte Gewicht beizumessen
wesentlich *substantially*:
    Er hat heute **wesentlich** besser gespielt

7.4.3 *sehr* is chiefly used as an adverb of degree (= 'very')

Er weiß es **sehr** gut.   Das ist **sehr** nett von dir.

However, it has a wider range of use than English *very*:

(a) It can modify a verb or phrase, corresponding to English 'very much'

Ich bewundere sie **sehr**   Er ist **sehr** dafür   Das interessiert mich **sehr**
Das ist **sehr** nach meinem Geschmack   Er hat sich **sehr** verändert

(b) After *so*, *wie* or *zu*, it can denote degree, like English 'much'

In such contexts *sehr* is used rather than *viel*:

Nicht **so sehr** die Handlung wie der Stil hat mich gefesselt
Wie sehr ich es bedaure, dass sie durchgefallen ist!
Er hat es sich **zu sehr** zu Herzen genommen

7.5 **Interrogative adverbs**

The German interrogative adverbs correspond to the English *wh*-words, and like them they introduce questions. They fall into similar groups to other adverbs:

Time:

wann? *when?*: **Wann** kommt der Zug in Gelsenkirchen an?
bis wann? *until when?, how long?*: **Bis wann** bleibt ihr hier?
   by when?: **Bis wann** seid ihr damit fertig?
seit wann? *since when?, how long?*: **Seit wann** spielen Sie Tennis?
wie lange? *how long?*: **Wie lange** wollt ihr heute noch spielen?
wie oft? *how often?*: **Wie oft** fährt der Zug nach Putbus?

Place and direction (see also 7.2.1):

wo? *where?*: **Wo** steckt die Angelika jetzt?
wohin? *where (to)?*: **Wohin** fahrt ihr heute?/**Wo** fahrt ihr heute **hin**?
woher? *where from?*: **Woher** kommt der Wagen?/**Wo** kommt der Wagen **her**?
von wo? *where from?*: **Von wo** kommt der Wagen?

Manner:

wie? *how?*: **Wie** habt ihr das nur gemacht?

Reason:

warum? *why?*: **Warum** wollt ihr nicht gehen?
was? *(coll.) why?*: **Was** rennst du denn so schnell? (see 5.3.3f)
wieso? *(coll.) why?*: **Wieso** wollt ihr nicht gehen?
weshalb? *(formal) why?*: **Weshalb** wollt ihr nicht gehen?
wozu? *what . . . for?*: **Wozu** benutzt man das?

These interrogative adverbs can also introduce indirect questions (see 16.6.4a and 19.2.4):

Er hat mich gefragt, **wann** ich morgen komme
Ich habe dir doch gesagt, **wie** man das macht

NB: For the interrogative pronouns *was* and *wer*, see 5.3.3. For the interrogative determiner *welcher*, see 5.3.1.

8 Comparison of adjectives and adverbs

Qualities can be compared using special forms of adjectives (and adverbs). These are called the comparative and superlative forms. Thus, for the adjective *groß*:

positive degree:	Mein Haus ist **groß**	*My house is big*
comparative degree:	Dein Haus ist **größer**	*Your house is bigger*
superlative degree:	Ihr Haus ist **das größte**	*Her house is the biggest*

Naturally, some adjectives or adverbs, such as *sterblich*, *einmalig* or *absolut*, have a meaning which excludes any possibility of comparison, and there are other ways of indicating degree, for example by modifying the adjective or adverb by an adverb of degree like *sehr*, see 7.4.

The **comparative** is normally used to compare two items, the **superlative** more than two:

der **größere** der beiden Brüder
Von den zwei Büchern über Berlin hat er das **billigere** gekauft
der **größte** von acht Jungen
Von diesen vielen Büchern hat er das **billigste** gekauft

As in English, this rule is not universally observed in everyday speech, and phrasings like *der größte der beiden Brüder* are often heard, although they are not considered to be correct.

This chapter deals with the formation and use of the comparative and superlative degree of adjectives and adverbs, and other various means of comparison in German:

- the **formation** of comparatives and superlatives (sections 8.1–8.2)
- the **uses** of the **comparative** and other means of comparison (section 8.3)
- the **uses** of the **superlative** (section 8.4)

8.1 Regular formation of the comparative and superlative

8.1.1 The comparative and superlative of adjectives are formed by adding the endings *-er* and *-st* to the positive form

This is shown for some common adjectives in Table 8.1. As the superlative almost always occurs in a declined form, with the definite article, *das* is included with all examples. The few exceptions to this regular pattern are explained in section 8.2.

TABLE 8.1 Regular formation of comparative and superlative

Positive	Comparative	Superlative
tief *deep*	tiefer	(das) tiefste
schön *beautiful*	schöner	(das) schönste
langsam *slow*	langsamer	(das) langsamste
freundlich *friendly, kind*	freundlicher	(das) freundlichste
unwiderstehlich *irresistible*	unwiderstehlicher	(das) unwiderstehlichste

In English we form comparatives and superlatives in two ways. With short adjectives, we use the endings '-er' and '-est', with longer adjectives we use 'more' and 'most'. In German, the endings *-er* and *-st* are used <u>no matter how long the adjective is</u>; *mehr* and *meist* are not normally used in comparatives and superlatives, except in the few special cases explained in 8.2.7.

Comparative and superlative forms decline in the same way as any adjective when used before a noun, with the same weak or strong endings (see 6.1–6.2).

ein schneller**er** Zug, der schnell**ste** Zug, in der tief**sten** Schlucht der Erde

8.1.2 **Comparative and superlative of adverbs**

The comparative of adverbs is formed with the ending *-er*, exactly like that of adjectives:

Vettel fährt aber schnell**er**

Kannst du bitte etwas laut**er** sprechen?

For the superlative of adverbs, a phrase is used formed using the stem in *-st*, with the ending *-en*, together with *am*

Schumacher fährt **am schnellsten**
Von der Burg aus sieht man es **am klarsten**

Schumacher drives fastest
You can see it most clearly from the castle

For further details about the form *am . . . sten*, see 8.4.1.

8.2 **Irregularities in the formation of comparatives and superlatives**

8.2.1 **Adjectives in *-el*, *-en*, *-er* can drop the *-e-* of the stem in the comparative**

dunkel – **dunkler** – das dunkelste
trocken – **trock(e)ner** – das trockenste

bitter – **bitt(e)rer** – das bitterste
teuer – **teurer** – das teuerste

(a) Those in *el* regularly drop the *-e-* of the stem

dunkel – dunk**ler**

edel – ed**ler**

(b) Those in *-en* and *-er* usually drop the *-e-* of the stem if they have an inflectional ending

trocken – der trock**nere** Wein

bitter – ein bitt**rerer** Geruch

If there is no ending, the *-e-* is usually kept in writing, although it is often dropped in speech:

Dieser Wein ist trock**ener**

Dieser Geruch war bitt**erer**

The *-e-* is always dropped in the comparative of adjectives in *-er* if it comes straight after a diphthong:

teuer – Diese Tasche ist teu**rer** – die teu**rere** Tasche

8.2.2 **Some adjectives add -*est* in the superlative as an aid to pronunciation**

(a) **Those whose stem ends in -*haft*, -*s*, -*sk*, -*ß*, -*x* and -*z* always have -*est***

boshaft – der boshaft**este**
lieblos – der lieblos**este**
brüsk – der brüsk**este**

süß – der süß**este**
fix – der fix**este**
stolz – der stolz**este**

(b) **Those with a stem ending in -*d*, -*t* and -*sch* usually add -*est***

mild – der mild**este**
sanft – der sanft**este**

berühmt – der berühmt**este**
rasch – der rasch**este**

However, longer words ending in these consonants have the ending -*st* if the last syllable is unstressed:

spannend – der spannend**ste**

komisch – der komisch**ste**

(c) **Those with a stem ending in a long vowel or diphthong can have the ending -*est* or -*st***

früh – der früh**ste**/früh**este**

treu – der treu**ste**/treu**este**

8.2.3 **A few adjectives and adverbs have *Umlaut* on the root vowel in the comparative and superlative, in addition to the ending**

arm – ärmer – der ärmste

klug – klüger – der klügste

Most of these adjectives are very common.

(a) **The following adjectives always have *Umlaut* in the comparative and superlative**

alt *old*
arg *bad*
arm *poor*
dumm *stupid*
fromm *pious*
grob *coarse*
hart *hard*
jung *young*
kalt *cold*
klug *clever*

krank *sick*
kurz *short*
lang *long*
oft *often*
rot *red*
scharf *sharp*
schwach *weak*
schwarz *black*
stark *strong*
warm *warm*

NB: (i) *groß, hoch* and *nah* also have *Umlaut* in the comparative and superlative, but they are otherwise irregular, see 8.2.4.
(ii) *fromm* occasionally lacks *Umlaut* in the comparative and superlative in written German.

(b) **A few adjectives have alternative forms with or without *Umlaut***

e.g.: *nass – nässer/nasser – der nässeste/nasseste*. These are:

bang *scared*
blass *pale*
gesund **healthy**
glatt *smooth*
karg *sparse*

krumm *crooked*
nass *wet*
schmal *narrow*
zart *tender*

In general, the forms without *Umlaut* are more frequent in writing, whereas those with *Umlaut* are more typical of spoken German, especially in the south.

8.2.4 **Some adjectives and adverbs have irregular comparative and superlative forms**

bald	**eher**	am **ehest**en	*soon*
gern	**lieber**	am **liebst**en	*willingly, gladly*
groß	**größ**er	das **größ**te	*big, large*
gut	**besser**	das **beste**	*good*
hoch	**höher**	das **höchste**	*high*
nah	**näher**	das **nächste**	*near*
viel	**mehr**	das **meiste**	*much, many*
wenig	**wenig**er/**minder**	das wenig**ste**/das **mindeste**	*little, few*

Further notes on these irregular forms:

(a) *mehr* and *weniger*

As these are adverbs, not adjectives, they do not have any endings even when used with a following noun: *Er hat* **weniger** *Geld als ich*; *Sie hat* **mehr** *Verstand als du*.

(b) *minder* and *mindest*

minder is only used in formal written German. It is only used to qualify adjectives, most commonly with a preceding *nicht*:

Anderswo zwischen Ostsee und Erzgebirge ist die Lage der Denkmalpflege nicht **minder** prekär (*Spiegel*)

mindest can be used for 'least' in the sense 'slightest':

Er hatte nicht die **mindesten** Aussichten zu gewinnen.

(c) *nichts weniger als* **normally means 'anything but'**

i.e. the same as *alles andere als*:

Er ist **nichts weniger als** klug   *He is anything but clever*

For 'nothing less than', German often uses a positive statement: *Das ist* **wirklich** *katastrophal* 'That is nothing less than catastrophic'. However, some Germans <u>do</u> now use *nichts weniger als* in the sense of 'nothing less than', and ambiguity is possible.

8.2.5 **Eight adjectives denoting position only have comparative and/ or superlative forms**

das äußere *outer, external*	das äußerste *outermost, utmost*
das innere *inner, internal*	das innerste *innermost*
das obere *upper*	das oberste *uppermost*
das untere *lower*	das unterste *lowest, bottom*
das vordere *front*	das vorderste *foremost, front*
das hintere *back*	das hinterste *back(most)*
das mittlere *central, middle; medium*	das mittelste *central, middle*

These adjectives are only used attributively, i.e. before a noun:

seine **äußere** Erscheinung   seine **innersten** Gedanken
mit der **äußersten** Höflichkeit   in der **vorderen**, **vordersten** Reihe

As equivalents for English 'external(ly)' and 'internal(ly)' in other contexts, i.e. after *sein* or as adverbs, German uses *äußerlich* and *innerlich*.

Seine Verletzungen sind nicht **äußerlich**,   Sie blieb **äußerlich/innerlich** ganz ruhig
sondern **innerlich**

8.2.6 **The comparative and superlative of compound adjectives**

(a) **Compound adjectives are treated as single words and form their comparative and superlative in the usual way**

This is always the case with those written as a single word:

altmodisch *old-fashioned*	altmodisch**er**	das altmodisch**ste**
schwerwiegend *serious, weighty*	schwerwiegend**er**	das schwerwiegend**ste**
vielsagend *meaningful*	vielsagend**er**	das vielsagend**ste**
vielversprechend *promising*	vielversprechend**er**	das vielversprechend**ste**

(b) **However, if both parts are felt to retain their original meaning, they are written as separate words and only the first has the comparative or superlative form**

The superlative then has the adverbial form *am . . . -sten*

die dicht bevölkerte Stadt *the densely populated city*
die **dichter bevölkerte** Stadt   die **am dichtesten bevölkerte** Stadt

die leicht verdauliche Speise *the easily digested food*
die **leichter verdauliche** Speise   die **am leichtesten verdauliche** Speise

A few frequent idiomatic combinations have **superlative** forms which are written as single words:

der hoch gelegene Ort *the place situated high up*
ein **höher gelegen**er Ort   der **höchstgelegen**e Ort

nahe liegende Gründe *obvious reasons*
näher liegende Gründe   **nächstliegend**e Gründe

die weit gehende Übereinstimmung *the far-reaching agreement*
die **weiter gehende** Übereinstimmung   die **weitestgehende** Übereinstimmung

Compound comparative forms of such adjectives with the suffixes added to the second part (*weitgehender, das weitgehendste*) are not uncommon, although they are sometimes thought of as incorrect. A few frequent words have alternative forms, in particular *schwerwiegend*, for which *schwerer wiegend* and *schwerstwiegend* are found as well as those given in (a) above.

8.2.7 *mehr* and *meist* in comparison

(a) **A very few adjectives form their comparative and superlative by means of a preceding** *mehr* or *am meisten*

This is restricted to (i) participles which are not normally used as adjectives, (ii) a few adjectives which are only used in the predicate (like *zuwider*, see 6.5.1b), and (iii) some unusually long and complex adjectives like *bemitleidenswert*:

Er verrichtet jetzt eine ihm **mehr**   *He is now performing a job which appeals to him*
zusagende Tätigkeit   *more*
Dresden ist die durch den Krieg **am**   *Dresden is the German city most completely*
meisten zerstörte deutsche Stadt   *destroyed in the war*

Er ist mir noch **mehr zuwider** als sein Bruder	*He is even more repugnant to me than his brother*
Er ist der **am meisten bemitleidenswerte** Kranke	*He is the most to be pitied of all the patients*

With past participles a prefixed *meist-* can be used rather than *am meisten*, e.g.: *die **meistzerstörte** Stadt, der **meistgekaufte** Geschirrspülautomat Deutschlands.*

(b) *mehr* **is also used if two qualities of the same object are being compared**

i.e. in the sense 'rather': *Diese Arbeit ist **mehr** langweilig als schwierig. eher* is an alternative to *mehr* in this meaning in more formal registers.

8.3 The use of the comparative and other types of comparison

8.3.1 The comparative particle (= 'than') is usually *als*

Peter ist älter **als** Thomas	Mein Wagen fährt schneller **als** deiner

(a) Alternatives to *als*

wie (or *als wie*) is common for *als* in (especially regional) colloquial speech, e.g. *Peter ist älter **(als)** wie Thomas*. This usage is not accepted as standard.

The use of *denn* instead of *als* is archaic, although it can be used in formal registers to avoid the sequence *als als*:

Die Mauer erscheint eher als Kunstwerk denn als Grenze (*Schneider*)	*The wall appears rather as a work of art than as a frontier*

NB: (i) *denn* <u>is</u> commonly used in some set phrases: *mehr denn je* 'more than ever', *Geben ist seliger denn nehmen* 'It is better to give than to receive'.
  (ii) Noun phrases after *als* and *wie* are in apposition to the noun they refer to, i.e. they are normally in the same case, see 2.6.

(b) Degree of difference is expressed by *um . . . als*, or by a noun phrase in the accusative case

Eine Fahrt im TGV-Atlantique kann **um** bis zu 50 Prozent teurer kommen **als** in einem herkömmlichen Schnellzug (*FR*)	*A trip on the TGV-Atlantique can work out up to 50% more expensive than in an ordinary express train*
Er ist (**um**) **einen Monat** jünger **als** ich	*He is a month younger than me*

(c) To express a greater degree (= 'even') *noch* is used with the comparative

London ist eine **noch schmutzigere** Stadt als Amsterdam	*London is an even dirtier city than Amsterdam*
Er hat gestern **noch weniger** gearbeitet	*He worked even less yesterday*
Es regnete **noch stärker**	*It was raining even harder*

8.3.2 Lower degrees of comparison are expressed by *weniger, am wenigsten*

These correspond to English 'less tall than', 'least tall', etc.:

Er war **weniger optimistisch** als sein Bruder	*He was less optimistic than his brother*

Er arbeitet **weniger fleißig** als ich	*He works less hard than me*
der **am wenigsten talentierte** Spieler	*the least talented player*
Er arbeitet **am wenigsten fleißig** von allen	*He works the least hard of all*

In practice, *am wenigsten* is felt to be awkward, and other constructions are often preferred. Compare:

die **uninteressanteste** Rede	*the least interesting speech*
der **billigste/preiswerteste** Wagen	*the least expensive car*
die **einfachste** Methode	*the least difficult method*
möglichst geringe Kosten	*the least possible expenditure*

NB: In formal German, *minder* is an occasional alternative to *weniger*, see 8.2.4b, e.g.: *Nicht minder virtuos ist dagegen die Vorstellung auf der gegenüberliegenden Reeperbahnseite*(HM).

8.3.3 The 'absolute' comparative

The comparative of some common adjectives or adverbs is used not to signal a direct comparison, but to indicate a fair degree of the relevant quality, e.g. *ein älterer Herr* 'an elderly gentleman', *eine größere Stadt* 'a fair-sized town'. This so-called 'absolute' comparative is possible with the following adjectives:

alt	dick	dünn	gut	jung	kurz	neu
bekannt	dunkel	groß	hell	klein	lang	oft

eine **bessere** Wohngegend	*a fairly good neighbourhood*
seit **längerer** Zeit	*for a longish time now*
ein **neueres** Modell	*a fairly new model*
Kommen Sie **öfter** (*coll. also*: öfters) hierher?	*Do you come here quite often?*

8.3.4 Progression is expressed by using *immer* with the comparative

This corresponds to English 'more and more':

Er lief **immer schneller**	*He ran faster and faster*
Der Sprit wird **immer teurer**	*Petrol is getting dearer and dearer*
Meine Arbeit wird **immer schwieriger**	*My work is getting more and more difficult*

NB: A construction like that of English, e.g. *Er lief schneller und schneller* is occasionally found, but it is much less frequent than that with *immer*.

8.3.5 Proportion (i.e. 'the more . . . the more')

Proportion is expressed in German by using a subordinate clause introduced by the conjunction *je*, followed by a main clause beginning with *umso* or (especially in formal written German) *desto*:

Je länger man Deutsch lernt, **desto/umso** leichter wird es	*The longer you learn German, the easier it gets*
je eher, **desto/umso** besser	*the sooner the better*
Je besser das Wetter, **desto/umso** mehr können wir wandern	*The better the weather, the more we can go hiking*

NB: (i) In older German, a second *je* could be used rather than *desto* or *umso*. This survives in a few set phrases such as *je länger, je lieber* and *je länger, je mehr*.
(ii) As an equivalent to 'all the more because', German uses *umso mehr, als/da/weil* . . . (see 19.4.3b).
(iii) In colloquial German the combination *umso . . . umso* is common, e.g. *umso größer, umso besser* 'the bigger, the better'.

8.3.6 **Equality is expressed by** *so . . . wie* (= 'as . . . as')

Peter ist **so** alt **wie** Thomas

Er arbeitet **so** fleißig **wie** ich

Mein neuer Wagen fährt nicht **so** schnell **wie** deiner

Er ist nur halb **so** alt **wie** seine Schwester

A number of variations on this construction occur:

(a) In colloquial German, *als* **is often used for** *wie*

Peter ist **so** alt **als** Thomas

Ich bin doch **so** groß **als** du

This is only regarded as acceptable in written registers in the following contexts:

(i) 'as well as' can be *sowohl wie* or *sowohl als* (see 19.1.4b), e.g.: *Ich will* **sowohl Anna als/wie (auch)** *Helga einladen*

(ii) 'as soon/little as possible' can be *so bald/wenig wie möglich* or *so bald/wenig als möglich.*

(iii) 'twice as . . . as' can be *doppelt so . . . wie* or *doppelt so . . . als: Die Ernte ist* **doppelt so groß als/ wie** *im vorigen Jahr*

NB: The combination *als wie*, e.g. *Ich bin doch so groß* **als wie** *du* is common in speech, but it is generally considered to be a non-standard regionalism.

(b) *so* **can be omitted in some common phrases and idioms**

Er ist (so) hart wie Stahl

Er ist (so) schlau wie ein Fuchs

(c) 'just as . . . (as)' is expressed by *ebenso . . . (wie)* or *genauso . . . (wie)*

Peter ist **ebenso/genauso** alt **wie** Thomas
Dort können wir **genauso** gutes Fleisch kaufen

(i) *ebenso* is also used to indicate equivalence between two qualities:

Er ist **ebenso** fleißig wie geschickt

He is (just) as industrious as he is skilful

(ii) *ebenso sehr* is used adverbially to indicate degree (= 'just as much'):

Die Brücke ist **ebenso sehr** ein Teil der Landschaft wie der Fluss

The bridge is just as much part of the scenery as the river

(iii) *nicht so sehr . . . wie* is used for 'not so much . . . as':

Er ist **nicht so sehr** dumm **wie** faul

He is not so much stupid as lazy

(d) *gleich* **can be used to indicate equality**

Peter und Thomas sind **gleich** alt
Diese Städte sind etwa **gleich** groß

Peter and Thomas are the same age
These towns are about the same size

8.4 **Types and uses of the superlative**

8.4.1 **The superlative form** *am . . . sten*

This form (see 8.1.2) is used in the following contexts:

(a) Always for adverbs

Von allen Gästen sprach er **am wenigsten**
Ich arbeite **am besten** nachts

Of all the guests he spoke least
I work best at night

Am einfachsten faxen Sie es ihr durch	*The simplest thing is to fax it to her*
Helmut läuft **am schnellsten**	*Helmut runs fastest*
Das hasse ich an den Schulmeistern **am meisten** (*Valentin*)	*That's what I hate most about schoolmasters*

(b) After the verb *sein*

Both superlative forms are found predicatively after *sein*, e.g.: *Welcher Junge ist **am stärksten**?* or *Welcher Junge ist **der stärkste**?*

(i) If a noun is understood, either can be used:

Diese Blume ist **die schönste/am schönsten**	*This flower is the most beautiful*
Unter den deutschen Flüssen ist die Donau **der längste/am längsten**	*Of the German rivers the Danube is the longest*

(ii) If there is no noun to be be understood or if something is being compared with itself (= 'at its most . . . '), only the form with *am* can be used:

Ein Mercedes wäre **am teuersten**	*A Mercedes would be the dearest*
Für meinen Geschmack ist eine Nelke schöner als eine Tulpe, aber eine Rose ist natürlich **am schönsten**	*For my taste a carnation is nicer than a tulip, but a rose is the nicest*
Hier ist die Donau **am tiefsten**	*The Danube is (at its) deepest here*
Der Garten ist **am schönsten** im Juni	*The garden is (at its) nicest in June*

8.4.2 Any superlative can be used in an absolute sense

i.e. not as a comparison but in the sense 'extremely'. This is known as the elative use of the superlative:

in **höchster** Erregung	*in great excitement*
mit **größter** Mühe	*with the greatest difficulty*
Es ist **höchste** Zeit, dass . . .	*It is high time that . . .*
Es herrschte das **rauheste** Wetter	*The weather was extremely raw*
Modernste Kureinrichtungen stehen zu Ihrer Verfügung (*FAZ*)	*You will have the use of the most up-to-date spa treatments*

8.4.3 An absolute adverbial superlative can be formed in *aufs . . .ste*

e.g. *aufs einfachste*, *aufs genaueste*, etc. The form can be spelled with a small or a capital letter: *aufs einfachste/aufs Einfachste* (see 23.2.1.). The preposition and definite article can be written out in full if emphasis is needed: *auf das einfachste/Einfachste*. It is common in formal writing:

Der große runde Tisch war **aufs festlichste/ Festlichste** geschmückt (*Dürrenmatt*)	*The large round table was decorated in a most festive way*
Herr Naumann war **aufs äußerste/ Äußerste** gereizt (*MM*)	*Mr Naumann was exceedingly irritated*
Lange Zeit hat der Ministerpräsident jeden Verdacht **auf das heftigste/Heftigste** dementiert	*For a long time the Prime Minister denied all suspicions most vehemently*

8.4.4 **A superlative adjective or adverb can be emphasised by prefixing *aller-***

This has the sense of the highest degree possible, e.g.:

der allerschnellste Wagen	*the fastest car of all*
Niemand in Deutschland muss sich auch nur im allergeringsten Sorgen machen (*HM*)	*Nobody in Germany needs to have even the slightest possible concern*
Nichts an der Blueserin ist authentisch, am allerwenigsten ihr Berner Dialekt (*SGT*)	*Nothing about the Blues singer is authentic, least of all her Bernese dialect*

8.4.5 **Some adverbial superlatives are formed in *-st*, *-stens* and *zu-* . . . *-st***

Only a few of each type of these are common, and they usually have an absolute or idiomatic meaning. New formations on these patterns are rare.

(a) Adverbial superlatives in *-st*

These consist simply of the superlative stem, whether regular or irregular. Some are in common use in speech and writing, often with special meanings:

äußerst *extremely*	meist *mostly*
höchst *highly, extremely*	möglichst *as . . . as possible; if at all possible*
jüngst (*elev.*) *recently*	unlängst *recently*
längst *for a long time, a long time ago*	

Die Situation ist **höchst** problematisch	*The situation is highly problematical*
Er ist **längst** gestorben	*He died a long time ago*
Du musst einen **möglichst** guten Eindruck machen	*You must make the best possible impression*
Sie ist **unlängst** zurückgekehrt	*She got back recently*

The following are typically used in formulaic idioms in formal registers:

eiligst *as quickly as possible*	höflichst *respectfully*
freundlichst *friendly*	schleunigst *as promptly as possible*
gefälligst, gütigst *kindly*	sorgfältigst *most carefully*
herzlichst *most cordially*	tunlichst *absolutely*

Ich danke Ihnen **herzlichst**	*I thank you most cordially*
Sie werden **höflichst** gebeten, diesen Irrtum ohne Verzug zu berichtigen	*You are respectfully requested to rectify this mistake without delay*
Wir machten uns **schleunigst** aus dem Staube (*Dönhoff*)	*We quickly got up off the floor*
Jeder Lärm ist **tunlichst** zu vermeiden	*Any noise is absolutely to be avoided*

New formations in *-st* are quite frequent, especially in journalism, where their conciseness can be exploited:

Die Böhmendeutschen sind nicht ausgesiedelt, sondern **brutalst** vertrieben worden (*Presse*)	*The Germans of Bohemia were not resettled, but driven out in the most brutal fashion*

Some forms in -*st*, i.e. *best-*, *größt-*, *höchst-*, *kleinst-*, *kürzest-* can be compounded with *möglich* to mean 'the best possible', etc.:

die **bestmögliche** Lösung   die **kleinstmögliche** Summe
der **größtmögliche** Schaden   der **kürzestmögliche** Weg

(b) A few in -*stens* are still used, typically with special idiomatic meanings

bestens *very well*   schnellstens *as quickly as possible*
frühestens *at the earliest*   spätestens *at the latest*
höchstens *at the most*   strengstens *strictly*
meistens *mostly*   wärmstens *most warmly*
mindestens *at least*   wenigstens *at least*
nächstens *shortly, soon*

Es kommen **höchstens** dreißig Gäste   *At most thirty guests are coming*
Ich stehe **meistens** früh auf   *I mostly get up early*
Ich brauche **mindestens** dreitausend Euro   *I need at least three thousand euros for this trip*
  für diese Reise
Wir kommen **spätestens** um sechs an   *We'll arrive at six at the latest*
Rauchen ist **strengstens** verboten   *Smoking is strictly prohibited*
Er könnte **wenigstens** anrufen   *He might at least ring up*

wenigstens and *mindestens* are often interchangeable, but *mindestens* emphasises the idea of the absolute minimum possible rather more strongly. It is used less often when no actual figure is mentioned, in which case *zumindest* (see (c) below) is a possible, rather more emphatic alternative to *wenigstens*.

(c) A few forms in *zu-* . . . -*st* are still current, with idiomatic meanings

zumindest *at (the very) least*   zutiefst *(very) deeply*
zunächst *at first, in the first place*   zuvorderst *(right) at the front*
zuoberst *(right) on top*

Some examples of use in context:

Er hätte uns **zumindest** grüßen können   *He could at least have said hello*
Das Angebot sah **zunächst** verlockend aus   *The offer looked attractive at first*
Sie nahm das Buch, das **zuoberst** lag   *She took the book which was lying on top*
Der Angeklagte bereut sein Fehlverhalten   *The accused deeply regrets his inappropriate*
  zutiefst (*NUZ*)   *behaviour*

9 Numerals

This chapter deals with all words for NUMBERS and NUMERALS in German and their associated forms and uses:

- **Cardinal numbers**, such as 'one', 'two', 'three', etc. (section 9.1)
- **Ordinal numbers**, such as 'first', 'second', 'third', etc. (section 9.2)
- **Fractions** and **decimals** (section 9.3)
- Other **numerical usages** (section 9.4)
- **Addresses** (section 9.5)

9.1 Cardinal numbers

CARDINAL NUMBERS are the numerals used in counting. Their form in German is shown on Table 9.1.

9.1.1 Notes on the forms of the cardinal numbers

(a) Long numbers are rarely written out in full

i.e. those with more than one element, like *zweiunddreißig*, *hundertzwanzig*. In practice, complex numbers are rarely written fully except on cheques, and, in general, figures are used in written German more often than is usual in English.

TABLE 9.1 The forms of the cardinal numbers

0	null	10	zehn	20	zwanzig	30	dreißig
1	eins	11	elf	21	einundzwanzig	40	vierzig
2	zwei	12	zwölf	22	zweiundzwanzig	50	fünfzig
3	drei	13	dreizehn	23	dreiundzwanzig	60	sechzig
4	vier	14	vierzehn	24	vierundzwanzig	70	siebzig
5	fünf	15	fünfzehn	25	fünfundzwanzig	80	achtzig
6	sechs	16	sechzehn	26	sechsundzwanzig	90	neunzig
7	sieben	17	siebzehn	27	siebenundzwanzig	91	einundneunzig
8	acht	18	achtzehn	28	achtundzwanzig	92	zweiundneunzig
9	neun	19	neunzehn	29	neunundzwanzig	93	dreiundneunzig

100	(ein)hundert	1000	(ein)tausend
101	hundert(und)eins	1099	tausend(und)neunundneunzig
102	hundertzwei	1100	(ein)tausendeinhundert/elfhundert
151	(ein)hunderteinundfünfzig	2305	zweitausenddreihundertfünf
200	zweihundert	10 000	zehntausend
535	fünfhundertfünfunddreißig	50 000	fünfzigtausend
999	neunhundertneunundneunzig	100 000	hunderttausend

564 297 fünfhundertvierundsechzigtausendzweihundertsiebenundneunzig

1 000 000	eine Million	1 000 000 000	ine Milliarde
2 000 000	zwei Millionen	1 000 000 000 000	eine Billion

5 276 423 fünf Millionen zweihundertsechsundsiebzigtausendvierhundertdreiundzwanzig

(b) Numbers higher than a thousand can be written with spaces every three digits

i.e. not commas as in English, i.e. *564 297*, not *564,297*. The comma is used in German for the English decimal point (see 9.3.3). Confusingly, a point is sometimes used instead of a space in German to separate thousands: *564.297*.

(c) *hundert* or *einhundert*; *tausend* or *eintausend*?

English speakers tend to overuse the longer form *einhundert* because of the similarity to English 'a hundred'. However, it is used less frequently than the shorter alternative *hundert*, and the long form *eintausend* is much less usual than simple *tausend*. However, *ein* is normally inserted in complex numbers, e.g. 101 100 *hunderteintausendeinhundert*.

(d) *und* **can be used between** *hundert* **and** *eins*

However, English speakers tend to overuse this, because of the similarity to English 'a hundred **and one'.** Nevertheless, *und* is wholly optional (and less frequent in practice), as in *hundert(und)eins*, *zweihundert(und)eins*, as also between *tausend* and tens or units, e.g. *tausend(und)eins*, *viertausend(und)elf*, *zwanzigtausend(und)zweiunddreißig*.

(e) *eine Million, eine Milliarde* **and** *eine Billion* **are treated as separate nouns**

They have a plural ending where necessary: *zwei Millionen*; *fünf Millionen vierhunderttausend*. Numbers higher than *eine Milliarde* are rare in normal use, so that, for instance, *tausend Milliarden* is more usual than *eine Billion*.

English speakers should note that *Milliarde* is the equivalent of what is nowadays usually referred to as 'a billion' in English (i.e. a thousand million), whilst *Billion* is a 'real' billion, i.e. a million million.

NB: The plural form is used when **one** million is followed by a decimal: *1,4 Millionen Euro*. This is spoken as *einskommavier Millionen Euro*.

(f) The otherwise archaic form *zwo* **is often heard for** *zwei*

This is used to avoid confusion with *drei*. *zwo* is particularly frequently used on the telephone, but it has become common in other spoken contexts and is sometimes extended to 2 in complex numbers, e.g. *zwounddreißig*, and the ordinal *der zwote*.

(g) The numbers from 2 to 12 have alternative forms with an additional *-e*

e.g. *sechse, neune, elfe*. These are common in spoken colloquial German (especially in the South) for emphasis, particularly when stating the time: *Ich bin um fünfe aufgestanden* and in counting scores in card games.

(h) Longer numbers are often stated in pairs

e.g. *4711* (a brand of eau de Cologne), spoken *siebenundvierzig elf*. This usage is particularly frequent (though optional) with telephone numbers (less frequently the dialling code). Thus, a number like *(0621) 54 87 23* is typically given as *null sechs zwo eins – vierundfünfzig siebenundachtzig dreiundzwanzig*.

(i) Years from *1100* **to** *1999* **are usually stated in hundreds**

This is similar to English usage, e.g. *1996: neunzehnhundertsechsundneunzig*.

(j) Years after *2000* **are given with** *zweitausend*

This differs from usage with 'twenty' which has become established in English. *2009* is thus *zweitausendneun* and *2015* is *zweitausendfünfzehn*.

(k) *beide* **is used in some contexts where English uses the numeral 'two'**

This is particularly the case where it is a question of 'two and only two' of the relevant items, see 5.5.3b, e.g. *Ich möchte diese beiden Hemden* 'I would like these two shirts'.

(l) *fünfzehn* and *fünfzig*

These are regularly pronounced *fuffzehn* and *fuffzig* in colloquial speech.

(m) As an indefinite large number, corresponding to English 'umpteen', colloquial German uses *zig*

Ich kenne sie schon **zig** Jahre	*I've known her umpteen years*
Die ist mit **zig** Sachen in die Kurve gefahren	*She took the bend at a fair old speed*

The compounds *zigmal* 'umpteen times', *zigtausend* 'umpteen thousand', etc. are also frequently used. All these forms can be written with an initial hyphen: *-zig, -zigmal*, etc.

(n) Cardinal numbers used as nouns

Where these refer to the numeral, they are feminine (see 1.1.2) and have a plural in *-en* if required:

Die Sieben ist eine Glückszahl	In Mathe habe ich nie **eine Fünf** gehabt
Die Hundert ist eine dreistellige Zahl	
Im Abitur hat er **drei Zweien** und **eine Eins** gekriegt	

The feminine nouns *die Hundert* and *die Tausend*, referring to the numbers as such, as illustrated above, are to be distinguished from the neuters *das Hundert* and *das Tausend*, which refer to quantities (see 9.1.5b).

(o) The numeral 7 is usually written in handwriting with a stroke

i.e. *7*. This helps to distinguish it from 1, which Germans write with an initial sweep, i.e. *1*.

9.1.2 *eins, ein, einer* 'one'

(a) The form *eins* **is used in isolation as a numeral**

i.e. in counting and the like:

Wir müssen mit der (Linie) eins zum Bahnhof fahren	*We've got to take the number one (i.e. tram, bus) to the station*

This form is also used with decimals (see 9.3.3): *einskommasieben*

(b) The form *ein* **is used with a following noun**

It agrees with the following noun for case and gender and has the same endings as the indefinite article, see Table 4.2.

ein Tisch	*one table*
eine Kirche	*one church*
ein Buch	*one book*
durch **einen** Fehler	*by one mistake*
aus **einem** Grund	*for one reason*

The **numerical** sense of *ein* (i.e. 'one') is distinguished from the **indefinite article** *ein* (i.e. 'a, an') in speech by always being pronounced in full, see 4.1.2b. In writing, if there is a possibility of ambiguity in context, the numerical sense can be made clear typographically, e.g.:

éin Buch   *ein* Buch   <u>ein</u> Buch   **ein** Buch   ein Buch

In practice this is only necessary in exceptional cases.

After *hundert* and *tausend*, e.g. *301, 2001*, there is considerable uncertainty as to how or whether to decline forms of *ein*. One possibility is to use a declined form of *-ein* with a **singular** noun, e.g. *ein Buch mit dreihundertundeiner Seite*. The combinations *hundertundeine Mark* and *Tausendundeine Nacht* 'The 1001 Nights' are well established idiomatically. However, many Germans feel this sounds odd in other contexts, but they are equally unhappy with the alternative of undeclined *-ein*, with a plural noun, e.g. *ein Buch mit dreihundertein Seiten*. A further alternative, using the invariant form *eins* with a plural noun, seems to be becoming predominant usage, e.g. *ein Buch mit dreihundertundeins Seiten, Wir haben hundertundeins tolle Ideen*.

(c) The form *einer* is used as a pronoun

Its declension is given in Table 5.10.

Wir haben einen Rottweiler, und ihr habt auch **einen**, nicht?
einer der Männer *one of the men*   **ein(e)s** der Häuser *one of the houses*

Further details on the use of *einer* are given in 5.5.4.

(d) After a determiner, *ein-* declines like an adjective

e.g. *der eine . . .* , 'the one . . .'

Das Dorf hatte bloß **die eine** Straße   Mit **seinem einen** Auge sieht er schlecht

(e) *ein* has no ending in a few constructions

(i) When followed by *oder* or *bis* and another number, e.g. *ein oder zwei, ein bis zwei*:

Ich pflückte **ein oder zwei** Rosen   Wir müssen **ein bis zwei** Tage warten
Er kam vor **ein oder zwei** Wochen   Ich sprach mit **ein oder zwei** anderen

(ii) When linked with *andere* or *derselbe*, the alternatives of declining *ein* or leaving it endingless are equally acceptable:

Ein(er) oder der andere machte eine kurze   *One or other made a brief remark*
    Bemerkung
An **ein(em)** und demselben Tag machten   *On one and the same day three firms went bankrupt*
    drei Firmen Pleite

With *mehrere*, *ein* is more commonly inflected: *vor einem* (rarely: *ein*) *oder mehreren Monaten* 'one or more months ago'.

(iii) *ein* is not inflected in *ein Uhr* 'one o'clock', see Table 11.1. (Compare *eine Uhr* 'a/one clock').

9.1.3 Declension of cardinal numbers

Apart from *ein* 'one', which is declined as explained in 9.1.2, cardinal numbers do not normally decline to show case or gender in German. Thus:

gegen sechs Kinder   die sechs Kinder
mit sechs Kindern   mit den sechs Kindern
wegen sechs Kindern   wegen der sechs Kinder

However, endings are found in one or two special contexts:

(a) *zwei* and *drei* have the GENITIVE forms *zweier* and *dreier*

These are used quite frequently in formal written German, but their use is not obligatory, e.g.:

Der Taufe **zweier** Kinder aus der Ehe stimmte er zu (*MM*)	*He agreed to the baptism of two children of the marriage*
die vielerlei Eindrücke **dreier** anstrengender Tage (*Zeit*)	*the various impressions from three strenuous days*

A following adjective has the strong ending *-er* (see 6.2.1a), as in the second example above, but an adjective used as a noun usually has the weak ending *-en*: *die Seligkeit zweier **Verliebten***. In less formal registers a phrase with *von* is used, e.g. *die Eindrücke von drei anstrengenden Tagen*, and in practice this is a perfectly acceptable alternative in most writing.

(b) **The numbers from 2 to 12 can have a** DATIVE **in** *-en* **when used in isolation**

i.e. when no noun follows:

Nur einer von **zweien** ist als gesund zu bezeichnen (*Zeit*)
als sich die Tür hinter den **dreien** geschlossen hatte (*Welt*)

This is a common alternative to the endingless form (i.e. *einer von **zwei***, etc.), even in spoken German, especially with the numbers 2, 3 and 4. It is most frequent for added emphasis and in set phrases such as *auf allen vieren* 'on all fours', *mit dreien* 'with three (Jacks)' (in the card game *Skat*), and in the formula *zu zweien, dreien, vieren* etc. 'in twos, threes, fours', e.g.: *dieser Spaziergang* **zu zweien**.

A rather more frequent alternative is a form in *-t* (using the stem of the ordinal, see 9.2.1), e.g. *zu zweit, zu dritt, zu viert*. However, a distinction can be made between *zu zweien* 'in pairs' and *zu zweit* 'as a pair' (i.e. when there are only two). Compare:

Sie gingen **zu zweien** über die Straße	*They crossed the road in pairs*
Sie gingen **zu zweit** über die Straße	*The two of them crossed the road together*

9.1.4 **Cardinals have an adjectival form in** *-er*

e.g. *fünfer, zehner*. This is used to denote value and measurement, or with reference to years. When they are used as adjectives, they do not decline (see 6.2.7e). When they are used as nouns, they have the dative ending *-n*:

Ich habe zwei Zehner und einen Hunderter	*I've got two ten euro notes and a hundred euro note*
zwei Fünfziger	*two fifty cent pieces* **or** *two fifty euro notes*
zehn achtziger Marken	*ten 80 cent stamps*
eine Achtziger	*an 80 cent stamp*
die Zehner und die Einer	*tens and units*
eine Sechserpackung	*a six-pack*
in den neunziger Jahren des 20. Jahrhunderts	*in the 1990s*
ein Mann in den Vierzigern	*a man in his forties*
eine Mittfünfzigerin	*a woman in her mid-fifties*
ein Dreitausender	*a mountain (over) 3000 metres high*
ein vierundneunziger Heppenheimer Krötenbrunnen	*a 94 Heppenheimer Krötenbrunnen* (i.e. a wine vintage 1994)

9.1.5 **hundert, tausend, Dutzend**

(a) *hundert* and *tausend* are used as normal numerals

They are not declined:

hundert, zweihundert Häuser	*a hundred, two hundred houses*
tausend Bücher, **sechstausend** Bücher	*a thousand books, six thousand books*

(b) *das Hundert*, *das Tausend* and *das Dutzend* are used as nouns of quantity

das zweite **Dutzend, Hundert, Tausend**	*the second dozen, hundred, thousand*
ein halbes **Dutzend,** ein halbes **Hundert**	*half a dozen, half a hundred* (i.e. fifty)
zwei **Dutzend** Eier	*two dozen eggs*
Hunderttausende von Menschen	*hundreds of thousands of people*
Die Menschen verhungerten zu **Hunderten** und **Tausenden**	*People were starving in hundreds and thousands*

(c) If these words refer to an indefinite quantity, they can be spelled with an initial capital or small letter

i.e. when they are used in the plural, especially after quantifiers such as *einige, mehrere, viele,* etc. In such contexts it is not clear whether they are nouns or numerals. They have a plural ending **if** the following phrase is introduced by *von* or is in the genitive (see 1.2.14 and 2.7.4):

In dem Stadion warten **Tausende/ tausende** von Menschen auf den Spielbeginn	*In the stadium thousands of people are waiting for the start of the match*
Mehrere **Hundert/hundert** Kinder waren an Typhus gestorben	*Several hundred children had died of typhus*
Diesen Stoff verkauft man in einigen **Dutzend/dutzend** Farben	*This material is sold in a few dozen shades*

In the genitive plural, they have the ending *-er* if no determiner precedes. A following adjective has the strong endings:

inmitten Tausender/tausender fröhlicher New Yorker (*HMP*)	*in the midst of thousands of happy New Yorkers*

However, they have the ending *-e* if a preceding determiner has the genitive plural ending *-er*: *die Ersparnisse vieler Tausende/tausende.*

NB: (i) *Dutzend* does not take a plural ending when used as a measurement noun in constructions such as *drei Dutzend* (*Eier*) 'three dozen (eggs)', see 1.2.14.
(ii) For the use of the genitive, apposition or a phrase with *von* after the nouns *Dutzend, Hundert, Tausend* see 2.7.4.

9.1.6 **Qualification of cardinal numbers**

(a) Numerals may be modified by certain adverbs of degree

bis zu *up to*	knapp *barely*	über *over*
unter *under*	zwischen *between*	
gegen, rund, um, ungefähr, circa/zirka (*abbrev.*: ca.) *about, approximately*		

Although most of these are prepositions which would be expected to require a particular case (dative or accusative), when they are used in these constructions with a following numeral they have no influence on the case of the following noun phrase:

Bis zu zehn Kinder können mitfahren	*Up to ten children can come with us*
Sie ist **zwischen 30 und 40 Jahre** alt	*She is between 30 and 40 years old*

However, when they are used as prepositions, the following noun phrase is in the case normally required by the preposition (dative or accusative):

Kinder **unter sieben Jahren** zahlen die Hälfte	*Children under seven years old pay half-price*
Kinder **über sechs Jahre** zahlen voll	*Children over six years old pay the full price*
geeignet für Kinder **zwischen sieben und zwölf Jahren**	*suitable for children between the ages of seven and twelve*

It is quite straightforward to work out whether these words are being used as **adverbs** (when they do not influence the selection of case) or **prepositions** (when they do), since in contexts where they are being used as adverbs the sentence would still be grammatically correct if they were left out: *Zehn Kinder können mitfahren*. But prepositions cannot be omitted: **Kinder sieben Jahren zahlen die Hälfte* is not a grammatical sentence.

(b) Other adverbials used with numbers:

Es dauert gut drei Stunden	*It lasts a good three hours*
Er gab mir **ganze** fünf Euro	*He gave me all of five euro*

9.2 Ordinal numbers

9.2.1 The formation of ordinal numbers

ORDINAL NUMBERS are those used as adjectives like English 'first', 'second', 'third', etc. The forms of ordinal numbers in German are given in Table 9.2. Most are formed by adding the suffix *-te* to the cardinals 2–19 and *-ste* to the cardinals from 20 upwards, but *der erste* 'first', *der dritte* 'third' and *der siebte* 'seventh' are exceptions to this pattern. All ordinal numbers are declined like adjectives.

TABLE 9.2 The forms of the ordinal numbers

1	der erste	**20**	der zwanzigste
2	der zweite	**21**	der einundzwanzigste
3	der dritte	**27**	der siebenundzwanzigste
4	der vierte		
5	der fünfte	**30**	der dreißigste
6	der sechste	**40**	der vierzigste
7	der siebte	**50**	der fünfzigste
8	der achte	**60**	der sechzigste
9	der neunte	**70**	der siebzigste
10	der zehnte	**80**	der achtzigste
11	der elfte	**90**	der neunzigste
12	der zwölfte		
13	der dreizehnte	**100**	der hundertste
14	der vierzehnte	**101**	der hundert(und)erste
15	der fünfzehnte	**117**	der hundertsiebzehnte
16	der sechzehnte		
17	der siebzehnte	**1000**	der tausendste
18	der achtzehnte		
19	der neunzehnte	**1 000 000**	der millionste
5437	der fünftausendvierhundertsiebenunddreißigste		

There are a few special forms and uses;

(a) *der x-te* and *der zigste* **are used as indefinite ordinals**

i.e. as equivalents of English 'the umpteenth', e.g.: *Das war mein x-ter/zigster Versuch.*

NB: *x-te* is pronounced [ɪkstə]. For the form *zig*, see 9.1.2l.

(b) The form *der wievielte* can be used to enquire about numbers

Das **wievielte** Kind ist das jetzt?	*How many children is that now?*
Den **Wievielten** haben wir heute?	*What's the date today?*
Zum **wievielten** Mal bist du schon hier?	*How many times have you been here?*

(c) The ordinal stems can be compounded with superlatives

die **zweitbeste** Arbeit   die **drittgrößte** Stadt   der **vierthöchste** Berg

(d) Ordinal numbers are indicated in writing by using a full stop after the numeral

am 14. Mai   das 275. Regiment   die 12. Klasse

This is nowadays the <u>only</u> usual means of indicating ordinal numbers in writing; abbreviations (e.g. *am 5ten Mai*) are no longer current.

(e) Ordinal numbers can be used as nouns

In this respect they are like other adjectives, and they are written with initial capitals:

jeder **Dritte**   Er kam als **Erster**   Wer ist der **Zweite**?

NB: As with other adjectives, a small initial letter is used if the noun is understood, e.g. *Anke war die erste Frau in unserem Kreis, aber wer war die zweite?* (see 6.2.5).

9.2.2 Equivalents for English 'to be the first to'

For 'to be the first to', German uses either *als Erster*, or *der Erste* followed by a relative clause:

Die Russen **waren die Ersten**, die einen künstlichen Erdsatelliten um den Globus schickten; sie brachten **als Erste** einen Menschen in den Weltraum (*Zeit*)	*The Russians were the first to send an artificial satellite around the earth; they were the first to put a man into space*
Dann musste Konstantin **als Erster** über den Graben (*Dönhoff*)	*Then Konstantin had to be the first to cross the ditch*

9.2.3 Equivalents for English 'first(ly)', 'secondly', etc.

For these, German uses the stem of the ordinal with the suffix *-ens*, e.g. *erstens* 'first(ly)', *zweitens* 'secondly', *drittens* 'thirdly', etc. Alternatively, the forms *zum Ersten, zum Zweiten, zum Dritten*, etc. are used.

9.3 Fractions and decimals

9.3.1 Fractions (*die Bruchzahlen*) are formed by adding *-el* to the ordinal stem

These are neuter nouns:

ein Drittel   ein Viertel   ein Fünftel   ein Achtel   ein Zehntel

They have an endingless plural, e.g. *zwei Drittel*. The ending *-n* is optional in the dative plural:

Die Prüfung wurde von **vier Fünftel(n)** der Schüler bestanden

If a fraction is the subject of a verb, then it takes a singular or plural ending as appropriate, see 12.1.4:

Ein Drittel **ist** schon verkauft   Zwei Drittel **sind** schon verkauft

When followed by a noun of measurement they are spelled with a small letter and an accompanying indefinite article takes its case and gender from the noun:

mit einer **drittel** Flasche   mit einem **viertel** Liter

If a fraction in the dative is followed by a phrase in the genitive, it sometimes lacks the expected ending:

in einem Drittel der Fälle (*less common*: in ein Drittel der Fälle)

In practice it is more usual to include it.

Fractions can be written together with measurement words, e.g. *ein Viertelliter*, *fünf Achtelliter*, *vier Zehntelgramm* and (especially) *eine Viertelstunde*. The following alternatives are thus all acceptable:

Er verfehlte den Rekord um **drei Zehntel einer Sekunde**
Er verfehlte den Rekord um **drei zehntel Sekunden**
Er verfehlte den Rekord um **drei Zehntelsekunden**

drei Viertel can be used in the same way, as a noun phrase: *der Topf ist zu drei Vierteln voll*, or, with a small letter, as an adverb: *der Topf ist drei viertel voll*. It can be compounded with *Stunde*, e.g. *in einer Dreiviertelstunde* 'in three-quarters of an hour' (alternatively: *in drei Viertelstunden*).

When used with full integers, fractions are read out as written, with no *und*: 3⅝ *drei fünfachtel*, 1⁷⁄₁₀ *eins siebenzehntel*.

9.3.2 'half' corresponds to the adjective *halb* and the noun *die Hälfte*

These are used as follows:

(a) 'half', used as a noun, is normally *die Hälfte*

Er hat mir nur **die Hälfte** gegeben   *He only gave me half*
die größere **Hälfte**   *the bigger half*

However, the form *das Halb*, from the adjective, is used in order to refer to the number as such:

(Ein) **Halb** ist mehr als ein Drittel   *Half is more than a third*

(b) 'half a': the usual equivalent is the indefinite article with *halb*

Ich aß einen **halben** Apfel   *I ate half an apple*
ein **halbes** Dutzend   *half a dozen*
ein **halbes** Brot   *half a loaf*

(c) 'half the/this/my'

The usual equivalent is *die Hälfte* with a following genitive, but the appropriate determiner can be used with *halb* if the reference is to a whole thing which can be divided cleanly in two:

Die Hälfte der/dieser Äpfel ist schlecht	*Half the/these apples are bad*
die Hälfte meines Geldes	*half my money*
Ich aß **die Hälfte des Kuchens** ⎱	*I ate half the cake*
Ich aß **den halben Kuchen** ⎰	

NB: The use of *halb* with a plural noun in such contexts, i.e. *die halben Äpfel* 'half the apples', is colloquial and not accepted as standard.

(d) English adverbial 'half' corresponds to German *halb*

halb angezogen	*half dressed*
Er weiß alles nur **halb**	*He only half knows things*

(e) German equivalents for English 'one and a half'

German uses either *eineinhalb* or (in more informal usage) *anderthalb*. 2½, 3½, etc. are *zweieinhalb*, *dreieinhalb*, etc. These are not declined:

Bis Walldürn sind es noch **eineinhalb**/ **anderthalb** Stunden	*It's another hour and a half to Walldürn*
Sie wollte noch **sechseinhalb** Monate bleiben	*She wanted to stay another six and a half months*

(f) Some other phrases and idioms:

Er hatte **halb so viel** wie ich	*He had half as much as me*
Kinder fahren **zum halben Preis**	*Children travel half price*
Er ist mir **auf halbem Wege** entgegengekommen	*He met me halfway* (literal and figurative sense)
Ich nehme noch **ein Halbes**	*I'll have another half*
Das ist **nichts Halbes** und nichts Ganzes	*That's neither flesh nor fowl*
Die Besucher waren **zur Hälfte** Deutsche	*Half the visitors were German*
nach der ersten **Halbzeit**	*after the first half* (sport)
halb Europa, **halb** München (see 6.2.7g)	*half Europe, half Munich*

9.3.3 Decimals are written with a comma

i.e. <u>not</u> with a point, e.g.:

0,7	nullkommasieben	4,75	vierkommasiebenfünf
1,25	einskommazweifünf	109,1	hundertneunkommaeins
3,426	dreikommavierzweisechs		

In everyday usage, two places of decimals are sometimes read out in terms of tens and units, e.g. 4,75 *vierkommafünfundsiebzig*.

9.4 Other numerical usages

9.4.1 Numerically equal distribution is expressed by *je*

Ich gab den Jungen **je** zehn Euro	*I gave each of the boys/each boy ten euros*
A. und B. wurden zu **je** drei Jahren verurteilt	*A and B were each sentenced to three years*
Sie erhielten **je** fünf Kilo Reis	*They each received five kilograms of rice*

9.4.2 **Multiples**

(a) German suffixes -*fach* to the cardinal number to form multiples

e.g. *einfach* 'single', *zweifach* 'twofold', *dreifach* 'threefold', etc.:

eine **einfach**e Karte	*a single ticket*
ein **vierfach**er Olympiasieger	*a four-time gold-medal winner*
. . . stiegen die Grundstückspreise zunächst aufs **Zehnfach**e (*Böll*)	*. . . the price of land first went up tenfold*

(b) *zweifach* **and** *doppelt*

zweifach is sometimes interchangeable in meaning with *doppelt* 'double', but more often refers to two <u>different</u> things, while *doppelt* refers to two of the same, e.g.: *ein zweifaches Verbrechen* 'two kinds of crime' but *Der Koffer hat einen doppelten Boden* 'the suitcase has a double bottom'. *zweifach* has the variant form *zwiefach* in older literary usage.

(c) -*fach* can also be suffixed to a few indefinites

e.g. *vielfach* or *mehrfach* 'manifold', 'frequent(ly)', 'repeatedly', *mannigfach* 'varied', 'manifold'.

(d) Forms in -*fältig* can also be used as multiples

e.g. *zweifältig*, *dreifältig*, *vielfältig*, etc. These are rather less common than forms in -*fach*. Note also (without *Umlaut*!) *mannigfaltig*, which is more frequent than *mannigfach*, and *die (heilige) Dreifaltigkeit* 'the (Holy) Trinity'. *einfältig* most often has the meaning 'simple(-minded)'.

(e) Equivalents for English *single*

When it is used in the sense 'individual', 'separate', *single* corresponds to *einzeln*, e.g. *Die Bände werden einzeln verkauft* 'The volumes are sold singly/separately'. In the sense 'sole', it corresponds to *einzig*, e.g. *Er hat keinen einzigen Freund* 'He hasn't got a single friend'.

9.4.3 *einmal, zweimal*, etc.

(a) Adverbs made up from -*mal* suffixed to the cardinals express the number of occasions

e.g. *einmal* 'once', *zweimal* 'twice', *dreimal* 'three times', *zehnmal* 'ten times', *hundertmal* 'a hundred times', *x-mal*, *zigmal* 'umpteen times', *dutzendmal* 'a dozen times', etc.

Ich habe ihn diese Woche **dreimal** gesehen	*I've seen him three times this week*
Ich habe es **hundertmal** bereut	*I've regretted it a hundred times*
Also, Herr Ober, **zweimal** Gulasch, bitte	*Right, waiter, goulash for two, please*
anderthalbmal so groß wie der andere Luftballon	*half as big again as the other balloon*

If particular emphasis is needed, the cardinal and the noun *Mal* 'times' can be written separately, e.g. *neun Mal!* '**nine** times!'

Adjectives are formed from these adverbs by suffixing -*ig* (see 22.3.1d), e.g. *einmalig, zweimalig*:

eine **einmalige** Gelegenheit	*a unique opportunity*
nach **dreimaligem** Durchlesen seines Briefes	*after reading his letter three times*

Formed in a similar way is *mehrmalig* 'repeated'.

(b) Forms and phrases with -mal and Mal

Mal (plural *Male*) is a neuter noun, and it is in most contexts written separately from any preceding adjectives or determiners, with an initial capital letter:

das erste **Mal**, als ich ihn sah	Das letzte **Mal** war das schönste
kein einziges **Mal**	ein um das andere **Mal** *time after time*
Ich werde es nächstes **Mal** tun	Das vorige **Mal** war es schöner
Zum wievielten **Mal bist du hier**?	Beim vorletzten **Mal** war sie schwer krank
Jedes **Mal** bist du zu spät gekommen	Er war nur ein paar **Mal** dort gewesen
Beide **Male** bin ich durchgefallen	viele (hundert) **Male**
Ich habe ihn oft besucht; das eine **Mal** zeigte er mir seine Sammlung	
Dieses **Mal** wird sie mich anders behandeln müssen	
Die letzten paar **Male** war sie nicht zu Hause	

The form *-mal* can be compounded in a few phrases:

diesmal *this time*	**dutzendmal** *a dozen times*
ein **paarmal** *a few times*	ein **andermal** *another time*

This possibility has been considerably limited in the reformed spelling. Only those given above are now accepted, and forms like *jedesmal* and *zum erstenmal* have been replaced by the full phrases, with each word written separately, as shown above.

(c) *vielmals* 'many times' is used in a few set constructions:

Ich danke Ihnen **vielmals** ⎫	*Many thanks*
Danke **vielmals** ⎭	
Ich bitte **vielmals** um Entschuldigung	*I do apologise*
Sie lässt Sie **vielmals** grüßen	*She sends you her kindest regards*

Cf. also *erstmals* 'for the first time', *mehrmals* 'repeatedly'.

9.4.4 The suffix -*erlei*

-erlei is added to the cardinal numbers to give forms which mean 'x kinds of', e.g. *zweierlei* 'two kinds of', *dreierlei* 'three kinds of', *vielerlei* 'many kinds of', etc. They can be used as nouns or adjectives and do not decline:

Ich ziehe **zweierlei** Bohnen	*I grow two kinds of beans*
Er hat **hunderterlei** Pläne	*He's got hundreds of different plans*
Ich habe ihm **dreierlei** vorgeschlagen	*I suggested three different things to him*

einerlei is most often used in the sense 'all the same' (i.e. = *egal*, *gleich*, etc.), e.g. *Das ist mir alles einerlei.*

9.4.5 Mathematical terminology

The common arithmetic and mathematical functions are expressed as follows in German. In some cases the symbols used in the German-speaking countries are slightly different from those current in the English-speaking countries:

$4 + 5 = 9$	vier und/plus fünf ist/macht/gleich neun
$8 - 6 = 2$	acht weniger/minus sechs ist/gleich zwei

$$3 \times 4 = 12 \atop 3 \cdot 4 = 12 \}$$ drei mal vier ist/gleich zwölf

$8 : 2 = 4$ acht (geteilt) durch zwei ist/gleich vier

$3^2 = 9$ drei hoch zwei (drei zum Quadrat) ist/gleich neun

$3^3 = 27$ drei hoch drei ist/gleich siebenundzwanzig

$\sqrt{9} = 3$ Quadratwurzel/zweite Wurzel aus neun ist/gleich drei

$5 > 3$ fünf ist größer als drei

9.5 **Addresses**

The format now recommended by the German, Swiss and Austrian postal services is as in the examples below:

Herrn
Dr. Ulrich Sievers
Sichelstraße 17
54290 Trier

Frau
Maria Jellinek
Maximiliansgasse 34
1084 Wien

Familie
Karl (und Ute) Schulz
Königsberger Straße 36
64711 Erbach/Odw.

Herrn
Beat Wernli
Gerechtigkeitsgasse 24
3011 Bern

Firma
Eugen Spengel
Rossgasse 7–9
07973 Greiz

Monsieur Alain Dubois
rue Napoléon 17
94320 THIAIS
FRANKREICH

(Herrn und Frau)
Peter und Eva Specht
Steinweg 2½
35037 Marburg/Lahn

Mr & Mrs Frank Johnson
27 Corsland Ave
GUILDFORD
GROßBRITANNIEN
GU3 4AY

An das
Katasteramt Westfalen
Bismarckallee 87
48151 Münster

Mr. Albert McEvoy
30987 – 31st Street SW.
CALGARY
CANADA
T3C 1E5

Contrary to previous practice, no blank line is left above the name of the postal town or city. The post code is regarded as essential and, for post to other countries, the name of the town and the name of the country should be written in capitals below the street name. Prefixed country codes, e.g. **A**-1084 Wien, **CH**-3011 Bern are no longer to be used.

On private letters the sender's name and address are written in a single line on the back of the envelope, preceded by *Abs.* (i.e. *Absender*), e.g.: *Abs.: Indermühle, Strohgasse 17, 8600 Düsendorf, Schweiz.*

10 Modal particles

MODAL PARTICLES **are words which express the speaker's attitude to what is being said.**

They are words like *aber, doch, ja, mal, schon*, etc., which alter the tone of what is being said and make sure that the speaker's intentions and attitudes are clearly understood. They can typically

- appeal for agreement
- express surprise or annoyance
- tone down a blunt question or statement
- sound reassuring

There is no full agreement as to which words can be classified as modal particles (called in German *Abtönungspartikeln* or *Modalpartikeln*). Their function is quite like that of adverbs of attitude (see 7.3.2), and like them they cannot be negated. In general, though, they are less independent and they cannot normally occur in first position in a main clause, before the main verb.

German has a far richer repertoire of these words than English, but English speakers have other ways of expressing their attitude to what is being said, especially intonation and tag questions like 'isn't it?' There is, though, a very marked tendency for German to use downtoners much more extensively than English. We have tried to give some idea of the flavour of each of the German modal particles in the translations by using equivalents like this, but they can only be a rough guide to usage. These equivalents should be understood in this sense, not as practical translation equivalents.

True modal particles relate to the clause or sentence as a whole, whereas scalar or focus particles (called *Gradpartikeln* in German), like *sogar*, focus attention on a particular word or phrase.

However, these distinctions are not clear-cut, and many of these words can be used in more than one way. *auch* and *nur*, for example, can be used both as modal and as focus particles, whereas *eigentlich* and *freilich* can function as adverbs of attitude as well as modal particles.

Many particles can be used to focus attention on a particular element in the sentence. In English this is often done by means of a so-called 'cleft sentence' (see 21.2.3), e.g. *Dieses Mal war **der Mann** aber schuld* 'This time **it was the man who** was to blame'. The examples in the sections below show typical instances where this is possible.

This chapter aims to give a practical account of the use in modern German of all those words which might be considered to be modal particles. They are listed in Table 10.1, which gives the section in which they are dealt with in this chapter. Many of these words have a range of uses besides those of modal particles; to avoid confusion, these uses are also explained here.

TABLE 10.1 German modal particles

aber	10.1	eigentlich	10.10	ja	10.19	ruhig	10.28
allerdings	10.2	einfach	10.11	jedenfalls	10.20	schließlich	10.29
also	10.3	erst	10.12	lediglich	10.21	schon	10.30
auch	10.4	etwa	10.13	mal	10.22	sowieso	10.31
bloß	10.5	freilich	10.14	man	10.23	überhaupt	10.32
denn	10.6	gar	10.15	noch	10.24	übrigens	10.33
doch	10.7	gleich	10.16	nun	10.25	vielleicht	10.34
eben	10.8	halt	10.17	nur	10.26	wohl	10.35
eh	10.9	immerhin	10.18	ohnehin	10.27	zwar	10.36

10.1 *aber*

10.1.1 In statements, *aber* expresses a surprised reaction

In effect, *aber* converts such statements to exclamations:

Das war aber eine Reise!	*That was quite a journey, wasn't it?*
Der Film war aber gut!	*The film <u>was</u> good*
Der Kaffee ist aber heiß!	*Oh! The coffee <u>is</u> hot*

aber can be given greater emphasis by adding *auch*. Compare:

Das war aber auch eine Reise!	*That really was some journey!*

ja is also used to express surprise (see 10.19.2), but surprise resulting from a difference in kind, where *aber* indicates a difference in degree. Compare:

Der Kaffee ist **aber** heiß (i.e. hotter than you had expected)
Der Kaffee ist **ja** heiß (you had expected <u>cold</u> coffee)

In this sense, *aber* is very similar in force to *vielleicht* (see 10.34.1): *Der Tee ist vielleicht heiß!*

10.1.2 *aber* is used within a clause to express a contradiction

In such contexts, *aber* has much the same sense it would have at the beginning of the clause (i.e. = English 'but', see 19.1.1). This sense is close to that of *doch* (see 10.7.1), and *though* is a close equivalent in English:

Mein Freund kam aber nicht	*My friend didn't come, though*
Sie muss uns aber gesehen haben	*But she must have seen us*
Jetzt kannst du etwas schneller fahren . . .	*You can go a bit quicker now . . . Look out at the*
Pass aber bei den Ampeln auf!	* lights, though!*
Dieses Mal war aber der **Mann** schuld	*This time it was the man who was to blame, though*

Used with *oder*, *aber* has the sense of 'on the other hand':

Seine Befürwortung könnte der Sache	*His support might help the affair or on the other*
helfen oder aber (auch) schaden	* hand it might harm it*

10.1.3 When used initially in exclamations, *aber* stresses the speaker's opinion

aber can sound scolding or reassuring, depending on the context:

Hast du was dagegen? Aber nein!	*Have you any objection? Of course not!*
Aber Kinder! Was habt ihr schon wieder	*Now, now, childen! What have you been doing?*
angestellt?	
Aber, aber! Was soll diese Aufregung?	*Oh now! What's all the excitement about?*

10.1.4 *aber* is also used as a coordinating conjunction

i.e. corresponding to English 'but', see 19.1.1.

10.2 *allerdings*

allerdings most often expresses a reservation about what has just been said. It usually corresponds to English 'admittedly', 'of course', 'to be sure', 'all the same', etc. *freilich* has a very similar meaning, see 10.14.

10.2.1 Within a sentence, the sense of *allerdings* is close to that of *aber*

However, *allerdings* is rather less blunt:

Es ist ein gutes Buch, allerdings gefallen mir seine anderen etwas besser	*It's a good book. Even so, I like his others rather better*
Wir haben uns im Urlaub gut erholt, das Wetter war allerdings nicht sehr gut	*The holiday was a good rest for us. All the same, the weather wasn't very good*
Ich komme gern, allerdings muss ich zuerst der Rita Bescheid sagen	*I want to come, of course I'll have to tell Rita first*

10.2.2 On its own in answer to a question, *allerdings* expresses a strongly affirmative answer

There may be a hint of a reservation of some kind which the speaker isn't making explicit:

Kennst du die Angelika? Allerdings!	*Do you know Angelika? Of course! (I know what she's like, too!)*
Ist der Helmut schon da? Allerdings!	*Is Helmut here yet? Oh, yes! (and you should see who he's come with!)*

10.3 *also*

10.3.1 *also* confirms something as the logical conclusion from what has just been said

also often corresponds to English 'so', 'thus' or 'then':

Du wirst mir also helfen können	*You're going to be able to help me, then*
Wann kommst du also genau?	*So, when are you coming precisely?*
Sie meinen also, dass wir uns heute entscheiden müssen	*So you think we're going to have to make a decision today*

10.3.2 Used in isolation, *also* links up with what has just been said

also can introduce a statement or a question:

Also, jetzt müssen wir uns überlegen, wie wir dahinkommen	*Well then, now we've got to think about how we're going to get there*
Also, besuchst du uns morgen?	*So, are you going to come to see us tomorrow?*
Also, gut!	*Well all right then!*
Also, so was!	*Well I never!*

10.4 *auch*

10.4.1 In statements, *auch* stresses the reasons why something is or is not the case

auch can be used to correct a false impression and is often used with *ja*:

Gerhard sieht heute schlecht aus	*Gerhard's not looking well today*
– Er ist (ja) auch lange krank gewesen	*– Well, he's been ill for a long time*
Jetzt möchte ich schlafen gehen	*I'd like to go to bed now*
– Es ist (ja) auch spät	*– Well, after all, it is late*
Das hättest du nicht tun sollen	*You ought not to have done that*
– Ich habe es (ja) auch nicht getan	*– But I didn't do it, you know*

10.4.2 In yes/no questions, *auch* asks for confirmation of something which the speaker thinks should be taken for granted

The English equivalent is very often a tag question:

Kann ich mich auch darauf verlassen?	*I can rely on that, can't I?*
Hast du auch die Rechnung bezahlt?	*You did pay the bill, didn't you?*
Bist du auch glücklich mit ihm?	*You're happy with him, aren't you?*

10.4.3 *auch* turns *w*-questions into rhetorical questions

auch confirms that nothing else could be expected:

Was kann man auch dazu sagen?	*Well, what can you say to that?*
Ich bin heute sehr müde	*I'm very tired today*
– Warum gehst du auch immer so spät ins Bett?	*– Well, why do you always go to bed so late?*

These questions can be turned into exclamations which emphasise the speaker's negative attitude:

Was war das auch für ein Erfolg?!	*Well, what sort of success do you call that?!*
Wie konnte er auch so schnell abreisen?!	*How could he have left as quickly as that?!*

10.4.4 *auch* reinforces commands

This is similar to the use of English 'Be/Make sure . . . !':

Bring mir eine Zeitung und vergiss es auch nicht!	*Bring me a paper and be sure you don't forget!*
Sei auch schön brav!	*Be sure you behave!*

10.4.5 Further uses of *auch*

(a) Before a noun *auch* has the force of English 'even'

It is an alternative to *sogar* or *selbst* as a focus particle:

Auch der beste Arzt hätte ihr nicht helfen können	*Even the best doctor wouldn't have been able to help her*

Auch der Manfred kann sich ab und zu mal irren	*Even Manfred can be wrong now and again*
Und wenn auch!	*even so, no matter*

NB: The usual equivalent for English 'not even' is *nicht einmal*.

(b) As an adverb, *auch* has the meaning 'too', 'also', 'as well'

Peter will auch mit	*Peter wants to come too*
Gisela ist auch nett	*Gisela's nice as well*
In Potsdam sind wir auch gewesen	*We also went to Potsdam*

(c) The combination *auch nur* expresses a restriction

It corresponds to English 'even', 'as/so little/much as', etc.:

wenn ich auch nur zwei Freunde hätte	*if I only had just two friends*
ohne auch nur zu fragen	*without even so much as asking*
Es war unmöglich, auch nur Brot zu kaufen	*You couldn't buy so much as a loaf of bread*

(d) *oder auch* has the sense 'or else', 'or even'

Du kannst Birnen kaufen oder auch Pfirsiche	*You can buy pears or else peaches*

(e) *auch nicht*, *auch kein* and *auch nichts* are often used for 'nor', 'neither', etc.

See 19.1.3d for details on German equivalents of 'neither' and 'nor':

Ich habe nichts davon gewusst – Ich auch nicht	*I didn't know anything about it – Nor me/Neither did I*
Sie kann nicht nähen, und stricken kann sie auch nicht	*She can't sew, and neither can she knit*
Das wird ihm auch nichts helfen	*That won't help him either*
Er liest keine Zeitungen und auch keine Bücher	*He doesn't read any newspapers or books*

(f) *auch* occurs in many concessive constructions

Its force is similar to that of English 'ever', e.g.: *Wer es auch sein mag* 'Whoever that may be'. Details are given in 19.6.2.

10.5 *bloß*

bloß usually has a restrictive sense (= English 'only', 'simply', 'merely'). In all its uses it is a rather less formal alternative to *nur*, see 10.26, where the uses of *nur* and *bloß* are compared:

Störe mich bloß nicht bei der Arbeit	*You'd better not disturb me while I'm working*
Wie spät ist es bloß?	*I wonder just what the time is?*
Wenn er bloß bald käme!	*If only he would come soon!*
Sie hatte bloß 100 Euro bei sich	*She only had 100 euros on her*
Sollen wir Tante Mia einladen? – Bloß nicht!	*Shall we invite aunt Mia? – No way!*

10.6 *denn*

10.6.1 As a modal particle, *denn* is used exclusively in questions

(a) *denn* most often serves to tone down the question

denn refers back to what has just been said, or to the general context, and makes the question sound rather less blunt and more obliging. In practice it is almost automatic in *w*-questions:

Hast du denn die Renate gesehen?	*Tell me, have you seen Renate?*
Geht der Junge denn heute nicht in die Schule?	*Isn't the boy going to school today, then?*
Ach, der Bus hält. Sind wir denn schon da?	*Oh, the bus is stopping. Are we already there, then?*
Warum muss er denn in die Stadt?	*Tell me, why has he got to go to town?*
Wie bist denn du gekommen?	*Tell me, how did you get here?*
Wie geht es dir denn?	*How are you then?*

NB: In colloquial speech, *denn* is often reduced to '*n* and suffixed to the verb, e.g. Hast'*n du die Renate gesehen? Wie bist'*n du gekommen?*

(b) If there is a negative element in the question, *denn* signals reproach

The negative element may not be explicit. The question itself expects a justification rather than an answer:

Hast du denn keinen Führerschein?	*Come on, haven't you got a driving licence?*
Bist du denn blind?	*Come on now, are you blind?*
Wo bist du denn so lange geblieben?	*Where on earth have you been all this time?*
Was ist denn hier los?	*What on earth's going on here?*

(c) *denn* can convert *w*-questions into rhetorical questions

A negative answer is expected:

Wer redet denn von nachgeben?	*Who's talking of giving in?* (prompting the answer: nobody!)
Was haben wir denn damit erreicht?	*And what have we achieved by that?* (prompting the answer: nothing!)

Adding *schon* makes it absolutely clear that the question is rhetorical:

Was hat er denn schon damit gewonnen?	*And what did he gain by that?* (prompting the answer: nothing!)

(d) Yes/no questions with *denn* can be used as exclamations of surprise

They often begin with *so*:

Ist das Wetter denn nicht herrlich?	*How lovely the weather is!*
So hat er denn die Stellung erhalten?	*So he did get the job!*

(e) The combination *denn noch* is used to recall a fact

Wie heißt er denn noch?	*What is his name again?*

NB: The force of *denn noch* is similar to that of *doch gleich* in section 10.7.4.

10.6.2 **Further uses of *denn***

(a) The combination *es sei denn, (dass)* is a conjunction meaning 'unless'

e.g.: *Sie kommt gegen ein Uhr, es sei denn, sie wird aufgehalten.* It is used chiefly in formal German; for further details see 16.5.3d.

(b) *geschweige denn* means 'let alone', 'still less'

It is used mainly in formal registers:

Er wollte mir kein Geld leihen, geschweige denn schenken	He wouldn't even <u>lend</u> me any money, let alone give me any

(c) *denn* is often used in place of *dann* 'then'

e.g.: *Na, **denn** geht es eben nicht.* This usage is common in North German colloquial speech, but is not accepted as standard.

(d) *denn* is used as a coordinating conjunction indicating a cause or reason

It corresponds to English 'for', 'because', e.g.: *Er kann uns nicht verstehen, denn er spricht kein Deutsch.* For details, see 19.1.2.

(e) *denn* is sometimes used in formal German and set phrases for *als* 'than' e.g. *mehr denn je* 'more than ever'.

For details, see 8.3.1a.

10.7 *doch*

doch is used typically in an attempt to persuade the listener of the speaker's point of view. It usually expresses a contradiction or disagreement and often corresponds to English 'though' or a tag question. The element of persuasion is given more force if *doch* is stressed.

10.7.1 In statements, *doch* indicates disagreement with what has been said

If *doch* is stressed, it clearly contradicts, and its meaning is close to that of *dennoch* or *trotzdem*. If it is unstressed, it appeals more politely and tentatively for agreement or confirmation:

Gestern hat es **doch** geschneit	All the same, it <u>did</u> snow yesterday
Gestern hat es doch geschneit	It snowed yesterday, didn't it?
Ich habe **doch** Recht gehabt	All the same, I <u>was</u> right
Ich habe doch Recht gehabt	I was right, wasn't I?
Wir müssen **doch** morgen nach Bremen	All the same, we <u>have</u> got to go to Bremen tomorrow
Ich habe ihm abgeraten, aber er hat es **doch** getan	I advised him against it, but he did it all the same
Du hast doch gesagt, dass du kommst	You did say you were coming, didn't you?

Unstressed *doch* may also mildly point out a reason for disagreement. In such contexts it has much the same force as *aber*, see 10.1.2:

Wir wollten doch heute Abend ins Theater gehen	Surely we were going to go to the theatre tonight (, weren't we?)
Die Ampel zeigt doch rot, wir dürfen noch nicht gehen	But the lights are red, we can't go yet

In literary German *doch* can be used with the verb first in the clause. This explains the preceding statement:

War ich doch so durch den Lehrbetrieb beansprucht, dass ich dafür keine Zeit fand (*Grass*)	After all, I was so busy with my lessons that I didn't have any time for that

NB: For the difference in meaning between *doch* and *ja* in statements appealing for the listener's agreement, see 10.19.1b.

10.7.2 **Unstressed *doch* can turn a statement into a question expecting a positive answer**

doch is then the equivalent of a following *oder?* or *nicht (wahr)?*, and one of these may be used as well:

Den Wagen kann ich mir doch morgen abholen?	*I can collect the car tomorrow, can't I?*
Du kannst mir doch helfen(, oder)?	*You can help me, can't you?*
Du glaubst doch nicht, dass ich es getan habe?	*Surely you don't think I did it?*
Es hat ihr doch Sandra gesagt	*It was Sandra who told her, wasn't it?*

10.7.3 ***doch* in commands**

The force of *doch* in commands can vary depending on the context. Sometimes it adds a note of impatience or urgency, and in this sense it can be strengthened by *endlich* or, in a negative sentence, by *immer*:

Reg dich doch nicht so auf!	*For heaven's sake, don't get so excited*
Bring den Wagen doch (endlich) in die Werkstatt!	*For goodness' sake, take the car to the garage*
Mach doch nicht (immer) so ein Gesicht!	*Don't keep making faces like that*
Freu dich doch!	*Do cheer up*

In other sentences, *doch* can moderate the force of the command, making it sound more advisory or encouraging. This can be made even more clear by adding *mal* or *ruhig*:

Lassen Sie mich doch (mal) das Foto sehen!	*Why don't you just let me see the photograph?*
Kommen Sie doch (ruhig) morgen vorbei!	*Why not drop by tomorrow?*

10.7.4 **In *w*-questions, *doch* asks for confirmation of an answer or the repetition of information**

doch can be strengthened by adding *gleich* (see 10.16), and its force is then similar to that of *denn noch*, see 10.6.1e:

Wie heißt doch euer Hund?	*What did you say your dog is called?*
Wer war das doch (gleich)?	*Who was that again?*
Wohin fahrt ihr doch auf Urlaub?	*Where did you say you were going on holiday?*

10.7.5 **In exclamations, *doch* emphasises the speaker's surprise**

In such sentences the force of *doch* is close to that of *ja*, see 10.19.2:

Wie winzig doch alles von hier oben aussieht!	*But how tiny everything looks from up here!*
Du bist doch kein kleines Kind mehr!	*You're not a baby any more, you know!*
Das ist doch die Höhe!	*That really is the limit!*
Wir haben doch Gulasch bestellt!	*But it was goulash we ordered!*

10.7.6 In wishes expressed with *Konjunktiv II*, *doch* emphasises the urgency of the wish

See also 16.7.6b. In such sentences *doch* is the equivalent of *nur* and may be used together with it, see 10.26.1c:

Wenn er doch jetzt käme!	*If only he would come now!*
Wäre ich doch zu Hause geblieben!	*If only I'd just stayed at home!*

10.7.7 Further uses of *doch*

(a) In reply to a question, *doch* contradicts a negative or emphasises an affirmative reply

Bist du nicht zufrieden? Doch!	*Aren't you satisfied? Yes, I am*
Kommt er bald? Doch!	*Is he coming soon? Oh, yes*
Er hat nie etwas für uns getan.	*He's never done anything for us.*
– Doch, er hat mir einmal 100 Euro geliehen	*– Oh, yes he has, he once lent me a hundred euros*

When used with *nein* or *nicht*, *doch* emphasises a negative reply:

Mutti, kann ich ein Stück Schokolade haben?	*Mummy, can I have a piece of chocolate?*
– Nein doch, du hast jetzt genug gegessen	*– Certainly not, you've had enough to eat*

(b) As a conjunction, *doch* is an alternative to *aber* 'but'

e.g.: *Sie wollten baden gehen, **doch** es hat geschneit*. Further details are given in 19.1.1.

10.8 *eben*

10.8.1 As a modal particle, *eben* typically expresses a confirmation that something is the case

eben often corresponds to English 'just'.

(a) In statements, *eben* emphasises an inescapable conclusion

Das ist eben so	*But there, that's how it is*
Ich kann ihn nicht überreden. Er ist eben hartnäckig	*I can't convince him. He's just obstinate*
Er zeichnet ganz gut	*He draws quite well*
– Nun, er ist eben ein Künstler	*– Well, he is an artist*
Ich mache es, so gut ich eben kann	*I'll do it as well as I can (given the circumstances)*
Eben das hat er schreiben wollen	*That's what he wanted to write*

(b) In commands, *eben* emphasises that there is no real alternative

These commands are often introduced by *dann*:

(Dann) bleib eben im Zug sitzen!	*Well, just stay on the train, then*
(Dann) fahr eben durch die Stadtmitte!	*Well, just drive through the town centre, then*

halt is a frequent alternative to *eben*, see 10.17. It was originally restricted to South Germany, but it has become more widely used recently.

10.8.2 **Further uses of *eben***

(a) *eben* **can be used in the sense of 'exactly', 'precisely', 'just'**

In this meaning it can be used as a focus particle before another word, or as a response to a statement or a question. *genau* is a common alternative:

Das wäre mir eben recht	*That would be just what I'd like*
Eben 'daran hatte ich nie gedacht	*That's the one thing I hadn't thought of*
Eben dieses Haus hatte mir zugesagt	*It was this house which attracted me*
Das wird sie doch kaum schaffen.	*She won't manage it, will she?*
– Eben!	*– Precisely!*

(b) Used with *nicht* before an adjective, *eben* lessens the force of *nicht*

gerade is a common alternative:

Sie ist nicht eben fleißig	*She's not exactly hard-working*
Der Zug war nicht eben pünktlich	*The train wasn't what you'd call on time*

(c) As an adverb, *eben* means 'just (now)'

gerade is very similar in its force:

Wir sind **eben** (erst) angekommen	**Eben** geht mir ein Licht auf
Mit zweitausend Euro im Monat kommen wir **eben** (noch) aus	

(d) As an adjective, *eben* means 'level'

e.g.: *Die Straße ist hier nicht **eben***

10.9 *eh*

eh has a very similar force to *ohnehin* or *sowieso*. Like them, it is an equivalent of English 'anyway' or 'in any case', but it is used predominantly in colloquial South German, especially in Austria and Bavaria. However, it has recently come to be used more widely:

Wenn ich arbeite, brauche ich eh immer mehr zum Essen (*Kroetz*)	*When I'm working I need more to eat anyway*
Für eine Markenpersönlichkeit wie Sie ist das neue Magazin der Süddeutschen eh ein Muss (*SZ*)	*It goes without saying that the new magazine of the "Süddeutsche Zeitung" is a must for a person of quality like you*

10.10 *eigentlich*

eigentlich emphasises that something is actually the case, even if it appears otherwise. It is often used to change the topic of conversation.

10.10.1 *eigentlich* **in questions**

(a) *eigentlich* can tone a question down and makes it sound more casual

In such cases it is relatively lightly stressed. It comes close to the sense of English 'actually' and is often used in conjunction with *denn*:

| Sind Sie eigentlich dieses Jahr schon in Urlaub gewesen? | *Tell me, have you been on holiday yet this year?* |
| Wohnt Eva eigentlich schon lange in Hameln? | *Has Eva actually been living a long time in Hameln?* |

(b) In *w*-questions, *eigentlich* implies that the question has not yet been answered fully or satisfactorily

In such contexts it is rather more heavily stressed and very close in meaning to *im Grunde genommen*, *tatsächlich* or *wirklich*, with the sense of 'at bottom', 'in actual fact', 'in reality':

| Wie heißt er eigentlich? | *What's his real name?* |
| Warum besuchst du mich eigentlich? | *Why, basically, did you come to visit me?* |

10.10.2 *eigentlich* in statements

(a) *eigentlich* indicates that something actually is the case, despite appearances

It moderates a refusal, an objection or a contradiction by indicating how strong the reasons are:

Er scheint manchmal faul, aber er ist eigentlich sehr fleißig	*He appears lazy sometimes, but in actual fact he's very hard-working*
Ich wollte eigentlich zu Fuß gehen	*In actual fact, I did want to walk*
Ich trinke eigentlich keinen Kaffee mehr	*Well, actually, I don't drink coffee now*

(b) Sometimes *eigentlich* can signal that the matter is still a little open

| Wir haben eigentlich schon zu | *Well, actually, we're already closed* (hinting that an exception might not be wholly out of the question) |
| Das darf man hier eigentlich nicht | *Strictly speaking, that's not allowed here* (but, possibly, . . .) |

10.10.3 As an adjective, *eigentlich* means 'real', 'actual', 'fundamental'

| Was ist die **eigentliche** Ursache? | Er nannte nicht den **eigentlichen** Grund |

10.11 *einfach*

einfach emphasises that alternative possibilities are excluded. It usually corresponds to English 'simply' or, especially in commands, 'just'. In commands it is frequently used in conjunction with *doch* and/or *mal*, and in exclamations it is often combined with *ja*:

Ich bin einfach weggegangen	*I simply walked away*
Ich werde ihm einfach sagen, dass es nicht möglich ist	*I'll simply tell him it's not possible*
Warum gehst du nicht einfach ins Bett?	*Why don't you simply go to bed?*
Leg dich (doch) einfach hin!	*Why don't you just go and lie down?*
Geh doch einfach mal zum Zahnarzt!	*Why not just simply go to the dentist?*
Heute ist das Wetter (ja) einfach herrlich!	*The weather is simply lovely today!*

einfach is used as a true adverb, as well as a particle, but there is a clear difference in meaning. As an adverb, *einfach* is always stressed and means 'in a simple manner'. Compare:

| Sie macht es **einfach** | *She is doing it simply* (in an uncomplicated way) |
| Sie **macht** es einfach | *She's simply doing it* ('just', 'without further ado') |

Du musst **einfach** anfangen	*You have to begin simply*
Du musst einfach **anfangen**	*You simply have to begin*

10.12 *erst*

10.12.1 As a modal particle, *erst* has intensifying force

(a) In statements and exclamations

Here *erst* implies that something really is the absolute limit and perhaps more than expected or desirable. It is often strengthened by adding *recht*:

Dann ging es erst (recht) los	*Then things really got going*
Das konnte sie erst recht nicht	*That she really couldn't manage*
Das macht es erst recht schlimm	*That really does make it bad*
Sie hat schon Hunger, aber das Kind erst (recht)!	*She may be hungry, but it's the kid who's really hungry*

(b) In wishes

Here, *nur* or *bloß* are alternatives to *erst* (and may be used with it):

Wäre er doch erst zu Hause!	*If only he were at home!*
Wenn er (bloß) erst wieder arbeiten könnte!	*If only he could start work again!*

10.12.2 As a focus particle, *erst* indicates that there are/were less or fewer than expected

(a) Before a number or an expression of quantity it corresponds to 'only'

Ich habe erst zehn Seiten geschrieben	*I've only written ten pages*
Er ist erst sieben Jahre alt	*He's only seven years old*
Ich habe erst die Hälfte fertig	*I've only got half of it finished*

Before other nouns the sense is 'nothing less than':

Erst mit einem Lehrstuhl in Berlin wird er sich zufrieden geben	*He'll only be satisfied with a professorship in Berlin*

(b) In time expressions, *erst* implies that it is later than expected or desirable

It usually corresponds to English 'only', 'not before', 'not until' or, in certain contexts, 'as late as':

Er kommt erst (am) Montag	{ *He's not coming till Monday* { *He's only coming on Monday*
Es ist erst acht Uhr	*It's only eight o'clock*
Ich kam erst im Sommer nach Heidelberg	*I didn't get to Heidelberg until the summer*
erst wenn/als (see 19.3.2b)	*not until, only when*
wenn er erst zu Hause ist, . . .	*once he's home . . .*
Es hatte eben erst zu schneien aufgehört (*Jünger*)	*It had only just stopped snowing*
Ich kann den Wagen erst Anfang nächste Woche abholen	*I shan't be able to collect the car till the beginning of next week*
Erst im September ist es mir aufgefallen	*It was only in September that I noticed it*

(c) *erst* 'only' must be carefully distinguished from *nur*
(see 10.26.2)

(i) With numbers, as in the examples in (a) above, *erst* implies that more are to follow. In English this can be made clear by adding 'as yet' to the sentence. *nur*, on the other hand, sets a clear limit, i.e. that number and no more. Compare:

Ich habe **erst** drei Briefe bekommen	*I've only received three letters (as yet)* (more are expected)
Ich habe **nur** drei Briefe bekommen	*I've only received three letters* (i.e. three and no more)

(ii) In time expressions, like the examples in (b) above, *erst* has the sense 'not before', etc., but *nur* means 'on that one occasion'. Compare:

Sie ist erst (am) Montag gekommen	*She only came on Monday* (i.e. not before Monday)
Sie ist nur (am) Montag gekommen	*She only came on Monday* (i.e. on no other day)

NB: (i)   The opposite of *erst* 'only' as a focus particle is *schon*, see 10.30.5.
(ii)   The distinction between *erst* and *nur* described above is not always consistently maintained in colloquial speech.

10.13 *etwa*

10.13.1 In yes/no questions, *etwa* implies that something is undesirable and suggests that the answer ought to be *nein*

A common English equivalent is a negative statement followed by a positive tag question or an exclamation beginning with 'Don't tell me . . .':

Hast du die Zeitung etwa schon weggeworfen?	*You haven't thrown the paper away already, have you?*
Ist das etwa dein Wagen?	*That's not your car, is it?*
Habt ihr etwa geschlafen?	*Don't tell me you've been asleep!*

Such questions with *etwa* can be in the form of statements, in which case they also contain *doch nicht*:

Sie wollen doch nicht etwa nach Paderborn umziehen?	*You don't want to move to Paderborn, do you?*

10.13.2 In negative sentences, *etwa* intensifies the negation

Sie müssen nicht etwa denken, dass ich ihn verteidigen will	*Now don't go and think I want to defend him*
Komm nicht etwa zu spät zum Flughafen!	*Make sure you don't get to the airport too late!*

10.13.3 In conditional sentences *etwa* stresses the idea of a possibility

Wenn der Zug etwa verspätet sein sollte, dann verpassen wir den Anschluss nach Gera	*If the train should be delayed we'll miss our connection to Gera*
Wenn das Wetter etwa umschlagen sollte, müssen wir die Wanderung verkürzen	*If the weather were to change, we'll have to shorten our walk*

10.13.4 Uses of *etwa* before a noun or noun phrase

In such contexts *etwa* is used as a focus or scalar particle.

(a) Before a number or expression of size or quantity, *etwa* expresses approximation

Ich komme etwa um zwei	*I'll come at about two*
Es kostet etwa dreißig Euro	*It costs about thirty euros*
Er ist etwa so groß wie dein Vater	*He is about as tall as your father*
Wir haben es uns etwa so vorgestellt	*We imagined it to be something like that*

(b) Before a noun or list of nouns, *etwa* suggests a possibility

It is often close in meaning to English 'for instance' or 'for example':

Er begnügte sich mit etwa folgender Antwort	*He was satisfied with, for instance, the following answer*
Bist du sicher, dass du den Jürgen gesehen hast, und nicht etwa seinen Bruder Thomas?	*Are you sure you saw Jürgen, and not perhaps his brother Thomas?*
Er hat viele Hobbys, (wie) etwa Reisen, Musik und Sport	*He has a lot of hobbies, for example travelling, music and sport*
Willst du etwa (am) Sonntag kommen?	*You're not thinking of coming on Sunday, are you?*
Hast du etwa Martina in Verdacht?	*Is it Martina you suspect?*

10.14 *freilich*

freilich usually has a concessive sense and its force is very similar to that of *allerdings*, see 10.2. It was originally typically South German, but it is now used more widely.

10.14.1 Within a clause *freilich* means 'admittedly', 'all the same'

Es scheint freilich nicht ganz so einfach zu sein	*Admittedly, it doesn't appear to be that simple*
Wir nehmen ihn mit, freilich muss er pünktlich am Treffpunkt sein	*We'll take him with us, even so he'll have to get to the meeting place on time*

10.14.2 In answer to a question, *freilich* stresses that the answer is yes

freilich is often used in conjunction with *ja*. It lacks the hint that there is some kind of reservation or qualification to the answer which is sometimes present with *allerdings*:

Kennst du die Angelika?	*Do you know Angelika?*
– (Ja,) freilich (kenne ich sie)!	*– Of course (I know her)!*
Kannst du auch alles besorgen?	*Can you see to it all?*
– (Ja,) freilich!	*– Certainly I can!*

NB: *freilich* can <u>never</u> mean 'freely', which is *frei* in most contexts.

10.15 *gar*

gar is used in a number of ways with an intensifying sense.

(a) The commonest use of *gar* is to intensify a negative

In these contexts *gar* is an alternative to *überhaupt*:

Sie hatte gar nicht gewusst, ob er abfahren wollte (*Johnson*)	*She hadn't even known whether he wanted to leave*
Ich habe doch heute gar keine Zeit	*I really haven't got any time at all today*

Less commonly, *gar* can intensify *so* or *zu* with an adjective (*allzu* is a more frequent alternative in this sense):

Du darfst das nicht gar so ernst nehmen	*You really mustn't take that quite so seriously*
Es waren gar zu viele Leute auf der Straße	*There were far too many people in the street*

(b) *gar* can be used to emphasise the following word and indicate surprise

In such contexts *gar* is the equivalent of English 'even' or 'possibly' and is a less frequent alternative to *sogar*, used mainly in literary registers:

Eher würde ich einem Habicht oder gar Aasgeier eine Friedensbotschaft anvertrauen als der Taube (*Grass*)	*I would rather entrust a message of peace to a hawk or even a vulture than to a dove*

10.16 *gleich*

As a modal particle *gleich* is used in *w*-questions to politely request the repetition of information. It is often used with *doch*, see 10.7.4:

Wie war Ihr Name (doch) gleich?	*What was your name again?*
Was hast du gleich gesagt?	*What was it you said?*

gleich is also used as a time adverb in the sense of 'immediately', e.g.: *Ich werde ihn **gleich** fragen*, or to mean 'at once' or 'at the same time', e.g. *Er hat **gleich** zwei Hemden gekauft.*

10.17 *halt*

halt is an alternative to *eben* in some senses (see 10.8). It was originally characteristic of South German speech, but it is now used much more widely:

Da kann man halt nichts machen	*There's just nothing to be done*
Dann nimm halt die U-Bahn!	*Just take the underground, then!*

10.18 *immerhin*

immerhin indicates that something might not have come up to expectations, but is acceptable at a pinch. It corresponds most often to English 'all the same' or 'even so' and can be used within a sentence or (very frequently) as a response:

Du hast immerhin tausend Euro gewonnen	*All the same, you won a thousand euros*
Wir haben uns immerhin einen neuen Blu-ray-Player anschaffen können	*Even so, we were able to buy a new blu-ray player*
Das Wetter im Urlaub war miserabel, aber wir hatten ein schönes Zimmer – (Na,) immerhin!	*The weather was lousy on holiday, but we did have a nice room.* *– Well, that was something, at least!*

10.19 *ja*

10.19.1 In statements, *ja* appeals for agreement

(a) By using *ja* the speaker insists that what s/he is saying is correct

A common English equivalent is the 'do' form of the verb, or a cleft sentence:

Wir haben ja gestern davon gesprochen	*We did talk about that yesterday (you know)*
Ihr habt ja früher zwei Autos gehabt	*Of course, you used to have two cars*
Hier im Gebirge ist es ja im Frühjahr am schönsten	*It's in spring when it's nicest here in the mountains*
Ich komme ja schon	*It's all right, I'm on my way*
Der katastrophale Zustand des Landes ist ja gerade das Erbe der Diktatur (*Spiegel*)	*It is the catastrophic state of the country which is the legacy of dictatorship*

(b) *ja* has a distinct meaning from *doch* when used to appeal for agreement

doch (see 10.7.1), implies that the listener might have a different opinion, but *ja* always presupposes that speaker and listener are agreed. Compare:

Du könntest dir **ja** Karls Rad leihen	*You could borrow Karl's bike, of course (we both know you can)*
Du könntest dir **doch** Karls Rad leihen	*Surely, you could borrow Karl's bike (you might have thought you couldn't)*
Das ist es **ja** eben	*Why, of course, that's the point*
Das ist es **doch** eben	*Don't you see, that's just the point*
Er kann unmöglich kommen,	*He can't possibly come,*
er ist **ja** krank	* he's ill, as you know*
er ist **doch** krank	* he's ill, don't you know*

10.19.2 In exclamations, *ja* expresses surprise

Heute ist es ja kalt!	*Oh, it is cold today!*
Er hat ja ein neues Auto!	*Why, he's got a new car!*
Das ist ja unerhört!	*That really is the limit!*
Da kommt ja der Arzt!	*Oh (good), here comes the doctor!*

By using *ja* (or *doch*, which has a very similar force in exclamations, see 10.7.5), the speaker can express surprise that something is the case at all. When *aber* or *vielleicht* are used in exclamations, though, surprise is expressed at the extent of a quality, see 10.1.1 and 10.34.1. Thus *die Milch ist ja/doch sauer!* would be said if the milk had been expected to be fresh, while *die Milch ist aber/vielleicht sauer* expresses surprise at <u>how</u> sour the milk is.

10.19.3 *ja* intensifies a command

There is often an implied warning or threat, especially if *ja* is stressed:

Bleib ja hier!	*Be sure to stay here!*
Geht ja nicht auf die Straße!	*Just don't go out onto the street!*
Er soll **ja** nichts sagen	*He really must not say anything (or else)*

NB: *nur* is an alternative to *ja* to intensify commands and sound a note of warning, see 10.26.1a.

10.19.4 *ja* can be used as a focus particle

In a string of nouns, verbs or adjectives, *ja* (sometimes in combination with *sogar*) emphasises the importance of the one (usually the last) before which it is placed. This often corresponds to English *indeed*, *even* or *nay*:

Es war ein Erfolg, ja ein Triumph	*It was a success, indeed a triumph*
Es war ein unerwarteter, ja ein sensationeller Erfolg	*It was an unexpected, indeed a sensational success*
Sie konnte die Aussage bestätigen, ja (sogar) beeiden	*She was able to confirm the testimony, even on oath*

10.19.5 *ja* is the affirmative particle

It corresponds to English 'yes', e.g.: *Kommst du morgen? – Ja!* It can also be used as a tag:

Es geht um acht los, ja?	*We're starting at eight, aren't we?*

10.20 *jedenfalls*

The phrases *auf jeden Fall* and *auf alle Fälle* are possible alternatives to the particle *jedenfalls*.

10.20.1 In statements *jedenfalls* stresses the reason why something should be the case

(or why something is not as bad as it may seem). In these contexts, *jedenfalls* corresponds to 'at least' or 'at any rate':

Vielleicht ist er krank, er sieht jedenfalls schlecht aus	*Perhaps he's ill, at least he doesn't look well*
Er ist nicht gekommen, aber er hat sich jedenfalls entschuldigt	*He didn't come, but at least he did apologise*

wenigstens or *zumindest* are alternatives to *jedenfalls* in this sense, see 8.4.4b.

10.20.2 In commands *jedenfalls* indicates that something should be done in any event

jedenfalls corresponds to English 'anyhow' or 'in any case':

Bei schönem Wetter gehen wir morgen baden. Bring jedenfalls deinen Badeanzug mit	*If it's fine we'll go swimming tomorrow. Bring your costume along anyhow*

10.21 *lediglich*

lediglich is used before another word to indicate a restriction or a limit. It is an emphatic alternative to *nur* in the sense of 'only', 'no more than'. It is used mainly in formal registers and can sound stilted:

Er hat lediglich zwei Semester in Münster studiert	*He only studied two semesters in Münster*
Ich verlange lediglich mein Recht	*I am only asking for what's due to me*

10.22 *mal*

10.22.1 *mal* moderates the tone of a sentence, making it sound less blunt

mal is frequent in commands, requests and questions. It can correspond to English 'just', (although in practice this is used far less than German *mal*):

Lies den Brief mal durch!	*Just read the letter through (will you?)*
Hol mal schnell den Feuerlöscher!	*Just quickly go and get the fire extinguisher*
Das sollst du mal probieren	*You just ought to try that*
Ich will ihr schnell mal simsen	*I just want to text her quickly*
Würden Sie mir bitte mal helfen?	*Could you just help me?*
Hältst du mir mal die Tasche?	*Just hold my bag for me, will you?*

mal is almost automatically added to a command in colloquial speech, especially if there is nothing else in the sentence apart from the verb:

Sieh mal her!   Hör mal zu!   Komm mal herüber!   Sag mal!

The tone of a request or a command may be moderated further by adding *eben*:

Reich mir eben mal das Brot!	*Just pass me the bread, would you?*
Lies den Brief eben mal durch!	*Won't you please just read the letter through?*

The combination *doch mal* makes a command sound more casual:

Nimm doch mal ein neues Blatt!	*Why don't you get another piece of paper?*
Melde dich doch mal beim Chef!	*Why not just arrange to see the boss?*

10.22.2 The particle *mal* is quite distinct from the adverb *einmal* 'once'

(see 9.4.3). In other words, *mal* is not simply a shortened form of *einmal*, which cannot be used for *mal* in any of the contexts explained in 10.22.1. However, in some contexts *einmal* is often shortened to *mal* in colloquial speech, e.g.:

(a) *noch einmal* '(once) again', 'once more'

Ich habe ihn noch (ein)mal gewarnt	*I warned him once again*

(b) *nun einmal* 'just'

This combination emphasises the lack of alternatives. It is a rather more forceful equivalent to *eben* or *halt*, see 10.8.1a:

Es wird nun (ein)mal lange dauern	*It's just going to take a long time*

(c) *nicht einmal* 'not even':

Er hat sie nicht (ein)mal gegrüßt	*He didn't even say hello to her*

10.23 *man*

man is a colloquial North German equivalent to *mal* in commands and requests

Geh du man vor!	*You just go ahead*
Seien Sie man bloß ruhig! (*Fallada*)	*Just keep calm*

10.24 *noch*

10.24.1 *noch* indicates something additional

In this sense *noch* can be used as a focus particle preceding a noun or pronoun, or as a modal particle within the clause:

Er hat noch drei Stunden geschlafen	*He slept another three hours*
Ich trinke noch eine Tasse Kaffee	*I'll have another cup of coffee*
Das wird sich noch herausstellen	*That will remain to be seen, too*
Wer war noch da?	*Who else was there?*
Und es hat auch noch geregnet!	*And apart from that, it rained too*

10.24.2 *noch* in time expressions

(a) *noch* **can indicate that something is going on longer than expected**

noch can be strengthened by *immer* and corresponds to English 'still 'or 'yet':

Angela schläft (immer) noch	*Angela's still asleep*
Klaus ist (immer) noch nicht gekommen	*Klaus hasn't come yet/Klaus still hasn't come*
Sie wohnen noch in Fritzlar	*They're still living in Fritzlar*
Ich habe sie noch nie gesehen	*I've never seen her (yet)*
Sie ist doch noch jung	*She's still young, isn't she?*

(b) If a particular point in time is indicated, *noch* **indicates that an event took place or will take place by then**

The implication may be that this is contrary to expectations:

Ich habe ihn noch vor zwei Tagen gesehen	*I saw him only two days ago*
Noch im Mai hat sie ihre Dissertation abgegeben	*She managed to hand her thesis in by the end of May*
Ich werde noch heute den Arzt anrufen	*I'll ring the doctor before tomorrow*

In this sense, *noch* can alternatively come after short time words and phrases as well as before them, e.g. *Ich werde* **heute noch** *den Arzt anrufen.*

10.24.3 Further uses of *noch*

(a) In *w*-questions, *noch* **asks for the listener to jog the speaker's memory**

i.e. suggesting that something has just slipped his/her mind:

Wie hieß er noch?	*Oh now, what <u>was</u> his name?*
Wann war das Spiel noch?	*Oh now, when <u>was</u> the game?*

(b) *noch* **is used with comparatives in the sense of 'even'**

e.g.: *Er ist* **noch** *größer als du.* For further details, see 8.3.1c.

(c) *noch* **is used with *weder* as the equivalent of English 'neither . . . nor'**

e.g.: *Er liest weder Bücher* **noch** *Zeitungen* (see 19.1.3d).

(d) *noch* **is used with *so* and an adjective in a concessive sense**

e.g.: *Wenn sie (auch)* **noch** *so fleißig ist, sie wird die Prüfung doch nicht bestehen* (see 19.6.2a).

10.25 *nun*

10.25.1 In questions, *nun* signals dissatisfaction with a previous answer

By using *nun* the speaker insists that the correct or complete information should be provided:

Wann kommt der Zug nun an?	When <u>does</u> this train get in, now?
Stimmt es nun, dass sie verheiratet ist?	Now, is it really true that she's married?

nun is commonly used on its own as a question to push the other speaker to give more information, cf. *Nun?* 'Well?', *Nun . . . und?* 'And then what?'

10.25.2 *nun* signals that the speaker considers the topic exhausted

In this sense *nun* occurs characteristically in isolation at the beginning of a sentence. It often corresponds to English 'well':

Nun, das ist alles schon wichtig, aber ich glaube, wir müssen zunächst das Wahlergebnis besprechen	Well, of course that's all very important, but I think we've got to discuss the election results first
Nun, natürlich hat er die besten Erfahrungen	Well, of course he's got the widest experience
Nun, wir werden ja sehen	Well, we shall see
Nun, meinetwegen!	All right then

10.25.3 *nun* is used as an adverb of time to mean 'now'

nun is rather less definite than *jetzt* and it is used less frequently to refer simply to the present moment as such:

Nun wollen wir umkehren	Now we'll turn back
Nun hat er mehr Zeit als früher	Now he's got more time than he used to have
Geht es dir nun besser?	Are you better now?

10.26 *nur*

nur is used as a modal particle with an intensifying sense, and as a focus particle with a restrictive sense (= 'only'). *bloß*, see 10.5, is a frequent alternative to *nur* in all its uses except where indicated below; it is slightly more emphatic than *nur*, and more characteristic of less formal registers.

10.26.1 As a modal particle, *nur* usually has intensifying force

(a) In a command, *nur* intensifies the basic meaning

Depending on the sense of the command, i.e. whether it is an urgent instruction or a request, *nur* can make it sound more of a threat <u>or</u> more reassuring respectively.

(i) 'threatening' or 'warning' *nur* is more common in negative commands or when *nur* is stressed. This sense is similar to that of *ja* (see 10.19.3):

Komm nur nicht zu spät!	You'd better not be late!
Nimm dich nur in Acht!	You'd better be careful!

Geh nur nicht in dieses Geschäft!	*Whatever you do, don't go into that shop*
Sehen Sie nur, was Sie gemacht haben!	*Just look what you've done!*

In this sense, *nur* (but **not** *bloß*) can be used initially in a positive or negative command using the infinitive or with no verb at all:

Nur nicht so schnell laufen!	*Just don't run so fast!*
Nur aufpassen!	*Just be sure to look out!*
Nur immer schön langsam!	*Take it nice and slow!*

(ii) The 'reassuring' sense of *nur* is close to that of *ruhig* (see 10.28):

Lass ihn nur reden!	*Just let him speak, do!*
Kommen Sie nur herein!	*Do come in!*
Hab nur keine Angst!	*Don't be afraid, will you!*
Nur weiter!	*Just carry on!* (implying: *It's all right so far*)

bloß is **not** used in this 'reassuring' sense, and commands with *bloß* always have a 'warning' tone. Compare *Lass ihn bloß reden!* 'Just let him speak (and you'll suffer the consequences)' with the first example in (ii) above.

(b) *nur* **intensifies *w*-questions and makes them sound more urgent**

Wie kann er nur so taktlos sein?	*How on earth can he be so tactless?*
Was können wir nur tun, um ihr zu helfen?	*Whatever can we do to help her?*
Wo bleibt sie nur?	*Where on earth is she?*

Such questions can be used as exclamations of reproach or astonishment, as no real answer is possible or expected:

Wie siehst du nur wieder aus?!	*What on earth do you look like?!*
Warum musste er nur wegfahren?!	*Why on earth did he have to go away?!*

(c) *nur* **intensifies a wish in the form of a *wenn*-clause**

See also 16.7.6b. The force of *nur* similar to that of *doch*, see 10.7.6, and they are often used together to add an even greater intensity to the wish:

Wenn sie (doch) nur anrufen würde!	*If only she would ring up!*
Hätte ich nur mehr Zeit!	*If only I had more time!*
Wenn er mir nur geschrieben hätte!	*If only he had written me!*

10.26.2 *nur* is used as a focus particle to express a restriction

i.e. with the force of English 'only'. *nur* is used in all kinds of sentences to qualify nouns, verbs or adjectives:

Ich wollte nur Guten Tag sagen	*I only/just wanted to say Hello*
Die Mittelmeerküste ist sehr schön, sie ist leider nur etwas dreckig	*The Mediterranean coast is very nice, only I'm afraid it's rather dirty*
Er geht nur bei schönem Wetter spazieren	*He only goes for a walk when it's fine*
Ich vermute nur, dass er gestern in Urlaub gefahren ist	*I'm only assuming that he went on holiday yesterday*
Man kann es nur dort kaufen	*It's only there you can buy it*
Dort kann man nicht nur Bücher kaufen, sondern auch allerlei Zeitschriften	*You can not only buy books there, but also magazines of all kinds*

NB: (i) For the difference between *erst* and *nur* as an equivalent of English 'only', see 10.12.2c.
  (ii) *nur dass* is used as the equivalent of the English conjunction 'only' (see also 19.7.6), e.g. *Die Zimmer waren in Ordnung, **nur** **dass** die Duschen fehlten*.
  (iii) *lediglich*, see 10.21, is a more formal alternative to *nur*.

10.27 *ohnehin*

ohnehin indicates that something is correct irrespective of any other reasons given or implied. A typical English equivalent is 'anyway' or 'in any case'. It is a more formal alternative to (southern) colloquial *eh* (see 10.9), or *sowieso* (see 10.31):

Er trinkt ohnehin zu viel	*He drinks too much anyway*
Der Zug hat ohnehin Verspätung	*The train's late anyway*
Du musst sofort zum Arzt	*You'll have to go to the doctor right away*
– Ich hätte ihn ohnehin morgen besucht	*– I would have gone to see him tomorrow in any case*

10.28 *ruhig*

ruhig lends a reassuring tone to what the speaker is saying. This meaning is clearly related to that of the adjective *ruhig* 'quiet'. It is used in commands (where it is an alternative to *nur*, see 10.26.1a), and in statements, especially with a modal auxiliary:

Bleib ruhig sitzen!	*Don't get up for me*
Arbeite ruhig weiter!	*Just carry on* (i.e. don't let me disturb you)
Auf dieser Straße kannst du ruhig etwas schneller fahren	*It's all right, you can go a bit faster on this road*
Sie dürfen ruhig hier im Zimmer bleiben	*You can stay here in this room, I don't mind*

10.29 *schließlich*

schließlich indicates that the speaker accepts the validity of a reason. It usually corresponds to English 'after all':

Es liegt schließlich nicht genug Schnee auf der Piste	*After all, there's not enough snow on the piste*
Wir wollen ihn schließlich nicht zu sehr reizen	*We don't want to annoy him too much, after all*
Schließlich kann das einem jeden passieren	*After all, it can happen to anybody*

10.30 *schon*

schon has the widest range of meaning of all the German particles.

10.30.1 **The use of *schon* as a modal particle in statements**

(a) In statements generally, *schon* expresses agreement or confirmation in principle, but with slight reservations

This sense is in practice concessive. *schon* often has (or implies) a following *aber*, *nur* or the like. *zwar* or, especially in North Germany, *wohl* are possible alternatives, see 10.35.3 and 10.36.1:

Das ist schon möglich (aber . . .)	*That's quite possible (but . . .)*
Ich wollte schon kommen	*Well, I did want to come*
Das stimmt schon, aber es könnte auch anders kommen	*That may be true, but things might turn out differently*
Ja, ich glaube schon (aber . . .)	*Well, I think so (but . . .)*
Der Film hatte schon wunderschöne Aufnahmen, nur war er etwas langweilig	*The movie may have had some lovely shots, only it was a bit boring*

In a response, *schon* corrects what has just been said and indicates why it was wrong:

Niemand fährt über Ostern weg – Mutter schon!	*Nobody's going away over Easter – But mother is*
Heute waren keine deiner Freunde da – Der Uli aber schon!	*None of your friends came today – But Uli did*
Er hat da ein sehr schönes Haus gekauft – (Das) schon, aber . . .	*He's bought himself a nice house there – Well yes, but . . .*

(b) In statements referring to the future, *schon* emphasises the speaker's confidence that something will happen

schon usually sounds reassuring, but in some contexts and situations it may take on a more threatening tone. English 'all right' has similar force:

Er wird uns schon helfen	*He'll help us all right*
Es wird schon gehen	*It'll be all right, don't worry*
Ich krieg's schon hin	*I'll manage it all right*
Dem werde ich's schon zeigen!	*I'll show him all right!*

10.30.2 *schon* gives persuasive force to a *w*-question which expects a negative answer or where the speaker has a negative attitude

Was sagt die Regierung zu Russland? – Nichts. Was sollen sie schon sagen?	*What does the government say about Russia? – Nothing. But then, what are they to say?*
Wer kann diesem Angebot schon widerstehen?	*Who can refuse this offer?* (i.e. 'nobody')
Warum kommt der schon wieder?	*What's he coming again for?* (implying: 'he's up to no good')
Na, und wenn schon?	*So what?*

10.30.3 In conditional sentences *schon* emphasises the condition

In addition, *schon* may point to the inescapability of the conclusion. It is normally used only in open conditions, with the indicative, see 16.5.2:

Wenn ich das schon mache, dann muss ich über alle Probleme informiert sein	*If I am going to do it, I'll need to be told about all the problems*
Wenn du schon ein neues Auto kaufst, dann aber kein so teures	*If you are going to buy a new car, then don't get such an expensive one*
Wenn sie schon ans Meer fährt, dann will sie auch baden	*If she's going to the seaside, she will want to go swimming*

10.30.4 **In commands, *schon* adds an insistent note**

The sentence often begins with *nun*:

(Nun,) beeile dich schon!	*Do hurry up (then)!*
Fang schon an!	*Do make a start!*
Sag mir schon, was du denkst! Ich werde es dir nicht übel nehmen	*Do tell me what you think. I shan't take it amiss*

10.30.5 ***schon* is used as a focus particle to express a restriction**

erst is the opposite of *schon* in the contexts dealt with under (a) and (b) below, see 10.12.2.

(a) Referring to time, *schon* indicates that something is happening or has happened sooner than expected or desirable

In some contexts, *schon* can stress that something actually has happened. In this meaning, it can correspond to English 'already', but it is much more widely used:

Er war schon angekommen	*He had already arrived*
schon am nächsten Tag	*the very next day*
Da bist du ja schon wieder	*There you are back again*
Sind Sie schon einmal in Köln gewesen?	*Have you been to Cologne before?*
Ich habe ihn auch schon in der Bibliothek gesehen	*I've sometimes seen him in the library*
Das habe ich schon 2005 geahnt	*I suspected that as early as 2005*
Schon im Mai ist es mir zum ersten Mal aufgefallen	*It was in May I noticed it for the first time*

(b) Before a number or an expression of quantity, *schon* indicates that this is more than expected or desirable

Sie hat schon dreißig Mails bekommen	*She has already received thirty e-mails*
Ich habe schon die Hälfte des Buches gelesen	*I've already read half the book*
Er wartet schon eine Stunde auf dich	*He's already been waiting for you for an hour*

(c) When used to qualify most nouns, *schon* expresses a restriction

schon can occasionally be used to qualify another part of speech:

Schon der Gedanke ist mir unsympathisch, schon wegen ihrer Kinder	*The very thought is repugnant to me, if only because of their children*
Das geht schon daher nicht, weil . . .	*That's impossible, not least because . . .*
Schon vor dem Krieg war die Eisenbahn in Schwierigkeiten geraten	*Even before the war the railways had run into difficulties*

10.31 *sowieso*

sowieso indicates that something is correct irrespective of any other reasons given or implied. It usually corresponds to English 'anyway' or 'in any case'. It is a rather more informal alternative to *ohnehin*, see 10.27:

Ich kann heute sowieso nicht arbeiten	*I can't work today anyway*
Der ist sowieso scharf auf sie	*He fancies her anyway*
Ich wäre sowieso nach Nürnberg gefahren	*I would have gone to Nuremberg in any case*

10.32 *überhaupt*

10.32.1 *überhaupt* makes statements and commands more general

The English equivalent is often 'at all' or 'anyhow':

Duisburg ist überhaupt eine grässliche Stadt	*Duisburg is a dreadful city anyhow*
Das ist überhaupt eine gefährliche Angelegenheit	*That's a risky business in any case*
Er liebte die italienische Sprache, ja die Sprachen überhaupt (*Goes*)	*He loved the Italian language, indeed, languages in general*
Seinen Mut müsste man haben, dachte ich. Oder überhaupt Mut (*Walser*)	*One ought to have his courage, I thought. Or any courage at all*
Ihr sollt überhaupt besser aufpassen!	*You ought anyway to pay more attention*

10.32.2 In questions, *überhaupt* casts doubt on the basic assumption

Er singt nicht besonders gut – Kann er denn überhaupt singen?	*He doesn't sing particularly well – Can he sing at all?*
Wie konntest du überhaupt so was tun?	*How could you do such a thing at all?*
Der Brief ist nicht da. Wo kann er überhaupt sein?	*The letter's not there. Wherever can it be?*
Was will er denn überhaupt?	*What the dickens does he want?*

10.32.3 *überhaupt* intensifies a negative

gar is a frequent alternative, see 10.15a:

Du hättest es überhaupt nicht tun sollen, und besonders jetzt nicht	*You ought not to have done it at all, and particularly not now*
Sie hat überhaupt keine Ahnung	*She's got no idea at all*
Ich weiß überhaupt nichts von seinen Plänen	*I don't know anything about his plans*

10.33 *übrigens*

übrigens is used in statements and questions to indicate a casual remark which is incidental to the main topic of conversation. It corresponds to English 'by the way', etc.:

Ich habe übrigens erfahren, dass er eine neue Stelle bekommen hat	*Incidentally, I've found out he's got a new job*
Sie hat übrigens vollkommen Recht	*She's perfectly right, by the way*
Wo wollt ihr übrigens dieses Jahr hin?	*By the way, where are you going this year?*

10.34 *vielleicht*

10.34.1 In exclamations unstressed *vielleicht* expresses surprise

These exclamations can have the form of statements or questions.

Siehst du vielleicht schlecht aus! Du siehst vielleicht schlecht aus!	*Oh, you really do look awful!*

Die Kiste ist vielleicht schwer!	*How heavy the crate is!*
Du bist vielleicht ein Idiot!	*You really are stupid!*
Das hat vielleicht gegossen!	*It really did pour!*
Ich habe vielleicht gestaunt!	*I wasn't half surprised!*

Like *aber* (see 10.1.1), *vielleicht* expresses surprise at a difference in **degree** from the speaker's expectation, whereas *ja* (see 10.19.2) relates to a difference in **kind**.

10.34.2 In yes/no questions, *vielleicht* signals that the speaker expects a negative answer

The sense of *vielleicht* is close to that of *etwa*, see 10.13.1. The English equivalent is often an exclamation beginning with 'Don't tell me . . .' or a negative statement followed by a positive tag question:

Willst du mir vielleicht erzählen, dass . . .?	*You don't mean to tell me that . . . , do you?*
Soll ich vielleicht bis 7 Uhr abends hier sitzen?	*I'm not supposed to sit here till seven at night, am I?*
Arbeitet er vielleicht?	*Don't tell me he's working?*

10.34.3 *vielleicht* is used as an adverb of attitude

i.e. corresponding to English 'perhaps':

Sie ist vielleicht 30 Jahre alt	*She is perhaps thirty years old*
Sie wird vielleicht morgen kommen	*She may come tomorrow*
Wird sie uns vielleicht morgen besuchen?	*Will she come to see us tomorrow, perhaps?*

vielleicht has a quite different meaning when it is used as an adverb from when it is used as a particle. The difference is often only clear from the intonation, with heavy emphases when it is being used as a particle:

Die Kiste ist vielleicht schwer	*Perhaps the case is heavy*
Die Kiste ist vielleicht schwer!	*How heavy this case is!*

In requests in the form of a question, *vielleicht*, like English 'perhaps', expresses polite reserve on the part of the speaker:

Könnten Sie mir vielleicht sagen, wo es zum Bahnhof geht?	*Could you perhaps tell me the way to the station?*
Würden Sie mir vielleicht helfen?	*Would you perhaps help me?*

10.35 *wohl*

10.35.1 In statements, *wohl* signals a fair degree of probability

The force of *wohl* is very similar to that of the future tense, see 14.4.3, and it is often used in conjunction with it. It corresponds to the English future tense or a positive statement followed by a negative tag question, or to formulae like 'I suppose', 'probably':

Das wird wohl der Briefträger sein	*That'll be the postman*
Sie sind wohl neu hier	*You're new here, aren't you?*
Sie hat wohl ihr Auto schon verkauft	*I suppose she's already sold her car*

Diese Probleme versteht er wohl nicht	*He probably doesn't understand these problems*
Ich habe ihn nie gesprochen, wohl aber oft gesehen	*I've never spoken to him, but I have often seen him*

The combination *ja wohl* sounds rather more certain, corresponding to English '(pretty) certainly' or 'no doubt':

Sie wird ja wohl noch in Potsdam sein	*She's pretty certainly still in Potsdam*
Das weißt du ja wohl	*No doubt you know that*

The combination *wohl doch* (or, for some speakers, *doch wohl*) sounds rather less certain, though the speaker hopes that it is the case:

Er hat wohl doch noch einen Schlüssel	*Surely he's got another key, hasn't he?*
Die Antje wird doch wohl noch das Abitur schaffen	*Antje's surely going to get through her Abitur, isn't she?*

10.35.2 In questions *wohl* signals uncertainty on the part of the speaker

wohl can make the question sound tentative, as if the speaker doubts whether the other can give a clear answer. The question can be in statement form.

Wer hat den Brief wohl geschrieben?	*Who can possibly have written the letter?*
Wie spät ist es wohl?	*I wonder what time it is*
Ist Peter wohl schon zu Hause?	*Peter is at home, isn't he?*
Darf ich wohl bei Ihnen telefonieren?	*Might I use your telephone?*
Horst ist wohl gestern Abend angekommen?	*Horst arrived last night, didn't he?*

10.35.3 In statements, stressed *wohl* has a concessive sense

wohl expresses agreement or confirmation in principle, but tinged with a slight reservation. It often has (or implies) a following *aber, nur* or the like. *zwar* or, especially in South Germany, *schon* are possible alternatives, see 10.30.1a and 10.36.1:

Er ist wohl mein Freund, aber ich kann ihm nicht helfen	*He may be my friend, but I can't help him*
Das ist wohl möglich(, aber . . .)	*That may be possible(, but . . .)*
Herbert ist wohl nach Basel gefahren, aber nur für eine Woche	*Herbert did go to Basle, but only for a week*

10.35.4 *wohl* intensifies a command, making it sound urgent, insistent and rather abrupt

wohl is often used with *werden* or *wollen*:

Hebst du wohl das Buch wieder auf!	*Pick that book up again right away!*
Wirst du wohl sofort wieder ins Bett gehen!	*Will you go straight back to bed!*
Wollt ihr wohl endlich still sein!	*Once and for all, will you be quiet!*

10.35.5 As an adverb, usually stressed, *wohl* has the sense 'well', 'fully'

wohl often strengthens an affirmative response (i.e. *jawohl!* 'yes, indeed'):

Ich fühle mich wohl	*I feel well*
Er hatte es sich wohl überlegt	*He had considered it fully*
Er weiß sehr wohl, dass er Unrecht hat	*He knows full well that he's wrong*
Schlaf wohl!	*Sleep well!*
Leb wohl!	*Farewell!*
Und er war so geartet, dass er solche Erfahrungen wohl vermerkte (*Th. Mann*)	*And his nature was such that he took full note of such experiences*

10.36 *zwar*

10.36.1 *zwar* can be used in a concessive sense

In this sense, *zwar* is typically followed by a clause with *aber* (or one is implied), and the combination *zwar . . . aber* can have the force of English '(al)though', see also 19.6.1b:

Er ist zwar krank, aber er kommt heute Abend noch mit	*Although he's ill, he's still coming with us tonight*
Er stand nach Kinkels Aussage „zwar in der Mitte, aber doch mehr nach rechts als nach links" (*Böll*)	*According to Kinkel he was 'politically in the centre, but tending all the same to the right rather than the left'*

In North Germany *wohl* is a possible alternative to *zwar* in this concessive sense, see 10.35.3, whilst in South and Central Germany *schon* is used, see 10.30.1a.

10.36.2 *und zwar* is used in the sense of English 'namely' to specify what has just been mentioned

Mein Entschluss fiel auf dem neuen Flugplatz in Mexico-City, und zwar im letzten Augenblick (*Frisch*)	*My decision was taken at the new airport in Mexico City, (in actual fact) at the very last minute*
Ich habe die wichtigsten Museen besucht, und zwar das kunsthistorische, das naturhistorische und die Albertina	*I visited the most important museums, namely the Museum of Art History, the Museum of Natural History and the Albertina*

11 Expressions of time

Usage in TIME EXPRESSIONS is characteristically idiomatic in all languages, involving special uses and meanings. German usage can differ quite markedly from English in the way in which various aspects of time are referred to, and particular attention is paid to these differences in this chapter, where the following aspects of time expressions are treated in detail:

- **clock times** (section 11.1)
- the **days of the week**, **months** and **public holidays** (section 11.2)
- dates (section 11.3)
- the use of **cases** (i.e. the accusative and the genitive) in time adverbials (section 11.4)
- the use of **prepositions** in time adverbials (section 11.5)
- simple time **adverbs** (section 11.6)

11.1 Times of the clock

11.1.1 In everyday speech the twelve-hour clock is the norm

As in English, the twelve-hour clock is used in everyday conversation, when reference is not being made to public events, official timetables and the like. The relevant forms are given in Table 11.1.

TABLE 11.1 Clock times

1.00	**Es ist ein Uhr**	*It's one (o'clock)*
	Es ist eins	
3.00	**Es ist drei (Uhr)**	*It's three (o'clock)*
3.05	**fünf (Minuten) nach drei**	*five (minutes) past three*
3.07	**sieben Minuten nach drei**	*seven minutes past three*
3.10	**zehn (Minuten) nach drei**	*ten (minutes) past three*
3.15	**Viertel nach drei**	*quarter past three*
	viertel vier (South and East Germany)	
3.20	**zwanzig nach drei**	*twenty past three*
	zehn vor halb vier	
3.25	**fünf vor halb vier**	*twenty-five past three*
3.30	**halb vier**	*half past three/half three*
3.35	**fünf nach halb vier**	*twenty-five to four*
3.40	**zwanzig vor vier**	*twenty to four*
	zehn nach halb vier	
3.45	**Viertel vor vier**	*quarter to four*
	dreiviertel vier (South and East Germany)	
3.47	**dreizehn Minuten vor vier**	*thirteen minutes to four*
3.50	**zehn (Minuten) vor vier**	*ten (minutes) to four*
3.55	**fünf (Minuten) vor vier**	*five (minutes) to four*

Note the striking difference between English and German when referring to the half hour: *halb vier* 'half past **three**'.

11.1.2 **In official contexts the twenty-four-hour clock is used**

This is the norm in timetables, for television and radio programmes, theatrical performances, official meetings, business hours, and in all other official contexts. Examples are given in Table 11.2:

TABLE 11.2 The twenty-four-hour clock

0.27	**null Uhr siebenundzwanzig**	*12.27 a.m.*
5.15	**fünf Uhr fünfzehn**	*5.15 a.m.*
10.30	**zehn Uhr dreißig**	*10.30 a.m.*
13.07	**dreizehn Uhr sieben**	*1.07 p.m.*
21.37	**einundzwanzig Uhr siebenunddreißig**	*9.37 p.m.*
24.00	**vierundzwanzig Uhr**	*12.00 midnight*

When these are used in speech, the word *Uhr* is only omitted in giving the full hours between 1 a.m. and noon, e.g. *Ihr Zug kommt um 9.00 an* (spoken: *um neun (Uhr)*). Otherwise the full forms, with *Uhr*, are used, e.g. *Die Vorstellung beginnt um 20.00* (spoken: *um zwanzig Uhr*), *um 20.15* (*um zwanzig Uhr fünfzehn*), *Der Zug fährt um 9.17* (spoken: *um neun Uhr siebzehn*), etc.

Even in everyday conversation it is common for 'official' times to be given using the twenty-four hour clock. Thus one would say *Mein Zug fährt um 19.35* (i.e. *um neunzehn Uhr fünfunddreißig*), but it would be odd to say *Tante Käthe hat uns für fünfzehn Uhr dreißig zum Kaffee eingeladen* – you would say: *halb vier*.

11.1.3 **Further phrases with clock times**

Wie viel Uhr ist es? ⎫	*What's the time?*
Wie spät ist es? (coll.) ⎭	
Wie viel Uhr haben Sie?	*What time do you make it?*
Um wie viel Uhr kommt sie?	*What time is she coming?*
Sie kommt um halb drei	*She's coming at half-past two*
um drei Uhr nachts	*at three in the morning*
um neun Uhr vormittags	*at nine in the morning*
um zwölf Uhr mittags	*at twelve noon*
um drei Uhr nachmittags	*at three in the afternoon*
um sieben Uhr abends	*at seven in the evening*
um Mitternacht	*at midnight*
Es ist Punkt/genau neun (Uhr)	*It is exactly nine (o'clock)*
Es ist gerade halb	*It is just half-past*
Es ist ungefähr neun (Uhr)	*It's about nine (o'clock)*
Es ist (schon) neun Uhr vorbei	*It's gone nine o'clock*
Er kommt ungefähr um neun Uhr	*He's coming at about nine o'clock*
Er kam gegen neun (Uhr) an	*He came at about nine/just before nine*

NB: *gegen* is ambiguous with clock times, see 11.5.7.

11.2 **Days of the week, months and public holidays**

11.2.1 **The days of the week**

The names of the days of the week in German are shown in Table 11.3.

TABLE 11.3 The days of the week

Sonntag	Sunday	Donnerstag	Thursday
Montag	Monday	Freitag	Friday
Dienstag	Tuesday	Samstag/Sonnabend	Saturday
Mittwoch	Wednesday		

As the equivalent for 'Saturday', *Samstag* was originally used only in the South and *Sonnabend* in the North (i.e. North of Frankfurt am Main). *Samstag* has recently come to be used much more widely at the expense of *Sonnabend*, which is now largely restricted to the far North and the former East Germany.

NB: For English 'on Sunday', etc. German uses *am Sonntag*, etc., see **4.5.3** and **11.5.2**.

11.2.2 The months

The German names of the **months** are shown in Table 11.4.

TABLE 11.4 The months of the year

Januar	January	Mai	May	September	September
Februar	February	Juni	June	Oktober	October
März	March	Juli	July	November	November
April	April	August	August	Dezember	December

NB: (i) In Austria, *Jänner* is always used for *Januar*, and, less commonly, *Feber* for *Februar*.
(ii) *Juni* and *Juli* are sometimes pronounced *Juno* and *Julei* to avoid confusion, especially on the telephone.
(iii) For English 'in January', etc., German has *im Januar*, etc., see **4.5.3** and **11.5.8**.

11.2.3 The major public holidays and religious festivals

Neujahr(stag)	*New Year's Day*
Dreikönigsfest/-tag	*Epiphany*
Rosenmontag	*Carnival Monday* (the day before Shrove Tuesday)
Aschermittwoch	*Ash Wednesday*
Gründonnerstag	*Maundy Thursday*
Karfreitag	*Good Friday*
Ostersonntag	*Easter Sunday*
Ostern	*Easter*
Ostermontag	*Easter Monday*
Fronleichnam	*Corpus Christi*
Pfingsten	*Whitsun*
Pfingstsonntag	*Whit Sunday*
Pfingstmontag	*Whit Monday*
(Christi) Himmelfahrt	*Ascension Day*
Mariä Himmelfahrt	*Assumption of the Virgin Mary* (15th August)
Tag der Deutschen Einheit	*Day of German Unity* (3rd October)
Allerheiligen	*All Saints' Day* (1st November)
Buß- und Bettag	*Day of Penitence and Prayer* (Wednesday before the last Sunday before Advent)
der Heilige Abend *or* Heiligabend	*Christmas Eve*

Weihnachten	*Christmas*
Erster Weihnachts(feier)tag	*Christmas Day*
Zweiter Weihnachts(feier)tag	*Boxing Day*
Silvester	*New Year's Eve*

NB: *Ostern, Pfingsten* and *Weihnachten* are usually treated as plurals, see 1.2.10b.

11.3 Dates

11.3.1 Ordinal numbers are used for the days of the month

i.e. *der fünfte April* 'the fifth of April'. This usage is similar to that in English, although there is no equivalent to English 'of'. In practice, numbers are always used for them in writing, i.e. they are never written out as words:

Der Wievielte ist heute? Den Wievielten haben wir heute? }	*What's the date today?*
Heute ist der 8. (*spoken:* achte) Mai Wir haben heute den 8. (achten) Mai }	*Today is the eighth of May*
Er kam am 5. (*spoken:* fünften) Juni, 2008	*He came on the fifth of June 2008*
am 5.6.2008 (*spoken:* am fünften, sechsten, zweitausendacht)	*on 5.6.2008*

NB: As the last example shows, the day is given **before** the month in German. This corresponds to usage in British English, but it is the reverse of American practice.

11.3.2 Usage where the day of the week precedes the date

i.e. equivalents of 'Monday, the fifth of June'. There are three alternative ways of expressing this in German.

(i) with the day of the week and the date in the accusative case:

Wir fliegen **Montag, den 5. Juni**(,) nach Australien

(ii) with the day of the week preceded by *am* and followed by the date in the accusative case:

Wir fliegen **am Montag, den 5. Juni**(,) nach Australien

(iii) with the day of the week preceded by *am* and followed by the date in the dative case:

Wir fliegen **am Montag, dem 5. Juni**(,) nach Australien

11.3.3 Usage in letter headings

In private correspondence (i.e. where the address is not printed on the notepaper), the writer's address is not usually written out in full at the head of the letter, as is the usual British practice. Instead, just the town is given, followed by the date, which may be written in various ways, i.e.:

Siegen, **(den) 5.6.11**	Siegen, **am 5.6.11**
Siegen, **(den/d.) 5. Juni 2011**	Siegen, **im Juni 2011**

When writing a formal letter to an unknown person, especially for the first time, some Germans put their full name and address in the top left-hand corner of the letter and the town and date, as given above, in the top right-hand corner.

11.4 **The accusative and genitive cases used in time adverbials**

In certain contexts the **accusative** and **genitive** cases of nouns can be used adverbially, without a preposition, to express ideas of time.

11.4.1 **Adverbial time phrases with the** ACCUSATIVE

A noun denoting time can be used in the accusative case to express duration of time or a specific point in time or period of time.

(a) The accusative can be used to indicate a length of time

The period of time lies entirely in the past, present or future, and the accusative usually corresponds to the English phrase with 'for '(see 11.5.6b). The word or phrase in the accusative may optionally be followed by *lang*, or, emphasising the duration, *über* or *hindurch*:

Ich war **einen Monat/drei Monate** (lang) in Kassel	*I was in Kassel for a month/for three months*
Dort blieb sie **viele Jahre** (lang)	*She stayed there for many years*
Jahre hindurch blieb er im Gefängnis	*He stayed in prison for years (on end)*
Ich bin jede Woche **einen Tag** (lang) in Kaiserslautern	*I am in Kaiserslautern one day every week*
Er lag **den ganzen Tag** (lang/über) im Bett	*He lay in bed the whole day/all day (long)*
den ganzen Sommer (lang)	*all summer, for the whole of the summer*
den ganzen Winter hindurch/über	*throughout the winter*
sein ganzes Leben (lang)	*all his life/for his whole life*
Wo warst du **die ganze Zeit**?	*Where were you the whole time?*
eine ganze Weile	*for quite a while*

(b) The accusative can be used to indicate a specific time

(i) Particularly in phrases denoting a period of time, corresponding to English 'last week', 'next year', etc.:

Einen Augenblick zuvor hätte sie ihn noch retten können	*A moment before she could still have saved him*
Er kommt **jeden Tag/jede Woche**	*He comes every day/every week*
Sie fährt **alle vierzehn Tage/alle paar Jahre** in die Schweiz	*She goes to Switzerland every two weeks/every few years*
Jede halbe Stunde kommt er vorbei	*Every half hour he comes past*
Wir besuchen sie **nächsten Dienstag/ kommenden Dienstag**	*We are visiting her next Tuesday*
Wir besuchen sie **kommende/nächste Woche**	*We are visiting her next week*
Wir werden **dieses Jahr** nicht verreisen	*We're not going away this year*
Sie ist **2011** wieder zur Vorsitzenden des Vereins gewählt worden	*In 2011 she was elected chair of the society again*
Ich sah sie **letzten Freitag/vorigen Freitag/vergangenen Freitag**	*I saw her last Friday*
Ich sah sie **letzte/vorige/vergangene Woche/den 5. Juni**	*I saw her last week/on the 5th of June (see 11.3.1)*

In many contexts a prepositional phrase (see 11.5) can be used as an alternative to a phrase in the accusative case, and the phrases below illustrate typical alternatives to the examples above:

am nächsten/kommenden Dienstag	*next Tuesday*
am letzten/vorigen/vergangenen Freitag	*last Friday*
in der nächsten/kommenden Woche	*next week*
in diesem Jahr	*this year*
im Jahre 2009	*in 2009*

In general, phrases with the accusative case are more frequent in everyday speech, whereas those with a preposition are rather commoner in writing. Further examples, with other prepositions:

Ich bin **Mittag** (*for*: um Mittag) wieder zu Hause	*I'll be back home at noon*
Fährst du **Ostern** (*for*: zu Ostern) zu deinen Eltern?	*Are you going to your parents at Easter?*
Sind Sie **das erste Mal** (*for*: zum ersten Mal) hier?	*Is this the first time you've been here?*

(ii) *Anfang*, *Mitte* and *Ende*, unlike their English equivalents, are used without a preposition, i.e. in the accusative, in time phrases:

Er ist **Anfang Januar/Mitte Januar/Ende Januar** gestorben	*He died at the beginning of January/in the middle of January/at the end of January*
Ich fahre schon **Anfang Ende** nächster Woche	*I'm leaving at the beginning at the end of next week*
Anfang 2009 fanden die Wahlen zum 18. hessischen Landtag statt	*At the beginning of 2009 the regional elections in Hesse took place*

If *Anfang* and *Ende* are used without a following time phrase, they are preceded by *am*, e.g. *am Anfang* 'at the beginning', *am Ende* 'at the end'.

11.4.2 Adverbial time phrases with the GENITIVE

The genitive case of nouns denoting time can refer to indefinite or habitual time. These are now mainly set expressions, and they are commonly extended by adjectives only in formal literary language:

eines Tages	*one day*
eines schönen Tages	*one fine day*
eines schönen Sommers	*one fine summer*
eines Sonntags	*one Sunday*
eines Morgens	*one morning*
eines Sonntagmorgens	*one Sunday morning*
eines nebligen Morgens	*one foggy morning*
eines Nachts	*one night*
dieser Tage	*in the next/last few days*

NB: Note the form *eines Nachts*, although *die Nacht* is feminine.

Some genitive phrases have become simple adverbs, and they are written with a small initial letter:

morgens, vormittags	*in the mornings*
nachmittags, abends	*in the afternoons, in the evenings*
tags, nachts	*by day, at night*
dienstags, freitags	*on Tuesdays, on Fridays*
wochentags, werktags	*on weekdays, on working days*
donnerstagabends/donnerstags abends	*on Thursday evenings*
von morgens bis abends	*from morning till night*
morgens und abends	*morning and evening*
sommers, winters	*in the summer, in the winter*
sommers wie winters	*all year round*

These adverbs are sometimes used to refer to single occasions, (e.g. *nachmittags* for *am Nachmittag*), especially in South German usage:

Wir kamen dort **sonntags** auf dem Spaziergang vorüber (*Gaiser*)
We came past there on Sunday during our walk

NB: The adverbs *morgens, abends*, etc. originated from noun phrases in the genitive with the definite article, e.g. *des Morgens, des Abends*. These full phrases are still sometimes used in formal written German.

11.5 Adverbial time phrases with prepositions

This section treats the most common prepositions used with nouns denoting time. Other uses of all prepositions are explained fully in Chapter 20.

11.5.1 *ab* (+ accusative or dative)

ab is used in the meaning 'from' and is an alternative to *von . . . an*, see 11.5.13. If it is used without a following determiner (as is usually the case, see 4.9.3c), both the dative and the accusative are found and considered equally correct:

ab neun Uhr, **ab** heute	*from nine o'clock, from today*
ab sofort	*with immediate effect*
ab ersten/erstem Mai	*from the first of May*
ab kommende(r) Woche	*from next week*
ab nächsten/nächstem Monat	*from next month*

However, if there is a definite article, then the dative must be used:

ab dem ersten Mai.	*from the first of May*
ab dem 21. Lebensjahr	*from the age of 21*

11.5.2 *an* (+ dative)

an is used with nouns denoting days and parts of the day. It is always followed by a noun in the dative case when referring to time, and the definite article is always used with nouns in the singular, see 4.5.3. In most contexts it corresponds to English 'in' or 'on':

am Tag	*in the daytime*
am Montag, **am** Dienstag, . . .	*on Monday, on Tuesday, . . .*

an Wochentagen	*on weekdays*
an besonderen Tagen	*on particular days*
am Morgen, **am** Nachmittag, **am** Abend	*in the morning, in the afternoon, in the evening*
am 31. Oktober (see 11.3.1)	*on the 31st of October*

Combinations of the days of the week and nouns denoting parts of the day are written together, e.g. *am Donnerstagabend.*

an is used with *Tag*, etc. even in contexts where English has no preposition:

am Tag nach seinem Tod	*the day after his death*
An diesem Morgen war er schlecht gelaunt	*That morning he was in a bad mood*
am anderen Tag, **am** anderen Morgen	*the next day, the next morning*

an occurs in a few other contexts:

Es ist **an** der Zeit, dass . . .	*It is about time that . . .*
am Anfang, **am** Ende (see **11.4.1b**)	*at the beginning, at the end*
gleich **am** Anfang	*at the very beginning*

NB: (i)   *in* is used with *Nacht*, see 11.5.8a.
(ii) An accusative time phrase is often an alternative to a phrase with *an*, especially in spoken German, see 11.4.1b.

11.5.3 *auf* (+ accusative)

auf indicates a period of time from 'now', corresponding to English 'for'. It is always used with a following accusative case in time phrases. In this sense it is a less common alternative to *für*, see 11.5.6, found mainly in formal registers, regionally and in some set phrases:

Sie fährt **auf** vier Monate in die Schweiz	*She is going to Switzerland for three months*
auf unbestimmte Zeit	*indefinitely*
auf ewig, **auf** immer	*for ever, for good*

NB: *auf* is used idiomatically in *auf die Minute (genau)* '(precisely) to the minute'.

11.5.4 *bei*

bei is used chiefly with nouns which do not of themselves express time to indicate the 'time when x took/was taking/will take place':

bei seiner Geburt	*at his birth*
bei dieser Gelegenheit	*on this occasion*
bei der Probe	*during the rehearsal*

It is also used in a similar meaning in a few set phrases with nouns expressing time:

Paris **bei** Tag, London **bei** Nacht	*Paris by day, London by night*
bei Tagesanbruch	*at daybreak*
bei Einbruch der Nacht	*at nightfall*
bei Sonnenuntergang	*at sunset*

11.5.5 *bis*

bis indicates an end-point in time and can correspond to English 'until' <u>or</u> 'by'. It can only be used on its own with adverbs and simple time phrases like dates and the days of the week, and it is <u>never</u> followed by a definite article:

Bis 1945 hat er in Wien gelebt	*Until 1945 he lived in Vienna*
Das Geschäft ist von 9 Uhr **bis** 18.30 Uhr durchgehend geöffnet	*The shop is open continuously from 9 a.m. until 6.30 p.m.*
Ich werde es **bis** heute Abend/**bis** Montag fertig haben	*I'll have it finished by tonight/by Monday*
bis nächste Woche, nächstes Jahr	*until next week, next year*
bis dahin/**bis** dann	*by then, until then*
bis jetzt, **bis** anhin (Sw.)	*up to now*
Bis dahin bin ich längst zurück	*I'll be back long before then*

With days of the week, months and dates, *bis* can be used with or without a following *zu* (and the definite article):

bis (zum) Freitag	*by/until Friday*
bis (zum) 11. Juni	*by/until the 11th of June*
Bis (zum) kommenden Montag kannst du mich hier erreichen	*You can reach me here till next Monday*

In other contexts *bis* <u>must</u> be followed by *zu* (or another appropriate preposition) with the definite article:

bis zum 18. Jahrhundert	*until/by the 18th century*
bis zu seinem Tode	*until his death*
bis zu den Ferien	*until the holidays*
bis vor kurzem	*until recently*
Bis vor zwei Wochen war er hier	*He was here until two weeks ago*
Ich arbeite **bis gegen** Mittag im Büro	*I'm working at the office until about noon*
Wir wollen es **bis auf** weiteres verschieben	*We'll postpone it for the present*
bis auf weiteres	*until further notice*
bis tief/spät **in** die Nacht hinein	*till late at night*

A date following a phrase with *bis* and a weekday is in the accusative, e.g. *bis Montag*, ***den*** *5. September*. In other contexts, the date is in the dative, e.g. *bis morgen*, ***dem*** *11. November*.

NB: (i) *erst* is used for 'not until', e.g. *Er kommt erst am Montag*, see 10.12.2.
 (ii) *bis* is frequently used in colloquial leave-taking phrases, e.g. *Bis gleich! Bis bald! Bis morgen! Bis nächste Woche!*

11.5.6 *für* and English 'for'

(a) *für* **indicates a period of time extending from 'now'**

In this sense, it corresponds to English 'for':

Ich habe das Haus **für** sechs Monate gemietet	*I've rented the house for six months*
Am nächsten Tag fuhren wir **für** einen Monat in den Schwarzwald	*The next day we went to the Black Forest for a month*

NB: (i) *auf* (+ accusative) is a less common alternative in this meaning, used chiefly in formal registers and set expressions, see 11.5.3.
 (ii) The use of *für* is idiomatic in *Tag für Tag* 'day by day'.

(b) English 'for' has the following main German equivalents

(i) a phrase in the accusative case, used to denote a period of time lying entirely in the past or future, e.g. *Er blieb einen Monat (lang) in Berlin* 'He remained in Berlin for a month'. See 11.4.1a for further details.

(ii) *seit* refers to a period of time which began in the past and extends up to the present, e.g. *Ich warte seit einer Stunde auf dich* 'I've been waiting for you for an hour'. See 11.5.10 for further details.

(iii) *für* (or more formal *auf*) to refer to a period of time extending from the present, as illustrated in (a) above.

In colloquial speech a phrase in the accusative is sometimes used instead of *für* to refer to a period of time extending from the present, e.g.: *Ich gehe eine halbe Stunde (lang) ins Cafe*. On the other hand, *für* is not unknown in the place of an accusative phrase to refer to a period of time lying entirely in the past or future, e.g. *Nur während der Wintermonate blieb er für längere Zeit an einem Ort (Bumke)*.

11.5.7 *gegen*

gegen means 'about' or 'towards'. It can be ambiguous, especially with clock times, as some Germans understand *gegen zwei Uhr* to mean 'at about two o'clock', while others interpret it as 'just before two o'clock'. In other phrases it usually has the meaning 'towards'. It is normally used without an article in time expressions:

gegen Mittag, **gegen** Abend	*towards noon, towards evening*
gegen Monatsende	*towards the end of the month*
gegen Ende des Jahrhunderts	*towards the end of the century*

11.5.8 *in* (+ dative)

in can refer to a specific period of time or a length of time. It is always used with the dative case in time expressions.

(a) *in* is used with most words denoting periods of time

It is used with all such words except those with which *an* is used (see 11.5.2), i.e. especially with the names of the months and seasons (<u>always</u> with a definite article, see 4.5.3), and with the following nouns:

der Augenblick	der Monat
die Epoche	die Nacht
das Jahr	die Woche
das Jahrhundert	das Zeitalter
die Minute	

Examples of use:

im Augenblick, **im** letzten Augenblick	*at the moment, at the last moment*
in der Frühe (*South German*)	*early in the morning*
im Jahre 2012	*in 2012*
in den letzten paar Jahren	*in the last few years*
in letzter Minute	*at the last moment*
im Mittelalter	*in the Middle Ages*

in der Nacht	*at night*
in der Nacht von Sonntag auf Montag ⎫	
in der Nacht zum/auf Montag ⎭	*during the night from Sunday to Monday*
zweimal in der Woche	*twice a week*
in der Woche vor Weihnachten	*in the week before Christmas*
in der Vergangenheit	*in the past*
in Zukunft	*in future*

The normal equivalent for English 'in 2015' in German is either *im Jahre 2015* or simply *2015*, with no preposition. However, the form *in 2015* is becoming widely used, in imitation of English usage, although many Germans consider this to be quite incorrect.

NB: For the use of *in* or *zu* with *Zeit* and *Stunde*, see 11.5.15b.

(b) *in* **indicates a period of time within which something happens**

Ich habe die Arbeit in zwei Stunden gemacht	*I did the work in two hours*
In zwei Jahren ist der Umsatz um 40 Prozent gestiegen	*In two years the turnover rose by 40%*
im Lauf(e) der Zeit	*in the course of time*
Das kann man in zwei Tagen schaffen	*You can do that in two days*

NB: *Das kann man **an** einem Morgen, Nachmittag, Abend schaffen.*

(c) *in* **can indicate the time after which something happens or is done**

Er kommt in einer halben Stunde zurück	*He's coming back in half an hour*
heute in acht Tagen	*a week today, in a week's time*
Sie fliegt in ein paar Tagen nach Sydney	*She's flying to Sydney in a few days (time)*

In some contexts, *in* can be ambiguous, like English 'in', so that *in drei Tagen* can mean 'in the course of three days' or 'in three days' time'. This ambiguity can be avoided by using *binnen* or *innerhalb*, which clearly mean 'within', e.g. *Der Rhein hat zum zweitenmal binnen 13 Monaten die Kölner Altstadt überschwemmt* (SZ).

11.5.9 *nach*

nach usually corresponds to English 'after' or 'later':

Nach vielen Jahren ließen sie sich scheiden	*After many years they got divorced*
Einen Monat nach seiner Verhaftung wurde er freigelassen	*A month after his arrest he was released*
Nach Ostern studiert sie in Erlangen Chemie	*After Easter she's going to study chemistry in Erlangen*
bald nach Anfang des 17. Jahrhunderts	*soon after the beginning of the 17th century*
nach einer Weile	*after a while*
nach Wochen, Jahren	*weeks, years later*

11.5.10 *seit*

seit marks a period of time beginning in the past and continuing to the present or a more recent point in the past. It corresponds to English 'since' or 'for', see 11.5.6b:

Er ist **seit** drei Wochen hier	*He's been here for three weeks*
Ich wartete **seit** einer halben Stunde auf dem Marktplatz	*I had been waiting in the market-place for half an hour*
Seit wann bist du wieder zu Hause?	*Since when have you been back home?*
Seit seiner Krankheit habe ich ihn nicht mehr gesehen	*I haven't seen him again since his illness*
Erst **seit** kurzem gibt es Sondertarife nach Ägypten	*There have only been special fares to Egypt for a short while*

NB: (i)   For the use of tenses with *seit* 'for', see 14.2.2 and 14.3.4a.
   (ii) An accusative phrase with *schon* is a possible alternative to *seit* 'for', e.g. *Er ist schon drei Wochen hier*, see 10.30.5a.

11.5.11 *über* (+ accusative)

über occurs in a few time expressions in the sense of 'over'. It is always used with the accusative case in time expressions:

Sie ist **über** Nacht/**übers** Wochenende geblieben	*She stayed overnight/over the weekend*
über kurz oder lang	*sooner or later*

It can be used **after** a noun in the accusative (see 11.4.1a) to emphasise duration:

Sie blieb die ganze Nacht **über**	*She stayed the whole night*
die Schwäne, die den Winter **über** geblieben waren (*Surminski*)	*The swans which had stayed the whole winter*

11.5.12 *um*

um is used with clock times (= 'at') and to express approximation.

(a) *um* corresponds to English 'at' with clock times

e.g. *um vier Uhr* 'at four o'clock', etc., see 11.1.3.

(b) With other time words *um* expresses approximation

It corresponds to English 'around' or 'about' and is often used with *herum* following the noun:

um Mitternacht (herum)	*around midnight*
um Ostern (herum)	*round about Easter time*
um 1890 (herum)	*around 1890*
die Tage **um** die Sommersonnenwende (herum)	*the days either side of the summer solstice*

NB: *um diese Zeit* is ambiguous. It can mean 'at this time' or 'around this time'. Adding *herum*, i.e. *um diese Zeit herum*, makes it clear that the second meaning is intended.

(c) Idiomatic time phrases with *um*

Stunde **um** Stunde	*hour after hour*
einen Tag **um** den anderen	*one day after the other*

11.5.13 *von*

von indicates a starting-point in time. It corresponds to English 'from' and is often linked with a following *an*:

Von 1991 an lebte sie in Rostock	*From 1991 she lived in Rostock*
Von kommendem Montag an kostet das Benzin 10 Cent mehr pro Liter	*From next Monday petrol will cost 10 cents a litre more*
von Anfang an	*(right) from the start*
von neun Uhr an	*from nine o'clock (on)*
von nun an	*from now on*
von <u>der</u> Zeit an	*from then on*
von Anfang bis Ende	*from beginning to end*
von heute auf morgen	*from one day to the next, overnight*
von vornherein	*from the outset, from the first*
von jeher/**von** alters her	*from time immemorial, always*
von Jugend auf	*from his (my, etc.) youth*
von Zeit zu Zeit	*from time to time*

NB: *ab* can be used in the sense 'from' in time expressions, e.g. *ab Montag den/dem 5. August, ab nächste(r) Woche*, see 11.5.1.

11.5.14 *vor* (+ dative)

vor corresponds to English 'ago' or 'before'. It is always used with the dative case in time expressions:

vor einem Jahr, **vor** mehreren Jahren	*a year ago, several years ago*
vor langer Zeit, **vor** einiger Zeit	*a long time ago, some time ago*
vor kurzem	*not long ago, recently* (see 11.6.5)
gestern **vor** acht Tagen	*a week ago yesterday*
die Verhältnisse **vor** der Krise	*the conditions before the crisis*

In many contexts *her* can be used in the sense of English 'ago', e.g. *Es ist schon lange, einen Monat her* 'It's a long time, a month ago'. *Wie lange ist es (schon) her?* 'How long ago is it?', see 7.2.5e.

11.5.15 *während*

während usually corresponds to English 'during':

Sie hat **während** der Aufführung geschlafen	*She slept during the performance*
während der Wintermonate (*Bumke*)	*during the winter months*
während des letzten Urlaubs, den sie in Italien verbracht hatten (*Walser*)	*during the last holiday which they had spent in Italy*

Unlike English 'during', *während* is not used with time words like *Tag, Abend, Nacht* or *Jahr* if these simply have a definite article with them. Compare:

am Tag, **am** Abend, **in** der Nacht	*during the day, during the evening, during the night*

However, *während* <u>can</u> be used with these nouns if there is an adjective with them, or if they are used with a determiner other than the definite article:

Während der letzten Nacht ist der Junge zweimal aufgewacht	*During the previous night the boy woke up twice*
während eines einzigen Tages	*during/in the course of a single day*

während indicates a period rather than simply duration, and it can be used in this sense in contexts where 'during' would be unusual or impossible in English:

während der ganzen Nacht	*throughout the night*
Andere Vogelarten wie der Star können **während** mindestens zweier Jahre Neues dazulernen (NZZ)	*Other species of birds like starlings can learn new things over the course of at least two years*
Während dreier Jahre verbrachten sie den Urlaub auf Sylt	*Three years running they spent their holidays on Sylt*

11.5.16 *zu*

zu is used with a number of time words, i.e.:

(a) with the major festivals

zu Weihnachten	zu Pfingsten
zu Ostern	zu Neujahr

NB: In south German, *an* is often used rather than *zu* with these festivals. In colloquial speech, there may be no preposition, e.g. *Sie kommt Weihnachten.*

(b) Both *zu* and *in* are used with *Zeit* and *Stunde*

(i) *zu* is used in contexts denoting one or more specific points or limited periods of time:

zur Zeit der letzten Wahlen	*at the time of the last election*
zu der Zeit, **zu** dieser Zeit	*at that time*
zu der Zeit, als du hier warst	*at the time when you were here*
zu einer anderen Zeit	*at some other time*
zu jeder Zeit	*at all times, at any time*
zu jeder Tageszeit	*at any time of the day*
zu gewissen Zeiten	*at certain times*
zur gewohnten Zeit	*at the usual time*
gerade noch **zur** rechten Zeit	*in the nick of time*
zu gleicher Zeit	*at the same time, simultaneously*
Zu meiner Zeit war das alles anders	*In my time that was all different*
zu dieser Stunde	*at this hour*
zu jeder Stunde	*at any time*
zur selben Stunde	*at the same hour*
zu später Stunde (*lit.*)	*at a late hour*

NB: (also) *zu diesem Zeitpunkt* 'at this point in time'.

(ii) *in* is used to denote a period within or after which something occurs, or in phrases which are felt to denote duration rather than a point or limited period in time:

In all **der** Zeit (*or:* In der ganzen Zeit) haben wir sie nicht gesehen	*In all that time we didn't see her*
In kurzer Zeit war er wieder da	*In a short time he was back again*
In unserer Zeit tut man das nicht mehr	*In our times that is no longer done*
in einer Zeit, in der die Städte wachsen	*at a time when towns are growing*
in einer solchen Zeit wie heute	*at a time like the present*
in früheren Zeiten	*in earlier times*
in künftigen Zeiten	*in times to come*
in der ersten Zeit	*at first*
in ruhigen Stunden	*in peaceful hours*
in elfter Stunde	*at the eleventh hour*

(c) zu is used with *Mal*

e.g.: ***zum** ersten Mal*, ***zum** zehnten Mal*, etc. (see 9.4.3)

11.6 Adverbs of time

Adverbs of time can indicate a **point in time** (e.g. *damals*), **duration** (e.g. *lange*) or **frequency** (e.g. *oft*). A selection of commonly used German time adverbs listed in terms of these categories is given in 11.6.1. Sections 11.6.2–11.6.5 deal with some time adverbs where German and English usage does not correspond.

11.6.1 Commonly used adverbs of time

Further information on some of these adverbs is given in other sections, as indicated. Note that the 'present' in terms of time adverbs can sometimes be a point of reference in the past or future rather than the actual present moment.

(a) indicating a point in time

(i) referring to the present:

augenblicklich	*at the moment*
derzeit	*at present*
gegenwärtig	*at present, currently*
gleichzeitig	*at the same time*
heuer (S. G.)	*this year*
heute (11.6.2)	*today*
heutzutage	*nowadays*
jetzt	*now*
momentan	*at present*
nun (10.25)	*now*
vorerst	*for the moment*
zugleich	*at the same time*
zurzeit	*at present*

(ii) referring to the past (or 'previously'):

damals (11.6.3a)	*then, at that time*
ehedem (*arch.*)	*formerly*
ehemals (*form.*)	*formerly*
einst	*once*
früher	*formerly, previously*
gerade	*just (now)*
gestern (11.6.2)	*yesterday*
jüngst (*elev.*)	*lately*
kürzlich (11.6.5)	*a short time ago*
neuerdings, neulich (11.6.5)	*recently*
seinerzeit	*at the time*
soeben	*just (now)*
unlängst (11.6.5)	*recently*
vordem (lit.)	*in olden times*
vorher (11.6.4)	*before(hand)*
vorhin	*just now*
zuvor (11.6.4)	*before(hand)*

(iii) referring to the future (or 'subsequently'):

alsbald (*lit.*)	*straightaway*
augenblicklich	*at once*
bald	*soon*
danach (11.6.4)	*afterwards*
darauf (11.6.4)	*after that*
daraufhin	*after that*
demnächst	*soon*
einst	*once*
gleich (10.16)	*at once*
hernach (*form.*)	*after(wards)*
morgen (11.6.2)	*tomorrow*
nachher (11.6.4)	*after(wards)*
nächstens (8.4.4)	*shortly*
sofort, sogleich	*at once, immediately*
später	*later*
vorher, zuvor (11.6.4)	*before(hand)*

(b) indicating duration

bisher, bislang	*up to now, hitherto*
fortan (*elev.*)	*henceforth*
indessen (*form.*), inzwischen	*meanwhile*
künftig	*in future*
kurz	*for a short time*
lange	*for a long time*
längst (8.4.4a)	*for a long time*
mittlerweile	*in the meantime*
momentan	*for an instant*
nunmehr (*elev.*)	*from now/then on*
seither, seitdem	*since then*
solange	*meanwhile*
unterdessen	*in the meantime*
vorerst, vorläufig, vorübergehend	*temporarily, for the time being, for the moment*
währenddem (*inf.*), währenddessen	*meanwhile*
zeitweilig	*temporarily*

lang can be suffixed to other time words to indicate duration, e.g. *stundenlang, monatelang, jahrelang* 'for hours, months, years (on end)', see also 11.4.1a.

(c) indicating frequency

abermals	*once more*
bisweilen (*elev.*)	*now and then*
gelegentlich	*occasionally*
häufig	*frequently*
immer	*always*
irgendwann (5.5.11b)	*sometime*
je	*ever*
jederzeit	*at any time*
manchmal	*sometimes*
mehrmals	*repeatedly*
meistens (8.4.4b)	*mostly*

mitunter	*now and then*
nie, niemals, nimmer (*lit.*)	*never*
nochmals	*again*
oft, öfters	*often*
selten	*seldom, rarely*
ständig	*continually*
stets	*always*
unaufhörlich	*incessantly*
wieder, wiederum (*elev.*)	*again*
zeitweise	*at times*
zuweilen	*from time to time*
zwischendurch	*in between times*

11.6.2 *gestern*, *heute* and *morgen*

These are used in conjunction with words indicating periods of the day to give the equivalent of English 'last night', 'this afternoon', etc.:

gestern Morgen	*yesterday morning*
gestern Abend	*last night* (before bedtime)
vorgestern	*the day before yesterday*
heute Nacht	*tonight* (after bedtime), *last night* (after bedtime)
heute Morgen/heute früh	*this morning*
heute Vormittag	*this morning* (after breakfast)
heute Nachmittag	*this afternoon*
heute Abend	*this evening, tonight* (before bedtime)
morgen früh	*tomorrow morning*
morgen Vormittag	*tomorrow morning* (after breakfast)
übermorgen	*the day after tomorrow*

11.6.3 German equivalents of English 'then'

(a) *damals* **refers to past time**

i.e. meaning 'at that time':

Sie war **damals** sehr arm	*She was very poor, then*
damals, vor dem großen Kriege (*Roth*)	*at that time, before the Great War*

(b) *dann* **is used for other meanings of 'then' referring to time**

especially in the sense of 'after that' with a series of actions or events:

Dann ist er weggefahren	*Then he left*
Erst bist du an der Reihe, **dann** ich	*First it's your turn, then mine*
Wenn er dir schreibt, **dann** musst du es deiner Mutter sagen	*If he writes to you, then you'll have to tell your mother*
Und wenn sie kommt, was machst du **dann**?	*And if she comes, what will you do then?*

dann is not used after a preposition, cf.: *bis dahin* 'till then, by then', *seither*, *seitdem* 'since then', *von da an* 'from then on', *vorher*, *zuvor* 'before then' (see also 11.6.4a).

(c) To intensify a question, the German equivalent is *denn*

e.g. *Was ist* **denn** *daran so komisch?* See 10.6.1 for further details.

11.6.4 German equivalents of English 'before' and 'after'

(a) *vorher* and *zuvor* are the commonest equivalents of 'before'

Both can be used with reference to past **or** future time:

Ich war ein Jahr **vorher/zuvor** da gewesen	*I had been there a year before*
Ich muss **vorher/zuvor** noch telefonieren	*I've got to make a phone call before then*
Er hatte uns am Tag **vorher/zuvor** besucht	*He had been to visit us the day before*
einige Zeit **vorher/zuvor**	*some time previously*

Referring to time up to the present moment, *früher* or *zuvor* is used (or, in a negative context, *noch*):

Sie hätten es mir **früher/zuvor** sagen sollen	*You ought to have told me before*
Ich habe sie **nie zuvor/noch nie** gesehen	*I've never seen her before*

(b) *danach* or *nachher* are the usual equivalents for 'after' (or 'later')

darauf is also often used after words expressing a period of time:

Ich habe sie einen Monat **danach/nachher** gesehen	*I saw her a month after/later*
Kurz **danach**/Kurz **nachher**/Kurz **darauf** sah ich sie wieder	*I saw her a short time after/shortly afterwards*
Am Tag **darauf/danach** gingen wir ins Theater	*The day after we went to the theatre*
Das werde ich dir **nachher** erzählen	*I'll tell you that afterwards*

im Nachhinein and *hinterher* are also frequently used for 'afterwards'.

11.6.5 German equivalents for English 'recent(ly)'

German has no single word with the range of meaning of English 'recent(ly)'. The following are the main equivalents, and the choice depends on the precise meaning to be expressed:

vor kurzem/kürzlich	*at a point in time not long ago*
unlängst/jüngst (*both elev., southern*)	
neulich/letztens (*elev.*)	*at a point in time not long ago* (recalled well by speaker and relevant to the present)
neuerdings	*up to and including the present* (sth. which started recently)
letzthin	*recently* (a point in the recent past or during a period up to the present)
in letzter Zeit	*latterly* (over a period of time up to and including the present)
seit kurzem	*not for very long* (continuing to the present)

As the above are all adverbial, they have to be used in paraphrases, etc. to give German equivalents for the English adjective 'recent', e.g.:

auf der **kürzlich stattgefundenen** Konferenz	*at the recent conference*
bei unserer Begegnung **neulich**	*at our recent meeting*
als er **vor kurzem** krank war	*during his recent illness*
eine **erst kürzlich eingeführte** Neuerung	*a (very) recent innovation*
sein **neuestes** Buch	*his most recent book*

Some other equivalents:

bis vor kurzem	*until recently*
Ich habe ihn noch später gesehen als Sie	*I have seen him more recently than you*
Kurt hat sie zuletzt gesehen	*Kurt has seen her most recently / just recently*

The word *rezent* is occasionally found, but at present it appears to be used predominantly in Austria and Switzerland, e.g *im Lichte der rezenten Erfahrungen* (*Presse*) 'in the light of recent experience', and in specialist geological or biological contexts, e.g. *rezente Amphibien* 'recent (i.e. still living) amphibians'.

12 Verbs: conjugation

Chapters 12–18 deal with the forms of VERBS in German and their uses:

- Chapter 12: the forms of verbs (their CONJUGATION)
- Chapter 13: the uses of the INFINITIVE (e.g. *machen, schlafen*) and the PARTICIPLES (e.g. *machend, schlafend; gemacht, geschlafen*)
- Chapter 14: the uses of the TENSES
- Chapter 15: the uses of the PASSIVE
- Chapter 16: the uses of the MOODS (the *imperative* and the *subjunctive*)
- Chapter 17: the MODAL AUXILIARY verbs (e.g. *dürfen, können, müssen*)
- Chapter 18: the VALENCY of verbs (i.e. which complements the need to make up a sentence)

Verbs typically express actions or activities (like *fallen, gehen, schreiben, stehlen*), processes (like *gelingen, sterben, wachsen*) or states (like *bleiben, leben, wohnen*). They constitute the core of the sentence and are usually accompanied by one or more noun phrases, i.e. the subject and the other complements of the verb:

Subject	Verb	Complement(s)
Der Lehrer	**redet**	Unsinn
Ihre Freundin	**unterrichtet**	die deutsche Sprache
Die Mutter	**gibt**	ihrer Tochter die Mappe
Der alte Mann	**wartet**	auf seine Frau

In German, verbs change their form (typically adding endings or changing the vowel) to express various grammatical ideas like TENSE, e.g. present and past; MOOD, e.g. the imperative and the subjunctive; and PERSON and NUMBER, e.g. *du* (second person singular), *wir* (first person plural). These are known as the grammatical categories of the verb. All the different forms of each verb make up its CONJUGATION. This chapter gives details on the conjugation of regular and irregular verbs in German, as follows:

- Basic principles of the **conjugation** of verbs in German (section 12.1)
- The conjugation of the simple **present** and **past** tenses and the **imperative** (section 12.2)
- The conjugation of the compound tenses: **future** and **perfect** (section 12.3)
- The conjugation of the **passive** (section 12.4)
- The conjugation of the **subjunctive** (section 12.5)

The forms of all strong and irregular verbs are given in Table 12.12, at the end of the chapter.

12.1 Verb conjugation

12.1.1 The forms and grammatical categories of German verbs

German verbs are usually given in dictionaries in the form of the INFINITIVE, which ends in *-en* or *-n*, e.g. *kaufen, singen, wandern*. If we take off this *-(e)n*, we obtain the basic core of the verb, which is called the ROOT, e.g. **kauf-, sing-, wander-**. The root carries the basic meaning of the verb (i.e. 'buy', 'sing' 'wander', etc.). By adding endings to this root, or by changing the vowel, we can show different grammatical categories, i.e.:

(a) Indicate the person and number of the subject of the verb

There is a particularly close link between a verb and its subject. This is indicated in German by adding special endings to the verb for each PERSON (i.e. **first**, **second** or **third** person, see Chapter 3) in the **singular** and **plural**.

	First person	Second person	Third person
Singular	**ich** kauf**e**	**du** sing**st**	**er/sie/es** wander**t**
Plural	**wir** kauf**en**	**ihr** sing**t**	**sie** wander**n**

In this way verbs are said to **agree** with the subject. Those forms of verbs which have an ending in AGREEMENT with the subject like this are known as FINITE verbs. For further details on the agreement between subject and verb, see 12.1.4.

(b) Indicate the time of the action, process or event expressed by the verb

We can add endings to the root of the verb (or change the vowel of some verbs) to show time:

Present tense	Past tense
ich kaufe	ich kauf**te**
du singst	du s**a**ngst
er wandert	er wander**te**

The various forms of the verb which express time relationships are known as the TENSES of the verb. German, like English, has two SIMPLE TENSES (i.e. with a single word), the PRESENT tense and the PAST tense, as illustrated above. The formation of these simple tenses is explained in section 12.2.

The other tenses are COMPOUND TENSES, formed by using the AUXILIARY VERBS *haben*, *sein* or *werden*, together with the PAST PARTICIPLE or the INFINITIVE of the verb:

Perfect tense	Pluperfect tense	Future tense
ich **habe** gekauft	er **hatte** gekauft	sie **werden** kaufen
ich **habe** gesungen	er **hatte** gesungen	sie **werden** singen
ich **bin** gewandert	er **war** gewandert	sie **werden** wandern

The **formation** of the compound tenses is explained in section 12.3, and the **use** of the tenses in German is treated in detail in Chapter 14.

(c) Show whether we are dealing with a fact, a possibility or a command

This is shown by the MOOD of the verb. German has three moods:

(i) The INDICATIVE mood states a fact

(ii) The SUBJUNCTIVE mood indicates a possibility or a report

(iii) The IMPERATIVE mood expresses a command

Indicative	Subjunctive	Imperative
sie kauft	sie kaufe	kaufe!
sie singt	sie sänge	singt!
Sie sind gewandert	Sie würden wandern	wandern Sie!

The indicative is the usual mood for statements or questions, and all the information about verb conjugation in sections 12.2–12.4 relates to the indicative mood. The formation of the subjunctive in German is detailed in section 12.5, and its use is dealt with in Chapter 16. The use of the imperative is explained in section 16.2, together with other ways of expressing commands.

(d) Change the relationship between the elements in the sentence

Using a different VOICE of the verb, i.e. the ACTIVE VOICE or the PASSIVE VOICE, allows different elements to appear as the subject of the verb and thus relates the action from a different perspective. German has two forms of the passive voice, formed by using the past participle with the auxiliary verb *werden* (the *werden*-passive), or the auxiliary verb *sein* (the *sein*-passive):

Active	*werden*-passive	*sein*-passive
Sie **schickt** die Mail ab	Die Mail **wird abgeschickt**	Die Mail **ist abgeschickt**
Er **verkaufte** das Buch	Das Buch **wurde verkauft**	Das Buch **war verkauft**

The conjugation of the passives is treated in section 12.4, and their uses are explained in Chapter 15.

(e) Construct the non-finite forms of the verb

Some forms of the verb do not show agreement with the subject of the verb, unlike the finite forms dealt with in (a) above. These are called the NON-FINITE forms of the verb, i.e. the INFINITIVE, the PRESENT PARTICIPLE and the PAST PARTICIPLE.

Infinitive	Present participle	Past participle
kauf**en**	kauf**end**	**ge**kauf**t**
sing**en**	sing**end**	**ge**sung**en**
wander**n**	wander**nd**	**ge**wander**t**

The non-finite parts of the verb can be combined with auxiliary verbs to form the compound tenses and the passive voice (see 12.3–4). They also have some other uses which are treated in Chapter 13.

12.1.2 How a verb is conjugated depends on whether it is WEAK or STRONG

There are two main types of conjugation for verbs in German, which are called WEAK and STRONG. The main difference between these is the way in which the **past tense** is formed:

(a) WEAK verbs form their past tense by adding -*te* to the root:

kauf-en   → kauf-**te**
mach-en   → mach-**te**
wander-n → wander-**te**

(b) STRONG verbs form their past tense by changing the vowel of the root:

flieg-en → fl**o**g
greif-en → gr**i**ff
sing-en   → s**a**ng

Most German verbs are weak; they are the regular verbs. There are far fewer strong verbs, but many of them are very common, so that half the verbs in a typical text will be strong. There is no way of telling from the infinitive of a verb whether it is weak or strong. Foreign learners therefore need to remember which verbs are strong, and learn their three most important forms, the **principal parts**, i.e. the **infinitive**, the **past tense** and the **past participle**. All the other forms can be built up from these three basic forms.

Infinitive	Past tense	Past participle
bleiben	blieb	geblieben
singen	sang	gesungen
fahren	fuhr	gefahren

The principal parts of all strong and irregular verbs are given in Table 12.12.

In practice, the vowel changes in most strong verbs (called *ABLAUT* in German) follow a number of recurrent patterns. It is useful to be aware of these patterns, which are shown in Table 12.1.

TABLE 12.1 Vowel changes in strong verbs

Vowel change	Example
ei – ie – ie	bleiben – blieb – geblieben
ei – i – i	greifen – griff – gegriffen
i – a – u	singen – sang – gesungen
i – a – o	schwimmen – schwamm – geschwommen
ie – o – o	fliegen – flog – geflogen
e – a – o	helfen – half – geholfen
e – a – e	geben – gab – gegeben
e – o – o	fechten – focht – gefochten
a – u – a	fahren – fuhr – gefahren
a – ie – a	fallen – fiel – gefallen

12.1.3 There are a few other irregular verbs

They fall into four groups:

(a) A few irregular weak verbs have vowel changes (and sometimes also consonant changes) in the past tense and the past participle

These changes are in addition to the usual endings of weak verbs:

kennen – kannte – gekannt   rennen – rannte – gerannt
bringen – brachte – gebracht   denken – dachte – gedacht

The principal parts of these irregular weak verbs are given in Table 12.12.

(b) A few irregular strong verbs have consonant changes as well as vowel changes in the past tense and the past participle

gehen – ging – gegangen   leiden – litt – gelitten
stehen – stand – gestanden   ziehen – zog – gezogen

The principal parts of these irregular strong verbs are given in Table 12.12.

(c) The modal auxiliary verbs and *wissen*

The six modal auxiliary verbs *dürfen, können, mögen, müssen, sollen, wollen* and the verb *wissen* 'know' have an irregular present tense with no ending -*t* in the third person singular and, in most cases, a different vowel in the singular and plural. Most of them also change the vowel in the past tense and the past participle:

können – er kann, wir **können** – konnte – gekonnt
müssen – er muss, wir **müssen** – musste – gemusst
wissen – er weiß, wir **wissen** – wusste – gewusst

All the forms of these verbs in the indicative tenses are given in Table 12.4.

(d) The verbs *haben, sein* **and** *werden*

These three verbs are wholly irregular. Aside from their basic meanings, i.e. *haben* 'have', *sein* 'be', *werden* 'become', they are used as AUXILIARY VERBS to form the compound tenses and the passives. The indicative forms of these verbs are given in Table 12.3.

12.1.4 Agreement of subject and finite verb

As explained in 12.1.1a, finite verbs have endings in agreement with the person and number (i..e. singular or plural) of the subject.

	First person	Second person	Third person
Singular	**ich** kauf**e**	**du** sing**st**	**er/sie/es** wander**t**
Plural	**wir** kauf**en**	**ihr** sing**t**	**sie/Sie** wander**n**

NB: The 'polite' form of the second person (with *Sie*) always has the same ending as the third person plural.

In some constructions there can be uncertainty about what the verb agrees with.

(a) If the subject of the verb is a clause, the verb has the third person singular endings

The clause can be a subordinate clause (see Chapter 19) or an infinitive clause (see 13.2.3):

Dass sie nichts tut, **ärgert** mich sehr	*I'm very annoyed that she isn't doing anything*
Sie wiederzusehen **hat** mich gefreut	*I was pleased to see her again*

(b) If the verb *sein* **is followed by a noun in the plural, the verb has a plural ending even if the subject is singular**

Mein Lieblingsobst **sind** Kirschen	*My favourite fruit is cherries*

This is in particular the case with *es, das* and other neuter pronouns (see 3.6.2b, 5.1.1h and 5.3.1a):

Was **sind** das für große Vögel?	*What kind of large birds are they?*
– Es **sind** Störche	*– They are storks*
Sind es deine Handschuhe?	*Are they your gloves?*
Welches **sind** deine Handschuhe?	*Which are your gloves?*

(c) If the subject consists of a series of linked nouns, the verb is usually plural

Helmut und sein Bruder **sind** gekommen	*Helmut and his brother have come*
Vater, Mutter, Tochter **saßen** beim Essen	*Father, mother and daughter were sitting down to a meal*

However, there are some constructions where it is possible to use a singular ending (although this is still less common than the plural ending):

(i) if the subject follows the verb:

Im Osten **winkte** das Völkerschlachtdenkmal, die Türme und die Essen von Leipzig	*In the east, the war memorial, the towers and chimneys of Leipzig beckoned*

(ii) if the parts of the subject are seen as separate or distinct (this is especially the case if the nouns are qualified by *jeder* or *kein*):

Wenig später **wurde** heiße Suppe und Weißbrot ausgeteilt	*A little later hot soup and white bread were distributed*
Ihm **konnte** kein Arzt und kein Apotheker mehr helfen	*No doctor and no chemist could help him now*

(iii) if the linked nouns are felt to form a single whole:

Diese Haltung und Miene **war** ihm eigentümlich (*Th. Mann*)	*This attitude and facial expression were peculiar to him*

(iv) with the conjunctions *sowie* and *sowohl . . . als/wie* (*auch*), see 19.1.4:

Sowohl Manfred als auch seine Frau **war** einverstanden	*Both Manfred and his wife agreed*

(d) If the subject consists of nouns linked by a disjunctive conjunction (= 'or') the verb is usually in the singular

(i) This applies in particular to (*entweder . . .*) *oder* and *nicht* (*nur*) *. . ., sondern* (*auch*)

Entweder Hans oder Karl **wird** mir helfen	*Either Hans or Karl will help me*
Mit dieser Lösung **wäre** nicht nur die Mehrheit der Partei, sondern auch Stöber selbst zufrieden gewesen	*Not only the majority of the party but Stöber too would have been satisfied with this solution*

A plural verb is sometimes used with these, especially if the nearest noun is plural, e.g.: *Entweder Karl oder seine Brüder* **werden** *mir helfen*.

(ii) With *weder . . . noch*, either a singular or a plural verb is possible, but the plural is more frequent:

In Berlin **waren** sich weder Kabinett noch Regierungsfraktionen einig	*In Berlin neither the cabinet nor the governing parties were agreed*

(e) If a coordinated subject includes a pronoun, the verb has the ending which corresponds to the combination

(i) This applies in particular with the conjunction *und* and its synonyms:

Mein Mann und ich (= wir) **trennten** uns im Frühjahr (*Spiegel*)	*My husband and I separated in the spring*
Du und sie (= ihr) **könnt** damit zufrieden sein	*You and she can be satisfied with that*
Sowohl sie als auch er (= sie) **haben** sich darüber gefreut	*Both she and he were pleased about it*

These combinations can sound artificial, especially if the second person plural *ihr* is involved, and they are often avoided by adding the appropriate plural pronoun, e.g.: *Ihr könnt damit zufrieden sein, du und sie.*

(ii) With disjunctive conjunctions, the verb usually agrees with the nearest pronoun, whether this precedes or follows:

Entweder du oder ich **werde** es ihnen sagen
Nicht ich, sondern ihr **sollt** es ihnen sagen
Dann **werden** nicht nur sie, sondern auch ihr es ihnen sagen
Ich, nicht du, **sollst** es ihnen sagen

These, too, can sound unnatural, and can be avoided by repeating the verb or splitting one pronoun off, e.g.:

Entweder du **sagst** es ihnen, oder ich **sage** es ihnen
Entweder du **sollst** es ihr sagen **oder ich**

(f) Usage with expressions of measure or quantity

(i) With singular nouns of indefinite quantity followed by a plural noun, the verb is normally plural:

Ein Dutzend Eier **kosten** 2 Euro	*A dozen eggs cost 2 euros*
Es **waren** eine Menge Leute da	*There were a lot of people there*
Eine Gruppe von Studenten **standen** vor dem Bahnhof	*A group of students were standing in front of the station*
Die Hälfte meiner Gedanken **waren** bei ihr (*Grass*)	*Half my thoughts were with her*

This is the predominant usage in speech and common in writing. Some authorities continue to insist that the use of the singular (e.g. *ein Dutzend Eier* **kostet** *2 Euro* or *Die Hälfte meiner Gedanken war bei ihr*) is still current, but it is in practice unusual.

(ii) With singular measurement words followed by a plural noun, the verb can be either singular or plural:

Ein Kilogramm Kartoffeln **reicht/reichen** aus
Ein Kubikmeter Ziegelsteine **wiegt/wiegen** fast zwei Tonnen

In these contexts the singular is rather more frequent.

(iii) With nouns of measurement used with a numeral or with a plural determiner, the verb is normally in the plural, although in such cases, masculine and neuter nouns of measurement have no plural ending (see 1.2.14):

Mehrere Liter Benzin **waren** verschüttet	*Several litres of petrol were spilled*
Fünf Kilo **kosten** fünfzehn Euro	*Five kilograms cost 15 euros*
Dafür **wurden** mir tausend Euro angeboten	*I was offered a thousand euros for it*
80 Prozent der Bevölkerung **waren** dagegen	*80% of the population was opposed to it*

However, a singular ending is often used in such contexts, especially in spoken German, as the quantity is thought of as a single whole: *Zwanzig Euro* **ist/sind** *zu viel; 80 Prozent der Bevölkerung war/waren dagegen*.

(g) Singular collective nouns are used with a singular verb

This contrasts strongly with English usage, where the plural is the norm (or at least frequent), and English-speaking learners need to pay careful attention to German usage in such contexts:

Die ganze Familie **ist** verreist   *The whole family have/has gone away*
Unsere Mannschaft **hat** wieder verloren   *Our team have/has lost again*

Die Polizei **kommt** gleich	*The police are coming straight away*
Die Regierung **hat** es beschlossen	*The government have/has decided it*

12.2 The simple present and past tenses, the non-finite forms and the imperative

These forms make up the basic conjugation of the German verb. They are all single words, formed by adding different prefixes or suffixes to the verb root, or by changing the form of the root, especially by altering the vowel.

12.2.1 Weak and strong verbs

Weak and strong verbs differ mainly in the way in which they form the PAST TENSE and the PAST PARTICIPLE (their 'principal parts'). Weak verbs have the ending -te in the past tense and -t in the past participle, while strong verbs change the vowel of the root in the past tense and have the ending -en (sometimes with a further change of vowel) in the past participle.

Otherwise, both weak and strong verbs have the same endings marking person and number in the two simple tenses and in the imperative mood, and the same affixes in the non-finite forms. Table 12.2 gives these forms for typical weak and strong verbs. The principal parts of all strong and irregular verbs are given in Table 12.12.

There are a few regular variations to the pattern of endings for strong and weak verbs as given in Table 12.2:

TABLE 12.2 Conjugation of the verb in the simple tenses

	Weak			Strong
Infinitive **Present participle** **Past participle**	kauf**en** kauf**end** **ge**kauf**t**	wart**en** wart**end** **ge**wart**et**	wander**n** wander**nd** **ge**wander**t**	sing**en** sing**end** **ge**sung**en**
Present tense	ich kauf**e** du kauf**st** es kauf**t** wir kauf**en** ihr kauf**t** Sie kauf**en** sie kauf**en**	ich wart**e** du wart**est** es wart**et** wir wart**en** ihr wart**et** Sie wart**en** sie wart**en**	ich wand(e)r**e** du wander**st** es wander**t** wir wander**n** ihr wander**t** Sie wander**n** sie wander**n**	ich sing**e** du sing**st** es sing**t** wir sing**en** ihr sing**t** Sie sing**en** sie sing**en**
Past tense	ich kauf**te** du kauf**test** es kauf**te** wir kauf**ten** ihr kauf**tet** Sie kauf**ten** sie kauf**ten**	ich wart**ete** du wart**etest** es wart**ete** wir wart**eten** ihr wart**etet** Sie wart**eten** sie wart**eten**	ich wander**te** du wander**test** es wander**te** wir wander**ten** ihr wander**tet** Sie wander**ten** sie wander**ten**	ich sang du sang**st** es sang wir sang**en** ihr sang**t** Sie sang**en** sie sang**en**

Imperative
  singular
  plural (familiar)
  plural (polite)
	kauf**(e)**!
	kauf**t**!
	kauf**en Sie**!
		wart**e**!
		wart**et**!
		wart**en Sie**!
			wand(e)r**e**!
			wander**t**!
			wander**n Sie**!
				sing**(e)**!
				sing**t**!
				sing**en Sie**!

(a) Verbs whose root ends in -*d* or -*t*, or in -*m* or -*n* after a consonant

These verbs add -*e*- before the endings -*t*, -*st*, and the -*te* of the past tense of weak verbs: *du arbeitest*, *er arbeitet*, *er arbeitete*, *gearbeitet*, etc. The full forms of *warten* 'wait' are given in Table 12.2 as illustration. Other examples:

finden *find*:   du findest, er findet, ihr findet; ihr fandet
regnen *rain*:   es regnet, es regnete, geregnet
atmen *breathe*: du atmest, sie atmet, ihr atmet, ich atmete, geatmet

These verbs also always have the ending -*e* in the imperative singular: *arbeite!, finde!, warte!*

NB: (i)   -*e*- is not added in the second person singular of the past tense of strong verbs: *du fandst*.
     (ii) Verbs with *l* or *r* before *m* or *n* do not need the linking -*e*-: *sie filmt* 'she is filming', *er lernt* 'he is learning'.
     (iii) Some strong verbs with a vowel change do not add -*t* in the third person singular of the present tense, see (e) and (f) below.

(b) Verbs whose root ends in -*s*, -*ß*, -*x* or -*z*

These drop the -*s*- of the ending -*st* in the second person singular of the present tense:

rasen *race* – du **rast**   grüßen *greet* – du **grüßt**
faxen *fax* – du **faxt**   sitzen *sit* – du **sitzt**

The use of the ending -*est* with these verbs, e.g. *du sitzest*, is archaic, except in Swiss usage. Strong verbs in -*s*, -*ß*, or -*z* add -*e*- before the ending -*st* in the second person singular of the present tense:

lesen *read* – du **lasest**   heißen *be called* – du **hießest**
sitzen *sit* – du **saßest**   wachsen *grow* – du **wuchsest**

Adding -*e*- before the ending -*t* of the second person plural of the past tense is now archaic, and *ihr last* is used rather than *ihr laset*.

(c) Verbs whose root ends in -*el* and -*er*

These verbs have some differences from the general pattern of endings, as illustrated by the forms of *wandern* given in Table 12.2.

They have the ending -*n* in the infinitive, and the first and third person plural of the present tense, e.g. *klingeln* 'ring', *wandern* 'wander'.

In the first person singular of the present tense and the imperative singular, the -*e*- of the root is always dropped with verbs in -*el* and frequently with verbs in -*er* (more commonly in speech than in writing), e.g.: *ich klingle, ich wand(e)re*.

NB: In spoken German forms are heard where the -*e*- of the root is kept, but the -*e* of the ending dropped, e.g. *ich klingel, ich wander*, etc.

(d) Verbs whose root ends in a long vowel or diphthong

These sometimes drop -*e*- in their endings, in particular:

(i) The present tense and infinitive of *tun* 'do': *ich tue, du tust, es tut, wir tun, ihr tut, sie tun*

(ii) The present tense of *knien* [kniːən] 'kneel' is as follows (see also 23.5.1):

ich knie [kniːə], du kniest [kniːst], er kniet [kniːt],
wir knien [kniːən], ihr kniet [kniːt], sie knien [kniːən].

The past tense of the strong verb *schreien* 'shout, scream' is similar, i.e.: *ich/er schrie, wir/sie schrien* [ʃriːən]. The past participle is *geschrieen* or *geschrien*.

(iii) Other such verbs generally lose the *-e-* of the ending *-en* in spoken German, and these forms are occasionally found in writing, e.g.: *schaun, gehn, gesehn* (for *schauen, gehen, gesehen*).

(e) Most strong verbs with *-e-* in the root change this to *-i-* or *-ie-* in the second and third person singular present, and in the imperative singular

In general, verbs in **short *-e-*** [ɛ] change this to *-i-*, whilst those in **long *-e-*** [eː] usually change this to *-ie-*:

essen *eat*:	du isst, es isst, iss!
helfen *help*:	du hilfst, es hilft, hilf!
lesen *read*:	du liest, es liest, lies!
stehlen *steal*:	du stiehlst, es stiehlt, stiehl!

There are some exceptions and further irregularities with these verbs, and full details are given for each verb in Table 12.12. However, the following general points may be noted:

(i) The following strong verbs in *-e-* do not change the vowel to *-i-* or *-ie-*:

bewegen *induce*	melken *milk*
gehen *go*	scheren *shear*
genesen *recover*	stehen *stand*
heben *lift*	weben *weave*

(ii) *erlöschen* 'go out' (of lights, fires) changes *-ö-* to *-i-*: *es erlischt*

(iii) Three strong verbs which have long *-e-* in their root change this to short *-i-* rather than long *-ie-* :

geben *give*:	du gibst, es gibt, gib!
nehmen *take*:	du nimmst, es nimmt, nimm!
treten *step*:	du trittst, es tritt, tritt!

(iv) Verbs with this vowel change whose root ends in *-d* or *-t* do not add *-et* in the third person singular of the present tense (see (a) above):

gelten *be worth*:	es gilt
treten *step*:	es tritt

(v) In colloquial speech, imperative forms without the vowel change are commonly heard: *ess!, geb!, nehm!* These are considered incorrect.

(f) Most strong verbs with *-a-* or *-au-* in their root have *Umlaut* in the second and third person singular of the present

fahren *go*:	du fährst, es fährt
lassen *let*:	du lässt, es lässt
wachsen *grow*:	du wächst, es wächst
laufen *run*:	du läufst, es läuft

There are some exceptions and further irregularities with these verbs:

(i) *stoßen* 'push' has *Umlaut* of *-o-*: *du stößt, es stößt*

(ii) *schaffen* 'create' and *saugen* 'suck' do not have *Umlaut*: *du schaffst, saugst; er schafft, saugt.*

(iii) Verbs whose root ends in *-d* or *-t* and which have *Umlaut* in these forms do not add *-et* in the third person singular (see (a) above):

halten *hold*:   es hä**lt**
laden *load*:   es lä**dt**
raten *advise*:   es rä**t**

Full details are given for each verb in Table 12.12.

NB: In spoken South German, *Umlaut* is often lacking with these verbs, and one hears, for example, *sie schlaft* instead of *sie schläft*. This is a non-standard regionalism.

(g) The ending *-e* of the imperative singular

(i) With most weak or strong verbs, this ending is optional: *Komm(e) in den Garten! Setz(e) dich! Stör(e) mich nicht!*. It is usually dropped in speech, but quite commonly used in written German.

(ii) The verbs with a vowel change of *-e-* to *-i-* or *-ie-* in the imperative (see (e) above) never have the ending: *Lies! Gib! Nimm!*

(iii) Verbs with roots ending in *-ig*, and *-m* or *-n* after another consonant (see (a) above) keep the ending *-e*: *Entschuldige bitte! Segne mich!*

(iv) Verbs in *-el* (see (c) above) drop the *-e-* of the root, but keep the ending: *Klinge laut!*.

(h) Some verbs lack the prefix *ge-* in the past participle

All these are verbs which are not stressed on the first syllable, i.e.:

(i) Verbs with inseparable prefixes (see 22.4):

bedeuten *mean*:	bedeutet	zerbrechen *smash*:	zerbrochen
erfinden *invent*:	erfunden	überlegen *consider*:	überlegt
gelingen *succeed*:	gelungen	unterdrücken *suppress*:	unterdrückt
misslingen *fail*:	misslungen	anvertrauen *entrust*:	anvertraut

(ii) Verbs in *-ieren*:

gratulieren *congratulate*: gratuliert   studieren *study*:   studiert

(iii) A few other verbs which are not stressed on the first syllable:

frohlocken *rejoice*:	frohlockt	posaunen *bellow*:	posaunt
interviewen *interview*:	interviewt	recykeln *recycle*:	recykelt
liebkosen *caress:*	liebkost	schmarotzen *sponge*:	schmarotzt
offenbaren *reveal*:	offenbart	stibitzen *nick, pinch*:	stibitzt
prophezeien *prophesy*	prophezeit		

NB: Some of these verbs can, alternatively, be pronounced with the first syllable stressed, and in this case the past participle has the prefix *ge-*: *'frohlocken – ge'frohlockt; 'liebkosen – ge'liebkost;'offenbaren – ge'offenbart*.

(i) Separable verbs

Separable verbs are made by adding a PREFIX to a simple verb to form a new verb with a distinctive meaning (as explained in 22.5 and 22.6). These verbs are called SEPARABLE VERBS because this prefix is separated from the main verb in certain contexts.

Separable verbs have exactly the same endings and forms, whether weak or strong, as the simple verbs from which they are derived. Thus, *ankommen* 'arrive' conjugates like *kommen*, *zumachen* 'shut' like *machen*.

(i) In main clauses, the prefix is separated from the verb and is placed at the end of the clause (see also 21.1.2):

ankommen *arrive*:	Ich komme morgen um zwei Uhr **an**. Ich kam gestern **an**
ausgehen *go out*:	Sie geht heute Abend **aus**.
nachahmen *imitate*:	Sie ahmten seine Bewegungen **nach**
totschlagen *kill*:	Er schlug das Tier mit einer Keule **tot**

(ii) The prefix remains joined to the verb in all the non-finite forms. The *ge-* of the past participle is inserted between the prefix and the verb:

ankommen – ankommend – an**ge**kommen
ausgehen – ausgehend – aus**ge**gangen
ausmachen – ausmachend – aus**ge**macht
vorstellen – vorstellend – vor**ge**stellt

If the simple verb has no *ge-* in the past participle (see (h) above), it is also lacking in all corresponding separable verbs:

einstudieren *rehearse*:	einstudiert
anerkennen *recognise*:	anerkannt

The *zu* of the expanded infinitive is also added between the prefix and the verb (see 13.1.4b):

ankommen – an**zu**kommen
ausgehen – aus**zu**gehen
anerkennen – an**zu**erkennen

(iii) In subordinate clauses, the prefix rejoins the finite verb in final position:

Ich weiß, dass sie heute Abend **ausgeht**
Er sah, wie sie seine Bewegungen **nachahmten**

(j) Usage in colloquial speech differs in some cases from that in writing

Although widespread in the spoken language, these forms are considered to be non-standard colloquialisms and they are rarely used in writing.

(i) Final *-e* tends to be dropped in all endings, e.g.: *ich kauf, ich fall, ich/es sucht* for *ich kaufe, ich falle, ich/es suchte*. If this occurs in written German, especially to give the impression of colloquial usage, or in dialogue, the missing ending is often indicated by using an apostrophe, e.g. *ich kauf', ich hätt'*.

(ii) The ending *-en* tends to be reduced to *-n*, e.g. *wir kaufn, sie falln, wir kauftn, sie botn, getretn* for standard German *wir kaufen, sie fallen, wir kauften, sie boten, getreten*.

(iii) *brauchen* is sometimes heard without the ending *-t* in the third person singular of the present tense, e.g. *er, sie brauch*.

(k) Recent loan words from English are typically fully integrated and have the regular endings of weak verbs

Thus *surfen* 'surf (the web)', *mailen* 'e-mail', *simsen* 'text', *bloggen* 'blog' or *googeln* 'google' have forms like *ich surfe, Hast du ihr gemailt, sie simst zu viel, wir bloggen täglich, Was wird in Deutschland am häufigsten gegoogelt?* etc.

12.2.2 **Irregular verbs**

The verbs *sein* 'be', *haben* 'have', *werden* 'become', the six modal auxiliary verbs *dürfen, können, mögen, müssen, sollen, wollen* and the verb *wissen* 'know' are wholly irregular in their conjugation. The conjugation of *sein, haben* and *werden* is given in full in Table 12.3 and that of the modal auxiliaries and *wissen* in Table 12.4. Some specific points about the forms of these verbs should be noted:

TABLE 12.3 Conjugation of *sein, haben, werden*

Infinitive	*sein*		*haben*		*werden*	
Present participle	seiend		habend		werdend	
Past participle	gewesen		gehabt		geworden	
Present tense	ich	bin	ich	habe	ich	werde
	du	bist	du	hast	du	wirst
	es	ist	es	hat	es	wird
	wir	sind	wir	haben	wir	werden
	ihr	seid	ihr	habt	ihr	werdet
	Sie	sind	Sie	haben	Sie	werden
	sie	sind	sie	haben	sie	werden
Past tense	ich	war	ich	hatte	ich	wurde
	du	warst	du	hattest	du	wurdest
	es	war	es	hatte	es	wurde
	wir	waren	wir	hatten	wir	wurden
	ihr	wart	ihr	hattet	ihr	wurdet
	Sie	waren	Sie	hatten	Sie	wurden
	sie	waren	sie	hatten	sie	wurden
Imperative						
singular	sei!		hab!		werde!	
plural (familiar)	seid!		habt!		werdet!	
plural (polite)	seien Sie!		haben Sie!		werden Sie!	

(a) Reduced forms of *sein* and *haben* are usual in colloquial speech

e.g.: *es is* for *es ist*; *wir/sie sin, ham* for *wir/sie sind, haben*; *simmer, hammer* for *sind wir, haben wir*.

(b) Special forms of *werden*

(i) The old form *ich/es ward* was sometimes used for *ich/es wurde* in elevated styles into the twentieth century, and it is still occasionally found in deliberately archaicising (especially biblical) contexts.

(ii) The past participle of *werden* has no *ge-* when used as an auxiliary to form the passive, see 12.4.2a, e.g.: *Er ist gelobt **worden**.* Compare its use as a full verb meaning 'become': *Er ist Schauspieler **geworden**.*

(c) The past participle of the modal auxiliaries is rarely used

When these verbs are used in the perfect tenses in conjunction with a main verb, the infinitive is used rather than the past participle (see 13.3.2):

Ich habe es machen **müssen**	Sie hatte es sehen **können**
Wir haben ihn lehren **sollen**	Sie hatten es uns sagen **wollen**

(d) The present participle and imperative of the modal auxiliaries are not used

Those of *wissen* are regular, i.e. present participle: *wissend.* Imperative: *wisse! wisst! wissen Sie!*

TABLE 12.4 Conjugation of the modal auxiliary verbs and *wissen*

Infinitive		*dürfen*	*können*	*mögen*	*müssen*	*sollen*	*wollen*	*wissen*
Present tense	ich	darf	kann	mag	muss	soll	will	weiß
	du	darfst	kannst	magst	musst	sollst	willst	weißt
	es	darf	kann	mag	muss	soll	will	weiß
	wir	dürfen	können	mögen	müssen	sollen	wollen	wissen
	ihr	dürft	könnt	mögt	müsst	sollt	wollt	wisst
	Sie	dürfen	können	mögen	müssen	sollen	wollen	wissen
	sie	dürfen	können	mögen	müssen	sollen	wollen	wissen
Past tense	ich	durfte	konnte	mochte	musste	sollte	wollte	wusste
	du	durftest	konntest	mochtest	musstest	solltest	wolltest	wusstest
	es	durfte	konnte	mochte	musste	sollte	wollte	wusste
	wir	durften	konnten	mochten	mussten	sollten	wollten	wussten
	ihr	durftet	konntet	mochtet	musstet	solltet	wolltet	wusstet
	Sie	durften	konnten	mochten	mussten	sollten	wollten	wussten
	sie	durften	konnten	mochten	mussten	sollten	wollten	wussten
Past part.		gedurft	gekonnt	gemocht	gemusst	gesollt	gewollt	gewusst

12.3 The compound tenses

12.3.1 The conjugation of the verb in the compound tenses

(a) The perfect and future are formed with the auxiliary verbs *sein*, *haben* and *werden*

The perfect tenses are formed with the past participle and *haben* or *sein*, and the future tense is constructed using *werden* and the infinitive, e.g.:

perfect:	ich habe gekauft *I have bought*	ich bin gekommen *I have come*
pluperfect:	ich hatte gekauft *I had bought*	ich war gekommen *I had come*
future:	ich werde kaufen *I shall/will buy*	ich werde kommen *I shall/will come*
future perfect:	ich werde gekauft haben *I shall/will have bought*	ich werde gekommen sein *I shall/will have come*

Full forms of all these tenses are given in Table 12.5 for the weak verb *machen* 'make' and the strong verb *singen* 'sing', which form their perfect tenses with the auxiliary *haben*, and for the strong verb *bleiben* 'remain' which forms its perfect tenses with the auxiliary *sein* (see 12.3.2). The uses of the tenses are explained in detail in Chapter 14.

(b) The non-finite parts of compound tenses are placed at the end of the clause in main clauses

i.e. they constitute the final part of the 'verbal bracket', see 21.1.2, e.g. *Ich **habe** sie gestern in der Stadt **gesehen**.* In subordinate clauses the auxiliary usually follows the non-finite part at the end of the clause, see 21.1.3, e.g. *Sie wissen, dass ich sie gestern in der Stadt **gesehen habe**.*

TABLE 12.5 Compound tenses of strong and weak verbs

		with *haben*				with *sein*	
Perfect	ich	habe	gemacht	habe	gesungen	bin	geblieben
	du	hast	gemacht	hast	gesungen	bist	geblieben
	es	hat	gemacht	hat	gesungen	ist	geblieben
	wir	haben	gemacht	haben	gesungen	sind	geblieben
	ihr	habt	gemacht	habt	gesungen	seid	geblieben
	Sie	haben	gemacht	haben	gesungen	sind	geblieben
	sie	haben	gemacht	haben	gesungen	sind	geblieben

		with *haben*				with *sein*	
Pluperfect	ich	hatte	gemacht	hatte	gesungen	war	geblieben
	du	hattest	gemacht	hattest	gesungen	warst	geblieben
	es	hatte	gemacht	hatte	gesungen	war	geblieben
	wir	hatten	gemacht	hatten	gesungen	waren	geblieben
	ihr	hattet	gemacht	hattet	gesungen	wart	geblieben
	Sie	hatten	gemacht	hatten	gesungen	waren	geblieben
	sie	hatten	gemacht	hatten	gesungen	waren	geblieben
Future	ich	werde	machen	werde	singen	werde	bleiben
	du	wirst	machen	wirst	singen	wirst	bleiben
	es	wird	macheån	wird	singen	wird	bleiben
	wir	werden	machen	werden	singen	werden	bleiben
	ihr	werdet	machen	werdet	singen	werdet	bleiben
	Sie	werden	machen	werden	singen	werden	bleiben
	sie	werden	machen	werden	singen	werden	bleiben
Future perfect	ich	werde	gemacht haben	werde	gesungen haben	werde	geblieben sein
	du	wirst	gemacht haben	wirst	gesungen haben	wirst	geblieben sein
	es	wird	gemacht haben	wird	gesungen haben	wird	geblieben sein
	wir	werden	gemacht haben	werden	gesungen haben	werden	geblieben sein
	ihr	werdet	gemacht haben	werdet	gesungen haben	werdet	geblieben sein
	Sie	werden	gemacht haben	werden	gesungen haben	werden	geblieben sein
	sie	werden	gemacht haben	werden	gesungen haben	werden	geblieben sein

12.3.2 *haben* or *sein* in the perfect?

Whether the perfect tenses are constructed with *haben* or *sein* depends on the meaning of the verb.

(a) The following groups of verbs form their perfect with *sein*

All these verbs are INTRANSITIVE, i.e. they do not have a direct object in the accusative case (see 18.3):

(i) Intransitive verbs of motion:

Ich **bin** in die Stadt gegangen
Wir **sind** aus dem Haus entkommen
Um die Zeit werden wir schon
    angekommen **sein**

Sie **war** zum Boden gefallen
Ihr **wart** auf die Mauer geklettert

NB: Some verbs of motion take *sein* **or** *haben* in different contexts, see (c) below.

(ii) Intransitive verbs expressing a change of state. This group includes a large number of verbs which point to the beginning or end of a process, including many with the prefixes *er-* and *ver-* (see 22.4):

Sie **ist** schon eingeschlafen
Die Bombe **ist** um zwei Uhr explodiert
Das Licht **ist** ausgegangen
Mein Buch **ist** verschwunden
Die Glocke **ist** erklungen

Die Blumen **sind** verwelkt
Der Reifen **war** geplatzt
Der Schnee **war** schon geschmolzen
Sie werden gleich danach ertrunken **sein**

NB: In colloquial North German, *anfangen* and *beginnen* form their perfect with *sein*. One thus hears *ich bin angefangen, begonnen* for standard German *ich habe angefangen, begonnen*.

(iii) Most verbs meaning 'happen', 'succeed', 'fail', i.e.:

begegnen *meet* (by chance)	misslingen *fail*
fehlschlagen *fail*	passieren *happen*
gelingen *succeed*	vorgehen *happen*
geschehen *happen*	vorkommen *occur*
glücken *succeed*	zustoßen *happen*
missglücken *fail*	

Ich **bin** ihr gestern begegnet

Der Plan **ist** fehlgeschlagen

Es **war** mir gelungen, ihn zu überzeugen

Das **war** schon einmal vorgekommen

Was wird mit ihr passiert **sein**?

NB: The colloquial verb *klappen* 'succeed' takes *haben*, e.g. *Hat's mit den Karten geklappt?* 'Did you manage to get the tickets?'

(iv) The verbs *bleiben* and *sein*:

Sie **ist** früher Lehrerin gewesen

War er mal Diplomat gewesen?

Wir **sind** in Dessau geblieben

Sie wird dort geblieben **sein**

(b) All other verbs form their perfect tenses with *haben*

This includes the majority of German verbs. The most important fall into the following groups:

(i) Transitive verbs, i.e. those taking an accusative object (see 18.3):

Ich **habe** sie gesehen

Er **hat** die Wohnung geputzt

Der Hund **hatte** die Mülltonne umgeworfen

Sie **hatte** mich geschlagen

Ich werde den Brief bis morgen früh geschrieben **haben**

A few compounds of *gehen* and *werden* are exceptions to this rule, e.g.:

Er ist die Strecke abgegangen	*He paced the distance*
Sie ist die Arbeit mit dem Schüler durchgegangen	*She went through the work with the pupil*
Er ist die Wette eingegangen	*He made the bet*
Ich bin ihn endlich losgeworden	*I have finally got rid of him*

(ii) Reflexive verbs:

Sie **hat** sich sehr gefreut

Ich **habe** mich schon erholt

Ich **hatte** mich aus dem Zimmer gestohlen

Ich **hatte** mir alles eingebildet

Sie wird sich müde gelaufen **haben**

When verbs which normally form their perfect with *sein* are used with a reflexive pronoun in the dative (= 'each other', see 3.2.7), the perfect is still constructed with *sein*, e.g.:

Sie sind sich ausgewichen	*They avoided each other*
Wir sind uns in der Stadt begegnet	*We met (each other) in town*

(iii) Intransitive verbs which do not express motion or a change of state, (see (a) above). Many of these verbs denote a continuous action or state, e.g.:

Ich **habe** gestern lange gearbeitet

Hast du in der Nacht gut geschlafen?

Sie **hatte** dabei gepfiffen

Sie **hatten** in Münster studiert

Dort **hat** jemand auf der Bank gesessen | Sie wird dort lange gewartet **haben**
Oben **hat** vorhin das Licht gebrannt | Gerhard wird ihr gesimst **haben**

The verbs *liegen*, *sitzen* and *stehen* form their perfect tenses with *haben* in standard German in Germany, e.g. *ich* **habe** *gelegen, gesessen, gestanden*. However, in South German, *sein* is commonly used (i.e. *ich* **bin** *gelegen*, etc.) and this usage is accepted as standard in Austria and Switzerland.

(iv) Most impersonal verbs:

Es **hat** geregnet, geschneit, gehagelt | Es **hatte** nach Benzin gerochen
An der Tür **hat** es geklopft | Da **hatte** es einen Krach gegeben

Impersonal expressions with verbs which form their perfect tenses with *sein* form an exception to this rule, e.g.: *Es* **ist** *mir kalt geworden; Wie* **war** *es Ihnen in Berlin gegangen?*

(v) The modal auxiliaries:

Ich **habe** es hinnehmen müssen | Wir **haben** es nicht gekonnt
Sie **hat** ihn besuchen wollen | Sie **hat** ihn nie gemocht

(c) The use of *haben* and *sein* with the same verb

(i) The choice of *haben* or *sein* depends on meaning, i.e. it is <u>not</u> an automatic feature of a particular verb. Several verbs which have more than one meaning can be used with *haben* or *sein* in the perfect if they have one meaning of the kind which requires *haben* for the perfect tense, and another which requires *sein*, as explained in (a) and (b) above. This variation between *haben* and *sein* is most common with verbs which can be used transitively or intransitively. Thus, *fahren*, used as an intransitive verb of motion (= 'go'), forms its perfect with *sein*:

Sie **ist** nach Stuttgart gefahren | Wir **sind** zu schnell gefahren

But when it is used transitively (= 'drive'), it takes *haben*:

Sie **hat** einen neuen Porsche gefahren | Ich **habe** ihn nach Hause gefahren

Some further examples with other verbs:

Ich **habe** eine Mail bekommen | *I have received an e-mail*
Das Essen **ist** mir gut bekommen | *The meal agreed with me*
Er **hat** das Rohr gebrochen | *He has broken the pipe*
Das Rohr **ist** gebrochen | *The pipe has broken*
Sie **hat** auf Zahlung gedrungen | *She has pressed for payment*
Wasser **ist** in das Haus gedrungen | *Water has penetrated into the house*
Er **hat** ihr gefolgt | *He has obeyed her*
Er **ist** ihr gefolgt | *He has followed her*
Es **hat** in der Nacht gefroren | *There was a frost in the night*
Der See **ist** gefroren | *The lake has frozen*
Da **haben** Sie sich geirrt | *You have made a mistake*
Er **ist** durch die Straßen geirrt | *He roamed through the streets*
Sie **hat** ihn zur Seite gestoßen | *She pushed him to one side*
Ich **bin** an den Schrank gestoßen | *I bumped into the cupboard*
Du **hast** mir den Spaß verdorben | *You have spoilt my fun*
Das Fleisch **ist** verdorben | *The meat has gone bad*
Sie **hat** viel Benzin verfahren | *She has used a lot of petrol/gas*
Wir **sind** nach diesem Grundsatz verfahren | *We acted according to this principle*

Sie **hat** in Künstlerkreisen verkehrt	*She moved in artistic circles*
Die Züge **sind** heute nicht verkehrt	*The trains didn't run today*
Ich **habe** die Vase zerbrochen	*I have broken the vase*
Die Vase **ist** zerbrochen	*The vase has broken*

(ii) A few verbs of motion form their perfect with *sein* if they express movement from one place to another, but *haben* if they just refer to the activity as such, without any idea of getting somewhere, e.g.:

Ich **habe** als junger Mann viel getanzt	*I danced a lot when I was a young man*
Er **ist** aus dem Zimmer getanzt	*He danced out of the room*
Sie **hat** den ganzen Morgen gesegelt	*She's been sailing the whole morning*
Sie **ist** über den See gesegelt	*She sailed across the lake*

This usage is more frequent in North Germany, and it is restricted to a few verbs, i.e. *flattern*, 'flutter', *paddeln* 'paddle', *reiten* 'ride', *rudern* 'row', *schwimmen* 'swim', *segeln* 'sail', *tanzen* 'dance', *treten* 'step'.

12.4 **The passive**

12.4.1 **There are two passives in German, the *werden*-passive and the *sein*-passive**

They are formed by combining the auxiliary verbs *werden* or *sein* with the past participle:

werden-passive:	Die Stadt **wird zerstört**	Ich **wurde verletzt**
sein-passive:	Die Stadt **ist zerstört**	Ich **war verletzt**

The *werden*-passive is often called the *Vorgangspassiv* in German, and the *sein*-passive the *Zustandspassiv*. The uses of both passives are dealt with in Chapter 15. The forms of the *werden*-passive are given in Table 12.6, and those of the *sein*-passive which are in current use are given in Table 12.7.

TABLE 12.6 The forms of the *werden*-passive

Present			Perfect				Future			
ich	werde	gelobt	ich	bin	gelobt	worden	ich	werde	gelobt	werden
du	wirst	gelobt	du	bist	gelobt	worden	du	wirst	gelobt	werden
es	wird	gelobt	es	ist	gelobt	worden	es	wird	gelobt	werden
wir	werden	gelobt	wir	sind	gelobt	worden	wir	werden	gelobt	werden
ihr	werdet	gelobt	ihr	seid	gelobt	worden	ihr	werdet	gelobt	werden
Sie	werden	gelobt	Sie	sind	gelobt	worden	Sie	werden	gelobt	werden
sie	werden	gelobt	sie	sind	gelobt	worden	sie	werden	gelobt	werden
Past			**Pluperfect**				**Future perfect**			
ich	wurde	gelobt	ich	war	gelobt	worden	ich	werde	gelobt	worden	sein
du	wurdest	gelobt	du	warst	gelobt	worden	du	wirst	gelobt	worden	sein
es	wurde	gelobt	es	war	gelobt	worden	er	wird	gelobt	worden	sein
wir	wurden	gelobt	wir	waren	gelobt	worden	wir	werden	gelobt	worden	sein
ihr	wurdet	gelobt	ihr	wart	gelobt	worden	ihr	werdet	gelobt	worden	sein
Sie	wurden	gelobt	Sie	waren	gelobt	worden	Sie	werden	gelobt	worden	sein
sie	wurden	gelobt	sie	waren	gelobt	worden	sie	werden	gelobt	worden	sein

TABLE 12.7 Current forms of the *sein*-passive

Present			Past			Imperative
ich	bin	verletzt	ich	war	verletzt	
du	bist	verletzt	du	warst	verletzt	Sei gegrüßt!
es	ist	verletzt	es	war	verletzt	
wir	sind	verletzt	wir	waren	verletzt	
ihr	seid	verletzt	ihr	wart	verletzt	Seid gegrüßt!
Sie	sind	verletzt	Sie	waren	verletzt	Seien Sie gegrüßt!
sie	sind	verletzt	sie	waren	verletzt	

12.4.2 The formation of the passive

(a) the *werden*-passive

(i) In the perfect tenses of the passive the past participle of *werden* has no prefix *ge-*, i.e. *worden*: *Das Haus ist 1845 gebaut **worden***.

(ii) Imperative forms of the *werden*-passive, e.g. *werde gelobt!* are rare. If a passive imperative is needed, the form with *sein* is used, see (b) below.

(b) the *sein*-passive

In practice, only the present and past tenses of the *sein*-passive, and the imperative, are at all frequently used. Other tenses, e.g. the perfect (*ich bin verletzt gewesen*, etc.) or the future (*ich werde verletzt sein*, etc.) are only used occasionally.

(c) The participle is placed at the end of the clause in main clauses

(as in other compound verb forms, see 21.1.2):

Das Haus wurde 1845 **gebaut**   Das Kind war schwer **verletzt**

In subordinate clauses the participle comes at the end, before the auxiliary, see 21.1.3:

Ich weiß, dass das Haus voriges Jahr **gebaut** wurde

12.5 The subjunctive

The SUBJUNCTIVE mood presents what the speaker is saying as **not necessarily true**, whereas the INDICATIVE presents what is said as a **fact**. Most modern German grammars and textbooks divide the forms of the German subjunctive into two major groups, which they refer to as KONJUNKTIV *I* and KONJUNKTIV *II*, since these terms make it simpler to explain their use. There are no English equivalents for them, and the German ones are used here. Table 12.8 shows how these groupings are related to the traditional 'tenses' of the subjunctive:

TABLE 12.8 The forms of *Konjunktiv I* and *Konjunktiv II*

Konjunktiv I	present subjunctive	es gebe
	perfect subjunctive	es habe gegeben
	future subjunctive	es werde geben
Konjunktiv II	past subjunctive	es gäbe
	pluperfect subjunctive	es hätte gegeben
	conditional	es würde geben

The subjunctive has the same compound tenses and passive forms as the indicative, formed in the same way, with the auxiliaries *haben*, *sein* and *werden*. In this section we give information about the various forms of the subjunctive. Their uses are treated in detail in Chapter 16.

12.5.1 *Konjunktiv I*

(a) The simple form of *Konjunktiv I* is regular for all verbs except *sein*

For all verbs except *sein* the endings are added to the root of the verb without any other changes or irregularities, as illustrated for a range of typical regular and irregular verbs in Table 12.9.

TABLE 12.9 The simple forms of *Konjunktiv I* and *Konjunktiv II*

		sein	*haben*	*können*	*werden*	*geben*	*machen*
Konjunktiv I	ich	sei	habe	könne	werde	gebe	mache
(present subjunctive)	du	sei(e)st	habest	könnest	werdest	gebest	machest
	es	sei	habe	könne	werde	gebe	mache
	wir	seien	haben	können	werden	geben	machen
	ihr	seiet	habet	könnet	werdet	gebet	machet
	Sie	seien	haben	können	werden	geben	machen
	sie	seien	haben	können	werden	geben	machen
Konjunktiv II	ich	wäre	hätte	könnte	würde	gäbe	machte
(past subjunctive)	du	wärest	hättest	könntest	würdest	gäbest	machtest
	es	wäre	hätte	könnte	würde	gäbe	machte
	wir	wären	hätten	könnten	würden	gäbe	machten
	ihr	wäret	hättet	könntet	würdet	gäbet	machtet
	Sie	wären	hätten	könnten	würden	gäben	machten
	sie	wären	hätten	könnten	würden	gäben	machten

Points to note about the simple form of *Konjunktiv I*:

(i) The second person singular and plural forms in *-est* and *-et* (e.g. *du sagest*, *ihr saget*), are felt to be artificial and are rarely used.

(ii) For most verbs except *sein*, the only difference in practice between the simple form of *Konjunktiv I* and the present indicative is in the third person singular, which has the ending *-e* as opposed to the ending *-t* of the indicative.

(iii) There are no vowel changes in the second or third person singular of any strong or irregular verbs. Compare subjunctive: *es gebe*, *es fahre*, with indicative: *es gibt*, *es fährt*.

(iv) Verbs with a root in *-el* (see 12.2.1c) usually drop the *-e-* of the root before the ending *-e*, e.g. *es segle*, *es lächle*, etc.

(b) Compound forms of *Konjunktiv I*

Compound perfect and future tenses of *Konjunktiv I*, and the *werden-* and *sein* passive, are constructed in exactly the same way as in the indicative, using subjunctive forms of the appropriate auxiliary verb, i.e. *haben*, *sein* or *werden*, together with the past participle or the infinitive. Examples are given in the third person singular, which is in practice the only form used.

perfect subjunctive with *haben*:	es **habe gekauft**
perfect subjunctive with *sein*:	es **sei gekommen**
future subjunctive:	es **werde kaufen**
werden-passive (present):	es **werde gekauft**
werden-passive (perfect):	es **sei gekauft worden**
werden-passive (future):	es **werde gekauft werden**
sein-passive:	es **sei gekauft**

12.5.2 *Konjunktiv II*

(a) There are three important and frequently used forms of *Konjunktiv II*

(i) The simple form, in one word, traditionally called the PAST SUBJUNCTIVE. Table 12.9 gives typical examples of its forms and endings with some common verbs. It is formed from the past indicative, as explained in paragraph (b) below and illustrated in Table 12.11.

(ii) The pluperfect subjunctive, formed from the past subjunctive of the auxiliary verbs *haben* or *sein* and the past participle, as illustrated in Table 12.10.

(iii) The conditional, formed from the past subjunctive of the auxiliary verb *werden* and the infinitive, as illustrated in Table 12.10.

TABLE 12.10 The pluperfect subjunctive and conditional forms of *Konjunktiv II*

	Pluperfect subjunctive (with *haben*)		Pluperfect subjunctive (with *sein*)		Conditional	
ich	hätte	gekauft	wäre	geblieben	würde	kaufen
du	hättest	gekauft	wärest	geblieben	würdest	kaufen
es	hätte	gekauft	wäre	geblieben	würde	kaufen
wir	hätten	gekauft	wären	geblieben	würden	kaufen
ihr	hättet	gekauft	wäret	geblieben	würdet	kaufen
Sie	hätten	gekauft	wären	geblieben	würden	kaufen
sie	hätten	gekauft	wären	geblieben	würden	kaufen

(b) The simple form of *Konjunktiv II* **is formed from the past tense of the indicative**

This is done in the following ways, as illustrated in Table 12.11. The forms are listed for each individual strong or irregular verb in Table 12.12.

(i) For regular weak verbs it is identical with the past indicative.

(ii) For regular strong verbs, it is formed by taking the form of the past tense, umlauting the vowel if possible, and adding -*e* to the endings if possible (although this -*e* of these endings is often dropped in speech).

(iii) A few strong verbs have an irregular *Konjunktiv II* form with a different vowel from that of the past tense. Only those given in Table 12.11 are at all commonly used nowadays.

(iv) Some other irregular verbs also have *Umlaut* in the simple *Konjunktiv II*. The most frequent are given in Table 12.11.

NB: In colloquial speech, *brauchen* 'need' also often has a *Konjunktiv II* form with *Umlaut*, e.g. *ich* **bräuchte**. This usage is not universally accepted as standard, but it is very widespread, and increasingly common in writing.

(c) The simple form of *Konjunktiv II* **and the compound form with** *würde*

The compound conditional form with *würde* is often used rather than the simple 'past subjunctive' form of *Konjunktiv II*, so that, for example, *ich würde kommen* is often used rather than *ich käme*. Which form is used depends on register, meaning and the individual verb involved. Current usage is explained fully in 16.4.4, but it can be summarised briefly here as follows:

(i) The simple forms of the weak verbs and those of many less frequent strong verbs are only used in formal writing. Indeed, several simple forms of strong verbs (e.g. *ich flöge, ich röche*) are felt to be stilted and avoided entirely. These are indicated in Table 12.12.

(ii) On the other hand, with the most common verbs, in particular *haben, sein, werden* and the modal auxiliaries, the simple form is much more common than the compound form in <u>both</u> writing <u>and</u> everyday speech.

(d) Passive forms of *Konjunktiv II*

The *werden-* and *sein*-passive of *Konjunktiv II* are constructed in exactly the same way as in the indicative, using subjunctive forms of the auxiliary verb *werden* or *sein* and the past participle:

werden-passive (past):	es **würde gekauft (werden)**
werden-passive (pluperfect):	es **wäre gekauft worden**
sein-passive:	es **wäre gekauft**

TABLE 12.11 Formation of the simple form of *Konjunktiv II* (past subjunctive)

	Verb	Past tense	*Konjunktiv II*
Regular weak verbs	kaufen	kaufte	kaufte
	machen	machte	machte
Regular strong verbs	bleiben	blieb	blieb**e**
	brechen	brach	bräch**e**
	fahren	fuhr	führ**e**
	gehen	ging	ging**e**
	kommen	kam	käm**e**
	lassen	ließ	ließ**e**
	sprechen	sprach	spräch**e**
	tragen	trug	trüg**e**
	tun	tat	tät**e**
	ziehen	zog	zög**e**
Strong verbs with irregular past subjunctive	helfen	half	hülf**e**
	stehen	stand	stünd**e**
	sterben	starb	stürb**e**
Irregular verbs	sein	war	wär**e**
	haben	hatte	hätte
	werden	wurde	würde
	dürfen	durfte	dürfte
	können	konnte	könnte
	mögen	mochte	möchte
	müssen	musste	müsste
	wissen	wusste	wüsste
	bringen	brachte	brächte
	denken	dachte	dächte

Notes on Table 12.12

Table 12.12 gives the principal parts, i.e. the infinitive, the past tense and the past participle, of all strong and irregular verbs, with the exception of the wholly irregular verbs and the modal auxiliaries whose forms are given in Tables 12.3 and 12.4.

(i) The third person singular of the present tense is given for those verbs which have vowel changes (see 12.2.1e/f).

(ii) The simple past subjunctive form of *Konjunktiv II* (see 12.5.2) is given for all verbs listed, but it is given in italics if it is obsolete, archaic or rarely used.

(iii) The auxiliary used to form the perfect tenses (i.e. *haben* or *sein*, see 12.3.2) is indicated by *hat* or *ist* alongside the past participle.

(iv) Less common alternative forms are given in brackets after the commoner ones.

(v) In principle, simple verbs (i.e. without prefixes) are given if they exist, even in cases when they are less frequent than compound verbs. As a rule, compound verbs conjugate in the same way as the simple verb from which they are derived; exceptions to this are given in the table.

TABLE 12.12 Principal parts of strong and irregular verbs

Infinitive 3rd person singular present	Past tense *Konjunktiv II*	Past participle
backen *bake* es bäckt (backt)	**backte** (buk) *büke*	hat **gebacken**
befehlen *command* es befiehlt	**befahl** *beföhle (befähle)*	hat **befohlen**
NB: *fehlen* 'lack' is weak, i.e. *fehlte, gefehlt.*		
beginnen *begin*	**begann** *begänne (begönne)*	hat **begonnen**
beißen *bite*	**biss** *bisse*	hat **gebissen**
bergen *rescue; hide* es birgt	**barg** *bärge*	hat **geborgen**
bersten *crack, burst* es birst (berstet)	**barst** *bärste*	hat **geborsten**
bewegen *induce*	**bewog** *bewöge*	hat **bewogen**
NB: *bewegen* 'move' is weak, i.e. *bewegte, bewegt*		
biegen *bend; turn*	**bog** *böge*	hat **gebogen**
bieten *offer*	**bot** *böte*	hat **geboten**
binden *bind*	**band** *bände*	hat **gebunden**
bitten *ask, request*	**bat** *bäte*	hat **gebeten**
blasen *blow* es bläst	**blies** *bliese*	hat **geblasen**
bleiben *stay, remain*	**blieb** *bliebe*	ist **geblieben**
braten *fry, roast* es brät (bratet)	**briet** *briete*	hat **gebraten**
brechen *break* es bricht	**brach** *bräche*	hat/ist **gebrochen**
brennen *burn*	**brannte** *brennte*	hat **gebrannt**
bringen *bring*	**brachte** *brächte*	hat **gebracht**
denken *think*	**dachte** *dächte*	hat **gedacht**
dreschen *thresh* es drischt	**drosch** *drösche*	hat **gedroschen**
dingen *hire, engage* (e.g. servant)	**dingte** (dang) *dingte/dänge*	hat **gedungen**
NB: Simple *dingen* is archaic, but the compound *sich (etwas) ausbedingen* 'make (sth.) a condition' is still used in formal registers. It always has strong forms, i.e. *bedang sich . . . aus, ausbedungen.*		
dringen *penetrate*	**drang** *dränge*	hat/ist **gedrungen**
empfehlen *recommend* es empfiehlt	**empfahl** *empföhle (empfähle)*	hat **empfohlen**

TABLE 12.12 (continued)

Infinitive 3rd person singular present	Past tense *Konjunktiv II*	Past participle
erkiesen *choose*	**erkor** *erköre*	hat **erkoren**

NB: Only the past tense and the past participle are now used, and then only in elevated registers.

erlöschen *go out* (lights) es erlischt	**erlosch** *erlösche*	ist **erloschen**

NB: Transitive *löschen* 'extinguish' is weak, i.e. *löschte, gelöscht*

erschrecken *be startled* es erschrickt	**erschrak** *erschräke*	ist **erschrocken**

NB: Transitive *erschrecken* 'frighten' is weak, i.e. *erschreckte, erschreckt.*

essen *eat* es isst	**aß** *äße*	hat **gegessen**
fahren *go, drive* es fährt	**fuhr** *führe*	ist/hat **gefahren**
fallen *fall* es fällt	**fiel** *fiele*	ist **gefallen**
fangen *catch* es fängt	**fing** *finge*	hat **gefangen**
fechten *fight, fence* es ficht	**focht** (fechtete) *föchte*	hat **gefochten**
finden *find*	**fand** *fände*	hat **gefunden**
flechten *plait, braid* es flicht	**flocht** (flechtete) *flöchte*	hat **geflochten**
fliegen *fly*	**flog** *flöge*	ist/hat **geflogen**
fliehen *flee*	**floh** *flöhe*	ist **geflohen**
fließen *flow*	**floss** *flösse*	ist **geflossen**
fragen *ask* er fragt (*S.G.* frägt)	**fragte** (*lit.* frug) *fragte*	hat **gefragt**
fressen *eat (of animals)* es frisst	**fraß** *fräße*	hat **gefressen**
frieren *freeze*	**fror** *fröre*	hat/ist **gefroren**
gären *ferment*	**gor/gärte** *göre/gärte*	hat/ist **gegoren/gegärt**

NB: Strong forms are usual when *gären* is used literally, the weak ones when it is used figuratively.

gebären *give birth* es gebiert (gebärt)	**gebar** *gebäre*	hat **geboren**
geben *give* es gibt	**gab** *gäbe*	hat **gegeben**
gedeihen *thrive*	**gedieh** *gediehe*	ist **gediehen**
gehen *go*	**ging** *ginge*	ist **gegangen**

TABLE 12.12 (continued)

Infinitive 3rd person singular present	Past tense *Konjunktiv II*	Past participle
gelingen *succeed*	**gelang** gelänge	ist **gelungen**

NB: *misslingen* 'fail' has similar forms, i.e. *misslang, misslungen.*

gelten *be valid* es gilt	**galt** gälte (gölte)	hat **gegolten**
genesen *recover* (elev.)	**genas** genäse	ist **genesen**
genießen *enjoy*	**genoss** genösse	hat **genossen**
geschehen *happen* es geschieht	**geschah** geschähe	ist **geschehen**
gewinnen *win*	**gewann** gewänne/gewönne	hat **gewonnen**
gießen *pour*	**goss** gösse	hat **gegossen**
gleichen *resemble*	**glich** gliche	hat **geglichen**
gleiten *glide, slide*	**glitt** glitte	ist **geglitten**

NB: *begleiten* 'accompany' is weak, i.e. *begleitete, begleitet.*

glimmen *glimmer* (elev.)	**glomm/glimmte** glömme/glimmte	hat **geglommen/geglimmt**
graben *dig* es gräbt	**grub** grübe	hat **gegraben**
greifen *grasp*	**griff** griffe	hat **gegriffen**
halten *hold; stop* es hält	**hielt** hielte	hat **gehalten**

NB: The compound verbs *beinhalten* 'comprise' and *haushalten* 'be economical' are weak.

hängen *hang* (intrans.)	**hing** hinge	hat **gehangen**

NB: The transitive verb *hängen* 'hang' is weak, i.e. *hängte, gehängt.*

hauen *hew, cut*	**haute** (hieb) haute (hiebe)	hat **gehauen** (*coll.* gehaut)

NB: The strong past form *hieb* is used in literary German in the meaning 'hew, cut (with a sword)'.

heben *lift*	**hob** (hub) höbe (hübe)	hat **gehoben**

NB: The forms *hub* and *hübe* are archaic, but they are still occasionally used in formal literary registers, particularly with the compound *anheben* 'commence'.

heißen *be called*	**hieß** hieße	hat **geheißen**
helfen *help* es hilft	**half** hülfe (hälfe)	hat **geholfen**
kennen *know*	**kannte** kennte	hat **gekannt**

TABLE 12.12 (continued)

Infinitive
    3rd person singular present
	Past tense
	    Konjunktiv II
		Past participle

klimmen *climb*	**klomm** (klimmte) *klömme*	hat **geklommen** (geklimmt)
klingen *sound*	**klang** *klänge*	hat **geklungen**
kneifen *pinch*	**kniff** *kniffe*	hat **gekniffen**
kommen *come*	**kam** *käme*	ist **gekommen**
kriechen *creep, crawl*	**kroch** *kröche*	ist **gekrochen**
küren *choose*	**kürte** (*elev.* kor) *kürte/köre*	hat **gekürt** (*elev.* gekoren)

laden *load; invite*
    es lädt (ladet)
	lud
	    lüde
		hat **geladen**

NB: *ladet* is regional, and only used in the sense 'invite', or with the compound *einladen*.

lassen *leave; let*
    es lässt
	ließ
	    ließe
		hat **gelassen**

NB: *veranlassen* 'cause' is weak, i.e. *veranlasste, veranlasst*.

laufen *run*
    es läuft
	lief
	    liefe
		ist/hat **gelaufen**

leiden *suffer*	**litt** *litte*	hat **gelitten**

NB: *verleiden* 'spoil' is weak, i.e. *verleidete, verleidet*.

leihen *lend; borrow*	**lieh** *liehe*	hat **geliehen**

lesen *read*
    es liest
	las
	    läse
		hat **gelesen**

liegen *lie*	**lag** *läge*	hat **gelegen**
lügen *tell lies*	**log** *löge*	hat **gelogen**
mahlen *grind*	**mahlte** *mahlte*	hat **gemahlen**
meiden *avoid*	**mied** *miede*	hat **gemieden**

melken *milk*
    es melkt (milkt)
	melkte (molk)
	    melkte
		hat **gemolken** (gemelkt)

messen *measure*
    es misst
	maß
	    mäße
		hat **gemessen**

nehmen *take*
    es nimmt
	nahm
	    nähme
		hat **genommen**

nennen *name, call*	**nannte** *nennte*	hat **genannt**
pfeifen *whistle*	**pfiff** *pfiffe*	hat **gepfiffen**

TABLE 12.12 (continued)

Infinitive 3rd person singular present	Past tense *Konjunktiv II*	Past participle
preisen *praise*	**pries** priese	hat **gepriesen**

NB: The compound *lobpreisen* can be weak (e.g. *lobpreiste*) or strong (e.g. *lobpries*).

quellen *gush, well up* es quillt	**quoll** *quölle*	ist **gequollen**
raten *advise* es rät	**riet** riete	hat **geraten**
reiben *rub*	**rieb** riebe	hat **gerieben**
reißen *tear*	**riss** risse	hat/ist **gerissen**
reiten *ride (a horse)*	**ritt** *ritte*	hat/ist **geritten**
rennen *run*	**rannte** rennte	hat/ist **gerannt**
riechen *smell*	**roch** röche	hat **gerochen**
ringen *wrestle*	**rang** ränge	hat **gerungen**
rinnen *flow, trickle*	**rann** ränne (rönne)	ist **geronnen**
rufen *call, cry*	**rief** riefe	hat **gerufen**
salzen *salt*	**salzte** *salzte*	hat **gesalzen** (gesalzt)
saufen *drink (of animals); booze* es säuft	**soff** söffe	hat **gesoffen**
saugen *suck*	**saugte/sog** *saugte/söge*	hat **gesaugt/gesogen**

NB: In technical language, only weak forms are used, especially in the compound *staubsaugen* 'vacuum'.

schaffen *create*	**schuf** *schüfe*	hat **geschaffen**

NB: *schaffen* is weak (*schaffte, geschafft*) in the meaning 'manage', 'work'.

scheiden *separate; depart*	**schied** schiede	hat/ist **geschieden**
scheinen *seem; shine*	**schien** schiene	hat **geschienen**
scheißen *shit* (vulg.)	**schiss** *schisse*	hat **geschissen**
schelten *scold* es schilt	**schalt** *schölte*	hat **gescholten**
scheren *shear, clip*	**schor** *schöre*	hat **geschoren**

NB: *scheren* is weak (i.e. *scherte, geschert*) in the meaning 'concern', as is the reflexive *sich scheren* 'bother about; clear off'.

schieben *push, shove*	**schob** *schöbe*	hat **geschoben**

TABLE 12.12 (continued)

Infinitive
    3rd person singular present
	Past tense
	    Konjunktiv II
		Past participle

schießen *shoot*	**schoss** schösse	hat/ist **geschossen**
schinden *flay, ill-treat*	[schindete (not used)]	hat **geschunden**

schlafen *sleep*
    es schläft
	schlief
	    schliefe
		hat **geschlafen**

schlagen *hit, beat*
    es schlägt
	schlug
	    schlüge
		hat **geschlagen**

schleichen *creep*	**schlich** schliche	ist **geschlichen**
schleifen *grind, sharpen*	**schliff** schliffe	hat **geschliffen**

NB: *schleifen* is weak (i.e. *schleifte, geschleift*) in the meaning 'drag'.

schließen *shut*	**schloss** schlösse	hat **geschlossen**
schlingen *wind, wrap*	**schlang** schlänge	hat **geschlungen**
schmeißen *chuck (coll.)*	**schmiss** schmisse	hat **geschmissen**

schmelzen *melt*
    es schmilzt (schmelzt)
	schmolz (schmelzte)
	    schmölze
		hat/ist **geschmolzen** (geschmelzt)

NB: The weak forms only occur if *schmelzen* is used transitively, and are colloquial.

schneiden *cut*	**schnitt** schnitte	hat **geschnitten**
schreiben *write*	**schrieb** schriebe	hat **geschrieben**
schreien *shout, scream*	**schrie** schriee	hat **geschrie(e)n**
schreiten *stride*	**schritt** schritte	ist **geschritten**
schweigen *not speak*	**schwieg** schwiege	hat **geschwiegen**

schwellen *swell*
    es schwillt
	schwoll
	    schwölle
		ist **geschwollen**

NB: *schwellen* is weak (i.e. *schwellte, geschwellt*) when used transitively.

schwimmen *swim*	**schwamm** *schwömme (schwämme)*	ist/hat **geschwommen**
schwinden *disappear*	**schwand** schwände	ist **geschwunden**
schwingen *swing*	**schwang** schwänge	hat **geschwungen**
schwören *swear*	**schwor** (*lit.* schwur) schwüre (schwöre)	hat **geschworen**

sehen *see*
    es sieht
	sah
	    sähe
		hat **gesehen**

senden *send*	**sendete/sandte** sendete	hat **gesendet/gesandt**

NB: The weak forms *sendete, gesendet* are used in technical senses, (i.e. = 'broadcast'). Otherwise the irregular forms are commoner.

TABLE 12.12 (continued)

Infinitive 3rd person singular present	Past tense *Konjunktiv II*	Past participle
sieden *boil* (*elev.; S.G.*)	**siedete/sott** *siedete (sötte)*	hat **gesotten** (gesiedet)
singen *sing*	**sang** *sänge*	hat **gesungen**
sinken *sink*	**sank** *sänke*	ist **gesunken**
sinnen *meditate* (*elev.*)	**sann** *sänne (sönne)*	hat **gesonnen**
sitzen *sit*	**saß** *säße*	hat **gesessen**
spalten *split, cleave*	**spaltete** *spaltete*	hat/ist **gespaltet** (gespalten)

NB: The strong past participle *gespalten* is used mainly as an adjective, e.g. *das gespaltene Deutschland.*

speien *spit, spew* (*elev.*)	**spie** *spiee*	hat **gespie(e)n**
spinnen *spin; be stupid*	**spann** *spönne (spänne)*	hat **gesponnen**
sprechen *speak* es spricht	**sprach** *spräche*	hat **gesprochen**
sprießen *sprout* (*elev.*)	**spross** *sprösse*	ist **gesprossen**
springen *jump*	**sprang** *spränge*	ist **gesprungen**
stechen *prick, sting* es sticht	**stach** *stäche*	hat **gestochen**
stehen *stand*	**stand** *stünde (stände)*	hat **gestanden**
stehlen *steal* es stiehlt	**stahl** *stähle (stöhle)*	hat **gestohlen**
steigen *climb; rise*	**stieg** *stiege*	ist **gestiegen**
sterben *die* es stirbt	**starb** *stürbe*	ist **gestorben**
stieben *fly up (like dust)* (*elev.*)	**stob** (stiebte) *stöbe*	ist **gestoben** (gestiebt)
stinken *stink*	**stank** *stänke*	hat **gestunken**
stoßen *bump; push* es stößt	**stieß** *stieße*	ist/hat **gestoßen**
streichen *stroke*	**strich** *striche*	ist/hat **gestrichen**
streiten *quarrel*	**stritt** *stritte*	hat **gestritten**
tragen *carry, wear* es trägt	**trug** *trüge*	hat **getragen**

NB: *beantragen* 'apply' and *beauftragen* 'commission' are weak.

treffen *meet; hit* es trifft	**traf** *träfe*	hat **getroffen**

TABLE 12.12 (continued)

Infinitive 3rd person singular present	Past tense *Konjunktiv II*	Past participle
treiben *drive; drift*	**trieb** triebe	ist/hat **getrieben**
treten *step* es tritt	**trat** träte	ist/hat **getreten**
triefen *drip* (*elev.*)	**triefte/troff** tröffe	hat **getrieft** (getroffen)
trinken *drink*	**trank** tränke	hat **getrunken**
trügen *deceive*	**trog** tröge	hat **getrogen**
tun *do*	**tat** täte	hat **getan**
verbleichen *fade*	**verblich** verbliche	ist **verblichen**

NB: Simple *bleichen* 'bleach' is weak (i.e. *bleichte, gebleicht*), as is *erbleichen* 'turn pale'.

verderben *spoil* es verdirbt	**verdarb** *verdürbe*	hat/ist **verdorben**
verdrießen *vex* (*elev.*)	**verdross** verdrösse	hat **verdrossen**
vergessen *forget* es vergisst	**vergaß** vergäße	hat **vergessen**
verlieren *lose*	**verlor** verlöre	hat **verloren**
verschleißen *wear out*	**verschliss** verschlisse	ist/hat **verschlissen**
verzeihen *excuse*	**verzieh** verziehe	hat **verziehen**
wachsen *grow* es wächst	**wuchs** wüchse	ist **gewachsen**
wägen *weigh (one's words)*	**wog/wägte** wöge	hat **gewogen/gewägt**

NB: Simple *wägen* is archaic. The compound *erwägen* 'consider' only has strong forms, *erwog, erwogen*.

waschen *wash* es wäscht	**wusch** wüsche	hat **gewaschen**
weben *weave*	**webte** (wob) webte	hat **gewebt** (gewoben)

NB: Usually weak, but the strong forms are used in literary German in figurative senses.

weichen *yield, give way*	**wich** wiche	ist **gewichen**

NB: The weak verb *weichen* (*weichte, geweicht*) means 'soften'. It has the compounds *einweichen* 'soak' and *aufweichen* 'make soft'.

weisen *point*	**wies** wiese	hat **gewiesen**
wenden *turn*	**wandte/wendete** wendete	hat **gewandt/gewendet**

NB: The irregular forms *wandte, gewandt* are generally more frequent, except in the sense 'turn over', 'turn round' (e.g. *das Auto, das Heu wenden*) and in the compounds *entwenden* and *verwenden*.

TABLE 12.12 (continued)

Infinitive 3rd person singular present	Past tense *Konjunktiv II*	Past participle
werben *recruit; advertise* es wirbt	**warb** *würbe*	hat **geworben**
werfen *throw* es wirft	**warf** *würfe*	hat **geworfen**
wiegen *weigh*	**wog** *wöge*	hat **gewogen**
NB: *wiegen* is weak (*wiegte, gewiegt*) in the meaning 'rock' (cradle, etc.).		
winden *wind, twist* (*elev.*)	**wand** *wände*	hat **gewunden**
winken *wave*	**winkte** winkte	hat **gewinkt/gewunken**
wringen *wring* (*N.G.*) *(clothes)*	**wrang** *wränge*	hat **gewrungen**
ziehen *pull; move*	**zog** zöge	hat/ist **gezogen**
zwingen *force*	**zwang** zwänge	hat **gezwungen**

13 The infinitive and the participles

This chapter deals with the main uses of the non-finite forms of the verb, i.e. the infinitive and the present and past participles:

Infinitive	Present participle	Past participle
kaufen	kaufend	gekauft
wandern	wandernd	gewandert
singen	singend	gesungen
aufmachen	aufmachend	aufgemacht
bestellen	bestellen	bestellt

As explained in 12.1.1e, these forms of the verb do not have endings to show agreement with the subject, or to express other categories of the verb such as tense and mood. They are used to form the compound tenses and the passive (see 12.3 and 12.4), and they occur in a number of constructions which depend on an element in a full clause with a finite verb. The formation of the infinitive and the participles of regular verbs is shown in Table 12.2. In German the present participle is often referred to as *Partizip I*, and the past participle as *Partizip II*.

Despite certain similarities, German differs quite markedly from English in respect of some non-finite constructions and their use, especially those with the present participle. The various uses and forms of these non-finite forms are explained in this chapter as follows:

- The **forms of the infinitive**: the compound infinitive; the infinitive with and without *zu* (section 13.1)
- The uses of the **infinitive with** *zu* (section 13.2)
- The uses of the **infinitive without** *zu* – the bare infinitive (section 13.3)
- Infinitives used as **nouns** (section 13.4)
- The uses of the **present** and **past participles** (section 13.5)
- **Clauses** with participles (section 13.6)
- Equivalents of the **English 'ing'-form** in German (section 13.7)

13.1 Forms of the infinitive

13.1.1 The simple infinitive

The simple INFINITIVE is the basic form under which verbs are listed in dictionaries, see 12.1. For most verbs it ends in -*en* (e.g. *kommen, machen, sehen*), but a few verbs have an infinitive ending in -*n*, i.e. *sein, tun* and verbs with a stem ending in -*el* and -*er*, see 12.2.1c.

13.1.2 The compound infinitive

The infinitive of the auxiliaries *haben, sein* and *werden* can be combined with the past participle of a verb to form compound infinitives:

perfect infinitive (with *haben* or *sein*):	gesehen haben	angekommen sein
passive infinitive (with *werden* or *sein*):	verletzt werden	verletzt sein
perfect passive infinitive:	verletzt worden sein	

The perfect infinitive is formed with *haben* or *sein* in accordance with the rules given in 12.3.2. For the use of *sein* or *werden* in the passive, see 15.2.2. The German perfect infinitive is used to show that an action took place before that of the main verb. This is similar to English:

Sie muss das Buch **lesen**	*She must **read** the book*
Sie muss das Buch **gelesen haben**	*She must **have read** the book*

13.1.3 **The infinitive with and without *zu***

In some constructions in German, the infinitive is accompanied by the particle *zu*, whilst in others a so-called **bare infinitive** is used, without *zu*:

Ich riet ihr zum Arzt **zu gehen**	*I advised her **to go** to the doctor*
Ich konnte nicht zum Arzt **gehen**	*I couldn't **go** to the doctor*

Constructions with *zu* (which are more frequent) are explained in section 13.2. Constructions with the bare infinitive are treated in section 13.3.

13.1.4 **The form of the infinitive with *zu***

(a) Simple verbs and verbs with inseparable prefixes

zu comes immediately before the verb and is separated from it in writing:

Sie fing an **zu schreiben**	Wir kamen auf dieses Thema **zu sprechen**
Ich war bereit **zu verhandeln**	Es gefiel mir mich mit ihr **zu unterhalten**

(b) Verbs with a separable prefix

zu is placed between the prefix and the verb. The whole is written as a single word (see 12.2.1i and 22.5):

Sie hatte vor ihn **anzurufen**	Es war schön euch **wiederzusehen**
Es wäre wohl besser ihr davon **abzuraten**	Sie wusste mit diesem Mann **umzugehen**

Similarly, if a verb has a separable prefix followed by an inseparable one, as in *anvertrauen*, *zu* comes between the prefixes:

Es fällt mir nicht ein mich ihm **anzuvertrauen**

NB: Although the verb *missverstehen* is inseparable, the *zu* is placed **after** the prefix, i.e. *misszuverstehen*. This is an alternative, if less frequent, possibility with a few other verbs with the prefix *miss-*, e.g. *zu missachten* or (less commonly) *misszuachten*, see 22.6.3.

(c) With compound infinitives

zu is placed between the participle and the auxiliary *haben*, *sein* or *werden*:

Er verleugnet es sie betrogen **zu** haben	*He denies having deceived her*
Ihr gefällt es nicht betrogen **zu** werden	*She doesn't like being deceived*
Sie behauptete betrogen worden **zu** sein	*She claimed to have been deceived*

Similarly, *zu* comes between the main verb and a modal auxiliary:

Es freut mich Sie hier begrüßen zu dürfen	*It is a pleasure to be able to welcome you here*

13.2 The use of the infinitive with *zu*

13.2.1 The infinitive with *zu* occurs in a reduced clause

In German this is called the *Infinitivsatz*. It can depend on a noun, verb or adjective in a full clause within the same sentence. The infinitive with *zu* comes at the end of its clause, i.e. in the same position as the finite verb in a subordinate clause (see 21.1.1c):

Er fing an **heftig zu weinen**	*He began to cry bitterly*
Er gab mir die Erlaubnis **in Berlin zu bleiben**	*He gave me permission to stay in Berlin*
Es ist nicht schwer **eine fremde Sprache zu lernen**	*It is not difficult to learn a foreign language*

If there are a number of infinitives, *zu* should be repeated with each, e.g.: *Es begann zu blitzen und zu donnern und zu stürmen.*

NB: For the use of the comma with infinitive clauses, see 23.6.3.

13.2.2 The position of the infinitive clause with *zu*

(a) The infinitive clause is usually quite separate from the main clause

i.e. it is <u>not</u> normally enclosed inside the clause it depends on (see 21.9.2), coming after whatever part of the verb comes in last position in that clause.

Sie hatten beschlossen **vor dem Rathaus zu warten**
 (NOT: *Sie hatten vor dem Rathaus zu warten beschlossen)
Wir hatten vor **im Urlaub nach Rom zu fliegen**
 (NOT: *Wir hatten im Urlaub nach Rom zu fliegen vor)
. . . weil er sich bemüht hat **rechtzeitig fertig zu sein**
 (NOT: *. . . weil er sich rechtzeitig fertig zu sein bemüht hat)

(b) In a few contexts the infinitive clause can be (or must be) enclosed within the main clause it depends on

These constructions are exceptions to the general rule given under (a), and the infinitive clause comes inside the main clause:

(i) Enclosure is the rule with the semi-auxiliary verbs (see 13.2.5):

 . . . bevor sein Duft ihn **zu ersticken drohte** (*Süßkind*)
 Seine Brutalität ist nicht mehr **zu ertragen gewesen** (*Wickert*)

(ii) Enclosure is possible with some other common verbs, although it is never obligatory. It is more typical of formal, especially written registers, and it is more common in subordinate clauses than with the compound tenses:

 Dass sie ihn **entdeckt zu haben** glaubte, war ein Beweis dafür, dass . . . (*Süßkind*)
 (**or**: Dass sie glaubte ihn entdeckt zu haben, . . .)
 Du hast mir **das zu tun** versprochen
 (**or**: Du hast mir versprochen das zu tun)

Verbs frequently used like this are *anfangen, beginnen, hoffen, meinen, trachten, vermögen, versuchen, wagen, wünschen*. In very formal registers, enclosed infinitive clauses are found with other verbs and phrases, but such constructions can sound stilted or clumsy.

(c) Incorporation of infinitive clause and main clause

If there is only the finite verb and its subject in the main clause, the infinitive clause can be incorporated with the main clause by splicing the object of the infinitive into it:

Er wagte **die Reise** aus diesem Grunde nicht **abzubrechen**	*He didn't dare to break his journey for this reason*
Diesen Vorgang wollen wir zu **erklären** versuchen	*We want to try to explain this series of events*

This construction is restricted to formal registers. It is usual only with those verbs which regularly enclose an infinitive clause, see (b) above.

(d) Infinitive clauses depending on relative clauses

The German equivalent of English constructions such as 'a man whom I tried to kill' typically has the infinitive clause enclosed within the relative clause, e.g. *ein Mann, den ich zu töten versuchte.* Other examples:

. . . die Person, **deren Gesicht** ich **zu erraten** versucht hatte (*Frisch*)	*. . . the person whose face I had tried to recognise*
. . . kein Mann, **den zu beseitigen** eine Revolution gelohnt hätte (*Spiegel*)	*. . . not a man whom it would have been worth a revolution to get rid of*

Alternatively, if there is only a simple infinitive clause (i.e. one consisting only of *zu* plus the infinitive), it can follow the finite verb, e.g. *ein Mann, den er versuchte zu töten.*

13.2.3 An infinitive clause with *zu* can be the subject of a verb

(a) A German infinitive clause used as the subject of a verb can correspond in English to an infinitive clause or to a clause with an 'ing'-form

In many contexts a choice exists in English between using the 'ing'-form or the infinitive with 'to' which is lacking in German, since German does not use present participles in the way the 'ing'-form is used in English (see 13.7.1). The finite verb has the ending of the third person singular:

Ihn zu überzeugen wird nicht leicht sein	*To convince him/Convincing him won't be easy*
So etwas zu erlauben ist unerhört	*To allow/allowing that kind of thing is outrageous*
Ihr Ziel ist **einen Roman zu schreiben**	*Her aim is to write/writing a novel*

(b) If a subject infinitive clause is short, it can, optionally, lack *zu*

This is most frequent with the verb *sein* and in set phrases:

Lange Auto (zu) fahren ist sehr anstrengend	*Driving a car for long periods is very strenuous*
Irren ist menschlich	*To err is human*

(c) A subject infinitive clause which follows the main verb is often anticipated by *es* in the main clause

(see 3.6.2e for further details of when this *es* is used):

Es war mir nicht möglich **ihm früher zu mailen**	*It wasn't possible for me to e-mail him earlier*
Ihm steht **(es)** nicht zu **ein Urteil zu fällen**	*It's not up to him to pass judgement*

13.2.4 **Many verbs can have an infinitive clause with *zu* as their object**

(a) A German infinitive clause used as the object of a verb can correspond to an English infinitive clause OR a clause with an 'ing'-form

In English the choice of infinitive or 'ing'-form depends on the individual verb used:

Ich hoffe **dich bald wiedersehen zu können**	*I hope to be able to see you again soon*
Ich gebe zu **das gesagt zu haben**	*I admit having said that*
Ich habe vor **sie morgen zu besuchen**	*I intend to visit them/am visiting them tomorrow*

(b) In some contexts, it is the SUBJECT of the main verb which is taken as the subject of the infinitive clause, but in other contexts it is the OBJECT

Compare the following sentence, where the **subject** of *versprechen* is understood as the subject of *mitzunehmen*:

Christian versprach Ellen **sie** mitzunehmen	*Christian promised Ellen to take her with him*

with this one, where the **object** of *bitten* is understood as the subject of *mitzunehmen*:

Christian bat Ellen **ihn** mitzunehmen	*Christian asked Ellen to take him with her*

What is understood to be the subject of the infinitive depends on the sense of the verbs involved and the context. In practice English and German generally agree on whether the subject or object of the main verb is to be understood as the subject of the infinitive. More examples:

Er gab zu **sich** geirrt zu haben	*He admitted having made a mistake*
Sie hat **ihm** geraten die Ausstellung zu besuchen	*She advised him to see the exhibition*

However, there are one or two contexts where there are significant differences between the two languages:

(i) There are fewer verbs in German than English which allow an object to be taken as the subject of a following infinitive clause. In particular, it is not possible with verbs of wishing, desiring, saying, knowing, thinking and the like. With these a *dass*- or *wenn*-clause has to be used in German, <u>not</u> an infinitive clause:

Sie will, **dass ich mit ihr gehe**	*She wants me to go with her*
Ich möchte nicht, **dass es irgendein Missverständnis gibt**	*I don't want there to be any misunderstanding*
Ich erwarte, **dass sie bald nach Flensburg umzieht**	*I expect her to move to Flensburg soon*
Mir wäre es lieber, **wenn Sie hier nicht rauchen würden**	*I would prefer you not to smoke here*
Sage ihm doch, **dass er warten soll**	*Tell him to wait, though*
Ich wusste, **dass es ein Irrtum war**	*I knew it to be a mistake*

It is not possible, either, to use these verbs in the passive with a following infinitive clause. Thus, there is no direct equivalent in German for English constructions of this type, and a subordinate clause has to be used:

Man erwartet, **dass sie bald nach Flensburg umzieht**	*She is expected to move to Flensburg soon*

Man sagte uns/Uns wurde gesagt, **dass wir warten sollten**	*We were told to wait*

(ii) With some verbs the subject of the infinitive has to be understood as indefinite (i.e. = *man*):

Der Präsident hat angewiesen alle Universitäten zu schließen	*The president has instructed that all the universities should be closed*
Er ordnete an die Gefangenen zu entlassen	*He ordered the prisoners to be released*
Helmut befahl früh aufzubrechen	*Helmut ordered an early start*

Other verbs commonly used this way are *anregen, auffordern, beantragen, befürworten, bitten, drängen, eintreten, empfehlen, ersuchen, fordern, plädieren, raten, veranlassen, verlangen, warnen.*

(iii) With a few verbs, the subject OR the object (or either) can be taken to be the subject of the infinitive:

Er schlug mir vor das Zimmer aufzuräumen	*He suggested that I/he/we should tidy the room up*

Other verbs which can be used like this are *anbieten, einreden, zusichern.*

(c) An infinitive clause can be used in German after some verbs denoting mental processes

The English equivalents typically require a subordinate clause:

Er behauptete (glaubte, meinte, war überzeugt) **mich gesehen zu haben**	*He maintained (believed, thought, was convinced) that he had seen me*

This construction is more usual in writing than in speech, where a subordinate clause (typically with the conjunction *dass* omitted, see 19.2.1b) will often be preferred, e.g. *Er meinte, er hätte mich gesehen/dass er mich gesehen hätte.*

(d) A following object infinitive is sometimes anticipated by *es*

(see 3.6.3a for details of when this *es* is used):

Ich konnte **es** kaum ertragen **ihn so leiden zu sehen**	*I could hardly bear to see him suffer like that*
Sie hat **(es)** versäumt **die Miete zu zahlen**	*She failed to pay the rent*

(e) When verbs which govern a prepositional object are followed by an infinitive clause, it is frequently anticipated by a prepositional adverb

(i.e. *da(r)*+preposition. See 18.5.14 for further details of when this is used):

Ich verlasse mich **darauf,** ihn zu Hause zu finden	*I am relying on finding him at home*
Ich erinnere mich **(daran)**, sie voriges Jahr in Bremen gesehen zu haben	*I remember having seen her in Bremen last year*

13.2.5 **Infinitive clauses with 'semi-auxiliary' verbs**

Some verbs have a closer link with a following infinitive clause than others. Their main role is to modify the meaning of the verb used in the infinitive in some way, like a modal auxiliary verb (see Chapter 17), and it is useful to think of them as **'semi-auxiliary'** verbs.

English has a much wider range of such 'semi-auxiliary' verbs than German. The natural German equivalent to many of these English verbs is a construction with an adverb, e.g. *Ich spiele **gern***

Tennis 'I **like** to play tennis', *Ich sah sie zufällig in der Stadt* 'I **happened** to see her in town'. A survey of these equivalences is given in 7.3.4.

A feature of these semi-auxiliary verbs in German is that they ALWAYS enclose the infinitive in dependent clauses or compound tenses (see 13.2.2b):

> . . . da er den eben Angekommenen **zu erkennen schien**
> . . . als das Boot **zu kentern drohte**
> Sie hat uns **zu verstehen gegeben**, dass sie morgen kommt

These verbs are also often incorporated with a dependent infinitive clause, see 13.2.2c.

The most important verbs which can be used as semi-auxiliaries in German are listed below. Many of them have other uses and meanings.

bekommen 'get':

> Und wenn ich dich **zu fassen bekomme** . . .   *And if I lay hands on you, . . .*

belieben 'like', 'wish'. Nowadays archaic except in an ironic sense:

> Sie **belieben zu scherzen**   *You must be joking*

bleiben 'remain'. The following infinitive has the force of a passive:

> Die Gesetzesvorlage **bleibt** noch **zu**   *The draft bill still remains to be discussed*
> **diskutieren**

NB: For the use of *bleiben* with a **bare infinitive**, see 13.3.1f.

brauchen 'need'. In this sense it only occurs with a negative (or with *nur* or *bloß*). This is the most common negative to *müssen* (see 17.5.1c):

> Du **brauchst** nur **anzurufen**, und ich   *You only need to call and I'll come straight away*
> komme sofort
> eine Sprache, die sie nie **zu erlernen**   *a language which they never needed to learn*
> **brauchten** (*Spiegel*)

NB: In colloquial speech, *brauchen* is commonly used without *zu* (see 13.3.1a): *Ich brauche nicht hingehen*. The infinitive is used rather than the past participle in the perfect tenses (see 13.3.2a): *Du hättest nicht hin(zu)gehen brauchen* and in this context it is considered acceptable to omit *zu*.

drohen 'threaten'. The subject is usually inanimate in this use:

> Oskars Herz **drohte** zu Stein **zu werden**   *Oskar's heart threatened to turn to stone*
> (*Grass*)

geben 'give'. Used mainly with *denken*, *erkennen*, *verstehen*:

> . . . weil sie uns **zu verstehen gab**, dass   *. . . because she gave us to understand that she*
> sie bald kommen würde   *would be coming soon*

NB: *es gibt* 'there is' (see 18.2.5) is also used as a semi-auxiliary, e.g. *. . . weil es hier wenig zu trinken gibt*.

gedenken 'propose'. It is restricted to elevated, formal registers:

> die Zahl der Truppen, die die Nato nach   *the number of troops which NATO proposes to send*
> Afghanistan **zu schicken gedenkt**   *to Afghanistan*

gehen 'go'. The use of *gehen* as a semi-auxiliary is colloquial. It expresses a possibility and the infinitive has passive force (see 15.4.5):

Die Uhr **geht zu reparieren**	*The clock can be repaired*

NB: For the use of *gehen* with a bare infinitive, see 13.3.1e.

haben 'have' expresses necessity or obligation. It is a (rather less frequent) alternative to *müssen* or *sollen*:

Was **habe** ich **zu bezahlen**?	*What have I got to pay?*
Ich **habe** mehrere Mails **zu schreiben**	*I have several e-mails to write*
Sie **haben** hier nichts **zu suchen**	*You have no business here*

With some verbs (especially *tun*), this use of *haben* is idiomatic and there is little sense of obligation or necessity:

Das **hat** mit dieser Sache nichts **zu tun**	*That's got nothing to do with this matter*
Das **hat** wenig **zu bedeuten**	*That doesn't mean very much*

NB: For the use of *haben* with a bare infinitive, see 13.3.1f.

kommen 'come' expresses a (chance) result:

Es war nicht meine Absicht, dass wir auf dieses Thema **zu sprechen kamen**	*It was not my intention for us to get onto this subject*
Wir arrangierten es so, dass ich neben ihr **zu sitzen kam**	*We arranged it so that I came to sit next to her*

NB: For the use of *kommen* with a bare infinitive, see 13.3.1e.

pflegen 'to be accustomed to' is restricted to formal registers:

Am Abend dann studierte Stefan die Sonntagsergebnisse der Bundesliga, wie er es immer zu tun pflegte (*HMP*)	*So in the evening Stefan studied the Sunday Bundesliga results, as he always used to do*

scheinen 'seem'

Ihm **schien** es **zu gefallen**	*He seemed to like it*
Das Dorf Lidiče, wohin die Spuren der beiden Attentäter **zu führen schienen**, wurde zerstört (*Presse*)	*The village of Lidiče, where the tracks of the two assassins seemed to lead, was destroyed*

sein 'be', as a semi-auxiliary, is the equivalent of *können* (or sometimes *müssen* or *sollen*). The following infinitive has the force of a passive, see 15.4.5:

Ist der Direktor heute **zu sprechen**?	*Can I see the manager today?*
Die Fahrausweise **sind** auf Verlangen **vorzuzeigen**	*The tickets are to be shown on demand*
Das Haus **ist zu verkaufen**	*The house is for sale*

NB: For the use of *sein* with a bare infinitive, see 13.3.1e.

stehen has a similar sense to *sein*, and the following infinitive also has the force of a passive. It is used chiefly with *befürchten, erwarten* and *hoffen*:

Es **steht zu erwarten**, dass er bald nachgibt	*It can be expected that he will soon give in*

suchen 'try', 'seek' is restricted to formal registers:

eine Ordnung, die die selbständige militärische Betätigung des Adels **einzuschränken suchte** (*Bumke*)	*a decree which sought to limit the independent military activities of the nobility*

versprechen 'promise'. In this sense, *versprechen* refers to an involuntary action with something desirable in the offing. The subject is normally **inanimate**:

Das Wetter **verspricht schön zu werden**	*The weather promises to be nice*
Wir sind froh, weil das Unternehmen **zu gedeihen verspricht**	*We are happy because the enterprise promises to prosper*

NB: As a full verb, in the sense of 'make a promise', *versprechen* is used with a separated infinitive clause and the subject is always **animate**, e.g. *Der Arzt versprach mir sofort zu kommen.*

verstehen 'be able to', 'know how to':

Sie war in Verhältnisse geschleudert worden, mit denen sie nicht **umzugehen verstand** (*Fleißer*)	*She had been catapulted into circumstances which she didn't know how to cope with*

wissen 'know how to'. In this sense *wissen* is similar to *verstehen*:

Er **weiß mit den Leuten umzugehen**	*He knows how to deal with people*
Wie soll zurechtkommen, wer sich in das Gegebene nicht **zu schicken weiß**? (*Wolf*)	*How is anyone going to manage who doesn't know how to come to terms with reality?*

13.2.6 **The infinitive with *zu* after adjectives**

In some infinitive constructions after *sein* used with an adjective, the **subject** of *sein* has to be understood as the **object** of the infinitive:

Diese Aufgabe ist **einfach zu lösen**	*This problem is simple to solve*
Er ist **leicht zu überzeugen**	*He is easy to convince*
Diese Frage ist **schwer zu beantworten**	*This question is difficult to answer*

This construction is common in English, but it is only possible with very few adjectives in German, i.e.: ***einfach, interessant, leicht, schwer, schwierig***. In German, too, the construction is only possible if the verb takes an accusative object, i.e. it cannot occur with verbs like *helfen* which govern a dative object. These other English constructions have quite different German equivalents:

Es war schön, sie zu kennen (i.e. NOT **Sie war schön zu kennen*)	*She was nice to know*
Meiner Schwester zu helfen war schwierig /Es war schwierig, meiner Schwester zu helfen (i.e. NOT **Meine Schwester war schwierig zu helfen*)	*My sister was difficult to help*
Zum Trinken war der Kaffee zu heiß (i.e. NOT **Der Kaffee war zu heiß zu trinken*)	*The coffee was too hot to drink*

In English we can also use these adjectives attributively (i.e. in front of a noun), with an infinitive depending on them, e.g. 'That is a **difficult** question **to answer**'. This construction does not exist in German, and other constructions are used:

Diese Frage zu beantworten ist schwer	
Das ist eine schwer zu beantwortende Frage	*That is a difficult question to answer*
Es ist ein leicht erreichbarer Ort	*It's an easy place to reach*
Es war dumm diese Frage gestellt zu haben	*That was a silly question to have asked*

13.2.7 **The infinitive with *zu* after prepositions**

An infinitive with *zu* can be used after a few prepositions, i.e. *um, ohne, (an)statt* and *außer*. Such constructions have special meanings and are the equivalent of adverbial clauses. These clauses are always preceded by a comma in writing, see 23.6.3b.

(a) The construction *um . . . zu*

This has a number of different uses:

(i) It can express purpose, often corresponding to English 'in order to'. It is the equivalent of a clause introduced by *damit* (see 19.5.1):

Ich konnte nichts tun, **um** ihn **zu** beruhigen	*I couldn't do anything to reassure him*
Er zündete das Haus an, **um** die Versicherung **zu** kassieren	*He set fire to the house (in order) to collect on the insurance*
Da war kein Wasser, **um** das Feuer **zu** löschen	*There was no water to put the fire out*

NB: The *um* is sometimes omitted, in elevated **and** colloquial registers, e.g. *Ich konnte nichts tun ihn zu beruhigen*.

(ii) It is used after an adjective qualified by *zu* or *genug*:

Er ist **zu jung, um** alles **zu** verstehen	*He is too young to understand everything*
Er ist alt **genug, um** alles **zu** verstehen	*He is old enough to understand everything*

NB: *um* is sometimes omitted, especially in colloquial speech, e.g. *Er ist zu jung alles zu verstehen*.

If the subject of the two clauses is different, the conjunction *als dass* is used, e.g. *Er ist zu jung/nicht alt genug, **als dass wir es ihm erklären können***. See 19.5.3 for further details.

(iii) It can be used simply to link clauses, as an equivalent to *und*:

Er betrat die Gaststätte, **um** sie nach kurzer Zeit wieder **zu** verlassen	*He went into the restaurant, only to leave it again after a short time*

NB: This construction is limited to formal writing and has been criticised by stylists, as it might be misunderstood to imply purpose, e.g. *Karl ging nach Australien, um dort von einem Auto überfahren zu werden*.

(b) *ohne . . . zu*

This corresponds to English 'without' followed by an 'ing'-form:

Er sollte den Gegner ablaufen, ohne ihn per Foul vom Ball zu trennen (*HMP*)	*He ought to run down his opponent without getting the ball off him by fouling him*
Er verließ das Haus, **ohne** gesehen **zu** werden	*He left the house without being seen*

With a change of subject, the conjunction *ohne dass* (see 19.7.7) is used, e.g.: *Er verließ das Haus, ohne dass ich ihn sah*.

(c) *(an)statt . . . zu*

This corresponds to English 'instead of' followed by an 'ing'-form:

Er hat gespielt, **(an)statt zu** arbeiten	*He played instead of working*

A clause with *(an)statt dass*, e.g. *Er hat gespielt, (an)statt dass er gearbeitet hat*, is an alternative to this construction. No change of subject is possible with either *(an)statt zu* or *(an)statt dass*.

(d) *außer . . . zu*

This corresponds to English 'except', 'apart from' or 'besides' with an infinitive:

Was konnten sie tun, **außer zu** protestieren? (*Zeit*)	*What could they do except protest?*

The use of *außer* with a following infinitive is quite recent. A common alternative is to use the preposition *außer* with an infinitive noun, e.g. *Sie tat nichts außer Schlafen*. With a different subject, a clause with the conjunction *außer dass* is used (see 19.7.2a).

(e) German equivalents for other English constructions with prepositions and a following infinitive

In German only the prepositions *um*, *ohne*, *(an)statt* and *außer* can be used with a following infinitive. English can use other prepositions, notably 'for' and 'with', with a following infinitive. These correspond to different constructions in German.

(i) English 'for' followed by a noun or a pronoun and an infinitive.

In a few contexts this corresponds in German to a noun with *für*, or a noun in the dative in the main clause:

Es ist Zeit für uns loszugehen	*It is time for us to leave*
Es war ihm unmöglich, das auch nur zu verstehen	*It was impossible for him even to understand that*

However, the most usual German equivalent is a construction with a subordinate clause, with the conjunction used depending on the sense:

Ihr lag es sehr daran, dass er die Stelle annahm	*She was very keen for him to take the job*
Hier sind ein paar Formulare, die Sie ausfüllen sollen	*Here are a few forms for you to fill in*
Er wartete darauf, dass sie ankam	*He was waiting for her to arrive*
Sie bringt die Fotos, damit wir sie uns ansehen können	*She's bringing the photographs for us to look at*
Sie muss schon sehr krank sein, wenn ihre Mutter den Arzt angerufen hat	*She must be very ill for her mother to have phoned the doctor*

(ii) English 'with' followed by a noun or a pronoun and an infinitive:

Depending on the sense, the German equivalent for this can be a subordinate clause with *da* or *weil*, a main clause with *und*, or a relative clause:

Da ich diesen Aufsatz schreiben muss, werde ich wohl nicht ins Kino gehen können	*With this essay to write, I probably shan't be able to go to the cinema*
Sie waren nur auf der Durchreise in München und konnten dort nur ein paar Stunden verbringen	*They were just passing through Munich, with no more than an hour or two to spend*
Auch der Sonntag, an dem sie nicht ins Büro ging, verging irgendwie	*Even Sunday, with no office to go to, passed somehow*

13.2.8 English uses infinitives in other constructions where an infinitive with *zu* is not used in German

(a) English infinitives in indirect statements and questions

e.g. 'He told me **how to do** it'. In German a subordinate clause (often with *sollen*, *müssen* or *können*) is used:

Er sagte mir, wie ich es machen soll	*He told me how to do it*
Ich weiß nicht, was ich tun soll/muss	*I don't know what to do*
Woher weiß man, welchen Knopf man drücken soll?	*How do you tell which button to press?*

(b) English infinitives used after a noun

e.g. 'the person **to apply to**'. A relative clause is used in German:

Ich möchte ein Paar Handschuhe, die zu meinem Wintermantel passen	*I want a pair of gloves to go with my winter coat*
das Einzige, was man tun kann	*the only thing to do*

These constructions are especially common after superlatives:

Er war der Erste (der Letzte, der beste Spieler), **der gekommen ist**	*He was the first (the last, the best player) to come*

13.2.9 Other uses of the infinitive with *zu*

(a) In comparative phrases with *als*

zu can be omitted, although it is more usual for it to be included:

Du kannst nichts Besseres tun **als zu Hause (zu) bleiben**
Man sollte lieber erst alles gründlich besprechen **als sofort (zu) streiten**

(b) In exclamations

These are very similar to the corresponding English constructions:

Und zu denken, dass es ihr nichts bedeutet hat!	*And to think it didn't mean anything to her!*
Ach, immer hier zu bleiben!	*Oh, to stay here for ever!*

(c) In small ads

Zwei-Zimmer-Wohnung ab 1. Mai zu vermieten	*Two-room flat to let from May 1st*

13.3 **The use of the infinitive without** *zu*

The **bare infinitive,** without *zu*, is used in fewer constructions than the infinitive with *zu*, but these are very frequent.

13.3.1 **A few verbs are followed by an infinitive without** *zu*

These infinitives are placed at the end of the clause: *Sie will diese Briefe morgen* **schreiben**. They are enclosed in subordinate clauses and compound tenses: *Ich weiß, dass sie diese Briefe morgen* **schreiben** *will* or *Sie hat diese Briefe heute* **schreiben** *wollen*. For further details see 21.1. The infinitive without *zu* is used with a small number of common verbs:

(a) The modal auxiliaries

i.e. *dürfen, können, mögen, müssen, sollen, wollen* (see Chapter 17):

Sie **darf** heute nicht **ausgehen**	Ich **musste** heute früh **aufstehen**
Wir **können** es nicht **verhindern**	Er wird mir nicht **helfen wollen**

In colloquial German, *brauchen* is often treated as a modal auxiliary and used with a bare infinitive, e.g. *Sie brauchen heute nicht hingehen.* However, many German speakers consider this to be unacceptable in standard, and *brauchen* is normally used with zu in writing: *Sie brauchen heute nicht hinzugehen.* Nevertheless, the omission of *zu* is acceptable in the perfect tense, when the infinitive of *brauchen* is used rather than a past participle, see 13.3.2a, e.g. *Das hättest du wirklich nicht (zu) lesen brauchen.*

(b) A few verbs of perception

fühlen, hören, sehen, spüren, e.g.:

Ich **sah** ihn ins Zimmer **kommen**	*I saw him come into the room*
Sie **hörte** das Kind **weinen**	*She heard the child crying*
Er **fühlte** sein Herz **klopfen**	*He felt his heart beat(ing)*
Ich **spürte** seinen Einfluss **wachsen**	*I sensed how his influence was growing*

With these verbs, a clause with *wie* is an alternative to the infinitive construction, e.g.:

Ich **hörte, wie** das Kind weinte	Ich **spürte, wie** sein Einfluss wuchs
Ich **sah, wie** der Polizist sich nach dem alten Mann umsah	

This tends to be more frequent than the infinitive construction in certain contexts, in particular if the sentence is long or complex, with the verbs *fühlen* and *spüren*, and in colloquial registers.

(c) *lassen*

lassen with a bare infinitive has two principal meanings:

(i) 'let', 'allow':

Er **ließ** mich das Buch **behalten**	*He let me keep the book*
Lass sie doch **hereinkommen**!	*Do let her come in!*

In this sense *lassen* is often used reflexively with a similar force to a passive construction (see 15.4.6):

Das **lässt sich** leicht **ändern**	*That can easily be changed*
Das Buch **lässt sich** leicht **lesen**	*The book is easy to read*

(ii) 'cause', 'make':

Sie **ließ** den Schlosser die Tür **reparieren**	*She had the locksmith fix the door*
Die Nachricht **ließ** ihn **erblassen**	*The news made him turn pale*
Er **ließ** sich die Haare **schneiden**	*He had his hair cut*

lassen is never followed by a passive infinitive, but in both meanings the infinitive after *lassen* can express the sense of a passive:

Er **lässt** die Bäume **fällen**	*He has the trees felled*
Er **ließ** sich **sehen**	*He allowed himself to be seen*
Sie **ließen** die Autobahnen **von den Gefangenen bauen**	*They had the motorways built by the prisoners*

(d) *tun*

The use of *tun* with a bare infinitive is typical of colloquial speech:

Er **tut** ja immer noch **essen**	*He's still eating*
Tust du mich auch **verstehen**?	*Do you understand me?*
Ich **täte** gern ins Kino **gehen**	*I would like to go to the cinema*

This usage is widespread and common in spoken German, but is not generally considered to be standard and not normally thought to be acceptable in writing. It is, however, permissible in written German to use *tun* in order to allow an emphasised verb to be placed first in the sentence:

Bewundern tue ich ihn nicht, aber er imponiert mir doch	*I don't admire him, but he does impress me*
Aber **schmerzen tat** es darum nicht weniger (*Reuter*)	*But it was no less painful for all that*

(e) Certain verbs of motion

gehen, kommen, fahren, schicken. The verb in the infinitive expresses the purpose of going:

Während ich **öffnen ging**, . . . (*Andersch*)	*While I went to open the door, . . .*
Kommst du heute **schwimmen**?	*Are you coming swimming today?*
Er **fährt** immer vormittags **einkaufen**	*He always goes shopping in the mornings*
Sie hat den Opa **einkaufen geschickt**	*She sent granddad shopping*

This usage is typically (but not only) colloquial. In everyday speech, too, the past tenses of *sein* can be used with a bare infinitive to mean 'go':

Ich **war** heute Morgen **schwimmen**	*I went swimming this morning*
Er **ist einkaufen gewesen**	*He went/has been shopping*

NB: *schicken* can alternatively be used with *zu* and an infinitive: *Sie hat den Großvater geschickt, Kartoffeln und Gemüse zu kaufen*. This is most usual if the infinitive clause is fairly long.

(f) *bleiben, finden* and *haben* followed by a verb of position

Er **blieb** im Zimmer **sitzen**	*He stayed sitting in the room*
Sie **ist** an den Ampeln **stehen geblieben**	*She stopped at the lights*
Er **hat** sein Auto vor der Tür **stehen**	*He's got his car at the door*
Sie **hat** einen Bruder in Köln **wohnen**	*She's got a brother living in Cologne*
Sie **fand** das Buch auf dem Boden **liegen**	*She found the book lying on the floor*

NB: (i)   *stehen bleiben* 'stop' and *sitzen bleiben* 'repeat a year' (at school) are sometimes understood to have a distinct lexical meaning and written as single words.
(ii)   For *finden* with the present participle, see 13.7.5c.
(iii)   *haben* is used with a bare infinitive in a few set constructions with adjectives, i.e. *Du hast gut/leicht reden* 'It's all very well for you to talk'.

(g) *heißen* 'command', *helfen*, *lehren*, *lernen*

These verbs can be followed by a bare infinitive OR an infinitive with *zu*:

Sie **hieß** ihn **schweigen**	*She bade him be silent*
Er **hieß** seine Truppen die Burg bis zum letzten Mann **zu verteidigen**	*He ordered his troops to defend the castle to the last man*
. . . und jetzt **hilf** mir **anpacken** (*Remarque*)	*. . . and now give me a hand*
Er **half** Carla die Weinflaschen **zu öffnen** (*Horbach*)	*He helped Carla to open the wine-bottles*
Sie **lehrte** mich **kochen**	*She taught me to cook*
Sie **lehrte** mich Suppe **zu kochen**	*She taught me how to make soup*
Er **lernte** beim Militär Russisch **sprechen/zu sprechen**	*He learnt to speak Russian in the army*

NB: (i)   This sense of *heißen*, i.e. 'command', is restricted to older literary language. In the sense 'mean', *heißen* is always followed by an infinitive without *zu*, see (h) below.
(ii)   *kennen lernen* 'meet', 'get to know' has developed a distinct lexical meaning and is sometimes written as a single word.

The construction with *zu* tends to be used with longer and more complex infinitive clauses. However, the bare infinitive is preferred if the alternative is an awkward construction, e.g.:

Es geht darum, die seit vierzig Jahren geforderte Freiheit der osteuropäischen Völker verwirklichen zu helfen (*FR*) (i.e. NOT *zu verwirklichen zu helfen*)	*It is a matter of helping the peoples of Eastern Europe to realise the freedom which has been demanded for forty years*

(h) A few other verbs in certain constructions or idioms

(i) With *machen* in a couple of idioms, i.e. *von sich reden machen* 'become a talking point' and *jdn. etwas glauben machen* 'convince sb. of sth.', and with a few other verbs, i.e. *jdn. gruseln, lachen, schwindeln, weinen, zittern machen* 'make sb. have the creeps', 'laugh', 'feel dizzy', 'cry', 'tremble'.

(ii) A bare infinitive is used as the complement of *heißen* 'be (the equivalent of)', 'mean' and *nennen* 'call', e.g.:

Das **heißt lügen**	*That amounts to lying*
Das **hieße** wieder von vorne **anfangen**	*That would mean starting again from scratch*
Das **nennst** du höflich **sein**!	*You call that being polite!*

NB: *heißen* in the meaning 'command' is followed by a bare infinitive or an infinitive with *zu*, see (g) above.

(iii) *legen* is followed by a bare infinitive in the idiom *sich schlafen legen* 'go to bed', e.g. *Ich legte mich schlafen.*

13.3.2 The use of the infinitive for a past participle

The infinitive is used rather than a past participle in the perfect tenses of some verbs used with a bare infinitive, e.g. *Sie hat kommen **wollen*** (NOT: *gewollt*), see 17.1.3. This is the case with the following verbs:

(a) the modal auxiliaries

Er hat heute ausgehen **dürfen**	Wir hätten Ihnen helfen **können**
Er hat ihn sehen **müssen**	Sie hätte es machen **sollen**
Karl hatte Sie sehen **wollen**	

brauchen also forms its perfect tenses with the infinitive rather than the past participle, whether used with an infinitive with *zu* or with a bare infinitive (see 13.3.1a), e.g.: *Wir haben nicht (zu) warten* **brauchen**.

NB: The past participle is occasionally used with these verbs in spoken German, e.g. *Sie hat arbeiten gemusst, gekonnt, gewollt*, etc. These forms are regarded as incorrect.

(b) *lassen*

Sie hat den Schlosser die Tür **reparieren lassen**
Er hat sich die Haare **schneiden lassen**
Er hat sie in das Zimmer **kommen lassen**

The infinitive of *lassen* is generally used rather than the past participle, but it is occasionally heard in the sense of 'leaving something somewhere', e.g. *Ich habe Kaffee und Kuchen stehen gelassen* (more usual: *stehen lassen*), and with the combinations *fallen lassen, liegen lassen*, etc.

(c) *sehen, hören* and other verbs of perception

With *sehen* and *hören*, the norm is to use the infinitive:

Ich habe sie hereinkommen **sehen**	*I have seen her come in*
Sie hatte ihn nicht kommen **hören**	*She hadn't heard him come*

In colloquial speech, the past participle is sometimes used with these verbs, e.g. *Sie hatte ihn nicht kommen gehört*. This is not usually regarded as standard, but it is occasionally encountered in writing. However, *fühlen* and *spüren* are now more often used with a past participle, e.g. *Sie hat die Katastrophe kommen gefühlt*.

(d) *helfen, heißen* and other verbs used with a bare infinitive

Both the infinitive and the past participle are accepted with all these verbs, but there are differences in frequency of usage.

(i) With *helfen*, the infinitive is more usual than the past participle:

Sie hat ihm den Koffer **tragen helfen** (*also common:* **tragen geholfen**)

(ii) With *heißen* the infinitive and the past participle are equally common:

Wer hat dich **kommen heißen/geheißen**?

(iii) With other verbs, i.e. *lehren, lernen, machen*, the past participle is the norm, rather than the infinitive:

Er hat sie **lachen gemacht** (*unusual:* **lachen machen**)

NB: In subordinate clauses the auxiliary normally precedes these double infinitives: *Er sagte, dass sie es* **hätte** *machen sollen /* . . ., *dass sie den Koffer* **hat** *tragen helfen*, etc. (see 17.1.4c and 21.1.3b).

13.3.3 Other uses of the bare infinitive

(a) in commands, in place of an imperative

The use of the infinitive with the force of a command is particularly frequent in official language and instructions, see also 16.2.2a:

Nicht rauchen! Bitte anschnallen!	*No smoking. Fasten seat-belts*

(b) in isolation, especially in elliptical questions, wishes and similar

Wie? Alles vergessen und vergeben?	*What? (Am I supposed to) forgive and forget?*
Wozu sich weiter bemühen?	*Why (should we) bother further?*
Was möchtest du jetzt?	*What would you like to do now?*
– Schlafen bis Mittag!	*– Sleep till lunchtime!*

13.4 Infinitives used as nouns

13.4.1 The infinitive of almost any verb can be used as a noun in German

(a) Infinitival nouns often correspond to English 'ing'-forms used as nouns

Such nouns from infinitives are neuter, see 1.1.3e, and they are spelled with a capital letter:

Ich hörte das laute **Bellen** eines Hundes	*I heard the loud barking of a dog*
Nach monatelangem **Warten** erhielt sie die Nachricht von seinem Erfolg	*After waiting for months she received news of his success*
Das **Mitnehmen** von Hunden ist polizeilich verboten	*Bringing dogs in is forbidden by law*
die Kunst des **Schreibens**	*the art of writing*

(b) With reflexive verbs, the pronoun *sich* is usually omitted

(i) This is especially the case if the use of the infinitive as a noun is well-established and frequent, e.g. *das Benehmen* 'behaviour' (from *sich benehmen* 'behave').

(ii) However, it may be included to avoid ambiguity, e.g. *die Kunst des Sichäußerns* 'the art of expressing oneself', where *das Äußern* could mean something different.

(iii) Increasingly, *sich* tends to be included with forms which have not yet become established usage, e.g. *dieses ständige Sichumschauen* 'this continual looking round', *das meditative Sichannähern an Gott* 'coming closer to God through meditation', *das Sichnichtbegnügenkönnen (Süßkind)* 'not being able to be satisfied'.

NB: The spelling of nouns from reflexive verbs produces uncertainties, and spellings like *das sich Äußern* are sometimes seen, although they are incorrect.

(c) Infinitival nouns are not normally used in the plural

This is because, like the English 'ing'-form, they simply express the action denoted by the verb. However, one or two established forms, with extended meanings, are commonly used in the plural, see 13.4.4.

(d) They can be compounded with the object or another part of the clause

e.g. *das Zeitunglesen* 'reading the newspaper', *das Rückwärtsfahren* 'reversing', *das Schlafengehen* 'going to bed'. If there are several words in these additional elements, they are normally written with hyphens, e.g. *dieses ständige Mit-sich-selbst-Beschäftigen (SWF)*, *das Auf-die-lange-Bank-Schieben*. The first word, the infinitive, and any nouns in the combination are all spelled with capital letters.

13.4.2 **Wide use of infinitival nouns is typical of written German**

They are especially frequent in technical registers, e.g.:

In der Bundesrepublik beginnt sich diese Basis humanen **Miteinanderlebens**, **Untereinanderaussprechens** und **Miteinanderwirkens** aufzulösen (*FAZ*)	*In the Federal Republic this basis of humanely living together, freely exchanging ideas and cooperating is beginning to dissolve*

But they are used in literary prose, too, e.g.:

Dann kam das Schiff, und ich beobachtete, wie so viele Male schon, das vorsichtige **Längsfahren**, **Stoppen**, **Zurückweichen** in dem **Sprudeln** und **Rauschen** und **Räderklatschen**, das **Taueschleudern** und **Festbinden** (*Strauß*).

13.4.3 **Infinitival nouns used with prepositions**

The preposition is usually fused with the appropriate form of the definite article in these constructions (see 4.1.1c).

(a) *beim* + **infinitival noun**

This usually corresponds to English 'on' with an 'ing'-form, or an adverbial time clause with 'when' or 'as':

Beim Erwachen am Morgen erschrak ich eine Sekunde lang (*Frisch*)	*On waking up/When I woke up in the morning I was frightened for an instant*
Die Brücke war so dicht mit vierstöckigen Häusern bebaut, dass man **beim Überschreiten** den Fluss nicht zu Gesicht bekam (*Süßkind*)	*The bridge was so densely built up with four-storey houses that you couldn't see the river as you crossed it*

(b) *zum* + **infinitival noun**

(i) This combination expresses purpose. It often corresponds to English 'for' with an 'ing'-form or an infinitive with 'to':

Zum Fußballspielen ist der Garten viel zu klein	*The garden is much too small for playing football in*
Ich gebrauche den Computer vor allem zum Spielen von Games	*I use the computer more than anything for playing games*
Der Kaffee ist zu heiß **zum Trinken**	*The coffee is too hot to drink*

(ii) Some combinations of infinitival nouns with *zum* are idiomatic:

Das ist doch **zum Lachen**, **zum Kotzen**, **zum Verrücktwerden**	*But that's laughable, enough to make you sick, enough to drive you mad*

(iii) *bis zum* with an infinitival noun is used for 'until':

Bitte bewahren Sie den Fahrschein **bis zum Verlassen** des Bahnhofs	*Please retain your ticket until you leave the station*

(iv) Combinations of infinitival nouns with *zum* are used with *bringen* or *kommen* to form phrasal verbs expressing the completion of an action:

zum **Halten** bringen/kommen   *bring/come to a stop*
zum **Kochen** bringen/kommen   *bring/come to the boil*

(c) *ins* + **infinitive**

This combination is frequent with *geraten* or *kommen* to form phrasal verbs denoting the beginning of an action, e.g.:

Der Ball geriet/kam **ins Rollen**   *The ball started rolling*
Der Turm kam/geriet **ins Schwanken**   *The tower started to sway*
Der Wagen kam **ins Schleudern**   *The car went into a skid*

13.4.4 Some infinitival nouns have extended meanings

These have lost their close link to the verb they originally came from and no longer simply express the action denoted by it. The following is a selection of the most frequent:

das Andenken	*souvenir*	das Schrecken	*terror*
das Benehmen	*behaviour*	das Unternehmen	*enterprise*
das Dasein	*existence*	das Verbrechen	*crime*
das Einkommen	*income*	das Vergnügen	*pleasure*
das Essen	*meal*	das Vermögen	*wealth*
das Gutachten	*reference*	das Versprechen	*promise*
das Guthaben	*credit balance*	das Vorhaben	*intention*
das Leben	*life*		

Such nouns are sometimes used in the plural, and plural forms of most of the above may be encountered (except for *das Benehmen* and *das Dasein*).

13.5 The present and past participles

Aside from the use of the past participle to form the perfect tenses and the passive (see 12.3–4), the German participles are chiefly employed as adjectives (see 13.5.2–4) or in participial clauses (see 13.6).

13.5.1 The names and meanings of the participles

In English, the two participles are usually called the **present participle** (e.g. *lesend, überwältigend*, etc.), and the **past participle** (e.g. *gestellt, geworfen*, etc.). These terms are rather misleading, as the participles do not necessarily refer to present or past time, and they are often referred to as *das erste Partizip* and *das zweite Partizip* in German (or simply *Partizip I* and *Partizip II*).

(a) The present participle usually indicates an action which is taking place at the same time as that of the finite verb

Den Schildern **folgend**, fanden sie das   *Following the signs, they found the hospital*
     Krankenhaus (*Walser*)

(b) The meaning of the past participle differs according to the verb

(i) With intransitive verbs, the past participle has an active (i.e. not passive) sense, and refers to an action which has taken place before that indicated by the finite verb:

Der neue Lehrer, in Freiburg **angekommen**,   *Having arrived in Freiburg, the new teacher*
     suchte das Humboldt-Gymnasium auf   *went to the Humboldt Secondary School*

(ii) With transitive verbs, the past participle has the force of a passive. If the verb denotes a continuous action, the participle refers to an action simultaneous with that of the main verb:

Der Zug, von zwei Lokomotiven **gezogen**,   *The train, which was being pulled by two engines,*
  fuhr in den Bahnhof ein   *came into the station*

With transitive verbs which denote a momentary action, the past participle refers to an action which has taken place before that of the main verb:

Der Flüchtling, von seinen Freunden   *The fugitive, who had been warned by his friends,*
  gewarnt, verließ sein Versteck   *left his hiding-place*

13.5.2 **The adjectival use of the participles**

(a) Most German present and past participles can be used as adjectives

This is their most frequent use outside the compound tenses:

die **schreienden** Vögel   mein **verlorener** Schirm
das **kochende** Wasser   der **gehasste** Feind

(b) Like other adjectives, they can be used as nouns

See 6.4 for more information on the use of adjectives as nouns.

die **Streikenden**   *the people on strike*   die **Gehasste**   *the detested woman*
der **Sterbende**   *the dying man*   das **Hervorragende**   *the outstanding thing*

ein bitterer Kampf zwischen **Habenden**   *a bitter struggle between the haves and the have-*
  und Habenichtsen, zwischen   *nots, between the overfed and those who have*
  Überfütterten und **Zukurzgekommenen**   *come off badly*
  (*Zeit*)

Many such participles used as nouns have taken on special meanings, e.g. *der/die Abgeordnete* 'member of parliament', *der/die Vorsitzende* 'chairperson', etc. More of these are given in 6.4.3.

(c) Like many other adjectives, they can also be used as adverbs

They mainly become adverbs of manner or viewpoint, see 7.3.1c:

Er hat die Sache **überraschend** schnell   *He settled the matter surprisingly quickly*
  erledigt

Sie rannten **schreiend** davon, als sie ihn   *They ran off screaming when they saw him*
  sahen (*Süßkind*)

Die alte Frau ging **gebückt** zum Rathaus   *The old woman was walking with a stoop towards*
  hin   *the town-hall*

(d) They are often compounded, especially in written German

See also 22.3.3. These compounds can then also be used as nouns or adverbs in the same way as simple participles:

Vancouver ist eine Stadt von   *Vancouver is a breathtakingly beautiful city*
  atemberaubender Schönheit

die **Arbeitsuchenden**   *the people looking for work*
ein **weichgekochtes** Ei   *a soft-boiled egg*
Tiefgefrorenes   *frozen food*

(e) Present participles can be used adjectivally with an accompanying *zu*

e.g. *das **abzufertigende** Gepäck* 'the baggage for checking'. This is an adjectival form of the construction with *sein* and an infinitive with *zu* expressing possibility or necessity (see 13.2.5). As in that construction the participle has passive force:

ein nicht **zu übersehender** Fehler	*a mistake which cannot be overlooked*
ihre **anzuerkennende** Leistung	*her achievement which must be acknowledged*
ein **Auszubildender**	*a trainee*

As the last example shows, these forms, too, can be used as nouns. This construction is common in formal, especially official registers.

13.5.3 **The extended participial phrase**

In German, a participle used adjectivally can be expanded leftwards by adding objects and/or adverbials. In this way, what in English would be a phrase or a relative clause placed **after** the noun can appear in German as an extended adjectival phrase placed **before** the noun:

Die **um ihre eigenen Arbeitsplätze fürchtenden** Stahlarbeiter wollten nicht streiken (*FR*)	*The steelworkers, who were afraid for their own jobs, did not want to strike*
Ich habe dieses von meinem Vetter **warm empfohlene** Buch mit Genuss gelesen	*I enjoyed reading this book which was strongly recommended to me by my cousin*
Wegen Überproduktion entlassene Arbeiter demonstrierten im Fabrikhof	*Workers who had been laid off on account of overproduction were demonstrating in the factory yard*
eine **von allen echten Demokraten zu begrüßende** Entwicklung	*a development which must be welcomed by all true democrats*

These extended adjectival phrases can be made into nouns, e.g. *das wirklich Entscheidende* 'what is really decisive', *die soeben Angekommenen* 'the people who have just arrived', etc.

This construction is common in formal written German, especially in non-literary registers (journalism, official writing, non-fiction, etc.), but it is not common in everyday speech. The following example shows that there can be a considerable distance between the article and the noun in phrases like this:

Zwar gilt **der** in den vergangenen vier Jahren auf der Basis einer deutsch-amerikanischen Regierungsvereinbarung für bislang 552 Millionen Mark entwickelte **Panzer** als Spitzenmodell seiner Klasse (*Spiegel*)

Although such constructions typically occur with participles, they are used with other adjectives, too: *eine für sie ganz typische **Haltung*** (see 6.6.3).

13.5.4 **Lexicalisation of participles used as adjectives**

Many participles used as adjectives have become **lexicalised**, i.e. they have developed a meaning distinct from that of the original verb, so that they are now felt to be independent adjectives rather than simply the participles of a particular verb. A clear indication of this is that lexicalised participles can be used with the usual comparative and superlative endings, e.g. *spannender, am spannendsten* 'more, most exciting'. With true participles, *mehr* and *meist* are used, see 8.2.7. Another indication of lexicalisation is the possibility of using the prefix *un-* with them, e.g. *(un)bedeutend* '(in)significant', (*un*)*angebracht* '(in)appropriate', etc. A selection of those most frequently used is given below.

(a) Lexicalised present participles

abstoßend	*repulsive*	empörend	*outrageous*
abwesend	*absent*	entscheidend	*decisive*
ansteckend	*infectious*	glühend	*glowing*
anstrengend	*strenuous*	reizend	*charming*
anwesend	*present*	rührend	*touching*
auffallend	*conspicuous*	spannend	*exciting*
aufregend	*exciting*	überraschend	*surprising*
bedeutend	*significant*	überzeugend	*convincing*
beruhigend	*reassuring*	umfassend	*extensive*
dringend	*urgent*	verblüffend	*amazing*
drückend	*oppressive*	verlockend	*tempting*
einleuchtend	*reasonable*	wütend	*furious*

These can be used not only before an adjective, but also after *sein*:

ein **spannender** Film	*an exciting film*
der Film war **spannend**	*the film was exciting*

True present participles cannot be used like this in German, and English speakers must beware of confusing these lexicalised participles with the 'ing'-forms of the English progressive tenses. Compare:

die **brennenden** Lichter	*the burning lights*
die Lichter **brannten**	*the lights were burning*

i.e. NOT: *die Lichter waren brennend*. German present participles <u>cannot</u> be used with *sein* to form progressive tenses like the English 'ing'-form with the verb 'be' (see also 14.6).

(b) Lexicalised past participles

angebracht	*appropriate*	belegt	*occupied*
angesehen	*respected*	erfahren	*experienced*
aufgebracht	*outraged*	gelehrt	*scholarly*
aufgeregt	*excited*	geschickt	*clever*
ausgezeichnet	*excellent*	verliebt	*in love*
bekannt	*famous*	verrückt	*insane*

Some lexicalised past participles are archaic and are no longer the current past participle of the verb in question, e.g.:

erhaben *illustrious*	(*erheben* 'raise' – modern past participle *erhoben*)
gediegen *solid, upright*	(*gedeihen* 'prosper' – modern past participle *gediehen*)
verhohlen *secret*	(*verhehlen* 'conceal' – modern past participle *verhehlt*)
verworren *confused*	(*verwirren* 'confuse' – modern past participle *verwirrt*)

A few adjectives which look like past participles are in fact not from verbs at all, e.g. *beleibt* 'portly' and *benachbart* 'neighbouring'. These come directly from the nouns *der Leib* 'body' and *der Nachbar* 'neighbour' – there are no verbs **beleiben* or **benachbaren*.

13.5.5 **Other uses of the past participle**

(a) Elliptical use of the past participle

The past participle is sometimes used in isolation as an exclamation or a depersonalised command. Many such forms have become idiomatic:

Verdammt! Verflucht (noch mal)!	*Blast!*
Frisch gewagt!	*Let's get on with it!*
Aufgepasst!	*Watch out!*

For further details, see 16.2.2b.

(b) The past participle after *finden*

This corresponds closely to the English construction:

Ich **fand** sie vor dem Ofen **zusammengesunken**	*I found her slumped in front of the stove*
Du wirst ihn dort **aufgebahrt finden**	*You will find him laid out there*

NB: For the use of *finden* with a present participle, see **13.7.5c**.

(c) The past participle after *kommen*

This corresponds to an English 'ing'-form:

Er **kam** ins Zimmer **gelaufen**	*He came running into the room*
Sie **kam herbeigeeilt**	*She came hurrying along*

(d) The past participle after *bleiben* and *scheinen*

These are similar to English constructions, e.g. *Ihr Brief blieb unbeantwortet* 'Her letter remained unanswered'; *Die Tür schien geschlossen* 'The door seemed/appeared closed'. The participle with these verbs has a similar force to that of the *sein*-passive, see 15.2.2c.

13.6 **Clauses with participles**

13.6.1 **Both participles can be used to construct non-finite clauses**

These can have the force of an adjective, qualifying a noun or pronoun, or of an adverb, giving the circumstances of the action. The participle is usually placed last in the clause, but, exceptionally, it may come earlier:

Ich putzte **auf dem Brett stehend** das Fenster von außen (*Spiegel*)	*I was cleaning the window from the outside, standing on the plank*
eine ständige Verbesserung des Automobils nach den Möglichkeiten der Zeit, **doch zugleich immer aufbauend auf das Erreichte** (*Mercedes advert*)	*a continuous improvement of the car according to the possibilities of the time, but at the same time always building on what has been achieved*
Zwar hatte dieses Mal der Dolch, **durch ein seidenes Unterkleid abgelenkt**, das Opfer nicht sogleich tödlich getroffen (*Heyse*)	*Although this time the dagger, deflected by a silk petticoat, had not immediately wounded the victim fatally*
Von der Wucht seiner Rede hingerissen, brachen die Zuhörer immer wieder in Beifall aus	*Carried away be the force of his speech, the audience continually broke out into applause*

| Da saß eine zarte Dame mit einem zarten Gesicht, **umrahmt von einem blonden Pagenkopf** | *There sat a delicate lady with a delicate face, which was framed by blond hair cut in the page-boy style* |

Participial clauses like these are restricted to formal written registers in German. In particular, those with present participles can sound stilted and they are used much less frequently than clauses with 'ing'-forms in English. In practice, English learners are best advised to avoid them entirely in German and use instead one of the alternatives detailed in 13.7.

13.6.2 Comparative clauses can be formed with *wie* and a past participle

| eine Betonburg, **wie** von einem anderen Stern in diesen Wald **gefallen** (*Walser*) | *a concrete castle, as if it had fallen into this forest from another star* |

In general, this construction is also typical of formal registers, but some have become established idioms and are more widely used:

Also, wie ausgemacht: Wir treffen uns um acht	*Well, then, as arranged, we'll meet at eight o'clock*
wie gesagt, wie erwartet, wie vorausgesehen	*as I said, as expected, as foreseen*
wie gehabt (*coll.*)	*as before, as usual*

13.6.3 A clause with a past participle can be introduced by *obwohl*

This is similar to the English construction with '(al)though':

| Obwohl von seinen Kollegen geachtet, war er nicht sehr beliebt | *Although respected by his colleagues, he was not very popular* |

No other conjunction can introduce a participial clause in German.

13.7 German equivalents of English constructions with the 'ing'-form

The English 'ing'-form is used much more widely than the German present participle, which is found mainly as an adjective (see 13.5). In other contexts, different constructions are usually preferred in German. In particular, the German present participle is not often used in participial clauses (see 13.6.1), and English learners are advised to avoid clauses with the present participle entirely in German. In general, the equivalents given below for constructions with the English 'ing'-form represent more idiomatic German usage.

13.7.1 The English 'ing'-form used as a noun

The usual German equivalent is one of the following. Often, more than one alternative is possible, as the examples in (a), (b) and (c) below show.

(a) An infinitive used as a noun, or another noun derived from a verb
(see 13.4 and 22.2):

Aufmerksames **Zuhören** ist wichtig	*Attentive listening is important*
die Freuden des **Skilaufens**	*the pleasures of skiing*
Warum hat man die **Eröffnung** der neuen Schule aufgeschoben?	*Why has the opening of the new school been delayed?*
Er ist einer solchen **Tat** nicht fähig	*He is not capable of doing such a thing*

(b) An infinitive clause with *zu*

Es ist wichtig aufmerksam zuzuhören	*Attentive listening is important*
Er gab zu das Fenster zerbrochen zu haben	*He admitted having broken the window*
Ich verlasse mich darauf, ihn zu Hause zu finden	*I rely on finding him at home*

(c) A *dass*-clause

Es ist wichtig, dass man aufmerksam zuhört	*Attentive listening is important*
Er gab zu, dass er das Fenster zerbrochen hatte	*He admitted having broken the window*
Ich verlasse mich darauf, dass ich ihn zu Hause finde	*I rely on finding him at home*

This alternative <u>must</u> be used if the English 'ing'-form has a different subject from that of the main verb:

Ich kann es mir nicht vorstellen, **dass sie ihren Ring verkauft**	*I can't imagine her selling her ring*
Ich verlasse mich darauf, **dass er alles arrangiert**	*I rely on his/him arranging everything*

NB: After verbs (or nouns and adjectives) governing a preposition, the infinitive clause or *dass*-clause of alternatives (b) and (c) above is often anticipated by a prepositional adverb (e.g. *darauf*), as the relevant examples show. For details see 6.6.2 and 18.6.14.

(d) A finite verb

Wer **kocht** bei Ihnen zu Hause?	*Who does the cooking at your house?*

The subjectless passive (see 15.1.4) can be used for an English 'ing'-form after 'there is/are':

Überall **wurde** laut **gesungen**	*There was loud singing everywhere*

For 'there is/are' followed by 'no' and an 'ing'-form, a construction with *sich lassen* (see 15.4.6) is often possible, e.g.:

Das **lässt sich** nicht leugnen	*There's no denying that*

13.7.2 The English 'ing'-form after prepositions

(a) 'by' (or 'through') + 'ing'-form

This construction usually corresponds to a clause with *dadurch, dass* or *indem* (see 19.7.3), or to *durch* followed by an infinitival noun. Thus the following are possible equivalents for the English sentence 'He escaped by jumping out of the window':

Er rettete sich **dadurch, dass er aus dem Fenster sprang**
Er rettete sich, **indem er aus dem Fenster sprang**
Er rettete sich **durch einen Sprung aus dem Fenster**

(b) 'for' + 'ing'-form

The commonest equivalents are (*um*) . . . *zu* (see 13.2.7a), or *zum* with an infinitival noun (see 13.4.3b):

Sie hat keine Zeit mehr, **(um) zu üben** Sie hat keine Zeit mehr **zum Üben** }	*She no longer has any time for practising*
Es ist zu kalt **zum Schwimmen**	*It's too cold for swimming*

(c) 'instead of' + 'ing'-form

For this, (*an*)*statt* . . . *zu* or (*an*)*statt dass* is used (see 13.2.7c):

Er spielt, **anstatt zu arbeiten/anstatt dass** **er arbeitet**	*He is playing instead of working*

(d) 'on' + 'ing'-form

This usually corresponds to a clause with *als* or *wenn*, or *beim* followed by an infinitival noun (see 13.4.3a):

Als sie den Brief las, wurde sie rot **Beim Lesen des Briefes** wurde sie rot }	*On reading the letter, she blushed*

(e) 'with' + 'ing'-form

This construction has a variety of possible equivalents in German, similar to those for participial clauses with 'ing'-forms (see 13.7.3):

Wenn der Berg nur als ein unbestimmtes Gebilde erscheint, **wobei** sich die Baumgruppen bloß als blasse Schatten zeigen, . . .	*If the hill only appears as an indefinite shape with the groups of trees showing only as faint shadows, . . .*
Es ist schön hier, **wenn** die Sonne durch die Bäume scheint	*It's lovely here with the sun shining through the trees*
Wir sahen die alte Stadt, **über die** die zerfallene Burg emporragte	*We could see the old town with the ruined castle towering above it*
Da der Fluss rasch stieg, mussten Notmaßnahmen getroffen werden	*With the river rising rapidly, emergency measures had to be taken*
Der Bürgermeister eröffnete die Sitzung **unter** Ausschluss der Öffentlichkeit	*The mayor opened the meeting, with the public being excluded*
Sie eilte durch die Stadt, **und dabei** wehten ihre Haare nach hinten	*She raced through the town with her hair streaming behind her*

(f) 'without' + ing'-form

This corresponds to *ohne . . . zu* or *ohne dass* (see 13.2.7b):

Der Zug fuhr durch, **ohne zu halten**	*The train went through without stopping*
Er bot uns seine Hilfe an, **ohne dass wir ihn darum bitten mussten**	*He offered us his help without our/us having to ask him for it*

(g) Other prepositions followed by 'ing'-forms

These correspond most often to a German subordinate clause or an appropriate preposition with an infinitival noun:

Nach seiner Ankunft/**Nachdem** er angekommen war, ging er sofort zum Rathaus	*After arriving he went straight to the town hall*

Vor dem Einschlafen/**Bevor** er einschlief, las er schnell die Zeitung	*Before going to sleep he read the newspaper quickly*
Trotz seiner Hilfe/**Obwohl** er mir geholfen hatte, kam ich zu spät an	*In spite of his/him having helped me, I arrived late*

NB: 'ing'-forms after prepositions governed by nouns, verbs or adjectives (e.g. 'I rely on finding him at home') are dealt with in 13.7.1.

13.7.3 Participial clauses with 'ing'-forms

The German equivalent depends on the sense of the clause.

(a) The participial clause and the main verb refer to consecutive or simultaneous actions

(i) The simplest German equivalent is to use main clauses joined by *und*. *dabei* can be used in the second to stress that the actions are taking place (or took place) at the same time:

Sie öffnete die Schublade **und** nahm das Testament heraus	*Opening the drawer, she took out the will*
Ich saß an seinem Tisch **und** schrieb einen Brief	*I was sitting at his table writing a letter*
Er erzählte seine Geschichte **und** machte (**dabei**) nach jedem Satz eine Pause	*He told his story, pausing after each sentence*

NB: In modern German, clauses with *indem* do NOT correspond to English participial clauses like those above, despite what some English handbooks of German claim. For the use of *indem*, see 19.7.3.

(ii) A clause introduced by *wobei* can be used if the actions in the two clauses are simultaneous, see also 19.3.8:

Er erzählte seine Geschichte, **wobei** er nach jedem Satz eine Pause machte.

(iii) If the action of the English participial clause precedes that of the main clause, the German equivalent can be a clause with *als*, *wenn* or *nachdem*:

Als wir zum Fenster hinausschauten, sahen wir einen Polizeiwagen heranfahren	*Looking out of the window, we saw a police car approaching*
Wenn man oben auf dem Kirchturm steht, sieht man das ganze Dorf	*Standing on top of the church tower, you can see the whole village*
Nachdem ich die Briefe beantwortet hatte, ging ich spazieren	*Having answered the letters, I went for a walk*

(b) Participial clauses which give a reason or cause

In German, a subordinate clause with *da* or *weil* can be used:

Da es schon spät war, gingen wir nach Hause	*It being late, we went home*
Weil ich wusste, dass sie verreist war, habe ich sie nicht angerufen	*Knowing that she was away, I didn't call her*

(c) Participial clauses introduced by a conjunction

Subordinate clauses with the appropriate conjunction are used in German:

Während ich auf dich wartete, habe ich einen schweren Unfall gesehen	*While waiting for you, I saw a bad accident*

13.7.4 **Clauses with 'ing'-forms used to qualify nouns**

These correspond in German to a relative clause or, especially in formal written German, to an extended participial phrase (see 13.5.3):

Er sah ein **in entgegengesetzter Richtung kommendes** Auto	
Er sah ein Auto, **das in entgegengesetzter Richtung kam**	*He saw a car coming in the opposite direction*
Einige Minuten später eilte der Arzt, **der einen kleinen Koffer trug**, zum Krankenhaus hin	*A few minutes later the doctor, carrying a small suitcase, was hurrying towards the hospital*

13.7.5 **English 'ing'-forms after some verbs**

The usual German equivalent of English 'ing'-forms after verbs is an infinitive with *zu* or a clause, see 13.7.1. However, a few verbs are special cases.

(a) verbs of perception

i.e. 'see', 'hear', 'feel'. The English 'ing'-form corresponds to a bare infinitive or a clause with *wie* (see 13.3.1b):

Ich höre die Vögel laut **singen**	
Ich höre, **wie die Vögel laut singen**	*I can hear the birds singing loudly*

(b) verbs of motion

e.g. 'go', 'come', 'send', etc. If the 'ing'-form expresses purpose, a bare infinitive is used in German (see 13.3.1e):

Wir gehen heute **schwimmen**	*We're going swimming today*
Kommst du heute mit **schwimmen**?	*Are you coming swimming with us today?*
Sie schickte ihn **einkaufen**	*She sent him shopping*

The past participle is used after *kommen*, e.g. *Sie kam herangelaufen* 'She came running up', see 13.5.5c.

(c) *ing*-form expressing position

i.e. *standing*, *sitting*, etc. after *find*, *have*, *remain*, *stay*.

(i) German uses a bare infinitive after *bleiben*, *finden*, *haben* and *lassen* (see 13.3.1):

Sie **blieb** neben dem Ofen **sitzen**	*She remained sitting by the stove*
Ich **fand** ihn am Fenster **stehen**	*I found him standing by the window*
Haben Sie einen Mantel in der Garderobe **hängen**?	*Have you got a coat hanging in the wardrobe?*
Sie **ließ** ihre Sachen **herumliegen**	*She left her things lying about*

(ii) *finden* can also be used with the present participle of many verbs, e.g. *Sie fand ihn schlafend*. *Er fand sie Pilze suchend im Wald*. This construction is also possible with verbs of place, as an alternative to the infinitive (see 13.3.1f): *Sie fand das Buch auf dem Boden liegend/liegen*.

(d) 'keep' + 'ing'-form

A frequent equivalent is *lassen* with a bare infinitive, see 13.3.1:

Sie **ließ** uns **warten**	*She kept us waiting*

(e) 'keep'/'go on' + 'ing'-form

The simplest idiomatic equivalent is *weiter* with the verb (see 7.3.4):

Sie sang **weiter**	*She kept/went on singing*

(f) 'need', 'want' + 'ing'-form

These most often correspond to *müssen*, see 17.5.1b:

Das muss noch erklärt werden	*That still needs/wants explaining*
Man muss sich um sie kümmern	*She needs/wants looking after*

(g) 'can't help' + 'ing'-form

einfach müssen is the commonest German equivalent, see 17.3.6:

Sie musste einfach lachen	*She couldn't help laughing*

14 Uses of the tenses

The grammatical category of TENSE involves the indication of time through special forms of the verb (see 12.1.1b). This chapter deals with the uses of the tenses of the INDICATIVE MOOD (i.e. not the subjunctive) in German:

- General notes on the **German tenses** (section 14.1)
- The **present tense** (section 14.2)
- The uses of the **past** and the **perfect tenses** (section 14.3)
- The **future tenses** (section 14.4)
- The **pluperfect tense** (14.5)
- German equivalents for the **English progressive tenses** (section 14.6)

The conjugation (i.e. the forms) of the tenses in German is explained in Chapter 12 and shown in full in the following tables:

- Table 12.2: the **simple tenses** of **regular verbs**
- Table 12.3: the **simple tenses** of the irregular verbs *haben, sein* and *werden*
- Table 12.4: the **simple tenses** of the **modal auxiliary** verbs and *wissen*
- Table 12.5: the **compound tenses**

14.1 The German tenses: general

14.1.1 There are six tenses in German

These are illustrated for the verb *kaufen* 'buy' in Table 14.1 (see also section 12.1.1b). There are, exactly as in English:

- two SIMPLE TENSES, with a single word: the PRESENT tense and the PAST tense
- four COMPOUND TENSES, formed with the AUXILIARY VERBS *haben*, *sein* and *werden*: the PERFECT tense, the PLUPERFECT tense, the FUTURE tense, and the FUTURE PERFECT tense.

In general, the forms and uses of the tenses in German and English are very similar, as shown in Table 14.1. For this reason this chapter concentrates on those aspects of the use of German tenses which differ significantly from those of the corresponding English tenses.

Table 14.1 illustrates the tenses of the active voice of *kaufen*. Exactly the same set of tenses are also found in the passive voice, with the same meanings, as shown in Chapter 15. This chapter only deals with the tenses of the indicative mood, which signal a fact. The subjunctive mood also has tense forms, but these are used in a rather different way, as explained in Chapter 16.

TABLE 14.1 German and English tenses

Present	ich kaufe	*I buy*
Past	ich kaufte	*I bought*
Perfect	ich habe gekauft	*I have bought*
Pluperfect	ich hatte gekauft	*I had bought*
Future	ich werde kaufen	*I shall/will buy*
Future perfect	ich werde gekauft haben	*I shall/will have bought*

14.1.2 **The German past tense**

What in this book is referred to as the **past tense** is sometimes called the **imperfect tense**. However, unlike the imperfect tense of some languages (e.g. French, Spanish and Latin), but like the English past tense, this German tense does <u>not</u> convey the idea of an incomplete or continuous action. It simply indicates that the action or event took place at some time in the past. For this reason, the less misleading term 'past tense' is preferable.

14.1.3 **There are no progressive tenses in German**

ich kaufe, for instance, normally corresponds to <u>both</u> English 'I buy' and 'I am buying'. However, in some contexts the difference in meaning between these English forms can (or must) be made clear in German in other ways, by using additional words or different constructions. Details are given in section 14.6.

14.2 **The present tense**

14.2.1 **The present tense is used to relate present, habitual or 'timeless' actions or events**

This corresponds to the normal use of the present tense (simple or progressive) in English:

Sie **singt** gut	*She sings/is singing well*
Ich **lese** die Zeitung von gestern	*I'm reading yesterday's newspaper*
Dankend **bestätigen** wir den Empfang Ihres Schreibens vom 30. Juni	*We gratefully acknowledge receipt of your letter of 30th June*
Ursula **spricht** ein wenig Spanisch	*Ursula speaks a little Spanish*
In Irland **regnet** es viel	*It rains a lot in Ireland*

14.2.2 **The present tense indicates an action or state which began in the past and is still going on at the moment of speaking**

Such sentences typically contain an adverb (*schon* or *bisher*), an adverbial phrase with *seit*, or an adverbial clause with *seit(dem)* or *solange*. These express the idea of 'up to now'.

(a) In 'up-to-now' contexts the PRESENT tense is used in German

This is different to English, where we use the **perfect** tense, typically the perfect progressive (e.g. 'have been doing', etc.):

Ich **stehe** schon lange hier vor dem Bahnhof	*I've been standing in front of the station for a long time*
Seit wann **kennst** du Frau Wiegand?	*How long have you known Mrs Wiegand?*
Ich **suche** sie seit vier Jahren zu verstehen (C. Weyden)	*I have been trying to understand her for four years*
Seitdem die Spanier die deutschen Finanzämter darüber **informieren**, wurden viele Villen rasch verkauft. (HMP).	*Since the Spanish have informed the German tax authorities about it, a lot of villas have been swiftly sold off*
Er **wohnt** in Hamburg, solange ich ihn kenne	*He's been living in Hamburg as long as I've known him*

(b) In a few 'up-to-now' contexts German uses the perfect tense

i.e. the perfect tense, rather than the present tense. These constitute exceptions to the general rule given in (a) above. There are two main types of such contexts:

(i) in negative statements:

Ich **habe** ihn seit Jahren nicht **gesehen**	*I haven't seen him for years*
Seitdem ich ihn kenne, **haben** wir uns nie **gestritten**	*Since I've known him, we have never quarrelled*

However, the present tense is used, even in negative statements, if there has been a continuous action or state lasting up to the present time:

Seit Weihnachten **arbeitet** er nicht mehr	*He hasn't worked since Christmas*
Seitdem ich hier im Dorf wohne, **bin** ich nie einsam	*Since I've been living here in the village, I've never been lonely*

(ii) when referring to a series of repeated actions or states

Er **ist** seit Weihnachten mehrmals krank **gewesen**	*He's been ill several times since Christmas*
Seit ihrer Erkrankung/Seitdem sie krank ist, **hat** sie viele Bücher **gelesen**	*Since she's been ill, she has read a lot of books*

However, the present tense is used to refer to a habit or state which has continued up to the present. English uses a different tense here, too, as can be seen by comparing this example with the one above:

Seit ihrer Erkrankung/Seitdem sie krank ist, **liest** sie viele Bücher	*Since she's been ill, she's been reading a lot of books*

(c) The present tense of *kommen* is often used to refer to the immediate past

Again, the idea is of an action continuing up to the present moment. English normally uses the perfect tense:

Ich **komme**, die Miete zu bezahlen	*I've come to pay the rent*

14.2.3 **The present tense can refer to future time**

(a) German often uses the present tense in contexts where a future tense is needed in English

This applies whether English uses the future tense with 'will/shall/'ll' or 'be going to':

In zwei Stunden **bin** ich wieder da	*I'll be back in two hours*
Wir **finden** es nie	*We're never going to find it*

In practice, the present tense is much more frequent than the future in German to refer to future time as long as it is clear from the context that the future is meant. This is especially the case if there is an adverbial in the sentence pointing to the future:

Ich **schreibe** den Brief heute Abend	*I'll write the letter tonight*
Morgen um diese Zeit **bin** ich in Wien	*This time tomorrow I'll be in Vienna*

But a present tense can always be used in German to refer to future time even when no adverbial is present, as long as the context points unambiguously to the future:

Astrid **holt** uns von der Bahn ab	*Astrid is going to meet us from the station*
Ich erwarte, dass sie **kommt**	*I expect she'll come*
Weitere Einzelheiten **erteilt** Ihnen unser Fachpersonal	*Our specialist staff will give you further information*
Vielleicht **sage** ich es ihm	*Perhaps I'll tell him*

The only contexts where a future tense needs to be used in German are those where the present tense could be interpreted as referring to the present, i.e. if the rest of the context does not make the reference to the future clear. Compare the following pairs of sentences, where we must use the future tense in German if we want to make it clear that the future is meant, because the present tense could only be understood to refer to the present:

Er **wird** wieder in der Bank **arbeiten**	*He's going to work for the bank again*
Er **arbeitet** wieder in der Bank	*He's working for the bank again*
Ich **werde** auf euch **warten**	*I'll be waiting for you*
Ich **warte** auf euch	*I'm waiting for you*
Sie weiß, was **geschehen wird**	*She knows what will happen*
Sie weiß, was **geschieht**	*She knows what is happening*

(b) If the future tense is used where it would be possible to use the present tense, it often emphasises the idea of a prediction, an intention or a supposition

This is particularly the case where reference to the future is clear, e.g. through an adverbial. In English we often use *be going to* (rather than *will*) in such contexts, as this tends to emphasise intention strongly:

Es **wird** morgen wieder **regnen**	*It is going to rain again tomorrow*
Ich **werde** den Brief heute Abend **schreiben**	*I am going to write the letter tonight*
Wir aber fliegen dorthin, wo die Sonne scheint, und keine Wolken **werden** uns jetzt noch **stoppen** (*Grzimek*)	*But we're flying to where the sun shines, and no clouds are going to stop us now*

14.2.4 The present tense is sometimes used to refer to the past

This so-called '**historic present**' is used more often in writing in German than English. It makes the past seem more immediate and it is a common stylistic device in narrative fiction and historical writing:

Mit zuckenden Nerven **marschieren** sie näher, noch immer **versuchen** sie sich gegenseitig zu täuschen, so sehr sie alle schon die Wahrheit **wissen**: dass die Norweger, dass Amundsen ihnen zuvorgekommen **ist**. Bald **zerbricht** der letzte Zweifel . . . (*Zweig*)

Similarly in newspaper headlines:

40-Tonner **zermalmt** Trabi – 2 starben (*BILD*)	*Forty-ton lorry squashes Trabi – two dead*

It is also a typical feature of narration in colloquial speech, as in English:

Gestern Abend **geh** ich ins Café und **seh** den Horst Brunner dort an der Theke sitzen	*Last night I go down the pub and see Horst Brunner sitting there at the bar*

14.3 The past tense and the perfect tense

14.3.1 The uses of the past and the perfect tenses in German: summary

In English there is a clear difference in meaning between the past and the perfect tenses, and the sentences 'I broke my leg' and 'I have broken my leg' are quite distinct in meaning. The English past tense simply tells us that something happened in the past, so that 'I broke my leg' tells us that it happened at some time in the past – and it's probably mended now. The English perfect tense, on the other hand, usually indicates that what happened in the past still has some relevance at the present. When we say 'I have broken my leg', for instance, it usually means that it is still broken at the moment of speaking.

The German sentences *Ich **brach** mir das Bein* and *Ich **habe** mir das Bein **gebrochen*** are deceptively similar to English. However, there is no clear-cut difference in meaning as in English, and in many contexts either is used without any real difference in meaning. Which one is used is often rather a matter of style or register. The main differences between the two German tenses can be summarised as follows:

- The PERFECT tense is used principally:
  - to refer to a past action or event which has relevance to the present
  - in spoken German, to refer to past actions and events

- The PAST tense is used principally:
  - in written German, to refer to past actions and events

More details on specific usage are given in the remainder of this section.

14.3.2 The use of the perfect and past tenses to refer to a past action or event which has continuing relevance in the present

(a) The PERFECT tense is usual in both spoken and written German to indicate a past action or event whose effect is relevant or apparent at the moment of speaking

Linking the past with the present is the typical function of the English perfect tense, and in practice the perfect tense is also normally used in German in such contexts, i.e.:

(i) where the result of a past action or event is still evident at the moment of speaking:

Es **hat** in der Nacht **geschneit** (there's snow on the ground)	*It has snowed in the night*
Sie **hat** sich das Bein **gebrochen** (her leg is still in plaster)	*She's broken her leg*
Meine Tante **ist** gestern **angekommen** (and she's still here)	*My aunt arrived last night*

As the last example above shows, the perfect tense is used in German to express the present relevance of a past action even if there is a past time adverbial in the sentence. English, on the other hand, **always** uses the past tense in sentences which contain adverbials expressing past time.

(ii) to refer to something which happened in the immediate past:

Jetzt **hat** Ballack den Ball **eingeworfen**	*Ballack has just thrown the ball in*
Damit **haben** wir diese kleine Führung **beendet**	*With this we have come to the end of this short guided tour*

(iii) to refer to states or repeated actions which have lasted up to the moment of speaking:

Ich **habe** immer **gefunden**, dass es nützlich ist, viel zu wissen	*I've always found it useful to know a lot*
Ich **habe** ihm wiederholt **gesagt**, dass er ihr schreiben sollte	*I've told him repeatedly that he ought to write to her*
Das Paket **ist** noch nicht **angekommen**	*The parcel hasn't arrived yet*

NB: The **present** tense is used in German to refer to activities or states which began in the past and continue into the present, where English typically uses a perfect progressive, see 14.2.2.

(b) The PAST tense is occasionally used to indicate a past action or event which has relevance for the present

i.e. in the kind of contexts given under (a) above. This use of the past tense is mainly restricted to the following contexts, almost exclusively in written German:

(i) in newspaper headlines and short announcements. In these contexts the past tense, with its single word, can sound neater and snappier:

Lastwagenfahrer **gaben** Blockade am Brenner nach einer Woche auf (*FR*)	*Lorry drivers have given up their blockade on the Brenner pass after a week*
Sie **sahen** soeben einen Bericht von unserem Korrespondenten in Moskau	*You have just been watching a report from our Moscow correspondent*

(ii) with common verbs, especially the auxiliary verbs, and in the passive:

In der letzten Zeit **war** sie sehr krank	*She has been very ill recently*
Er **musste** heute kommen	*He has had to come today*
Noch nie **wurde** ein Auto so oft gebaut (*VW advert*)	*No car has ever been produced in such numbers*

(iii) in relative clauses:

Das sind die ersten Bilder der Unruhen in Birma, die uns **erreichten**	*These are the first pictures which have reached us of the disturbances in Burma*

In all the above examples the perfect tense would be equally possible.

14.3.3 The use of the past and perfect tenses to relate past actions or events

Narrations of past actions and events are typically in the PAST tense in <u>written</u> German and in the PERFECT tense in <u>spoken</u> German. In English, we typically use the past tense to relate an action or event lying entirely in the past. In German, however, while the past tense is usual in such contexts in the written language, the perfect predominates in everyday speech, especially in south Germany.

The characteristic use of the past tense for a written narrative can be seen in the following passage from Bernhard Schlink's novel *Der Vorleser*:

Den Sommer nach dem Prozess **verbrachte** ich im Lesesaal der Universitätsbibliothek. Ich **kam**, wenn der Lesesaal **öffnete**, und **ging**, wenn er **schloss**. An den Wochenenden **lernte** ich zu Hause. Ich **lernte** so ausschließlich, so besessen, dass die Gefühle und Gedanken, die der Prozess betäubt hatte, betäubt **blieben**. Ich **vermied** Kontakte. Ich **zog** zu Hause aus und

mietete ein Zimmer. Die wenigen Bekannten, die mich im Lesesaal oder bei gelegentlichen Kinobesuchen **ansprachen**, **stieß** ich zurück.

In Franz Xaver Kroetz's *Chiemgauer Gschichten*, by contrast, where ordinary people (from South Germany) are telling their stories to the author, the narrative is in the perfect tense:

> Ja, und dann **hats** wieder ein bisschen **gedauert**, bis sie wieder eine Arbeit **gekriegt hat**, also Lohn von ihr **ist** praktisch nichts **eingegangen**. **Hab** ich alles selbst verdienen **müssen**. Da wo wir dann **geheiratet haben**, da **hab** ich zwei Monate so noch **gearbeitet** auf Montage, und dann **bin** ich gekündigt **worden**.

Nevertheless, there are some exceptions to this general tendency for the past tense to be used in written narrative and the perfect tense in spoken narrative:

(a) The past tense in spoken German

In South Germany (and Austria and Switzerland) the past tense is practically never used in everyday speech. However, this is much less true in North Germany (i.e. north of the river Main), where the past tense is quite frequently used in everyday speech, especially in the following contexts:

(i) with commonly used verbs, i.e.:

- *sein, haben, bleiben, gehen, kommen, stehen* and *es gibt*
- the modal auxiliaries
- verbs of saying, thinking and feeling

In this way, the following would be equally frequent in North German speech:

Ich **war** vorige Woche in Bremen	Ich **bin** vorige Woche in Bremen **gewesen**
Sie **konnte** gestern nicht kommen	Sie **hat** gestern nicht kommen **können**
Was **sagten** Sie?	Was **haben** Sie **gesagt**?

The past tense of other verbs can be heard in spoken North German, but, in general, rather less often than the perfect tense.

(ii) with the passive, e.g. *Das alte Haus* **wurde** *abgerissen* or *Das alte Haus* **ist** *abgerissen* **worden**

(iii) in clauses introduced by *als* or *wie*, and in any sentence with the adverb *damals*:

Ich habe sie gesehen, als sie aus der Straßenbahn **ausstieg**	*I saw her when she got out of the tram*
Ich habe gehört, wie sie die Treppe **herunterkam**	*I heard her coming down the stairs*
Damals **mussten** alle Russisch lernen	*At that time everybody had to learn Russian*

(iv) to record a state, or a habitual or repeated action in the past:

Die Rechnung **lag** auf dem Tisch	*The bill was lying on the table*
Bei uns in der alten Heimat **dauerten** die Sommerferien länger als hier	*In our old homeland the summer holidays used to last longer than they do here*
Ich habe gewusst, dass sein Vater **trank**	*I knew his father used to drink*

(b) There is a tendency for a longer narrative to start with a perfect tense, and then continue in the past tense

The perfect is used to set the scene, as it were. This usage is especially frequent in newspaper reports:

10 Tage nach der Jumbo-Katastrophe in Japan **ist** schon wieder eine Boeing **explodiert**. 54 Urlauber **starben** gestern in einem flammenden Inferno auf dem Flughafen Manchester (England). Als ihr Jet nach Korfu (Griechenland) starten **wollte**, **wurde** das linke Triebwerk krachend zerfetzt. Sofort **brannte** die Maschine wie eine Riesenfackel. Im Rumpf eingeschlossene Urlauber **trampelten** andere tot. (*BILD*)

(c) The perfect is sometimes used as a narrative tense in written German

The perfect tense is sometimes used deliberately to give a more colloquial tone. However, particularly outside fiction, it is often treated simply as an alternative to the past and seems to be used for reasons which relate to style, emphasis and sentence rhythm, as in the following text from Grzimek's *Serengeti darf nicht sterben*:

Ein tüchtiger Mann namens Rothe, der Verwalter bei den Siedentopfs **war**, **hat** 1913 die Reste einer uralten Siedlung und eines Friedhofs aus der Jungsteinzeit am Nordende des Kraters **entdeckt**. Schon diese Leute, die einige Jahrhunderte vor Christus **gelebt haben**, **weideten** als Hirten ihr Vieh wie heute die Massai. Rothe **hieß** eigentlich anders, er **war** 1905 bei der ersten finnischen Revolution kurze Zeit Minister **gewesen**, . . . In Ägypten **stellte** ihm die russische Geheimpolizei nach, und so **kam** er als Tierpfleger mit Maultieren nach Deutsch-Ostafrika.

In practice, the past tense could be substituted for any of the perfect tenses in this passage, or vice versa, without any real difference in meaning.

14.3.4 Other uses of the past tense

The perfect tense cannot be used in any of these contexts.

(a) to relate a state or activity which began in the past and was still in progress at a more recent point in the past

This is the equivalent in past time of the use of the present with *seit* phrases, etc. (see 14.2.2). In English the pluperfect tense (especially the pluperfect progressive) is used in such contexts:

Ich **wartete** schon zwei Stunden/seit zwei   *I had been waiting for her for two hours*
   Stunden auf sie
Das Schloss **gehörte** seit Jahrhunderten den   *The castle had belonged to the Counts of Solms*
   Grafen von Solms   *for centuries*

However, as with the use of the perfect tense rather than the present (see 14.2.2), the pluperfect tense, not the past tense, is used in **negative statements** or when referring to a **series** of actions or states:

Ich **hatte** ihm seit Jahren **zugeredet**, sein   *I had been urging him for years to sell his house*
   Haus zu verkaufen

(b) with the sense of a future-in-the-past

In such contexts, the past tense is an uncommon alternative to the *würde*-form of *Konjunktiv II* (the 'conditional', see 16.4.5):

Nachdem er sicher war, dass der Vorgang   *When he was sure that the curtain would not*
   nicht mehr **hochging** (*more usual:*   *go up again, he left the theatre*
   hochgehen würde), verließ er das Theater

(c) to refer to the present moment

This is a special usage to recall information which has already been given in the past:

Wie **war** ihr Name doch gleich?	*What was your name again?*
Wer **erhielt** das Eisbein?	*Who is getting the knuckle of pork?*
Herr Ober, ich **bekam** noch ein Bier	*Waiter, I did order another beer*

14.3.5 **Further uses of the perfect tense**

The past tense cannot be used in any of these contexts.

(a) as an alternative to the future perfect tense

(i) The perfect tense is often used in the sense of a future perfect:

Bis morgen um diese Zeit **habe** ich alles **geregelt**	*By this time tomorrow I shall have settled everything*
Bald **habe** ich den Brief **geschrieben**	*I'll have written the letter soon*

As with the use of the present tense to refer to future time (see 14.2.3), the perfect tense can only substitute for the future perfect if it is clear from the context (e.g. from a time adverbial) that the reference is to the future. There is no comparable usage in English, where the future perfect tense is always used in such contexts. When the future perfect tense is used in such sentences in German, e.g. *Bis morgen um diese Zeit **werde** ich alles **geregelt haben***, there is often an additional sense of a prediction or a supposition, see 14.4.2.

(ii) The perfect is the usual tense in subordinate time clauses with future reference. In these contexts English and German correspond in the use of the perfect tense.

Wenn ich von ihm **gehört habe**, werde ich dir schreiben	*When I've heard from him, I shall write to you*

Very occasionally a future perfect is used in such sentences in written German:

Ich will fortgehen, wenn ich genug **gelesen haben werde** (*Andersch*)	*I intend to leave when I have read enough*

(b) to indicate a characteristic state

The perfect tense can be used in German to indicate an action whose completion can be taken to define a particular person or thing. This usage is particularly common in technical and legal language and has no equivalent in English.

Ein Unglück **ist** schnell **geschehen**	*Accidents happen quickly* (i.e. if you don't watch out)
Ein Akademiker **hat studiert**	*A graduate is a person who has completed a course of studies*
Die Mannschaft, die zuerst 50 Punkte **erreicht hat**, ist Sieger	*The first team to reach 50 points is the winner*

14.4 **The future tense and the future perfect tense**

The future tense in German is formed with the auxiliary verb *werden* and the **infinitive** (e.g. *Ich werde sie am Montag sehen*). The future perfect is formed with *werden*, the **past participle** of the main verb, and the **infinitive** of the auxiliary verb *haben* or *sein* (depending on what main verb is involved, e.g. *Ich werde den Brief geschrieben haben; Sie wird schon gegangen sein*). The conjugation of these tenses is explained and shown in detail in 12.3.1 and Table 12.5.

The English future has two forms, one with the auxiliary *will* (in some contexts, especially in British English, *shall*), which is usually reduced to *'ll* in speech (e.g. *I'll probably see her on Monday*), and one with the phrase *be going to* (e.g. *I'm going to see her on Monday*). The difference in meaning between these English forms is slight, although *be going to* is rather less frequent, more typical of informal registers, and tends to emphasise immediacy or intention more strongly.

14.4.1 The basic uses of the future tense and the future perfect tense are to refer to future time

The **future tense** (sometimes called *Futur I* in German) relates an action or event which will happen after the time of speaking:

Ich **werde** sie nicht mehr **sehen**	*I won't/shan't see her again*
Wirst du ihr helfen **können**?	*Will you be able to help her?*

The **future perfect** tense (sometimes called *Futur II* in German) is a 'relative' tense; it indicates an action or event which will take place **before** another action or event in the future:

Gewiss **wird** sie den Brief bis morgen Abend **geschrieben haben**	*She will certainly have written the letter by tomorrow evening*

However, if the reference to future time is otherwise clear from the context, German often prefers the present tense to the future (see 14.2.3), and the perfect tense to the future perfect (see 14.3.5a). However, there are contexts where these tenses must be used simply to indicate futurity, since the present or the perfect would have their basic meaning:

Ich mag sie nicht und **werde** sie nie **mögen**	*I don't like her and I'll never like her*
Hat er Ihnen nicht gesagt, dass er Sie **besuchen wird**?	*Didn't he tell you that he's going to visit you?*
Am Montag **wird** sie den Gipfel **erreicht haben**	*On Monday she'll have reached the summit*

14.4.2 The future and future perfect tenses often convey the idea of an intention or an assumption

This is generally the case when future time reference is otherwise clear from the context, and the present or the perfect tense could be used rather than the future tenses:

Morgen **wird** es bestimmt **schneien**	*It will definitely snow tomorrow*
Ich **werde** es heute Abend noch **erledigen**	*I am going to finish it tonight*
Morgen **wird** er die Arbeit **beendet haben**	*He'll have finished the work tomorrow*

14.4.3 The future tenses often simply express an assumption in the present

In these contexts these tenses do not refer to future time at all; the future refers to the present and the future perfect to the past. English uses its future tenses in a similar way:

Sie **wird** bereits zu Hause **sein**	*She'll be home already*
Er ist nicht gekommen. Er **wird** wieder zu viel zu tun **haben**	*He hasn't come. He'll have too much to do again*

Sie **wird** den Zug **verpasst haben**	*She'll have missed the train*
Sie **wird** sich gestern ein neues Handy **gekauft haben**	*She'll have bought a new mobile/cellphone yesterday*

When used like this to express a supposition, these tenses are often accompanied by the particle *wohl* (see 10.35.1):

Sie wird **wohl** bereits zu Hause sein
Sie wird **wohl** den Zug verpasst haben

NB: This sense of the future and future perfect is very similar to the meaning of *dürfte* (see 17.2.2), so that *Sie wird bereits zu Hause sein* means much the same as *Sie dürfte bereits zu Hause sein.*

14.5 The pluperfect tense

The German pluperfect tense is formed with the **past tense** of *haben* or *sein* (depending on the verb involved) and the **past participle**: *Ich hatte sie nicht gesehen; Ich war schon gegangen*, see 12.3 and Table 12.5. This is similar to the formation of the pluperfect in English (e.g. 'I hadn't seen her').

14.5.1 The German pluperfect tense mainly indicates a past within the past

(a) The German pluperfect tense is a relative tense

Like the English pluperfect, it places an action or event further back in the past than the time of the context. It is characteristically used in clauses introduced by *nachdem* (see 19.3.4):

Nachdem sie **gegangen war**, fiel ihr ein, was sie **vergessen hatte**	*After she had gone she remembered what she had forgotten*
Das bemerkte man erst, nachdem man Platz **genommen hatte** (*Morgner*)	*You only noticed that after you had sat down*

But it is used in many other types of context to indicate a more **remote past**:

Wir warteten, bis der Zug **abgefahren war**	*We waited until the train had left*
Sie kamen zu spät, denn das Hochwasser **hatte** den Damm schon **überflutet**	*They came too late, as the high water had already flooded over the embankment*

(b) The perfect tense is occasionally used where one would expect a pluperfect

This may emphasise the immediacy of a state or an action. The effect is rather similar to that of the 'historic present', see 14.2.4:

Dann seufzte sie auf eine Weise, die mir deutlich machte, wie alt sie **geworden ist** (*Böll*)	*Then she sighed in a way which made it clear to me how old she had become*

This usage is quite frequent in writing, and it is increasingly common in everyday speech.

(c) The past tense is sometimes used for an expected pluperfect

This usage is mainly literary and is usually motivated by stylistic reasons, the one-word form being preferred in context:

. . . doch ergab der Befund jene hoffnungslose Krankheit, die man **vermutete** (*Dürrenmatt*)	*. . . but the investigation revealed the terminal disease which had been suspected*

14.5.2 **The pluperfect tense is sometimes used in colloquial German simply to refer to the past**

i.e. the pluperfect occurs where a past or perfect tense would be expected:

Eva **hatte** dich **gesucht**	*Eva was looking for you*
Wer **war** das **gewesen**?	*Who was that?*

This 'pseudopluperfect', is increasingly common in everyday speech, but it is not accepted as standard.

14.5.3 **Complex pluperfect tense forms**

In colloquial speech in South Germany the **pluperfect** tense is commonly formed with the **perfect** tense of the auxiliaries *haben* or *sein*. For example, *Ich habe ihn gesehen gehabt*, is used for standard German *Ich hatte ihn gesehen*. Forms like this are now widespread in spoken German and no longer restricted to the South. Indeed, if an extra dimension of remoteness in time is needed, the **pluperfect** tense of the auxiliary is sometimes used, e.g.: *Sie hatte ihn gesehen gehabt, bevor er sie bemerkt hatte*. This form is very common in speech if the action has been reversed again, e.g.:

Sie hatte ihren Schlüssel vergessen gehabt	*She had forgotten her key*
	(but she's remembered it again now)

These complex pluperfects are mainly typical of informal colloquial registers and considered to be non-standard. However, they are not unknown in writing:

Er dachte: Du kannst jetzt nichts gesehen haben, du kannst wegdrücken . . . und **hast** bloß den Anschluss **verloren gehabt** und bist kein Jäger (*Gaiser*)	*He thought 'You can't have seen anything now, you can sneak off . . . You had just got left behind and you're not a rifleman'*
Wir **haben** uns alle schon daran **gewöhnt gehabt**, dass nichts geschieht, aber immer etwas geschehen soll (*Musil*)	*We had all got used to the idea that nothing was going to happen but that something always ought to happen*

14.6 **German equivalents for the English progressive tenses**

14.6.1 **There are _no_ progressive tenses in German**

The distinction between the English **progressive present** tense 'He is singing well' (i.e. at the moment) and the **simple present** tense 'He sings well' (i.e. usually) cannot be expressed by using different forms of the verb in German. In most contexts the distinction is simply ignored in German and 'Er singt gut' is used for both these English sentences.

NB: The English perfect progressive can indicate that an action beginning in the past is still going on at the moment of speaking, e.g. *I have been waiting here for an hour*. German uses the simple present tense in these contexts, see 14.2.2.

14.6.2 **Indicating continuous action in German**

Nevertheless, there are contexts where we need to make it clear in German that we are dealing with a continuous action. For instance, an English sentence like 'He was reading *War and Peace* yesterday' implies that he didn't finish reading it, whereas to say in German *Gestern las er „Krieg und Frieden"* or *Gestern hat er „Krieg und Frieden" gelesen* could imply that he <u>did</u> finish it (which is unlikely in a single day). In such contexts, German has a number of possibilities for making it clear that the action was continuous or unfinished, i.e.:

(a) By using an appropriate adverb

(i) especially *eben* or *gerade*:

Ich schreibe **eben** einen Brief an Anja	*I'm writing a letter to Anja*
Er rasiert sich **gerade**	*He's shaving*

(ii) With verbs of motion, *schon* or *gleich* can often be used:

Ich fahre **schon**	*I'm leaving*
Sie kommt **gleich**	*She's coming*

(iii) Other adverbs or particles can be used in other contexts:

Ich habe ihn **letzthin** zweimal in der Woche gesehen	*I've been meeting him twice a week (recently)*
Ich kümmere mich **eben mal** darum	*I'm seeing to it now*

(iv) The sense of habitual or repeated action which is expressed by a simple (i.e non-progressive) tense in English can be indicated by an adverb in German:

Ich stehe **immer** um sechs auf	*I always get up at six*
Sie spielt **meistens** gut	*She (usually) plays well*

(b) By using (*gerade/eben*) *dabei sein* followed by an infinitive with *zu*

Ich bin **gerade dabei**, das Zimmer ein bisschen aufzuräumen	*I'm just tidying the room up a bit*
Gestern war er **gerade dabei**, „Krieg und Frieden" zu lesen	*He was reading* War and Peace *yesterday*

(c) By using a construction with an infinitival noun

(i) In standard German *beim* is used with an infinitival noun (see 13.4.3a):

Als seine Frau zurückkam, war er **beim Kochen**	*When his wife returned, he was cooking*
Wir waren **beim Kartenspielen**, als er klingelte	*We were playing cards when he rang the bell*

(ii) In Northwest Germany, *am* is used with an infinitival noun to express continuous action:

Wir sind **am Arbeiten**	*We are working*
In Köln ist es immer **am Regnen**	*It's always raining in Cologne*
Diese Lobby ist ständig **am Wachsen** (*FAZ - Leserbrief*)	*This lobby is growing all the time*

This usage was originally regional, and characteristic of the Northwest. It has recently become much more widely used in colloquial speech everywhere, but it is still considered non-standard and is rarely found in writing.

(d) by using a noun with a prepositional phrase

Wir sind **an der Arbeit**	*We're working*
Er liest **in der Zeitung**	*He's reading the newspaper*
Sie strickte **an einem Strumpf**	*She was knitting a stocking*

(e) by using a different verb

Some German verbs, especially those with prefixes (see 22.4–22.5), imply the completion of an action. The corresponding unprefixed verbs do not necessarily imply that the action has finished and can in certain contexts correspond more closely to the sense of an English progressive tense:

Sie **erkämpften** die Freiheit ihres Landes	*They fought for their country's freedom* (i.e. they were successful)
Sie **kämpften** für die Freiheit ihres Landes	*They were fighting for their country's freedom*
Sie **erstiegen** den Berg	*They climbed the mountain*
Sie **stiegen** auf den Berg	*They were climbing the mountain* (i.e. in the process of climbing, or only part of the way)
Wir **haben** die Würste **aufgegessen**	*We ate the sausages (up)*
Wir **haben** die Würste **gegessen**	*We were eating the sausages*

15 The passive

We typically express actions by using the ACTIVE VOICE, both in English and in German. The active sentence tells us what is happening and who or what is doing it. But we can present a different perspective on an action by using the PASSIVE VOICE, which places the emphasis on what is going on, without necessarily saying who or what is doing it.

active voice: Die Schlange frisst **den Frosch**
passive voice: **Der Frosch** wird (von der Schlange) gefressen

Most active sentences with a TRANSITIVE VERB (i.e. a verb which has an accusative object, see 18.3) can be turned into passive sentences. The **accusative object** of the **active sentence** becomes **the subject** of the **passive sentence**. The subject of the active sentence (the person or thing carrying out the action, called the **agent**) can also appear in a phrase using *von* or *durch* (= English 'by'), but it is often left out altogether. The possibility of talking about an action without saying who or what did it is a major motivation for using the passive rather than the active.

There are <u>two</u> passive forms in German, using the auxiliary verbs *werden* or *sein* together with the past participle:

- The *werden*-**passive** (e.g. *die Stadt wurde zerstört*) expresses a process (German: *Vorgangspassiv*) and is closely related to the corresponding active voice.
- The *sein*-**passive** (e.g. *die Stadt war zerstört*) expresses a state (German: *Zustandspassiv*). Its use is more restricted than that of the (much more frequent) *werden*-passive.

The use of these, and other German constructions which are the equivalent of passives, is explained in this chapter:

- The *werden*-**passive** (section 15.1)
- The *sein*-**passive**, and the differences between it and the *werden*-passive (section 15.2)
- The use of *von* and *durch* for English 'by' with the passive (section 15.3)
- Other German constructions with **passive meaning** (section 15.4)
- The use of the active and passive voice in German and English (section 15.5)

TABLE 15.1 Active and passive sentences

Tense	Active	Passive
Present	Der Arzt **heilt den Patienten** *The doctor **heals the patient***	**Der Patient wird** (vom Arzt) **geheilt** ***The patient is healed** (by the doctor)*
Past	Die Bauleute **rissen das Haus ab** *The builders **pulled down the house***	**Das Haus wurde** (von den Bauleuten) **abgerissen** ***The house was pulled down** (by the builders)*
Perfect	Die Firma **hat den Angestellten entlassen** *The company **has sacked the employee***	**Der Angestellte ist** (von der Firma) **entlassen worden** ***The employee has been sacked** (by the company)*
Future	Der Computer **wird das Buch verdrängen** *The computer **will replace the book***	**Das Buch wird** (vom Computer) **verdrängt werden** ***The book will be replaced** (by the computer)*

15.1 The *werden*-passive

15.1.1 The *werden*-passive has the same range of tenses and moods as the active voice

The conjugation of these tenses in the indicative is given in Table 12.6. For passive forms in the subjunctive mood, see section 12.5. Table 15.1 shows the relationship between the tenses of the active and passive voice.

(a) The use of the passive tenses is in general the same as in the active

(see Chapter 14). There is slight variation in use in a few instances:

(i) The future tense is little used in the passive, and the present tense is preferred unless there is a risk of being misunderstood (see 14.4). Thus, in the sentence

Das Buch **wird** nächste Woche **gelesen werden**	*The book will be read next week*

normal usage will prefer the present tense *Das Buch* **wird** *nächste Woche* **gelesen** rather than the future, and this is possible because the phrase *nächste Woche* makes the time reference clear. However, in the sentence

Das Haus **wird abgerissen werden**	*The house will be pulled down*

we cannot replace the future tense by the present tense without changing the meaning. *Das Haus* **wird abgerissen** can only mean 'The house is being pulled down'.

(ii) The past tense of the passive is quite common in both written and spoken German, even in contexts where the perfect tense might be expected in the active voice (see 14.3.2).

(b) The *werden*-passive is hardly ever used in commands

To give commands in the passive, the *sein*-passive is used, e.g. *Sei gegrüßt! Sei beruhigt!* (see 15.2.1).

15.1.2 The *werden*-passive can be formed from most transitive verbs

i.e. verbs which are used with a direct object in the accusative case, see 18.3.1.

(a) The accusative object of the active verb becomes the subject of the corresponding passive construction

Mein Vater liest **diesen Roman**	→	**Dieser Roman** wird von meinem Vater gelesen
My father is reading this novel		*This novel is being read by my father*

Further examples are shown in Table 15.1.

(b) A few transitive verbs cannot be used in the *werden*-passive

This group consists in particular of certain verbs of knowing, containing, possessing and receiving, i.e. *bedeuten, bekommen, besitzen, enthalten, erhalten, haben, kennen, kriegen, umfassen, wissen*. These are not used in the passive in German, although some of the English equivalents of these verbs do have passive forms. In German other constructions are used for these verbs, in particular active forms of another verb or a construction with *man*:

Dieses Schloss gehört dem Grafen von Libowitz	*This palace **is owned** by Count von Libowitz*
(i.e. NOT *wird . . . besessen)	

Ihr Brief traf gestern ein (i.e. NOT **wurde . . . erhalten*)	*Your letter **was received** yesterday*

Man wusste nicht, wie viele Kinder
   kommen würden
   (i.e. NOT **es wurde . . . gewusst*)
	*It **was not known** how many children would
	   come*

NB: *enthalten* can be used with *sein*, e.g. *Wieviel Essig ist in diesem Gefäß enthalten?* but this is not really a passive construction. A passive of *erhalten* can be formed with *bleiben*, see 15.2.2c.

(c) No passive can be formed with the verbs of perception followed by a bare infinitive

(see 13.3.1). These verbs can be used in the passive with an 'ing'-form in English, but the equivalent sentences in German must use alternative constructions, usually with the active voice:

Man hörte ihn singen	*He was heard singing*
Ein Vorbeigehender sah ihn in das Haus einbrechen	*He was seen breaking into the house by a passer-by*

15.1.3 Passive constructions with verbs governing a dative object, a genitive object or a prepositional object

In German <u>only</u> the **accusative (direct) object** of a transitive verb can become the **subject** of a passive construction. This is an important restriction which does not apply in English. It means that the dative object, the genitive object or the prepositional object of a verb can never become the subject of a passive construction in German:

(a) If a verb which takes a dative object is used in the passive, the dative object remains in the dative case

This is the case with all those verbs which govern the dative case, and have no accusative object (see 18.4.1).

Astrid dankte **ihm** für seine Hilfe
   Astrid thanked him for his help
	→ **Ihm** wurde für seine Hilfe gedankt
	   He was thanked for his help

As the dative object remains in the dative, the verbs in these passive constructions are **subjectless** (or **impersonal**) and the verb has the endings of the third person singular. Further examples:

Die Polizei kann **Ihnen** helfen
   The police can help you
	→ **Ihnen** kann geholfen werden
	   You can be helped

Er empfahl **mir**, eine Kur zu nehmen
   *He recommended me to take a course
   of treatment at a spa*
	→ **Mir** wurde empfohlen, eine Kur zu nehmen
	   *I was recommended to take a course
	   of treatment at a spa*

The dative object does not need to be placed before the verb, but if it is placed later in the sentence the pronoun *es* (see 3.6.2a) has to be used in first position in the clause, before the verb. Compare the following (equally acceptable) alternatives to the examples above:

Es kann Ihnen geholfen werden
Es wurde mir empfohlen, eine Kur zu nehmen

(b) With verbs which have both an accusative object and a dative object, the dative object remains in the dative in the passive

Details on these *einem etwas* verbs are given in 18.4.2. In German, only an accusative object can become the subject of a passive verb. This differs from English, where, with many verbs which have two objects, either can become the subject of the passive. Thus, an English sentence like *He gave the old man the money* can be converted into the passive in two ways, with the direct object *the money* or the indirect object *the old man* as the subject. Compare the following sentences and their German equivalents:

The money (direct object) was given to the old man   *Das Geld wurde dem alten Mann gegeben*

The old man (indirect object) was given the money   *Dem alten Mann wurde das Geld gegeben*

The direct object *das Geld* of the equivalent German sentence *Er gab dem alten Mann das Geld* can be the subject of the passive sentence in German, as in English. However the indirect (dative) object *dem alten Mann* must remain in the dative case in German. As these are effectively impersonal or 'subjectless' constructions, see 15.1.4, the verb is always in the form of the third person singular. Compare:

The old men **were** given the money   *Den alten Männern **wurde** das Geld gegeben*

Note that a dative object can become the subject of a passive construction with *bekommen* or *kriegen*, see 15.4.2.

(c) The passive infinitive of a verb which governs the dative case cannot be used in an infinitive clause with *zu*

Sentences like 'He could not hope to be helped' are quite usual in English. In German, though, we cannot say **Er konnte nicht hoffen geholfen zu werden*, since *helfen* governs a dative and its object cannot be used as the subject of a passive construction. We have to use a *dass*-clause in such cases:

Er konnte nicht hoffen, dass ihm geholfen   *He could not hope to be helped*
wurde
Er besteht darauf, dass ihm geantwortet wird   *He insists on being answered*

(d) Subjectless passives are also used with verbs which govern a genitive object or a prepositional object

See 18.5 and 18.6 for details on these verbs. Like dative objects, genitive objects and prepositional objects remain in the same form in the passive:

Sie gedachten **der Toten**   →   **Der Toten** wurde gedacht
    They remembered the dead   *The dead were remembered*
Meine Mutter sorgt **für die Kinder**   →   **Für die Kinder** wird gesorgt
    My mother is taking care of the children   *The children are being taken care of*

With these verbs, too, the genitive or the prepositional phrase can be placed later in the sentence rather than at the beginning, but, similarly, *es* then has to be inserted before the verb:

Es wurde der Toten gedacht   **Es** wird für die Kinder gesorgt

As with the constructions with a dative object (see (b) above), the verb is always in the form of the third person singular.

NB: In practice, *gedenken* is the only verb governing the genitive which is used in the passive in modern German.

15.1.4 The 'subjectless' *werden*-passive

(a) The *werden*-passive can be used without a subject to denote an activity in general

A sentence like *Es wird getanzt* simply means 'There is dancing going on' without any indication of who is doing it. No comparable construction exists in English. The verb has the third person singular endings:

Sie hörten, wie im Nebenzimmer **geredet wurde**	*They heard people talking in the next room*
Hier darf nicht **geraucht werden**	*Smoking is not allowed here*
Vor Hunden **wird gewarnt**	*Beware of dogs*
Heute **ist** mit den Bauarbeiten **begonnen worden** (*ARD*)	*They started building today*

(b) A subjectless passive can be formed from any verb which expresses a continuous activity

This construction can be used not only with transitive verbs, but also with verbs which otherwise cannot form a passive, i.e. intransitive verbs and, in colloquial German, even reflexive verbs:

Im Flugzeug darf ab Herbst **gesurft** und **gesimst werden**	*From the autumn it will be permitted to use the internet and send text messages in aeroplanes*
An dem Abend **wurde** viel **gesungen**	*There was a lot of singing that evening*
Jetzt **wird sich gewaschen**	*It's time to get washed*

NB: This is basically the same construction as that used with verbs which do not govern an accusative object (and which, strictly speaking, are also intransitive), see 15.1.3.

(c) The pronoun *es* is inserted in a main clause if there is no other word or phrase before the verb

(see 3.6.2a for further details on this use of *es*):

Es wurde auf den Straßen getanzt	*There was dancing in the streets*
Es wird besonders rücksichtslos geparkt (*ARD*)	*People are parking in a particularly inconsiderate way*

(d) The subjectless passive is often used to give commands

(see 16.2 for further details on commands):

Jetzt wird gearbeitet!	*Let's get down to work now*
Jetzt wird nicht gelacht!	*No laughing now!*

15.2 The *sein*-passive

15.2.1 Forms of the *sein*-passive

The conjugation of verbs in the indicative mood of the *sein*-passive is given in Table 12.7. Subjunctive forms are explained in section 12.5. In practice, only a limited range of tenses and moods is in use:

Present tense:	Ich **bin** beruhigt	**Past tense:**	Ich **war** beruhigt
Konjunktiv I:	Ich **sei** beruhigt	*Konjunktiv II:*	Ich **wäre** beruhigt
Imperative:	**Sei** beruhigt		

The past tense tends to be used rather than the perfect tense, although the perfect tense is sometimes heard in spoken German and is occasionally found in writing:

Vierzig Lehrer **sind** gestern als krank **gemeldet gewesen** (*Zeit*)	*Forty teachers were reported sick yesterday*

The future tense (e.g. *Die Bilder **werden** morgen entwickelt **sein***) is very rare.

15.2.2 **The *sein*-passive and the *werden*-passive**

The existence of two quite distinct passive forms in German, and the fact that the less frequently used of them looks deceptively like the English passive with *be*, means that English learners need to pay particular attention to the distinction between the two, which is explained in full in this section.

(a) The *sein*-passive indicates the state which the subject of the verb is in as the result of a previous action

This is reflected in its German name: *Zustandspassiv*. The *werden*-passive, on the other hand, relates an action or process, hence its German name: *Vorgangspassiv*.

(i) The following sentence illustrates the difference between the two passives:

Als ich um fünf kam, **war** die Tür **geschlossen**, aber ich weiß nicht, wann sie **geschlossen wurde**	*When I came at five the door was shut, but I don't know when it was shut*

In the first case, someone had **already shut** the door by the time I arrived, i.e. it was in a **state** of being shut, and for this reason the *sein*-passive is used. In the second case I am referring to the time when the **action** of shutting the door occurred, and the *werden*-passive is used.

(ii) As with the *werden*-passive, see 15.1.3, only the accusative object of a transitive verb can become the subject of a *sein*-passive. With verbs which take a dative, genitive or prepositional object, a 'subjectless' construction must be used in the *sein*-passive too:

Damit ist **den Kranken** nicht geholfen	*The patients have not been helped by that*
Für die Verletzten ist gesorgt	*The wounded have been taken care of*

NB: In practice, few intransitive verbs are used in the *sein*-passive, chiefly *dienen, helfen, nützen, schaden, sorgen für.*

(iii) The *werden*-passive is more frequent than the *sein*-passive and it can be used with more verbs. Nevertheless, the *sein*-passive can be quite common in some registers, e.g. in newspaper reports, which often have reason to refer to states or to the results of actions, and also in narrative fiction:

Deutschland **ist** fest in die NATO **eingebunden** (*Welt*)
Dass die Wahlergebnisse in der DDR **gefälscht waren**, bestreitet auch Modrow nicht (*Spiegel*)

(b) Examples of the difference between the *sein*-passive and the *werden*-passive

A possible source of confusion for English learners is that the English passive, which uses the auxiliary 'be', <u>looks</u> like the *sein*-passive. The examples below show that the two passives have distinct meanings and are rarely interchangeable:

Der Tisch **wird gedeckt**	*The table is being laid* (i.e. someone is performing the action of laying the table)
Der Tisch **ist gedeckt**	*The table is laid* (i.e. someone has already laid it)
Die Stadt **wurde** 1993 **zerstört**	*The town was destroyed in 1993* (i.e. the action took place in 1993)
Die Stadt **war zerstört**	*The town was destroyed* (i.e. someone had already destroyed it)

Das Rathaus **wurde** allmählich von Demonstranten **umringt**	*The town hall was gradually (being) surrounded by demonstrators* (i.e. the demonstrators were in the process of surrounding it)
Das Rathaus **war** von Demonstranten **umringt**	*The town hall was surrounded by demonstrators* (i.e. the demonstrators were already all round the town hall)

(c) Indicators pointing to the use of the *werden*-passive or the *sein*-passive

In practice, there are a number of indicators which can prove helpful in determining whether to use the *sein*-passive or the *werden*-passive:

(i) The *werden*-passive often corresponds to an English progressive tense, while this is never the case with the *sein*-passive. As the examples in (b) above show, this is especially the case in the present tense.

(ii) As the *sein*-passive relates the state resulting from a previous action, its meaning is close to that of the perfect tense, since the perfect tense often presents a result (see 14.3.2). This means, for example, the following pairs of sentences are very close in meaning:

Das Haus **ist gebaut**	Das Haus **ist gebaut worden**
Die Stadt **war zerstört**	Die Stadt **war zerstört worden**

As a consequence, the natural English equivalent of a German *sein*-passive is often a perfect or pluperfect tense rather than a present or a past tense:

Das Auto **ist repariert**	*The car has been repaired*
Rund 2500 Polizeibeamte riegelten die Stadt ab, über die ein umfassendes Demonstrationsverbot **verhängt war** (*Welt*)	*About 2500 police officers cordoned off the city, which had been made subject to a comprehensive ban on demonstrations*

(iii) In the *sein*-passive, the past participle is essentially descriptive, being used with the force of an adjective describing the state of the subject of the verb. For example, *geöffnet* in the sentence *Die Tür ist geöffnet* has much the same function as *offen* in *Die Tür ist offen*. Compare also:

Der Brief **ist geschrieben**	Der Brief ist fertig
Die Stadt **war zerstört**	Die Stadt war kaputt

The past participles of many reflexive verbs (which cannot form a passive) can similarly be used with *sein* with the force of an adjective:

Das Mädchen **ist verliebt**	(compare: *Das Mädchen hat sich verliebt*)
Ich **bin erholt**	(compare: *Ich habe mich erholt*)

The past participle can be used in a similar way with the verbs *bleiben* and *scheinen*:

Das Museum **bleibt geschlossen**	*The museum remains closed*
Der Wagen **schien** leicht **beschädigt**	*The car seemed slightly damaged*
Nur Bruchstücke dieser Skulptur **sind erhalten geblieben**	*Only fragments of this sculpture have been preserved*

(iv) As the *sein*-perfect expresses a state resulting from a previous action, it is normally only used with verbs whose action produces a clear result, e.g. *bauen, begraben, beunruhigen, brechen, öffnen, reparieren, schreiben, verletzen, waschen, zerstören*, etc. These are typically verbs which express a change in location or a change of state. Compare the following examples on page 304:

Meine Hand ist verletzt	*My hand is injured* (and you can see the resulting injury)
Mein Wagen ist beschädigt	*My car is damaged* (and you can see the resulting damage)

By contrast, verbs whose action produces no tangible or visible result, like *bewundern* or *zeigen*, cannot be used in the *sein*-passive at all, as admiring or showing do not involve any kind of result. Other verbs which are not used in the *sein*-passive include:

anbieten	*offer*	brauchen	*need*
begegnen	*meet*	erinnern	*remind*
bemerken	*notice*	loben	*praise*
betrachten	*look at*	sehen	*see*

(d) The *sein*- and *werden*-passive with *geboren*

Current usage with this verb is as follows:

(i) *Ich bin geboren* is used when no other circumstances or only the place of birth are mentioned:

Wann **sind** Sie **geboren**?
Ich **bin** in Hamburg **geboren**

(ii) *Ich wurde geboren* is used if further circumstances, or the date, are mentioned:

Ich **wurde** im Jahre 1985 in Hamburg **geboren**
Als ich **geboren wurde**, schneite es

(iii) Referring to people who are dead, either passive may be used:

Goethe **wurde/war** im Jahre 1749 in Frankfurt **geboren**

15.2.3 The *sein*-passive can indicate a continuous state

Diese Insel **ist** von Kannibalen **bewohnt**	*The island is inhabited by cannibals*
Die Oberrheinebene **ist** durch ihre Randgebirge vor rauhen Winden **geschützt** (*Brinkmann*)	*The Upper Rhine plain is protected from harsh winds by the hills which fringe it*
Die Häuser **sind** nur durch einen Drahtzaun von der Müllverbrennungsanlage **getrennt**	*The houses are only separated from the incinerating plant by a wire fence*
Das Esszimmer **ist** von einem großen Kronleuchter **beleuchtet**	*The dining-room is lit by a large chandelier*
Die Bücher in der alten Bibliothek **sind** mit Staub **bedeckt**	*The books in the old library are covered with dust*

Here we are not dealing with the result of a process, but with a lasting state, often a permanent one. In such sentences, the *werden*-passive and the *sein*-passive are interchangeable as long as the *werden*-passive cannot be interpreted as referring to an action. Thus, the following are equally acceptable alternatives to the first four examples above:

Diese Insel **wird** von Kannibalen bewohnt
Die Oberrheinebene **wird** durch ihre Randgebirge vor rauhen Winde geschützt
Die Häuser **werden** nur durch einen Drahtzaun von der Müllverbrennungsanlage getrennt
Das Esszimmer **wird** von einem großen Kronleuchter beleuchtet

But NOT: *Die Bücher in der alten Bibliothek **werden** mit Staub bedeckt*, as this would mean someone is covering them with dust.

15.3 *von, durch* and *mit* with the passive

A major motivation for using the passive rather than the active is to avoid mentioning who is performing the action, and this is the case with 90% of passive sentences in German. However, if required, the **agent** (i.e. the person or thing carrying out the action) can be included in a passive construction by adding a prepositional phrase introduced by *von* or *durch*, which correspond to English *by*.

The traditional rule of thumb is that *von* is used with persons, *durch* with things. This is a useful guideline, but it is not fully reliable. Phrases with the agent occur chiefly with the *werden*-passive. With the *sein*-passive they occur mainly when it is a matter of a continuing state, as in 15.2.3.

15.3.1 *von* indicates the AGENT who actually carries out the action

This is usually a person, but can be an inanimate force:

Ich war **von meinem Onkel** gewarnt worden	*I had been warned by my uncle*
Sie wurde **von zwei Polizeibeamten** verhaftet	*She was arrested by two police officers*
Die Stadt wurde **von einem großen Waldbrand** bedroht	*The city was threatened by a huge forest fire*

15.3.2 *durch* indicates the MEANS by which the action is carried out

This is most often a thing which is the involuntary cause of the occurrence, but it can be a person acting as an intermediary. Thus, we would say *Ich wurde **durch einen Boten** benachrichtigt* 'I was informed by a messenger', not *von einem Boten*, because the messenger was bringing a message from someone else.

Die Ernte wurde **durch den Hagel** vernichtet	*The crop was destroyed by hail*
Ich wurde **durch den starken Verkehr** aufgehalten	*I was held up by the heavy traffic*
Die Hühnerpest wird **durch ein mikroskopisch nicht nachweisbares Virus** verursacht (*ND*)	*Fowl pest is caused by a virus which is not detectable under the microscope*

15.3.3 The distinction between *von* and *durch* is not always upheld

(a) In practice there is considerable hesitation between *von* and *durch*

It is often not wholly clear whether we are dealing with the 'agent' or the 'means'. *von* is always usual for persons who obviously carried out the action themselves. However, when this might be a matter of interpretation, or with 'things' (like storms and earthquakes) which people might think of as actually carrying out an action, either *von* or *durch* can be acceptable, as in the following sentences:

Sie ist **von den Demonstranten/durch die Demonstranten** aufgehalten worden	*She was held up by the demonstrators*
Der Baum ist **von dem Blitz/durch den Blitz** getroffen worden	*The tree has been struck by lightning*

In the first sentence *von den Demonstranten* could imply that the demonstrators held her up deliberately, whereas *durch die Demonstranten* could mean that it just happened to be the case that she was held up by them. However, such fine distinctions are not always made in practice.

(b) The difference between *von* **and** *durch* **is most clear when both are used in the same sentence**

Ich war v**on meinem Onkel durch seinen Sohn** gewarnt worden	*I had been warned by my uncle through his son* (My uncle is doing the warning, his son is the intermediary)
Das Gebäude wurde **von Terroristen durch einen Sprengstoffanschlag** zerstört	*The building was destroyed by terrorists in a bomb attack* (Terrorists destroyed it, the bombs were the means)

15.3.4 A phrase with *mit* can be used to indicate the INSTRUMENT used to perform an action

Das Schloss musste **mit einem Hammer** geöffnet werden	*The lock had to be opened with a hammer*
Dieser Brief ist **mit der Hand** geschrieben	*This letter was written by hand*

15.4 Other passive constructions

German has a wide range of alternative means of expressing the passive.

15.4.1 *man* is often used in German where English naturally uses a passive

See 5.5.18 for details on the use of *man*:

Man sagt, dass . . .	*It is said that . . .*
Man hatte ihn davor **gewarnt**	*He had been warned about it*
Das **macht man** nicht	*That's not done*

15.4.2 A passive construction is possible with *bekommen* and *kriegen*

(a) By using the verbs *bekommen* **or** *kriegen* **a dative object can be made into the subject of a passive construction**

As explained in 15.1.3, a dative object cannot be turned into the subject of the *werden*-passive. However, if *bekommen* or *kriegen* is used with the past participle of another verb, a dative object can be converted into the subject:

Ich schenke **meinem Bruder** das Buch → **Mein Bruder kriegt/bekommt** das Buch (von mir) **geschenkt**

Ich widerspreche **meinem Bruder**   →   **Mein Bruder kriegt/bekommt** (von mir) **widersprochen**

This construction is chiefly found in speech (especially with *kriegen*), and not all Germans accept it as correct in writing, although it is increasingly frequent. The conditions under which it is possible are not fully clear, but in general it appears that it can only be used with verbs which express an action and where the original dative object can be interpreted in some way as receiving something.

NB: Less commonly, the verb *erhalten* is used rather than *bekommen* or *kriegen*, e.g. *Sie erhält die Kosten erstattet*.

(b) The *bekommen/kriegen*-passive can be formed from various kinds of dative object

Specifically:

(i) from the dative object of a verb which governs both a dative and an accusative object (see 18.4.2). In practice this passive occurs most frequently with this type of verb, and these constructions are now generally accepted. The English equivalent may be a passive, or a construction with 'have' and a past participle. Active sentences like

Man zahlt **mir** das Geld regelmäßig aus   OR   Man hat **uns** viel gezeigt
Somebody pays me the money regularly   *Somebody showed us a lot*

can be rephrased with the *bekommen/kriegen*-passive as:

Ich **bekomme/kriege** das Geld regelmäßig   Wir haben viel **gezeigt bekommen/gekriegt**
  ausgezahlt
I am paid the money regularly/   *We were shown a lot/*
I have the money paid to me regularly   *We had a lot shown to us*

This construction is possible with verbs which have an accusative and a dative object, with the notable exception of *geben*.

(ii) from the dative object of verbs which only govern a dative object (see 18.4.1). The use of the *bekommen/kriegen* passive with these verbs is common in colloquial speech, but not (yet) widely accepted in writing:

Sie bekam gratuliert   *She was congratulated*
Vera bekommt von dir geholfen   *Vera is being helped by you*
Er bekam von niemandem widersprochen   *He was contradicted by nobody*

This construction is not possible with verbs which do not denote an activity or whose dative object cannot be interpreted as a recipient, e.g. *ähneln, begegnen, gefallen, gehören* or *schaden*.

(iii) from the dative of advantage or the dative of possession (see 2.5.3 and 2.5.4). This often corresponds to an English construction with 'get'. As in the previous case, this use of the *bekommen/kriegen* passive with these verbs is colloquial and not widely accepted in writing:

Sie **kriegte** den Wagen **repariert**   *She got her car repaired*
Man **bekommt** den Schlips **abgeschnitten**   *You get your tie cut off*
  (*Grzimek*)
Er **bekam** von mir die Wohnung **renoviert**   *He got his flat renovated by me*
Das Haus **bekam** einen Balkon **angebaut**   *The house got a balcony built on*

(c) In a few instances, the subject of a construction with *kriegen/bekommen* does not relate to a dative

(i) It can be used with verbs which take two accusatives, e.g. *lehren* 'teach' and *schimpfen* 'tell off', 'bawl out' (see 18.3.3). The conditions are the same, i.e. that the verb denotes an action and the subject of the *kriegen/bekommen* construction is a recipient. This usage is strictly colloquial:

Er **bekommt** (von mir) **geschimpft**	*He's getting told off (by me)*
Der Junge **bekommt** die Vokabeln **gelehrt**	*The boy is getting the words taught him*

(ii) It can be used in other contexts where English can use a construction with 'get':

Ich **kriege** den Brief bis heute Abend **geschrieben**	*I'll get the letter written by tonight*

15.4.3 A reflexive verb can often be an alternative to a passive

With verbs which denote accomplishments or activities a verb can be used with *sich* to give the sense of a passive, e.g. *Das erklärt sich leicht* 'That is easily explained' (see 18.3.6 for further details on reflexive verbs). A sense of ability (= *können*) is often implied, but not with all verbs.

(a) Reflexive constructions from transitive verbs

In most instances an adverbial of manner is needed to complete the sense:

Das **lernt sich** rasch	*That is/can be quickly learned*
Das Buch **verkaufte sich** in Rekordauflagen	*The book was sold in record numbers*
Mein Verdacht **hat sich bestätigt**	*My suspicions have been confirmed*

(b) Reflexive constructions from intransitive verbs

An adverbial of manner **and** an adverbial of place or time are usually needed to complete the sense. These are impersonal constructions:

Es **fährt sich** gut auf der Autobahn	*You can drive well on the motorway*
In der Hauptstadt **lebt es sich** besser als anderswo (*Zeit*)	*You can live better in the capital than anywhere else*

(c) A reflexive verb is the natural German equivalent of many English passives or constructions which look like passives

sich ärgern	*be annoyed*	sich schämen	*be ashamed*
sich freuen	*be pleased*	sich verbinden	*be associated*

15.4.4 Many phrasal verbs have a passive meaning

Such phrasal verbs comprise a verbal noun (especially in -*ung*) and a verb which has little real meaning in the context. The following verbs are frequently used to form such complex verb phrases with a passive sense: *erfahren, erhalten, finden, gehen, gelangen, kommen, stehen*:

eine große Vereinfachung erfahren (= sehr vereinfacht werden)	*be greatly simplified*
seine Vollendung finden (= vollendet werden)	*be completed*
in Vergessenheit geraten (= vergessen werden)	*be forgotten*

zur Anwendung kommen (= angewendet werden)	*be used*

Unsere Arbeit hat **Anerkennung gefunden**	*Our work was appreciated*
Der Wunsch **ging in Erfüllung**	*The wish was fulfilled*
Das Stück **gelangte/kam zur Aufführung**	*The play was performed*
Diese Frage **steht zur Diskussion**	*This question is being discussed*

Such phrasal verbs are very characteristic of modern written non-literary German. They have been criticised by stylists as verbose, but they make it possible to express nuances lacking in the simple verb. For example, *Das Stück gelangte zur Aufführung* emphasises the start of the action, whilst *Das Stück wurde aufgeführt* simply records that the action took place.

15.4.5 **The infinitive with *zu* with some auxiliary and semi-auxiliary verbs has the force of a passive**

This has been termed the 'modal infinitive' construction, and further details are given in 13.2.5. Depending on the verb, these constructions can express possibility, obligation or necessity, i.e. have the sense of *können*, *müssen* or *sollen* followed by a passive infinitive. The following verbs occur in this construction:

(a) *sein*: **the construction has the sense of** *können, müssen* **or** *sollen*

The English construction with 'be to' has a very similar meaning:

Die Anträge **sind** im Rathaus **abzuholen**
   (= Die Anträge können/müssen im
   Rathaus abgeholt werden)
	*The applications may/must be collected from the
	   town hall/are to be collected from the town hall*

Diese Frage **ist** noch **zu erörtern**
   (= Diese Frage muss/soll noch
   erörtert werden
	*This question must still be discussed/is still to
	   be discussed*

Dieser Text **ist** bis morgen **zu übersetzen**
   (= Dieser Text muss/soll bis morgen
   übersetzt werden)
	*This text must be translated by tomorrow/
	   This text is to be translated by tomorrow*

This construction can be turned into an extended adjective using a present participle, e.g. *diese noch zu erörternde Frage* (see 13.5.2e).

(b) *bleiben*: **the construction has the sense of** *müssen*

Vieles bleibt noch zu erledigen (= Vieles muss noch erledigt werden)	*Much still remains to be done*

(c) *gehen*: **the construction has the sense of** *können*

Das Bild geht nicht zu befestigen (= Das Bild kann nicht befestigt werden)	*The picture cannot be secured*

This construction is colloquial and not accepted as standard.

(d) *stehen*: **the construction has the sense of** *müssen*

It is only used impersonally, with a limited number of verbs, principally *befürchten* and *erwarten*:

Es **steht zu befürchten**, dass sich diese
   Vorfälle häufen
   (= Es muss befürchtet werden, dass
   sich diese Vorfälle häufen)
	*It is to be feared that these incidents will occur
	   increasingly*

(e) *es gibt*: the construction has the sense of *müssen*

Es **gibt** noch vieles **zu tun**   *There's still a lot to be done*
   (= Vieles muss noch getan werden)

15.4.6 *sich lassen* with a following infinitive can have the force of a passive

It expresses possibility and thus means much the same as using *können* with a passive infinitive. This construction is very frequent in all registers, with transitive verbs:

Das lässt sich aber erklären   *But that can be explained*
   (= Das kann aber erklärt werden)
Das Problem lässt sich leicht lösen   *The problem can be solved easily*
   (= Das Problem kann leicht gelöst werden)
Das ließe sich aber ändern   *That might be altered, though*
   (= Das könnte geändert werden)
Ein Ende lässt sich nicht absehen (*Lenz*)   *There is no end in sight*

This construction can be used impersonally with transitive or intransitive verbs. The impersonal subject *es* can be omitted if it is not in initial position in a main clause, see 3.6.2:

Es **lässt sich** dort gut **leben**   *It's a good life there*
Darüber **lässt** (es) **sich streiten**   *We can argue about that*

In general, this construction is only possible if the subject is a thing rather than a person. Reflexive *lassen* with a person as subject usually has the sense of 'cause' or 'permit', see 13.3.1c.

15.4.7 *gehören* with a past participle has passive force and the sense of obligation or necessity

This construction is found mainly in colloquial South German speech:

Dieser Kerl **gehört eingesperrt**   *That bloke ought to be locked up*
   (= Dieser Kerl sollte eingesperrt werden)
Dem **gehört** das deutlich **gesagt**   *He ought to be told that clearly*
   (= Ihm sollte das deutlich gesagt werden)

15.4.8 Adjectives in *-bar* from verbs can be used with *sein* to express a possibility with a passive sense

They correspond to English adjectives in '-able'/'-ible', see 22.3.1a:

Diese Muscheln sind nicht **essbar**   *These shellfish are not edible/cannot be eaten*
   (= Diese Muscheln können nicht
   gegessen werden)
Das Argument ist nicht **widerlegbar**   *The argument is irrefutable/cannot be refuted*
   (= Dieses Argument kann nicht
   widerlegt werden)
Man ist einfach **unerreichbar** (*Frisch*)   *One simply cannot be reached*

Adjectives with the suffixes *-lich* (from some verbs, see 22.3.1f) or *-fähig* (from some verbal nouns) can have similar force:

Seine Antwort war **unverständlich**
  (= Seine Antwort konnte nicht
  verstanden werden)

His answer was incomprehensible/could not be
  understood

Dieser Apparat ist nicht weiter
  entwicklungsfähig
  (= Dieser Apparat kann nicht weiter
  entwickelt werden)

This apparatus cannot be developed further

15.5 The use of active and passive in German

The passive is used quite frequently in German, particularly in formal writing (especially in technical registers and journalism), and it is certainly <u>not</u> to be 'avoided' as a matter of course, as some English manuals and handbooks of German suggest. However, it does tend to be rather less frequent than in English. One reason for this is that we often use a passive in English to manoeuvre something other than the subject to the beginning of the sentence. In German, with its more flexible word order, this can be achieved simply by shifting the elements in the sentence round. Thus, the following sentences probably represent the most natural equivalents in the two languages:

Diesen Roman hat Thomas Mann
  während eines Aufenthaltes in Italien
  geschrieben

*This novel **was written by Thomas Mann***
  during a stay in Italy

In German, the accusative object can be placed before the verb and the subject after it, in order to change the emphasis of the sentence, without needing to use a passive construction, as in English. More details on this are given in 21.2.3b.

16 Mood: the imperative and the subjunctive

The grammatical category of MOOD makes it possible for speakers to signal their attitude to what they are saying, in particular to indicate whether what they are saying is to be understood as a fact, a possibility or a command. The different moods of the verb are shown by special endings or forms. German has three moods:

- The INDICATIVE mood states a **fact**
- The SUBJUNCTIVE mood indicates a **possibility** or a **report**
- The IMPERATIVE mood expresses a **command**

Indicative	Subjunctive	Imperative
sie ist	sie sei	sei!
sie kauft	sie kaufe	kaufe!
sie kam	sie käme	kommt!
sie ist gewandert	sie würde wandern	wandern Sie!

This chapter gives details on the **use** of the moods in German:

- The **three moods** of German (section 16.1)
- The **imperative** mood and other means of expressing commands (section 16.2)
- The **subjunctive** mood, its forms and tenses (sections 16.3–16.7)

The FORMS of the indicative and the imperative in the active voice are given in Tables 12.2–12.5, and in the passive in Tables 12.6 and 12.7. The formation of the subjunctive mood is explained in section 12.5 and the most important forms are shown in Tables 12.9–12.11.

16.1 Indicative, imperative and subjunctive

16.1.1 The INDICATIVE mood presents what the speaker is saying as a fact

The **indicative** is the most frequent mood, used in all kinds of statements and in questions – in effect in all contexts where speakers do not want to give a command or to signal that what they are saying may not be the fact. As it is the 'normal' or default mood, its use is not treated specifically in this chapter.

16.1.2 The IMPERATIVE mood is used in commands and requests

As we normally address these to the person we are talking to, the **imperative** mood is restricted to the second person (i.e. the 'you'-form). The uses of the imperative in German are treated in section 16.2, together with the other ways of giving commands and requests.

16.1.3 The SUBJUNCTIVE mood presents what the speaker is saying as not necessarily true

If we use the **subjunctive**, we are characterising an activity, an event or a state as unreal, possible or, at best, not necessarily true (hence its old German name of *Möglichkeitsform*). English has kept very few distinct subjunctive forms, and even these, like *If she were a teacher . . .*, often sound very archaic or artificial even in the most formal registers. These ideas are expressed in other ways in English, typically by using a 'modal auxiliary' verb like 'may' or 'should', or an adverb of attitude like 'perhaps' or 'presumably'. German has these possibilities too, with modal auxiliaries like *können* or *müssen* (see Chapter 17), adverbs of attitude like *vielleicht* and *vermutlich* (see 7.3.2) or modal particles (see Chapter 10). But the subjunctive mood is still widely used in German, in particular to signal a hypothetical possibility and in indirect speech. Full information is given in sections 16.3–16.7.

16.2 Commands and the imperative

16.2.1 The imperative mood is used in all kinds of commands and requests

(a) The imperative mood only has special forms for the second person

i.e. the person to whom the request or command is being directly addressed. For its forms, see Tables 12.2 and 12.3:

Hans, **sei** doch nicht so dumm!
Angela, **stell(e)** dich nicht so an!
Kinder, **bringt** mal die Stühle zu uns in den Garten!
Kommen Sie doch bitte herein und **nehmen Sie** Platz, Frau Meier!

In speech the imperative is characteristically used with the modal particles *mal* (see 10.22.1) and/ or *doch* (see 10.7.3). Without one of these, a spoken command may sound insistent or harsh. Other modal particles which are commonly used with the imperative and alter the tone of a command are *ja* (10.19.3), *nur* (10.26.1a), *ruhig* (10.28) and *schon* (10.30.4).

(b) Stressed *du* or *ihr* is sometimes added to the simple imperative form

A pronoun is normally only present in the *Sie*-form of the imperative, but the other pronouns are occasionally added to give strong emphasis:

Bestell <u>du</u> inzwischen das Frühstück! (Wendt)	*Meanwhile, you order breakfast*
Kinder, wir kommen gleich. **Geht** <u>ihr</u> **schon vor!**	*Children, we're just coming. You go first.*

16.2.2 Other ways of expressing commands and requests

German has a range of constructions besides the imperative which express commands, requests, instructions and the like.

(a) The infinitive is commonly used in official commands and instructions

Using the infinitive makes the command sound more general and less directed at a particular person or group (see also 13.3.3a):

Nicht **rauchen**! Bitte **anschnallen**!	*No smoking. Fasten seat belts*
Erst **gurten**, dann **starten**	*Fasten your safety belt before setting off*
	(official advice to motorists)
Bitte **einsteigen**!	*Please get in*
	(railway announcement)
4 Eiweiß zu sehr steifem Schnee **schlagen**	*Beat 4 egg whites until stiff*
	(cooking instruction)

With reflexive verbs, the reflexive pronoun is omitted, e.g. *Nicht* **hinauslehnen**! (from *sich hinauslehnen* 'lean out').

(b) The past participle is sometimes used for depersonalised commands

In practice, this construction is limited to idiomatic usage with a small number of verbs (see also 13.5.5a):

Abgemacht!	*Agreed!*
Aufgepasst!	*Look out!*
Stillgestanden!	*Attention!* (military command)

(c) The subjectless passive can have the force of a command

See also 15.1.4d. The speaker can include him/herself in the instruction:

Jetzt wird gearbeitet!	*Let's get down to work now*
Hier wird nicht geraucht!	*No smoking here!*

(d) Statements or questions in the present or future can serve as commands

i.e. by being given the characteristic intonation of a command, as in English. These always sound more blunt than the simple imperative. In this way, any of the following could be used for English 'Are you going to listen now?!' or 'You're going to listen now!':

Hörst du jetzt zu?!	Du hörst jetzt zu!
Wirst du jetzt zuhören?!	Du wirst jetzt zuhören!

(e) The modal auxiliary *sollen* can be used with the force of a command

This usage is linked to the basic meaning of *sollen*, which expresses obligation, see 17.6.1b:

Du **sollst** das Fenster zumachen	*(I want you to) shut the window*
Sie **sollen** ihr sofort schreiben	*(You should) write to her at once*

sollen is often used to repeat a command to someone who appears not to have heard the first time: *Du* **sollst** <u>sofort</u> *nach Hause kommen!*

Commands in indirect speech are most often given with *sollen*, e.g. *Sie sagte ihm, dass er sie am Dienstag anrufen* **sollte** 'She told him to call her on Tuesday'. For details see 16.6.4b. *sollen* is also commonly used in third person commands (see (g) below).

(f) Commands and requests in the first person plural

In English, these are typically in the form 'Let's . . .'. German has a number of equivalents for this, i.e.:

(i) the first person plural form of *Konjunktiv I*, with the verb first:

Seien wir dankbar, dass nichts passiert ist! *Let's be thankful that nothing happened!*
Na, also, **gehen wir** ganz langsam (*Fallada*) *Well then, let's walk quite slowly*
Also, **trinken wir** doch noch ein Glas Wein! *All right, let's have another glass of wine then!*

Only the verb *sein* shows that a subjunctive is used in this construction, as this is the only verb with a distinctive first person plural *Konjunktiv I* form.

(ii) the imperative of *lassen*. This construction is rather formal:

Lass uns jetzt ganz langsam gehen! **Lasst uns** dankbar sein!
Lassen Sie uns doch noch ein Glas Wein trinken!

(iii) the modal auxiliary *wollen*:

Wir wollen doch noch ein Glas Wein trinken!

Questions with *wollen*, e.g. *Wollen wir jetzt nach Hause gehen?* have the force of a suggestion, rather like English 'Shall we . . .?' (see 17.7.1b).

(g) Commands and requests in the third person

We use these, for instance, to ask someone else to tell a third person to do something, as in English 'Let/Have her come in', or when issuing general instructions to anyone concerned.

(i) Third person commands are most often expressed using the modal auxiliary *sollen*, see 17.6.1b:

Er **soll** hereinkommen *Let him come in/Tell him to come in*
Sie **sollen** draußen bleiben *Tell them to stay outside*
Man **soll** hier nicht parken *There's no parking here*

(ii) *Konjunktiv I* is sometimes used in third person commands (see 16.7.6d):

Es **sage** uns niemand, es gebe keine *Let nobody tell us that there is no longer any*
  Alternative mehr (*Augstein*) *alternative*
Er **komme** sofort *Let him come at once*

A generalised command (i.e. 'to whom it may concern') can be expressed by using *Konjunktiv I* with the pronoun *man*:

Man **schlage** 4 Eiweiß zu steifem Schnee *Beat 4 egg whites until stiff*

These constructions with *Konjunktiv I* now sound stilted and rather old-fashioned. *sollen* is preferred for third person commands, and the infinitive for generalised commands and instructions (see (a) above).

(iii) *Konjunktiv I* of the modal auxiliary *mögen* can express a command to a third person: *Er möge sofort kommen* (see 17.4.4). This usage is formal and rather old-fashioned.

(h) A *dass*-clause in isolation can be used as a command

These are emotive in tone and are normally heard exclusively with the particle *ja* (see 10.19.3) and/or with an 'ethic' dative (see 2.5.3d):

Dass du **mir (ja)** gut aufpasst! *Be careful for my sake*
Dass ihr **ja** der Mutter nichts davon *Just don't tell your mother anything about it*
  erzählt!

16.3 The subjunctive mood: general

Although the subjunctive mood is widely used in modern German, some forms and uses are nowadays restricted to formal written German, while others have become obsolete. Even educated native speakers are often uncertain and insecure about what constitutes 'good' or 'correct' usage, and there is often a gulf between what people think they **ought** to say or write and what they actually **do** say or write.

Few other aspects of German grammar have attracted so much attention from self-appointed guardians of the language and sundry pedants, and information in German grammar books and even teaching manuals for foreign learners is often at variance with actual usage. This does not make it easy to describe modern usage clearly for the English-speaking learner, but in the following sections we shall try to explain as accurately as possible how the subjunctive is actually used in modern German, concentrating on those usages which are most likely to be encountered in practice or needed when speaking and writing German, as follows:

- The forms and tenses of the subjunctive: *Konjunktiv I* and *Konjunktiv II* (section 16.4)
- The use of the subjunctive in **conditional** sentences (section 16.5)
- The use of the subjunctive in **indirect speech** (section 16.6)
- **Other uses** of the subjunctive (section 16.7)

16.4 Forms and tenses of the subjunctive

16.4.1 The German subjunctive has two main sets of forms: *Konjunktiv I* and *Konjunktiv II*

The forms of the subjunctive are traditionally referred to by the names of the tenses, e.g. present subjunctive (*er komme*), past subjunctive (*er käme*), perfect subjunctive (*er sei gekommen*), etc. However, the six forms of the subjunctive do not correspond to time differences in the same way as the tenses of the indicative, and these traditional terms are misleading. Many modern German grammars group the subjunctive forms into two sets which they call *Konjunktiv I* and *Konjunktiv II* as set out in Table 16.1, and these terms will be adopted here since they also make it easier to explain how the subjunctive is used in German.

TABLE 16.1 The forms of *Konjunktiv I* and *Konjunktiv II*

Konjunktiv I	present subjunctive perfect subjunctive future subjunctive	es gebe es habe gegeben es werde geben
Konjunktiv II	past subjunctive pluperfect subjunctive conditional	es gäbe es hätte gegeben es würde geben

16.4.2 *Konjunktiv I* and *Konjunktiv II* have largely distinct uses

These have nothing to do with time or tense, and the so-called 'present subjunctive' and 'past subjunctive' can both refer to the present time, as the following examples show:

(a) present subjunctive

Gisela sagt ihrer Mutter, sie **komme** um sechs in Berlin an	*Gisela is telling her mother that she is arriving in Berlin at six*

The main use of the present subjunctive – and all the other *Konjunktiv I* forms – is to mark indirect speech, see 16.6.

(b) past subjunctive

Wenn ich es jetzt **wüsste, könnte** ich es dir sagen	*If I knew it now, I would be able to tell you*

The main use of the past subjunctive – and all the other *Konjunktiv II* forms – is to indicate an unreal condition or a possibility, see 16.5.

16.4.3 Time differences are indicated by using compound forms

The difference between present and past time is expressed in *Konjunktiv I* and *Konjunktiv II* by using the 'perfect' or 'pluperfect' subjunctives:

(a) The perfect subjunctive functions as a past tense in *Konjunktiv I*

Gisela sagt ihrer Mutter, sie **sei** um sechs in Berlin **angekommen**	*Gisela is telling her mother that she arrived in Berlin at six*

(b) The pluperfect subjunctive functions as the past tense of *Konjunktiv II*

Wenn ich es damals **gewusst hätte, hätte** ich es dir sagen **können**	*If I had known it then, I would have been able to tell you*

16.4.4 The CONDITIONAL form with *würde* often replaces the simple past subjunctive

Konjunktiv II has three forms:

Past subjunctive	Pluperfect subjunctive	Conditional
ich hätte	ich hätte gehabt	ich würde haben
ich wäre	ich wäre gewesen	ich würde sein
ich käme	ich wäre gekommen	ich würde kommen
ich schliefe	ich hätte geschlafen	ich würde schlafen
ich machte	ich hätte gemacht	ich würde machen

The conditional form is often used instead of the simple past subjunctive, in exactly the same meanings and contexts, so that people say or write *ich würde schlafen* rather than *ich schliefe*. Which one is used depends on the individual verb involved and on register (i.e. whether we want to sound formal or informal). The use of the simple forms is still often encouraged by German school teachers and traditionalists as a mark of good style, but in practice they often sound stilted or archaic, and they are avoided. Modern usage can be summarised as follows:

(a) With weak verbs the simple form is only used if the subjunctive meaning is otherwise clear from the context

This is because their past subjunctive form is exactly the same as the past indicative. For example:

Wenn ich das Fenster **aufmachte, hätten** wir frische Luft im Zimmer	*If I opened the window, we would have some fresh air in the room*

Although *aufmachte* could be ambiguous (in isolation we would have no way of knowing whether it is indicative or subjunctive), the clear *Konjunktiv II* form *hätte* in the other half of the sentence makes it clear that the whole sentence is to be understood as expressing possibility.

However, the past subjunctive forms of weak verbs are hardly ever used in everyday speech, which usually prefers the conditional: *Wenn ich das Fenster **aufmachen würde**, hätten wir frische Luft im Zimmer.*

Even in writing, the conditional is used <u>if</u> the subjunctive meaning is not otherwise clear from the context:

Bei der Hitze **würde** ich das Fenster **aufmachen**	*With this heat I would open the window*

(b) With the common irregular verbs only the past subjunctive form is usual

This applies in particular to *sein, haben, werden* and the modal auxiliaries. With these, the past subjunctive forms *wäre, hätte, würde, könnte, müsste*, etc. are preferred in <u>both</u> spoken <u>and</u> written German. The conditional forms *würde sein, würde haben*, etc. are quite infrequent in any register, unless there is a sense of 'future-in-the-past', see 16.4.5.

(c) The past subjunctive forms of a few other common strong or irregular verbs are quite frequent

With the following verbs the past subjunctive forms and the conditional are roughly equally frequent in written German:

finden	geben	gehen	halten	heißen	kommen	lassen	stehen	tun	wissen
fände	**gäbe**	**ginge**	**hielte**	**hieße**	**käme**	**ließe**	**stünde**	**täte**	**wüsste**

käme, täte and *wüsste* are also quite common in spoken German, as well as in writing, and those of the others in this group are sometimes heard, too.

(d) The past subjunctive forms of the other strong or irregular verbs are infrequent

In practice, they only ever occur in formal written German, and even there they are less common than the conditional forms, so that, for example, *sie würde schlafen* or *sie würden hier sitzen* are significantly more frequent than *sie schliefe* or *sie säßen hier*

In fact, the past subjunctive forms of many less common strong verbs, in particular most of the irregular ones and others in -ö- and -ü- (e.g. *begönne, flösse, verdürbe*), are felt to be impossibly archaic, stilted and even comical. Many Germans do not even know the forms, and they are generally avoided even in writing. The forms which are no longer used in practice are given in italics in Table 12.12.

(e) Pluperfect forms with *würde . . . haben/sein* are unusual

The pluperfect subjunctive normally has *hätte* or *wäre* (depending on whether the verb forms its perfect tenses with *haben* or *sein*) together with a past participle:

Ich **hätte geschlafen**	*I would have slept*
Ich **wäre gekommen**	*I would have come*

The longer forms (e.g.: *ich würde geschlafen haben, ich würde gekommen sein*) are occasionally used, but they are much less common than the shorter forms with *hätte* or *wäre*, especially in writing.

16.4.5 **The conditional is often used in the sense of a future-in-the-past**

i.e. where the speaker or writer is looking forward within a narrative in the past tense, e.g.:

Er wusste viel besser als Chénier, dass er keine Eingebung **haben würde**; er hatte nämlich noch nie eine gehabt (*Süßkind*)	*He knew much better than Chénier that he would not have an inspiration; because he had never had one*
Ich beschloss, sobald ich groß **sein würde**, Spengler zu lesen (*Dönhoff*)	*I decided I would read Spengler as soon as I was grown up*
Ich war sicher, dass ich den Job nicht **kriegen würde**	*I was sure I wouldn't get the job*

The simple past subjunctive is <u>not</u> normally used in contexts of this type.

16.5 **Conditional sentences**

Typical CONDITIONAL SENTENCES consist of a subordinate clause, introduced by the conjunction *wenn* (= English 'if'), expressing a condition, and a main clause, expressing the consequence, as shown in Table 16.2:

TABLE 16.2 Conditional sentences

Condition	Consequence
Wenn ich genug Zeit hätte,	käme ich gern mit
If I had enough time	*I would gladly come with you*
Wenn sie mich fragen würde,	würde ich ihr alles sagen
If she asked me	*I would tell her everything*
Wenn ich gewonnen hätte,	wäre ich nach Amerika gefahren
If I had won	*I would have gone to America*

16.5.1 *Konjunktiv II* **is used in sentences which express unreal conditions**

(a) The past subjunctive or conditional form of *Konjunktiv II* is used to express an unreal condition relating to the present

Wenn wir Zeit **hätten**, **könnten** wir einen Ausflug machen	*If we had time, we would be able to go on an excursion*
Die Europäer **wären** erleichtert, wenn England wieder **austreten würde** (*Zeit*)	*The Europeans would be relieved if England pulled out again*
Wenn ich 200 000 Euro im Lotto **gewinnen würde**, **würde** ich eine Villa auf Teneriffa **kaufen**	*If I won 200,000 euros in the lottery I would buy a villa on Tenerife*

Konjunktiv II is used in <u>both</u> the *wenn*-clause <u>and</u> the main clause in German. This contrasts with English, which uses the past tense in the 'if'-clause, and the conditional (with 'would') in the main clause. Either form – past subjunctive or conditional – can be used in German in either of the clauses. Which one is used depends on register and on the individual verb used, as explained in 16.4.4.

Stylists have long argued that sentences with two *würde*-forms should be avoided as they are clumsy. However, this prescription is widely ignored in both spoken and written German, especially if the simple *Konjunktiv II* forms of the verbs involved are obsolete or not used, as in the last example above and the following:

Was **würden** wir sagen, wenn die Gletscher immer größer und die Eiskappen am Süd- und Nordpol immer dicker **würden**? (*MM*)	*What would we say if the glaciers kept on getting bigger and the ice-caps on the South and North Poles kept getting thicker?*

Nevertheless, all things being equal, the most common pattern in conditional sentences is with a simple *Konjunktiv II* form to be used in the *wenn*-clause and a *würde*-form in the main clause:

Ich **würde** den schönen Top **kaufen**, wenn ich genug Geld **hätte**	*I would buy that nice top if I had enough money*

(b) Conditional sentences with the pluperfect subjunctive express a hypothetical possibility in the past

The pluperfect subjunctive is used in <u>both</u> the *wenn*-clause <u>and</u> the main clause:

Wenn ich es nicht mit eigenen Augen **gesehen hätte**, **hätte** ich es nicht **geglaubt**	*If I hadn't seen it with my own eyes, I wouldn't have believed it*
Wenn mich jener Anruf nicht mehr **erreicht hätte**, **wären** wir einander nie **begegnet** (*Frisch*)	*If that call hadn't reached me, we would never have met*
Es **wäre** besser für mich **gewesen**, wenn ich **hätte** absagen **können** (*Böll*)	*It would have been better for me if I had been able to refuse*

(c) Time differences between the main clause and the *wenn*-clause can be indicated by using the past subjunctive/conditional forms or the pluperfect forms as appropriate

Wäre Sarkozy schon im ersten Wahlgang **gewählt worden**, **würde** die französische Bevölkerung schon jetzt das Datum **kennen**	*If Sarkozy had been elected in the first ballot the French people would already know the date*
Ich **säße** hier nicht auf demselben Stuhl, wenn wir bisher diesen Punkt nicht **erreicht hätten** (*Zeit*)	*I wouldn't be sitting here in the same chair if we hadn't already reached this point*

(d) Other auxiliary verbs used in sentences expressing unreal conditions

(i) The *Konjunktiv II* of *sollen* is often used in the *wenn*-clause. These normally point to the future, and the meaning is similar to using 'should' or 'were to' in English:

Wenn sie mich **fragen sollte**, würde ich ihr alles sagen	*If she were to ask me, I would tell her everything*
Er hält sich bereit, aus der Bodenluke zu springen, wenn sich nachts ein Auto der Sägemühle **nähern sollte** (*Strittmatter*)	*He is ready to jump out of the skylight if a car should approach the sawmill at night*

(ii) The *Konjunktiv II* of *wollen* also occurs frequently in the *wenn*-clause, often with only a faint suggestion of its basic meaning of 'want', 'intend':

Wenn du schneller **arbeiten wolltest**, könntest du mehr verdienen	*If you worked a bit faster you could earn more*
Wie wäre es, wenn wir ihr **helfen wollten**?	*What about us helping her?*

It is particularly common in formal written German if the conjunction *wenn* is omitted (see 16.5.3a):

Es würde uns zu lange aufhalten, **wollten wir** alle diese Probleme ausführlich behandeln	*It would detain us too long if we were to treat all these problems in detail*

(iii) The *Konjunktiv II* of *tun* is common in colloquial speech instead of *würde*, especially in the South, see 13.3.1d. This usage is not accepted as standard:

Wenn ich jetzt **losfahren täte**, so könnte ich schon vor zwölf in Augsburg sein	*If I set off now, I could be in Augsburg by twelve*

16.5.2 The indicative is used in conditional sentences which express 'open' conditions

i.e. where there is a real possibility of the conditions being met. These correspond to conditional sentences without 'would' in English. In English, the future tense is the norm in the main clause of such sentences, but in German the present is at least as frequent, see 14.2.3:

Wenn sie immer noch krank **ist**, **muss** ich morgen allein kommen	*If she's still ill, I'll have to come on my own tomorrow*
Wenn ich ihr jetzt **schreibe**, **bekommt** sie den Brief morgen	*If I write to her now, she'll get the letter tomorrow*
Wenn wir jetzt **losfahren**, **werden** wir schon vor zwölf in Augsburg **sein**	*If we set off now, we'll be in Augsburg by twelve*

If one half of a conditional sentence is seen as hypothetical, but the other as factual, the first can be in the subjunctive and the second in the indicative:

Was **würdet** ihr **tun**, wenn ihr **mitbekommt**, dass euer Freund mit anderen Frauen **simst**?	*What would you do if you find out that your boyfriend has been texting other women?*

With the past tense, the sense is that the conditions have been met, and *wenn* typically is very close to the meaning 'whenever', see 19.3.1e:

Wenn meine Eltern mir Geld **schickten**, **kaufte** ich mir sofort etwas zum Anziehen	*If/Whenever my parents sent me money I immediately bought something to wear*

16.5.3 Alternative forms for conditional sentences

A typical conditional sentence has a *wenn*-clause and a main clause, as shown in Table 16.2, but there are a number of possible variations on this pattern.

(a) The conjunction *wenn* can be omitted

If this is done, the subordinate clause begins with the verb:

Hätte ich Zeit, käme ich gern mit	*If I had time, I should like to come with you*
Ist sie krank, muss ich morgen allein kommen	*If she's ill, I'll have to come on my own tomorrow*
Sollte ich nach Berlin kommen, würde ich sie sicher besuchen	*If I should get to Berlin I'd be sure to visit her*

This construction can be compared to the similar, rather old-fashioned English construction, e.g. '**Had** I time, . . .'. In German it is commoner in formal writing than in speech, and it is very often used in legal or quasi-legal contexts. Occasionally, the main clause comes first:

Das Bild wäre unvollständig, **würden** nicht die vielen Gruppen erwähnt, die den Einwanderern das Leben leichter machen (*FR*)

The picture would be incomplete if the many groups were not mentioned who make life easier for the immigrants

(b) If the *wenn*-clause comes first in the sentence, it can be picked up by *so* or *dann* at the start of the main clause

This 'correlating' *so* or *dann* is optional, but quite common:

Wenn ich Zeit hätte, (**so/dann**) käme ich gern mit
Wenn ich ihr heute schreibe, (**so/dann**) bekommt sie den Brief morgen

This is particularly frequent if *wenn* is omitted (see (a) above):

Hätte ich Zeit, (**so**) käme ich gern mit
Ist sie krank, (**so**) muss ich morgen allein kommen
Sollte ich nach Berlin kommen, (**so**) würde ich sie sicher besuchen

(c) The condition may appear in another form than in a *wenn*-clause

e.g. in an adverbial or another kind of clause. In such contexts *Konjunktiv II* signals a hypothetical condition:

Dieser Unbekannte würde mich **wahrscheinlich** besser verstehen (*Böll*)

This stranger would probably understand me better

Ohne die Notlandung in Tamaulipas wäre alles anders gekommen (*Frisch*)

But for the emergency landing in Tamaulipas everything would have turned out differently

Wer diese Entwicklung vorausgesehen hätte, hätte viel Geld verdienen können

Anyone foreseeing this development would have been able to make a lot of money

In some sentences the condition is implicit:

Lieber **bliebe** ich zu Hause (i.e. an deiner Stelle)

I would rather stay at home

Ich **hätte** dasselbe **getan** (i.e. wenn ich die Wahl hätte)

I would have done the same

(d) Other conjunctions used in conditional sentences

wenn is the predominant conjunction in conditional sentences, but there are other possibilities:

(i) *falls* 'if' unambiguously introduces a condition.

wenn, which can also mean 'when(ever)' (see 19.3.1e), and *falls* can be useful to make the sense clear in contexts where a misunderstanding would be possible. A sentence like:

Wenn ich nach Berlin komme, besuche ich sie

could mean 'When(ever) I get to Berlin I visit her' **or** 'If I get to Berlin I shall visit her'. But *Falls ich nach Berlin komme, besuche ich sie* can only mean 'If I get to Berlin I shall visit her'.

falls is most often used to introduce 'open' conditions, with the indicative (see 16.5.2), although it does occasionally occur with *Konjunktiv II*, and it is particularly frequent with *sollte*:

Sie kann niemanden ins Oberhaus befördern lassen, **falls** er einen unsicheren Wahlkreis vertritt (*FAZ*)	*She cannot elevate anybody into the Upper House if he hasn't got a safe seat*
Falls diese Hinweise zuträfen, wäre das eine eindeutige Verletzung der Abmachungen (*MM*)	*If these indications were correct, that would be a clear infringement of the agreements*
Man hielt eine Ratskonferenz für denkbar, jedoch nur, **falls** Frankreich dem Haushalt die Zustimmung verweigern sollte (*FAZ*)	*A meeting of the Council was considered conceivable, but only if France should refuse to give its consent to the budget*

Even if it is used with the subjunctive, it still leaves the possibility open that the consequence can be realised – unlike *wenn*, which can indicate a completely hypothetical and unfulfillable condition.

(ii) *angenommen, dass . . ., vorausgesetzt, dass . . .* 'assuming that', 'provided that' mainly introduce open conditions.

Angenommen, dass er den Brief erhalten hat, wird er bald hier sein	*Assuming he got the letter, he'll be here soon*
Vorausgesetzt, dass nichts dazwischen kommt, ziehen wir im Frühjahr nach Graz um	*Provided that all goes well, we'll be moving to Graz in the spring*

The *dass* can be omitted, and then the following clause has the word order of a main clause, e.g. *Angenommen, er hat den Brief erhalten, wird er bald hier sein.*

(iii) *sofern* and *soweit* are used in the sense of 'if' or 'provided that' in open conditions:

Sofern/Soweit es die Witterungsbedingungen erlauben, findet die Aufführung im Freien vor der alten Abtei statt	*If weather conditions permit, the performance will take place in the open air in front of the old abbey*

(iv) *selbst wenn, auch wenn, sogar wenn, wenn . . . auch* all correspond to English 'even if'. For example, the German equivalent of 'Even if I wrote to him today, he wouldn't get the letter until Tuesday', could be any of the following:

Selbst wenn ich ihm heute schriebe, **Auch wenn** ich ihm heute schriebe **Sogar wenn** ich ihm heute schriebe, **Wenn** ich ihm **auch** heute schriebe,	würde er den Brief erst Dienstag bekommen

or with *wenn* omitted, in formal written German only (often with an optional *doch* in the main clause):

Schriebe ich ihm **auch** heute, würde er den Brief (**doch**) erst Dienstag bekommen

(v) *es sei denn, (dass) . . .* 'unless' is chiefly used in 'open' conditions.

The *dass* can be omitted, and then the following clause has the word order of a main clause:

Ich komme um zwei, **es sei denn**, ich werde aufgehalten/dass ich aufgehalten werde	*I'll come at two, unless I'm held up*

In old-fashioned literary usage *denn* on its own can have this meaning:

| „Ich lasse dich nicht fort", rief sie, „ du sagst mir **denn**, was du im Sinn hast" (*Wiechert*) | *'I shan't let you go', she cried, 'unless you tell me what you have in mind'* |

(vi) *wenn . . . nicht* is the most frequent equivalent for English 'unless'. It is used with open or unreal conditions, in the latter case with *Konjunktiv II*:

| **Wenn** er **nicht** bald kommt, wird es zu spät sein | *Unless he comes soon, it will be too late* |
| Er hätte es nicht gesagt, **wenn** er **nicht** schuldig wäre | *He wouldn't have said it unless he was guilty* |

In some contexts, *wenn . . . nicht* can mean 'if not'. Compare:

| Du brauchst die Suppe nicht zu essen, **wenn** du sie wirklich **nicht** magst | *You needn't eat the soup if you really don't like it* |

16.6 Indirect speech

16.6.1 Indirect and direct speech

(a) In indirect speech we report what someone said by putting it into a sentence of our own

This is sometimes called 'reported speech'. It contrasts with direct speech, where we quote what someone said in the original spoken form. Compare the following English examples:

| Direct speech: | She said, 'I am writing a letter' |
| Indirect speech: | She said **that she was writing a letter** |

There are marked differences in English between direct and indirect speech. In particular, we put what was said in a subordinate clause of its own, often introduced by 'that', the pronoun can be altered (especially from the first person to the third person) and the tense is shifted to the past.

(b) In German, instead of shifting the tense, forms of *Konjunktiv I* mark indirect speech

| Direct speech: | Sie sagte: „Ich schreibe einen Brief" |
| Indirect speech: | Sie sagte, **dass sie einen Brief schreibe** |

This is the most important use of *Konjunktiv I* – so much so that *Konjunktiv I* on its own is often enough to indicate indirect speech.

However, the use of the subjunctive to mark indirect speech varies considerably. It is used much less in informal registers, and there is much uncertainty among native speakers about correct usage.

The conjunction *dass*, like English 'that', can be left out after the verb of saying, see 19.2.1b. In this case, the following clause has the order of a main clause, with the verb in second place (see 21.1.1a), e.g. *Sie sagte, sie **schreibe** einen Brief*.

16.6.2 Standard rules for the use of the subjunctive in indirect speech

All modern grammars of German prescribe the following rules, as summarised with examples in Table 16.3, as correct in formal writing.

(a) Rule 1: *Konjunktiv I* is used to mark indirect speech wherever possible

i.e. as long as the forms of *Konjunktiv I* are clearly distinct from those of the present indicative tense.

TABLE 16.3 *Konjunktiv I* and *Konjunktiv II* in indirect speech – standard rules

Rule	Tense of direct speech	Direct speech	Indirect speech
Rule 1: Use *Konjunktiv I* in indirect speech, keeping the same tense as in the origi- nal direct speech	present	„Sie weiß es" *She knows it'*	Er sagte, sie wisse es *He said she knew it*
	past	„Sie wusste es" *'She knew it'*	Er sagte, sie habe es gewusst *He said she had known it*
	perfect	„Sie hat es gewusst" *'She knew/has known it'*	Er sagte, sie habe es gewusst *He said she had known it*
	future	„Sie wird es wissen" *'She will know it'*	Er sagte, sie werde es wissen *He said she would know it*
Rule 2: If the *Konjunktiv I* form is the same as the indicative, use *Konjunktiv II*	present	„Sie wissen es" *'They know it'*	Er sagte, sie wüssten es *He said they knew it*
	past	„Sie wussten es" *'They knew it'*	Er sagte, sie hätten es gewusst *He said they had known it*
	perfect	„Sie haben es gewusst" *'They knew/have known it'*	Er sagte, sie hätten es gewusst *He said they had known it*
	future	„Sie werden es wissen" *'They will know it'*	Er sagte, sie würden es wissen *He said they would know it*

(i) In practice, for all verbs except *sein*, this is the case only in the third person singular, where the *-e* ending of *Konjunktiv I* (e.g. *sie schreibe*) contrasts with the present indicative ending *-t* (e.g. *sie schreibt*)

(ii) The basic principle is that the same tense of *Konjunktiv I* is used for the indirect speech as was used in the indicative in the original direct speech, as shown in the examples in Table 16.3.

The only exception to this principle is that if the original direct speech was in the past or the pluperfect tense, the perfect subjunctive is used in indirect speech. In this way the following sentences of direct speech:

„Ich **wusste** es nicht"   „Ich **habe** es nicht **gewusst**"   „Ich **hatte** es nicht **gewusst**"

are all converted into indirect speech as *Sie sagte, sie **habe** es nicht gewusst.*

NB: Complex pluperfect forms are sometimes used if the original direct speech was in the pluperfect, e.g: *Sie sagte, sie **habe** es nicht gewusst gehabt.* Such constructions are not considered acceptable.

(iv) If the present tense of the original direct speech refers to the future (see 14.2.3), the future subjunctive is often used in indirect speech, as an alternative to the present subjunctive. In this way, there are two possibilities for converting the following sentence into indirect speech:

„Sie **heiratet** bald"   →   Sie sagte, sie **heirate** bald *or* Sie sagte, sie **werde** bald **heiraten**

(b) Rule 2: If the form of *Konjunktiv I* is the same as that of the indicative, *Konjunktiv II* is used

The principle underlying this **replacement rule** is that indirect speech should be marked by a distinct subjunctive form if possible. This is typically needed in the third person plural, where only *sein* has a *Konjunktiv I* form (*sie seien*) which differs from the form of the present indicative (see Table 12.9).

For example, to turn the sentence „*Wir wissen es nicht*" into indirect speech, we cannot use the *Konjunktiv I* form *sie wissen*, because it is not different from that of the present indicative. It is replaced by the *Konjunktiv II* form: *Sie sagten, sie **wüssten** es nicht*. Table 16.3 gives more examples of the application of this rule for the other tenses.

(c) The standard rules for the use of the subjunctive in indirect speech are adhered to with particular consistency in newspapers

By using *Konjunktiv I* we can indicate that we are simply reporting what someone else said, without committing ourselves to saying whether we think it is true or not. This makes it a handy device for journalists (especially when reporting politicians?!) and newspapers make wide use of it:

Der Bundespressechef verwies darauf, dass in den kommenden Gesprächen noch manches verfeinert werden **könne** (FAZ)	*The Federal information officer pointed out that some things could be refined in future discussions*
Mehdorn erklärte, die Bahn **könne** das Betriebsrisiko nicht übernehmen, auch wenn es zusätzliche öffentliche Mittel für den Bau der Strecke **gebe** (*Presse*)	*Mehdorn explained that the Federal Railways could not take on the operational risks even if there were additional public funds to build the line.*

Konjunktiv I is such a clear indication of indirect speech that it can be used on its own to show that a statement is simply reported. This means that in German we can often dispense with the repeated cues like 'He said that . . .', 'He went on to say that . . .' which we usually need in English. Almost any newspaper report provides examples of how this possibility is exploited:

Der Regierungssprecher bedauerte die Veröffentlichung. Die Dokumente **seien** „auf illegale Art und Weise an die Öffentlichkeit gelangt". Die robusten und festen Beziehungen zu den USA **würden** aber in „keiner Weise" betrübt. Es **gebe** eine in Jahrzehnten gewachsene tiefe Freundschaft, die auf gemeinsamen Werten **beruhe** und durch die Publikation „nicht ernsthaft beschädigt wird". Passagen über deutsche Politiker **hätten** eher das „Niveau des Lästerns". (*SZ 30.11.2010*)

Note the alternation of *Konjunktiv I* and *Konjunktiv II* forms according to the 'replacement rule' and that, even in such a sequence of main clauses without any verb of saying the subjunctive on its own is enough to signal indirect speech. Interspersing a few stretches of direct speech in quotation marks, in the indicative, is also very typical in this style of presentation in newspapers.

TABLE 16.4 Indirect speech in spoken German

Formal writing *Konjunktiv I*	Everyday speech Indicative or *Konjunktiv II*
Er sagte, sie wisse es Er hat gesagt, sie wüsste es	Er hat gesagt, sie weiß es
Er sagte, sie habe es gewusst Er hat gesagt, sie hätte es gewusst	Er hat gesagt, sie hat es gewusst

16.6.3 Alternative current usage in indirect speech

where they occur most commonly. A summary is given for quick reference in Table 16.4.

(a) *Konjunktiv II* is used rather than *Konjunktiv I*, even where a distinct *Konjunktiv I* form is available

i.e. in contexts – notably in the third person singular of most verbs except *sein* – where it is not required by the 'replacement rule' explained in 16.6.2b. This occurs:

(i) in everyday speech:

Sie hat gesagt, sie **käme** heute nicht	*She said she wasn't coming today*
Sie hat gesagt, sie **hätte** es verstanden	*She said she had understood it*
Sie hat gesagt, sie **würde** den Brief noch heute schreiben	*She said she'd get the letter written today*

In spoken German *Konjunktiv II* is an alternative to the indicative (see (c) below), and it is often preferred when the main verb is in the past tense. *Konjunktiv II* also tends to be used if there is a longer stretch of indirect speech covering more than one sentence:

Er sagt, er hat eben einen neuen Wagen gekauft. Der **hätte** über 80 000 Euro gekostet und **hätte** eine Klimaanlage	*He says he's just bought a new car. It cost more than 80,000 euros and it's got air-conditioning*

Konjunktiv I can sound very stilted and affected in informal registers and it is rarely used in colloquial German. The only exception is that forms of *sein* are occasionally heard, but these often imply that the speaker has doubts. If someone says *Gertrud hat mir gesagt, sie **sei** heute krank* it often indicates that s/he thinks that Gertrud might not have been telling the whole truth.

(ii) in writing: *Konjunktiv II* is less usual than *Konjunktiv I*, but it is by no means unknown.

Sie sagte, ihr Vater **schliefe** erst gegen Morgen richtig ein und **würde** bis neun im Bett **bleiben**, und sie müsse den Laden aufmachen (*Böll*)	*She said that her father didn't get to sleep properly till the morning and he would stay in bed till nine and that she had to open the shop*
Tante Sissi schrieb uns, es gehe Onkel Heinrich nicht gut und sie **säße** oft an seinem Bett (*Dönhoff*)	*Aunt Sissi wrote telling us that Uncle Heinrich wasn't well and she often sat at his bedside*

('Standard' usage in the above examples would be *schlafe*, *bleibe* and *sitze*.)

(b) The conditional with *würde* is used in place of the past subjunctive form of *Konjunktiv II*

The use of *würde* in indirect speech as a substitute for the simple past subjunctive is potentially confusing for English speakers, as they could interpret it as having the same meaning as an English conditional with 'would'.

(i) The use of *würde* is frequent in colloquial spoken German, especially since the simple past subjunctive is restricted to a few common verbs (see 16.4.4):

Er sagte, ich **würde** zu schnell **reden**	*He said I talk too fast*
Er wirft mir vor, ich **würde** ihm nicht **vertrauen**.	*He tells me off, saying I don't trust him*

(ii) In writing the use of the conditional in indirect speech is frowned on by purists, but it does occur, most often with those strong verbs whose simple *Konjunktiv II* forms are obsolete, or with weak verbs (see 16.4.4).

- It can be used for a *Konjunktiv II* required by the 'replacement rule':

Immer häufiger, berichtet Professor N. von der Uni Hamburg, **würden** Studenten abends oder nachts **jobben**. Tagsüber seien sie dann furchtbar erschöpft (*Spiegel*)	*Professor N. from the University of Hamburg reports that more and more often students take on casual work in the evenings or at night. During the day they are then terribly exhausted, he said*

| Sieben Leser gaben an, sie **würden** regelmäßig Fachzeitschriften **lesen** (*MM*) | *Seven readers declared that they regularly read specialist journals* |

(The conditionals are used here rather than the ambiguous past subjunctive of *jobben* (i.e. *jobbte*) or the obsolescent *läsen*.)

- It can be used even where a distinct *Konjunktiv I* form is available:

| Gleichzeitig informierte man die Presse, die Polizei **würde** auch die Namen zweier Komplizen **kennen** (*Horizont*) | *At the same time the press was informed that the police also knew the names of two accomplices* |

(The past subjunctive *kennte* is obsolete, but by the standard rule one would expect the unambiguous *Konjunktiv I* form *kenne*.)

- It can be used in place of the *Konjunktiv I* form *werde* if the meaning is 'future-in-the-past' (see 16.4.5):

| Er glaubte, er **würde** schon eine Lösung **finden** | *He thought he would surely find a solution* |

In practice, this last usage is very frequent, and it is accepted in formal writing even by the most fastidious stylists.

(c) The indicative is used rather than the subjunctive

If the main verb is in the past tense, the verb in indirect speech is usually in the tense of the original direct speech. However, it is sometimes shifted to the past tense, as in English. The indicative is used:

(i) in spoken German:

Sie hat gesagt, sie **weiß** es schon	*She said she knew it already*
Sie hat gesagt, sie **hat** es verstanden	*She said she had understood it*
Sie hat gesagt, sie **wird** den Brief noch heute schreiben	*She said she'd write the letter today*

In practice, the indicative is the most frequent alternative in informal registers, although *Konjunktiv II* also occurs (see (a) above).

(ii) in writing. There are a few contexts where the indicative is fairly regular in indirect speech in written German, as a permissible alternative to the subjunctive, i.e.:

- if the indirect speech is in a clause introduced by *dass*:

| Der Kanzler erklärte, dass er zu weiteren Verhandlungen bereit **ist/war** | *The Chancellor declared that he was prepared to enter into further negotiations* |
| Es wurde erzählt, dass der Verwalter ihnen persönlich das Mittagessen **auftrug** (*Wiechert*) | *It was recounted that the administrator served them lunch in person* |

If *dass* is included, the indicative is almost as frequent as the subjunctive even in written German. However, if *dass* is omitted (see 19.2.1b), then the subjunctive is regarded as obligatory in writing: *Der Kanzler erklärte, er **sei** zu weiteren Verhandlungen bereit.*

- if a **first** or **second person** is involved:

Er sagte ihr, von wo ich gekommen **bin**	*He told her where I had come from*
Er hat mir erzählt, dass der Fluss hier tief **ist**	*He told me that the river was deep here*
In deinem letzten Brief hast du mir geschrieben, seine Tochter **studiert** schon vier Semester in Hamburg	*In your last letter you wrote that his daughter had already been studying in Hamburg for four semesters*

The function of *Konjunktiv I* is to distance the speaker from what is being reported, i.e. to make it clear that s/he isn't willing to vouch for whether it is true or not. For this reason it may not make sense to use it in contexts where the speaker or the listener is directly involved.

- if the 'replacement rule' (see 16.6.2b) is ignored:

Die Verfügung des letzten deutschen Kaisers besagte, dass im Ruhrgebiet weder Universitäten noch Kasernen gebaut werden **dürfen** (*v. d. Grün*)	*The decree by the last German emperor declared that neither universities nor barracks were allowed to be built in the Ruhr*

The standard rule would require *dürften*, as the form *dürfen* is identical with the indicative and not a clear subjunctive. However, these ambiguous third person plurals are not unusual. They are sometimes used, too, if the 'replacement rule' produces an obsolete past subjunctive form, as in the following example:

Der Unterhändler sagte, er hoffe, dass die Vernunft siege und Verhandlungen **beginnen**	*The negotiator said he hoped that reason would prevail and talks would begin*

Applying the replacement rule would result in the obsolete form *begönnen*.

- for stylistic reasons, to render the flavour of colloquial speech:

Seit der Wende denken die Nazis, sie **bestraft** ohnehin keiner	*Since unification the Nazis have thought that nobody would punish them anyway*

(d) There is no consistent distinction in meaning between *Konjunktiv I*, *Konjunktiv II* and the indicative when used in indirect speech

Some authorities have claimed that there is a difference between the three possible forms, i.e.:

(i) Manfred sagte, dass er krank **gewesen sei**

(ii) Manfred sagte, dass er krank **gewesen wäre**

(iii) Manfred sagte, dass er krank **gewesen ist**

According to this theory, (i) *Konjunktiv I* is used merely to report Manfred's statement neutrally, without offering any personal opinion as to whether it is true or false. Using (ii) *Konjunktiv II*, on the other hand, would make it clear that the speaker thinks Manfred's statement is untrue, while in (iii) the speaker's use of the indicative would acknowledge that it is a fact that he had been ill.

However, although some writers may try to operate with such a distinction, it is never consistently maintained. In practice the use of the three forms is determined not by meaning, but by register, stylistic considerations and norms of usage, as outlined in this section.

16.6.4 Indirect questions and commands

(a) Usage in indirect questions follows the same pattern as in indirect statements

i.e. as outlined in 16.6.2 and 16.6.3:

(i) In written German *Konjunktiv I* (or *Konjunktiv II*, by the 'replacement rule') is used:

Sie fragte ihn, wie alt sein Vater **sei**	*She asked him how old his father was*
Der Lehrer fragte uns, ob wir **wüssten**, was das **bedeute** (*Böll*)	*The teacher asked us if we knew what that meant*
Die Dame fragte, ob denn die Typen einer bestimmten Sorte von Schreibmaschinen alle ununterscheidbar gleich **wären** (*Johnson*)	*The lady asked whether the characters of a particular make of typewriter were all the same and indistinguishable from each other*

As in statements, *Konjunktiv II* is sometimes used even if a distinct *Konjunktiv I* form is available: *Sie fragte ihn, wie alt sein Vater **wäre***.

The indicative occasionally occurs in indirect questions in formal writing, although it is less frequent than the subjunctive:

Warum ich nicht fragte, ob Hanna noch **lebt**, weiß ich nicht (*Frisch*)	*I don't know why I didn't ask whether Hanna was still alive*

(ii) In spoken German, the indicative, *Konjunktiv II* or the *würde*-form are found:

Sie hat ihn gefragt, wie alt sein Vater **ist/wäre**
Tante Emma hat sie gefragt, ob sie Hunger **hat/hätte**
Der Lehrer hat gefragt, ob sie es **wissen/wüßten/wissen würden**

(b) Commands are reported in indirect speech by using a modal verb

Konjunktiv I is used in writing, but both *Konjunktiv II* and the indicative are frequent, and these are more usual in spoken German.

(i) *sollen* is the most frequent verb in indirect commands, see 17.6.1b. Thus the direct command *Rufe mich morgen im Büro an!* would correspond to the indirect command:

Herr Hempel sagte ihr, sie **solle/sollte/ soll** ihn morgen im Büro anrufen	*Mr Hempel told her to call him at the office tomorrow*

(ii) *müssen* indicates a rather more forceful command, e.g. *Herr Hempel sagte ihr, sie **müsse/müsstel muss** ihn (unbedingt) morgen im Büro anrufen*

(iii) *mögen* sounds less peremptory. It is most often used in the *Konjunktiv II* form *möchte*: *Herr Hempel sagte ihr, sie **möchte** ihn morgen im Büro anrufen*. The *Konjunktiv I* form *möge* is also found, especially in literary registers. Elsewhere it can sound old-fashioned and stilted (or facetious):

der junge Kleiderverkäufer, der mich bat, ich **möge** doch auch bei ihm etwas kaufen (*Biehl*)	*the young clothing salesman who asked me please to buy something from him, too*

16.7 Other uses of the subjunctive

16.7.1 Hypothetical comparisons: 'as if'-clauses

(a) Clauses expressing a hypothetical comparison are typically introduced by *als ob* in German

This corresponds to English clauses with 'as if':

Er tat, **als ob** er krank wäre	*He acted as if he was/were ill*
Das Kind weint, **als ob** es Schmerzen hätte	*The child is crying as if it is in pain*

There are one or two alternatives to using **als ob**:

(i) The *ob* can be left out. The finite verb then moves into the position immediately after the *als*:

Er tat, **als wäre** er krank   Das Kind weint, **als hätte** es Schmerzen

This is more frequent than **als ob** in writing, but it is rare in speech.

(ii) *als wenn* and *wie wenn* are less frequent alternatives to *als ob*:

Er tat, **als wenn/wie wenn** er krank wäre

Das Kind weint, **als wenn/wie wenn** es Schmerzen hätte

(b) The verb in German 'as if'-clauses is usually in a form of *Konjunktiv II*

(i) If the action in the 'as if'-clause is simultaneous with the action in the main clause, the simple past subjunctive is used:

Er tat, als ob er krank **wäre**   Das Kind weint, als ob es Schmerzen **hätte**

The conditional can be used if the simple past subjunctive is obsolete or unusual (see 16.4.4). See also (c) below:

Sie hatten den Eindruck, als **würde** sich Diana um die Rolle in einem Kostümfilm **bewerben** (*Spiegel*) (*Simple* bewürbe *is obsolete*)	*They got the impression that Diana was trying for a part in a period film*

(ii) If the action in the 'as if'-clause took place before the action in the main clause, the pluperfect subjunctive is used:

Sie sieht aus, als ob sie seit Tagen nicht **gegessen hätte**	*She looks as if she hasn't eaten for days*
Er tat, als ob nichts **passiert wäre**	*He acted as if nothing had happened*

(iii) If the action in the 'as if'-clause will take place after the action in the main clause, the conditional is used:

Es sieht aus, als ob es **regnen würde**	*It looks as if it will rain*
Es sah aus, als ob er gleich **hinfallen würde**	*It looked as if he was about to fall down*

(c) In written German, *Konjunktiv I* can be used in 'as if'-clauses

It is less frequent than *Konjunktiv II* even in writing, and some Germans even consider it incorrect. It can be used <u>if</u> its form is distinct from that of the present indicative:

Er tat, als ob er krank **sei**   Es sah aus, als **werde** er hinfallen

Sie sieht aus, als ob sie seit Tagen nicht gegessen **habe**

There is no difference in meaning between using *Konjunktiv I* and *Konjunktiv II* in 'as if'-clauses. *Konjunktiv I* is sometimes used, rather than a conditional (see (b) above), to avoid an obsolete or unusual past subjunctive form (see 16.4.4):

Der Eindruck, als **befände** sich die Partei auf dem Weg zurück in ihre beschwerliche Vergangenheit – als **kämpfe** sie nicht für die Überwindung akuter Probleme (*Zeit*)	*The impression that the party was on the road back to its problematic past, that it wasn't fighting to overcome immediate problems*

The *Konjunktiv II* form *kämpfte* is not distinguishable from the past tense, and so the writer has preferred to use *Konjunktiv I* – although s/he **did** use the past subjunctive *befände* earlier in the same sentence.

(d) In spoken German the indicative is commonly used in 'as if'-clauses

The indicative is at least as frequent as the subjunctive in spoken German, especially in the North (Austrians consider it a 'Prussianism') but it is much less common in writing. The *ob* is never omitted (see (a) above) if the verb is in the indicative.

Er tat, als ob er krank **war** Es ist mir, als ob ich hinfallen **werde**
Sie sieht aus, als ob sie seit Tagen nicht gegessen **hat**

16.7.2 The subjunctive in clauses of purpose

(a) Clauses with *damit* 'so that' sometimes have a verb in the subjunctive

Konjunktiv I or *Konjunktiv II* is used without any difference in meaning:

Konstantin musste als Erster über den Graben, um die Flinte in Empfang zu nehmen, damit sie nicht womöglich mir ins Wasser **fiele** (*Dönhoff*)	*Konstantin had to cross the ditch first to take hold of the shotgun so that I shouldn't let it drop into the water*
Einmal schickte Dionysos dem Aristippos drei Mädchen, damit er sich eine davon als Geliebte aussuchen **könne** (*SZ*)	*Dionysus once sent three girls to Aristippos so that he could choose one of them as a lover*

This usage is typical of elevated registers and can sound rather old-fashioned. The indicative is nowadays more frequent in all registers, e.g.:

Ich habe ihm auch Bücher gebracht, damit er sich nicht **langweilte** und nicht immer gezwungen **war**, an seine Verschwörungen zu denken (*Bergengruen*)	*I brought him some books too, so that he didn't get bored and wasn't always compelled to be thinking of his plots*

The modal verbs *können* or *sollen* are often used in *damit*-clauses, especially (but not only) in spoken German, e.g.

Dieses Jahr vermietete ein Hausbesitzer einen Teil des Dachs an einen Mobilfunkbetreiber, damit dieser dort eine Antenne aufstellen **konnte** (*MM*)	*This year a house-owner rented out part of his roof to a mobile telephone company, so that it could set up an aerial there.*

(b) The conjunction *auf dass* 'so that'

auf dass is an alternative to *damit*. It sounds archaic and solemn and is usually followed by a subjunctive (usually *Konjunktiv I* if the form is unambiguous):

Der Häuptling eines Eingeborenenstammes verfluchte sie, auf dass ihnen nichts von allem, was sie dem Boden und den Gewässern abgewinnen würde, je zum Nutzen **gereiche** (*Spiegel*)	*The chief of a native tribe cursed them, that they might never derive benefit from anything they gained from the soil or the waters*

16.7.3 *Konjunktiv II* can moderate the tone of an assertion, a statement, a request or a question

It sounds less blunt than the indicative. This usage is very frequent, especially in spoken German, and the conditional is often used in similar contexts with a similar effect in English. The simple past subjunctive of the common verbs is used, or the conditional form of others (see 16.4.4):

Ich **wüsste** wohl, was zu tun **wäre**	*I think I know what's to be done*
Eine Frage **hätte** ich doch noch	*There's one more thing I'd like to ask*
Da **wäre** er nun aufgewacht	*He seems to have woken up*
Ich **würde** auch **meinen**, dass es jetzt zu spät ist	*It seems a little late to me, too*
Diese Sache **hätten** wir also geregelt	*That would appear to be sorted out*
Das **wär**'s für heute	*I think that's enough for today*
Hätten Sie sonst noch einen Wunsch?	*Is there anything else you would like?*
Würden Sie bitte das Fenster **zumachen**?	*Would you be so kind as to shut the window?*
Könnten Sie mir bitte sagen, wie ich zum Bahnhof komme?	*Could you please tell me how to get to the station?*

16.7.4 *Konjunktiv II* is sometimes used in time clauses introduced by *bis, bevor* or *ehe*

The use of the subjunctive in these clauses is restricted to formal written German and is an optional (and much less usual) alternative to the indicative. It can stress that it was still in doubt whether the action or event in question would actually take place:

Sie beschlossen zu warten, bis er **käme**	*They decided to wait till he came*
Er weigerte sich, den Vertrag zu unterzeichnen, bevor wir ihm weitere Zugeständnisse **gemacht hätten**	*He refused to sign the contract before we had made further concessions*

16.7.5 The subjunctive in negative contexts

Konjunktiv II can be used in contexts where an event, action or state was possible, but in fact did not take place or was not the case. The indicative is almost always a possible alternative, especially in speech, but it can sound less tentative. Such contexts are:

(a) After the conjunctions *nicht dass, ohne dass* and *als dass*

Nicht, dass er faul **wäre** (*or:* ist), aber er kommt in seinem Beruf nicht voran	*Not that he's lazy, but he's not getting on in his career*

Es wurden auch häppchenweise private Daten gesammelt, angeblich ohne dass das Unternehmen davon **wüsste** (**ist** would sound more definite)	*Private data was also collected little by little – allegedly without the company knowing anything about it*
Die Auswahl war zu klein, als dass ich mich **hätte** schnell entscheiden mögen (*Grass*)	*The choice was too small for me to have wanted to decide quickly*

NB: The set phrase *nicht dass ich (es) wüsste* 'not that I know of' is <u>always</u> used with a subjunctive.

(b) In other subordinate clauses where the main clause and/or the subordinate clause have a negative element

So gab es keine menschliche Tätigkeit, die nicht von Gestank begleitet gewesen **wäre** (*Süßkind*)	*So there was no human activity which was not accompanied by stench*
Es gibt nichts, was schwieriger **wäre** (*or*: ist), als der Gebrauch des Konjunktivs	*There's nothing more difficult than the use of the subjunctive*
nicht eine einzige Großstadt, die nicht ihr Gesicht in zwei Jahrzehnten gründlich gewandelt **hätte** (*Zeit*) (**hat** would sound much more positive)	*not a single city that has not changed its appearance totally in twenty years*

(c) In sentences with *fast* or *beinahe*

In these the pluperfect subjunctive can be used to emphasise that something almost happened, but didn't:

Er **wäre** (*or*: ist) **beinahe hingefallen**	*He almost fell down*
Ich **wäre** (*or*: bin) **fast nicht gekommen**	*I nearly didn't come*
Wir **hätten** (*or*: haben) das Spiel **beinahe gewonnen**	*We almost won the match*

16.7.6 The subjunctive in wishes, instructions and commands

(a) *Konjunktiv I* can be used in the third person to express a wish

In modern German this is largely restricted to set phrases, e.g.:

Gott **segne** dich/dieses Haus!	*God bless you/this house!*
Es **lebe** die Freiheit!	*Long live freedom!*
Gott **sei** Dank!	*Thank God!*
Behüte dich Gott!	*God protect you!*

NB: The use of the *Konjunktiv I* of *mögen* in wishes, e.g. *Möge er glücklich sein!* 'May he be happy!' is archaic.

(b) A conditional clause with *Konjunktiv II* can express a wish

The clause can have the form with or without *wenn*, see 16.5.3a. The force of the wish is often strengthened by adding *doch* and/or *nur* or *bloß* (see 10.7.6 and 10.26.1c):

Wenn er doch nur **käme**!	*If only he would come!*
Wenn er bloß fleißiger **arbeiten würde**!	*If only he would work harder!*
Wenn ich bloß/nur/doch zu Hause **geblieben wäre**!	*If only I'd stayed at home!*
Hätte mein Vater doch dieses Haus nie **gekauft**!	*If only my father hadn't bought this house!*

(c) The *Konjunktiv I* of *sein* or the *sein*-passive can be used in technical German to express a proposition

Gegeben **sei** ein Dreieck ABC	*Given a triangle ABC*
In diesem Zusammenhang **sei** nur darauf verwiesen, dass diese Hypothese auf Einstein zurückgeht	*In this context we merely wish to point out that this hypothesis goes back to Einstein*

NB: In mathematical contexts the indicative is nowadays at least as common as the subjunctive, e.g. *Gegeben **ist** ein Dreieck ABC.*

(d) *Konjunktiv I* is used for commands or instructions in the third person and the first person plural

Also, **spielen** wir jetzt Karten!	*Well, let's play cards*
Im Notfall **wende** man sich an den Hausmeister!	*In case of emergency please apply to the caretaker*

Details are given in 16.2.2f/g.

17 The modal auxiliaries

Six verbs are usually referred to as MODAL AUXILIARY verbs:

dürfen	mögen	sollen
können	müssen	wollen

They are called 'modal' verbs because they indicate the attitude of the speaker with regard to what is being said, expressing ideas like ability, possibility, permission, necessity, obligation and volition. This meaning is very similar to that of the MODAL PARTICLES (see Chapter 10) and the category of MOOD (see Chapter 16). They are referred to as 'auxiliary' verbs because they are mainly used with other verbs.

The modal auxiliary verbs are all irregular (see 12.1.3c), and their forms are given in full in Table 12.4.

This chapter explains the **uses** of the modal auxiliaries:

- Common features of all the modal auxiliary verbs (section 17.1)
- Individual modal auxiliary verbs, treated in alphabetical order (sections 17.2–17.7)

17.1 The modal auxiliaries: form and syntax

The modal auxiliary verbs have several special features which distinguish them from other German verbs, and from their English equivalents. The most important of these are listed briefly below and explained in the sections indicated:

- Their forms are quite **irregular** in similar ways (see 12.1.3c and Table 12.4)
- They have a full range of **tense** and **mood** forms (see 17.1.1)
- They are used with a **'bare' infinitive**, without *zu* (e.g. *Ich kann ihn **sehen**,* see 13.3.1a and 17.1.2)
- Their **perfect tenses** are constructed with the **infinitive** (called in German the *Ersatzinfinitiv*), not with the past participle (e.g. *Ich habe ihn sehen **können**,* see 13.3.2a and 17.1.3)

17.1.1 The German modal auxiliaries have a full range of tense and mood forms

In this they differ from the corresponding English verbs (*can, may, must,* etc.), which have at most only a present tense and a past tense (which often has conditional meaning). German *können,* for example, can be used in the future tense:

Er **wird** es morgen nicht machen können *He won't be able to do it tomorrow*

English 'can' is impossible here, as it has no future tense, and we have to use the paraphrase 'be able to'. Similarly, there is a clear difference in German between the past tense *konnte,* which means 'was able to', and the subjunctive *könnte,* which means 'would be able to'. English 'could', on the other hand, is often used in either sense, depending on the context:

Ich **konnte** sie gestern nicht besuchen, weil ich keine Zeit hatte	*I couldn't visit her yesterday, as I didn't have time*
Ich **könnte** sie morgen besuchen, wenn ich das Auto nehmen dürfte	*I could visit her tomorrow if you were to let me take the car*

Because of this, the German modal auxiliaries can seem complicated for the English learner. But they are easy to master if the various combinations of tense and mood with a following simple or compound infinitive are treated independently and learned with their usual English equivalents. The examples in sections 17.2 to 17.7 are set out to facilitate this, and Table 17.1 illustrates the various possible combinations with *können*.

TABLE 17.1 The tenses and moods of *können* with an infinitive

Tense	Infinitive type	Example	
present	+ infinitive	Er **kann** es **machen**.	*He can do it.*
	+ perfect infinitive	Er **kann** es **gemacht haben**.	*He can have done it.*
future	+ infinitive	Er **wird** es **machen können**.	*He will be able to do it.*
past	+ infinitive	Er **konnte** es **machen**.	*He was able to do it.*
perfect	+ infinitive	Er **hat** es **machen können**.	*He has been able to do it.*
pluperfect	+ infinitive	Er **hatte** es **machen können**.	*He had been able to do it.*
past subj.	+ infinitive	Er **könnte** es **machen**.	*He could do it.*
past subj.	+ perfect infinitive	Er **könnte** es **gemacht haben**.	*He could have done it.*
pluperf. subj.	+ infinitive	Er **hätte** es **machen können**.	*He would have been able to do it.*

17.1.2 The modal verbs are followed by a 'bare' infinitive, without *zu*

(see 13.3.1a). This is similar to the typical English equivalents of these verbs. As Table 17.1 shows, they can be followed by a simple or a compound infinitive:

Ich kann **schwimmen**	*I can swim*
Darf ich **gehen**?	*May I go?*
Sie muss es **gesehen haben**	*She must have seen it*

17.1.3 In the perfect tenses, the infinitive of the modal verbs is used instead of the past participle

Wir haben meinen Onkel nicht besuchen **können**	*We weren't able to visit my uncle*
Ich habe es ihr versprechen **müssen**	*I had to promise her*
Sie hätte das Buch lesen **sollen**	*She ought to have read the book*

The past participle is used, however, if the modal auxiliary is used on its own, without another verb, see 13.3.2 and 17.1.5, e.g. *Ich habe es nicht **gewollt**.*

NB: The use of the past participle if the modal auxiliary has another infinitive with it, e.g. *Herbert hat arbeiten gemusst*, is not unknown in colloquial speech, but it is not accepted as standard.

17.1.4 The position of the modal auxiliary and the infinitive

For further information on word order and the modals, see 21.1.

(a) In main clauses the infinitive of the main verb is in final position

Darf ich heute Tennis **spielen**?	*May I play tennis today?*
Ich möchte das Buch gern **lesen**	*I would like to read that book*

In compound tenses, the infinitive of the modal verb comes **after** the infinitive of the main verb at the end of the clause:

Sie wird morgen nicht **kommen können**	*She won't be able to come tomorrow*
Sie hätte ihrem Mann doch **helfen sollen**	*She really ought to have helped her husband*

(b) In infinitive clauses with *zu*, the modal verb comes after the infinitive of the main verb

i.e. at the **end** of the infinitive clause, with the infinitive particle *zu* coming between the main verb and the modal verb:

Es scheint **regnen zu wollen**	*It looks as if it's going to rain*
Sie gab vor, meine Handschrift **nicht lesen zu können**	*She claimed not to be able to read my handwriting*

(c) In subordinate clauses, the modal verb comes after the infinitive of the main verb at the end of the clause

Wenn Sie diesen Ring nicht **kaufen wollen**, ...	*If you don't want to buy this ring, ...*
Obwohl ich gestern Abend **ausgehen durfte**, ...	*Although I was allowed to go out last night, ...*
die Frau, die ich **besuchen sollte**	*the woman I ought to visit*

If a modal verb is used in a compound tense in a subordinate clause, the tense auxiliary *werden* or *haben* comes **before** the two infinitives:

Obwohl ich ihn morgen **werde** besuchen können, ...	*Although I'll be able to visit him tomorrow*
Es war klar, dass er sich **würde** anstrengen müssen	*It was clear that he would have to exert himself*
Das Buch, das ich **hätte** kaufen sollen, kostete dreißig Mark	*The book I ought to have bought cost thirty marks*
Sie hat mir gesagt, dass sie es **hat** machen müssen	*She told me she had had to do it*

NB: In Austrian usage, the tense auxiliary is frequently placed between the main verb and the modal verb, e.g. *am Flughafen Wien-Schwechat, wo die Luftraumsperre von 0.00 Uhr bis 5.00 Uhr dauern hätte sollen* (Standard). This usage is not accepted as standard outside Austria.

A similar order is usual with a passive infinitive:

... weil der Vertrag **hätte** überprüft werden sollen	*... because the contract should have been checked*

If there are two modals in the clause, the finite one may come before **or** after the two infinitives:

... weil sie ihrem Bruder **müsste** helfen können/ ... weil sie ihrem Bruder helfen können **müsste**	*... because she should be able to help her brother*

17.1.5 **The omission of the main verb after the modal auxiliaries**

The infinitive of the main verb can be left understood and omitted in the following contexts:

(a) The main verb is a verb of motion

(i) If there is an adverbial or, very commonly, a separable prefix in the sentence which conveys the idea of movement, a specific verb of motion can be omitted after the modal verbs. This usage is especially common in colloquial speech, but it is found in writing, too:

Wo wollen Sie morgen hin?	*Where do you want to go tomorrow?*
Ich will nach Frankfurt	*I want to go to Frankfurt*
Ich sollte zu meinem Onkel	*I ought to go to my uncle's*
Ich kann heute Abend nicht ins Kino	*I can't go to the cinema tonight*
Sie will ihm nach	*She wants to go after him*
Ich möchte jetzt fort	*I'd like to leave now*

If the modal is at the end of the clause, a separable prefix is written together with it, e.g. *Sie wissen ja, dass Sie jetzt zu Fuß nach Elberfeld **zurückmüssen**.*

(ii) The verb understood is usually *gehen, kommen* or *fahren*, as in the above examples, but other verbs can be omitted if the idea of movement is sufficiently clear from the adverbial or the prefix:

Er wollte über die Mauer [klettern]	*He wanted to climb over the wall*
Die Strömung war so stark, dass er nicht bis ans Ufer [schwimmen] konnte	*The current was so strong that he couldn't swim to the bank*

(iii) The omission of a verb of motion is most common with simple tenses of the modals, but it is also frequently found with the future and perfect tenses of *können* and *müssen*:

Er hat ins Geschäft gemusst	*He's had to go to work*
Ich glaube schon, ich werde vorbeikönnen	*I think I'll be able to get past*

(b) The main verb is *tun*

Das kann ich nicht	*I can't do that*
Das darfst/sollst du nicht	*You mustn't/ought not to do that*
Was soll ich damit?	*What am I supposed to do with it?*
Ich kann nichts dafür	*I can't help it*
Er kann was	*He is very able*

(c) The main verb has just been mentioned

This often corresponds to English usage. Optionally, *es* can be added to make it clear that a previous phrase is being referred to, see 3.6.1a:

Ich wollte Tennis spielen, aber ich konnte/ durfte (es) nicht	*I wanted to play tennis, but I couldn't/wasn't allowed to*
Der junge Spieler könnte niemanden erkennen, auch wenn er es wollte	*The young player wouldn't be able to recognise anyone even if he wanted to*

(d) In some idiomatic phrases

Ich kann nicht mehr [weitermachen]	*I can't go on*
Was soll das eigentlich [bedeuten]?	*What's the point of that?*
Sie hat nicht mehr gewollt	*She didn't want to go on*
Er kann mich [am Arsch lecken] (vulg.)	*He can get stuffed*
Mir kann keiner [was antun]	*No-one can touch me*

17.1.6 **In German two modals can be used in the same sentence**

Rechnen **muss** doch jeder **können**	*But everyone has to be able to add up*
Wir **müssten** hier spielen **dürfen**	*We should be allowed to play here*
Wie **kannst** du das nur machen **wollen**?	*How can you want to do that?*

17.2 *dürfen*

17.2.1 *dürfen* **most often expresses permission**

(a) In this sense *dürfen* **corresponds to English 'be allowed to' or 'may'**

Sie dürfen hereinkommen	*They may/can come in* / *They are allowed to come in*
Sie durfte ausgehen, wenn sie wollte	*She was allowed to go out when she wanted to*
Endlich durfte er die Augen wieder aufmachen	*At last he could open his eyes again*
Sie wird erst heute Nachmittag mit uns spielen dürfen	*She won't be allowed to play with us till this afternoon*

In English, 'can' often expresses permission and is often preferred to 'may', which can sound affected. *können* is sometimes heard for *dürfen* in everyday speech in this sense (see 17.3.4), but it is less common than English 'can'.

(b) Negative *dürfen* **has the sense of English 'must not'**

i.e. it expresses a prohibition (= 'not be allowed to'):

Sie **dürfen nicht** hereinkommen	*They mustn't come in* / *They're not allowed to come in*
Aber ich **darf** mich **nicht** loben (*Langgässer*)	*But I mustn't praise myself*
Wir **dürfen** es uns **nicht** zu leicht machen (*Brecht*)	*We mustn't make it too easy for ourselves*

Note that *nicht müssen* usually means 'doesn't have to', 'needn't', not 'mustn't', see 17.5.1c.

(c) *Konjunktiv II* forms of *nicht dürfen* **often correspond to English 'shouldn't', 'ought not to'**

dürfen keeps its basic sense of permission in such contexts and thus sounds more incisive than *sollen*, see 17.6.4a:

Das **dürfte** sie doch gar **nicht** wissen (it shouldn't be allowed)	*She ought not to know that*
Er **hätte** so etwas **nicht** machen **dürfen** (someone should have forbidden it)	*He ought not to have done anything like that*

(d) *dürfen* is commonly used in polite formulas

It usually corresponds to English 'can' in such contexts. The tone is that of a polite request or a tentative suggestion:

Das **darf** als Vorteil betrachtet werden	*That can/may be seen as an advantage*
Was **darf** sein? (in shop)	*How can/may I help you?*
Der Wein **dürfte** etwas trockener sein	*The wine could just be a bit drier*
Dürfte ich Sie um das Salz bitten?	*Could I ask you to pass the salt?*
Wir freuen uns, Sie hier begrüßen zu **dürfen**	*We are pleased to be able to welcome you here*

17.2.2 *dürfen* can express probability

The *Konjunktiv II* of *dürfen* expresses an assumption that something is likely:

Das **dürfte** reichen	*That'll be enough*
Manchester United **dürfte** unser bisher schwerster Gegner in der Champions League werden	*Manchester United will probably be our most difficult opponent so far in the Champions League*
Das **dürfte** ein Vermögen gekostet haben	*That'll have cost a fortune*

This sense of *dürfen* is very close to that of the future tense with *werden* (see 14.4), or that of the modal particle *wohl* (see 10.35.1).

17.3 *können*

17.3.1 *können* is most often used to express ability

Its usual English equivalents are 'can' or 'be able to':

Sie **kann** ihn heute besuchen	*She can/is able to visit him today*
Ich **konnte** sie nicht besuchen Ich **habe** sie nicht besuchen **können** }	*I couldn't visit her/I wasn't able to visit her*
Ich **werde** sie morgen besuchen **können**	*I'll be able to visit her tomorrow*
Ich **könnte** sie morgen besuchen, wenn ich Zeit hätte	*I could visit her tomorrow if I had time*
Ich **hätte** sie gestern besuchen **können**, wenn ich Zeit gehabt hätte	*I would have been able to/could have visited her yesterday, if I'd had time*

17.3.2 *können* can have the sense of possibility

In this sense *können* usually corresponds to English 'may':

Das **kann** sein	*That may be*
Ich **kann** mich irren	*I may be wrong*
Er **kann** krank sein	*He may be ill*

(a) The use of *können* to express possibility is limited

In general *können* can only be used in this sense in contexts where it cannot be understood to mean 'be able to'. This is most frequently the case:

(i) with a perfect or passive infinitive:

Er **kann** den Schlüssel verloren haben	*He may have lost the key*
Die Straße **kann** gesperrt sein	*The road may be blocked*
Er **kann** krank gewesen sein	*He may have been ill*

(ii) in the *Konjunktiv II* form *könnte* (= English 'might' or 'could'), to indicate a remote possibility:

Sie **könnte** jetzt in Wien sein	*She could be in Vienna now*
Wir **hätten** umkommen **können**	*We might/could have been killed*
Er **könnte** krank sein	*He might/could be ill*
Er **könnte** krank gewesen sein	*He might/could have been ill*

(iii) *könnte* can also be used to express a tentative request (see 16.7.3):

Könnten Sie mir bitte helfen?   *Could you please help me?*

(b) Other German equivalents for English 'may', 'might'

Since *können* can only be used in the sense of possibility in contexts where it cannot be understood to mean 'be able to', we often need to express the idea of possibility in German in other ways, i.e.:

(i) with the adverbs *vielleicht* or *möglicherweise*, or a paraphrase (e.g. *Es ist möglich, dass . . .*).

Compare the following possibilities for English 'He may be working in the garden':

Vielleicht arbeitet er im Garten
Es ist möglich, dass er im Garten arbeitet
Möglicherweise arbeitet er im Garten

Note that *Er kann im Garten arbeiten* can only mean 'He is able to work in the garden'.

(ii) In sentences with a negative, the phrasings given under **(i)** above can be used, or the sense of possibility can be made clear by adding *auch* to *nicht können* (see 10.4.1), especially if you are contradicting something just said. *nicht* is stressed in these contexts:

Sie **kann auch <u>nicht</u>** kommen
Möglicherweise kommt sie nicht } *She may not come*

Er **kann auch <u>nicht</u>** krank gewesen sein
Vielleicht ist er gar nicht krank gewesen } *He may not have been ill*

Sie **kann** das Auto **auch <u>nicht</u>** gesehen haben
Vielleicht hat sie das Auto gar nicht gesehen } *She may not have seen the car*

17.3.3 *können* is used in the meaning 'know' of things learnt

This applies especially to languages, school subjects, the rules of games, etc. In practice, *können* is a full verb in these contexts, not an auxiliary:

Er **kann** Spanisch   *He can speak Spanish*
Ich **kann** die Melodie der österreichischen   *I know the tune of the Austrian national anthem*
   Nationalhymne   (i.e. 'I've learnt it')
Kann der Manfred Skat?   *Does Manfred know how to play Skat?*
Ich **kann** den Trick   *I know that trick*

   (i.e. 'I can do it'. Compare *Ich **kenne** den Trick* 'I've seen it before')

17.3.4 *können* is used to express permission

i.e. in the sense of *dürfen* (see 17.2.1) This usage is primarily colloquial:

Kann ich herein?   *Can I come in?*
Du **kannst** den Bleistift behalten   *You can keep the pencil*

Even in colloquial German *können* is less frequent to express permission than is 'can' in English.

17.3.5 *können* is used less often than English 'can' with verbs of sensation

The verbs 'see', 'hear', 'feel' and 'smell' are often used with 'can' in English without any real idea of being able. *können* is not necessary in German unless the idea of ability is being emphasised:

Ich sehe die Kirche	*I can see the church*
Ich höre Musik	*I can hear music*
Sie sahen die Stadt im Tal liegen	*They could see the town lying in the valley*

17.3.6 German equivalents for English 'I couldn't help . . .'

There are a number of alternative possibilities, e.g., for English 'I couldn't help laughing':

(i) Ich **musste einfach** lachen
(ii) Ich **konnte nicht anders, ich musste** lachen
(iii) Ich **konnte nichts dafür, ich musste** lachen
(iv) Ich **konnte nicht umhin zu** lachen

Alternative (i) is the simplest and most usual in speech, although (ii) and (iii) are quite current. Alternative (iv) is restricted to formal registers.

17.3.7 *könnte . . . gemacht haben* and *hätte . . . machen können*

These two constructions have different meanings in German. The English equivalents for both are 'could have done' or 'might have done', but German makes distinctions which we ignore in English, e.g.:

Sie **könnte** den Brief nicht **geschrieben haben**	*She couldn't have written the letter* (i.e. it isn't possible that it was she who wrote it)
Sie **hätte** den Brief nicht **schreiben können**	*She couldn't have written the letter* (i.e. she wouldn't have been able to)
Er **könnte umgekommen sein**	*He might have been killed* (i.e. it is possible that he was killed)
Er **hätte umkommen können**	*He might have been killed* (i.e. it was possible, but he wasn't)

17.4 *mögen*

17.4.1 The most frequent sense of *mögen* is to express liking

(a) It most commonly occurs in the *Konjunktiv II* form *möchte*

This expresses a polite request and usually corresponds to English 'would like' or 'want'. It is often linked with the adverb *gern*:

Sie **möchte** (gern) nach Rom fahren	*She would like to go to Rome*
Ich **möchte** nichts mehr davon hören	*I don't want to hear any more about it*
Ich **möchte** ihr Gesicht gesehen haben	*I would have liked to see her face*
Ich **möchte** nicht, dass er heute kommt	*I don't want him to come today*

The pluperfect subjunctive is also used occasionally in this sense, e.g.:

Baldini **hätte** ihn erwürgen **mögen**   *Baldini would have liked to strangle him*
(*Süßkind*)

In general, though, German more often simply uses *gern* with the pluperfect subjunctive of the verb than this, e.g., for 'I would have liked to read the book', *Ich **hätte gern** dieses Buch **gelesen**.*

(b) Other tenses of *mögen* are used in the sense of English 'like'

(i) As a full verb, on its own, it occurs most often (although not exclusively) in the negative, chiefly with reference to people, places and food:

Sie **mag** keinen Tee	*She doesn't like tea*
Was sie an dem Rapper aus Berlin **mögen**	*What they like about the rapper from Berlin*
Ich **mag** ihn nicht	*I don't like him*
Sie **hat** ihn nie **gemocht**	*She never liked him*

(ii) With a following infinitive it is only used in the negative:

Wie es im Winter werden soll, daran **mag** er noch gar nicht denken (*Zeit*)	*He doesn't want to think about what it's going to be like in winter*
Ich **mag** das Wort gar nicht aussprechen	*I don't even like saying that word out loud*
Ich **mag** diese Fragen nicht beantworten (*BILD*)	*I don't want to answer these questions*
Er **mochte** nicht allein an der Straße stehen (*Johnson*)	*He didn't want to stand on the street alone*

17.4.2 *mögen* sometimes expresses possibility or probability

The use of *mögen* to express possibility is largely limited to formal written registers and set phrases (although it is more widely used in spoken South German). When it is used it tends to express a rather higher degree of probability than *können*, see 17.3.2.

(a) When indicating possibility *mögen* often has a concessive sense

i.e. there is an expected qualification by a following *aber* (which may or may not be present). This usage is similar to English 'That may well be (, but . . .)':

Das **mag** vielen nicht einleuchten, (aber . . .)	*That may not be clear to many, (but . . .)*
Das Tief **mag** über Italien weiterwandern und den Balkan einnässen. Wir aber fliegen dorthin, wo die Sonne scheint (*Grzimek*)	*The low may drift over Italy and make the Balkans wet. But we're flying to where the sun shines*
Eine Zeitlang **mochte** es scheinen, dass es gelänge, das Absinken der deutschen Währung abzubremsen, doch schien es nur so (*Heuss*)	*For a time it might have appeared that the attempt to stop the German currency falling would be successful, but that appearance was deceptive*

(b) In other contexts *mögen* indicates a reasonable degree of probability

i.e. somewhere between 'possible' and 'probable':

Sie **mag/mochte** etwa sechzig sein	*She is/was probably about sixty*
Die parteipolitischen Attacken der Opposition **mögen** auch eine Rolle gespielt haben (*MM*)	*The party political attacks of the opposition probably also played a part*

An einem Sonntag im März – es **mochte**
etwa ein Jahr seit seiner Ankunft in
Grasse vergangen sein (*Süßkind*)

*On a Sunday in March – a year or so had probably
gone by since his arrival in Grasse*

(c) Some idiomatic phrases with *mögen* express possibility

The following set phrases are used in spoken German as well as in formal writing:

Das mag (wohl) sein
Wer mag das (schon) sein?
Wie mag das (nur) gekommen sein?

That may well be
Who can that be?
How can that have happened?

A few phrases with *möchte* convey a **doubt** or a supposition:

Ich möchte meinen, dass . . .
Dabei möchte man verrückt werden

I should think that . . .
It's enough to drive you mad

könnte can be used for *möchte* in such contexts, but it sounds less tentative.

17.4.3 *mögen* in concessive clauses

i.e. the German equivalent of English clauses like 'whatever/whoever that may be', etc. (see also
19.6.2). *mögen* can be used in these clauses in German, especially in writing:

Wann er auch ankommen mag, . . .
Was auch immer geschehen mag, . . .
Wer er auch sein mag, . . .

Whenever he may arrive . . .
Whatever happens . . .
Whoever he may be . . .

Alternatively, the main verb can simply be used on its own, and in practice this is more frequent
in less formal registers, especially in spoken German:

Wann er auch **ankommt**, . . .   Was auch immer **geschieht**, . . .   Wer er auch **ist**, . . .

However, *mögen* is <u>always</u> used in the set phrase *Wie dem auch sein mag* 'However that may be'.

17.4.4 *mögen* in wishes and commands

(a) *Konjunktiv I* of *mögen* can express a wish or a command in the third person

Möge er glücklich sein!
Die Herren **mögen** bitte unten warten

May he be happy!
*Would the gentlemen be so kind as to wait
downstairs?*

This usage is limited to formal German and sounds old-fashioned, see 16.2.2g.

(b) The subjunctive of *mögen* is used in indirect commands

Sagen Sie ihr, sie **möchte** zu mir kommen
Er sagte mir, ich **möchte** einen Augenblick
auf ihn warten

Ask her to be kind enough to come and see me
He asked me to wait for him a moment

The *Konjunktiv I* of *mögen* (e.g. . . ., *sie* **möge** *zu mir kommen*) is also used in indirect commands in
formal registers. For further details, see 16.6.4b.

17.5 *müssen*

17.5.1 *müssen* most often expresses necessity or compulsion

(a) The most frequent English equivalent is 'must', 'have (got) to'

Wir **müssen** jetzt abfahren	*We must leave now/We have (got) to leave now*
Wir **werden** bald abfahren **müssen**	*We'll have to leave soon*
Ich **musste** um acht abfahren ⎫ Ich **habe** um acht abfahren **müssen** ⎭	*I had to leave at eight*
Ich **muss** den Brief bis heute Abend **geschrieben haben**	*I've got to have the letter written by tonight*
Wir **mussten** die Anträge bis zum 15. Januar **abgegeben haben**	*We had to have the applications handed in by the 15th of January*
Sie **muss** sich beeilen, wenn sie den Zug erreichen will	*She'll have to hurry if she wants to catch the train*

(b) With a passive infinitive or a passive equivalent, 'need' is sometimes a more natural English equivalent for *müssen*

Das **muss** gut überlegt werden	*That needs thinking about properly*
Man **muss** sich um sie kümmern	*She needs looking after*

(c) Negative *müssen* keeps the sense of necessity

(i) It usually has the sense of English 'needn't' or 'don't have to':

Wir **müssen** noch **nicht** gehen	*We needn't go yet/We don't have to go yet*
Er **hat** es **nicht** tun **müssen**	*He didn't need to/didn't have to do it*
Du **musst nicht** hier bleiben, du kannst auch gehen	*You needn't stay here, you can leave*

In practice *nicht brauchen* (see 13.2.5) is rather more frequent as *nicht müssen* in this meaning, e.g. *Du brauchst nicht hier zu bleiben.*

(ii) English 'mustn't' expresses a prohibition, and usually corresponds in German to *nicht dürfen*, see 17.2.1b. *nicht müssen* is sometimes used in this sense in speech, e.g. *Sie müssen hier nicht parken* 'You mustn't park here', but this is considered to be a non-standard (northern) regionalism.

17.5.2 *müssen* can express a logical deduction

(a) This corresponds to English 'must' or 'have to'

Sie spielt heute Tennis, also **muss** es ihr besser gehen	*She's playing tennis today, so she must be better*
Das **muss** ein Fehler sein	*That must/has to be a mistake*
Sie **muss** den Unfall gesehen haben	*She must have seen the accident*

If *müssen* could be taken in context to express necessity where logical deduction is intended, the meaning can be made clear by using the adverb *sicher* rather than *müssen*, e.g.:

Er ist heute **sicher** in Frankfurt	*He must be in Frankfurt today*

Er muss heute in Frankfurt sein would naturally be understood to mean 'He has to be in Frankfurt today'.

(b) German uses the past tense *musste* with a simple infinitive to express a logical deduction in the past

In such contexts English uses 'must' with a compound infinitive:

Er schuftete, dass ihm heiß sein | *He was working hard, so he must have been hot*
musste (*Grass*)

(c) A logical deduction can be queried by *nicht brauchen*

This is commoner than *nicht müssen*, e.g.: *Er war heute nicht im Büro, aber er* **braucht nicht** *deshalb krank zu sein* (less often: *aber er muss nicht . . .*)

(d) A negative logical deduction is expressed by *nicht können*

This corresponds to English 'can't':

Sie spielt heute Tennis, also **kann** sie **nicht** | *She's playing tennis today, so she can't be ill*
krank sein

17.5.3 The *Konjunktiv II* of müssen

(a) The *Konjunktiv II* form *müsste* can express a possible compulsion or necessity, and in this sense it corresponds to English 'would have to' or 'need to':

Er weiß ja nicht, was er tut – ich **müsste** | *He doesn't know what he's doing – otherwise I*
ja sonst meine Hand von ihm | *would have to disown him*
zurückziehen (*Böll*)
Es sind Felsen, Gestein, wahrscheinlich | *They are rocks and stones, probably volcanic, that*
vulkanisch, das **müsste** man nachsehen | *would need to be checked and established*
und feststellen (*Frisch*)

In negative sentences the *Konjunktiv II* of *nicht brauchen* is more usual than that of *nicht müssen*, see 17.5.2c:

Du hättest **nicht** hinzugehen **brauchen**, | *You wouldn't have had to go there if . . .*
wenn . . .

(b) *müsste* can express a logical probability or necessity

(i) In this sense, 'should' or 'ought to' are the usual English equivalents:

Deutschlands Kohle ist teurer, als sie sein | *Coal in Germany is dearer than it ought to be/*
müsste (*Zeit*) | *should be*
Das **müsste** eigentlich reichen | *That really ought to be enough*
Ich **hätte** mich vielleicht anders ausdrücken | *Perhaps I ought to/should have expressed myself*
müssen | *differently*

(ii) This sense of *müsste* is close to that of *sollte*, which also corresponds to English 'should' or' ought to', see 17.6.4. There is a difference, though, as *sollte* always expresses an obligation (often laid on a person by someone else), whereas *müsste* expresses a logical probability or necessity. Compare:

Sie **sollte** heute im Büro sein | *She ought to be at the office today*
(i.e. she is obliged to be if she doesn't want to get into trouble)

Sie **müsste** heute im Büro sein	*She ought to be at the office today*
(i.e. I assume that is the most likely place for her to be)	
Das **hätte** er eigentlich wissen **sollen**	*He ought to have known that*
(i.e. he was obliged to – it could have stopped him making a mistake)	
Das **hätte** er eigentlich wissen **müssen**	*He ought to have known that*
(i.e. I would have thought it was a pretty fair assumption that he did)	
Wo ist der Brief? Er **müsste** in dieser Schublade sein	*Where's the letter? It ought to be/should be in this drawer*
(A logical deduction: *sollte* would not be possible)	

müsste nicht is not normally used as an equivalent for English 'shouldn't' or 'ought not to'; we usually find *sollte nicht* or *dürfte nicht*, see 17.2.1c and 17.6.4.

(c) *müsste . . . gemacht haben* and *hätte . . . machen müssen*

The English equivalent for both these constructions is usually 'should/ought to have done', but there is often a clear distinction between them in German. Compare, for English *He ought to have written the letter yesterday*:

Er **müsste** den Brief schon gestern **geschrieben haben**
    (i.e. it is a fair deduction that he did)
Er **hätte** den Brief schon gestern **schreiben müssen**
    (i.e. he ought to have done it, but he didn't)

17.6 *sollen*

17.6.1 *sollen* most commonly expresses an obligation

(a) This corresponds to 'be to', 'be supposed to' or (in a few special contexts) 'shall'

Um wie viel Uhr **soll** ich kommen?	*What time am I to/shall I come?*
Ich **soll** nicht so viel rauchen	*I'm not supposed to smoke so much*
Was **soll** ich in Greifswald tun?	*What am I (supposed) to do in Greifswald?*
Sie wusste nicht, was sie tun **sollte**	*She didn't know what to do*
Wir **sollten** uns gestern treffen	*We were (supposed) to meet yesterday*

The meaning of *sollen* is close to that of *müssen*, and 'must', 'have to' is often a possible English equivalent. However, *sollen* always conveys the idea that some other person is making an obligation. Compare:

Ich **soll** hier bleiben	*I am to/have (got) to stay here*
	(i.e. someone's told me to)
Ich **muss** hier bleiben	*I've got to stay here*
	(i.e. it is necessary for me)

In questions, the past tense of *sollen* can be used to prompt a strong reaction (negative or positive, depending on the context). It can sound ironic:

Wie **sollte** ich das wissen?	*How was I (supposed) to know that?*
Sollte das nun fertig sein?	*Is that supposed to be finished?* (ironic)
Sollte er wirklich nichts davon wissen?	*Is he really supposed not to know anything about it?*

(b) *sollen* often has the force of a command

See also 16.2.2e. This use is related to the basic sense of obligation:

Du **sollst** nicht stehlen	*Thou shalt not steal*
Du **sollst** das Fenster zumachen	*(I want you to) shut the window*
Man **soll** sofort den Saal verlassen	*Everyone has to leave the room immediately*
Das **soll** dir eine Warnung sein	*Let that be a warning to you*
Er **soll** sofort kommen	*He is to/has got to come at once/Tell him to come at once*

sollen is the most frequent modal auxiliary in indirect commands (see 16.6.4b):

Er sagte ihr, sie **solle/sollte** unten warten	*He told her to wait downstairs*
Ich habe ihm gesagt, er **soll** seinem Vater helfen	*I told him to help his father*

17.6.2 *sollen* can express an intention or prediction

(a) In this sense *sollen* corresponds to 'be to', 'be supposed/meant to'

Eine zweite Fabrik **soll** bald hier gebaut werden	*A second factory is to be built here soon*
Soll das ein Kompliment sein?	*Is that meant as a compliment?*
Es **sollte** eine Überraschung sein	*It was intended to be a surprise*
Was **soll** das heißen?	*What's that supposed to mean?*
Es **soll** nicht wieder vorkommen	*It won't happen again*
Das **sollst** du noch bereuen	*You're going to regret that*

(b) The sense of intention is common in first person plural questions

In such contexts *sollen* is an alternative to *wollen*, although there is a slight difference of meaning, see 17.7.1b. Whereas *sollen* leaves the decision entirely to the other person(s), *wollen* indicates that the speaker is in favour:

Was **sollen wir** uns heute in der Stadt ansehen?	*What are we going to look at in town today?*
Sollen wir heute Abend ins Kino gehen?	*Shall we go to the cinema tonight?*

(c) The past tense of *sollen* can indicate what was destined to happen

This sense is essentially that of a 'future-in-the-past':

Diese Meinung **sollte** sie noch oft zu hören bekommen	*She would often hear this opinion again*
Er **sollte** früh sterben	*He would/was (destined) to die young*
Er **sollte** niemals nach Deutschland zurückkehren	*He would never return to Germany*

In these contexts *sollte* differs slightly from *würde* (see 16.4.5), since it indicates that this is a prediction by the speaker.

17.6.3 *sollen* can express a rumour or report

i.e. 'It is said that . . .'. Only the present tense of *sollen* is used in this sense, with a compound infinitive to refer to past time if necessary:

Er **soll** steinreich (gewesen) sein	*He is said to be (have been) enormously rich*
Bei den Unruhen **soll** es bisher vier Tote gegeben haben (*FAZ*)	*So far four people are reported to have been killed in the course of the riots*

Das Auto **soll** eine rote Ampel überfahren
haben (*MM*)

The car is reported to have gone through a red light

17.6.4 The *Konjunktiv II of sollen*

(a) The *Konjunktiv II* of *sollen* conveys the idea of a possible obligation

These forms are the commonest equivalents to English 'should (have)', 'ought to (have)':

Warum **sollte** ich denn nicht ins Theater gehen?	*Why shouldn't I go to the theatre?*
Das **solltest** du mal probieren	*You ought just to try that*
Das **sollte** ihm inzwischen klar geworden sein	*He ought to have realised that by now*
Das **hätten** Sie mir aber gestern sagen **sollen**	*You ought to have told me that yesterday*

NB: (i)   For negative 'shouldn't', 'ought not to', *dürfte nicht* can be used as a more incisive alternative to *sollte nicht*, see 17.2.1b.
(ii)   For the distinction between *sollte* and *müsste* as equivalents of English 'should'/'ought to', see 17.5.3b.

(b) *sollte . . . gemacht haben* and *hätte . . . machen sollen*

The English equivalent for both these constructions is usually 'should'/'ought to have done', but German can make a distinction between them. Thus, for English 'He ought to have written the letter yesterday':

Sie **sollte** den Brief gestern **geschrieben haben**
    (i.e. I would expect her to have done so)
Er **hätte** den Brief gestern **schreiben sollen**
    (i.e. he ought to have done, but he didn't)

(c) In questions, *sollte* is often used as an alternative to *könnte*

There is no significant difference in meaning:

Wie **sollte/könnte** ich das wissen?	*How could I know that?*
Warum **sollte/könnte** er nicht einmal in London gewesen sein?	*Why shouldn't he have been to London some time?*

(d) *sollte* is often used in conditional sentences and clauses of purpose

(i)   In 'if'-sentences it corresponds to 'should' or 'were to', see 16.5.1d:

Wenn/Falls es regnen **sollte**, so komme ich nicht	*If it should rain, I shan't come*
Sollten Sie ihn sehen, dann grüßen Sie ihn bitte von mir	*If you were to see him, please give him my regards*

(ii)   *sollen* is often used in clauses of purpose with *damit* (see 19.5.1a):

Ich trat zurück, damit sie mich nicht sehen **sollten**	*I stepped back, so that they shouldn't see me*

For alternative usage in clauses of purpose see 16.7.2.

17.7 *wollen*

17.7.1 *wollen* most often expresses desire or intention

(a) In many contexts it expresses a wish

(i) It usually corresponds to English 'want/wish (to)':

Sie **will** ihn um Geld bitten	*She wants to ask him for money*
Sie **wollte** ihn um Geld bitten	*She wanted to ask him for money*
Sie **hat** ihm um Geld bitten **wollen**	
Hättest du kommen **wollen**?	*Would you have wanted to come?*
Willst du nicht deinem Vater helfen?	*Don't you want to help your father?*

(ii) In this sense, *wollen* is often used without a dependent infinitive, as a full verb:

Was **wollen** Sie von mir?	*What do you want from me?*
Der Arzt **will**, dass ich mehr Bewegung mache	*The doctor wants me to take more exercise*
Mach, was du **willst**	*Do what you like*

(iii) The sense of 'wish' is often given by *Konjunktiv II*:

Ich **wollte**, ich hätte sie nicht so beleidigt	*I wish I hadn't offended her so much*
Ich **wollte**, ich wäre zu Hause	*I wish I was at home*

(iv) *wollen* can correspond to English 'will', 'would':

Er **will** es nicht zugeben	*He won't admit it*
Ich bat sie, es zu tun, aber sie **wollte** nicht	*I asked her to do it, but she wouldn't*
Willst du mir helfen? Ja, ich **will** dir helfen	*Will you help me? Yes, I will help you*

wollen in this sense is distinct in meaning from the future tense. **Wirst** *du mir helfen? Ja, ich* **werde** *dir helfen*, sounds more impersonal and lacks the sense of active intention on the part of the speaker which is conveyed by *wollen*.

(v) *wollen* is common in second person questions with the sense of an insistent request:

Willst du bitte noch mal nachsehen?	*Will you have another look, please?*
Wollen Sie bitte die Frage wiederholen?	*Will you repeat the question, please?*

In such requests, *Konjunktiv II* (e.g. **Würden** *Sie bitte noch mal nachsehen?*, see 16.7.3) sounds less blunt and direct than *wollen*.

(b) *wollen* **can express intention**

(i) In such contexts it often corresponds to English 'be going to', but *wollen* stresses the notion of intention more forcefully than the future with *werden*:

Wir **wollen** uns bald einen HD-fähigen Fernseher anschaffen	*We're going to buy ourselves an HD-ready TV set soon*
(The future *Wir* **werden** *uns bald einen HD-fähigen Fernseher anschaffen* has more the sense of a prediction than a definite intention)	
Wie **wollen** Sie ihm das klarmachen?	*How are you going to explain that to him?*
Ich **wollte** Sie darüber fragen	*I was going to ask you about it*
Was **wollen** Sie damit sagen?	*What do you mean by that?*
Das **will** nicht viel sagen	*That doesn't mean much*

Ich **will** sie erst morgen anrufen	*I don't intend phoning her/I'm not going to phone her until tomorrow*
Es scheint regnen zu **wollen**	*It looks as if it's going to rain*

(ii) In first person plural questions *wollen* has the sense of English 'Shall we . . .?':

Wollen wir eine Tasse Kaffee trinken?	*Shall we/Let's have a cup of coffee*
Was **wollen wir** heute machen?	*What shall we do today?*
Na, dann **wollen wir** mal (anfangen)?	*Well then, let's get on with it!*

sollen is an alternative to *wollen* in such constructions, see 17.6.2b. However, there is a slight difference in meaning. *wollen* clearly indicates that the speaker is in favour of the proposal, but *sollen* leaves the decision entirely to the other person(s).

(c) With an inanimate subject, *wollen* **corresponds to English 'need'**

The sense of *wollen* in these contexts is similar to that in (a) and (b) above, but English 'want' and 'wish' are not normally used with an inanimate subject:

Tomaten **wollen** viel Sonne	*Tomatoes need a lot of sun*
Eine solche Arbeit **will** Zeit haben	*A piece of work like that needs time*
Das **will** gut überlegt werden	*That needs proper consideration*

Negative *wollen* with an inanimate subject has the sense of 'refuse':

Der Koffer **wollte** nicht zugehen	*The suitcase refused to/wouldn't close*
Meine Beine **wollen** nicht mehr	*My legs won't carry me any further*
Das **will** mir nicht in den Kopf	*I can't grasp that*

17.7.2 *wollen* can be used in the sense of 'claim'

In this sense, *wollen* is usually linked with a perfect infinitive, typically with the implication that the claim is false:

Er **will** eine Villa auf Mallorca **gekauft haben**	*He claims to have bought a villa on Majorca*
Sie **wollen** dich in Berlin **gesehen haben**	*They say they saw you in Berlin*
. . . eine ehemalige Geliebte, die nichts gesehen haben weil sie „schockiert" war (*MM*)	*who claims not to have a former lover, seen anything because she was 'shocked'*

A few set phrases are an extension of this sense of *wollen*:

Keiner will es getan haben	*No-one admits doing it*
Ich will nichts gesagt haben	*Go on as if I hadn't said anything*
Ich will nichts gehört/gesehen/gemerkt haben	*I'll go on as if I hadn't heard/seen/noticed anything*

18 Verbs: valency

Different verbs need different elements to make a grammatical sentence. The elements which a particular verb needs to form a grammatical sentence are called the COMPLEMENTS of the verb, and the type and number of complements required by a particular verb to construct a grammatical sentence is known as the VALENCY of the verb.

The valency of verbs can involve significant differences between English and German. In particular, German typically shows the relationship between the complements and the verb through the use of CASES (see Chapter 2). English noun phrases do not have endings to show case, and the relationship of the complements to the verb is indicated more often by their position (see Chapter 21).

This chapter explains about the valency and the complements of verbs, paying attention to those verbs and constructions which are different from their nearest English equivalents:

- verb **valency, complements** and **sentence patterns** (section 18.1)
- the **subject** of the verb, in the nominative case (section 18.2)
- the **accusative** or direct object of the verb (section 18.3)
- verb objects in the **dative** case (section 18.4)
- **prepositional** objects (section 18.5)
- **predicate complements** (section 18.6)
- verb objects in the **genitive** case (section 18.7)
- **place** and **direction** complements (section 18.8)

18.1 Valency, complements and sentence patterns

18.1.1 The COMPLEMENTS of the verb

The complements of a particular verb are the elements it needs to construct a grammatical sentence. Different verbs need different elements – the action of giving, for instance, involves a person handing a thing over to another person. The verb *geben*, therefore, needs three elements to form a sentence: a **subject** (in the nominative case), a **direct object** (in the accusative case) and an **indirect object** (in the dative case):

Gestern hat **mein Vater** (NOM) **seinem Bruder** (DAT) **das Geld** (ACC) gegeben

If we omitted any of these, the sentence would be ungrammatical. Other verbs, like *telefonieren*, only need one element, i.e. a subject:

Ich habe eben telefoniert　　　　　　　*I've just made a phone call*

Many verbs, like *schlagen*, need two, i.e. a subject and a direct object:

Sie hat **den Ball** geschlagen　　　　　　*She hit the ball*

Some verbs have other types of construction, for example with a subject and a phrase with a particular preposition (a 'prepositional object'), like *warten*:

Ich habe lange **auf dich** gewartet　　　　*I waited a long time for you*

Apart from the subject, which all but a few verbs must have and which is dealt with in 18.2, there are four main types of complement in German, and these are shown in Table 18.1. A few less common ones are explained separately. Further detail on all the complements is given in sections 18.3–18.8.

TABLE 18.1 Verb complements in German

accusative object	a noun phrase in the **accusative** case	Er trinkt **schwarzen Tee** **Diesen Mann** sah er in der Stadt
dative object	a noun phrase in the **dative** case	Sie verkaufte **mir** zwei DVDs **Ihrem Mann** teilte sie es nicht mit
prepositional object	a **phrase** introduced by a **preposition** determined by the verb	Sie warnte mich **vor dem Polizisten** Er starb **an einer Lungenentzündung**
predicate complement	a noun phrase in the **nominative** case or an **adjective** with a copular verb	Er ist **ihr Bruder** Das Heft war **teuer**

German has a number of less frequent complements. The most important of these are:

(a) the GENITIVE **complement, i.e. a noun phrase in the genitive case**

Diese Errettung bedurfte **des Mutes**   Sie erinnerte sich **des Vorfalls**

There are very few verbs in modern German which have a genitive complement, see 18.7.

(b) DIRECTION **complements**

Sie ist **in die Stadt** gefahren   Er legt das Buch **auf den Tisch**

Verbs of motion always imply a direction (e.g. where somebody or something is going, or where something is being put), and any phrase indicating direction used with them (which is often obligatory) is a complement. More details on these are given in 18.8.1.

18.1.2 The VALENCY of the verb is the type and number of complements required by a particular verb to construct a grammatical sentence

Every German verb <u>governs</u> a specific number of complements of a particular type. *geben*, for instance, has three: a subject, an accusative object and a dative object, whereas *telefonieren* has only a subject (see 18.1.1). This property of each verb to govern a certain number of complements of a particular type is the VALENCY of the verb.

We have to know the valency of a German verb to be able use it correctly. This is sometimes different from the valency of what may seem to be the equivalent English verb:

Das hat er **mir** gestern mitgeteilt   *He informed me of that yesterday*
Ich fürchte **mich vor dem Zahnarzt**   *I'm afraid of the dentist*
Er riet **ihr von dieser Reise** ab   *He advised her against (making) this journey*

<u>English learners need to learn the valency of each verb</u> carefully in order to be able to use it in context. It is good practice to learn German verbs in typical sentences containing them. A number of verbs, especially the most frequent, are used with different valencies. This is often associated with differences in meaning:

jdn. achten   *respect somebody*
auf jdn. achten   *pay attention to somebody*

Further examples are given in the remainder of this chapter.

18.1.3 German sentence patterns

All German verbs require one, two or three of the complements listed in Table 18.1 to form a complete clause or sentence. How many there are, and of what type, is determined by the valency of the verb.

There are a limited number of combinations of complements which occur commonly with German verbs, since many verbs have the same valency. In this way, we can say that German possesses a restricted number of possible sentence structure types or **sentence patterns** (the German term is *Satzbaupläne*). For example, many verbs are *einem etwas* verbs, like *geben*, and need an accusative object and a dative object besides a subject (pattern D in Table 18.2).

The most frequent sentence patterns of German are given in Table 18.2. They are explained in the remainder of this chapter under the heading of the individual complements.

TABLE 18.2 German sentence patterns

A	Subject + **Der Mann**	Verb + *schwimmt*		
B	Subject + **Der Mann**	Verb + *kauft*	Accusative Object **den neuen Fernseher**	
C	Subject + **Der Mann**	Verb + *hilft*	Dative Object **seinem Bruder**	
D	Subject + **Der Mann**	Verb + *gibt*	Dative Object + **seinem Bruder**	Accusative Object **den neuen Fernseher**
E	Subject + **Der Mann**	Verb + *wartet*	Prepositional Object **auf seinen Bruder**	
F	Subject + **Der Mann**	Verb + *hindert*	Accusative Object + **seinen Bruder**	Prepositional Object **an seiner Arbeit**
G	Subject + **Der Mann**	Verb + *dankte*	Dative Object + **seinem Bruder**	Prepositional Object **für seine Hilfe**
H	Subject + **Der Mann**	Verb + *ist*	Predicate Complement **nett/ein netter Mensch**	

18.1.4 Complements and adverbials

The complements are those elements which are required by the verb to form a complete grammatical sentence. However, a sentence can contain other elements:

Mein Vater hat seinem Bruder **gestern** das Geld gegeben
Heute habe ich diesen Mann **in der Stadt** gesehen
Sie wohnte **lange** in Halle
Gestern ging sie **schnell** in die Stadt

Words and phrases like those in bold type provide additional information, often about the time, manner or place of the action or event. They may be important in context, but they are not closely bound up with the basic meaning of the verb like the complements. If we leave them out, the sentence is still grammatical. These elements are called ADVERBIALS (in German *freie Angaben*).

They can be single words (adverbs) or adverb phrases, and they can be classified into types as shown in Table 7.1.

As a rule, **complements are necessary** to make a complete grammatical sentence, whilst **adverbials are optional**. But the distinction is not always as clear-cut as this. Certain complements of some verbs can be omitted without this resulting in an ungrammatical sentence. Compare:

Er trinkt **viel Kaffee**   Er trinkt
Sie fährt **in die Stadt**   Sie fährt

We still have grammatical sentences even when the phrases in bold are left out. However, the action of *trinken* must involve consuming some liquid (the direct object), and the action of *fahren* always implies going somewhere (the direction complement). These elements are so closely bound up in meaning with the action of the verb that, even if we can leave them out in some contexts, we have to regard them as complements rather than as adverbials. They are not simply extra pieces of information about the circumstances of the action.

It can happen that the same word or phrase is a complement in some contexts, but an adverbial in others. Compare:

Sie wohnte **in Köln**:   *in Köln* is a **complement** to the verb of position *wohnen*; it cannot be omitted

Sie starb **in Köln**:   *in Köln* can be omitted; it is an **adverbial** adding extra information to the sentence

18.2 The subject

18.2.1 Most German verbs require a subject

Characteristically, the **subject** of verbs in the active voice is the agent, i.e. the animate being carrying out the action, e.g. *der Räuber hat das Geld gestohlen*, *die Studenten singen*, *der Bär frisst das Fleisch*.

(a) The subject is in the nominative case if it is a noun phrase

The finite verb AGREES with the subject, see 12.1.4:

Ich reise nach Italien
Das hat uns **die Geschichte** gelehrt
Wer ruft mich?
Kommen **deine Geschwister** morgen?

NB: For the use of *es* as a 'dummy subject' in order to permit the real subject to occur later, e.g. **Es** *saß eine alte Frau am Fenster*, see 3.6.2d.

(b) The subject can be a subordinate clause or an infinitive clause

In this case, the verb has the third person singular ending, see 12.1.4a.

Dass du hier bist, freut mich
Dich wiederzusehen hat mich gefreut

Subordinate subject clauses are introduced by *dass* or an interrogative, see 19.2. For further information on subject infinitive clauses see 13.2.3. If such a clause is not in first position in the sentence, it can be anticipated by *es*, e.g. *Es freut mich, dass du hier bist*, see 3.6.2e.

(c) The subject can be 'understood' in certain contexts

In German as in English, we can leave out the subject of the verb in some contexts. In particular, if the verbs in two (or more) main clauses linked by the coordinating conjunctions *und* and *oder* (see 19.1) have the same subject, the second (or subsequent subject) is often omitted. We say that the subject is 'understood' in the second clause:

Er kam herein und sah seine Frau in der Ecke sitzen	*He came in and saw his wife sitting in the corner*
Meine Schwester geht oft ins Kino oder besucht ein Konzert	*My sister often goes to the cinema or attends a concert*

18.2.2 A few verbs do not need a subject

These verbs just have an **accusative** or a **dative object** (depending on the verb), but **no subject**. The verb is in the third person singular form, e.g. *mich hungert, mir bangt*. Most of these verbs express an emotion or a sensation, and almost all are now limited to formal or literary registers, or to regional (especially southern) usage. The following are still used (more frequently used equivalents are given where appropriate):

Mir **bangt** vor etwas (dat.)	*I am afraid of sth.*
(More usual: *Ich habe Angst vor etwas*)	
Mich **dürstet, hungert**	*I am thirsty, hungry*
(More usual: *Ich habe Durst, Hunger*)	
Mich/Mir **ekelt** vor etwas (dat.)	*I am disgusted at sth.*
(More usual: *Es ekelt mich/Ich ekele mich vor etwas* or: *Etwas ekelt mich*)	
Mich **friert**	*I am cold*
(More usual: *Es friert mich* or, more colloquially: *Ich friere*)	
Mir **graut** vor jdm./etwas (dat.)	*I have a horror of sb./sth.*
(More usual: *Es graut mir vor etwas*)	
Mich/Mir **schaudert** vor etwas (dat.)	*I shudder at sth.*
(More usual: *Es schaudert mich vor etwas*)	
Mich/Mir **schwindelt**	*I feel dizzy*
(More usual: *Mir ist schwindlig*)	
Mir **träumte** von etwas (dat.)	*I dream of sth.*
(More usual: *Ich träumte von etwas*)	
Mich **wundert**, dass . . .	*I am surprised that . . .*
(Still quite frequent, but there are also common alternatives: *Es wundert mich/Ich wundere mich, dass . . .*)	

18.2.3 German is more restrictive than English in respect of the noun which can occur as the subject of the verb

In English nouns which do not denote an agent can often be used as the subject of the verb. This is less frequent in German, where the subject of the verb is usually the agent actually performing the action. In such cases, the noun which is the subject in English typically appears in a prepositional phrase in German:

In diesem Hotel sind Hunde verboten	***This hotel** forbids dogs*
In diesem Zelt können vier schlafen	***This tent** sleeps four*
Mit dieser Anzeige verkaufen wir viel	***This advertisement** will sell us a lot*

Wir können **mit dem Prozess** nicht fortfahren	*The trial cannot proceed*
Damit haben wir unseren besten Mittelstürmer verloren	*This has lost us our best striker*
In Berlin wird es wieder ziemlich heiß sein	*Berlin will be rather hot again*

Logically, things like 'hotels' cannot really 'forbid'. Neither do 'tents' actually 'sleep' or 'advertisements' do any 'selling', etc., and, in the last example, Berlin is <u>where</u> 'it' is hot rather than a person or thing feeling the heat. The German constructions reflect this more clearly than do the corresponding English sentences.

18.2.4 The impersonal subject *es*

Many verbs are exclusively or commonly used impersonally, with the indefinite subject *es*, (see also 3.6.2a), which corresponds to English 'it' or 'there'. The *es* cannot be omitted except in the cases indicated under (e) and (f) below.

(a) Verbs referring to weather (which are only used impersonally)

Es regnet, hagelt, schneit	*It is raining, hailing, snowing*
Es blitzte	*There were flashes of lightning*
Es dämmert	*It is growing light/dusk*

(b) Verbs used with impersonal *es* to refer to an indefinite agent

These are verbs which **can** be used with a specific subject, but are used impersonally if the agent is vague or unknown:

(i) verbs referring to natural phenomena:

Es zieht	*There's a draught*
Es brennt	*Something's burning*
Da riecht **es** nach Teer	*There's a smell of tar there*

(ii) verbs denoting noises:

Es läutet, klingelt	*Someone's ringing the bell*
Es klopfte an der Tür	*There was a knock at the door*
Es kracht, zischt, knallt	*There is a crashing, hissing, banging noise*

Many other verbs can be used with an impersonal *es* to bring out the idea of a vague impersonal agent, see 3.6.2a.

(c) Verbs denoting sensations and emotions

Many verbs denoting sensations can be used with an impersonal *es* as subject to give the idea of an unspecified force causing the sensation. The person involved appears as an accusative object:

Es juckt mich	*I itch*
Es überlief mich kalt	*A cold shiver ran up my back*
Es zog mich zu ihr	*I was drawn to her*
Es hält mich hier nicht länger	*Nothing's keeping me here any more*

Most verbs which can be used without a subject in formal or older German are now more usually constructed like this, e.g.: *Es friert mich, Es wundert mich*, etc. See 18.2.2 for details.

(d) Impersonal *es* with *sein* or *werden* followed by a noun or an adjective

This usually corrresponds to English 'it':

Es ist, wurde spät	*It is, got late*
Es ist dein Vater	*It's your father*

Further details on this use of *es* are given in 3.6.2b. The use of *es ist* in the sense of English 'there is/are' is treated in detail in 18.2.5.

(e) *sein* and *werden* can be used impersonally with a personal dative and some adjectives expressing a sensation

Es ist mir heiß, kalt, schwindlig, übel, warm, etc.

For details see 2.5.5c. *es* is usually left out unless it is in first position in a main clause.

Ist (es) dir kalt? Ja, mir ist (es) kalt
Ich merkte, dass (es) mir schwindlig wurde.

(f) Impersonal passive and reflexive constructions

Es lebt sich gut in dieser Stadt	*You can live well in this city*
Es wurde im Nebenzimmer geredet	*People were talking in the next room*

es is usually deleted unless it is in initial position in a main clause. Details are given in 3.6.2a and 15.1.3–4.

(g) Other impersonal verbs and constructions

Many of these are idiomatic and the verbs involved are also used in other constructions with a definite subject. A selection of the most common:

Dafür bedurfte es einer Sonderregelung (*HMP*)	*A special provision was required for that*
Es fehlt mir an etwas (dat.) (see also 18.4.1d)	*I lack sth.*
Es gefällt mir in Heidelberg (see also 18.4.1d)	*I like it in Heidelberg*
Es gibt (For *es gibt* and *es ist* as equivalents of 'there is/are', see 18.2.5)	*There is/are*
Es geht	*It can be done; OK (in answer to Wie geht es (dir/ Ihnen)?)*
Wie geht es (dir/Ihnen)?	*How are you?*
Es geht um Leben und Tod	*It's a matter of life and death*
Es gilt, etwas zu tun	*The thing is to do something*
Es geschah ihm recht	*It served him right*
Es handelt sich um etwas (*acc.*)	*It is a question of sth.*
Es heißt, dass . . .	*It is said that . . .*
Es kommt auf etwas (*acc.*) an	*It depends on sth.*
Es kommt zu etwas (*dat.*)	*Something occurs*
e.g.: Am Abend **kam es zu** neuen Zusammenstößen	*e.g. There were fresh clashes in the evening*
Es liegt an etwas (*dat.*)	*It is due to sth.*
e.g.: **Woran liegt es**, dass . . .?	*e.g. Why is it that . . .?*
Es macht/tut nichts	*It doesn't matter*

Es steht schlecht/besser um ihn	*Things look bad/better for him*
Wie steht es mit ihr?	*How's she doing?*
Es verhält sich so	*Things are like that*
e.g.: Ähnlich **verhält es sich** an der Universität Münster	*Things are similar at the University of Münster*

18.2.5 *es ist/sind* and *es gibt* as equivalents of English 'there is/are'

es ist/sind and *es gibt* have rather different meanings. The following is a guide to choosing the correct one for the context.

(a) *es gibt* indicates existence in general

It is a real impersonal construction, and the *es* is never omitted.

(i) *es gibt* is typically used in broad, general statements, denoting existence in general, without necessarily referring to a particular place:

Es gibt Tage, wo alles schief geht	*There are days when everything goes wrong*
So etwas **gibt es** nicht	*There's no such thing*
Es gibt verschiedene Gründe dafür	*There are various reasons for that*
Dort **hat** es schon häufig Ärger **gegeben** (*HMP*)	*There has often been trouble there*

(ii) *es gibt* is used to point in a general way to permanent existence in a large area (i.e. a city or a country):

Es gibt drei alte Kirchen in unserer Stadt	*There are three old churches in our town*
In Trier **gibt es** ja so viel zu sehen	*There's so much to see in Trier*
Es dürfte in der Bundesrepublik wenige **geben**, die so gut wie er informiert sind (*Zeit*)	*There are probably not many people in the Federal Republic who are as well informed as he is*

(iii) *es gibt* records the consequences of some event:

Wenn du das tust, **gibt's** ein Unglück	*If you do that, there'll be an accident*
Bei den Unruhen **soll es** bisher vier Tote **gegeben haben** (*FAZ*)	*It is reported that there have been four killed in the disturbances so far*

NB: In everyday speech in Southwest Germany, *es hat* is used for *es gibt*. This is a non-standard regionalism.

(b) *es ist/sind* indicates the presence of something at a particular time and place

The *es* of *es ist/sind* is a 'dummy' subject (see 3.6.2e), allowing the real subject of the verb to occur later in the sentence. It drops out when it is not in initial position in a main clause. Compare:

Es war eine Maus in der Küche	*There was a mouse in the kitchen*
BUT: In der Küche **war** eine Maus	*In the kitchen there was a mouse*
Er hat gemerkt, dass eine Maus in der Küche **war**	*He noticed that there was a mouse in the kitchen*

es ist/sind is used:

(i) to refer to permanent or temporary presence in a definite and limited place, or temporary presence in a large area:

Es war noch ein kleines Café in der Berliner Straße	*There was still a little cafe in the Berliner Strasse*

Es ist irgendjemand an der Tür	*There's someone at the door*
Es waren noch viele Menschen auf den Straßen	*There were still a lot of people in the streets*
Es sind keine Wolken am Himmel **gewesen**	*There were no clouds in the sky*

Sentences with *es ist/sind* **must** contain an indication of place. This is often quite simply *da*:

Es ist ein Brief für Sie **da**	*There's a letter for **you***

es gibt is sometimes used in contexts like this, but it emphasises the thing rather than the place and underlines its distinctive character:

In dieser Diele **gab es** gegenüber der Tür einen offenen Kamin (*Wendt*)	*In this lounge there was an open fireplace opposite the door*

(ii) to record events and when speaking of weather conditions:

Letzte Woche **war** in Hamburg ein Streik	*There was a strike in Hamburg last week*
In Mainz **war** ein Aufenthalt von fünf Minuten	*There was a five-minute stop in Mainz*
Am nächsten Morgen **war** dichter Nebel	*Next morning there was thick fog*
Gestern **war** ein Gewitter in Füssen	*There was a thunderstorm in Füssen yesterday*

Usage varies in this type of context, and *es gibt* is often used without any real difference of meaning:

Letzte Woche **gab es** einen Streik in Hamburg
In Mainz **gab es** einen Aufenthalt von fünf Minuten
Gestern **gab es** ein Gewitter in Füssen

es gibt is particularly frequent when a need is felt to emphasise the exceptional nature of the event or to refer to the future:

Es gab eine Explosion in der Fabrik	*There was an explosion in the factory*
Morgen **wird es** wieder schönes Wetter **geben**	*It will be fine again tomorrow*

18.3 **The accusative object**

18.3.1 **Transitive verbs govern a direct object in the accusative as one of their complements**

Verbs which govern an accusative object are called TRANSITIVE VERBS. This accusative object is called the DIRECT OBJECT. With many of these verbs, the accusative is the only complement apart from the subject (sentence pattern B in Table 18.2):

Er hat **sie** besucht
Christian hat **seine Freundin** besucht
Seine Worte haben **mich** verletzt
Den Arzt hat sie nicht gesehen

Table 18.2 shows that some transitive verbs can have other complements in addition to the accusative object, most commonly a dative object (sentence pattern D), and a prepositional object (sentence pattern F). A few verbs also have an accusative object with a genitive object or a direction complement. Details about these sentence patterns are given in the sections dealing with these other complements.

Verbs which do not have a direct object in the accusative case are called INTRANSITIVE VERBS.

NB: The accusative case is used in some time and place phrases, e.g.: *Es hat **den ganzen Tag** geschneit* (see 2.2.5). These are **not** complements of the verb, but adverbials.

18.3.2 The direct object can have the form of a clause

(a) Many verbs can have a clause as their direct object

Because these clauses function as complements of the verb, they are called COMPLEMENT CLAUSES. These clauses can be:

(i) A subordinate clause with *dass, ob* or an interrogative (see 19.2):

Ich bedauerte, **dass ich nicht kommen konnte**
Sie fragte mich, **ob ich dort übernachten wollte**

(ii) An infinitive clause with *zu* (see 13.2.4):

Ich hoffe **dich bald wiedersehen zu können**
Ich habe vor **sie morgen zu besuchen**

Many verbs which have a clause as object can have either a subordinate clause or an infinitive clause, depending on context. However, a few verbs only allow an infinitive clause (especially verbs denoting an intended action, like *versuchen, vorhaben, wagen, sich weigern, zögern*), whereas others only allow a subordinate clause (especially verbs of saying and hearing, e.g. *erleben, fragen, mitteilen, verfügen*). In practice, usage in German is similar to that with the nearest English equivalents; exceptions are detailed in 13.2.4.

(b) A direct object clause is sometimes anticipated by *es*

This can be the case whether the complement is a subordinate clause or an infinitive clause, e.g.:

Sie sah **es** als gutes Zeichen an, dass keine Leute mehr vorbeikamen
Ich konnte **es** kaum ertragen, ihn so leiden zu sehen

Details on the use of this 'anticipatory' *es* are given in 3.6.3a.

18.3.3 A few verbs are used with two accusative objects

In general, only one accusative (direct) object is possible in a sentence. However, a small number of verbs allow two accusative objects.

(a) Verbs with two accusative objects

(i) *kosten* and *lehren* are normally used with two accusatives:

Der Flug hat **meinen Vater 5000 Euro** gekostet	*The flight cost my father 5000 euros*
Sie hat **mich Deutsch** gelehrt	*She taught me German*

In colloquial German both these verbs are commonly used with a dative of the person, e.g. *Sie hat **mir** Deutsch gelehrt; Das hat **mir** viel Geld gekostet*. This is not generally considered standard, but it is acceptable with *kosten*, as an alternative to the accusative, in figurative contexts:

Das kann **ihn/ihm** den Hals kosten	*That may cost him his life*

(ii) *abfragen* and *abhören* 'test sb. orally' can be used <u>either</u> with two accusative objects <u>or</u> a dative of the person and an accusative:

Der Lehrer hat **ihn/ihm** die englischen Vokabeln abgefragt/abgehört	*The teacher tested him on his English vocabulary*

If only the person is mentioned in the sentence, only the accusative is used, e.g. *Der Lehrer hat **ihn** abgefragt/abgehört*

(iii) *bitten* and *fragen* can be used with two accusatives. One denotes the person asked, the other is an indefinite pronoun or a subordinate clause:

Hast du **ihn etwas** gefragt?	*Did you ask him something?*
Das möchte ich **dich** bitten	*I would like to request that of you*
Sie fragte **ihn, ob er mitkommen wollte**	*She asked him if he wanted to come with her*

NB: *bitten* is more commonly used with a prepositional object introduced by *um*, see 18.6.10, e.g. *Ich möchte dich **darum** bitten*.

(iv) *angehen* is used with an accusative of the person and an indefinite expression of quantity, e.g.:

Das geht **dich nichts** an	*That doesn't concern you at all*

Similarly: *Das geht **mich** viel/wenig/einen Dreck an*. The use of *angehen* with a dative of the person (e.g. *Das geht **dir** nichts an*) is a North German regionalism which is not accepted as standard.

(b) A few verbs have a predicate complement in the accusative

i.e. an additional element which relates back to the accusative object, describing or identifying it:

Er nannte **mich einen Lügner**	*He called me a liar*

This construction is restricted in German to verbs of calling, i.e. *heißen, nennen* and *schimpfen*. A similar construction is possible with more verbs in English than in German. The German equivalents of these most often have a phrase with *als* in apposition (see 2.6), or a prepositional complement, usually with *zu*, although some verbs select other prepositions:

Ich sehe es **als eine Schande** an	*I consider it a shame*
Er erwies sich **als Feigling**	*He proved himself a coward*
Er machte sie **zu seiner Frau**	*He made her his wife*
Man erklärte ihn **zum Verräter**	*He was declared a traitor*
Wir hielten ihn **für einen Idioten**	*We considered/thought him an idiot*

18.3.4 Some German transitive verbs have English equivalents with different constructions

Common examples are:

etwas beantragen	*to apply for sth.*
jdn. beerben	*to inherit from sb.*
etwas bezahlen	*to pay for sth.*
etwas ekelt mich (see also 18.2.2)	*I am disgusted at sth.*
etwas dauert mich	*I regret sth.*
etwas freut mich	*I am pleased/glad about sth.*
jdn./etwas fürchten	*to be afraid of sb./sth.*

18.3.5 **Fewer verbs can be used both transitively and intransitively in German than in English**

English learners need to be aware that German verbs are often less flexible than their nearest English counterparts and more restricted to use in certain constructions only. A few German verbs can be used both transitively and intransitively, e.g.:

Ich brach den Zweig	*I broke the branch*
Der Zweig brach	*The branch broke*

Far fewer German than English verbs have this facility, and this means that many English verbs have two (or more) German equivalents depending on whether the English verb is being used transitively or intransitively. These can take a number of forms:

(a) **The transitive and intransitive uses of some English verbs can correspond to different verbs in German**

grow
Er **züchtet** Blumen	*He grows flowers*
Die Blumen **wachsen** im Garten	*The flowers grow in the garden*

leave
Sie **verließ** das Haus	*She left the house*
Ich **ließ** den Brief im Fach (**liegen**)	*I left the letter in the pigeonhole*
Der Zug **fährt** schon **ab**	*The train is already leaving*
Er **ging** früher als ich (**weg**)	*He left before me*

open (see also (c) below)
Ich **machte** die Tür **auf**	*I opened the door*
Die Tür **ging auf**	*The door opened*

(b) **The transitive and intransitive uses of some English verbs can correspond to related verbs in German**

The prefix *be-* (see 22.4.1) often forms transitive verbs from intransitive verbs, but other prefixes (e.g. *er-* and *ver-*) can sometimes have this function, and there are some pairs of verbs with vowel changes:

answer
Sie **beantwortete** die Frage	*She answered the question*
Sie **antwortete**	*She answered*

climb
Ich **bestieg** den Berg	*I climbed the mountain*
Ich **erstieg** den Berg	*I climbed the mountain (to the top)*
Die Maschine **stieg**	*The plane climbed*

drown
Man **ertränkte** die Hexe	*The witch was drowned*
Die Matrosen **ertranken**	*The sailors drowned*

sink
Wir **versenkten** das Schiff	*We sank the ship*
Das Schiff **sank**	*The ship sank*

sit
Sie **setzt** sich auf den Stuhl	*She sits down on the chair*
Sie **sitzt** auf dem Stuhl	*She is sitting on the chair*

(c) Some transitive German verbs can be used reflexively as the equivalent of the English verb used intransitively

change

Das hat nichts **geändert**	*That has changed nothing*
Das hat **sich geändert**	*That has changed*

feel

Sie **fühlte** etwas unter ihren Füßen	*She felt something under her feet*
Sie **fühlte sich** unwohl	*She felt unwell*

open (see also (a) above)

Ich **öffnete** die Tür	*I opened the door*
Die Tür **öffnete sich**	*The door opened*

turn

Ich **drehte** das Rad	*I turned the wheel*
Das Rad **drehte sich**	*The wheel turned*

(d) A construction with *lassen* and a German intransitive verb can correspond to the transitive use of the verb in English

For this 'causative' use of *lassen*, see 13.3.1c:

drop

Ich **ließ** den Stein **fallen**	*I dropped the stone*
Der Stein **fiel**	*The stone dropped*

fail

Sie **haben** den Kandidaten **durchfallen lassen**	*They failed the candidate*
Der Kandidat **ist durchgefallen**	*The candidate failed*

run

Ich **habe** das Wasser in die Badewanne **laufen lassen**	*I've run the bathwater*
Der Wasserhahn **läuft**	*The tap's running*

(e) A construction with *sich lassen* and a German transitive verb sometimes corresponds to the intransitive use of the verb in English

For this construction with *sich lassen*, see 15.4.6:

cut

Sie **hat** das Papier **geschnitten**	*She cut the paper*
Das Papier **lässt sich** leicht **schneiden**	*The paper cuts easily*

18.3.6 Reflexive verbs

Many German verbs are always used with a reflexive pronoun in the accusative case (see 3.2), e.g. *sich beeilen* 'hurry', *sich erkälten* 'catch a cold'. These REFLEXIVE VERBS have no direct equivalent in English – reflexive pronouns like 'myself' in English are used in a quite different way – and they can correspond to a variety of English verb constructions and verb types.

A number have English equivalents quite different from the simple verb (and the English equivalent is often an intransitive verb), e.g. *sich setzen* 'sit down' (cf. *setzen* 'put'), etc. In some instances the nearest English equivalent is a passive (or passive-like) construction (see 15.4.3).

Many verbs used with a reflexive accusative also have other complements, e.g. a dative, genitive or prepositional object. They are treated in the sections dealing with these other complements.

It is helpful to distinguish two types of reflexive verb in German:

(a) 'True' reflexive verbs, which are ONLY used with a reflexive pronoun

With these, the reflexive pronoun is an integral part of the verb:

sich bedanken	*say 'thank you'*	sich erholen	*recover*
sich beeilen	*hurry*	sich erkälten	*catch a cold*
sich befinden	*be (situated)*	sich irren	*be mistaken*
sich benehmen	*behave*	sich verabschieden	*say 'goodbye'*
sich eignen	*be suited*	sich verneigen	*bow*
sich entschließen	*decide*	sich weigern	*refuse*

(b) Other transitive verbs used reflexively, with the accusative object appearing as a reflexive pronoun

(i) Many transitive verbs can be used with a reflexive pronoun. The agent is then performing the action on him-/herself. Compare:

non-reflexive	**reflexive**
Das habe ich **meinen Bruder** gefragt	Das habe ich **mich** gefragt
Ich setzte **den Koffer** auf den Stuhl	Ich setzte **mich** auf den Stuhl
Ich habe **den Hund** gewaschen	Ich habe **mich** gewaschen
Ich habe **ihn** nicht überzeugen können	Ich habe **mich** nicht überzeugen können

(ii) Many transitive verbs denoting activities and accomplishments can be used reflexively with a subject which is not the person carrying out the action. These usually correspond to English passive constructions:

Das **erklärt sich** leicht	*That is easily explained*
Mein Verdacht **hat sich bestätigt**	*My suspicions were confirmed*

Intransitive verbs denoting activities and accomplishments can also be used in a similar way with a reflexive pronoun. These constructions are always impersonal and have a sense similar to a construction with *man* (see also 15.4.3).

Dort **wohnt** es **sich** gut	*One can live well there*
Hier **arbeitet** es **sich** bequem	*One can work comfortably here*

(iii) A few verbs have reflexive and non-reflexive forms where the reflexive variant is a 'true' reflexive, with a slightly different meaning, see also 18.3.5c:

Das erinnert mich an etwas	*That reminds me of something*
Ich erinnere mich an etwas	*I remember something*
Das habe ich ihr versprochen	*I promised her that*
Ich habe mich versprochen	*I made a slip of the tongue*

18.4 The dative object

A DATIVE OBJECT occurs in three main sentence patterns (see Table 18.2), and these are explained in the sections indicated:

- C: Subject + verb + dative object (section 18.4.1)
- D: Subject + verb + accusative object + dative object (section 18.4.2)
- G: Subject + verb + dative object + prepositional object (section 18.4.1)

The prepositions used with individual verbs in sentence pattern G are treated in 18.5. Verbs with a dative reflexive are dealt with in 18.4.3. The dative case has a wide range of other uses in German, as detailed in 2.5. As explained in 15.1.3, the dative object can never be converted into the subject of a corresponding passive sentence.

NB: Besides dative objects, there are also 'free' datives, which are not closely linked to particular verbs and are not complements. These are explained in detail in section 2.5.3.

18.4.1 **Verbs governing the dative**

A fair number of German verbs have a dative object, but no accusative object.

These have no direct equivalent in English, and English learners need to learn these verbs with their constructions. No general rules can be given as to which verbs govern a dative object, but it is helpful to be aware that these dative objects often relate to persons who are advantaged or disadvantaged in some way through the action expressed by the verb.

(a) Common verbs which govern a dative object

abraten *advise against*
   Sie hat **ihm** davon abgeraten   *She advised him against it*
ähneln *resemble, look like*
   Er ähnelt **seinem Bruder**   *He looks like his brother*
applaudieren *applaud*
   Sie applaudierten **dem Solisten**   *They applauded the soloist*
ausweichen *get out of the way of, evade, avoid*
   Er ist **der Gefahr** ausgewichen   *He avoided the danger*
begegnen *meet* (by chance)
   Ich bin **ihr** in der Stadt begegnet   *I met her in town*
bekommen *agree with one* (of food)
   Fleisch bekommt **mir** nicht   *Meat doesn't agree with me*
NB: *bekommen* with an accusative object means 'receive', e.g. *Er bekam **einen langen Brief** von seinem Vater.*

danken *thank*
   Ich dankte **ihnen** sehr dafür   *I thanked them very much for it*
dienen *serve*
   Er diente **dem König von Italien**   *He served the king of Italy*
drohen *threaten*
   Sie drohte **ihm** mit einem Stock   *She threatened him with a stick*
einfallen *occur*
   Das ist **mir** nicht eingefallen   *That didn't occur to me*
erliegen *succumb to*
   Er **erlag** seinen Wunden   *He succumbed to his injuries*
folgen *follow*
   Er ist **ihr** ins Exil gefolgt   *He followed her into exile*
NB: *folgen* is used with *auf* (acc.) in the sense 'succeed, come after': *Auf den Sturm folgten drei sonnige Tage.*

gehorchen *obey*
   Sie gehorcht **ihrem Vater**   *She obeys her father*
gehören *belong*
   Der Mercedes gehört **mir** nicht   *The Mercedes doesn't belong to me*
NB: (i)   In the sense 'be part of, be one of', *gehören* is used with *zu: Das gehört zu meinen Aufgaben.* See 18.6.13b.
   (ii) In the sense 'be a member of', *angehören* is used. It also takes a dative: *Ich gehöre dem Verein an.*

gelten *be meant for, be aimed at, be for*
   Gilt diese Bemerkung **mir**?   *Is that comment meant for me?*

Der Beifall galt **den Schauspielern**	The applause was for the actors

gleichen *be equal to, resemble*

Jeder Tag glich **dem anderen**	One day was like the next

gratulieren *congratulate*

Sie haben **ihr** zum Geburtstag gratuliert	They congratulated her on her birthday

helfen *help*

Er half **seinem Vater** in der Küche	He helped his father in the kitchen

imponieren *impress*

Sie hat **ihm** sehr imponiert	She impressed him a lot

kündigen *fire, give notice*

Der Chef hat **ihm** gestern gekündigt	The boss gave him notice yesterday

NB: In colloquial spoken German, *kündigen* is used with an accusative object, e.g. *Sie hat **ihn** gekündigt*. In the meaning 'cancel', it is <u>always</u> used with an accusative, e.g. *Er hat **den Vertrag** gekündigt*.

nutzen/nützen *be of use*

Das nutzt **mir** doch gar nichts	But that's no use to me

passen *suit*

Das neue Kleid passt **dir** gut	The new dress suits you

NB: *zu jdm./etwas passen* 'go with sb./sth.' (see 18.5.13b)

schaden *harm*

Rauchen schadet **der Gesundheit**	Smoking is harmful to your health

schmeicheln *flatter*

Der Student wollte **dem Professor** schmeicheln	The student wanted to flatter the professor

trauen *trust*

Ich traute **meinen Augen** nicht	I couldn't believe my eyes

NB: *misstrauen* 'distrust' also governs a dative object.

trotzen *defy*

Er trotzte **der Gefahr**	He defied/braved the danger

unterliegen *be defeated by, be subject to*

Er unterlag **seinem Gegner**	He lost to his opponent

vertrauen *have trust in*

jdm. blind vertrauen	have a blind trust in somebody

wehtun *hurt*

Der Wespenstich hat **ihm** wehgetan	The wasp sting hurt him

(b) Most verbs with the meaning 'happen', 'occur' govern a dative

Es wird **dir** doch nichts geschehen	But nothing will happen to you
Was ist **ihm** gestern passiert?	What happened to him yesterday?
So etwas ist **mir** noch nie vorgekommen	Nothing like that has ever happened to me

Similarly: *bevorstehen, widerfahren, zustoßen*, etc.

(c) Verbs with certain prefixes usually take a dative

i.e. those with *bei-, ent-, entgegen-, nach-, wider-, zu-*:

Er ist **der SPD** beigetreten	He joined the SPD
Das entsprach **meinen Erwartungen**	That came up to my expectations
Sie kam **mir** entgegen	She came towards me
Er eilte **ihr** nach	He hurried after her
Das Kind widersprach **seiner Mutter**	The child contradicted its mother
Er hat **dem Gespräch** zugehört	He listened to the conversation

Similarly (among many others):

beistehen	*give support to*	nachlaufen	*run after*
beiwohnen	*be present at*	nachstellen	*follow, pester*
entsagen	*renounce*	nachstreben	*emulate*
entstammen	*originate from*	sich widersetzen	*oppose*
entgegengehen	*go to meet*	widerstehen	*resist*
entgegenwirken	*counteract*	zulaufen	*run up to*
nachgeben	*give way to*	zustimmen	*agree with*
nachkommen	*follow*	zuvorkommen	*anticipate*

The verbs prefixed with *ent-* meaning 'escape' (*entgehen, entfliehen, entkommen, entrinnen, entwischen*, etc.) also all govern a dative.

NB: A few verbs with these prefixes have a dative <u>and</u> an accusative object (see 18.4.2), e.g. *jdm. etwas beibringen* 'teach somebody something', *jdm. etwas zutrauen* 'credit somebody with something'.

(d) The dative object of some verbs corresponds to the subject of the usual English equivalent

Etwas fällt mir auf	*I notice something*
Etwas entfällt mir	*I forget something*
Es fällt mir leicht, schwer	*I find something easy/difficult*
Etwas fehlt, mangelt mir/Es fehlt, mangelt mir an etwas	*I lack something*
Etwas gefällt mir	*I like something*
Etwas geht mir auf	*I realise something*
Etwas gelingt mir	*I succeed in something*
Etwas tut mir Leid	*I am sorry about something*
Das leuchtet mir nicht ein	*I don't understand that*
Es liegt mir viel an etwas (dat)	*I am keen on something*
Etwas liegt mir	*I fancy something*
Das genügt, reicht mir	*I have had enough of that*
Etwas schmeckt mir	*I like something* (i.e. food)

NB: With these verbs, there is a strong tendency for the dative object to precede the verb in main clauses, e.g. *Mir hat das nicht gefallen.*

18.4.2 **Verbs governing a dative and an accusative object**

These are transitive verbs with two complements, i.e. an accusative (direct) object, which is usually a thing, and a dative object, called the indirect object, which is usually a person. It is helpful to remember them as *einem etwas* verbs.

The German dative commonly corresponds to an English prepositional phrase with 'to' or 'from', or to an English indirect object (e.g. *He gave me the book*). In German, though, the indirect object is indicated by the dative case, not by a preposition, so that 'He gave the money to his uncle' is *Er gab seinem Onkel das Geld*, NOT **Er gab das Geld zu seinem Onkel*.

With many verbs (e.g. *geben*) the dative object is essential to construct a grammatical sentence, with others (e.g. *beweisen*) it can be dropped in some contexts.

(a) Verbs of giving and taking (in the widest sense) govern a dative and an accusative object

There are a large number of such verbs:

Sie haben **mir eine Stelle** angeboten	*They offered me a job*
Das wollte er (**mir**) beweisen	*He wanted to prove that (to me)*
Er brachte (**ihr**) **einen Blumenstrauß**	*He brought (her) a bunch of flowers*

Ich kann (**dir**) **diesen Roman** empfehlen	*I can recommend this novel (to you)*
Er hat **dem Lehrer einen Bleistift** gegeben	*He gave the teacher a pencil*
Sie will **mir** jetzt **etwas Ruhe** gönnen	*She is now willing to let me have some peace and quiet*
Kannst du **mir hundert Franken** leihen?	*Can you lend me a hundred francs?*
Wir haben (**ihr**) **die Tasche** genommen	*We took the bag (from her)*
Ich habe (**ihr**) **das Paket** geschickt	*I've sent (her) the parcel*
Du schuldest **mir** noch **hundert Euro**	*You still owe me a hundred euros*
Er verkaufte (**mir**) **seinen alten Golf**	*He sold (me) his old Golf*
Er zeigte **ihr seine Kupferstiche**	*He showed her his etchings*

(b) Most verbs involving an act of speaking are used with a dative and an accusative object

(i) With most of these verbs the accusative object can only be either a neuter or indefinite pronoun (e.g. *es, das, etwas, nichts*) or a clause (a subordinate clause introduced by *dass, ob* etc., or an infinitive clause). The equivalent English verbs often have quite different constructions:

Sie hat (mir) geantwortet, dass sie morgen kommen wollte	*She answered me, and said she was going to come tomorrow*
Wer hat (dir) befohlen, die Geiseln zu erschießen?	*Who gave (you) the order to shoot the hostages?*
Das habe ich ihm schon gestern erzählt	*I already told him that yesterday*
Er hat mir geraten, mein Haus zu verkaufen	*He advised me to sell my house*
Er versicherte mir, dass er alles erledigt hätte	*He assured me he had taken care of everything*
Das wird er (dir) nie verzeihen können	*He'll never be able to forgive you that*

NB: With *antworten*, the dative is only used for persons. Cf.: *Er hat* **auf** *meinen Brief,* **auf** *meine* **Frage** *geantwortet.*

sagen is normally used in this way, with an optional dative of the person:

Was wollen Sie (ihm) sagen?	*What do you want to say (to him)?*
Sie sagte mir, dass sie es auf keinen Fall machen würde	*She told me that on no account would she do that*

However, it is used with *zu* when introducing direct speech or for a person addressing himself:

„Nun komm doch!" sagte sie zu Christian	*'Come along now', she said to Christian*
„Wie kannst du das nur machen", sagte er zu sich selbst	*'How on earth can you do that?', he said to himself*

(ii) With a few verbs the accusative object or the dative object can be omitted, as the context requires. This is not possible with all the nearest equivalent verbs in English:

Die irakische Regierung erlaubte (der Delegation) die Einreise	*The Iraqi government allowed the delegation into the country*
Sie hat mir (einen langen Brief) geschrieben	*She wrote me (a long letter)*
Hat sie dir gestern gemailt	*Did she e-mail you yesterday?*
Das hat sie mir vorhin gesimst	*She texted me that just now*

(iii) *glauben* has a dative of the person and/or an accusative of the thing:

Er glaubt **dem Lehrer**
Er glaubt **jedes Wort**
Er glaubt **dem Lehrer jedes Wort**

NB: *glauben an* (acc.) (see 18.6.2b), is used for 'believe in', e.g. *Ich* **glaube an** *seinen Erfolg.*

(c) With some verbs the German dative and accusative construction differs from the construction used with the nearest equivalent English verb

The following are common:

Man merkt ihm die Anstrengung an	*One notices the effort he's making*
Sie fügte es dem Brief bei	*She enclosed it with the letter*
Das hat ihm das Studium ermöglicht/ erschwert	*That made it possible/difficult for him to study*
Das hat sie mir gestern mitgeteilt	*She informed me of that yesterday*
Die Polizei konnte ihm nichts nachweisen	*The police couldn't prove anything against him*
Das hat sie mir aber verschwiegen	*She didn't tell me about that, though*
Das hätte ich ihr nicht zugetraut	*I wouldn't have believed her capable of that*

(d) With verbs of sending or transferring, a phrase with *an* is often used instead of a noun phrase in the dative

The effect is to emphasise the recipient more strongly:

Ich habe ein Paket **an meinen Vater** geschickt
Ich habe einen Brief **an deinen Vater** geschrieben
Er hat seinen alten Opel **an seinen Vater** verkauft

(e) A few reflexive verbs have a dative object

With these the reflexive pronoun is the accusative object:

Sie mussten sich **dem Feind** ergeben	*They had to surrender to the enemy*
Sie näherten sich **der Stadt**	*They approached the city*

18.4.3 **Some verbs are used with a dative reflexive pronoun**

(a) Many verbs governing a dative may be used with a dative reflexive pronoun if the action refers back to the subject

Both types of verbs governing the dative can be used in this way, i.e.:

(i) Verbs where the dative is the sole object (see 18.4.1):

Ich habe **mir** mehrmals widersprochen	*I contradicted myself several times*
Du schadest **dir** mit dem Rauchen	*You're harming yourself by smoking*

(ii) *einem etwas* verbs (see 18.4.2):

Ich erlaubte **mir**, ihm zu widersprechen	*I allowed myself to contradict him*
Ich muss **mir** Arbeit verschaffen	*I must find work*
Ich habe **mir** zu viel zugemutet	*I've taken on too much*

(b) A few other verbs occur with a dative reflexive pronoun

These are 'true' reflexive verbs (see 18.3.6), where the reflexive pronoun is an integral part of the verb. All also have an accusative object:

Das habe ich **mir** angeeignet	*I acquired that*
Das habe ich **mir** eingebildet	*I imagined that*
Das verbitte ich **mir**	*I refuse to tolerate that*
Ich habe **mir** vorgenommen, das zu tun	*I have resolved to do that*
Das kann ich **mir** gut vorstellen	*I can imagine that well*
Ich habe **mir** eine Grippe zugezogen	*I contracted flu*

Similarly: *sich etwas anmaßen* 'claim sth. for oneself', *sich etwas ausbedingen* 'make sth. a condition'.

18.5 Prepositional objects

18.5.1 Many verbs are followed by an object introduced by a preposition

The PREPOSITION used in prepositional objects is wholly idiomatic and determined by the individual verb. The fact that German has *Ich warte* **auf** *Sie* for English 'I am waiting **for** you', for example, is not related in any way to the usual meaning of the German preposition *auf* or the English preposition 'for'. For this reason, the foreign learner has to treat each combination of verb and preposition separately and remember them as a whole.

There are three main sentence patterns with prepositional objects, see Table 18.2, i.e.:

- Verbs with a prepositional object as their only object (sentence pattern E)
- Transitive verbs with an accusative object and a prepositional object (sentence pattern F)
- Verbs with a dative object and a prepositional object (sentence pattern G).

A few verbs have two prepositional objects. All prepositional objects are treated in this section under the individual prepositions, with other complements governed by the verb indicated as appropriate.

18.5.2 *an*

an is most often followed by the dative case in prepositional objects, but a few verbs govern *an* with the accusative case.

(a) **Used in prepositional objects with the DATIVE case,** *an* **often conveys the idea of 'in respect of, in connection with'**

Ich erkannte sie **an ihrem knallroten Haar**	*I recognised her by her bright red hair*
Er ist **an einer Lungenentzündung** gestorben	*He died of pneumonia*
Ich zweifle **an seiner Ehrlichkeit**	*I doubt his honesty*

A selection of other verbs:

arbeiten an	*work at*
mitwirken an	*play a part in*
erkranken an	*fall ill with*
teilnehmen an	*take part in*
gewinnen an (*e.g.*: an Bedeutung gewinnen)	*gain (in)*
verlieren an (*e.g.*: an Boden verlieren)	*lose (some)*
leiden an	*suffer from*
sich an jdm./etwas freuen	*take pleasure in sb./sth.*

NB: *sich freuen auf* (acc.) 'look forward to' (18.5.3a), *sich freuen über* 'be glad/pleased about' (18.5.9).

jdn. an etwas hindern	*prevent sb. from (doing) sth.*
Es fehlt mir an etwas	*I lack sth.* (see 18.4.1d)
Es liegt mir viel an etwas	*I am very keen on sth.* (see 18.4.1d)
sich an etwas orientieren	*orientate oneself by sth.*
etwas an jdm. rächen	*avenge sth. on sb.*
sich an jdm. für etwas rächen	*take revenge on sb. for sth.*

(b) **Most of the few verbs which govern a prepositional object with** *an* **and a following** ACCUSATIVE **case denote mental processes**

Du erinnerst mich **an ihn**	*You remind me of him*
Ich erinnere mich **an ihn**	*I remember him* (see 18.7.2)
Ich glaube **an den Fortschritt**	*I believe in progress* (see 18.4.2b)

Also:

denken an	*think of*
sich an etwas halten	*stick to sth.*
sich an etwas gewöhnen	*get used to sth.*

18.5.3 *auf*

auf most often occurs with the accusative case in prepositional objects. Very few verbs govern *auf* with the dative.

(a) *auf* **with the** ACCUSATIVE **case is the commonest preposition in prepositional objects**

Ich werde **auf deine Kinder** aufpassen	*I'll mind your children*
Seine Bemerkung bezog sich **auf dich**	*His comment related to you*
Das läuft **auf das Gleiche** hinaus	*It amounts to the same thing*
Er wies (mich) **auf die Schwierigkeiten** hin	*He pointed the difficulties out (to me)*

Other verbs:

achten, Acht geben auf	*pay attention to*
sich berufen auf	*refer to*
drängen auf	*press for*
sich erstrecken auf	*extend to*
folgen auf	*follow* (see 18.4.1a)
sich freuen auf	*look forward to* (see 18.5.2a, 18.5.9a)
hoffen auf	*hope for*
sich konzentrieren auf	*concentrate on*
pfeifen auf (*coll.*)	*not care less about*
pochen auf	*insist on*
reagieren auf	*react to*
rechnen auf	*count on*
schimpfen auf/über	*curse about*
schwören auf	*swear on/by*
sich spezialisieren auf	*specialise in*
sich stützen auf	*lean, count on*
sich verlassen auf	*rely on*
sich verstehen auf	*be expert in*
(jdn.) verweisen auf	*refer (sb.) to*
verzichten auf	*do without*
warten auf	*wait for*
zählen auf	*count on*
zurückkommen auf	*come back to, refer to*
Es kommt (mir) auf etwas an	*sth. matters (to me)*
etwas auf etwas beschränken	*limit/restrict/confine sth. to sth.*
sich auf etwas beschränken	*limit oneself/be limited to sth.*
etwas auf etwas zurückführen	*put sth. down to sth.*

(b) A few verbs which convey the idea of immovability govern *auf* **with the** DATIVE **case**

Er beharrte **auf seiner Meinung**	*He didn't shift from his opinion*
Ich bestehe **auf meinem Recht**	*I insist on my right*

NB: *bestehen aus* 'consist of' (18.5.4), *bestehen in* 'consist in' (18.5.6b); *bestehen auf* with a following accusative is now old-fashioned.

Similarly *beruhen auf, fußen auf*, which all mean 'be based on', 'rest on'. Note, however, *sich gründen auf* (**acc.**) 'be based on', e.g. *Der Vorschlag gründet sich auf diese Annahme.*

basieren auf, when used intransitively, in the meaning 'be based on' is followed by the dative, e.g. *Das basiert auf genauer Kenntnis dieser Methode.* When used transitively, in the meaning 'base (sth.) on' it can be followed by the dative <u>or</u> the accusative, although the accusative is more frequent, e.g. *Sie basierte ihre Aussage auf zahlreiche Beispiele* (less common: *zahlreichen Beispielen*).

18.5.4 *aus*

aus usually has the meaning 'of', 'from' in prepositional objects.

Ihr Essen bestand **aus trockenem Brot**	*Their food consisted of dry bread*

Other verbs:

etwas aus etwas entnehmen, ersehen	*infer, gather sth. from sth.*
sich aus etwas ergeben	*result from sth.*
etwas aus etwas folgern, schließen	*conclude sth. from sth.*

NB: (i) *bestehen auf* 'insist on' (see 18.5.3), *bestehen in* 'consist in' (18.5.6b).
(ii) *entnehmen* can alternatively be constructed with a dative, e.g. *Ich entnehme (aus) Ihrem Brief, dass Sie das Geschäft aufgeben wollen.*
(iii) *sich in etwas ergeben* 'submit to sth.' (see 18.5.6a), *sich jdm./etwas ergeben* 'surrender to sb./sth.' (see 18.4.2e).

18.5.5 *für*

für usually has the meaning 'for' in prepositional objects.

Ich habe ihm **für seine Mühe** gedankt	*I thanked him for his trouble*
Ich habe mich **für den Audi** entschieden	*I decided on the Audi*
Ich halte deine Freundin **für hochbegabt**	*I consider your friend to be very gifted*

Other verbs:

sich (bei jdm.) für etwas bedanken	*give thanks for sth. (to sb.)*
sich für etwas begeistern	*be enthusiastic about sth.*
sich für jdn./etwas eignen	*be suitable for sb./sth.*
sich für jdn./etwas interessieren	*be interested in sb./sth.*
sich für jdn./etwas schämen	*be ashamed of sth./for sb.*
für jdn./etwas sorgen	*take care of/look after sb./sth.*

NB: (i) Non-reflexive *interessieren* is used with *für* <u>or</u> *an* (dat.), e.g. *Er interessierte sie für das/an dem Unternehmen.*
(ii) *sich eignen zu/als* means 'be suitable as' (see 18.5.13).
(iii) *sich (wegen) jds./etwas schämen* (see 18.7.2) 'be ashamed of sb./sth.', *sich vor jdm. schämen* 'feel ashamed in front of sb.' (see 18.5.12a).
(iv) *sich um jdn./etwas sorgen* 'be worried about sb./sth.'.

18.5.6 *in*

(a) *in* **is most often used with the** ACCUSATIVE **case in prepositional objects**

Sie willigte **in die Scheidung** ein	*She agreed to the divorce*
Er verliebte sich **in sie**	*He fell in love with her*

Other verbs:

jdn. in etwas einführen	*introduce sb. to sth.*
sich ergeben in	*submit to (see 18.5.4)*
sich mischen in	*meddle in*
sich vertiefen in	*become engrossed in*

(b) Very few verbs govern *in* **with the** DATIVE **case**

Meine Aufgabe besteht **in der Erledigung** der Korrespondenz (see also 18.5.3b)	*My duties consist in dealing with the correspondence*
Ich habe mich nicht **in ihr** getäuscht	*I was not mistaken in (my judgement of) her*

NB: (i) *bestehen auf* 'insist on' (18.5.4), *bestehen aus* 'consist of' (18.5.5).
  (ii) *sich täuschen über* 'to be mistaken about' (18.5.9a).

18.5.7 *mit*

mit usually has the sense of 'with' in prepositional objects.

Sie hat **mit ihrer Arbeit** angefangen	*She made a start on her work*
Willst du bitte **damit** aufhören?	*Please stop doing that*
Sie hat ihm **mit der Faust** gedroht	*She threatened him with her fist*
Mein Freund simst **mit anderen Frauen**	*My boyfriend texts other women*
Ich habe gestern **mit ihm** telefoniert	*I spoke to him on the telephone yesterday*
sich abfinden mit	*be satisfied with*
sich befassen mit	*deal with*
sich begnügen mit	*be satisfied with*
sich beschäftigen mit	*occupy oneself with*
rechnen mit	*count on*
sprechen mit (*or:* jdn. sprechen)	*speak to/with*
übereinstimmen mit	*agree with*
sich unterhalten mit	*converse with*
vergleichen mit	*compare with*
sich verheiraten mit	*marry*
versehen mit	*provide with*
zusammenstoßen mit	*collide with*

18.5.8 *nach*

(a) *nach* **often has the sense of English 'after', 'for' with verbs of calling, enquiring, longing, reaching, etc.**

Haben Sie sich nach seinem Befinden erkundigt?	*Have you enquired how he is?*
Plötzlich griff das Kind nach der Katze	*Suddenly the child made a grab for the cat*
Sie schrie nach ihrem Cousin	*She yelled for her cousin*
Ich telefonierte nach einem Arzt	*I rang for a doctor*

Other verbs:

fragen nach	*ask after, for*
hungern nach	*hunger after, for*
rufen nach	*call after, for*
sich sehnen nach	*long for*
streben nach	*strive for*
suchen nach	*search for*
verlangen nach	*ask, long for; crave*

NB: *sich erkundigen über* 'enquire about'; *fragen über* 'ask about'.

(b) *nach* **often has the sense of English 'of' with verbs of smelling, etc.**

Es riecht **nach Teer**	*It smells of tar*
Es schmeckte **nach Fisch**	*It tasted of fish*

Similarly: *duften nach, stinken nach*, etc., and: *Es sieht nach Regen aus* 'It looks like rain'.

18.5.9 *über*

über always governs the **accusative** case in prepositional objects.

(a) *über* **corresponds to English 'about' with verbs of saying, etc.**

Ich habe mich sehr **über sein Benehmen** geärgert	*I was very annoyed at his behaviour*
Sie musste lange **darüber** nachdenken	*She had to think it over for a long time*
Ich sprach gestern mit dem Chef **über diese Bewerbung**	*I talked to the boss about this application yesterday*

Many verbs can be used with *über* in this sense, e.g.:

sich bei jdm. über etwas beklagen/ beschweren	*complain to sb. about sth.*
sich über jdn./etwas freuen	*be pleased about sth. (see 18.5.2a, 18.5.3a)*
jdn. über etwas informieren	*inform sb. about sth.*
über jdn./etwas spotten	*mock sb./sth.*
sich täuschen über etwas	*be mistaken about sth. (see 18.5.6b)*
über etwas urteilen	*judge sth.*
sich über jdn./etwas wundern	*be surprised at sb./sth.*

Some verbs, i.e. *denken, erzählen, hören, lesen, sagen, schreiben, sprechen* and *wissen* can be used with *über* or *von* in the sense of 'about'. *über* tends to refer to something more extensive than *von*.

Compare:

Was denken Sie **darüber**?	*What is your view of that?*
Was denken Sie **von ihm**?	*What do you think of him?*
Er wusste viel **über Flugzeuge**	*He knew a lot about aeroplanes*
Er wusste nichts **von ihrem Tod**	*He knew nothing of her death*

(b) Other verbs governing a prepositional object with *über*

es nicht über sich bringen, etwas zu tun	*not bring oneself to do sth.*
sich über etwas hinwegsetzen	*disregard sth.*
über etwas verfügen	*have sth. at one's disposal*

18.5.10 *um*

um usually has the meaning 'concerning', 'in respect of' in prepositional objects.

Sie hat sich **um ihre Schwester** in Dresden geängstigt	*She was worried about her sister in Dresden*
Es handelte sich **um eine Wette**	*It was a question of a bet*
Ich kümmerte mich **um meine Enkelkinder**	*I took care of my grandchildren*

Other verbs:

sich um etwas bemühen	*take trouble over sth.*
jdn. um etwas beneiden	*envy sb. sth.*
jdn. um etwas betrügen	*cheat sb. out of sth.*
jdn. um etwas bitten, ersuchen (*elev.*)	*ask sb. for sth., request sth. from sb.*
jdn. um etwas bringen	*make sb. lose sth.*
Es geht um etwas (see 18.2.4g)	*Something is at stake*
um etwas kommen	*lose sth., be deprived of sth.*
sich um jdn./etwas sorgen	*be worried about sth.*
sich um/über etwas streiten	*argue about/over sth.*

NB: *sich ängstigen vor* 'be afraid of' (18.5.12).

18.5.11 *von*

von usually has the sense of English 'of' or 'from' in prepositional objects.

Ich will dich nicht **von der Arbeit** abhalten	*I don't want to keep you from your work*
Wir müssen **davon** ausgehen, dass . . .	*We must start by assuming that . . .*
Ich muss mich **von meinem Kollegen** distanzieren	*I have to dissociate myself from my colleague*
Das Kind träumte **von einer schönen Prinzessin**	*The child was dreaming of a beautiful princess*

Other verbs:

etwas hängt von jdm./etwas ab	*sth. depends on sb./sth.*
jdm. von etwas abraten	*advise sb. against sth.*
von etwas absehen	*refrain from sth., disregard sth.*
jdn. von etwas befreien	*liberate sb. from sth.*
sich von etwas erholen	*recover from sth.*
von etwas herrühren	*stem from sth.*
jdn. von etwas überzeugen	*convince sb. of sth.*
jdn. von etwas verständigen	*inform sb. of sth.*
von etwas zeugen	*show, demonstrate sth.*

18.5.12 *vor*

vor is always used with the **dative** case in prepositional objects.

(a) *vor* often corresponds to English 'of' with verbs of fearing, etc.

Ich ekele mich **vor diesen großen Spinnen**	*I have a horror of these big spiders* (see 18.2.2)
Er fürchtete sich **vor dem Rottweiler**	*He was afraid of the Rottweiler*
Er warnte mich **vor dem Treibsand**	*He warned me about the quicksand*

Other verbs:

sich vor jdm./etwas ängstigen	*be afraid of sb./sth.* (see 18.5.10)
Angst vor jdm./etwas haben	*be afraid, scared of sb./sth.*
sich vor etwas drücken (*coll.*)	*dodge sth.*
vor jdm./etwas erschrecken	*be scared by sb./sth.*
sich vor jdm./etwas hüten	*beware of sb./sth., be on one's guard against sb./sth.*
sich vor jdm. schämen	*feel ashamed in front of sb.* (see 18.5.5)
sich vor etwas scheuen	*be afraid of, shrink from sth.*

(b) *vor* **often corresponds to English 'from' with verbs of protecting, etc.**

Sie bewahrte ihn **vor der Gefahr**	*She protected him from danger*
Sie flohen **vor der Polizei**	*They fled from the police*

Other verbs:

jdn. vor jdm./etwas beschützen, beschirmen (*elev.*)	*protect sb. from sb./sth.*
jdn. vor etwas retten	*save sb. from sth.*
sich vor jdm./etwas verbergen	*hide from sb./sth.*

18.5.13 *zu*

(a) *zu* **often corresponds to English '(in)to' with verbs of empowering, leading, persuading, etc.**

All these verbs are transitive, i.e. they have an accusative object besides the prepositional object with *zu*:

Er ermutigte sie **zum Widerstand**	*He encouraged them to resist*
Er trieb sie **zur Verzweiflung**	*He drove her to despair*
Er überredete mich **zu einem Glas Wein**	*He talked me into having a glass of wine*
Er zwang mich **zu einer Entscheidung**	*He forced me into a decision*

Other verbs used similarly:

autorisieren *authorise*		nötigen *invite*
berechtigen *entitle*		provozieren *provoke*
bewegen *induce*		raten *advise*
einladen *invite*		veranlassen *cause*
ermächtigen *empower*		verführen *seduce*
herausfordern *challenge*		verhelfen *help*

(b) Some other verbs have a prepositional object with *zu*

Das hat **zu seinem Erfolg** sehr beigetragen	*That contributed a lot to his success*
Sie entschloss sich **zur Teilnahme**	*She decided to take part*
Ich rechne/zähle ihn **zu meinen Freunden**	*I count him among my friends*

Other verbs:

es zu etwas bringen	*attain sth.* (see 3.6.3c)
zu etwas dienen	*serve as sth.*
sich zu etwas eignen	*be suitable as sth.* (see 18.5.5)
zu etwas führen	*lead to sth.*

zu etwas gehören	*be part of sth., be one of sth.* (see 18.4.1a)
jdm. zu etwas gratulieren	*congratulate sb. on sth.*
zu etwas neigen	*tend to sth.*
zu jdm./etwas passen	*go with sb./sth.* (see 18.4.1a)
sich zu etwas verhalten	*stand in a relationship to sth.*

18.5.14 If a prepositional object is in the form of a CLAUSE it is frequently anticipated by a prepositional adverb

i.e. the form *da(r)+preposition*, see 3.5. The prepositional object can be a subordinate clause (usually introduced by *dass*), or an infinitive clause with *zu*, for example:

Sie hat ihm **dafür** gedankt, **dass er ihr geholfen hatte**
Ich verlasse mich **darauf, dass er alles arrangiert**
Er hinderte mich **daran, den Brief zu schreiben**
Ich verlasse mich **darauf, ihn zu Hause zu finden**

The prepositional adverb is optional with some verbs, e.g.:

Ich ärgerte mich (**darüber**), dass er so wenig getan hatte
Sie haben (**damit**) angefangen, die Ernte hereinzubringen

There are no precise rules for contexts when the prepositional adverb is used or not, and it is often left out with some common verbs. If it is used, it tends to emphasise the following clause more strongly. In general, it is more commonly included than omitted in written German (and it is never incorrect to include it), whilst omission is more typical of everyday speech.

The following list gives the common verbs with which the prepositional adverb is often left out:

abhalten von	sich ekeln vor	raten zu
abraten von	sich entscheiden für	sich scheuen vor
Acht geben auf	sich entschließen zu	sich schämen über
anfangen mit	sich erinnern an	sich sehnen nach
(sich) ärgern über	fragen nach	sorgen für
aufhören mit	sich freuen auf/über	sich sorgen um
aufpassen auf	sich fürchten vor	sich streiten über
beginnen mit	glauben an	träumen von
sich beklagen über	hindern an	überzeugen von
sich bemühen um	hoffen auf	urteilen über
sich beschweren über	sich hüten vor	sich wundern über
bitten um	klagen über	zweifeln an

In addition, the prepositional adverb can be omitted with all the transitive verbs used with *zu* (see 18.5.13a).

18.6 Predicate complements

PREDICATE COMPLEMENTS are used with very few verbs, but these are common and important, like *sein* and *werden*. These verbs typically have a noun phrase or an adjective with them which describes the subject in some way (sentence pattern H in Table 18.2):

Er ist **mein Freund**	Das scheint mir **ratsam**
Das Buch ist **langweilig**	Er wurde **Katholik**
Sie ist **blass** geworden	Du bist ganz **der Alte** geblieben

These verbs are known as COPULAR (i.e. 'linking') VERBS, because the verb simply links the subject with the noun phrase or adjective which is the predicate complement. We can see this by comparing the following sentences:

Holger fährt einen Bus   *Holger drives a bus*
Holger ist Busfahrer   *Holger is a bus-driver*

In the first sentence, *Holger* and *Bus* refer to clearly different things, but in the second *Holger* and *Busfahrer* refer to one and the same person. Because the complement simply describes the subject, it is in the **nominative** case if it is a noun.

The following verbs are used with a predicate complement:

bleiben	*remain*	sein	*be*
heißen	*be called*	werden	*become*
scheinen	*seem*		

werden is used in two sentence patterns. When used with a predicate complement, it has the meaning 'become' and is typically used with nouns denoting professions and beliefs, etc. (e.g. *Er wurde Katholik, Kommunist; Sie werden Soldaten*). When used with a prepositional object introduced by *zu*, it means 'change, develop, turn into', e.g.:

Die Felder waren **zu Seen** geworden   *The fields had turned into lakes*
Das ist mir **zur Gewohnheit** geworden   *That has become a habit of mine*
Es wurde **zur Mode**   *It became a fashion*
Er wurde **zum Verbrecher**   *He became a criminal*

18.7 Genitive objects

A small number of verbs have an object in the genitive case. With a very few this is the only object, i.e. they are intransitive verbs with no accusative object. Others are transitive verbs with an accusative object and a genitive object. Many of the latter are reflexive verbs.

All these verbs are uncommon in modern German and restricted to formal writing. A few more are used only in set phrases. In the following lists of verbs which are still used with a genitive, the more usual alternatives are given wherever possible.

18.7.1 Non-reflexive verbs with a noun phrase in the genitive case as the only object

bedürfen *need, require* (more common: *brauchen, benötigen*)
Die Ursache des Unfalls bedarf **weiterer**   *The cause of the accident requires*
  Ermittlungen (*SZ*)   *further investigation*

entbehren *lack* (more commonly used with an accusative object)
Der Staat konnte **eines kraftvollen**   *The state could not do without a*
  Monarchen nicht entbehren (*v. Rimscha*)   *powerful monarch*

ermangeln *lack* (more usual *fehlen*, see 18.4.1d)
Sein Vortrag ermangelte **jeglicher**   *His lecture was lacking in any kind*
  Sachkenntnis   *of knowledge of the subject*

gedenken *remember* (elev. for *denken an* (acc.), with reference to the dead)
Der Bundespräsident hat **der Opfer** des   *The Federal President remembered the*
  Nationalsozialismus gedacht   *victims of National Socialism*

harren *await* (elev. for *warten auf* (acc.); has a biblical ring)
   Wir harren **einer Antwort** (*Zeit*)   *We are awaiting an answer*

18.7.2 Reflexive verbs with a genitive object

Most of these are 'true' reflexive verbs, with an accusative reflexive pronoun (see 18.3.6):

sich annehmen *look after, take care of* (more usual: *sich kümmern um*)
   Er hätte sich **dieses Kindes** angenommen   *He would have looked after that child*
   (*Walser*)

sich bedienen *use* (more usual: *benutzen, gebrauchen, verwenden*)
   Die Firma bediente sich nur **schmutziger**   *The firm only used dirty ships*
   Schiffe (*Böll*)

sich bemächtigen *seize* (various alternatives, e.g. *ergreifen, nehmen*)
   Sie bemächtigten sich **des Bürgermeisters**   *They seized the mayor of Le Mans*
   von Le Mans (*Zeit*)

sich entsinnen *remember* (more usual: *sich erinnern an* (acc.), see 18.5.2b)
   Ich entsann mich **des Anblicks** der   *I remembered the sight of the long huts*
   langgestreckten Baracken (*Andersch*)

sich erfreuen *enjoy* (more usual: *genießen, sich freuen über* (acc.))
   Sie erfreuten sich **des schönen**   *They were enjoying the fine summer*
   Sommerwetters (*OH*)   *weather*

sich erinnern *remember* (more usual: *sich erinnern an* (acc.), see 18.5.2b)
   Ich erinnere mich **bestimmter Details**   *I still remember certain details*
   noch (*Böll*)

sich erwehren *refrain from* (more usual: *abwehren*)
   Ich konnte mich **eines Lächelns** kaum   *I could scarcely refrain from a smile*
   erwehren

sich rühmen *boast about/of* (more usual: *stolz sein über*)
   Die meisten Länder Europas rühmen sich   *Most European countries can boast*
   einer tausendjährigen Geschichte   *of a thousand years of history*
   (*Haffner*)

sich schämen *be ashamed of* (more usual: *sich schämen für/wegen*, see 18.5.5)
   Er schämte sich **seines Betragens**   *He was ashamed of his behaviour*

sich vergewissern *make sure* (more usual: *nachprüfen, überprüfen*)
   Sie vergewisserte sich **der Zuverlässig-**   *She made sure about this man's reliability*
   keit dieses Mannes

18.7.3 Verbs used with a genitive and an accusative object

anklagen *accuse* (outside formal legal parlance: *anklagen wegen*)
   Man klagte ihn der fahrlässigen Tötung an   *He was accused of manslaughter through*
                                         culpable negligence

berauben *rob* (more commonly: *einem etwas rauben*)
   Er beraubte ihn der Freiheit   *He robbed him of his freedom*

versichern *assure* (more commonly: *einem etwas zusichern*)
   Ich versichere Sie meines   *I assure you of my absolute trust*
   uneingeschränkten Vertrauens

The following verbs are used with a genitive in legal language, but with a following clause in everyday speech:

jdn. einer Sache beschuldigen/bezichtigen	*accuse sb. of sth.*
jdn. einer Sache überführen	*convict sb. of sth.*
jdn. einer Sache verdächtigen	*suspect sb. of sth.*

18.7.4 Set phrases with a genitive object

Many more verbs were used with a genitive object in older German, and some of these still occur in idiomatic phrases, although they, too, are mainly used in formal writing:

der Gefahr nicht **achten**	*pay no heed to danger*
jdn. eines Besseren **belehren**	*teach someone better*
sich eines Besseren **besinnen**	*think better of something*
jeder Beschreibung **spotten**	*beggar description*
jdn. des Landes **verweisen**	*expel someone from a country*
seines Amtes **walten**	*discharge one's duties*
jdn. keines Blickes **würdigen**	*not to deign to look at someone*

18.8 Direction complements

Direction complements differ from adverbials, even if they can sometimes be left out, because they are closely linked with the meaning of the verb, as explained in 18.1.4. The difference between them and adverbials is particularly important in respect of word order, see 21.8.1.

18.8.1 Most verbs expressing motion can occur with a direction complement

DIRECTION COMPLEMENTS are words or phrases used with verbs of motion which indicate where someone or something is moving. A direction complement usually takes the form of a prepositional phrase or an equivalent word. It can be omitted with many verbs.

Some verbs of motion – typically verbs of coming and going – are INTRANSITIVE and only have a direction complement with them.

Gestern fuhr sie **nach Italien**
Der Junge fiel **hinein**

Other verbs of motion – typically verbs of putting – are TRANSITIVE and have an accusative object as well as the direction complement:

Ich warf den Ball **dorthin**
Sie legte das Buch **auf den Tisch**

18.8.2 Complements of place

Some verbs indicating position need a phrase to denote where someone or something is located, e.g.:

Sie wohnte lange **in der Pfeilgasse**	*She lived a long time in the Pfeilgasse*
Der Brief befand sich **dort**	*The letter was there*

Nach der Party übernachtete er **bei ihr**	*He spent the night with her after the party*
Sie hielt sich **in Hamm** auf	*She stayed in Hamm*

These phrases are similar to direction complements with verbs of motion, because they are closely linked to the meaning of the verb, and in practice the sentences would be ungrammatical if they were omitted. Common verbs which have such place complements are:

sich aufhalten *stay*	stattfinden *take place*
bleiben *stay, remain*	stehen *stand*
hängen *hang*	übernachten *spend the night*
leben *live*	sich verlieren *get lost*
liegen *lie, be lying*	wohnen *live, dwell*
parken *park*	zelten *camp*
sitzen *sit*	

19 Conjunctions and subordination

If sentences contain more than one clause, the clauses can be related to one another in two ways.

- There may be two (or more) parallel clauses of equal status. Typically, MAIN CLAUSES (German *Hauptsätze*) with the finite verb in second position are linked by a **coordinating conjunction** like *und* or *aber*.
- Alternatively, one or more clauses can be embedded inside another. These are SUBORDINATE CLAUSES (sometimes also called 'embedded clauses' or 'dependent clauses': German *Nebensätze*). In German they have the finite verb in final position and they are introduced by a **subordinating conjunction**.

SUBORDINATE CLAUSES form part of another clause, and we can distinguish three main types of subordinate clause according to their function in the clause which they are part of:

(i) Noun clauses play the same part as a noun phrase, for example as the subject or object of a verb, e.g. *Ich weiß, **dass sie morgen kommt***. As they are typically used as complements to the verb they are sometimes termed COMPLEMENT CLAUSES, see 18.3.2.

(ii) Adjective clauses have the function of adjectives, e.g. *die Frau, **die morgen kommt***. They are introduced by a relative pronoun and are often called RELATIVE CLAUSES.

(iii) Adverbial clauses, which have the same function as adverbs, i.e. they indicate time, cause, manner, etc., e.g. (for time): *Die Frau kam, **als die Sonne aufging***. They can be classified according to their meaning like adverbs (see Table 7.1).

This chapter gives details about the clauses of German and the conjunctions used in them as follows:

- **Coordinating conjunctions** (section 19.1)
- **Noun clauses** (section 19.2)
- **Adverbial clauses** (sections 19.3–19.7)
  - Conjunctions of **time** (section 19.3)
  - **Causal** conjunctions (section 19.4)
  - Conjunctions of **purpose** and **result** (section 19.5)
  - **Concessive** conjunctions (section 19.6)
  - Conjunctions of **manner** and **degree** (section 19.7)

Relative pronouns and **relative clauses** are dealt with in section 5.4. Conjunctions used to introduce **conditional clauses** (= 'if') are explained in section 16.5.

19.1 Coordinating conjunctions

Coordinating conjunctions link clauses of the same kind. If both the clauses they join are main clauses, they are followed by regular main clause word order, i.e. the verb is the second element, see 21.1.4:

Er ist gestern Abend angekommen, **aber** ich **habe** ihn noch nicht gesehen.

They can also join subordinate clauses:

Ich weiß, dass sie morgen kommt **und** dass sie mich sehen möchte.

Most of them can also link single words or phrases:

Ich finde diese CD schön, **aber** etwas zu teuer.
Sie hat ein Buch **und** zwei Zeitschriften gekauft.

A few, like *sowie*, are only used like this, i.e. they cannot link clauses.

Table 19.1 lists the coordinating conjunctions of German, with the section indicated in which their use is explained.

TABLE 19.1 Coordinating conjunctions

aber	but	19.1.1	nämlich	as, for	19.1.2
allein	but	19.1.1	oder	or	19.1.3
bald . . . bald	now . . . now	19.1.5	sondern	but	19.1.1
beziehungsweise	or	19.1.3	sowie	as well as	19.1.4
denn	as, for	19.1.2	sowohl . . . als	as well as	19.1.4
doch	but	19.1.1	teils . . . teils	partly . . . partly	19.1.5
entweder . . . oder	either . . . or	19.1.3	und	and	19.1.4
jedoch	but	19.1.1	weder . . . noch	neither . . . nor	19.1.3

19.1.1 *aber, allein, doch, jedoch, sondern* 'but'

These conjunctions all indicate restrictions of some kind.

(a) *aber* **is the usual equivalent of English 'but'**

Er runzelte die Stirn, **aber** sie sagte noch   *He frowned, but she still didn't say anything*
nichts

NB: For *aber* with *zwar* in the preceding clause, see 19.6.1b.

(b) *allein, doch* and *jedoch* **are mainly literary alternatives to** *aber*

(i) *allein* is only used in formal literary German. It usually introduces a restriction which is unwelcome or unexpected:

Ich hatte gehofft, ihn nach der Sitzung zu   *I had hoped to speak to him after the meeting, but*
sprechen, **allein** er war nicht zugegen   *he wasn't present*

(ii) *jedoch* is rather more emphatic than *doch*:

Der Lohn ist karg, **doch** man genießt die   *The wages are meagre, but one enjoys the evening*
abendlichen Stunden (*Jens*)   *hours*
Im Allgemeinen war er kein guter Schüler,   *In general he was not a good pupil, but he was better*
jedoch in Latein war er allen überlegen   *than any in Latin*

(c) *aber, doch* and *jedoch* **are also used as modal particles or adverbs**

(For *aber*, see 10.1.2, for *doch*, see 10.7.1). They have much the same meaning when used like this as when they are used as conjunctions, but they form part of the clause rather than introduce it, and the word order is different. Compare these alternatives to the sentences in (a) and (b):

Er runzelte die Stirn, sie **aber** sagte noch nichts
Er runzelte die Stirn, sie sagte **aber** noch nichts

Der Lohn ist karg, **doch** genießt man die abendlichen Stunden
Der Lohn ist karg, man genießt **doch** die abendlichen Stunden
. . ., in Latein **jedoch** war er allen überlegen
. . ., in Latein war er **jedoch** allen überlegen

Constructions like this highlight the contrast rather more than when these words are simply used as conjunctions. *aber* is often used like this if the verbs in the two clauses have the same subject, and the subject is then omitted in the second clause: *Er runzelte die Stirn, sagte aber noch nichts.*

(d) *sondern* **'but'**

(i) *sondern* contradicts a preceding negative

Er ist nicht reich, **sondern** arm	*He is not rich, but poor*
Wir sind nicht ins Kino gegangen, **sondern** wir haben im Garten gearbeitet	*We didn't go to the cinema, but worked in the garden*

sondern is distinct from *aber*, which is only used after a negative if it doesn't contradict, i.e. if the linked elements are equally true:

Er ist nicht reich, **aber** ehrlich (i.e. he is *both* 'not rich' *and* 'honest')	*He is not rich, but (he is) honest*

(ii) *nicht nur . . . sondern auch* corresponds to 'not only . . . but also':

Er ist **nicht nur** reich, **sondern auch** großzügig	*He is not only rich, but generous, too*
Sie besorgten **nicht nur** ihren Haushalt, **sondern** sie waren **auch** berufstätig	*They didn't only run the household, they had a job, too*

NB: (i) See 12.1.4 (d)/(e) for the agreement of the finite verb if the subject consists of more than one noun or pronoun linked by *nicht nur . . . sondern auch.*

(ii) Initial *nicht nur* is followed immediately by the finite verb, e.g. **Nicht nur hat** Helmut kräftig mitgeholfen, sondern Franziska hat auch ihren Teil dazu beigetragen.

19.1.2 *denn, nämlich* 'as', 'because', 'for'

denn and *nämlich* are coordinating, not subordinating conjunctions, i.e. they are used in main clauses, with the verb in second position. Clauses with them give the reason for the event or action in the preceding clause, so they are never in first position in the sentence.

(a) *denn*

Wahrscheinlich hatte ich den Fremden angestarrt, **denn** er sah auf und lächelte (*R. Schoof*)	*I had probably been staring at the stranger because he looked up and smiled*

denn is no longer common in colloquial speech, and *weil* is often heard in its place as a coordinating conjunction, followed by a main clause with the verb second. This is not regarded as acceptable in standard German, see 19.4.1.

(b) *nämlich* **is always placed within the clause, after the verb**

Er konnte sie nicht verstehen, er war **nämlich** taub	*He couldn't understand her, as he was deaf*

19.1.3 *oder, beziehungsweise* 'or', *entweder . . . oder* 'either . . . or', *weder . . . noch* 'neither . . . nor'

These are **disjunctive** conjunctions, giving alternatives. See 12.1.4 for the agreement of the finite verb if the subject consists of two or more nouns or pronouns linked by them.

(a) *oder* **is the most usual equivalent for English 'or'**

Ich weiß, was passiert, wenn eine Warmfront **oder** eine Kaltfront vorbeiziehen (*Grzimek*)	*I know what happens when a warm front or a cold front go past*
Morgen können wir zu Hause bleiben, **oder** wir können einen Spaziergang machen, wenn du willst	*Tomorrow we can stay at home, or we can go for a walk if you want to*
Wir können in Heidelberg **oder** in Mannheim umsteigen	*We can change trains in Heidelberg or Mannheim*
Sie wollten das Haus aus- **oder** umbauen	*They wanted to extend or alter the house*

oder can be ambiguous, like English 'or', since the alternatives linked by it can be **exclusive** (one or the other, but not both) or **inclusive** (i.e. 'and/or', as in the last example above). In order to confirm that exclusion is meant, *aber (auch)* can be added to *oder* (see 10.1.2), e.g.: *Wir können in Heidelberg, **oder aber (auch)** in Mannheim umsteigen.* Alternatively, *beziehungsweise* or *entweder . . . oder* can be used to signal exclusion (see (b) and (c) below).

(b) *beziehungsweise* **indicates mutually exclusive alternatives**

In writing it is usually abbreviated to *bzw.*:

Sie haben lange in Deutschland gewohnt, **bzw.** sie haben dort oft Urlaub gemacht	*They lived a long time in Germany, or (else) they often took their holidays there*
Es kostet 300 Euro, **bzw.** 250 Euro mit Rabatt	*It costs 300 euros, or 250 euros with the discount*

beziehungsweise was originally restricted to formal registers, but it is now commonly used in spoken German.

(c) *entweder . . . oder* **'either . . . or' signals mutually exclusive alternatives**

Entweder er wird entlassen, **oder** er findet gar keine Stellung (*BILD*)	*He will either be dismissed or not find a job at all*

Less usually, *entweder* can be immediately followed by the verb, e.g. *Entweder wird er entlassen, oder . . .*

(d) *weder . . . noch* **'neither . . . nor'**

Er liest **weder** Bücher **noch** Zeitungen	*He reads neither books nor newspapers*
Ich habe **weder** seinen Brief bekommen, **noch** habe ich sonst von ihm gehört	*Neither have I received his letter, nor have I heard from him in any other way*

A common alternative to *weder . . . noch* is to use *und auch nicht/kein*. This is often felt to be less clumsy and more natural, especially in spoken German:

Er liest keine Bücher **und auch keine** Zeitungen.
Ich habe seinen Brief nicht bekommen, **und** ich habe **auch nicht** sonst von ihm gehört.

noch cannot be used on its own in the sense of 'nor' without a preceding *weder*. As an equivalent for English 'nor' without a preceding 'neither' (or 'or' preceded by a negative) German uses *und auch nicht/kein*:

Sie hat mir noch nicht geschrieben, **und** ich erwarte **auch nicht**, dass ich bald von ihr höre	*She hasn't written to me yet, nor do I expect to hear from her soon*
Ich höre die Nachrichten im Radio nicht **und** kaufe **auch keine** Zeitungen	*I don't listen to the news on the radio or buy newspapers*

19.1.4 *und* 'and'; *sowie, sowohl . . . als* 'as well as'

(a) *und* **is the common equivalent for English 'and'**

Angela **und** Gudrun wollen auch kommen	*Angela and Gudrun want to come too*
Einer der Verdächtigten durchbrach eine Straßensperre **und** konnte erst nach einer Verfolgungsjagd gestoppt werden (NZZ)	*One of the suspects broke through a road block and could only be stopped after a chase*

(b) *sowie, sowohl . . . als* **'both . . . and', 'as well as'**

These are frequent stylistic alternatives to *und*, especially in written German, although they are not unknown in speech. They emphasise the connection between the elements more than *und*, and they are often used with a following *auch*:

Dürrenmatt hat **sowohl** Dramen **als (auch)** Kriminalromane geschrieben	*Dürrenmatt wrote both plays and detective novels*

NB: Less commonly, *wie* is used for *als* with *sowohl*.

sowie puts rather more stress on the second element than *sowohl . . . als*, e.g.:

Dürrenmatt hat Dramen **sowie (auch)** Kriminalromane geschrieben.

NB: See 12.1.4 for the agreement of the finite verb if the subject consists of more than one noun or pronoun linked by *sowohl . . . als* or *sowie*.

19.1.5 **Less frequent coordinating conjunctions**

(a) *bald . . . bald* **'one moment . . . the next', 'now . . . now'**

This is mainly found in formal writing. *bald* is followed immediately by the verb in both clauses:

Bald weinte das Kind, **bald** lachte es	*One moment the child was crying, the next it was laughing*

(b) *teils . . . teils* **'partly . . . partly'**

Wir haben unseren Urlaub **teils** in Italien verbracht, **teils** in der Schweiz	*We spent our holiday partly in Italy, partly in Switzerland*
teils heiter, **teils** wolkig	*cloudy with sunny intervals*

When clauses are linked with *teils*, the verb follows immediately after *teils* in both clauses:

Teils war man sehr zuvorkommend, **teils** hat man mich völlig ignoriert	*Sometimes people were very helpful, at others I was completely ignored*

19.2 **Noun clauses**

Noun clauses have the same function in the sentence as nouns or noun phrases. They are most often found as complements of a verb, and for this reason they are also called COMPLEMENT

CLAUSES. They can be the subject (*Dass sie kommt, freut mich*), object (*Sie sah, wie er sich anstrengte*) or one of the other **complements** of a verb (see Table 18.1). Noun clauses in German can be introduced by *dass, ob, wenn* or the interrogative *w*-words (see 7.5).

NB: If a noun clause is used as the **subject**, the verb has the third person singular endings, see 12.1.4a.

19.2.1 *dass* 'that'

(a) *dass* is the commonest conjunction used to introduce noun clauses

It corresponds closely to English 'that':

subject:	**Dass sie morgen kommt**, erstaunt mich
accusative object:	Sie versicherte mir, **dass alles in Ordnung war**
genitive object:	Man klagt ihn an, **dass er das Geld gestohlen hat**
prepositional object:	Er wartete darauf, **dass Peter ihn grüßte**
predicate complement:	Tatsache ist, **dass er gelogen hat**

Noun clauses with *dass* can also depend on adjectives, e.g. *Ich bin froh, dass du kommen konntest* or on nouns related to verbs, e.g. *Ihn quälte die Angst, dass etwas passieren könnte*

(b) The omission of *dass*

The conjunction *dass* can be omitted in some contexts and some types of noun clause, and then the dependent clause has the order of a main clause, with the verb second. Compare the following alternatives:

Sie sagte, **dass** sie einen Brief **schreibe**
Sie sagte, sie **schreibe** einen Brief

However, it is far less frequent for German *dass* to be dropped than English *that*. It is possible to leave *dass* out:

(i) after verbs (and other expressions) of saying, when introducing indirect speech (see 16.6):

Ich sagte, sie sei das einzige Mädchen, mit dem ich „diese Sache" tun wollte (*Böll*)	*I said she was the only girl I wanted to do "that" with*
Bei denen herrscht die Meinung vor, die Universitäten litten an der Überlast ungeeigneter Studenten (*Spiegel*)	*With these people the idea is dominant that universities are suffering from being overloaded with unsuitable students*

In practice, the alternative without *dass* is rather more frequent in both spoken and written German. However, *dass* is usually retained if the main verb is negative. Thus *Er sagte nicht, dass er sie nach Hause fahren werde* is more usual than *Er sagte nicht, er werde sie nach Hause fahren*.

(ii) after verbs (and other expressions) of perceiving, feeling, hoping, thinking and believing (in the widest sense). The omission of *dass* here is commoner in spoken than in written German.

Ich hatte gehofft, er würde es auf zehn Mark abrunden (*Böll*)	*I had hoped he would round it down to ten marks*
die Ahnung, sie könnte noch unterwegs sein	*the idea that she could still be on her way*

(c) Initial *dass*-clauses are more frequent in German than in English

Especially in written German, it is much more usual to find sentences which begin with a subject or object *dass*-clause than is the case in English, where we tend to provide a noun (especially 'the fact') for the 'that'-clause to link to. Compare:

Dass die Wahlergebnisse der DDR gefälscht waren, bestreitet auch Modrow nicht (*Spiegel*)	*The fact that the election results in the GDR were falsified is not disputed even by Modrow*
Dass er einmal nicht mehr wollen würde, wagte er nicht zu hoffen (*Walser*)	*The possibility that at some time he wouldn't want to any more, was something he didn't dare to hope*

(d) It is considered poor style for *dass* to be followed immediately by another conjunction

For example:

(i) Sie sagte, dass er, wenn er am Wochenende kommen sollte, bei ihrer Mutter übernachten könnte

(ii) Sie sagte, dass er bei ihrer Mutter übernachten könnte, wenn er am Wochenende kommen sollte are considered preferable to the following ordering (although it is not unknown, even in writing):

(iii) Sie sagte, dass, wenn er am Wochenende kommen sollte, er bei ihrer Mutter übernachten könnte

Ordering similar to (iii) is very frequent in English, with an adverbial clause (especially one introduced by 'as', 'if' or 'when') often following straight after 'that', e.g.: 'She said that if he were to come at the weekend he would be able to stay with her mother'. English learners are strongly advised to avoid this type of construction in German, and to use only type (i) or (ii).

(e) *dass*-clauses can be used in isolation

(i) in commands or wishes (often with an 'ethic' dative, see 2.5.3d):

Dass du (mir) rechtzeitig nach Haus kommst!	*Make sure you're not too late home!*

(ii) in exclamations:

Dass die es heute so eilig haben!	*They are in a hurry today!*

19.2.2 *ob* 'whether', 'if'

(a) *ob* typically indicates a question or a doubt

ob-clauses are all indirect questions and can have the following functions:

subject:	**Ob sie morgen kommt**, ist mir gleich
accusative object:	Sie vergaß, **ob sie eine Karte gekauft hatte**
prepositional object:	Ich erinnere mich nicht daran, **ob ich eine gekauft habe**
predicate complement:	Die Frage ist, **ob wir eine Tankstelle erreichen**

(b) Isolated *ob*-clauses

ob-clauses are often used in isolation, especially in spoken German to ask a question:

Ob es in Schwerin noch Glocken gibt? (*Surminski*)	*Are there still bells in Schwerin?*

They are used particularly frequently to pick up or repeat a question, or to express a general query or supposition:

Ja, **ob** das wirklich stimmt?	*I wonder whether that's really right*

19.2.3 *wenn* 'when', 'if'

Noun clauses introduced by *wenn* can function as:

subject:	Mir ist es recht, **wenn sie heute nicht kommt**
accusative object:	Sie mag es nicht, **wenn ich sie bei der Arbeit störe**

The verb in noun clauses introduced by *wenn* can be in the *Konjunktiv II* form if an unreal condition is involved, see 16.5.1, e.g. *Mir wäre es recht, wenn sie heute nicht käme*. Noun clauses with *wenn* **always** have a correlating *es* in the main clause, see 19.2.5.

19.2.4 Interrogatives

All the *w*-words which can be used to ask questions (see 7.5) can also be used as conjunctions to introduce noun clauses. Noun clauses with *w*-words are all indirect questions and can function as:

subject:	**Was sie dort macht**, ist mir gleich
accusative object:	Sie vergaß, **wie man es macht**
prepositional object:	Ich erinnere mich nicht daran, **wann ich es gehört habe**
predicate complement:	Die Frage ist, **wo sie es gekauft hat**

19.2.5 Correlates to complement clauses

In German, a noun clause is often linked to a pronoun in the main clause which anticipates it. Such pronouns are called **correlates**, and their form differs depending on the function of the clause.

(a) The pronoun *es* functions as a correlate to subject and object clauses

Dann fiel **es** mir auf, dass sie plötzlich fehlte	*Then I noticed that all at once she wasn't there*
Ich bedaure **es**, dass sie nicht kommen konnte	*I regret that she couldn't come*

More details on this 'correlating' *es* are given in 3.6.2e and 3.6.3a.

(b) The prepositional adverb can act as a correlate to noun clauses functioning as prepositional objects

i.e. the form *da(r)* + preposition (see 3.5) can appear in the main clause:

die Angst **davor**, dass er vielleicht nicht entkommen könnte	*the fear of perhaps not being able to escape*
Er verlässt sich **darauf**, dass wir rechtzeitig kommen	*He's relying on us arriving on time*

With many nouns, adjectives and verbs this use of the prepositional adverb is optional, see 6.6.2 and 18.6.14.

(c) The pronoun *dessen* can function as a correlate to noun clauses with the function of a genitive object

These constructions are infrequent in modern German, and *dessen* is in all cases optional:

Ich bin mir (**dessen**) bewusst, dass ich ihn strafen sollte	*I am aware that I should punish him*

19.3 **Conjunctions of time**

The main conjunctions which introduce adverbial clauses of time in German are given in Table 19.2.

TABLE 19.2 Conjunctions of time

als	when	19.3.1	seit(dem)	since	19.3.5
bevor	before	19.3.2	sobald	as soon as	19.3.6
bis	until, till; by the time	19.3.2	solange	as long as	19.3.6
da	when	19.3.1	sooft	as often as, whenever	19.3.6
ehe	before	19.3.2	sowie	as soon as	19.3.6
indem	as	19.3.1	während	while, whilst	19.3.7
indes, indessen	while, whilst	19.3.7	wann, wenn	when(ever)	19.3.1
kaum dass	hardly, scarcely	19.3.3	wie	as	19.3.1
nachdem	after	19.3.4	wobei	when	19.3.8

19.3.1 *als, da, indem, wann, wenn, wie* 'when', 'as'

(a) Clauses with *als* refer to a single event in the past

als corresponds to English 'when' or 'as':

Als ich in Passau ankam, habe ich sie auf dem Bahnsteig gesehen — *When I arrived in Passau, I saw her on the platform*

Als ich weiterging, wurde ich immer müder — *As I went on, I grew more and more tired*

Als die Frau später ihre Arbeitspapiere vorlegen musste, kam die Wahrheit an den Tag (*BILD*) — *When, later on, the woman had to show her work documents, the truth came to light*

A main clause following an *als*-clause is sometimes (optionally) introduced by a correlating *da*, e.g. *Als ich in Passau ankam, **da** habe ich sie auf dem Bahnsteig gesehen.*

(b) *da* is a literary (and rather old-fashioned) alternative to *als*

Die Sonne schien an einem wolkenlosen Himmel, **da** er seinen Heimatort verließ (*Dürrenmatt*) — *The sun was shining in a cloudless sky as/when he left his home village*

(c) *wie* can be used for 'when' with a verb in the present tense referring to a past action

i.e. with a 'historic' present (see 14.2.4). *wie* is an alternative to *als* in such contexts:

Als/Wie ich das Fenster öffne, schlägt mir heftiger Lärm entgegen — *As/When I opened the window, I was confronted by an intense noise*

The use of *wie* in place of *als* with a past or perfect tense is common in colloquial spoken German, especially in the south, e.g. ***Wie** ich in Passau ankam/angekommen bin, . . .* This usage is occasionally found in writing, but it is not generally accepted as standard.

(d) *wann* is used in questions

wann is an interrogative adverb (= 'when?'), see 7.5. As such, it is used to introduce questions in direct speech, e.g. ***Wann** kommst du heute Abend nach Hause?* or in indirect speech (see 19.2.4), e.g. *Er hat mich gefragt, **wann** ich heute Abend nach Hause komme.*

(e) *wenn* **introduces clauses referring to the present, the future, or to repeated actions in the past**

Ich bringe es, **wenn** ich morgen vorbeikomme	*I'll bring it when I drop by tomorrow*

A main clause following a *wenn*-clause is often introduced by *dann*. This *dann* is always optional:

Wenn das Wasser ausgelaufen ist, **(dann)** schließt sich die Klappe automatisch	*When the water has run out, the valve shuts off automatically*

wenn often conveys the sense of English 'whenever', especially in the past, where *als* must be used if a single action is involved (see (a) above):

An den Bahnhöfen standen Grenzsoldaten und bewachten die Gleise, **wenn** die U-Bahn langsam mit geschlossenen Türen durchfuhr (*MM*)	*Border guards stood on the stations and watched the tracks when(ever) an underground train went through slowly with its doors closed*

wenn, not *als*, is used if there is a sense of a future-in-the-past:

Ich wollte zu Hause sein, **wenn** Karl ankam	*I wanted to be at home when Karl arrived*

wenn is also used in conditional clauses, i.e. = 'if' (see 16.5). If there is a possibility of ambiguity, *immer wenn* can be used to emphasise that the sense is that of 'whenever'. Alternatively, *falls* can be used to make it clear that 'if' is meant (see 16.5.3d).

(f) *indem* **'as' can only link simultaneous actions**

Anna küsste ihre Mutter, **indem** sie die Palette und den nassen Pinsel in ihren Händen weit von ihr abhielt (*Th. Mann*)	*Anna kissed her mother, holding the palette and the wet brush well away from her in her hands*

This use of *indem*, where the *indem*-clause corresponds to an English 'ing'-phrase, now sounds old-fashioned. See 13.7 for German equivalents of English phrases with an 'ing'-form. In modern German, *indem* is mainly used in the sense of English 'by + . . .ing', see 19.7.3.

(g) **Equivalents of English 'when' introducing relative clauses**

e.g. *zu einer Zeit, wo* . . . 'at a time **when** . . .'. For these, see 5.4.6b.

19.3.2 *bevor, ehe* 'before'; *bis* 'until, till', 'by the time'

For the occasional use of the subjunctive in clauses introduced by these conjunctions, see 16.7.4.

(a) *bevor* **and** *ehe* **'before'**

There is no real difference in meaning between these. *bevor* is far more frequent; *ehe* is typical of more formal registers, although it does occasionally occur in speech.

Der Kanzler muss das Volk befragen, **bevor** er einen Friedensvertrag unterzeichnet (*Presse*)	*The Chancellor has to ask the people before he signs/ before signing a Peace Treaty*
Es bestand, **ehe** die Erde geschieden war von den Himmeln (*Heym*)	*It existed before the earth was separated from the heavens*

bevor or *ehe* can be strengthenend by *noch* to give the sense of '**even** before', e.g. **Noch** *bevor/ehe sie zurückkkam* 'Even before she got back'.

(b) German equivalents for English 'not . . . before', 'not . . . until'

(i) The most straightforward equivalent is *erst . . ., wenn/als*:

Ich will **erst** nach Hause gehen, **wenn** Mutter wieder da ist	*I don't want to go home before/until mother gets back*
Das Kind hörte **erst** zu weinen auf, **als** es vor Müdigkeit einschlief	*The child didn't stop crying until it was so tired that it fell asleep*

(ii) *Nicht . . . bevor* (or *ehe*) and *nicht . . . bis* are only used if the dependent clause implies a condition. An extra (redundant) *nicht* is often added:

Bevor er sich (nicht) entschuldigt hatte, wollte sie das Zimmer nicht verlassen	*She didn't want to leave the room before/until he had apologised*
Du darfst nicht gehen, **bis** du (nicht) deine Hausaufgaben fertig hast	*You can't go out until you've finished your homework*

The rule given by some authorities that this second *nicht* is only added if the subordinate clause precedes is not always followed in practice.

(c) *bis* has two main English equivalents

(i) 'until, till':
Ich warte hier, **bis** du zurückkommst	*I'll wait here till you get back*

(ii) 'by the time (when)', e.g.:
Bis du zurückkommst, habe ich das Fenster repariert	*I'll have fixed the window by the time you get back*

19.3.3 *kaum (dass)*, etc. 'hardly/scarcely . . . when', 'no sooner . . . than'

The most usual German equivalent for these English combinations is to use two main clauses, the first introduced by *kaum*, the second by *so* or *da*:

Kaum hatten wir das Wirtshaus erreicht, **so/da** begann es zu regnen	*We had hardly reached the inn when it began to rain/ No sooner had we reached the inn, than it began to rain*

Alternatively, a main clause introduced by *kaum* followed by a subordinate clause with *als* can be used: *Kaum hatten wir das Wirtshaus erreicht, **als** es zu regnen begann*. In formal written German, the phrasal conjunction *kaum dass* is sometimes used, e.g. *Kaum **dass** wir das Wirtshaus erreicht hatten, begann es zu regnen*. This alternative now sounds rather old-fashioned.

19.3.4 *nachdem* 'after'

Er wollte wissen, was mit Valette geschehen war, **nachdem** er sie das letzte Mal gesehen hatte (*Schneeweiß*).	*He wanted to know what had happened to Valette after he had seen her last*

nachdem is sometimes used in a causal sense, as an alternative to *da* (= 'as, since', see 19.4.1):

Er musste zurücktreten, **nachdem** ihm verschiedene Delikte nachgewiesen wurden	*He had to resign, as various offences had been proved against him*

This usage is typical of South Germany and Austria and is considered non-standard elsewhere.

NB: For *je nachdem* 'according as', see 19.7.5

19.3.5 *seit, seitdem* 'since'

The shorter form *seit* was formerly restricted to colloquial registers, but it is now at least as frequent as *seitdem*, even in writing:

Seit(dem) er sein Haus verkauft hat, wohnt er in einem Hotel	*Since he sold his house, he's been living in a hotel*
Vertraut er ihr an, dass er unter Schreibstörungen leidet, **seit** er diesen Drehbuchauftrag bekommen hat? (*Schoof*)	*Will he confess to her that he has been suffering from writer's block since he got that commission for a screen-play?*

NB: For the use of tenses in sentences with *seit*(*dem*), see 14.2.2 and 14.3.4a.

19.3.6 *sobald, sowie* 'as soon as', *solange* 'as long as', *sooft* 'as often as'

These conjunctions are always spelled as single words and are not normally followed by *als* or *wie*.

(a) *sobald* 'as soon as'

Sobald ich merkte, dass er gar nicht zuhörte, griff ich ihn am Ärmel (*Frisch*)	*As soon as I noticed he wasn't listening I grabbed him by the sleeve*

sowie is commonly used for *sobald* in colloquial registers, e.g. *Das hat sie auch getan, sowie sie nach Hause gekommen ist.*

(b) *solange* 'as long as'

(i) *solange* can refer purely to time:

Wir haben gewartet, **solange** wir konnten	*We waited as long as we could*
Solange Leute da sind, werden wir Musik machen und ausschenken (*MM*)	*As long as there are people here we'll make music and pour drinks*

NB: The sense of *solange* can approach that of *seit*(*dem*), as in the second example, and tense use is similar, see 14.2.2 and 14.3.4a.

(ii) It may also have a conditional sense (= 'provided that'), e.g.:

Solange er sein Bestes tut, bin ich zufrieden	*As long as he does his best, I shall be satisfied*

(iii) The conjunction *solange* is distinguished from the phrase *so lange* 'so long', which is written as two words:

Du hast uns **so lange** warten lassen, dass wir den Zug verpasst haben	*You kept us waiting so long that we missed the train*
So lange er auch wartete, es kam kein Zug mehr	*However long he waited, no more trains came*

(c) *sooft* corresponds to English 'as often as' or 'whenever'

Du kannst kommen, **sooft** du willst	*You can come as often as you want to*

| Sooft er kam, brachte er uns immer Geschenke mit | *Whenever he came, he always brought us presents* |

19.3.7 *während* 'while', 'whilst' and alternatives

(a) *während* **is the usual equivalent of English 'while', 'whilst'**

Like 'while', it can express time **or** a contrast (i.e. = 'whereas'):

| Die Zollprobleme löste Boris, **während** wir in Urlaub waren (*Bednarz*) | *Boris solved the problems with the customs while we were on holiday* |
| Klaus Buch müsste auch sechsundvierzig sein, **während** der vor ihm Stehende doch eher sechsundzwanzig war (*Walser*) | *Klaus Buch ought to be forty-two as well, whereas the man standing in front of him was more like twenty-six* |

NB: (i)   noch während is used for 'even as/whilst', e.g. **Noch während** sie schlief . . . 'Even as she slept . . .'
    (ii)   während is sometimes used with main clause word-order (i.e. with the verb second) in colloquial speech. This usage is not accepted as standard.

(b) *indes* **and** *indessen* **are mainly literary alternatives to** *während* **in both senses**

| Seine Glieder zitterten, **indes** er diese grauenvolle Lust in sich erwürgte (*Süßkind*) | *His limbs were trembling as he throttled this terrible desire in himself* |

(c) *wohingegen* **is an alternative to** *während* **to signal a contrast**

It occurs mainly in formal writing and stresses the contrast more strongly:

| Er ist sehr zuvorkommend, **wohingegen** sein Bruder oft einen recht unfreundlichen Eindruck macht | *He is very obliging, while/whereas his brother often makes a very unpleasant impression* |

19.3.8 *wobei* introduces a clause with an action taking place at the same time as that of the main clause

It has no precise English equivalent, but a clause with *wobei* often corresponds to an English participial clause with an 'ing'-form, or a main clause joined with 'and':

| Nach Angaben der Polizei schlug der Mann sie ins Gesicht, **wobei** er sie verletzte (*MM*) | *According to the police the man struck her in the face, injuring her* |
| Es kam zur Kollision mit dem Wagen einer 24-Jährigen, **wobei** sich beide Fahrzeuge überschlugen (*SGT*) | *A collision occurred with a car driven by a 24 year old woman, and both vehicles overturned* |

wobei is often used with a following main clause construction (i.e. with the verb in second position rather than at the end), especially when it is used in a meaning close to that of 'but' or 'although': e.g. *Sie ist immer sehr freundlich, wobei ich muss sagen, dass das nicht jedem gefällt.* This is a feature of colloquial speech and is considered to be non-standard.

19.4 Causal conjunctions

German conjunctions expressing a cause or a reason are given in Table 19.3.

TABLE 19.3 Causal conjunctions

da	as, since	19.4.1
nun (da/wo)	*now that, seeing that*	19.4.2
umso mehr, als	*all the more because*	19.4.3
weil	*because*	19.4.1
zumal	*especially as*	19.4.3

19.4.1 *da* and *weil*

The distinction between *da* and *weil* parallels that between English 'as' (or 'since'), 'because'. *da*-clauses, like those with 'as' or 'since', usually precede the main clause and typically indicate a reason which is already known.

Ich musste zu Fuß nach Hause gehen, **weil** ich die letzte Straßenbahn verpasst hatte	*I had to walk home because I had missed the last tram*
Da er getrunken hatte, wollte er nicht fahren	*As he'd had something to drink, he didn't want to drive*

A *weil*-clause can be anticipated by *darum, deshalb* or *deswegen* in the preceding main clause, especially in spoken German. The effect is to give greater emphasis to the reason given in the *weil*-clause:

Er konnte **darum/deshalb/deswegen** nicht kommen, **weil** er krank war	*He wasn't able to come because he was ill*

In colloquial German *weil* is frequently heard with main clause word order, i.e. with the finite verb second rather than at the end of the clause:

Du musst langsam sprechen, **weil** der **versteht** nicht viel	*You'll have to speak more slowly because he doesn't understand a lot*

This usage is now very common, but it is universally regarded as non-standard and unacceptable in written German.

NB: *denn* and *nämlich* are also used to indicate a cause or a reason (i.e. in the sense of English 'because'). They are, however, **coordinating** conjunctions, with main clause word-order, see 19.1.2.

19.4.2 *nun da*, etc. 'now that', 'seeing that'

Nun da wir alle wieder versammelt sind, können wir das Problem weiter besprechen	*Seeing/Now that we're all gathered together again, we can carry on talking about the problem*

There are a number of alternatives to *nun da*. Simple *nun* is occasionally found in formal written registers:

Nun alles geschehen ist, bleibt nur zu wünschen, dass . . . (*FAZ*)	*Now that everything has been done, one can only wish that . . .*

Other alternatives, i.e. *nun wo, wo . . . (doch), da . . . nun (mal)*, are typical of colloquial registers:

Nun wo du sowieso in die Stadt fährst, kannst du uns wohl mitnehmen, oder?	*Seeing as you're going into town anyway, you'll be able to take us with you, won't you?*

Ich muss es wohl tun, **wo** ich es dir (**doch**) versprochen habe

I'll have to do it, seeing that I promised you

Da er das **nun (mal)** schon weiß, (so) muss ich ihm wohl das Weitere erzählen

Seeing that he already knows that, I'll have to tell him the rest

19.4.3 Other causal conjunctions

(a) *zumal* **is a stronger alternative to** *da*

It corresponds to English 'especially as':

Sie wird uns sicher helfen, **zumal** sie dich so gern hat

She's sure to help us, especially as she's so fond of you

Mehr verriet sie nicht, **zumal** es Stiller gar nicht wunderte, warum sie dieses Bedürfnis hatte (*Frisch*)

She didn't reveal any more, especially as Stiller was not at all surprised why she felt this need

(b) *umso mehr . . ., als/da/weil* **correspond to 'all the more . . . because'**

Ich freute mich **umso mehr** über seinen Erfolg, **als/da/weil** er völlig unerwartet war

I was all the more pleased about his success because it was totally unexpected

Du musst früh ins Bett gehen, **umso mehr als** du morgen einen schweren Tag hast

You've got to go to bed early, all the more because you've got a busy day tomorrow

The construction with *umso . . ., als* can be used with other comparatives:

Die Sache ist **umso** dringlicher, **als/da** die Iraner den Ölhahn zudrehen könnten

The matter is all the more urgent because the Iranians might turn off the oil tap

19.5 Conjunctions of purpose and result

German conjunctions indicating purpose or result (also called **final conjunctions** and **consecutive conjunctions** respectively) are given in Table 19.4:

TABLE 19.4 Conjunctions of purpose and result

als dass	*for . . . to*	19.5.3
auf dass	*so that* (purpose)	19.5.1
damit	*so that* (purpose)	19.5.1
derart dass	*so that* (consecutive)	19.5.2
so dass	*so that* (consecutive)	19.5.2

English learners need to be aware that 'so that' has two distinct senses, with different German equivalents, i.e.:

(i) Final 'so that' expresses purpose and is an alternative to 'in order that'. The usual German equivalent is *damit*, see 19.5.1.

(ii) Consecutive 'so that' expresses a result and has the sense of '(in) such (a way) that' and corresponds to German *so dass*, see 19.5.2.

19.5.1 Clauses of purpose

(a) *damit* **is the most frequent conjunction in final clauses**

Diese Tüte ist aus Papier, **damit** sie nicht aus Kunststoff ist	*This bag is made of paper so that it shouldn't be made of plastic*
König Ludwig ließ Wagner 40 000 Gulden auszahlen, **damit** sich der total verschuldete Meister bei seinen Gläubigern freikaufen konnte (*SZ*)	*King Ludwig had 40,000 guilders paid to Wagner so that the totally debt-ridden maestro could pay off his creditors*

NB: (i) The verb in *damit*-clauses is usually in the indicative in modern German. For the occasional use of the subjunctive, see 16.7.2a.
    (ii) Infinitive clauses with *um . . . zu* have a final meaning (= 'in order to'), see 13.2.7a.

(b) *auf dass* **is an old-fashioned sounding alternative to** *damit*

It has a formal, even biblical ring and is used principally for stylistic effect. It is always followed by a subjunctive, see 16.7.2b:

Schenke du ihr ein reines Herz, **auf dass** sie einstmals eingehe in die Wohnungen des ewigen Friedens (*Th. Mann*)	*Give her a pure heart, so that she may some day enter into the dwellings of eternal peace*

(c) Simple *dass* **is sometimes used for** *damit*

This usage is most often encountered in colloquial speech, but it is not unknown in formal writing, where it is sometimes used with a subjunctive:

Ich mache dir noch ein paar Brote, **dass** du unterwegs auch was zu essen hast	*I'll make you a couple of sandwiches so that you've got something to eat on the journey*
Er entfernte sich leise, **dass** niemand ihn sehe, niemand ihn höre (*Süßkind*)	*He withdrew quietly, so that no-one should see him, no-one should hear him*

NB: In colloquial German, *so dass* is sometimes used to introduce clauses of purpose. This usage is not considered standard.

19.5.2 Clauses of result

(a) *so dass* **is the most frequent conjunction introducing clauses of result**

Sein Bein war steif, **so dass** er kaum gehen konnte	*His leg was stiff, so that he could hardly walk*
Das Wetter war schlecht, **so dass** wir wenig wandern konnten	*The weather was bad, so that we couldn't do much hiking*
Er schob den Ärmel zurück, **so dass** wir die Narbe sehen konnten	*He pushed his sleeve back, so that we were able to see the scar*

The difference between consecutive clauses and final clauses is clear if we replace *so dass* by *damit* in the last example. *Er schob die Ärmel zurück, **damit** wir die Narbe sehen konnten* implies that he did it with the express intention that we should see the scar. With *so dass*, the fact that we could see the scar is only the (possibly unintentional) result of his action.

NB: *so dass* can alternatively be written as a single word (i.e. *sodass*), and this is the usual form in Austria.

(b) In clauses of result with adjectives or adverbs, the *so* **can precede these**

These correspond to similar constructions in English. Compare the examples below to the first two examples in (a) above:

Sein Bein war **so** steif, **dass** er kaum gehen konnte	*His leg was so stiff that he could hardly walk*

| Das Wetter war **so** schlecht, **dass** wir wenig wandern konnten | *The weather was so bad that we weren't able to do much hiking* |

derart and (in some contexts) *dermaßen* are more emphatic alternatives to *so* in such contexts:

| Er fuhr **so/derart/dermaßen** langsam, **dass** Frieda uns leicht einholte | *He drove so slowly that Frieda caught us up easily* |
| Es hat **so/derart/dermaßen** geregnet, **dass** wir schon Montag nach Hause gefahren sind | *It rained so much that we came home as early as Monday* |

dermaßen is only possible if some idea of quantity is involved. Thus, only *derart* could replace *so* in: *Er hat den Ärmel **so/derart** zurückgeschoben, dass wir die Narbe sehen konnten.*

19.5.3 *als dass*

als dass is only used to introduce a clause after an adjective modified by *zu, nicht genug* or *nicht so*. The equivalent English sentences usually have an infinitive with 'for'. *Konjunktiv II*, particularly of a modal verb, is commonly used in these clauses, see 16.7.5a.

Er ist **zu** vernünftig, **als dass** ich das von ihm erwartet hätte	*He's too sensible for me to have expected that of him*
Es ist noch **nicht so** kalt, **als dass** wir jetzt schon die Heizung einschalten müssten	*It's not so cold for us to have to turn the heating on yet*
Das Kind ist **nicht** alt **genug, als dass** wir es auf einer so langen Reise mitnehmen könnten	*The child is not old enough for us to be able to take it with us on such a long journey*

In everyday speech, simpler constructions are preferred to sentences with *als dass*, e.g. *Es ist noch nicht so kalt, also brauchen wir die Heizung noch nicht einschalten.*

NB: If the subject of the two clauses is the same, an infinitive clause with *um . . . zu* is used rather than an *als dass*-clause (see 13.2.7a).

19.6 **Concessive conjunctions**

Concessive conjunctions typically include the equivalents for English '(al)though' (see section 19.6.1), and the forms which correspond to English 'however', 'where(so)ever', etc. (see section 19.6.2). Conditional concessive conjunctions (*selbst wenn, auch wenn, sogar wenn, wenn . . . auch* = English 'even if') are treated in 16.5.3d.

19.6.1 **German equivalents for English '(al)though'**

(a) *obwohl* **is the commonest concessive conjunction in current usage**

| **Obwohl** sie Schwierigkeiten mit dem Reißverschluss hatte, stand ich nicht auf, ihr zu helfen (*Böll*) | *Although she was having difficulties with her zip, I didn't stand up to help her* |

If the *obwohl*-clause comes first, the contrast can be emphasised by using (*so*) . . . *doch* in the main clause:

| **Obwohl** ich unterschrieben hatte, (**so**) blieb sie **doch** sehr skeptisch | *Although I had signed, she still remained very sceptical* |

Less commonly, the contrast may be stressed by putting the verb second in the following main clause:

Obwohl er mein Cousin ist, ich **kann** nichts für ihn tun	*Although he is my cousin, I can't do anything for him*

NB: *obwohl* is occasionally used with the word order of a main clause, i.e. with the verb second: *Sie kann ihn sehen,* **obwohl** *es* **ist** *sehr dunkel*. This usage is increasing, especially in spoken German, but it is not accepted as standard.

(b) Other concessive conjunctions

(i) *obschon* is quite common in Swiss usage:

Ivy hatte drei Stunden lang auf mich eingeschwätzt, **obschon** sie wusste, dass ich grundsätzlich nicht heirate (*Frisch*)	*Ivy had kept on at me for three hours although she knew that I wasn't getting married on principle*

(ii) *trotzdem* is sometimes used as a conjunction to mean 'although':

Ich hab die jungen Herrschaften auch gleich erkannt, **trotzdem** es ein bisschen dunkel ist (*Th. Mann*)	*I recognised the young master and mistress immediately although it is a little dark*

The use of *trotzdem* as a conjunction is considered colloquial, and many Germans think it should be avoided in writing.

(iii) A common alternative way to express concession is a construction with *zwar . . . aber*, i.e. with two main clauses. The first one contains the particle *zwar* (see 10.36.1), and the second is introduced by *aber*:

Bei den Hotlines gab es **zwar** laufend Anrufe, **aber** keine größeren Störfälle (*Presse*)	*Although there was a stream of calls to the hotlines, there weren't any major breakdowns*

(iv) Some other alternatives to *obwohl* are used occasionally in written German, roughly in the following descending order of frequency: *obgleich, wenngleich, wiewohl, obzwar*.

19.6.2 Clauses of the type 'however', 'whoever', 'whenever', etc.

(a) The usual German equivalent for these is *wie . . . auch, wer . . . auch*, etc.
i.e. the clause is introduced by one of the interrogative pronouns (see 5.3) or the interrogative adverbs (see 7.5), and the particle *auch* is placed later in the clause:

Wer er **auch** ist, ich kann nichts für ihn tun	*Whoever he is, I can't do anything for him*
Wann sie **auch** ankommt, ich will sie sofort sprechen	*Whenever she arrives, I want to speak to her immediately*
Wohin sie **auch** hingeht, ich werde ihr folgen	*Wherever she may go, I shall follow her*
Wo er sich **auch** zeigte, er wurde mit Beifall begrüßt	*Wherever he showed himself, he was greeted with applause*

As the examples show, a main clause following these concessive clauses usually has normal word order, with the verb second, see 21.2.1c. Other features of this type of concessive clause:

(i) The modal verb *mögen* often occurs in these clauses in more formal registers, e.g. *Wer er auch sein* **mag**, . . .; *Wann sie auch ankommen* **mag**, . . . etc. (see 17.4.3).

(ii) In modern German, the indicative mood is used in clauses of this type. The subjunctive still occurs occasionally, but it can sound affected, except in the set phrase *Wie dem auch sei* 'However that may be'.

(iii) *auch* can be strengthened by adding *immer*, e.g. *Wo er sich **auch immer** zeigte*, . . . Alternatively, *immer* can be used on its own. It always follows the interrogative, e.g.: *Wo **immer** er sich zeigte*. . .

(b) *so/wie . . . auch* **corresponds to English 'however' followed by an adjective or an adverb**

So/Wie gescheit er **auch** sein mag, für diese Stelle passt er nicht	*However clever he may be, he's not right for this job*
So/Wie teuer das Bild **auch** ist/sein mag, ich will es doch kaufen	*However dear the picture is, I'm still going to buy it*
So höhnisch die Antwort Vittlars **auch** sein mochte, gab sie mir dennoch mehr Gewissheit (*Grass*)	*However scornful Vittlar's answer may have been, it still gave me more certainty*

Similarly *sosehr . . . auch* is usual for 'however much':

Sosehr das Publikum die feurigen Latinorhythmen **auch** beklatschte, getanzt wurde nicht (*MM*).	*However much the public clapped in time to the fiery Latin rhythms, nobody danced*

noch so can be used in a concessive sense with a following adjective. Compare the following alternative for the first example above: *Er mag **noch so** gescheit sein, für diese Stelle passt er nicht.*

(c) *was für (ein)* **or** *welcher . . . auch* **corresponds to 'whatever' with a noun**

Was für Schwierigkeiten du **auch** hast, es ist der Mühe wert	*Whatever difficulties you may have, it's worth the trouble*
diese Vorgänge, von **welcher** Seite man sie **auch** betrachtet (*SZ*)	*these events, from whatever side one considers them*
aus **welchem** Land **auch immer**	*from whatever country*
aus **welchem** Grund **auch immer**	*for whatever reason*

19.7 **Conjunctions of manner and degree**

Table 19.5 lists the principal conjunctions of manner and degree.

TABLE 19.5 Conjunctions of manner and degree

als	*than*	19.7.1
als ob/wenn	*as if*	16.7.1
(an)statt dass	*instead of*	13.2.7c
außer dass	*except that*	19.7.2
außer wenn	*except when*	19.7.2
dadurch dass	*by + . . .ing*	19.7.3
indem	*by + . . .ing*	19.7.3
insofern (als)	*inasmuch as*	19.7.4
insoweit (als)	*inasmuch as*	19.7.4
je . . . umso/desto	*the more . . . the more*	8.3.5
je nachdem (ob/wie)	*according to*	19.7.5
nur dass	*only that*	19.7.6
ohne dass	*without + . . .ing*	19.7.7
sofern/soviel	*provided that*	19.7.4
soweit	*as/so far as*	19.7.4
wie	*as, like*	19.7.1

NB: That some of these are treated in other sections rather than here.

19.7.1 *als* and *wie* introduce comparative clauses

For the use of *als* and *wie* generally in comparatives, see 8.3:

Wir fahren schneller, **als** du denkst	*We're travelling faster than you think*
Der Vortrag war nicht so interessant, **wie** ich erwartet hatte	*The lecture was not as interesting as I had expected*

Clauses expressing unreal comparisons with *als ob/wenn* (= 'as if') are explained in 16.7.1. For *je . . . umso/desto* 'the more . . . the more', see 8.3.5.

19.7.2 *außer dass* and *außer wenn*

(a) *außer dass* **corresponds to English 'except that'**

Ich habe nichts herausfinden können, **außer dass** er erst im April zurückkommt	*I didn't find anything out, except that he's not coming back till April*

NB: An infinitive clause with *außer . . . zu* can be used if the subjects of the two clauses are the same, see 13.2.7d.

(b) *außer wenn* **corresponds to English 'except when' or 'unless'**

Wir gingen oft im Gebirge wandern, **außer wenn** es regnete	*We often used to go hiking in the mountains, except when/unless it was raining*
Du brauchst die Suppe nicht zu essen, **außer wenn** du sie wirklich magst	*You don't need to eat the soup, unless you really like it*

außer is often used for *außer wenn*, especially in colloquial speech. It is followed by the word order of a main clause, with the verb second, e.g. *Wir gehen morgen im Gebirge wandern, **außer** es regnet.*

NB: (i)   For other equivalents for English 'unless', see 16.5.3d.
    (ii) For *anstatt dass* 'instead of', see 13.2.7c.

19.7.3 *dadurch dass* and *indem* have instrumental meaning

Their usual English equivalent is 'by' followed by the 'ing-'form of the verb, see also 13.7.2a:

Er hat sich **dadurch** gerettet, **dass** er aus dem Fenster sprang/Er hat sich gerettet, **indem** er aus dem Fenster sprang	*He saved himself by jumping out of the window*
Man kann **dadurch** Unfälle vermeiden helfen, **dass** man die Verkehrs-vorschriften beachtet/Man kann Unfälle vermeiden helfen, **indem** man die Verkehrsvorschriften beachtet	*One can help to avoid accidents by observing the highway code*

NB: This is the only current use of *indem* in modern German. Its use in time clauses, see 19.3.1f, is now obsolete.

19.7.4 *insofern (als)*, *insoweit (als)*, *sofern*, *soviel*, *soweit*

These are all quite close in meaning.

(a) *insofern (als)* **and** *insoweit (als)* **correspond to English '(in) so/as far as' or 'inasmuch as'**

Ich werde dir helfen, **insofern (als)** ich kann/**insoweit (als)** ich kann	*I'll help you in so far as I'm able to*

insofern and *insoweit* can be placed within a preceding main clause, especially qualifying an adjective or adverb. In this case they **must** be used with a following *als*:

Diese Verhandlungen werden **insofern/ insoweit** schwierig sein, **als** es sich um ein ausgesprochen heikles Problem handelt	*These negotiations will be difficult, inasmuch as we're dealing with an extremely delicate problem*

NB: The use of *insofern* with a following *weil* or *dass* rather than *als* is frequent in colloquial registers, but not accepted as standard.

(b) *soweit* **usually has the sense of '(in) so'/'as far as'/'as much as'**

In this sense *soweit* is an alternative to *insofern/insoweit (als)*:

Ich werde dir helfen, **soweit** ich kann	*I'll help you as much as I can*
Soweit ich die Lage beurteilen kann, muss ich ihm Recht geben	*In so far as I can judge the situation, I've got to admit he's right*

soweit can sometimes be used with a conditional sense. In such contexts it is an alternative to *sofern*, see (c) below and 16.5.3d:

Soweit/Sofern noch Interesse besteht, wollen wir schon morgen damit anfangen	*Provided there's still interest, we're going to make a start tomorrow*

NB: *soviel ich weiß* 'as far as I know'.

(c) *sofern* **usually has a conditional sense, corresponding to English 'provided that' or 'if'**
See also 16.5.3d.

Sofern wir es im Stadtrat durchsetzen können, wird die neue Straße bald gebaut	*Provided (that)/If we can get it through the town council, the new road will soon be built*

19.7.5 *je nachdem* 'according to', 'depending on'

je nachdem is normally used with a following *ob* or an interrogative:

Je nachdem, ob es ihm besser geht oder nicht, wird er morgen verreisen	*Depending on whether he's better or not, he'll leave tomorrow*
Je nachdem, wann wir fertig sind, werden wir hier oder in der Stadt essen	*Depending on when we get finished, we'll eat here or in town*
Je nachdem, wie das Wetter wird, werden wir am Montag oder am Dienstag segeln gehen	*According to what the weather is like, we'll go sailing on Monday or Tuesday*

je nachdem often occurs in isolation, e.g.:

Kommst du morgen mit? Na, **je nachdem**	*Are you coming tomorrow? Well, it depends*

19.7.6 *nur* dass 'only (that)'

In der neuen Schule hat er sich gut eingelebt, **nur dass** seine Noten etwas besser sein könnten	*He's settled down well at his new school, only his marks could be a bit better*

A main clause introduced by *nur* is often preferred to *nur dass* in spoken German, e.g. . . ., **nur könnten seine Noten etwas besser sein.**

19.7.7 *ohne dass* 'without'

ohne dass must be used for English 'without' followed by an 'ing'-form if the subordinate clause has a different subject from the main clause:

Er verließ das Zimmer, **ohne dass** wir es merkten	*He left the room without our noticing*
Sie haben mir sofort geholfen, **ohne dass** ich sie darum bitten musste/müsste	*They helped me immediately without my having to ask them*

If the subjects of the two clauses are the same, an infinitive clause with *ohne . . . zu* can be used for English 'without' + 'ing', see 13.2.7b.

NB: The subjunctive is often used in *ohne dass* clauses, see 16.7.5a.

20 Prepositions

PREPOSITIONS are a small class of words which combine with a following **noun phrase** to form a PREPOSITIONAL PHRASE. Prepositional phrases often express notions of time, place and direction and are typically (but not only) used as **adverbials**.

In German, the noun phrase following each preposition is in a particular case – we say that the preposition 'governs' a particular case. Most German prepositions govern the dative or the accusative case; prepositions governing the genitive are mainly confined to formal language. One important group of common prepositions is followed by the accusative **or** the dative case, with a difference in meaning.

All the prepositions of German are dealt with in this chapter, ordered according to the case they govern:

- prepositions with the **accusative** case (section 20.1)
- prepositions with the **dative** case (section 20.2)
- prepositions with the **dative** or the **accusative** case (section 20.3)
- prepositions with the **genitive** case (section 20.4)
- German equivalents for **English 'to'** (section 20.5)

The most important literal and figurative senses of each preposition are treated together. Some uses of prepositions are dealt with in more detail elsewhere in the book, as indicated below:

- the use of prepositions in **time phrases** (section 11.5)
- the use of prepositions after **adjectives** (section 6.6)
- prepositions with verbs – **prepositional objects** (section 18.6)
- the **contraction** of some prepositions with the definite article, e.g. *am, ins* (section 4.1.1c)
- the **prepositional adverb**, e.g. *darauf, damit* (section 3.5)

Table 20.1 lists the most frequent German prepositions with their cases.

TABLE 20.1 The most frequent German prepositions and their cases

Prepositions governing the:			
accusative	dative	accusative or dative	genitive
bis	aus	an	(an)statt
durch	außer	auf	trotz
für	bei	hinter	während
gegen	gegenüber	in	wegen
ohne	mit	neben	
um	nach	über	
	seit	unter	
	von	vor	
	zu	zwischen	

20.1 **Prepositions governing the accusative case**

Six common prepositions are used with the accusative:

bis   durch   für   gegen   ohne   um

The following are less frequent and are treated together in 20.1.7:

à   betreffend   eingerechnet   pro   wider

20.1.1 *bis*

In practice, *bis* is rarely used as a preposition in its own right. It is **never** followed by an article (or any determiner), and it is used on its own only with names, adverbs and a few time words. Otherwise it is followed by another preposition which determines the case of the following noun.

(a) Referring to place, *bis* means 'as far as', '(up) to'

(i) Followed by names of places and adverbs *bis* is used **without an article**. In practice the case of the following noun is never obvious:

Ich fahre nur **bis** Frankfurt	*I'm only going as far as Frankfurt*
Bis dahin gehe ich mit	*I'll go that far with you*
bis hierher und nicht weiter	*so far and no further*

(ii) If the following noun has an article, an appropriate preposition must follow, usually the appropriate equivalent of English 'to', see 20.5:

Wir gingen **bis zum** Waldrand	*We went as far as the edge of the forest*
Sie ging **bis zur** Tür	*She went up to the door*
Sie ging **bis an** die Tür	*She went right up to the door*
Wir fuhren **bis an** die Grenze	*We went as far as/up to the border*
Sie standen im Wasser **bis an** die Knie	*They were standing in water up to their knees*
Sie standen im Wasser **bis über** die Knie	*They were standing in water coming up over their knees*
bis hin zu den Wanzen im Gesicht (*Borst*)	*right down to the warts on his face*
Er stieg **bis aufs** Dach	*He climbed right onto the roof*
bis über die Ohren verschuldet	*up to one's ears in debt*

bis zu can be used in the sense of 'up to' with quantities, e.g. *Bis zu dreißig Kinder nahmen an dem Ausflug teil.* See 9.1.6 for further details of this usage and the distinction between the adverbial and prepositional usage of *bis zu* with quantities.

(iii) With names of towns, cities and countries, *bis* or *bis nach* can be used. The latter is more emphatic: *Wir fahren **bis (nach)** Freiburg, von Köln **bis (nach)** Aachen.*

(b) Referring to time, *bis* means 'until' or 'by'

e.g. *bis nächste Woche, bis nächstes Jahr*, see 11.5.4. If the noun is used with a determiner, *zu* (or another appropriate preposition) is inserted: ***bis zum** Abend, **bis zum** 4. Mai, **bis zu** seinem Tod, **bis zu** diesem Augenblick, **bis auf** den heutigen Tag.*

(c) *bis auf* (+ acc.) means 'down to (and including)' or 'all but', 'except'

Die Kabinen waren mit 447 Passagieren **bis auf** das letzte Klappbett belegt (*Zeit*)	*With 447 passengers, the cabins were full down to the last camp bed*
Bis auf drei kamen alle Insassen um	*All but three of the passengers were killed*

bis auf can be ambiguous: *Der Bus war **bis auf** den letzten Platz besetzt* can mean 'The bus was full down to the last seat' or 'The bus was full except for the last seat'.

20.1.2 *durch*

(a) *durch* means 'through', referring to place

Sie ging **durch** die Stadt	*She went through the city*
Er atmete **durch** den Mund	*He was breathing through his mouth*
mitten **durch** den Park (see 7.1.3)	*through the middle of the park*

durch is often strengthened by adding *hindurch*, see 7.2.4, e.g.: *Wir gingen **durch** den Wald **hindurch*** 'We went (right) through the forest'.

It can also be used for English 'across', especially with a preceding *quer*. This can give the sense of 'crosswise', 'diagonally', but it is often used simply to strengthen *durch* (i.e. = 'right through'):

Wir wateten (**quer**) **durch** den Fluss	*We waded across the river*
im Rahmen ihrer Frühlingstournee **quer** **durch** Deutschland (*MM*)	*in the course of their spring tour right across Germany*

(b) *durch* can also be used for English 'throughout'

(i) This is its usual sense when it refers to time, in which case it can be strengthened by adding *hindurch*, e.g. **durch** *viele Generationen* (***hindurch***) 'throughout many generations'.

(ii) *hindurch* can be used without a preceding *durch* for 'throughout' after an accusative phrase of time with *ganz*, see 11.4.1a:

den ganzen Winter **hindurch**	*throughout the winter*
die ganze Nacht **hindurch**	*throughout the night*

durch can also be used on its own after the noun in this meaning: *die ganze Nacht **durch***.

(iii) A phrase with *ganz* and an appropriate preposition is needed to give the sense of English 'throughout' referring to place, e.g.:

im **ganzen** Land	*throughout the country*
durch die **ganze** Stadt	*throughout the town*

(c) *durch* is used to express means

This use of *durch* is related to its use for 'by' in passive sentences, see 15.3.

(i) *durch* introduces the agent or means through whom or which an action is carried out:

Durch harte Arbeit hat er sein Ziel erreicht	*He attained his aim by (means of) hard work*
Er ist **durch** einen Unfall ums Leben gekommen	*He was killed through an accident*
durch seine eigene Schuld	*through his own fault*
Ich habe es **durch** Zufall erfahren	*I learnt of it by chance*

(ii) *durch* in this sense corresponds to 'by' with a verbal noun:

die Annahme des Kaisertitels **durch** den König	*the assumption of the title of emperor by the king*
die Erfindung des Verbrennungsmotors **durch** Benz und Daimler	*the invention of the internal combustion engine by Benz and Daimler*

(iii) *durch* with a verbal noun often corresponds to English 'by' with an 'ing'- form, see 13.7.2a, e.g.: *durch Betätigung des Mechanismus* 'by activating the mechanism'

(iv) The prepositional adverb *dadurch* often has the sense of 'thereby':

Was willst du **dadurch** erreichen?	*What do you hope to gain by that?*
Meinst du, **dadurch** wird alles wieder gut?	*Do you think that will make everything all right again?*

NB: For the compound conjunction *dadurch, dass* 'by . . .ing' see 19.7.3.

20.1.3 *für*

(a) *für* **corresponds to English 'for' in a wide range of senses**

i.e. where 'for' has the meaning of 'on behalf of' and the like, e.g.:

Er hat viel **für** mich getan
Das wäre genug **für** heute
Das war sehr unangenehm **für** mich (6.5.1a)
Für einen Ausländer spricht er recht gut Deutsch
Das ist kein Buch **für** Kinder
Ich habe es **für** zehn Euro gekriegt

NB: (i) *für* is used idiomatically in *ein Sinn, ein Beispiel für etwas* 'a sense, an example of sth.'.
    (ii) Where English 'for' expresses **purpose**, its usual German equivalent is *zu*, see 20.2.9d.

(b) *für* **indicates a period of time**

e.g. *für sechs Wochen* 'for six weeks'. For this, and other German equivalents for English 'for' referring to time, see 11.5.5.

20.1.4 *gegen*

(a) **Referring to place or opposition,** *gegen* **means 'against'**

Er warf den Ball **gegen** die Mauer	*He threw the ball against the wall*
gegen den Strom schwimmen (in literal <u>and</u> figurative senses)	*swim against the current*
Sie verteidigte sich **gegen** diese Leute	*She defended herself against those people*

The prepositional adverb *dagegen* is commonly used to indicate opposition, e.g.:

Hast du was **dagegen**, wenn wir früher anfangen?	*Do you have any objection to our starting earlier?*

Note the different idiomatic usage between German and English in *Ich brauche Tabletten* **gegen** *Kopfschmerzen* 'I need tablets **for** a headache'.

(b) *gegen* **can indicate direction**

(i) *gegen* often corresponds to 'into':

Er fuhr **gegen** einen Baum	*He drove into a tree*
Wir müssen aufpassen, dass wir nicht **gegen** die Kraterwände fliegen (Grzimek)	*We've got to watch out that we don't fly into the sides of the crater*

(ii) In some contexts *gegen* has the sense of 'towards':

Michael will die Maschine mit dem Propeller **gegen** die flache Böschung am Seeufer drehen (Grzimek)	*Michael is going to turn the aeroplane with the propellor towards the slight incline on the lake shore*

The use of *gegen* in the sense of 'towards' with the points of the compass is now old-fashioned. For *gegen Norden fahren* one now finds **nach** *Norden fahren*, see 20.2.6. The form *gen* (e.g. *gen Norden fahren*) is even more restricted to elevated literary registers and sounds archaic and biblical.

NB: Note the difference from English usage in *etwas gegen das Licht halten* 'hold sth. **up to** the light'.

(c) *gegen* **can express a contrast (= 'contrary to', 'compared with')**

Ich handelte **gegen** seinen Befehl	*I acted against/contrary to his orders*
gegen alle Erwartungen	*against/contrary to all expectations*
Gegen meine Schwester bin ich groß	*I'm tall compared to my sister*
gegen früher	*compared to formerly*

(d) *gegen* **can have the sense of '(in exchange/return) for'**

Er gab mir das Geld **gegen** eine Quittung	*He gave me the money in exchange for a receipt*
Ich will meine Digitalkamera **gegen** einen HD-Camcorder eintauschen	*I want to exchange my digital camera for an HD camcorder*

(e) *gegen* **can express approximation (= 'about')**

Es waren **gegen** (*or* etwa, *or* an die) 500 Zuschauer im Saal	*There were about 500 spectators in the hall*

(f) *gegen* **is used after a number of nouns and adjectives**

See also 6.6.1. These nouns or adjectives mostly involve a mental attitude 'towards' something or someone, e.g.:

die Abneigung gegen	*aversion towards*	die Grausamkeit gegen	*cruelty towards*
der Hass gegen	*hatred of*	das Misstrauen gegen	*distrust of*
argwöhnisch gegen	*suspicious of*	gleichgültig gegen	*indifferent to*
gesichert gegen	*secure against*		

seine Pflicht gegen seine Eltern	*his duty towards his parents*
sein Verhalten gegen seinen Chef	*his attitude to(wards) his boss*
rücksichtslos/rücksichtsvoll gegen	*(in)considerate towards*

With these nouns and adjectives *gegenüber* is often a possible alternative to *gegen*, see 20.2.4d. Some adjectives can be followed by *zu* or *gegen*, see 20.2.9g.

(g) Referring to time, *gegen* **means 'about', 'towards'**

e.g. *Sie kam gegen Abend, gegen vier Uhr an.* For details, see 11.5.6.

20.1.5 *ohne*

In most contexts *ohne* corresponds to English 'without':

Das tat er **ohne** mein Wissen
Er geht selten **ohne** Hut
Das haben wir **ohne** große Schwierigkeiten erledigt

ohne can be used idiomatically on its own in colloquial speech:

Der Wein ist nicht **ohne**	*The wine's got quite a kick*
Er ist gar nicht so **ohne**	*He's got what it takes*

After the combination *mit oder ohne* it is nowadays acceptable to ignore the usual rule that the noun phrase must be repeated after prepositions which govern different cases. It is thus not necessary to say or write *mit Kindern oder ohne Kinder* or *mit ihm oder ohne ihn* as *mit oder ohne Kinder* or *mit oder ohne ihn* is acceptable.

NB: (i) *ohne* is used with no determiner in many contexts where English has an indefinite article or a possessive, see 4.9.3b.
   (ii) For the use of *ohne* in infinitive clauses (i.e. *ohne . . . zu*), see 13.2.7b; for the conjunction *ohne dass*, see 19.7.7.

20.1.6 *um*

(a) Referring to place, *um* means '(a)round', 'about'

Wir standen **um** den Teich	*We were standing (a)round the pond*
Er kam **um** die Ecke	*He came (a)round the corner*
Sie sah **um** sich	*She looked round (in all directions)*

um is often strengthened by adding *rund*, *rings* or *herum* (see 7.2.4b), e.g.:

Wir standen **rings/rund um** den Tisch *or* **um** den Tisch **herum**
Er kam **um** die Ecke **herum**
Sie sah um sich **herum**

(b) *um* means 'at' with clock times, but 'about' with other time expressions

e.g. *Ich komme um zwei Uhr*, see 11.5.11.

um can also be used adverbially with numerals in the sense of 'about', 'approximately', see 9.1.6. It is then often followed by a definite article, but a following adjective has **strong** endings, e.g. *um die vierzig ausländische Gäste*.

(c) *um* is used to denote the degree of difference

This usually corresponds to English 'by':

Ich werde meinen Aufenthalt **um** zwei Tage verlängern	*I shall extend my stay by two days*
Sie hat sich **um** 20 Euro verrechnet	*She was 20 euros out in her calculations*
um die Hälfte mehr	*half as much again*
eine Erweiterung der EU **um** Rumänien	*an expansion of the EU by the inclusion of Romania*

When *um* is used in this sense with a comparative adjective and a measurement phrase (see 8.3.1c), an alternative to *um* is simply to put the measurement phrase in the **accusative** case, e.g.: *Sie ist (um) einen Kopf größer als ich.*

(d) *um* can convey the idea of 'in respect of', 'concerning'

This sense is common when *um* is used in a prepositional object, see 18.6.10, but it occurs in other constructions, especially after some nouns and adjectives, e.g.:

der Kampf **ums** Dasein	*the struggle for existence*
Er tat es nur **um** das Geld	*He only did it for the money*
Er wandte sich an mich **um** Rat	*He turned to me for advice*
Es ist schade **um** den Verlust	*It's a pity about the loss*
Es steht schlecht **um** ihren Bruder	*Her brother's in a bad way*
ein Streit **um** etwas	*an argument about sth.*
die Angst **ums** Leben	*fear for one's life*
Es ist recht still **um** ihn geworden	*You don't hear anything about him now*

Idiomatically also *Auge um Auge, Zahn um Zahn* 'an eye for an eye, a tooth for a tooth'

(e) The prepositional adverb *darum* is used in the meaning 'therefore', 'that's why'

It is an alternative to *deshalb*:

Darum habe ich nicht schreiben können	*That's why I couldn't write*
Sie hatte eine Panne, **darum** ist sie so spät gekommen	*She had a breakdown, that's why she was so late coming*

20.1.7 Less frequent prepositions which govern the accusative

(a) *à* is used in the sense of 'at' (i.e. @), with prices

e.g.: *zehn Paar Schuhe à 150 Mark*. This usage is now rather old-fashioned, and *zu* is now more frequent than *à*, see 20.2.9h.

(b) *betreffend* 'with regard to' is used mainly in commercial German

It is an alternative to *betreffs* (+ gen.) and may precede or follow the noun it governs: *betreffend Ihr Schreiben vom 23. Mai* or *Ihr Schreiben vom 23. Mai* **betreffend**.

(c) *eingerechnet* 'including' is limited to commercial language

It follows the noun it governs: *meine Unkosten eingerechnet* 'including my expenses'.

(d) *pro* 'per'

pro was originally restricted to commercial language, but it has increasingly come to be used in speech. A common alternative is *je*, see 9.4.1:

Die Pfirsiche kosten 80 Cent **pro** Stück	*The peaches cost 80 cents each*
Was ist der Preis **pro** Tag?	*What is the cost per day?*
zwanzig Euro **pro** Person	*twenty euros per person*
Unsere Reisekosten betragen 3000 Euro **pro**/**je** Vertreter **pro**/**je** Monat	*Our travel expenses amount to 3000 euros per representative per month*

As *pro* is most often used without a following adjective or determiner, the case it governs may not be obvious. This has given rise to uncertainty. In practice, when the case used is clear, *pro* is seen to be used quite frequently with the dative rather than the accusative, e.g. *pro neuem Mitarbeiter*. Occasionally it is used with a nominative, especially with an adjective used as a noun, e.g. *pro Angestellter*. All these alternatives are accepted as correct.

(e) *wider* 'against' is an obsolete alternative to *gegen*

It is occasionally used in elevated registers, but most often in a few set phrases:

Diese Unterlassung relativiert alle markigen Worte **wider** den Terrorismus (*Zeit*)	*This omission qualifies all the vigorous speeches against terrorism*
wider (alles) Erwarten	*against (all) expectations*
wider Willen	*against my (his, her, etc.) will*
wider besseres Wissen (*MM*)	*against my (his, her, etc.) better judgement*

20.2 Prepositions governing the dative case

Nine common prepositions are used with the dative:

aus	außer	bei	gegenüber	mit	nach	seit	von	zu

The following are less frequent and are treated together in 20.2.10:

ab	binnen	dank	entgegen	entsprechend	fern	gemäß	laut
(mit)samt	nahe	nebst	per	zufolge	zuliebe	zuwider	

20.2.1 *aus*

(a) *aus* most commonly denotes direction 'out of' or 'from' a place

(i) Examples of the use of *aus* in the sense of 'out of':

Er kam **aus** dem Haus	*He came out of the house*
Ich sah **aus** dem Fenster	*I looked out of the window*
(*or*: zum Fenster hinaus)	
Er trank Wodka **aus** einer Tasse	*He was drinking vodka from a cup*
Sie ging mir **aus** dem Weg	*She avoided me*
aus der Mode kommen/sein	*go/be out of fashion*
aus der Übung kommen	*get out of practice*

(ii) In practice, *aus* more often corresponds to English 'from'

English learners need to distinguish between *aus* and *von*, which can also mean 'from' (see 20.2.8a). *aus* is used with reference to places one has been **in**, with the idea of origin. Its opposite is *in* (+ acc.). *von*, by contrast, is used for 'from' with reference to places one has been **at**, i.e. it expresses the idea of direction. Its opposite is *zu*. Examples of *aus*:

Er kommt **aus** Hamburg	*He comes from Hamburg*
(i.e. he lives in Hamburg).	
Er kommt **von** Hamburg	*He is travelling from Hamburg*
(i.e. on this occasion)	
aus dieser Richtung	*from that direction*
(compare: *in diese(r) Richtung* 'in that direction')	
Dieser Schrank ist **aus** dem 18.	*This cupboard is from the 18th century*
Jahrhundert	
(i.e. it was made **in** the 18th century)	
ein Mädchen **aus** unserer Klasse	*a girl from our class*
(i.e. she is **in** our class)	

(b) *aus* denotes 'made of' referring to materials

Die Kaffeekanne war **aus** Silber	*The coffee pot was made of silver*
aus Holz, Stahl, Eisen	*made of wood, steel, iron*
ein Kleid **aus** Wolle	*a woollen dress*

(c) *aus* is used to denote a cause, a reason or a motive

Sie tat es **aus** Dankbarkeit, **aus**	*She did it out of gratitude,*
Mitleid, **aus** Überzeugung	*out of sympathy, from conviction*
Ich weiß es **aus** (der) Erfahrung	*I know it from experience*
Ich frage nur **aus** Interesse	*I'm only asking out of interest*
aus Furcht vor, Liebe zu etwas	*for fear, love of sth.*
aus diesem Grund(e)	*for that reason*

NB: For the distinction between *aus* and *vor* (+ dat) to indicate cause, see 20.3.15d.

(d) Some idiomatic uses of *aus*

aus erster Hand	*at first hand*
Daraus werde ich nicht klug	*I can't make it out*
Aus dir wird nichts werden	*You'll never come to anything*

20.2.2 *außer*

(a) *außer* usually expresses a restriction (= 'except (for)', 'besides')

Niemand hat ihn gesehen **außer** dem Nachtwächter	*No-one saw him except for the nightwatchman*
Niemand wird es machen können **außer** mir	*No-one will be able to do it except for me*
Ich konnte nichts sehen **außer** Straßenlichtern	*I couldn't see anything besides street lights*

außer can also be used with the same case as the word to which it refers back, rather than with the dative. The following are acceptable alternatives to the examples above:

Ich konnte **nichts** sehen außer **Lichter**
Niemand wird es machen können außer **ich**

In effect *außer* is used in such contexts to introduce a phrase in apposition (see 2.6) rather than as a preposition. It can be used in a similar way to introduce another preposition, e.g.: *Außer bei Regen kann man hier spielen.*

(b) *außer* is used in the meaning 'out of', 'outside'

This sense now occurs chiefly in set phrases, in most of which *außer* is used without a following article:

Die Maschine ist **außer** Betrieb	*The machine is out of service*
außer Kontrolle sein/geraten	*be/get out of control*
etwas **außer** Acht lassen	*disregard sth.*
Ich war **außer** mir	*I was beside myself*
Aber dies war etwas, was ganz **außer** seiner Macht lag (*Musil*)	*But this was something which lay completely beyond his power*

Similarly:

außer Atem	*out of breath*	außer Gefahr	*out of danger*
außer Reichweite	*out of range*	außer Sicht	*out of sight*
außer Übung	*out of practice*	außer Zweifel	*beyond doubt*

In one or two obsolescent phrases *außer* is used with a genitive, notably in *außer Landes gehen* 'leave the country'. More usual for this would be *ins Ausland gehen*, or simply *auswandern*.

With verbs of motion, *außer* can be used with the accusative, although this is only obvious in those rare contexts where a determiner or an adjective is used, e.g. *etwas außer jeden Zweifel setzen*.

20.2.3 *bei*

(a) Referring to place, *bei* usually corresponds to English 'by' or 'at'

(i) In this sense *bei* is less precise than *an* (+ dat.), see 20.3.2a, meaning 'in the vicinity of' rather than 'adjacent to':

Er stand **bei** mir	*He was standing by/near me*
(= Er stand in meiner Nähe)	
Bad Homburg liegt **bei** Frankfurt	*Bad Homburg is by/near Frankfurt*
(dicht) **bei** der Kirche	*(right) by the church*
Ich habe ihn neulich **beim** Fußballspiel gesehen	*I saw him recently at the football match*

NB: *bei* is always used with battles, e.g. *die Schlacht* **bei** *Hastings.*

(ii) Used with reference to people, *bei* usually means 'at (the house of)'. It is also used to indicate place of employment:

Sie wohnt **bei** ihrer Tante	*She lives at her aunt's*
Ich habe dieses Fleisch **beim** neuen Metzger gekauft	*I bought this meat at the new butcher's*
Sie arbeitet **bei** der Post, **bei** Bayer	*She works at the post office, at Bayer's*
bei uns	*at our house*
bei uns in der Fabrik	*at our works*

bei is not used in standard German to indicate motion **to** somebody's house. Compare *Sie geht zu ihrer Tante* 'She's going to her aunt's house'.

(iii) *bei* is also used in a number of extended senses with reference to people. This often corresponds to English 'with':

Ich habe mich **bei** ihm entschuldigt beschwert	*I apologised/complained to him*
Er hat großen Einfluss **beim** Minister	*He has a lot of influence with the minister*
Mathe haben wir **bei** Frau Gerstner	*We have Frau Gerstner for maths*
Hast du deinen Ausweis **bei** dir/dabei?	*Have you got your identity card on you?*
Bei Goethe liest man . . .	*In Goethe's works one reads . . .*

(b) *bei* **is frequently used to indicate attendant circumstances**

This usage has a range of English equivalents, i.e.:

(i) *bei* can mean 'in view of', 'with', etc., e.g.:

bei den immer steigenden Preisen	*in view of the constantly rising prices*
Bei diesem Gehalt kann ich mir keinen neuen Wagen leisten	*With this salary I can't afford a new car*
Bei all seinen Verlusten bleibt er ein Optimist	*Despite all his losses he remains an optimist*

(ii) *bei* can mean 'on the occasion of', 'at'. This sense is related to its use in time expressions, see 11.5.3:

bei dieser Gelegenheit	*on this occasion*
bei dem bloßen Gedanken	*at the very thought*
Sie erblasste **bei** der Nachricht	*She turned pale at the news*
Acht Menschen kamen **bei** diesem Verkehrsunfall ums Leben (*FAZ*)	*Eight people were killed in this road accident*
bei diesem Anblick	*at the sight of this*
bei einem Glas Wein	*over a glass of wine*

Similarly:

bei der Arbeit	*at work*	beim Fußball	*when playing football*
bei Tisch	*at table*	bei seinem Tod	*at his death*
bei schönem Wetter	*if it's fine*	bei diesen Worten	*at these words*

Both *bei* and *auf* (see 20.3.4b), can be used for English 'at', referring to formal occasions, functions and the like, e.g.:

Ich habe sie **bei/auf** ihrer Hochzeit kennen gelernt	*I met her at their wedding*

The difference of meaning is often slight, but in general *bei* points more clearly to the time, rather than the place, of the event.

(iii) *bei* is used with the infinitive or other verbal nouns in the sense of English 'on . . .ing' or a subordinate time clause, see 13.4.3a and 13.7.2d. This usage is frequent in non-literary written German, but it is not restricted to that register:

beim Schließen der Türen	*on shutting the doors*
beim Schlafen, **beim** Essen	*while sleeping, eating*
bei seiner Ankunft	*on arrival/when he arrived*
bei näherer Überlegung	*on closer consideration*

(c) Some idiomatic uses of *bei*

Sie war bei guter/schlechter Laune	*She was in a good/bad mood*
Sie nannte mich beim Vornamen	*She called me by my first name*
Sie nahm mich beim Wort	*She took me at my word*
Sie nahm mich bei der Hand	*She took me by the hand*

20.2.4 *gegenüber*

NB: In writing, *gegenüber* is increasingly used with a following genitive, e.g. *gegenüber des Theaters*. This is not (yet) considered correct.

(a) The position of *gegenüber* before or after the noun or pronoun

(i) *gegenüber* always follows a pronoun, e.g.:

Sie saß **mir gegenüber**	**Ihr gegenüber** stand ein alter Herr

(ii) *gegenüber* can come before or after a noun, e.g. *gegenüber alten Menschen* or *alten Menschen gegenüber* The position before the noun is now more frequent except in elevated registers.

seine Verantwortung **gegenüber** den chinesischen Web-Nutzern (*MM*)	*its responsibility towards Chinese web users*
Gegenüber dem Rathaus liegt ein Krankenhaus	*Opposite the town hall there is a hospital*

(b) Referring to place, *gegenüber* means 'opposite'

Ich setzte mich ihr **gegenüber**	*I sat down opposite her*
Ich wohne **gegenüber** dem Krankenhaus	*I live opposite the hospital*

In this sense, *gegenüber* is often used with a following *von*, especially in speech: *Ich saß **gegenüber von ihr**/Ich wohne **gegenüber vom** Krankenhaus*.

gegenüber is often used on its own, as an adverb, e.g. *Sie wohnt gegenüber / das Haus gegenüber/die Leute von gegenüber*.

(c) *gegenüber* **can express a comparison (= 'compared to')**

Depending on the context, *gegen*, see 20.1.4c, or *neben*, see 20.3.10d, may be alternatives to *gegenüber* in this sense:

Gegenüber meiner Schwester bin ich groß	*I'm tall compared to my sister*
gegenüber dem Vorjahr	*compared to last year*

(d) *gegenüber* **can mean 'in relation to', in respect of', 'towards'**

mein Verhalten Astrid **gegenüber**	*my attitude towards Astrid*
Heinrich war vollkommen hilflos	*Heinrich was completely helpless in*
Maries Ängsten **gegenüber** (*Böll*)	*the face of Marie's fears*

In this sense, *gegenüber* is particularly frequent after nouns and adjectives, where it is an (often more common) alternative to *gegen*, see 20.1.4f, or, in some contexts, *zu*, see 20.2.9g:

Er handelte durchaus gerecht mir **gegenüber** (*or:* gegen mich)	*He acted absolutely fairly towards me*
Seine Güte mir **gegenüber** (*or:* zu mir) war rührend	*His kindness towards me was touching*

Similarly:

das Misstrauen gegenüber/gegen	*distrust of*
eine Pflicht gegenüber/gegen	*a duty towards*
gleichgültig, gegenüber/gegen	*indifferent towards*
rücksichtsvoll/-los gegenüber/gegen	*(in)considerate to*
freundlich gegenüber/zu	*kind to(wards)*

20.2.5 *mit*

(a) *mit* **corresponds most often to English 'with'**

ein Paar Würstchen **mit** Kartoffelsalat	*a pair of sausages with potato salad*
Mit ihr spiele ich oft Tennis	*I often play tennis with her*
Was ist **mit** dir los?	*What's up with you?*
mit großer Freude	*with great pleasure*
mit meinem Bruder zusammen	*together with my brother*

(b) *mit* **indicates the instrument with which an action is performed**

This most often corresponds to English 'with':

Er hat **mit** einem Filzstift geschrieben	*He wrote with a felt-tip*
Er hat den Frosch **mit** einem Messer getötet	*He killed the frog with a knife*

German usage sometimes differs from English:

mit Tinte schreiben	*write in ink*
mit leiser Stimme	*in a low voice*
mit der Maschine schreiben	*type*

To refer to a means of transport German uses *mit* for English 'by':

mit der Bahn/dem Zug	*by rail/train*	mit dem Auto	*by car*
mit dem Flugzeug	*by plane*	mit der Post	*by post*
Ich bin mit dem Fahrrad gekommen	*I came by bike/on a bike*		

NB: Whereas *mit* indicates the **instrument**, the **means** by which an action is carried out is usually given by *durch*, see 20.1.2c.

(c) *mit* **is common in phrases involving parts of the body, where English does not have a preposition or uses a simple verb**

Sie hat mich **mit** dem Fuß gestoßen	*She kicked me*
mit den Achseln zucken	*shrug one's shoulders*

(d) Some common idiomatic uses of *mit*

mit vierzig Jahren	*at the age of forty*
mit der Zeit	*in (the course of) time*
etwas mit Absicht tun	*do sth on purpose*
mit anderen Worten (m.a.W.)	*in other words*
Her damit! (*coll.*)	*Give it here!*
Schluss damit!	*That's enough!*
mit oder ohne Kinder	*with or without children* (see 20.1.5)

20.2.6 *nach*

(a) *nach* **is used to denote direction, in the sense of English 'to'**

See also 20.5.3. In this sense *nach* is only used with:

(i) neuter names of countries and towns used without an article:

Er ging **nach** Amerika, **nach** Irland, **nach** Bacharach.

NB: *in* is used with names of countries which have an article, see 4.4.1: *Sie ging in die Schweiz.*

(ii) points of the compass used without an article:

Wir fuhren **nach** Norden, Süden, Westen, Osten.

NB: *in* is used if an article is present, as is usual when one of these nouns is qualified by an adjective: *Wir fuhren in den sonnigen Süden.*

(iii) with adverbs of place:

Sie ging **nach** oben, **nach** unten, **nach** vorne, **nach** rechts, links

NB: also *nach Hause gehen* 'go home'.

(iv) in North Germany *nach* is often used for *zu, an, auf* or *in*: *Ich gehe nach* (standard German: *zu*) *meiner Schwester*; *Wir gingen nach dem* (standard German: *auf den, zum*) *Bahnhof*. This usage is regional and non-standard, but North Germans sometimes use it in writing.

(b) *nach* **can be used in the sense of 'towards', 'in the direction of'**

It is frequently strengthened by adding *hin*, see 7.2.3, e.g.:

Er bewegte sich langsam **nach** der Tür	*He moved slowly towards the door*
Ich sah **nach** der Tür (hin)	*I looked towards the door*
nach allen Seiten (hin)	*in all directions*

NB: *auf . . . zu* is a frequent alternative for 'towards', see 20.3.5a.

(c) Referring to time, *nach* **means 'after'**

e.g. *nach vier Uhr, nach dem Sommer*, etc., see 11.5.8. The prepositional adverb *danach* can be used to mean 'after(wards)' or 'later', see 11.6.4b.

(d) *nach* **can be used in the sense of 'according to', 'judging by'**

Nach meiner Uhr ist es schon halb elf	*By my watch it's already half past ten*
nach italienischer Art	*in the Italian manner*
nach Ansicht meines Bruders	*in my brother's view*
etwas **nach** dem Gewicht verkaufen	*sell sth. by weight*
nach besten Kräften	*to the best of one's ability*
nach Wunsch	*just as I (he, she, etc.) wanted*

In this sense, *nach* can **follow** the noun. In general, this is usual only with certain nouns (most of which it may precede **or** follow), in set phrases, and in the meaning 'judging by':

allem Anschein **nach**	*to all appearances*
diesem Bericht **nach**	*according to this report*
(in less formal registers usually: *nach diesem Bericht*)	
der Größe **nach**	*according to size*
(also commonly: *nach der Größe*)	
meiner Meinung **nach**	*in my opinion*
(also: *nach meiner Meinung*)	
Ich kenne sie nur dem Namen **nach**	*I only know her by name*
der Reihe **nach**	*in turns*
Seiner Aussprache **nach** kommt Herr Oettinger aus Schwaben	*Judging by his accent Herr Oettinger comes from Swabia*

NB: A few other prepositions are used to mean 'according to' in formal registers, i.e. *entsprechend, gemäß, laut* and *zufolge*, see 20.2.10e.

20.2.7 *seit*

seit is used only with reference to time, in the meaning of English 'since' (e.g. **seit** *dem achtzehnten Jahrhundert*) or 'for' (e.g. *Ich warte* **seit** *einer halben Stunde auf meine Schwester*), see 11.5.9. For the use of tenses in *seit* phrases, see 14.2.2 and 14.3.4a.

20.2.8 *von*

(a) *von* **indicates direction 'from' a place**

(i) In this sense, *von* is the opposite of *zu*, which indicates direction towards, see 20.2.9. For the difference between *von* and *aus* as equivalents of English 'from', see 20.2.1a:

Ich fuhr **von** Frankfurt nach München	*I travelled from Frankfurt to Munich*
Sie bekam einen Brief **von** mir	*She received a letter from me*
Sie kommt **von** ihrer Schwester	*She's coming from her sister's*
Ich wohne zehn Minuten **vom** Bahnhof (entfernt)	*I live ten minutes from the station*
Die Blätter fallen **von** den Bäumen	*The leaves are falling from the trees*

(ii) *von* can be strengthened by adding *aus* after the noun to emphasise the point of origin, e.g.:

Von meinem Fenster (**aus**) kann ich die Paulskirche sehen	*I can see St. Paul's church from my window*
Wir sind **von** Madrid (**aus**) mit der Bahn nach Barcelona gefahren	*We travelled by train from Madrid to Barcelona*

von . . . aus also occurs in a few idiomatic phrases:

Er war **von** Haus **aus** Lehrer	*He was originally a teacher*
von mir **aus**	*as far as I'm concerned*
von Natur **aus**	*by nature*

(iii) Direction from a point can be emphasised by adding *her* (see 7.2.3):

Eine Stimme kam **von** oben **her**	*A voice came from above*
Ich komme **von** meiner Schwester **her**	*I am coming from my sister's*

von . . . her is now commonly (and fashionably) used in the sense 'in respect of', 'from the point of view of', 'regarding'. In practice this represents a contraction of the phrase *von . . . her betrachtet*:

Von Beruf **her** ist er Schlosser	*As for his job, he's a mechanic*
Besonders raffiniert **von** der Farbe **her**	*Particularly subtle in respect of the colouring*
Von der Zielsetzung **her** sind wir der gleichen Meinung	*We're of the same opinion in respect of our objectives*

Occasionally, *her* is omitted in these contexts: *Von der Zielsetzung sind wir der gleichen Meinung.*

(b) *von* **also means 'from' referring to time**

It is often strengthened by *an* after the noun, e.g. *von neun Uhr (an)*, see 11.5.12.

(c) *von* **is used to introduce the agent in passive constructions**

See 15.3 for details about *von* with the passive, and on the distinction between *von* and *durch* as equivalents of English 'by'.

(d) **A phrase with** *von* **is often used in place of a genitive**

i.e. for English 'of', e.g. *ein Ereignis* **von** *weltgeschichtlicher Bedeutung*. This usage is covered in 2.4.

(e) *von* **has a wide range of figurative uses**

(i) It often corresponds to English 'of' in the sense of 'on the part of':

Das war sehr nett, liebenswürdig, vernünftig **von** ihr	*That was very nice, kind, sensible of her*
Das war doch dumm **von** mir	*That was silly of me, wasn't it?*
Er tat es **von** selbst	*He did it of his own accord*

(ii) Some common idiomatic phrases with *von*:

Das ist nicht von ungefähr passiert	*It didn't happen by accident*
Das kommt davon	*That's what comes of it*
Das gilt nicht von ihm	*That's not true of him*
Ich kenne sie nur vom Sehen	*I only know her by sight*
von ganzem Herzen	*with all my heart*

20.2.9 *zu*

(a) *zu* **expresses direction**

It is a common equivalent for English 'to', particularly:

(i) for going to a person('s house):

Er ging **zu** seinem Onkel, **zu** Müllers, **zum** Frisör.

NB: For 'at' (a person's house), *bei* is used, see 20.2.3.

(ii) for going to a place or an occasion:

Dieser Bus fährt **zum** Bahnhof	*This bus goes to the station*
Ich ging **zur** Kirche und wartete dort auf sie	*I went to the church and waited for her there*
Wir machten einen Ausflug **zum** Dorf	*We went on an outing to the village*
Sie kehrte **zu** ihrer Arbeit zurück	*She returned to her work*
eine Expedition **zum** Mond	*an expedition to the moon*
Sie geht morgen **zu** einem Kongress	*She's going to a conference tomorrow*

zu is the opposite of *von*, see 20.2.8a and puts the emphasis on the **general direction** rather than reaching the destination. For the distinction between it and the more specific prepositions *an*, *auf* or *in* (with the accusative) as an equivalent of English 'to', see 20.5.

zu can be strengthened by adding *hin* after the noun, see 7.2.3, e.g. *Sie ging zur Post (hin). Er blickte zur Decke (hin).* The effect is to emphasise the direction, so that *zu . . . hin* is a common equivalent for English 'towards'.

(iii) in some idiomatic phrases:

Sie sah **zum** Fenster/**zur** Tür **hinaus**	*She looked out of the window/the door*
Setzen Sie sich doch **zu** uns!	*Do come and join us*

(b) *zu* **sometimes refers to a place**

i.e. with the meaning of English 'at' or 'in'. This sense of *zu* used to be common, especially with names of towns, but it is now only used in elevated styles, as modern German prefers *in*:

J.S. Bach wurde **zu** (*more usually*: in) Eisenach geboren	*J.S. Bach was born in Eisenach*
der Dom **zu** Köln (*more usually*: der Kölner Dom)	*Cologne cathedral*

However, *zu* is still used in this sense in some common set phrases, e.g.:

zu Hause	*at home*
zu beiden Seiten	*on either side*

(c) *zu* **is used in certain time expressions**

See 11.5.15 for details. It usually corresponds to English 'at', e.g. *zu Ostern, zu dieser Zeit*.

(d) *zu* **is the usual equivalent of English 'for' to express purpose**

(i) Examples:

zu diesem Zweck	*for this purpose*
Das ist kein Anlass **zur** Klage	*That is no cause for complaint*
Was gibt es heute **zum** Nachtisch?	*What's for dessert today?*
Stoff **zu** einem neuen Anzug	*material for a new suit*
Zum Geburtstag hat er mir eine Uhr geschenkt	*He bought me a watch for my birthday*
Wir hatten keine Gelegenheit **zu** einem Gespräch	*We didn't have a chance for a talk*

The prepositional adverb *dazu* is commonly used in the sense of 'for that purpose', e.g. **Dazu** *soll man ein scharfes Messer gebrauchen.* Compare also *Wozu?* 'To what purpose?', 'What for?'.

(ii) In this sense, *zu* is very common with an infinitive used as a noun, or with other verbal nouns, where English uses 'for . . .ing' or an infinitive with 'to', see 13.4.3b and 13.7.2b. It is typical of written non-literary German, but it is by no means confined to that register.

Wozu gebraucht man dieses Messer? **Zum** Kartoffelschälen.	*What do you use this knife for? For peeling potatoes/To peel potatoes*
Hier gibt es viele Möglichkeiten **zum** Schilaufen	*There are lots of possibilities for skiing here*
Ich sage dir das **zu** deiner Beruhigung	*I'm telling you this to reassure you*

(iii) In certain contexts, this sense of *zu* approaches that of *als*, i.e. 'by way of', as:

Er murmelte etwas **zur** Antwort	*He muttered something by way of reply*
Er tat es mir **zu** Gefallen	*He did it as a favour to me*

Similarly:

zur Abwechslung	*for a change*	zum Scherz	*as a joke*
zum Andenken an	*in memory of*	zum Spaß	*as a joke*
zum Beispiel	*for example*	zur Strafe	*as a punishment*
zur Not	*if necessary, at a pinch*	zum Vergnügen	*for pleasure*

(e) In some contexts *zu* indicates a result or an effect

The English equivalent is most often 'to':

Zu meinem Erstaunen hat sie die Prüfung bestanden	*To my surprise she passed the exam*

Similarly:

zu meiner Befriedigung	*to my satisfaction*
zu meiner großen Freude	*to my great pleasure*
Es ist zum Lachen, zum Heulen, zum Verrücktwerden	*It is laughable, enough to make one weep, enough to drive one mad*

NB: *zu* commonly occurs in this sense in the prepositional object of many verbs, see 18.6.13a.

(f) *zu* can express a change of state

This usage is associated with a small number of verbs or nouns with appropriate meanings:

Sie wählten ihn **zum** Präsidenten	*They elected him President*
Er wurde **zum** Major befördert	*He was promoted to major*
Ich habe es mir **zur** Regel gemacht, dies zu tun	*I've made it a rule to do this*

Similarly with *bestimmen* 'destine to be', *degradieren* 'demote', *ernennen* 'appoint', *krönen* 'crown', *weihen* 'ordain', *werden* 'become' (see 18.8), etc. and the nouns *die Beförderung* 'promotion', *die Ernennung* 'appointment', *die Wahl* 'election', etc.

(g) *zu* can express a mental attitude towards someone or something

(i) This is frequent with adjectives, see 6.6.1, e.g.:

Sie war sehr freundlich **zu** mir	*She was very kind to me*

Similarly:

frech zu	*impudent towards*	nett zu	*nice to*
gut zu	*good, kind to*	respektvoll zu	*respectful to*
(un)höflich zu	*(im)polite to*	unfreundlich zu	*unkind to*

(ii) also with a number of nouns, e.g.:

Er hatte keine freundschaftlichen Beziehungen **zu** diesen Menschen	*He was not on friendly terms with these people*
ihre Einstellung **zur** Wiedervereinigung	*her attitude to reunification*
seine Liebe **zu** ihr	*his love for her*
das Verhältnis des Einzelnen **zum** Staat	*the relationship of the individual to the state*

gegen (see 20.1.4f) and *gegenüber* (see 20.2.4d) can also denote attitude towards or relations with someone or something. Whether *gegen* or *zu* is used depends on the particular noun or adjective, though *gegen* tends to occur with those which denote hostile attitudes, *zu* with those which denote friendly attitudes. A few adjectives can be used with either, e.g.:

gerecht zu/gegen	*fair, just to*	hart zu/gegen	*hard towards*
grausam zu/gegen	*cruel to*		

gegen is used with some nouns although the related adjective has *zu*, e.g. *die Frechheit, die Gerechtigkeit, die Grausamkeit, die Härte, die (Un)höflichkeit gegen jdn. gegenüber* is a common alternative to *gegen* or *zu* with most adjectives or nouns which occur with these prepositions, see 20.2.4.

(h) Uses of *zu* with numbers

(i) to indicate price or measure:

10 Stück Seife **zu** je 4 Euro	*10 bars of soap at 4 euros each*
5 Päckchen Kaffee **zu** hundert Gramm	*5 hundred gram packs of coffee*
zum halben Preis	*at half price*

Also with fractions, etc.: *zur Hälfte, zum Teil, zu einem Drittel fertig*

(ii) With the dative of the cardinal or the stem of the ordinal to indicate groups, e.g *zu zweien, zu zweit*, see 9.1.3b.

(iii) With the declined ordinal number for 'first(ly)', 'secondly', etc., e.g. *zum Ersten, zum Zweiten*, etc., see 9.2.3.

(i) Selected idiomatic uses of *zu*

jdn. zum Besten haben	*make a fool of sb.*
zu Boden fallen	*fall to the ground*
sich (dat.) etwas zu eigen machen	*adopt sth.*
zu Ende gehen	*draw to a close*
zu Fuß	*on foot*
jdn. zu Rate ziehen	*ask sb.'s advice*
jdn. zur Rechenschaft ziehen	*call sb. to account*
zur Sache kommen	*come to the point*
jdm. zur Seite stehen	*give sb. one's support*
zur Welt kommen	*be born*

20.2.10 **Less frequent prepositions governing the dative**

(a) *ab* 'from'

ab was originally restricted to commercial and official German, but has become common in all registers. The case use with *ab* varies. When referring to place, it is always used with the dative, but when referring to time, the accusative is used as frequently as the dative if no article follows.

(i) Referring to place, it is an alternative to *von*, but it emphasises the starting point more strongly:

Ab Jericho folgten wir einer langen Kolonne israelischer Touristenbusse (*Zeit*)	*From Jericho we followed a long convoy of Israeli tourist buses*
Dieser Sondertarif gilt **ab** allen deutschen Flughäfen	*This special fare applies from all airports in Germany*
ab Fabrik	*ex works*

(ii) For the use of *ab* in time phrases, e.g. *ab heute* 'from today', see 11.5.1

(b) *binnen* indicates a period of time (= 'within')

It is used mainly in formal registers to avoid the potential ambiguity of *in*, see 11.5.7:

binnen einem Jahr, drei Jahren	*within a year, three years*
binnen kurzem	*shortly*

NB: (i) In formal registers *binnen* is occasionally used with a following genitive, e.g. *binnen eines Jahres*.
(ii) In Switzerland *innert* is commonly used for *binnen*, with a following dative or (occasionally) a genitive, e.g. *innert einem/ eines Jahres*.

(c) *dank* 'thanks to'

It is mainly found in formal German and is often used with a genitive, especially with a following plural noun:

dank seinem Einfluss/seines Einflusses	*thanks to his influence*
dank seiner Sprachkenntnisse	*thanks to his knowledge of languages*

(d) *entgegen* 'contrary to'

It can occur before or (rather less frequently) after the noun:

entgegen allen Erwartungen/allen Erwartungen **entgegen**	*contrary to all expectations*

In writing, *entgegen* is occasionally used with a genitive. This is not (yet) regarded as correct.

(e) *entsprechend, gemäß, laut, zufolge* 'according to'

These prepositions are used chiefly in formal German. They all mean 'according to', as does the more frequent *nach*, see. 20.2.6d, but they are not interchangeable in all contexts. It is not uncommon to see *entsprechend* and *gemäß* used with a genitive in writing. This is not (yet) regarded as correct:

(i) *entsprechend* means 'in accordance with'. It can precede or (more commonly) follow the noun:

unseren Anordnungen **entsprechend**/ **entsprechend** unseren Anordnungen	*in accordance with our instructions*

(ii) *gemäß* usually follows the noun, but occasionally precedes it. It means 'in accordance with':

Die Maschine wurde den Anweisungen **gemäß** in Betrieb gesetzt	*The machine was put into operation in accordance with the instructions*

(iii) *laut* introduces a verbatim report of something said or written. It is commonly used without a following article, see 4.9.3:

Laut Berichten soll der Präsident neue Verhandlungen vorgeschlagen haben	*According to reports the president has proposed fresh negotiations*
laut Gesetz	*according to the law*
laut Angela Merkel	*according to Angela Merkel*

If the following noun has an article (or an adjective) with it, *laut* often governs the genitive rather than the dative:

laut des Berichtes/dem Bericht aus Berlin	*according to the report from Berlin*
laut neuer Berichte/neuen Berichten	*according to recent reports*
laut ämtlichem Nachweis/ämtlichen Nachweises	*according to an official attestation*

(iv) *zufolge* follows the noun. In accepted usage it indicates a consequence:

Dem Vertrag **zufolge** werden nun große Mengen von Rohöl geliefert	*In accordance with the contract large quantities of crude oil are now being delivered*

zufolge is also used where there is no sense of a consequence or a result:.

unbestätigen Berichten **zufolge**	*according to unconfirmed reports*
einem Regierungssprecher **zufolge**	*according to a government spokesman*

The use of *zufolge* with a following noun in the genitive, e.g. *zufolge des Vertrages*, is now obsolete and *infolge* (+ gen.) is used instead.

(f) *fern* 'far from' is restricted to elevated registers

It can occur before or (rather less frequently) after the noun:

Sie blieben **fern** der Heimat/der Heimat **fern**	*They remained far from home*
Europa liegt immer noch **fern** dem britischen Horizont (*Zeit*)	*Europe is still far removed from British horizons*

In practice, *fern von* or *weit von* are more frequent for English 'far from'.

(g) *mitsamt* and *samt* 'together with'

These are restricted to elevated styles and are sometimes seen with a following genitive in writing. The usual equivalent for 'together with' is *zusammen mit*, or often simply *mit*:

Ich fahre dich **mitsamt** dem Fahrrad nach Hause (H. Fischer)	*I'll drive you home together with your bike.*

(h) *nahe* 'near (to)' is used chiefly in formal registers

ein altes Haus **nahe** dem freien Feld (*FR*)	*an old house near the open field*

When used in an abstract sense *nahe* commonly follows the noun:

Sie war der Verzweiflung **nahe**   *She was close to despair*

(i) *nebst* 'together with', 'in addition to' occurs in formal registers

eine gut gekühlte Flasche Champagner nebst dem nötigen Zubehör (R. Müller)

(j) *per* 'per', 'by'

per was originally only used in commercial language, but it is used increasingly in spoken and other less formal registers. When used with a means of transport it is an alternative to more usual *mit*, see 20.2.5b:

per Post (= mit der Post)	*by post*
per Bahn (= mit der Bahn)	*by rail*
per Luftfracht	*by air*
per Einschreiben	*by recorded mail*
per Adresse (p.A.)	*c/o*
per Anhalter fahren	*to hitchhike*
mit jdm. per du sein	*be on first-name terms with sb.*
Sie bezahlen erst per 31. Dezember	*You do not pay until 31 December*
Die Waren sind per 1. Mai bestellt	*The goods are ordered for 1 May*

As *per* is most often used without a following adjective or determiner, the case it governs is often not obvious. This has given rise to uncertainty, and in practice, when a case is clear, *per* is actually seen to be used with the accusative as well as the dative, e.g. *per zweiten/zweitem Bildungsweg*. Either usage is regarded as correct.

(k) *zuliebe* 'for the sake of' follows the noun it governs

Ich habe es meiner Mutter **zuliebe** getan	*I did it for my mother's sake*
Dir **zuliebe** gibt es Spargel	*Just for you, we're having asparagus*
wahrscheinlich dem Wald **zuliebe** (Walser)	*probably for the sake of the forest*

(l) *zuwider* 'contrary to' follows the noun it governs

It is an emphatic alternative to *gegen* in formal registers:

Karl handelte seinem Befehl **zuwider**   *Karl acted contrary to his order*

20.3 Prepositions governing the accusative or the dative case

Ten prepositions govern the accusative *or* the dative, i.e.:

an	auf	entlang	hinter	in
neben	über	unter	vor	zwischen

General rules governing the use of the two cases are given in 20.3.1, and the individual prepositions are dealt with in the following sections. For the more common ones (i.e. *an, auf, in, über, unter* and *vor*) the use with the accusative and the dative is treated separately.

20.3.1 **These prepositions govern the accusative case if they express direction, but the dative if they express position**

It is often claimed that the accusative case is used with these prepositions when motion is involved, but it is more precise to say that the **accusative case** is used with a phrase expressing the **direction** in which someone or something is moving or being put.

Ich hänge das Bild an **die** Wand	*I'm hanging the picture on the wall*
Das Bild hängt an **der** Wand	*The picture is hanging on the wall*
Wir gingen in **dieses** Zimmer hinein	*We went into this room*
Wir essen in **diesem** Zimmer	*We eat in this room*

In some contexts the reason for the choice of case is less obvious, or usage is variable:

(a) Even if direction is involved, the dative case is used if there is no movement in relation to the person or thing denoted by the following noun

Er ging neben **seiner** Frau	*He was walking next to his wife*
Er ging zwischen **seinen** Eltern	*He was walking between his parents*
(His position is constant in relation to his wife or his parents)	
Ein Flugzeug kreiste über **der** Stadt	*A plane was circling over the town*
(Though it was moving, it stayed over the town)	

Usage where two prepositional phrases occur in the same sentence with a verb of motion follows the basic principle, e.g.: *Elke legte sich auf* **eine** *Bank* **im** *Schatten hin*. Elke is moving in the direction of the bench, but the bench is stationary in relation to the shadow.

(b) The dative is usual with verbs of arriving, appearing and disappearing

German does not consider that such verbs indicate a direction:

Sie kamen **am** Bahnhof an	*They arrived at the station*
Sie landeten auf **dem** Mond	*They landed on the moon*
Er kroch unter **dem** Tisch hervor	*He crept out from under the table*
Sie erschien hinter **der** Theke	*She appeared behind the counter*
Der Reiter verschwand hinter **dem** Berg	*The horseman disappeared behind the hill*
Sie verbarg sich unter **der** Decke	*She hid under the sheet*

Occasionally with these verbs the sense of movement in a particular direction may be felt so strongly that the accusative <u>is</u> used, e.g. *Er verschwand über* **das** *Dach*. Nevertheless, this is quite infrequent.

(c) In a few contexts, these prepositions are used with the accusative after a simple verb, but with the dative after a related prefixed verb

With the prefixed verbs, the action is seen as already completed, whereas with the simple verbs it is visualised as continuing:

(an/fest)binden *tie, fasten*
    Das Pferd war an **einen** Baum gebunden
    Das Pferd war an **einem** Baum an-/festgebunden

(vor)fahren *drive up*
    Der Wagen fuhr vor **den** Bahnhof
    Der Wagen fuhr vor **dem** Schloss vor

(auf)hängen *hang (up)*
    Sie hängte das Bild an **die** Wand
    Sie hängte das Bild an **der** Wand auf

sich (fest)klammern *cling to*
 Er klammerte sich an **sie**
 Er klammerte sich an **ihr** fest

sich (nieder)legen, -setzen *lie, sit down*
 Sie legte/setzte sich auf **die** Bank
 Sie legte/setzte sich auf **der** Bank nieder

(auf)schreiben *write (down)*
 Ich schrieb ihre Adresse in **mein** Notizbuch
 Ich schrieb ihre Adresse in **meinem** Notizbuch auf

(d) Usage with verbs with the prefix *ein-*

(i) These verbs are often used with *in*, usually followed by a noun phrase in the accusative case:

Sie stieg in **den** Zug ein   Wir weihten ihn in **das** Geheimnis ein
Ich trug den Namen in **die** Liste ein   Er wickelte sich in **eine** Decke ein

(ii) A noun in the accusative case is used even in the *sein*-passive, although here usage is variable:

Er war in **eine** Reisedecke eingehüllt   Sie ist in **das** Geheimnis eingeweiht
Sein Name war in **die/der** Liste eingetragen

(iii) *sich einschließen* is used with either case depending on whether the movement in a particular direction is emphasised: *Sie schloss sich in **ihr/ihrem** Zimmer ein.*

(iv) *sich einfinden, einkehren* and *eintreffen* are followed by a preposition with a noun phrase in the dative case, as they denote arrival (see (a) above):

Wir trafen in **der** Hauptstadt ein   *We arrived in the capital*
Sie kehrten in **einer** Gaststätte ein   *They turned in at an inn*

(e) With a few verbs usage is idiomatic

In the main these are verbs which do not denote movement as such. The choice of case depends on how native speakers envisage the action, and it can vary. If no preposition is indicated in the examples below, the verb is commonly used with more than one (e.g. *sehen*, which occurs with *an, auf, in*, etc.)

(i) A noun phrase in the dative case is usual in conjunction with the following verbs:

anbringen *fix*   befestigen an *fasten*   drucken *print*   notieren *note*

(ii) A noun phrase in the accusative case is usual in conjunction with the following verbs:

anbauen an	*build on to*	kleiden in	*clothe in*	verteilen	*distribute*
anschließen	*add on*	münden in	*flow into*	vertieft in	*engrossed in*
gebeugt über	*bent over*	sehen, schauen	*look*	verwickelt in	*involved in*
grenzen an	*border on*	stützen auf	*support*		

(f) The dative and the accusative have different meanings with a few verbs

aufnehmen   A noun phrase in the accusative case implies complete acceptance; in the dative case it implies that the acceptance is temporary:

Er ist **in den** Chor aufgenommen worden   *He was admitted into the choir*
Ich wurde **in seiner** Familie sehr   *I was amicably received in his family*
 freundlich aufgenommen

einführen If there is an idea of direction, a noun phrase in the accusative case is used, whereas a noun phrase in the dative puts the stress on the place:

Waren **in ein** Land einführen (i.e. **nach** Italien)	*import goods into a country*
Er will die Sitte **in diesem** Land einführen (i.e. **in** Italien)	*He wants to introduce the custom in that country*

halten If the gesture is emphasised, a noun phrase in the accusative is used; a noun phrase in the dative emphasises the position:

Er hielt das Buch in **die** Höhe	*He held the book up in the air*
Er hielt das Buch in **der** Hand	*He held the book in his hand*

klopfen A noun phrase in the accusative is the norm, but in the context of knocking on doors, etc., the dative can be used if the emphasis is on the place rather than the action:

Er klopfte **an die** Tür/**auf den** Tisch	*He knocked on the door/the table*
Da klopfte es **an der** Haustür (i.e. the front door rather than somewhere else)	*There was a knock at the front door*

schreiben A noun phrase in the accusative case refers to the action of writing down; the dative case is used if the place where something is written is uppermost:

Er schrieb es **in sein** Heft	*He wrote it (down) in his notebook*
In seinem Brief schreibt er, dass . . .	*He writes in his letter that . . .*

(g) In contexts where these prepositions do not have their literal meaning, they are used only or predominantly with a single case

In idiomatic uses, *auf* and *über* are used only with the accusative, all the other prepositions mainly with the dative. This is particularly evident where these prepositions are used to refer to time, see 11.5, where they are used in prepositional objects, see 18.6, with adjectives, see 6.6, and in all other contexts where they are not used in their literal senses.

20.3.2 *an* (+ dative)

(a) The basic meaning of *an* with the dative is 'on (the side of)'

(i) This contrasts with *auf* (+ dat.), which means 'on (top of)'. *an* (+ dat.) can correspond to English 'on', or, if the person or thing is not actually touching, 'at', 'by' or 'along'. See 20.2.3a for the distinction between *an* (+ dat.) and *bei* in the sense of 'at':

Das Bild hing **an** der Wand	*The picture was hanging on the wall*
am Berg (compare: *auf* dem Berg 'on the mountain-top')	*on the mountain(side)*
An der Grenze wird kontrolliert	*There's a check at the border*
Wir warteten **an** der Bushaltestelle	*We were waiting at/by the bus stop*
am Fluss (compare: *auf* dem Fluss 'on the river' (i.e. in a boat))	*on the river(side)*
Ich stand **am** Fenster	*I was standing by/at the window*
Sie wohnt **am** See	*She lives by the lake*

(ii) *an* (+ dat.) is also used for 'on (the underside of)':

Die Lampe hängt **an** der Decke	*The lamp was hanging from the ceiling*
am Himmel (compare: *im* Himmel 'in heaven')	*in the sky*

(iii) In older German, *an* was often used in the sense of 'down on', and this is still apparent in phrases like *am Boden, an der Erde* 'on the ground', where *auf* is a possible alternative. Compare also *am Strand* 'on the beach', *am Ufer* 'on the bank', etc.

(iv) *an* (+ dat) is used in three phrases in conjunction with an adverb following the noun. In all these the dative is used since, although movement is involved, there is no indication of direction.

With a following *hin*, see 7.2.3, *an* expresses movement alongside:

Sie gingen **an** der Mauer **hin**	*They were walking along the wall*

an (+ dat.) . . . *vorbei* means 'past':

Wir gingen **an** seinem Haus **vorbei**	*We walked past his house*

an (+ dat.) . . . *entlang* means 'along', see 20.3.6c.

(b) *an* (+ dat.) is used with academic and other institutions at which a person is employed

Sie lehrt **an** der Universität Augsburg	*She teaches at the University of Augsburg*
Er ist Intendant **am** Staatstheater	*He is director at the State Theatre*
Er ist Pfarrer **an** der Peterskirche	*He is the pastor at St. Peter's*

(c) *an* (+ dat.) is used in a number of time expressions

In particular with dates and days of the week, e.g. *am Dienstag, **am** 31. August*, see 11.5.2.

(d) *an* (+ dat.) is used with many nouns, adjectives and verbs meaning 'in respect of', 'in connection with'

Further details of the use of *an* in this sense with adjectives are given in 6.6.1. For its use in the prepositional object of verbs, see 18.6.2a.

Der Bedarf **an** Arbeitskräften verringert sich	*The demand for labour is decreasing*
Wir haben mehrere Millionen Euros **an** Aufträgen vorliegen	*We have several million euros worth of orders on the books*
Sie hat etwas Eigenartiges **an** sich	*There's something strange about her*
Das Schönste **an** der Sache ist, dass . . .	*The best thing about it is that . . .*

an (+ dat.) often indicates the feature **by** which one recognises or notices something:

Ich bemerkte **an** seinem Benehmen, dass . . .	*I noticed from his behaviour that . . .*
Sie erkannte ihn **an** seinem Bart	*She recognised him by his beard*

(e) *an* (+ dat.) indicates a partially completed action

This often provides a way of indicating progressive action, see 14.6.2d:

Sie strickt **an** einem Pullover	*She's knitting a pullover*
Er arbeitet **an** seiner Dissertation	*He's working on his thesis*

(f) Other uses of *an* (+ dat.)

(i) *am* is used to form the superlative of adverbs and predicate adjectives, e.g. *am schönsten, am einfachsten*, see 8.4.1.

(ii) *am* is used colloquially with the infinitive to express a continuous action, e.g. *Sie ist am Schreiben*, see 14.6.2c.

20.3.3 *an* (+ accusative)

(a) *an* (+ acc.) **indicates direction if the destination is** *an* **(+ dat.)**

i.e. in contexts where the ultimate goal of the person or thing will be a position 'on', 'at' or 'by' something.

(i) It most often corresponds to English 'to' (see 20.5.1c) or 'on':

Sie hängte das Bild **an** die Wand	*She hung the picture on the wall*
Sie fuhr **an** die Küste	*She drove to the coast*

Similarly:

Ich ging **ans** Fenster, **an** die Tür, **an** seinen Platz
Er kam **an** die Bushaltestelle, **an** den Waldrand

(ii) The idea of right up to somebody or something can be indicated by adding *heran*, see 7.2.4b. e.g.:

Sie trat **an** mich, **an** den Tisch **heran**	*She walked up to me, to the table*

(iii) *an* occurs commonly with the person to whom one addresses something:

Er richtete diese Frage **an** mich	*He addressed this question to me*
eine Bitte **an** den Bundeskanzler	*a request to the Federal Chancellor*
Ich werde mich **an** ihn um Rat wenden	*I shall turn to him for advice*

(b) Verbal nouns from verbs which take a dative usually govern *an* **(+ acc.)**

See 18.4. The dative object of the verb appears in a prepositional phrase with *an*:

die Anpassung **an** die neuen Verhältnisse	*adaptation to new circumstances*
Compare: *Er passt sich **den neuen Verhältnissen** an.*	
sein Befehl **an** die Truppen	*his order to the troops*
Compare: *Er befahl **den Truppen** . . .*	

Similarly:

eine Antwort **an** mich	ein Bericht **an** die Akademie
viele Grüße **an** Onkel Robert	die Kriegserklärung **an** Japan
der Verkauf des Hauses **an** meinen Sohn	sein Vermächtnis **an** seine Tochter

NB: For the use of *an* (+ acc.) in this sense with verbs in place of a dative, see 18.4.2d.

(c) *an* **(+ acc.) is used to indicate indefinite quantity**

Er verdient **an die** 5000 im Monat	*He earns getting on for 5000 a month*

an in this sense is often followed by the definite article. A following adjective has **strong** endings: *an die vierzig **ausländische** Gäste*.

(d) Some idiomatic uses of *an* **(+ acc.)**

etwas ans Licht, an den Tag bringen	*bring sth. to light*
an (und für) sich	*actually*
die Erinnerung an seine Jugend	*the memory of his youth*
der Glaube an den Sieg	*the belief in victory*

NB: For the use of *an* (+ acc.) in prepositional objects with verbs denoting mental processes, see 18.6.2b.

20.3.4 *auf* (+ dative)

(a) The basic meaning of *auf* (+ dat.) is 'on (top of)'

For the distinction between *auf* and *an* (+ dat.), see 20.3.2a.

Das Buch liegt **auf** dem Tisch	*The book is lying on the table*
Sie sind **auf** dem Mond gelandet	*They landed on the moon*
Die Katze spielt **auf** dem Rasen	*The cat is playing on the lawn*
auf dem Weg nach Stuttgart	*on the way to Stuttgart*

(b) *auf* (+ dat.) is used for English 'at' or 'in' in some contexts

(i) for formal occasions, e.g. weddings, conferences, parties, etc.:

Ich traf sie **auf** einem Empfang	*I met her at a reception*
Wir lernten uns **auf** ihrer Hochzeit kennen	*We met at their wedding*
Sie ist **auf** einer Tagung	*She's at a conference*

bei is a common alternative to *auf* in this sense, but there may be a slight difference in meaning, see 20.2.3b.

(ii) with a few other nouns, where idiomatic usage may differ from English:

Die Schafe sind **auf** der Wiese	*The sheep are in the meadow*
Er ist **auf** seinem Zimmer	*He is (up) in his room*
auf dem Land(e)	*in the country*
Die Kinder spielten **auf** der Straße	*The children were playing in the street*

NB: *in* (+ dat.) is used to refer to a particular street, e.g. *Wir wohnen in der Schillerstraße.*

Similarly:

auf dem (Bauern)hof	*on the farm*	auf dem Gang	*in the corridor*
auf ihrer Bude	*in her bedsit*	auf seinem Gut	*on his estate*
auf dem Feld	*in the field*	auf dem Hof	*in the yard*
auf dem Flur	*in the (entrance) hall*	auf der Toilette	*on the toilet*

(iii) with a few nouns denoting public buildings and places. With several of these, *auf* is nowadays going out of use (although it is often still current in Austria). The preposition which is more often used nowadays is given in brackets:

auf dem Bahnhof (an)	auf dem Markt(platz)	auf dem Rathaus (in)
auf der Bank (in)	auf der Post	auf der Universität (an)
auf der Bibliothek (in)		

(c) Some idiomatic uses of *auf* (+ dat.)

blind auf einem Auge	*blind in one eye*
Das hat nichts/viel auf sich	*There's nothing/a lot to that*
etwas auf dem Herzen haben	*have sth. on one's mind*
Sie liefen auf dem Feld herum	*They were running all over the field*
auf der anderen Seite	*on the other hand*
auf der Stelle	*immediately*

20.3.5 *auf* (+ accusative)

(a) *auf* **(+ acc.) indicates direction if the destination is** *auf* **(+ dat)**

i.e. in contexts where the ultimate goal of the person or thing will be a position 'on (top of)' or 'at' something.

(i) *auf* (+ acc.) usually corresponds to English 'on(to)':

Sie legte das Buch **auf** den Tisch	*She put the book on the table*
Die Katze sprang **auf** das Dach	*The cat leapt onto the roof*

(ii) Where German uses *auf* (+ dat.) for English 'at' or 'in', *auf* (+ acc.) usually corresponds to English 'into' or 'to':

Wir gingen **auf** das Feld	*We went into the field*
Er ging **auf** sein Zimmer	*He went (up) to his room*
Er geht **auf** die Toilette	*He's going to the toilet*

For further details on this use of *auf* (+ acc.) see 20.5.1b.

(iii) *auf* (+ acc.) . . . *zu* indicates direction (i.e. = 'towards'):

Sie kam **auf** mich **zu**	*She came towards me/approached me*
Sie ging **auf** die Tore des Friedhofs **zu**	*She went towards the cemetery gates*

(b) *auf* **(+ acc.) indicates a period of time extending from 'now'**

e.g. *Ich fahre auf vier Wochen in die Schweiz.* For details see 11.5.3. The prepositional adverb *darauf* is used in the sense of 'after(wards)', see 11.6.4b, e.g. *am Tag darauf* 'the day after'.

NB: *auf* (+ acc.) is similarly used to indicate a distance **from** here, e.g.: *Kurven auf fünf Kilometer* 'bends for 5 kilometres'.

(c) *auf* **(+ acc.) is used after a large number of adjectives and verbs**

e.g. *Sie ist neidisch auf ihn. Ich wartete vor dem Bahnhof auf sie.* For the use of *auf* with adjectives, see 6.6.1, with verbs in prepositional objects, see 18.6.3a.

(d) *auf* **(+ acc.) can denote 'in response to', 'as a result of'**

In this sense it is often strengthened by a following *hin*, see 7.2.3c:

Auf meine Bitte (**hin**) hat er die Sache für sich behalten	*At my request he kept the matter to himself*
Er hat sofort **auf** meinen Brief **hin** gehandelt	*He acted immediately following my letter*

Similarly:

auf Anfrage	*on application*
auf meine Empfehlung (hin)	*on my recommendation*
auf einen Verdacht hin	*on the strength of a suspicion*
auf Wunsch, auf meinen Wunsch (hin)	*by request, at my request*
daraufhin	*as a result, thereupon*

(e) Other uses of *auf* **(+ acc.)**

(i) with languages:

Sie hat mir **auf Deutsch** geantwortet	*She answered me in German*

in (+ dat.) is also used, especially with extended phrases:

Er hält seine Vorlesungen **in Deutsch/auf Deutsch**	*He gives his lectures in German*
Er sagte es **in gebrochenem Deutsch**	*He said it in broken German*
Wie heißt das **in Ihrer Sprache**?	*What's that called in your language?*

(ii) to form absolute superlatives, e.g. *aufs angenehmste/Angenehmste*. See 8.4.3 for further details.

(iii) Some common idiomatic expressions with *auf*:

jdn. auf den Arm (S.G.)/auf die Schippe (N.G.) nehmen	*pull somebody's leg*
etwas auf die lange Bank schieben	*put sth. off*
auf den ersten Blick	*at first sight*
Das kommt, läuft auf dasselbe hinaus	*It comes down to the same thing*
auf jeden Fall, auf alle Fälle	*in any case*
auf eigene Gefahr	*at one's own risk*
auf eigene Kosten	*at one's own expense*
jdm. auf die Nerven gehen, auf den Wecker gehen, fallen	*get on somebody's nerves*
Das geht auf meine Rechnung	*This one's on me*
auf diese Weise	*in this way*

20.3.6 *entlang*

entlang (often shortened to *lang* in colloquial speech in North Germany) corresponds to English 'along'. There is much variation in its use, both in respect of the position of the noun and the case used with it.

(a) Indicating position alongside an extended object

The most frequent usage in this meaning is *entlang* followed by a noun phrase in the dative case:

im Sommer, wenn **entlang den** Boulevards und in den Vorgärten Rosen blühen (*Zeit*)	*in summer when roses are blooming along the boulevards and in the front gardens*
Bäume standen **entlang der** Bahnlinie	*Trees stood along the railway line*

Alternatively, *entlang* is often used in written German with a following noun phrase in the genitive case to express position:

die Uferpromenade **entlang des** Rheins (*MM*)	*the promenade along the bank of the Rhine*

Very occasionally, *entlang* follows a noun phrase in the dative or accusative case to express position:

die Straße, die Mussolini **der Küste entlang** gebaut hat (*Grzimek*)	*the road which Mussolini built along the coast*
Flaschen und Gläser standen **die lange Tafel entlang** (*Welt*)	*Bottles and glasses were standing along the long table*

(b) Indicating movement alongside an extended object, or down the middle of a road or river

The most frequent usage in this meaning is for *entlang* to **follow** a noun phrase in the **accusative** case:

Gehst du die Reihen der Maschinen
  entlang (*ND*)
Sie gingen den Bach **entlang**
Sie hastete den Flur **entlang** bis zum
  Ende des Ganges (*Johnson*)

If you walk along the rows of machines

They were walking along the stream
She hurried along the entrance hall
  to the end of the corridor

In Swiss usage, *entlang* can follow a noun phrase in the dative case in this meaning:

Wir flogen gar nicht der Küste **entlang**
  (*Frisch*)

We were not flying along the coast at all

(c) *an* **(+ dat.)** *. . . entlang* **is a common alternative to simple** *entlang*

It can be used with reference to position or movement alongside an extended object, but not for 'down the middle' of roads, rivers, etc.:

Da gab es **an** der nördlichen
  Friedhofsmauer **entlang** den Bittweg
  (*Grass*)
Er steuerte **am** Ufer **entlang**, bis die
  Stelle gefunden war (*Frisch*)

Along the north wall of the cemetery
  was the Bittweg

He steered along the bank until he
  had found the spot

(d) Alternatives to *entlang* **in the meaning 'along'**

entlang is used much less frequently than English *along*, and the following are common equivalents:

(i) *an* (+ dat.), see 20.3.2a, often appears in contexts where English naturally uses 'along', e.g.:

An der Küste war das Wetter schön

The weather was fine along the coast

an (+ dat.) *. . . hin* can refer to movement alongside something, especially when one is very close to it or in contact with it:

Sie ging **an der Mauer hin**
Er rutschte **am Boden hin**

She went along the wall
He slid along the floor

(ii) *längs*, see 20.4.3, only expresses position. It governs a following genitive or (less commonly) a dative, e.g. *längs der Küste, längs des Flusses/dem Fluss*.

20.3.7 *hinter*

(a) *hinter* **is used to refer to place and usually corresponds to English 'behind' or 'beyond'**

(i) Used with a following noun phrase in the dative case, *hinter* indicates position:

Der Wagen steht **hinter** der Garage
Ich habe das Schlimmste **hinter** mir
100 Kilometer **hinter** der Grenze

The car is behind the garage
I've got the worst behind me
100 kilometres beyond the border

(ii) Used with a following noun phrase in the accusative case, *hinter* indicates direction:

Er fuhr den Wagen **hinter** die Garage
Sie trieben ihn **hinter** die Kirche

He drove the car round the back of the garage
They drove him round the back of the church

(b) To indicate movement in relation to another person or thing, *hinter* **is used with** *her*

See also 7.2.3b. The noun phrase is always in the dative case:

Er rannte **hinter** ihr **her**	*He was running after her*
Ich ging **hinter** meinen Eltern **her**	*I was walking behind my parents*

(c) *hinter* **is used in a few idiomatic expressions**

Ich konnte nicht dahinter kommen	*I couldn't get to the bottom of it*
Es muss etwas dahinter stecken	*There must be something in it*
Schreib dir das hinter die Ohren!	*Will you get that into your thick head!*

20.3.8 *in* (+ dative)

(a) The basic meaning of *in* **(+ dat) is 'in(side)'**

Sie ist **im** Haus/**im** Freien/**in** der Kirche/**im** Kino/**in** der Stadt/ **im** Wald/**im** Tal/**in** ihrem Zimmer	*She is in the house/in the open air/in the church/in the cinema/in town in the forest/in the valley/in her room*
Sie sind **in** Bremen/**in** Deutschland/ **in** der Schweiz/**im** Ausland	*They are in Bremen/in Germany/in Switzerland/abroad*
Die Milch ist **im** Kühlschrank	*The milk is in the fridge*
Die Sonne geht **im** Westen unter	*The sun sets in the west*

NB: In colloquial German, *in* is often strengthened by adding *drin*, e.g.: *Die sind in der Hütte drin.*

In some contexts, German usage is at variance with English, e.g.:

Ihr Büro ist **im** vierten Stock	*Her office is on the fourth floor*
Das habe ich **im** Fernsehen gesehen/ **im** Radio gehört	*I saw it on the television/heard it on the radio*

In particular, German uses *in* with reference to attendance at public buildings and the like, where English often uses 'at':

Die Kinder sind heute **in** der Schule	*The children are at school today*
Meine Eltern sind **in** der Kirche	*My parents are at church*
Elke ist **im** Kino/**im** Theater/**in** einem Konzert/**im** Rathaus/**in** der Bibliothek	*Elke is at the cinema/at the theatre/at a concert/at the town hall/at the library*

(b) *in* **(+ dat.) indicates a period of time**

e.g. *In drei Wochen sind wir wieder da.* Full details are given in 11.5.8.

(c) Some common idiomatic phrases with *in* **(+ dat.)**

in der Absicht, etwas zu tun	*with the intention of doing something*
im Allgemeinen	*in general*
Ist dein Chef im Bilde?	*Is your boss in the picture?*
im Durchschnitt	*on average*
nicht im Geringsten/Entferntesten	*not in the slightest*
in dieser Hinsicht	*in this respect*
in gewissem Maße	*to a certain extent*
in dieser Weise (*also*: **auf diese** Weise)	*in this way*
in diesem Zusammenhang	*in this context*

20.3.9 *in* (+ accusative)

(a) *in* **(+ acc.) indicates direction if the destination is *in* (+ dat.)**

i.e. in contexts where the ultimate goal of the person or thing will be a position 'in(side)' something.

(i) *in* often corresponds to English 'into':

Sie ging **ins** Haus/**in** die Kirche/**in** den Wald/**in** das Tal/**in** ihr Zimmer	*She went into the house/the church/ the forest/the valley/her room*
Ich habe die Milch **in** den Kühlschrank gestellt	*I put the milk in the fridge*

NB: With *Richtung* the accusative or the dative case are equally acceptable: *in diese/dieser Richtung.*

(ii) *in* is a common equivalent of English 'to', if, on arrival, one will be <u>in</u> the place concerned, see 20.5.1a:

Sie ging **in** ein Konzert/**ins** Kino/ **in** den vierten Stock	*She went to a concert/to the cinema/to the fourth floor*
Wir sind **in** die Schweiz/**ins** Ausland gefahren	*We went to Switzerland/abroad*
Die Kinder gehen heute **in** die Schule	*The children are going to school today*

(b) Some frequent idiomatic phrases with *in* (+ acc.):

Der Vorteil springt ins Auge	*The advantage is obvious*
sich in Bewegung setzen	*begin to move*
mit jdm. ins Gespräch kommen	*get into conversation with sb.*
aus dem Französischen ins Deutsche übersetzen	*translate from French into German*

20.3.10 *neben*

(a) *neben* **is most often used with reference to place, corresponding to English 'next to' or 'beside':**

(i) Used with a following dative case, *neben* indicates position:

Die Blumen standen **neben** dem Schrank	*The flowers were next to the cupboard*
Er saß **neben** seiner Frau	*He was sitting next to his wife*

(ii) Used with a following accusative case, *neben* indicates direction. It can be strengthened by adding *hin*, see 7.2.3a:

Er stellte die Blumen **neben** den Schrank (hin)	*He put the flowers (down) next to the cupboard*
Er setzte sich **neben** seine Frau (hin)	*He sat down next to his wife*

(b) To indicate relation of movement to another person or thing moving in the same direction, *neben* **is used with a following** *her*

See also 7.2.3b. The noun phrase is always in the dative case:

Er ging **neben** seiner Frau **her**	*He was walking next to his wife*

(c) *neben* **(+ dat.) can be used in the sense of 'besides', 'apart from'**

Its sense is close to that of *außer*, see 20.2.2a:

Neben zwei Franzosen waren alle Anwesenden aus Deutschland	*Apart from two Frenchmen all those present were from Germany*

(d) *neben* **(+ dat.) can be used to express a comparison**

It is a common alternative to *gegen* or *gegenüber*, see 20.2.4c:

Neben ihrer Mutter ist sie groß	*She's tall compared with her mother*

(e) The prepositional adverb *daneben* is used with verbs to express the idea of failing to hit a target

daneben is usually interpreted as a separable prefix, see 22.5.2, and written together with the verb:

Er hat danebengeschossen	*He shot wide of the mark*
Sie hat sich danebenbenommen	*She behaved quite abominably*

20.3.11 *über* (+ dative)

With a following noun phrase in the dative case, *über* is only used to refer to position. It corresponds to English 'over', 'above' or, in certain contexts, 'across' or 'beyond':

Das Bild hängt **über** meinem Tisch	*The picture hangs over my desk*
Briançon liegt 1400 Meter **über** dem Meeresspiegel	*Briançon lies 1400 metres above sea level*
Der Baum lag mir (quer) **über** dem Weg	*The tree lay across my path*
Er wohnt **über** der Grenze	*He lives over/across the border*
Sie wohnt **über** dem See	*She lives across/beyond the lake*

20.3.12 *über* (+ accusative)

(a) *über* **(+ acc.) indicates movement over a person or object**

über corresponds to English 'above', 'over', 'across' or (with reference to a journey) 'via':

Sie hängte das Bild **über** meinen Tisch	*She hung the picture over/above my desk*
Wir gingen **über** die Straße	*We crossed the road*
die neue Brücke **über** den Inn	*the new bridge over/across the Inn*
Der Baum fiel uns (quer) **über** den Weg	*The tree fell across our path*
Er ist **über** die Grenze geflüchtet	*He fled over the border*
Es lief mir eiskalt **über** den Rücken	*An ice-cold shiver went down my back*
Wir sind **über** die Schweiz nach Italien gefahren	*We drove to Italy through Switzerland*
Dieser Zug fährt nach Stralsund **über** Rostock	*This train goes to Stralsund via Rostock*
Der Kaiser herrschte **über** viele Länder	*The emperor ruled over many countries*

If the movement involved is parallel to a surface, *über* (+ acc.) can be strengthened by adding *hin*, see 7.2.3a:

Die Enten flogen **über** den See (**hin**)	*The ducks were flying over the lake*

(b) *über* **(+ acc.) is used in more abstract senses of 'above' or 'beyond'**

In the sense of going 'beyond', a limitation *über* can be strengthened by adding *hinaus*:

Diese Aufgabe geht **über** meine Fähigkeiten (**hinaus**)	*This task goes beyond my capabilities*
Er liebt die Ruhe **über** alles	*He likes quiet above all things*
darüber hinaus	*over and above that*

(c) *über* **(+ acc.) occurs in a few time expressions in the sense of 'over'**

For details, see 11.5.10.

(d) *über* **(+ acc.) has the sense of 'over', 'more than' with quantities**

e.g. *Es hat über tausend Euro gekostet; Kinder über zehn Jahre*, etc. See 9.1.6 for further details of this usage and the distinction between the adverbial and prepositional usage of *über* with quantities.

(e) *über* **(+ acc.) is used in the sense of 'about', 'concerning'**

ein Buch **über** die europäischen Vögelarten	*a book about European bird species*
meine Freude **über** ihren Erfolg	*my delight at her success*
Er beschwerte sich **über** den kaputten Fernsehapparat	*He complained about the broken television set*
Sie war ärgerlich **über** ihn	*She was annoyed at him*

This usage is particularly frequent with nouns, adjectives (see 6.6.1) and in the prepositional object of verbs of saying, etc. (see 18.6.9a).

20.3.13 *unter* (+ dative)

(a) With reference to place, *unter* **(+ dat.) corresponds to English 'under(neath)', 'beneath', 'below'**

Manfred lag **unter** dem Tisch	*Manfred was lying under(neath) the table*
200 Meter **unter** dem Gipfel	*200 metres below the summit*
Das Land steht **unter** Wasser	*The land is under water*
Sie trug die Tasche **unter** dem Arm	*She was carrying her bag under her arm*
unter dem Schutz der Dunkelheit	*under cover of darkness*
unter Zwang handeln	*act under duress*

(b) *unter* **(+ dat.) is a common equivalent for English 'among(st)'**

Hier bist du **unter** Freunden	*You're among friends here*
Ich fand das Rezept **unter** meinen Papieren	*I found the prescription among my papers*
Unter den Zuschauern waren viele Ausländer	*There were a lot of foreigners among the spectators*
unter uns gesagt	*between ourselves*
unter vier Augen	*in private*
unter anderem (u.a.)	*amongst other things*

zwischen can also correspond to English 'among(st)', see 20.3.17a. It is preferred if *unter* could be understood to mean 'under'. Compare:

Das Haus steht **unter Bäumen**	*The house stands under some trees*
Das Haus steht **zwischen Bäumen**	*The house stands amongst some trees*

(c) *unter* (+ dat.) is used to indicate circumstances

unter diesen Umständen	*under these circumstances*
unter allen Umständen	*in any case*
unter den größten Schwierigkeiten	*with the greatest difficulty*
unter diesen Bedingungen	*on these conditions*
unter Vorspiegelung falscher Tatsachen	*on false pretences*

(d) *unter* (+ dat.) has the sense of 'under', 'below' with reference to quantity

e.g. *Es hat unter tausend Euro gekostet.* See 9.1.6 for further details of this usage and the distinction between the adverbial and prepositional usage of *unter* with quantities.

20.3.14 *unter* (+ accusative)

(a) *unter* (+ acc.) indicates direction if the destination is *unter* (+ dat.)

i.e. where English has 'under(neath)', 'below', 'among':

Manfred kroch **unter** den Tisch	*Manfred crawled under the table*
Sie steckte die Tasche **unter** ihren Arm	*She put her bag under her arm*
Er tauchte den Kopf **unter** das Wasser	*He dipped his head under the water*
Wir gingen **unter** die Brücke hindurch	*We walked under the bridge*
Sie ging **unter** die Menge	*She went among the crowd*

(b) Some common idiomatic expressions with *unter* (+ acc.)

jdn. unter die Arme greifen	*come to sb.'s assistance*
sein Licht unter den Scheffel stellen	*hide one's light under a bushel*
etwas unter den Tisch fallen lassen	*let sth. go by the board*

20.3.15 *vor* (+ dative)

(a) With reference to place, *vor* (+ dat.) means 'in front of', 'ahead of'

Das Auto steht **vor** der Garage	*The car is in front of the garage*
Der Himalaja lag **vor** uns	*The Himalayas lay before us*
vor ihm in einiger Entfernung	*some distance ahead of him*
vor Gericht erscheinen	*appear in court*
Die Insel liegt **vor** der deutschen Ostseeküste	*The island lies off the Baltic coast of Germany*

(b) To indicate relation of movement to another person or thing moving in the same direction, *vor* (+ dat.) is used with *her*

See also 7.2.3b:

Vor uns **her** fuhr ein roter BMW	*A red BMW was driving along ahead of us*

(c) *vor* is used in time expressions with the sense of 'ago' or 'before'

e.g. *vor zwei Jahren, vor Weihnachten*. For details, see 11.5.13.

(d) *vor* can be used to indicate cause or reason

In this sense, *vor* (+ dat.) normally occurs without a following article:

Man konnte **vor** Lärm nichts hören	*You couldn't hear anything for the noise*
Ich konnte **vor** Aufregung nicht einschlafen	*I couldn't get to sleep with the excitement*

Vor Nebel war nichts zu sehen	*You couldn't see anything for the fog*
Sie warnte mich **vor** dem Hund	*She warned me of the dog*
blass **vor** Furcht, gelb **vor** Neid	*pale with fear, green with envy*

In contrast to *aus*, see 20.2.1c, which points to a voluntary cause or reason, *vor* (+ dat.) always expresses a cause which is involuntary. This use of *vor* (+ dat.) is very common with adjectives, see 6.6.1, and in the prepositional object of verbs, see 18.6.12.

20.3.16 *vor* (+ accusative)

(a) *vor* (+ acc.) **indicates movement to the front of something or someone**

Ich fuhr den Wagen **vor** die Garage	*I drove up in front of the garage*
Sie stellte sich **vor** mich	*She stood in front of me*
Alle traten **vor** den Vorhang	*Everyone stepped out in front of the curtain*
Die Sache kommt **vor** Gericht	*The case is coming to court*

(b) *vor sich hin* **means 'to oneself'**

See 7.2.5, e.g.:

Sie las **vor** sich **hin**	*She was reading to herself*
Ich murmelte etwas **vor** mich **hin**	*I muttered something to myself*

20.3.17 *zwischen*

(a) *zwischen* **is used with reference to place or time in the sense of English 'between'**

(i) *zwischen* (+ dat.) indicates position:

Ich saß **zwischen** dem Minister und seiner Frau	*I was sitting between the minister and his wife*
Die Tagung fand **zwischen** dem 4. und dem 11. Oktober statt	*The conference took place between the 4th and the 11th of October*
zwischen den Zeilen lesen	*read between the lines*

zwischen can also correspond to English 'among(st)' if more than two objects are involved:

Pilze wuchsen **zwischen** den Bäumen	*Toadstools were growing among(st) the trees*

NB: See 20.3.13b for the distinction between *unter* and *zwischen* to mean 'among'.

(ii) *zwischen* (+ acc.) indicates direction:

Ich setzte mich **zwischen** den Minister und seine Frau	*I sat down between the minister and his wife*
Wir legen die Tagung **zwischen** den 4. und den 11. Oktober	*We are putting the conference between the 4th and the 11th of October*

(b) **To indicate relation of movement to another person or thing moving in the same direction,** *zwischen* (+ dat.) **is used with** *her*

See also 7.2.3b. The noun phrase is always in the dative case:

Ich ging **zwischen** meinen Eltern **her**	*I was walking between my parents*

(c) *zwischen* (+ dat.) **has the sense of 'between' with reference to quantity**

e.g. *Kinder zwischen dem 10. und dem 15. Lebensjahr*. See 9.1.6 for further details of this usage and the distinction between the adverbial and prepositional usage of *zwischen* with expressions of quantity.

20.4 **Prepositions governing the genitive case**

The prepositions governing the genitive fall into three main groups:

(i) four common prepositions, dealt with in 20.4.1:

(an)statt	trotz	während	wegen

These are normally used with the genitive case in formal German, but are often found with a dative case in colloquial speech.

(ii) eight prepositions expressing place relationships, see 20.4.2:

außerhalb	oberhalb	diesseits	unweit
innerhalb	unterhalb	jenseits	
		beid(er)seits	

These are often used with a following *von* rather than a genitive.

(iii) a large number of prepositions with rather specialised meanings which are hardly used outside very formal (often official) registers. They are listed and explained in 20.4.3.

20.4.1 **The four common prepositions which govern the genitive**

(a) *(an)statt* **'instead of'**

(i) Examples of the use of *(an)statt*:

Statt eines Fernsehers hat sie sich eine neue Stereoanlage gekauft	*Instead of a television she bought herself a new stereo system*
Statt eines Briefes schickte er ihr eine Postkarte	*Instead of a letter he sent her a postcard*

(ii) *(an)statt* can be used as a conjunction rather than a preposition, i.e. as an alternative to *und nicht*. In this construction the noun or pronoun has the same case as the noun or pronoun immediately preceding *(an)statt* with which it is linked:

Ich besuchte meinen Onkel **statt** (= und nicht) meinen Bruder	*I visited my uncle instead of my brother*
Ihr Haus hat sie mir **statt** (= und nicht) ihm vermacht	*She left her house to me instead of to him*

(an)statt is always used in this way if it links prepositional phrases or personal pronouns:

Ich schreibe jetzt mit einem Filzstift **statt** mit einem Füller	*I write with a felt-tip now instead of with a fountain pen*

(iii) *anstelle von* is a common alternative to *(an)statt*. It often sounds less stilted:

Wir gebrauchen jetzt Margarine **anstelle von** Butter	*We use margarine instead of butter now*

NB: (i) The longer form *anstatt* is less frequent; it occurs chiefly in formal written German.
    (ii) For infinitive phrases with *(an)statt . . . zu* and the conjunction *(an)statt dass* see 13.2.7c.

(b) *trotz* **'despite', 'in spite of'**

Wir sind am Sonntag **trotz** des starken Regens nach Eulbach gewandert	*We walked to Eulbach on Sunday despite the heavy rain*

(c) *während* **'during'**

e.g. *während des Sommers* 'during the summer'. Details on the use of *während* are given in 11.5.15.

(d) *wegen* **'because of', 'for the sake of'**

(i) *wegen* normally precedes the noun it governs, but it sometimes follows in more elevated registers:

Wir konnten **wegen** des Regens nicht kommen	*We couldn't come because of the rain*
Er musste **wegen** zu schnellen Fahrens eine Geldstrafe bezahlen	*He had to pay a fine because he had been driving too fast*
Er wich jeder Schafherde aus, nicht der Schafe **wegen**, sondern um den Geruch der Hirten zu umgehen (*Süßkind*)	*He kept away from all the flocks of sheep, not because of the sheep, but to avoid the smell of the shepherds*

(ii) *wegen* is sometimes used in the sense of 'about', 'concerning':

Wegen deiner Reise muss ich noch mit Astrid sprechen	*I've still got to talk to Astrid about your trip*

(iii) The combination *von* (+ gen.) . . . *wegen* occurs in a few set phrases:

von Amts wegen	*ex officio*
von Berufs wegen	*by virtue of one's profession*
von Rechts wegen	*legally, by rights*

(iv) The combination *von wegen* (+ dat.) is common in colloquial German to mean 'because of' or 'concerning'. This usage is considered to be non-standard:

Jetzt hört mir nur auf **von wegen** Idealismus (*Valentin*)	*For goodness' sake stop talking about idealism*

von wegen is very frequent in isolation to challenge a previous statement:

Also, heute Abend bezahlst du alles. – **Von wegen**!	*So, you're paying for everything tonight. – No way!*

NB: For the forms of personal pronouns and demonstrratives with *wegen* (*meinetwegen, ihretwegen*, etc.), see 3.1.2c and 5.1.1

(e) The use of (*an*)*statt*, *trotz*, *während* and *wegen* with a dative

Although these prepositions are normally followed by a noun phrase in the genitive case in standard German, in certain conditions they are used with a following noun phrase in the dative.

(i) They are very frequently used with a following dative in everyday colloquial speech. This reflects the general avoidance of the genitive in informal registers, see 2.3:

Ich konnte **wegen dem Regen** nicht kommen
Während dem Mittagessen hat sie uns etwas über ihren Urlaub erzählt

(ii) They are more often used with a following dative in writing in Switzerland, e.g. *Die Koalition wird deshalb vorerst wahrscheinlich trotz **dem neuerlichen Scheitern** überleben* (NZZ).

(iii) Although the use of the dative case with these prepositions is not generally accepted as standard in writing in Germany, it is accepted (or at least tolerated) in a number of constructions, i.e.:

Prepositions

- if they are followed by a plural noun which is not accompanied by a declined determiner or adjective: *während fünf **Jahren**, wegen ein paar **Hindernissen***
- if the noun they govern is preceded by a possessive genitive: *während Vaters **kurzem Urlaub**, wegen des ehemaligen Bundeskanzlers **langem Schweigen***
- to avoid the use of the genitive of the personal pronouns, see 3.1.2: *Langsam fahren – **wegen uns**!* (on a road sign outside a kindergarten)
- to avoid consecutive genitives in *-(e)s*, see 2.4.2a: ***trotz dem Rollen** des Zuges* (Th. Mann)
- if the following noun has no determiner with it: *trotz Geldmangel(s), wegen Amtsmissbrauch(s)*
- to achieve a particular stylistic effect: *Freies Denken **statt starrem Lenken*** (election slogan)
- a relative pronoun with these prepositions can be in the dative: *seit dem Ende des Zweiten Weltkriegs, während **dem** die Stadt Salzburg zahlreiche Bombenangriffe erleiden musste* (Baedeker)

20.4.2 **The eight prepositions denoting position**

(a) Meaning and use

(i) *außerhalb* 'outside' and *innerhalb* 'inside', 'within' can be used with reference to place or time:

Sie wohnt **außerhalb** der Stadt	*She lives outside the city*
Das liegt **außerhalb**/**innerhalb** meines Fachgebietes	*That lies outside/within my specialist field*
Das kann sie **außerhalb** der Arbeitszeit erledigen	*She can finish that outside working hours*
Das wird **innerhalb** eines Jahres geändert werden	*That will be changed within a year*

NB: (i) *außerhalb* and *innerhalb* only denote position, not direction. Compare *Wir gingen aus der Hütte hinaus/in die Hütte hinein* 'We went outside/inside the hut'.
   (ii) Like *binnen* (see 20.2.10b), *innerhalb* can be used to avoid any potential ambiguity with *in*, see 11.5.8c.

(ii) *oberhalb* 'above' and *unterhalb* 'below', 'underneath' refer to position and are more specific in meaning than *über* and *unter*:

Oberhalb der Straße war ein Felsenvorsprung	*Above the road there was a rocky ledge*
Ich habe mich **unterhalb** des Knies verletzt	*I injured myself below the knee*
der Rhein **oberhalb**/**unterhalb** der Stadt Basel	*the Rhine above/below the city of Basle*

(iii) *beid(er)seits* 'on either side of', *diesseits* 'on this side of, *jenseits* 'beyond', 'on the other side of':

in den Bauten **beidseits** des Flusses (*FR*)	*in the buildings on either side of the river*
diesseits, **jenseits** der niederländischen Grenze	*on this side, the other side of the Dutch border*

NB: *hinter* is more commonly used for 'beyond' than *jenseits*, especially in everyday German, e.g. *Das Dorf liegt hinter der Grenze, hinter Hannover*.

(iv) *unweit* 'not far from'

Wir standen auf einer Höhe **unweit** des Dorfes	*We were standing on a hill not far from the village*

NB: *unfern*, with the same meaning as *unweit*, is now obsolete. It could be used with the genitive or the dative case.

(b) All these prepositions are often used with *von* rather than the genitive

(i) This is usual in colloquial speech, but it is also quite common in writing, although many Germans prefer to use the genitive in formal registers:

Sie wohnt **außerhalb von** der Stadt
Innerhalb von einem Jahr wird alles anders werden
Jenseits von der Grenze standen vier Vopos
ein Dorf **unweit von** Moskau (*Bednarz*)

(ii) The use of *von* is the norm even in written German in those contexts where the common prepositions taking the genitive are commonly used with the dative (see 20.4.1e), e.g. *innerhalb von fünf Jahren*. A following relative pronoun is also often in the dative, e.g. *die Zone, innerhalb der* (less commonly: *derer*) *Autos verboten sind*.

20.4.3 **Other prepositions governing the genitive**

The large number of other prepositions with the genitive are largely limited to formal, especially written registers, the majority in official and commercial language. Elsewhere they can sound stilted. Many of them were originally adverbs, participles or phrases which have fairly recently come to be used as prepositions, and similar new ones are constantly entering the language. With this proviso, the following list is as complete as possible.

†NB: These prepositions are used with a following dative case in the same contexts as the common prepositions, see 20.4.1e.

abseits *away from*
 eine Speisekarte abseits jeglicher Tradition (*Presse*)
†**abzüglich** *deducting, less*:
 abzüglich der Unkosten
anfangs *at the beginning of*:
 anfangs dieses Jahres (or with the acc.: *anfangs nächsten Monat*)
angesichts *in view of*:
 angesichts der wachsenden Konkurrenz aus Fernost (*MM*)
anhand (*also* **an Hand**) *with the aid of/from*:
 anhand einiger Beispiele
anlässlich *on the occasion of*:
 anlässlich seines siebzigsten Geburtstages
anstelle (*also* **an Stelle**) *in place of, instead of*:
 anstelle einer Antwort (in speech often anstelle *von*)
aufgrund (*also* **auf Grund**) *on the strength of*:
 aufgrund seiner juristischen Ausbildung (*in speech often* aufgrund von)
†**ausschließlich** *exclusive of*
 die Miete ausschließlich der Heizungskosten
ausweislich *according to*
 Im Lesen sind die Deutschen ausweislich dieser Studie keineswegs Spitze (*SZ*)
behufs *for the purpose of*
 behufs einer Verhandlung
betreffs, bezüglich *with regard to*
 betreffs, bezüglich Ihres Angebotes
eingangs *at the beginning of*
 eingangs dieses Jahres
eingedenk (*may precede or follow the noun*) *bearing in mind*
 eingedenk seiner beruflichen Fehlschläge

†einschließlich *including*
  einschließlich der Angehörigen (*SZ*)
†exklusive *excluding*
  exklusive Versandkosten
fernab *far from*
  fernab des Lärms der Städte
gelegentlich *on the occasion of*
  gelegentlich seines Besuches
halber (*following the noun*) *for the sake of*
  der Wahrheit halber

NB: (i) *halber* can be compounded with nouns to form adverbs, e.g. *sicherheitshalber* 'for safety's sake', *urlaubshalber* 'for a holiday', *vorsichtshalber* 'as a precaution'.
   (ii) When used with pronouns *halber* appears as *-halben* and is compounded with forms of the pronoun in *-t*, e.g. *meinethalben* 'for my sake' 'for all me', see 3.1.1c and 5.1.1..

hinsichtlich *with regard to*
  hinsichtlich Ihrer Anfrage
infolge *as a result of*
  infolge der neuen Steuergesetze (often with *von: infolge von den Steuergesetzen*)
†inklusive *including*
  inklusive Bedienung
inmitten *in the middle of*
  ein neues Möbelhaus inmitten der Fußgängerzone (*HAZ*)
kraft *in virtue of*
  kraft seines Amtes
längs *along(side)*
  längs des Flusses (*less frequently*: längs dem Fluss)
links *on/to the left of*
  links der Donau
†mangels *for want of*
  Freispruch mangels Beweises
†mittels *by means of*
  mittels eines gefälschten Passes
namens *in the name of*
  Ich möchte Sie namens unseres Betriebes einladen
ob *on account of*
  die Besorgnisse des sowjetischen Staatspräsidenten ob der deutschen Frage (*Zeit*)
plus *plus* (*commercial registers*)
  5 Prozent plus einer Topdividende von 0,75 Prozent (*HAZ*)
rechts *to/on the right of*
  rechts der Isar
seitens *on the part of*
  seitens der Bezirksverwaltung
seitlich *to/at the side of*
  seitlich der Hauptstraße
um . . . willen *for the sake of*
  um meiner Mutter willen

NB: *um . . . willen* forms compounds with special forms of the personal pronouns, e.g. *um meinetwillen*, see 3.1.1c and 5.1.1

unbeschadet (*may precede or follow the noun*) *regardless of*
  unbeschadet des enttäuschenden Ergebnisses (*Presse*)
ungeachtet (*may precede or follow the noun*) *notwithstanding*
  ungeachtet unserer üblichen Skepsis (*Dönhoff*)

vermöge *by dint of*
   vermöge seines unermüdlichen Fleißes
vorbehaltlich *subject to*
   vorbehaltlich seiner Zustimmung
zeit (*only used in set phrases with* das Leben) *during*
   zeit seines Lebens
zugunsten (*also* **zu Gunsten**) *for the benefit of*
   eine Sammlung zugunsten/zu Gunsten der Opfer des Faschismus
zuungunsten (*also* **zu Ungunsten**) *to the disadvantage of*
   Die Richter urteilen meist zuungunsten der Skisportler (*MM*)
⁺zuzüglich *plus*
   Es kostet 2000 Euro zuzüglich der Versandkosten
⁺zwecks *for the purpose of*
   Er besuchte sie zwecks einer gründlichen Erörterung der Situation

20.5 German equivalents for English 'to'

English 'to' has a number of possible German equivalents depending on context, and the use of each of these is summarised here. Fuller details and further examples can be found in earlier sections under the relevant German prepositions.

20.5.1 *an*, *auf* or *in* (+ accusative) are frequent equivalents for 'to'

The choice between *an*, *auf* or *in* with a noun phrase in the accusative case to mean 'to' depends on which of these prepositions would be used with the dative to express position 'in' or 'at' the place concerned after you get there. Thus:

(a) *in* **(+ accusative) is used for going 'to' places which one will then be inside, i.e. (*in* + dative)**

Sie ging **ins** Büro/**ins** Dorf/**ins** Kino/**in** die Kirche/**in** ein Museum/**ins** Restaurant/**in** die Schule/**in** die Stadt/**in** den Zoo, etc.

In this way, *Ich gehe **in** die Kirche* means 'I am going to church' in the sense of going in to a service. If one is just going up to the church, one says *Ich gehe **an** die Kirche* or *Ich gehe **zur** Kirche*.

(b) *auf* **(+ accusative) is used for going 'to' certain places and events, in particular those where** *auf* **(+ dative) is used to say you are 'at' them**

(i) The use of *auf* is fixed with a number of nouns:

Die Schafe gingen **auf** die Wiese	*The sheep went into the meadow*
Wir fuhren **aufs** Land	*We went into the countryside*
Die Kinder gingen **auf** die Straße	*The children went into the street*

Similarly:

auf den Berg	*up the mountain*	auf sein Gut	*to his estate*
auf den (Bauern)hof	*to the farm*	auf den Hof	*into the yard*
auf ihre Bude	*to her bedsit*	auf die Jagd gehen	*go hunting*
auf den Flur	*into the hall*	auf die Toilette	*to the toilet*
auf den Gang	*into the corridor*		

With all these, *auf* (+ dative) is used to denote presence 'in' or 'on' them, see 20.3.4b.

(ii) *auf* (+ accusative) is also sometimes used for going 'to' formal occasions (e.g. weddings, conferences, parties, etc.):

Sie ging **auf** einen Empfang, **auf** eine Hochzeit, **auf** eine Party, **auf** eine Tagung.

Although *auf* (+ dative) is still used to denote presence 'at' such functions, see 20.3.4b, *zu* is now more usual than *auf* (+ acc.) to express going 'to' them, especially in less formal registers.

(iii) *auf* (+ accusative) is used for going 'to' certain public buildings:

Sie ging **auf** den Bahnhof, **auf** die Bank, **auf** die Bibliothek, **auf** die Post, **auf** das Rathaus, **auf** die Universität

With many of these words, *auf* occurs chiefly in more formal registers or in Austrian usage (see 20.3.4b and 20.3.5a). *zu* is regularly used in its place, although *an* (+ accusative) is frequent with *Universität*.

(c) *an* **expresses direction 'to' a precise spot or objects which extend lengthways (i.e. rivers, shores, etc.)**

an expresses movement to a point adjacent to the object concerned. One is then *an* (+ dative) that point, i.e. 'at' it, see 20.3.2a. Examples:

Er ging **an den** Tisch	→	Er steht an dem Tisch
Sie kam **an die** Bushaltestelle	→	Sie traf ihn an der Haltestelle
Sie ging **an die** Grenze	→	An der Grenze wurde kontrolliert
Wir fahren **ans** Meer	→	Wir verbringen unseren Urlaub am Meer

Similarly:

Er eilte **ans** Fenster   Er ging **an die** Kasse
Wir kamen **an die** Front   Sie ging **ans** Ufer
Sie geht **ans** Mikrophon/**an** ihren Platz/**an** die Straßenkreuzung/**an** die Tür/**an** die
    Tafel/**an** die Stelle/wo der Tote aufgefunden wurde
Sie gingen **an** den Fluss/**an** die Mosel/**an** den Strand/**an** den See/**an** die Theke/**an**
    den Zaun

20.5.2 *zu* commonly has the meaning of English 'to'

(a) *zu* **is used in many contexts in place of the more precise prepositions** *an*, *auf* **and** *in*

(see 20.5.1). It is rather vaguer than these three prepositions and tends to emphasise general direction rather than reaching the objective. It is particularly frequent in colloquial registers.

(i) *zu* is used rather than *in* if one is just going up to the place involved (but not necessarily going inside), or to emphasise the general direction rather than reaching the place:

Ich ging **zum** neuen Kino und wartete auf ihn
Die Straßenbahn fährt **zum** Zoo

(ii) *zu* is in practice more common than *auf* in current (especially informal) usage with reference to functions and public buildings:

Er geht **zu** einem Empfang/**zu** einer Tagung/**zu** einer Party
Wir gehen **zum** Bahnhof/**zur** Bank/**zur** Post/**zum** Rathaus/**zur** Universität

(iii) *zu* can be used rather than *an* if the emphasis is on general direction rather than arriving adjacent to the place concerned:

Ich begleitete sie **zur** Fabrik   Er ging **zum** Fenster, **zur** Tür
Sie ging **zu** ihrem Platz   Er schlenderte **zur** Theke

(b) *zu* **is always used with reference to people**

i.e. going up to someone, or to their house or shop

Sie ging **zu** ihrem Onkel/**zu** ihrer Freundin
Er ging **zu** Fleischers/**zu** seinem Chef
Wir gehen **zum** Bäcker frische Semmeln kaufen

20.5.3 Equivalents for English 'to' with geographical names

(a) *nach* **is used with neuter names of continents, countries and towns which are used without an article**

Wir fahren **nach** Amerika, **nach** Frankreich, **nach** Duisburg (see 20.2.6a)

(b) *in* **(+ accusative) is used with names of countries, etc. which are used with an article**

Most of these are feminine, but a few are masculine, neuter or plural, see 4.4.1:

Sie reist morgen **in** die Schweiz, **in** den Jemen (or nach Jemen), **in** das Elsass, **in** die USA

(c) **Various prepositions are used with other geographical names**

In particular *in*, *an* or *auf* (+ acc.) are used in the same way as with other nouns, see 20.5.1, depending on whether one will be *in*, *an* or *auf* (+ dat.) on arrival:

Wir fahren **in** die Alpen, **in** den Harz
Wir gingen **auf** den Feldberg, **auf** die Jungfrau
Wir wollen im Sommer **an** den Bodensee, **an** die Riviera fahren

21 **Word order**

German word order is different to English and it has a different role in determining how sentences are constructed. English uses word order to identify the subject and the object(s) of the verb. In English, the subject must come first, before the verb, and the objects after it, in the order indirect object + direct object. In a sentence like

My father lent our neighbour the old lawnmower

we cannot move the elements round without saying something quite different, so that, for example, *Our neighbour lent my father the old lawnmower* has another meaning. In German, various permutations are possible without changing the essential meaning:

(i) **Mein Vater** hat *unserem Nachbarn* den alten Rasenmäher geliehen
(ii) *Unserem Nachbarn* hat **mein Vater** *den alten Rasenmäher* geliehen
(iii) *Den alten Rasenmäher* hat **mein Vater** *unserem Nachbarn* geliehen
(iv) **Mein Vater** hat *den alten Rasenmäher* *unserem Nachbarn* geliehen

In German it is the **case endings,** not the word order, which tell us **who is doing what to whom**, i.e. what is the subject and what are the objects (for explanations of these, see Chapter 18). The order of the words and phrases can be changed round to give a different emphasis to the elements without altering the basic meaning. Sentence (iv), for example, stresses who is being lent the lawnmower. In German, the position of the verb is relatively fixed, and the other elements can be moved in order to show different emphases.

Nevertheless, the various elements do tend to come in a particular order – but this is a tendency rather than a rule of grammar. This chapter shows first this 'neutral' basic order, and then how it can be varied to give a different emphasis:

* the **three basic clause structures**, with the finite verb in different positions (section 21.1)
* the use of **first position** in main clauses to highlight an important element (section 21.2)
* the position of the **other elements** in the clause (sections 21.3–21.8)
    – the position of **pronouns** (section 21.4)
    – the position of **noun subject** and **objects** (section 21.5)
    – the position of **adverbials** (section 21.6)
    – the position of *nicht* and other negative elements (section 21.7)
    – the position of other verb **complements** (section 21.8)
    – placing elements **after the verb** at the end of the clause (section 21.9)

Although we usually speak of '**word** order', what is involved is often a **phrase** of some kind rather than a single word. For example, time adverbials tend to come in a particular place whether they are single words, like *heute*, or phrases like *den ganzen Tag* or *am kommenden Dienstag*. In order to cover these possibilities, we refer to these segments of the clause as **elements**. In German they are called *Satzglieder*.

21.1 **Clause structure and the position of the verb**

The basic feature of German word order is that the various parts of the verb have a fixed position in the clause.

21.1.1 **The three basic clause structures of German**

There are three clause types in German which differ in the place of the finite verb:

   (i)   main clause statements: *Petra **kommt** nach Erfurt*
          The finite verb is the **second** element
  (ii)   questions and commands: ***Kommt** Petra nach Erfurt? Kommen Sie nach Erfurt!*
          The finite verb is the **first** element
 (iii)   subordinate clauses: *Ich weiß, dass Petra nach Erfurt **kommt***
          The finite verb is the **last** element

(a) Main clause statements: the finite verb is the SECOND element

Only **one** element, whether it is a single word, a phrase, or a whole clause, can normally come before the finite verb in main clauses (see 21.2). All other parts of the verb, i.e. infinitives, past participles or separable prefixes, are placed at the end of the clause:

Initial position	Verb¹	Other elements	Verb²
Helga	kommt	eben aus der Bäckerei	
Morgen	muss	ich mit dem Zug nach Trier	fahren
Nach einiger Zeit	blickte	sie zum Fenster	hinaus
Gestern	habe	ich fünf neue Apps	gekauft
Als er klein war,	hat	er oft mit Werner	gespielt

Noun clauses with *dass* omitted (see 19.2.1b) have the same structure as main clause statements: *Sie glaubt, **sie hat ihn gestern in der Stadt gesehen**.*

NB: (i)   Exceptions to the rule that the finite verb must be the second element are explained in 21.2.1c.
     (ii) The order of infinitives and participles at the end of the clause when there is more than one of these is explained in 21.1.3.

(b) Questions and commands: the finite verb is the FIRST element

As in main clause statements, any other parts of the verb are in final position. In some questions, the verb is preceded by an interrogative (e.g. *was, was für ein . . .*, etc.):

w-word	Verb¹	Other elements	Verb²
	Kommt	sie bald?	
	Musst	du schon	gehen?
	Hat	dich Peter schon	gesprochen?
	Fangen	Sie sofort	an!
	Pass	doch an der Kreuzung	auf!
Was	hast	du da schon wieder	angestellt?
Welches Buch	sollen	wir zuerst	lesen?
Was für eine Stadt	ist	Bochum?	

Conditional clauses with no *wenn* (see 16.5.3a), and comparative clauses introduced simply by *als*, see 16.7.1a, have a similar structure, with the finite verb in first position, e.g. ***Hätte ich Zeit**, so würde ich gern mit Ihnen nach Italien fahren; Es war mir, **als wäre ich** hoch in der Luft.*

(c) Subordinate clauses: the finite verb is the FINAL element

The clause is introduced by a conjunction in first position, see Chapter 19. Other parts of the verb come immediately before the finite verb at the end of the clause (see 21.1.3):

Conjunction	Other elements	Verb²	Verb¹
weil	ich gestern krank		war
(der Mann), der	in der Ecke allein		steht
ob	sie diesen neuen Top	gekauft	hat?
dass	er den Brief sofort	tippen	soll
dass	er morgen		kommt
	den Stuhl in die Ecke		zu stellen
ohne	ihrem Freund	helfen	zu können

As the table shows, non-finite clauses with an infinitive with *zu* (see 13.2.1) have a similar structure to that of other subordinate clauses, with the verb last (although there is not necessarily a conjunction at the beginning of the clause). Clauses with participles follow the same pattern, with the verb last: *Den Schildern folgend*, *fanden sie das Krankenhaus* (Walser); *eine Betonburg*, *wie von einem anderen Stern in diesen Wald gefallen* (Walser).

NB: Exclamations introduced by an interrogative word may have the form of questions **or** subordinate clauses, e.g.: *Wie der Chef darüber geschimpft hat!* **or**: *Wie hat der Chef darüber geschimpft!*

21.1.2 The 'verbal bracket'

A typical feature of German is that most elements in the clause are sandwiched between the various parts of the verb in main clauses, or between the conjunction and the parts of the verb in subordinate clauses. This construction is known as the 'verbal bracket'. This bracket forms a framework for German clauses, and the order of all the other elements in the clause can be described in relation to it:

Initial position	Bracket¹ [	Other elements	Bracket² [
Heute	darf	sie mit uns ins Kino	kommen
Ich	habe	sie zufällig in der Stadt	gesehen
Ich	komme	morgen gegen zwei Uhr noch	vorbei
	Darf	sie heute mit uns ins Kino	kommen?
	Hast	du sie zufällig in der Stadt	gesehen?
	Komm	doch morgen gegen zwei Uhr	vorbei?
. . .,	ob	sie heute mit uns ins Kino	kommen darf
. . .,	weil	ich sie heute zufällig in der Stadt	gesehen habe
. . .,	dass	du morgen gegen zwei Uhr noch	vorbeikommst

More examples of verbal brackets can be seen in the tables in 21.1.1. The construction has some characteristic features:

(i)   In main clauses there is only **one element** in initial position before the first 'bracket' formed by the verb. This position is called the *Vorfeld* in German; its function is explained in 21.2.

(ii)   All other elements (and this means all elements in questions, commands and subordinate clauses) are positioned within the bracket. In German, this is called the *Mittelfeld*. As the examples above show, the order of elements in the *Mittelfeld* is exactly the same for all clause types. The order of elements within it is explained in 21.3 to 21.8.

(iii)   Under certain conditions elements can be placed after the closing bracket, i.e. after the part of the verb which is at the end, e.g. *Ich rufe an* **aus London**; *Hat sie dich angerufen* **aus London**?; *Ich weiß, dass sie dich angerufen hat* **aus London**. This position is called the *Nachfeld* in German. Its use is explained in section 21.9.

21.1.3 **The order of verbs at the end of the clause**

If there is more than one part of the verb at the end of the clause, the order of these is fixed.

(a) In main clause statements, questions and commands the auxiliary verb comes after the main verb

Initial	Finite verb	Other elements	Main verb	Auxiliary verb
Ich	**werde**	es ihr doch	**sagen**	**müssen**
Sie	**hat**	ihn voriges Jahr	**schwimmen**	**gelernt**
	Ist	dir das schon	**erklärt**	**worden?**
	Soll	dieser Brief heute noch	**geschrieben**	**werden?**

(b) In subordinate clauses the finite verb usually follows all infinitives and participles

The main verb comes before the infinitive or past participle of an auxiliary verb:

Conjunction	Other elements	Main verb	Auxiliary	Finite verb
Da	ich sie zufällig	gesehen		habe
. . ., dass	er mir das Geld	leihen		wird
. . ., dass	sie mit uns ins Kino	gehen		darf
. . ., wie	sie den Brief	fallen		ließ
(das Haus), das	sie	verkaufen		ist
. ., dass	mir das schon	erklärt	worden	sollte
(das Haus), das	heute noch	verkauft	werden	muss

However, if there are two infinitives at the end of the clause (the 'double infinitive' construction, see 13.3.2 and 17.1.4c), the finite verb comes before them both:

Conjunction	Other elements	Finite verb	Main verb	Auxiliary
(Ich weiß), dass	ich es bald	werde	erledigen	müssen
(der Brief), den	sie	hat	fallen	lassen
. . ., weil	er die Probleme	soll	lösen	können
(das Haus), das	sie	hätte	verkaufen	sollen
. . ., dass	Paul ihn	hat	kommen	hören

NB: (i) In Austrian usage, the finite verb is often placed **between** the main verb and the auxiliary: *der Flughafen, wo die Luftraumsperre von Mitternacht bis 5 Uhr dauern hätte sollen* (*Standard*).

(ii) This rule only applies with *lassen, hören* and *sehen* **if** the infinitive is substituting for a past participle (see 13.3.2). With *lassen* the order with the auxiliary in final position is also acceptable, e.g. *der Brief, den sie fallen lassen hat.* Otherwise, the finite verb is placed at the end of the clause *Weil Norwegen die Isländer in einem Stück internationalen Gewässers nicht fischen lassen will, . . .* (*Presse*).

(iii) The auxiliary *werden* is sometimes placed after the other verbs, e.g. *dass ich es bald erledigen müssen werde.* This sequence is also regarded as acceptable.

21.1.4 **Coordinated clauses have the same structure**

Coordinated clauses are linked by a coordinating conjunction such as *aber, oder* or *und* (see 19.1).

(a) In coordinated main clauses, the verb is in second position in both

Zu Hause **schreibt** Mutter Briefe und Vater **arbeitet** im Garten
Am Abend **blieb** ich in meinem Zimmer, aber ich **konnte** nicht arbeiten
Du **kannst** mit uns ins Kino kommen oder du **kannst** zu deiner Freundin gehen

If the subject of clauses linked by *sondern* or *und* is identical, it can be omitted ('understood'):

Wir **gingen** nicht ins Kino, sondern **arbeiteten** im Garten
Jürgen **kam** um vier Uhr in Soest an und **ging** sofort zu seiner Freundin

However, if the second clause has another element in initial position, the subject **must** be inserted again after the verb and cannot be omitted. This is different from English, where the subject can still be understood even if another element comes before the verb. Compare:

Ich schrieb ein paar Briefe und dann ging
   ich zu meiner Tante

I wrote a few letters and then went to my aunt's

If an element other than the subject comes in initial position, before the verb, it can be left out (and taken as understood) in following coordinated clauses. The following clauses begin with the verb, and the subject is repeated after it. This stresses that the initial element applies equally to all the clauses:

Schon im April demonstrierten die Bauern, blockierten **sie** Straßen in Ost-Berlin und protestierten **sie** vor der Volkskammer (*Zeit*)
(*Schon im April* is here taken to apply to **all three** coordinated clauses)

As early as April the farmers demonstrated, blocked streets in East Berlin and protested in front of the Volkskammer

However, if no need is felt to emphasise that the initial phrase also applies to the second clause, the subject is placed before the second verb. In practice this is more usual, especially outside formal written German:

Am Abend blieb ich zu Hause und **meine Schwester ging** ins Kino

That night I stayed at home and my sister went to the cinema

(b) In parallel subordinate clauses linked by coordinating conjunctions the verb is in final position

Ich weiß, dass sie gestern krank **war** und dass ihr Mann deswegen zu Hause geblieben **ist**

I know that she was ill yesterday and that her husband stayed at home because of that

Wenn deine Familie dagegen **ist** oder wenn du keine Zeit **hast**, dann wollen wir den Plan fallen lassen

If your family is against it or if you don't have time, then we'll drop the plan

If the two clauses have compound tenses with the same auxiliary, the auxiliary can be omitted in the first one:

Nachdem ich Tee **getrunken** und eine Weile **gelesen hatte**, machte ich einen kurzen Spaziergang

After I had had tea and read for a while, I went for a short walk

21.2 Initial position in main clause statements

21.2.1 Only one element precedes the finite verb in main clause statements

This means that the finite verb is normally the **second element** in a main clause, forming the first part of the verbal bracket, see 21.1.1a and 21.1.2.

(a) This clause structure is quite different to English

In English the subject has to come before the verb, because that is the only way we can tell it is the subject. In English, too, other elements can come before the subject, so that there can be several elements in front of the verb:

(i) *Then she began to read the letter*
(ii) *Then, unwillingly, she began to read the letter*
(iii) *Then, unwillingly, when she had shut the door, she began to read the letter*

In the equivalent German sentences, all but one of these elements has to be moved to another position, so that the **verb stays in second place**, e.g. (among numerous possible permutations):

(i) **Dann** begann sie den Brief zu lesen/**Sie** begann dann den Brief zu lesen
(ii) **Widerwillig** begann sie dann den Brief zu lesen/**Dann** begann sie widerwillig den Brief zu lesen
(iii) **Nachdem sie die Tür geschlossen hatte**, begann sie dann widerwillig den Brief zu lesen/ **Dann** begann sie widerwillig den Brief zu lesen, nachdem sie die Tür geschlossen hatte

Because of this fundamental difference in clause structure, corresponding sentences in English and German often have a very different form.

(b) Many types of element can occur in initial position

The subject is often the most natural element to occur in initial position, and it has been estimated that two thirds of main clause statements in German in all registers begin with the subject:

Tobias zog heftig an seiner Pfeife. **Die Spucke im Mundstück** prasselte; **man** hörte es, obwohl jetzt, immer deutlicher, auch noch das Schießen der anderen hinzukam... **Sie** waren am Kahn. **Tobias** bückte sich und ließ das Kettenschloss aufschnappen. **Die Luft überm See** flimmerte. **Der Milan hoch oben** tat keinen Flügelschlag. (*Schnurre*)

However, it is quite wrong to think of the order subject + finite verb as the 'normal' order (as it is in English), and thus imply that it is 'abnormal' for something else to come before the verb. Almost all types of element except the negative *nicht* and the modal particles (see Chapter 10) can naturally come first in a main clause. To demonstrate this, examples are given below of those elements, aside from the subject, which are common at the start of main clause.

(i) an accusative or dative object. Occasionally, only in writing, this can be a (stressed) pronoun, but it is more usually a noun phrase:

Ihn nahm er zuletzt nach Prag mit (*Hildesheimer*)
Ihr war das Bett viel zu klein
Das Verfahren gegen ihn deutet er als weiterer Beleg für die politische Verfolgung (*Spiegel*)
Mariken hat es sehr Leid getan (*Surminski*)

(ii) an adverbial (a single adverb or a phrase):

Natürlich kannte er sämtliche Parfum- und Drogenhandlungen der Stadt (*Süßkind*)
Trotz den feierlichen Londoner Erklärungen wird weiter gekämpft (*NZZ*)

Time and **place adverbials** are especially frequent in initial position:

An dem Abend kam ich mit Mahler in den „Kronenkeller" (*Bachmann*)
In vielen Städten sind kostenlose Parkplätze Mangelware

(iii) another complement of the verb, i.e. a genitive object, a prepositional object, a place or direction complement or a predicate complement (see Table 18.1)

> **Zu einem bedauerlichen Zwischenfall** kam es, als . . . (*Zwerenz*)
> **Ins Theater/Dahin** komme ich jetzt nur sehr selten
> **Ein guter Kerl** ist er trotz alledem

(iv) a prepositional phrase qualifying a noun later in the clause

> **Über den Ernst der Lage** hat aber auch er keinen Zweifel (*FR*)

(v) the non-finite part of a compound tense. This gives particularly strong emphasis to the verb:

> **Anzeigen** wird sie ihn (*Fallada*)
> **Abgefunden mit ihrer Lage** haben sich 16,6 Prozent der Frauen (*LV*)

(vi) a noun belonging with a quantifying determiner later in the clause. This gives particular emphasis to the noun:

> **Personen** wurden nach Polizeiangaben keine verletzt (*NZZ*)
> **Menschen** sind um diese Zeit wenige unterwegs (*Gaiser*)

Occasionally this construction is found with adjectives, e.g.:

> **Beweise** hat er äußerst triftige gebracht

(vii) part of a phrasal verb

> **Sehr leid** hat es mir getan
> **Zur Abstimmung** ist dieser Vorschlag nicht gekommen

(viii) a subordinate clause. This can be a finite or non-finite clause

> **Wohin sie dich gebracht haben**, weiß ich nicht (*Surminski*)
> **Den Schildern folgend**, fanden sie das Krankenhaus (*Walser*)
> **Ihr Geld zu leihen**, habe ich doch nie versprochen

(c) Constructions with more than one element in initial position

There are a few possible exceptions to the rule that the verb is always the second element in main clauses. In practice, these are only apparent exceptions in special kinds of construction, i.e.:

(i) Interjections, the particles *ja* and *nein*, and names of persons addressed are regarded as standing outside the clause proper and are placed before the initial element and followed by a comma, e.g.:

> **Ach**, es regnet schon wieder
> **Du liebe Zeit**, da ist sie ja auch
> **Ja**, du hast Recht
> **Nein**, das darfst du nicht
> **Karl**, ich habe dein Buch gefunden
> **Lieber Freund**, ich kann nichts dafür

(ii) Some other words or phrases link up a clause with what has just been said or the general context. They are seen as standing outside the clause and placed before the initial element with a comma:

Kurzum, die Lage ist nun kritisch
Wissen Sie, ich habe sie nie richtig kennen gelernt

The most frequent of these words and phrases are:

das heißt (d.h.)	*that is (i.e.)*	so	*well now, well then*
im Gegenteil	*on the contrary*	unter uns gesagt	*between ourselves*
kurz, kurzum, kurz gesagt,	*in short*	weiß Gott	*Heaven knows*
kurz und gut		wie gesagt	*as I said*
mit anderen Worten	*in other words*	wissen Sie, weißt du	*you know*
nun, na	*well*	zugegeben	*admittedly*
sehen Sie, siehst du	*d'you see*		

A few such words or phrases can be used like the group above, or on their own in initial position as part of the clause, e.g.:

Er ist unzuverlässig. **Zum Beispiel,** er kommt immer spät *or* **Zum Beispiel** kommt er immer spät.

The following words and phrases can be used like this:

zum Beispiel	*for instance*	natürlich	*of course*
erstens, zweitens, etc. (see 9.2.3)	*first, secondly*, etc.	offen gesagt	*to be frank*

(iii) A few adverbs and particles can be used together with another element in initial position, i.e.:

Am Ende **freilich** ist etwas Unerwartetes und etwas Neues da (*Borst*)	*To be sure at the end something new and unexpected is there*
Der Buchfink **jedoch** ist nur in den ersten Lebensmonaten lernfähig (*NZZ*)	*Chaffinches, on the other hand, are only able to learn in the first months of their life*
Selbst in den Chroniken der Städter **schließlich** hat sich die Stadt als revolutionäre Neuheit in die Feudalwelt gestellt (*Borst*)	*After all, even in the chronicles of the burghers the city appears as a revolutionary innovation in feudal society*

The following adverbs can be used in this way:

allerdings	*to be sure, admittedly*	jedenfalls	*at any rate*
also	*thus*	jedoch	*however*
freilich	*to be sure, admittedly*	wenigstens	*at least*
höchstens	*at most*	sozusagen	*so to speak*
immerhin	*all the same*	übrigens	*incidentally*

Alternatively, these can occur on their own in initial position in the usual way, e.g. *Freilich ist am Ende etwas Unerwartetes und etwas Neues da*. In practice, this is more frequent.

NB: The function of these adverbs is like that of a coordinating conjunction in such constructions, and the conjunctions *aber* and *doch* have a similar flexibility in their positioning, see 19.1.1c.

(iv) Some types of subordinate clause are seen as separate from the main clause and are followed by another element before the finite verb, in particular:

a *was*-clause which relates to the following clause as a whole:

Was so wichtig ist, das Buch verkauft sich gut	*What is so important, the book is selling well*

concessive clauses of the 'whatever' type, see 19.6.2:

> **Es mag noch so kalt sein,** die Post muss ausgetragen werden
> **Wer er auch ist,** ich kann nichts für ihn tun
> **Wie schnell er auch lief,** der Polizist holte ihn ein

(v) Two (or more) elements of the same kind can occur together in initial position if they complement or extend one another. In effect, they are seen as a single element. This is most frequent with adverbials of time and place, e.g.:

> **Gestern um zwei Uhr** wurde mein Mann operiert
> **Auf dem alten Marktplatz in der Marburger Stadtmitte** findet diese Woche ein Fest statt
> **Gestern Abend in Leipzig** fand eine große Demonstration statt

(vi) A highlighted element can occur in isolation from the clause and dislocated from it. It is usually picked up by a pronoun or the like in initial position in the clause proper, e.g.:

> **Nach Kanada auswandern**, das haben sie ja immer gewollt
> **Die Gudrun**, der traue ich ja alles zu
> **Der Nachbar**, der hat uns ja immer davon abhalten wollen
> **Als ich davon hörte**, da war es schon zu spät
> **Mit Andreas**, da wird es bald Ärger geben

Alternatively, the highlighted element may be placed after the clause, with a pronoun within the clause which refers forward to it, e.g. *Der traue ich doch alles zu, der Gudrun*. These constructions are typical of everyday colloquial language and are rarely encountered in formal writing.

21.2.2 The initial element functions as the TOPIC of the clause

The topic is the element in a sentence which we mention first to say something more about it:

> **Der Kranke** hat die ganze Nacht nicht geschlafen
>   (Information is being given about the patient)
> **In Frankfurt** findet jedes Jahr die internationale Buchmesse statt
>   (We are being told what happens in Frankfurt)
> **In diesem Zimmer** kannst du dich nicht richtig konzentrieren
>   (We are given information about this room)
> **In zwei Tagen** wird die Reparatur fertig sein
>   (We are informed about what will be happening in two days)

The topic, in initial position, functions as a starting point for the clause. It comes first because we want to give the listener or reader some piece of new information about it. The following general observations can be made about the topic in a German main clause statement.

(a) The element in initial position is often known or familiar to both speaker and listener

A clause often starts off with something which is known in this way, and some piece of new information is given about it later in the clause. This is shown by the examples above and the following:

> **Trotz des Poststreiks** ist der Brief rechtzeitig angekommen
>   (You knew about the postal strike, but it's news to you that the letter still got there on time)
> **An den meisten deutschen Gymnasien** ist Englisch die erste Fremdsprache
>   (You know about German schools but this is something you didn't know about the curriculum)

It is because a clause often begins with an element which is familiar to both speaker and listener that time adverbials are so common in initial position.

(b) The initial element often refers back to something just mentioned

Very often we want to pick up something which has just been referred to and give further information about it. The initial element often takes up a preceding word or phrase in continuous texts or dialogue:

Wir haben ihn im Garten gesucht, aber **im Garten** war niemand zu sehen
Ich sehe ihn oft. **Seinen Bruder** aber sehe ich jetzt recht selten
Ich war drei Wochen auf Sylt. – **Darum** siehst du auch so gut aus.

The answer to a question often repeats an element in the question in initial position and gives the answer later in the clause. Compare:

Was ist gegen Kriegsende geschehen?	– **Gegen Kriegsende** wurden viele Städte zerstört
Wann wurden diese Städte zerstört?	– **Diese Städte** wurden gegen Kriegsende zerstört

(c) The element in initial position is hardly ever the main piece of new information in the clause

Most main clauses begin with something familiar and the new information appears later. In this way, the following sentences sound odd because they start off with an important piece of new information:

?? **In einem kleinen Dorf** in Böhmen ist Stifter im Jahre 1805 geboren
?? **Ein neues Schloss** kaufte dieser Mann gestern
?? **Scharlachrot** ist ihr neues Kleid

These examples show that it is not true that 'any' element can be placed first 'for emphasis'. The first element must be a suitable topic or starting point for the clause. The strongest emphasis is usually on the most important piece of new information which appears later in the clause, see 21.3.

(d) In many clauses, the subject may not be suitable for initial position

The subject is often a natural choice as topic of a clause. However, if the subject involves new information, it is often more natural to begin with another element which is known and delay the subject until later in the clause:

Vor deiner Tür steht doch **ein neues Auto** (With strong emphasis on the surprise at seeing the new car)	*But there's a new car by your front door*
Zwei Tage darauf wurde gegen die Streikenden **Militär** eingesetzt (*Brecht*) (*Militär* is the crucial new information; it would sound odd to begin the sentence with it)	*Two days later the military was deployed against the strikers*

It is unusual for a sentence to begin with an indefinite noun, as they normally involve new pieces of information. For similar reasons, the subject rarely occurs in initial position with verbs of happening, since the event is usually the main new information (see also 21.5.3), e.g.: *Gestern ereignete sich **ein schwerer Unfall** in der Mariahilfer Straße.*

A 'dummy subject' *es* (see 3.6.2d) is often used to shift the subject to later in the clause and give it heavier emphasis as important new information, e.g.:

Es kamen **viele Gäste**	*There were many guests*
Es möchte Sie **jemand** am Telefon sprechen	*There's somebody who wants to speak to you on the telephone*

(e) The topic of the sentence can be changed readily

The emphasis in a clause can be altered by changing the element in initial position. What we choose to place in first position depends on how we want to present the information and what we assume the listener already knows. Thus, if we say:

Das Konzert findet heute Abend im Rathaus statt

we assume the listener knows that there is a concert on, and we are telling him or her where it is. On the other hand, if we say:

Heute Abend findet ein Konzert im Rathaus statt

we are telling the listener what's happening tonight. We are assuming that he or she doesn't know that there's a concert on in the town hall, and we are giving him or her this information. We can begin with *heute Abend*, because that is information which the speaker and the listener share. Finally, if we say:

Im Rathaus findet heute Abend ein Konzert statt

we are telling the listener something about the town hall, i.e. that there's a concert on there tonight.

21.2.3 English equivalents for German constructions with an element other than the subject in initial position

The ease with which an element can be moved into the initial position in German to serve as the topic, as shown in 21.2.2e, is not shared by English, where the order SUBJECT + VERB is fixed. If we want to convert something other than the natural subject of the verb into the topic of a main clause in English, we often have to use a more complex construction. This is unnecessary in German. The following gives examples of such English constructions and their German equivalents.

(a) Cleft sentences

If we want to bring an element other than the subject into first position in English, we often put it in a clause of its own with 'it' and the verb 'be', e.g. *It was Angela (who) I gave the book to*. These are called **cleft sentence** constructions. They are not needed in German, where the topic can simply be shifted into initial position before the verb:

Erst gestern habe ich es ihr gesagt	*It was only yesterday that I told her*
Dort habe ich sie getroffen	*It was there that I met her*
Weil sie oft schwimmt, ist sie fit	*It's because she swims a lot that she's fit*
Was man sagt, zählt	*It's what you say that counts*

There are many variants of this construction, all with simpler equivalents in German:

Dieses Auto da muss ich kaufen	*That's the car I've got to buy*
Dort/Hier wohnt sie	*That/This is where she lives*
Das meine ich (auch)	*That's what I mean*
So macht man das	*That's the way to do it*

Dann ist es passiert	*That's when it happened*
Dem gehört es	*That's whose it is*
Im Frühjahr ist es hier am schönsten	*Spring is when it's loveliest here*
Zu diesem Schluss gelangt Haas in ihrer neusten Arbeit	*This is the conclusion reached by Haas in her most recent work*

With the exception of the type *Er war es, der mich davon abhielt*, i.e. with the subject of the sentence in the cleft to emphasise it (see 3.6.2c), cleft sentence constructions rarely sound natural in German and are best avoided.

(b) English often uses a passive construction where an active is possible or preferable in German

Passive constructions are often used in English to shift the object of the verb to initial position (as the subject of the verb) and function as its topic. Although passives are not unusual in German, a construction using the active voice, with the object in initial position, is often preferred (see also 15.5). For example:

Meinem Vater hat der Chef sehr freundlich gratuliert	*My father was congratulated by the boss in a very kindly way*
Auf diese Worte müssen nun Taten folgen (*Zeit*)	*These words must now be followed by deeds*

(c) English can use a construction with 'have' and a participle

This construction brings the relevant element to the beginning of the sentence by making it the subject of 'have'. There is no equivalent construction in German, where the relevant element is simply placed in initial position:

In diesem Buch fehlen zwanzig Seiten	*This book has (got) twenty pages missing*
In diesem Wald haben voriges Jahr viele Nachtigallen genistet	*This wood had a lot of nightingales nesting in it last year*
Ihm wurde eine Golduhr gestohlen	*He had a gold watch stolen*
Ihnen wurden die Fenster eingeworfen	*They had their windows smashed*

21.3 The order of other elements in the sentence: general principles

Most elements in all clause types come within the verbal bracket explained in 21.1. The relative order of the elements inside the verbal bracket is the same for all clause types:

Initial position	Bracket[1] [	Other elements	Bracket[2]]
Sie	hat	**ihn heute zufällig in der Stadt**	gesehen
	Hat	**sie ihn heute zufällig in der Stadt**	gesehen?
. . .,	weil	**sie ihn heute zufällig in der Stadt**	gesehen hat

This order is determined by two basic principles:

(i) Elements which are more heavily stressed and convey important new information tend to follow elements which are less stressed.

The elements inside the verbal bracket are usually put in order of increasing importance, passing from unstressed elements like pronouns to those elements which represent the main new information and are given most emphasis. The element nearest the end of the bracket is typically the most important piece of new information and typically carries the heaviest stress.

(ii) Elements which are more closely linked to the verb tend to come after elements with a less strong link.

Many verb complements usually appear immediately before the final part of the verbal bracket. Similarly, direct objects, if they are nouns, normally come after the indirect objects, whose link with the verb is less 'direct'.

Following these general principles, the elements within the verbal bracket tend to occur in the order given in Table 21.1.

The order given in Table 21.1 reflects general guidelines for the English-speaking learner, and it should not be taken to represent rigid rules of German word order. However, following these guidelines will almost always produce an acceptable German sentence, if they can be varied in certain ways for reasons of emphasis. Details on the position of each of the groups of elements are outlined in sections 21.4 to 21.8.

However, English-speaking learners need to be aware of the effect, in terms of emphasis and presentation, of changing the position of elements in a sentence. It is quite possible to end up saying something rather different to what you mean.

21.4 The position of pronouns

21.4.1 Pronouns normally follow immediately after the finite verb or the conjunction

Pronouns refer to persons and things already mentioned, or well known to the speaker and listener. They are typically unstressed and occupy the least prominent position within the verbal bracket, before everything else:

> Gestern hat **ihn** mein Mann in der Stadt gesehen
> Hat **ihn** dein Mann gestern in der Stadt gesehen?
> Da **ihn** mein Mann gestern in der Stadt gesehen hat, . . .
> Dann hat **es** mein Bruder meinem Vater gegeben
> Dann hat **mir** mein Bruder den Brief gegeben

The only exception to this rule is that pronouns can be placed **before** OR **after a noun subject**. It is more usual for them to come first, but the following are quite usual alternatives to the first three examples above:

> Gestern hat mein Mann **ihn** in der Stadt gesehen
> Hat dein Mann **ihn** gestern in der Stadt gesehen?
> Da dein Mann **ihn** gestern in der Stadt gesehen hat, . . .

However, a pronoun does more usually follow a noun subject if the endings do not show nominative and accusative case clearly:

Gestern hat meine Mutter **sie** in der Stadt gesehen	*My mother saw her in town yesterday*
Da das Mädchen **sie** in der Stadt gesehen hat, . . .	*As the girl has seen her in town* . . .

> (*Da sie das Mädchen in der Stadt gesehen hat* would normally be taken to mean 'As she has seen the girl in town')

If there are two pronoun objects, it is more usual for them to follow a noun subject, e.g.:

TABLE 21.1 Basic order of the elements in the German sentence

	Topic	Bracket¹	Pronouns N	A	D	Noun subject	Dative noun object	Most adverbials	Accusative noun object	Manner adverbials	Complements	Bracket²
Main clause	Heute Jan Wir	hat soll wurden			ihr	mein Freund	dem Chef	heimlich jetzt nachher	eine E-Mail den Bericht			geschickt. bringen. erinnert.
Question/ command		Hat Soll Geben	sie er Sie	es	ihm Ihnen mir			denn trotzdem sofort	den Weg das Geld	höflich richtig	daran	erklärt? zeigen? zurück!
Subordinate clause		..., weil ..., da ..., dass	sie			der alte Herr meine Tante	dem Mann	meistens	den Brief	vorsichtig schnell	für seine Hilfe in die Tasche	gedankt hat. fährt. stecken wollte.

Weil der Lehrer **es ihnen** gezeigt hat, . . .   *Because the teacher has shown it to them, . . .*

Nevertheless, other orders are also possible, e.g. *Weil es der Lehrer ihnen gezeigt hat, . . . Weil es ihnen der Lehrer gezeigt hat, . . .*

21.4.2 **Personal pronouns precede other pronouns**

Thus, *er, dir, Ihnen, ihm*, etc. (and *man*) come before demonstrative pronouns such as *der, das, dieser*, etc., irrespective of case, e.g.:

Wollen **Sie die** gleich mitnehmen?   *Do you want to take those away with you?*
Hat **ihn dieser** denn nicht erkannt?   *Didn't that person recognise him, then?*
Eben hat sie **mir das** gezeigt   *She's just shown me that*

21.4.3 **Personal pronouns occur in the order nominative + accusative + dative**

This order is usual if there is more than one personal pronoun within the verbal bracket:

Da **sie dich ihm** nicht vorstellen wollte, . . .   *As she didn't want to introduce you to him . . .*
Hast **du es uns** nicht schon gesagt?   *Haven't you already told us that?*
Gestern hat **er sie ihm** gegeben   *He gave them to him yesterday*
Heute will **sie ihm** helfen   *She's going to help him today*
Heinz hat **es mir** gezeigt   *Heinz showed it to me*

This order is relatively fixed. The only common variation on it is that the pronoun *es*, in the reduced form *'s*, often follows a dative pronoun in colloquial speech, e.g. *Heinz hat **mir's** gezeigt*.

21.4.4 **The position of the reflexive pronoun** *sich*

sich normally occurs in the same position as other accusative or dative pronouns, i.e. immediately after the finite verb or the conjunction (and after a pronoun in the nominative, if there is one):

Gestern hat **sich** der Deutsche über das Essen beschwert
Gestern hat **sich** jemand darüber beschwert
Gestern hat er **sich** darüber beschwert
Er hatte es **sich** (*dat*.!) so vorgestellt
Er hat **sich** (*acc*.!) mir vorgestellt

However, it is occasionally placed after a noun subject, e.g.: *Gestern hat der Deutsche **sich** über das Essen beschwert*. Very occasionally, it is placed even later in the clause, e.g.: *Gestern hat der Deutsche über das Essen **sich** beschwert*. In general, this is only possible with 'true' reflexive verbs used with an accusative reflexive, see 18.3.6a.

21.5 **The position of noun subject and objects**

21.5.1 **The usual order for noun subject and objects within the verbal bracket is nominative + dative + accusative**

This group of elements includes not only noun phrases in the nominative, accusative or dative case, but also indefinite pronouns such as *etwas, jemand, niemand, nichts*. As Table 21.1 shows, they usually follow personal and demonstrative pronouns (but see 21.4.1 for exceptions), and precede other verb complements. The position of adverbials in relation to them is explained in 21.6.1. Examples:

Gestern hat **jemand meinem Vater eine Kettensäge** geliehen
Warum hat **Manfred seiner Freundin nichts** gebracht?
Ich weiß, dass **mein Freund seiner Frau diese Bitte** nicht verweigern konnte
Heute hat **der Chef den Mitarbeitern** für ihre Mühe gedankt

Variations on this order usually involve special circumstances of some kind, as explained in 21.5.2 and 21.5.3.

21.5.2 The dative object sometimes follows the accusative object

(a) If the dative object refers to a person, this order indicates it is much more important in context and emphasises it very strongly

This possibility is used sparingly:

Er hat sein ganzes Vermögen **seinem**   *He left his whole fortune to his nephew*
     Neffen vermacht
     (We already know about the fortune, what is surprising is who he left it to; *Neffen* is heavily stressed to indicate this)

Er stellte seinen Neffen **dem Pfarrer** vor   *He introduced his nephew to the parson*
     (**Who** the nephew was introduced to is the important fact. Compare the sentence *Er stellte dem Pfarrer seinen Neffen vor*)

als mein Vater diese merkwürdige   *when my father told this remarkable story*
     Geschichte **einem ihm völlig**   *to a gentleman whom he didn't know*
     unbekannten Herrn erzählte   *at all*
     (The dative object is indefinite and thus previously unknown to the listener. It is more newsworthy and significant in context than 'this story', which must have been mentioned before)

(b) If both accusative and dative objects refer to things, the more important of them in context is placed second

dass er uns nicht alle zwingt, unsere   *that he's not forcing us all to subject our higher aims*
     höheren Zwecke **seinem Interesse** zu   *to his personal interest*
     unterwerfen (*Wolf*)
Er hat sein Glück **seiner Karriere** geopfert   *He sacrificed his happiness to his career*

     (Compare the different emphasis in *Er hat seiner Karriere **sein ganzes Glück** geopfert*)

(c) A dative object referring to a thing usually follows an accusative object referring to a person

It is rarely possible for the dative object to come first in such contexts:

Sie überantworteten die Verbrecher **der**   *They delivered up the criminal to justice*
     Justiz
Sie haben den armen Jungen **der**   *They exposed the poor boy to ridicule*
     Lächerlichkeit preisgegeben

21.5.3 The noun subject can follow an accusative and/or a dative object (and other elements) if it constitutes the major piece of new information

See also 21.2.2d. In practice the subject in such contexts is usually a noun with an indefinite article or no article, or an indefinite pronoun:

Glücklicherweise wartet nun in Wien an jeder Ecke **ein Kaffeehaus** (*Zweig*)	*Luckily there is a coffee house waiting for you on every corner in Vienna*
Nun begrüßte den Dirigenten und den Virtuosen **lautes Händeklatschen** (*Kapp*)	*Now the conductor and the virtuoso were met with loud applause*
Gestern hat meinen Bruder Gott sei dank **niemand** gestört	*Thank goodness nobody disturbed my brother yesterday*
Er wusste, dass dieser Gruppe **etwas Unangenehmes** bevorstand	*He knew that something unpleasant was in store for this group*

Occasionally a subject with a definite article is placed late in the clause if it needs strong emphasis:

Die Tatsache, dass der EU unausweichlich **das Geld** ausgeht	*The fact that the EU's money will inevitably run out*

The late position of an indefinite subject is almost regular with verbs of happening and the like, and it is also frequent in passive sentences:

Er wusste, dass seinem Chef **eine große Ehre** zuteil geworden war	*He knew that a great honour had been bestowed on his boss*
Zum Glück ist meinem Bruder da **nichts** passiert	*Luckily nothing happened to my brother*
Deshalb können den Asylbewerbern **keine Personalausweise** ausgestellt werden	*For this reason no identity cards can be issued to the asylum-seekers*

21.6 The place and order of adverbials

An adverbial can be a single word (e.g. *trotzdem, heute*), or a phrase with or without a preposition (e.g. *den ganzen Tag, mit großer Mühe*). This difference in form has no effect on word order. The classification of adverbs in Chapter 7 applies equally to all adverbials.

The placing of adverbials is more flexible than that of any other element in the clause. This reflects their general freedom of occurrence as elements optionally added to give additional information, see 18.1.4. This section deals first with the placing of adverbials in relation to other elements (chiefly the noun subject and objects), and then explains the ordering of adverbials where more than one is present.

21.6.1 The position of adverbials in relation to the noun subject and objects

As shown in Table 21.1, most adverbials occur after a noun subject and dative object, but before an accusative object. However, the relative position of adverbials and noun subjects and objects depends very much on their relative importance in the clause. Specifically, that element appears later in the clause which is most strongly stressed or conveys the most important new information.

(a) Unstressed adverbials (usually single words) can precede the noun subject and/or the dative object

This applies in particular to adverbs of attitude (and modal particles, see Chapter 10), e.g. *bestimmt, sicher, vielleicht*, etc. Unstressed short adverbs of time and place like *da, dort, hier, gestern, heute, morgen, dann, damals, daher* also often occur early in the clause, immediately after the personal pronouns, e.g.:

Sie wird **wohl gleich** ihrer Freundin simsen	*She'll probably text her friend straightaway*
Ich weiß, dass sie es **sicher** meinem Vater empfehlen wird	*I know she'll be sure to recommend it to my father*
Sie ist **heute** ihrem Freund aus Bonn begegnet	*She met her friend from Bonn today*
Hat sie **schon damals** ihrem Großvater die ganze Geschichte erzählt?	*Did she tell her grandfather the whole story at that time?*

In most of the above contexts the adverb could follow the noun subject or objects, and it would then be more strongly emphasised. Compare *Hat sie ihrem Großvater **schon damals** die ganze Geschichte erzählt?* However, such permutation is not possible in contexts where the noun subject or object is a vital piece of new information (especially if it is indefinite) and needs to be placed where it carries most stress, e.g.:

Das hat **bisher** keiner gemerkt	*Nobody's noticed it up to now*
Da war **doch** niemand	*Nobody was there, though*
Ich bin **dort** einem Freund von deinem Bruder begegnet	*I ran into a friend of your brother's there*

A sentence like *Da war niemand doch* sounds quite odd.

(b) The order of adverbials and noun objects (accusative or dative) usually depends on emphasis

i.e. how important they are in the context of the whole clause or sentence. The element which is being presented as more important comes later. Compare the following:

Er hat diese neuen Wagen **im Sommer** gekauft
    (The stress is on **when** he bought the new car)
Er hat im Sommer **diesen neuen Wagen** gekauft
    (The emphasis is on **what** he bought)

Sie haben Fußball **im Park** gespielt
    (This tells us **where** they were playing)
Sie haben im Park **Fußball** gespielt
    (This tells us **what** they were playing)

Das hat **gestern** ihr Kollege meinem Verlobten erzählt
    (**Who** was told is the point at issue)
Das hat ihr Kollege **gestern** meinem Verlobten erzahlt
    (Who did the telling is seen as relatively unimportant)
Das hat ihr Kollege meinem Verlobten **gestern** erzählt
    (prominence is given to the time when the fiancé was told)

Although, from a grammatical point of view, there is flexibility in the order of these elements, in a particular context only one may be appropriate. Thus, in answer to the question *Wann hat er diesen neuen Wagen gekauft?* one would most naturally use the first of the alternatives above, and the second would sound strange.

(c) Adverbials of manner follow the noun objects

(and **all** other adverbials, see 21.6.2). This is because they usually convey the most important new information:

Meiner Meinung nach hat das Quartett dieses Stück **viel zu schnell** gespielt	*In my opinion the quartet played that piece much too fast*
Er warf den Ball **sehr vorsichtig** über den Gartenzaun	*He threw the ball very carefully over the garden fence*

21.6.2 **The relative order of adverbials**

(a) If a clause contains more than one adverbial, they most frequently occur in the order:

attitude – time – reason – viewpoint – place – manner

These groups correspond to the classification in Chapter 7

(i) Adverbials of attitude. This group includes all the modal particles (see Chapter 10) and other adverbials which express some attitude on the part of the speaker towards what is being said (see 7.3.2), e.g. *angeblich, leider, vermutlich, zum Glück, zweifellos*, etc.:

Sie wollte **doch** vor zwei Uhr in Magdeburg sein
Er ist **vielleicht** schon am Montag abgereist

(ii) Time adverbials. As explained in 11.6 these can indicate a point in time (e.g. *bald, voriges Jahr, am kommenden Sonntag*), frequency (e.g. *stündlich, jeden Tag*) or duration (e.g. *lange, seit Montag, ein ganzes Jahr*). If there is more than one time adverbial in a clause, they are usually placed in the order

point of time – duration – frequency

Within these categories the general precedes the particular, e.g. *jeden Tag um vier Uhr*. Examples:

Sie ist **vor zwei Tagen** trotz des Sturms nach Reutte gewandert
Die Streikenden blieben **vier Stunden lang** vor dem Rathaus versammelt

(iii) Adverbials of reason i.e. adverbials expressing circumstance (e.g. *zu unserem Erstaunen*), condition (e.g. *gegebenenfalls*), purpose (e.g. *zur Durchsicht*) or reason (e.g. *wegen des Unfalls*), see 7.3.3. The passive agent introduced by *von* or *durch* (see 15.3) also occurs in this position:

Sie hat den Brief **trotzdem** mit der Maschine geschrieben
Der Brand wurde **von der freiwilligen Feuerwehr** schnell gelöscht

(iv) Viewpoint adverbials e.g. *finanziell* 'from a financial point of view', see 7.3.1b. Phrases with *mit* and *ohne* also occur in this position:

Deutschland ist in den letzten Jahren **wirtschaftlich** stärker geworden
Sie geht **mit Begeisterung** in die Tanzschule

(v) Place adverbials. See 7.1. Place adverbials should be distinguished from direction complements, see (c) below.

Sie geht mit Begeisterung **in die Tanzschule**
Ich habe bis 18 Uhr **im Büro** gearbeitet

(vi) Manner adverbials i.e. those which indicate how an action is carried out, see 7.3.1. Adverbs of manner are almost always the final element in the clause before any complements:

Sie ist heute mit ihrem Porsche **viel zu schnell** in die Kurve gefahren
Der Vorschlag wurde von den Anwesenden **einstimmig** angenommen

(b) The order of adverbials can be varied for emphasis

The relative order given in (a) above is only a guide to a 'neutral' order of the adverbs, assuming they all have roughly similar emphasis, and it is not a rigid rule. As with the relative order of adverbials and the noun subject and objects, variation in the order of adverbials follows the general principle given in 21.3, i.e. an adverbial can be given more or less emphasis by being placed later or earlier in the clause. This often depends on what is regarded as the main new information in context, which needs to be emphasised, e.g.:

Paula ist zum Glück **gestern** nicht zu schnell gefahren
Paula ist gestern **zum Glück** nicht zu schnell gefahren
   (The adverbial in bold is made more prominent in each case by being placed later. The manner adverbial, as the major information, is the last element in both cases.)

Viele deutsche Städte wurden gegen Kriegsende **von den Alliierten** zerstört
Viele deutsche Städte wurden von den Alliierten **gegen Kriegsende** zerstört
   (Placing the time adverbial after the *von*-phrase in the second example gives it particular prominence, possibly in reply to a question about when it happened.)

Sie hat sehr lange **dort** auf ihre Mutter gewartet
Sie hat dort **sehr lange** auf ihre Mutter gewartet
   (Time adverbials usually precede place adverbials, but they can follow if they need to be given prominence. The prepositional object always follows both adverbials.)

(c) The traditional rule that adverbials occur in the order time – manner – place can be misleading

As shown in (a) above, adverbials normally occur in the order **time – place – manner**:

Der junge Tenor hat gestern in Berlin **gut** gesungen
Die Kinder wollten heute auf der Wiese **ungestört** spielen

Elements indicating direction or place at the end of the verbal bracket, immediately before the final part of the verb, are complements of the verb, not adverbials, see 18.8 and 21.8.1. These complements follow **all** adverbials, including those of manner:

Paula ist gestern viel zu schnell **in die Kurve** gefahren
Andreas wollte gestern mit seiner Freundin gemütlich **nach Freising** wandern
Sie hat die schöne Vase sehr vorsichtig **auf den Tisch** gestellt
Müllers wohnen einsam in einem großen Haus **im Wald**
Astrid lag erschöpft **auf der Couch**
Sie sind wegen des schlechten Wetters widerwillig **zu Hause** geblieben

The elements in bold in the above examples are **direction complements** depending on verbs of motion, or **place complements** depending on verbs of position. As explained in 18.1.4, complements are more closely linked to the verb than adverbials, which simply give additional circumstantial information. Following the principles given in 21.3, they are placed at the end of the verbal bracket.

21.7 **The position of *nicht* and other negative elements**

Other negative elements like *nie* 'never' and *kaum* 'hardly, scarcely' occupy the same position in the clause as *nicht*, and the following applies equally to them.

21.7.1 **The position of *nicht* if it negates the content of the whole clause**

In this case, *nicht* is placed near the end of the clause, just **before any adverbs of manner and verb complements**. *Nicht* is similar to an adverb of manner, and this determines its position if it relates globally to the whole content of the clause. However, it usually precedes manner adverbials.

(a) *nicht* follows any noun objects

Er hat seine neue Stelle **nicht** erwähnt	*He didn't mention his new job*
Er hat mir das Buch **nicht** gegeben	*He didn't give me the book*
Verkaufe die Bücher **nicht**!	*Don't sell the books*
Ich weiß, dass sie ihren Bruder gestern **nicht** gesehen hat	*I know she didn't see her brother yesterday*

However, *nicht* precedes objects with no article which are part of a fixed verb phrase (see 21.8.2):

Sie hatte damals **nicht** Klavier gespielt	*She didn't play the piano then*

(b) *nicht* follows all adverbials except those of manner

Sie haben sich seit langem **nicht** gesehen	*They haven't seen each other for a long time*
Den Turm sieht man von hier aus **nicht**	*You can't see the tower from here*
Ich wollte es ihr trotzdem **nicht** geben	*I didn't want to give it to her all the same*
Das ist mir in diesem Zusammenhang **nicht** aufgefallen	*That didn't occur to me in that context*
Wir sind wegen des Regens **nicht** nach Bernau gewandert	*We didn't walk to Bernau because it was raining*
Sie haben gestern **nicht** gut gespielt	*They didn't play well yesterday*
Ich weiß es **nicht** ausführlich	*I don't know it in detail*

(c) *nicht* precedes most verb complements

i.e. all complements of the verb **except** the subject and the objects of the verb, see 21.8:

Sie sind gestern **nicht** nach Aalen gefahren	*They didn't go to Aalen yesterday*
Sie legte das Buch **nicht** auf den Tisch	*She didn't put the book on the table*
Wir konnten uns **nicht** an diesen Vorfall erinnern	*We couldn't remember the incident*
Er blieb **nicht** in Rostock	*He didn't stay in Rostock*
Sie ist sicher **nicht** dumm	*She's certainly not stupid*
Sie war heute **nicht** im Büro	*She wasn't at the office today*

nicht can follow prepositional objects or direction complements **if** it is relatively unstressed and the complement has to be emphasised. Compare:

Das kann ich doch **nicht von ihm** verlangen	*I <u>can't</u> ask that of him*
Das kann ich doch **von ihm nicht** verlangen	*I can't ask that of <u>him</u>*

21.7.2 **If *nicht* applies to ONE particular element in the clause it precedes it**

Sie hat mir **nicht** das Buch gegeben (not the book, but something else)	*She didn't give me the book*
Sie sind **nicht** am Freitag nach Kreta geflogen (not Friday, but some other day)	*They didn't fly to Crete on Friday*

Nicht mir hat er das Buch gegeben, sondern meiner Schwester

It wasn't me he gave the book to, it was my sister

Compare the 'partial' negation in the first example above with 'global' negation of the whole clause, with *nicht* in its usual position: *Sie hat mir das Buch nicht gegeben* simply means 'She didn't give me the book'.

NB: Alternatively, the stressed element can appear on its own in the initial position, with the *nicht* later in the clause, e.g. *Mir hat er das Buch **nicht** gegeben*. This is common if the contrast is implicit, i.e. if there is no following *sondern* clause.

Unstressed *nicht* is often used in this way in tentative or rhetorical questions or exclamations, e.g.:

Hast du **nicht** die Königin gesehen?

Didn't you see the Queen?

War **nicht** dein Vater eigentlich etwas enttäuscht?

Wasn't your father really a bit disappointed?

Was du **nicht** alles weißt!

Don't you know a lot!

21.8 The position of complements

Apart from the subject and objects of the verb, which have their own position in the clause (see 21.4–21.5), the other complements of the verb (see 18.5–18.8) are always placed towards the end of the verbal bracket. This position is relatively fixed, irrespective of emphasis, and only very exceptionally are the complements found earlier in the clause.

21.8.1 The following complements are placed at the end of the verbal bracket

(a) prepositional objects

Nun wird er sich sicher **um seine beiden Kinder** kümmern können

Now he will certainly be able to look after his two children

Sie hat in der Ankunftshalle lange **auf ihren Mann** gewartet

She waited for her husband in the arrivals hall for a long time

Wir haben uns vorgestern lange und ausführlich **darüber** unterhalten

We talked about it in detail for a long time the day before yesterday

(b) the predicate complement of copular verbs

i.e. *sein, werden, bleiben, scheinen, heißen*, see 18.8. This complement may be a noun or an adjective:

Herbert war immerhin längere Zeit **der beste Schüler** in unserer Klasse

All the same, Herbert was top of our class for a long time

Sie wurde plötzlich **blass**

She suddenly turned pale

Dann scheinen mir diese Bedingungen jedoch **etwas hart**

In that case these conditions seem rather hard to me, though

(c) genitive objects

weil der Verletzte dringend **eines Arztes** bedurfte

because the injured man urgently needed a doctor

(d) direction complements with verbs of motion

Warum hat Peter den Stein plötzlich **in den Bach** geworfen?

Why did Peter suddenly throw the stone into the stream?

Sie ist mit ihrem Porsche zu schnell **in die Kurve** gefahren

She took the bend too fast in her Porsche

Wir möchten nächste Woche **nach Emden zu meinen Eltern** fahren	*We want to go to my parents' in Emden next week*

(e) place complements with verbs of position

Er befand sich plötzlich **in einem dunklen Saal**	*He suddenly found himself in a dark room*
Er wollte unter keinen Umständen **in Duisburg** bleiben	*He didn't want to remain in Duisburg under any circumstances*
Sie haben lange **in dieser Hütte** gewohnt	*They lived in that hut for a long time*

21.8.2 **The position of the noun portions of phrasal verbs**

Extended verb phrases can consist of a noun (often an infinitive or other verbal noun) used in a set phrase with a verb, e.g. *Abstand halten, Abschied nehmen, ins Rollen geraten*. The noun portion of these is always placed in the last position in the verbal bracket. They are similar to separable prefixes, and could be considered as forming part of the final portion of the verb bracket rather than as separate elements within the clause.

Er hat sie durch seine Unvorsichtigkeit **in die größte Gefahr** gebracht	*He brought her into very great danger through his carelessness*
Ich habe ihr alle meine Bücher **zur Verfügung** gestellt	*I put all my books at her disposal*
Gestern hat uns der Minister von seinem Entschluss **in Kenntnis** gesetzt	*The Minister informed us of his decision yesterday*
Sein Chef hat ihn vorige Woche sehr **unter Druck** gesetzt	*His boss put him under a lot of pressure last week*
Ich merkte, wie der Wagen langsam **ins Rollen** kam	*I noticed the car slowly starting to roll forwards*

21.9 *Ausklammerung*: placing elements after the end of the verbal bracket

The last element in a German clause is usually the final part of the verb, whether this is a separable prefix, an infinitive or a past participle (in main clause statements, questions and commands) or the finite verb (in subordinate clauses).

However, there are some contexts where it is usual or possible to place an element after the final part of the verb. This construction is called *Ausklammerung* in German, and it is becoming increasingly frequent, even in formal writing. This section explains where *Ausklammerung* is preferable or acceptable in modern German.

21.9.1 **Subordinate clauses are not normally enclosed within the verbal bracket**

Sentences with clauses enclosed within one another and a cluster of verbs at the end (called *Schachtelsätze*, because they are like sets of boxes inside each other) can be cumbersome and are best avoided. Taken to extremes they can be quite impenetrable, like the following example:

Das „Vorsicht-Glatteis"-Verkehrszeichen, das letzte Nacht, die Frostbildung, was für den Autofahrer, der etwas getrunken und ein Auto gefahren, das abgefahrene Reifen hat, hat, erhöhte Gefahren mit sich bringt, brachte, total beschädigt wurde, wird nicht mehr aufgestellt.

As a general rule it is preferable to complete one clause, with the final part of its verbal bracket, before starting another. In the following pair of sentences, the second alternative, though not ungrammatical, is nowadays generally regarded as clumsy:

Ich konnte den Gedanken nicht loswerden, **dass wir ihn betrogen hatten**
Ich konnte den Gedanken, **dass wir ihn betrogen hatten**, nicht loswerden

A relative clause can be separated from the noun it refers to in order to avoid enclosing it:

Und wie dürfte man eine Zeitung verbieten, **die sich wiederholt und nachhaltig für die Wahl der staatstragenden Partei eingesetzt hat**? (*Spiegel*)

Enclosing the relative clause would result in an unwieldy sentence: *Und wie dürfte man eine Zeitung, die sich wiederholt und nachhaltig fur die Wahl der staatstragenden Partei eingesetzt hat, verbieten?*

21.9.2 Infinitive clauses

In general, infinitive clauses are not enclosed within the verbal bracket:

Sie haben beschlossen **vor dem Rathaus zu warten**
Er hat versucht **sein Geschäft zu verkaufen**

However, enclosure is usual or possible in some constructions, notably with some 'semi-auxiliary' verbs. Details are given in 13.2.2.

21.9.3 Comparative phrases introduced by *als* or *wie*

These are usually placed outside the verbal bracket:

Gestern haben wir einen besseren Wein getrunken **als diesen**	*Yesterday we drank a better wine than this one*
Ich wusste, dass sie ebenso ärgerlich war **wie ich**	*I knew she was just as annoyed as me*

However, enclosure of these phrases within the verbal bracket is not unusual:

Die Volkstracht hat sich in Oberbayern stärker **als anderswo in Deutschland** erhalten (*Baedeker*)	*Local costumes have been retained in Upper Bavaria longer than elsewhere in Germany*
ein Mann, der **wie ein Italiener** aussah	*a man who looked like an Italian*

Enclosure is especially frequent within longer clauses, especially in writing:

da die Orangen und Zitronen von den Kindern **wie Schneebälle** über die Gartenmauern geworfen wurden (*Andres*)

21.9.4 Other elements are sometimes placed after the verbal bracket

There are three main reasons for such *Ausklammerung*:

(i) to emphasise the element placed last:

Du hebst das auf **bis nach dem Abendessen** (*Baum*)

(ii) as an afterthought:

Ich habe sie doch heute gesehen **in der Stadt**

(iii) In order not to overstretch the verbal bracket, e.g.:

Seitdem Rodrigue seine Chronik begonnen hatte, freute er sich darauf, sie zu
beschließen **mit der Darstellung der Regierung dieses seines lieben Schülers und Beichtkindes**

The following elements are commonly placed outside the verbal bracket:

(a) Adverbials which have the form of prepositional phrases
These are commonly excluded for the reasons given above:

Hallo, ich rufe an **aus London** (*Telecom advert*)
Vieles hatte Glum schon gesehen **auf seinem Weg von seiner Heimat bis über den Rhein
hinweg** (*Böll*)

In general, these constructions are more typical of colloquial speech than formal writing.
However, *Ausklammerung* is not uncommon in writing, especially if the prepositional phrase is
quite long or if a further clause (usually a relative clause) depends on the element excluded, e.g.
*Von hier aus konnte man noch wenig sehen **von der kleinen Stadt**, die am anderen Ufer im Nebel lag.*

(b) Prepositional objects
Prepositional objects are the only complement of the verb to be regularly excluded in standard
German:

Er hätte das merken können **an den gelegentlichen Rückblicken und dem Arm**,
der entspannt auf der freien Vorderlehne lag (*Johnson*)
Er darf sich entschädigt fühlen **für ganze Jahre Underdog-Dasein im Straßenverkehr** (*Zeit*)
Du solltest dich nicht zu sehr freuen **auf diese Entwicklung**

Not all prepositional objects can be excluded in this way and sentences like, e.g., *Ich habe vor dem
Bahnhof gewartet auf meine Freundin* are unacceptable to many native speakers. No clear rules have
yet been identified about the prepositional objects which can or cannot be excluded.

(c) Other verb complements
i.e. the subject or the accusative and dative objects, or place and direction complements. These
are not usually excluded in standard German, although *Ausklammerung* of lengthy elements is
occasionally found in writing, e.g.:

Wir haben aus Steuergeldern gebaut **Wohnungen für nahezu zwanzigtausend Menschen**

Otherwise, such exclusions are restricted to non-standard colloquial speech (and then only nouns,
never pronouns), e.g. *Gestern habe ich gesehen **Manfred Schuhmacher und Angela Hartmann**.*

(d) Adverbs
Exclusion of simple adverbs is common in colloquial speech, but generally avoided in formal
written German:

Bei uns hat es Spätzle gegeben **heute**
Sie sollen leise reden **hier**
Ich bin nach Trier gefahren **deshalb**
Hat es euch gefallen **dort**?

22 Word formation

We can distinguish in German between SIMPLE WORDS (or 'root words') like *Kind*, *dort* and *schön*, which cannot be broken down, and COMPLEX WORDS like *kindisch*, *dortig* and *Schönheit*, which are obviously made up of more than one component and are derived from simple words in some way. Knowing about German word formation (called 'DERIVATION'), i.e. how these complex words are made up, is invaluable for extending the learner's vocabulary. The importance of being able to work out the meaning of a whole word from its parts, and to recognise patterns like *Dank – danken – dankbar – Dankbarkeit – Undankbarkeit* cannot be overestimated. Such series of words are often much more transparent in German than in English, as we can see when we compare this set to English *thanks – to thank – grateful – gratitude – ingratitude*.

This chapter explains the most frequent means of word formation in German:

- methods of **word formation** (section 22.1)
- the formation of **nouns** (section 22.2)
- the formation of **adjectives** (section 22.3)
- the formation of **verbs** (sections 22.4–22.7)
    - with **inseparable prefixes** (section 22.4)
    - with **separable prefixes** (section 22.5)
    - with **variable prefixes** (section 22.6)
    - other means of **verb formation** (section 22.7)

22.1 Methods of word formation

22.1.1 Complex words are formed from simple words in three main ways

(a) by means of a prefix or suffix

In general, prefixes and suffixes do not occur as words in their own right, but are only used with root-words to form other words, e.g.:

(i) prefixes:

die Sprache	→ die **Ur**sprache	schön	→ **un**schön
stehen	→ **be**stehen	besser	→ **ver**bessern

(ii) suffixes:

gemein	→ die Gemein**heit**	bedeuten	→ die Bedeu**tung**
der Freund	→ freund**lich**	denken	→ denk**bar**
der Motor	→ motor**isieren**	die Kontrolle	→ kontroll**ieren**

Prefixes are most often used to create nouns from nouns, adjectives from adjectives, or verbs from other verbs or from nouns and adjectives. Suffixes are most common to make nouns from adjectives or verbs or adjectives from nouns or verbs; they are seldom used to form verbs.

(b) by means of vowel changes

These vowel changes are often linked with particular suffixes, but they can occur on their own. The following vowel changes are used in word formation:

(i) *Umlaut*:

| der Arzt | → die Ärztin | der Bart | → bärtig |
| der Druck | → drücken | scharf | → schärfen |

(ii) *Ablaut*, i.e. vowel changes like those of the strong verbs, see 12.1.2. *Ablaut* in word formation is chiefly restricted to use with strong verb roots:

| aufsteigen | → der Aufstieg | werfen | → der Wurf |
| beißen | → bissig | schließen | → schlüssig |

These vowel changes, especially *Ablaut*, are barely still productive (see 22.1.2) in modern German.

(c) by forming compound words
In compounding, a new word is made up from two (or more) existing words:

| der Staub + saugen | → der Staubsauger | hell + blau | → hellblau |
| der Rat + das Haus | → das Rathaus | die Brust + schwimmen | → brustschwimmen |

Sometimes there is a linking sound between the two words, e.g.:

| der Bauer + der Hof | → der Bauernhof |
| das Land + der Mann | → der Landsmann |

The ease with which compounds can be formed is a distinctive feature of German (and the source of the notorious long words), and the extensive use of compounds is typical of modern German, especially in technical registers.

22.1.2 Productive and unproductive word formation patterns

If new words are still being created by means of a particular pattern (e.g. by adding a particular prefix or suffix), that pattern is called **productive**. For example, the suffix *-bar* is commonly used to make adjectives from nouns (= English '-able', '-ible', see 22.3.1a), and new words in *-bar* are regularly found, like *machbar* 'do-able' or even from recent English loans like *downloadbar*.

On the other hand, many abstract nouns from adjectives are found with the suffix *-e*, and *Umlaut* of the root vowel where possible, see 22.2.1b, e.g.:

| groß → die Größe | gut → die Güte | hoch → die Höhe | lang → die Länge |

However, no new nouns are created from adjectives in this way; the pattern is **unproductive**. Nevertheless, it is still important to know about it, because there are so many words in the language which have been formed with this pattern. This chapter deals with the commonest patterns of word formation in German, whether they are productive or unproductive.

22.2 The formation of nouns

22.2.1 Noun derivation by means of suffixes

The following suffixes are common, although not all of them are still fully productive. Most are linked to a particular gender, see 1.1.

(a) *-chen*, *-lein* (neuter)
These suffixes are very productive and used to form **diminutives** from nouns:

| das Auge | → das Äuglein *little eye* | die Karte | → das Kärtchen *little card* |
| das Buch | → das Büchlein *little book* | die Stadt | → das Städtchen *little town* |

The vowel of the stressed syllable usually has *Umlaut* if possible, although exceptions are common, especially with names, e.g. *Kurtchen*. *-chen* is commoner than *-lein*, which is mainly restricted to words ending in *-ch*, *-g* or *-ng*, and to archaic or poetic language. It was originally south German, but, in practice, colloquial south German speech now uses other forms from the local dialects to form diminutives, e.g. *-li* (Switzerland), *-(e)le* (Swabia), *-la* (Franconia), *-(er)l* (Austria and Bavaria).

In some cases, derivations with both *-chen* and *-lein* from the same noun are used with a difference in meaning, e.g. *Fräulein* 'girl', *Frauchen* 'mistress' (e.g. of a dog).

NB: In non-standard colloquial speech, *-chen* is sometimes added to plurals in *-er*, e.g. *Kinderchen*.

(b) *-e* (feminine)

(i) Nouns in *-e* from verbs denote an **action** or an **instrument**. The latter is still productive, especially in technical registers:

| absagen | → die Absage *refusal* | bremsen | → die Bremse *brake* |
| pflegen | → die Pflege *care* | leuchten | → die Leuchte *light* |

(ii) Nouns in *-e* from adjectives denote a quality. The vowel has *Umlaut* if possible. This pattern is no longer productive, having been replaced by *-heit* or *-(ig)keit* (see (e) below):

| groß→ die Größe *size* | | stark | → die Stärke *strength* |

(c) *-ei, -erei, -elei* (feminine)

These suffixes are productive and form nouns from verbs or from other nouns. The suffix *-ei* is always stressed, see 23.1.6b.

(i) Nouns in *-erei* from verbs are mainly pejorative, indicating a repeated, irritating action:

| fragen | → die Fragerei *lots of annoying questions* |

The basis can be a whole phrase, e.g.:

Rekorde haschen → die Rekordhascherei *record hunting*.

-ei is used in the same sense from verbs in *-eln* and *-ern*, e.g.:

lieben → die Liebelei *flirtation*

-elei and *-erei* also have pejorative meaning if used with a noun base:

| Fremdwörter | → die Fremdwörtelei *using (too) many foreign words* |
| die Sklave | → die Sklaverei *slavery* |

(ii) Nouns in *-ei* from nouns denote the place where something is done. The base is often a noun in *-er*:

| das Datum | → die Datei *(computer) file* (i.e. where data are kept) |
| der Bäcker | → die Bäckerei *bakery* |

(d) *-er, -ler, -ner* (masculine)

These productive suffixes form nouns from verbs or nouns. The root vowel occasionally has *Umlaut*:

(i) Most nouns in -*er* from verbs denote the person who does something, often indicating a profession:

einbrechen	→ der Einbrech**er** *burglar*	schreiben	→ der Schreib**er** *writer*
lehren	→ der Lehr**er** *teacher*	betteln	→ der Bettl**er** *beggar*

The base may be a whole phrase, e.g : *einen Auftrag geben* → *der Auftraggeber* 'client, customer'

New formations can also be formed from foreign, especially English roots, e.g. *der Blueser* (from *die Blues*) 'blues singer/fan'.

(ii) -*ler* (less commonly -*ner*) is used to derive nouns from other nouns to indicate the person who does something. Some are pejorative:

das Bühnenbild	→ der Bühnenbild**ner**	die Rente	→ der Rent**ner** *pensioner*
stage designer		der Sport	→ der Sport**ler** *sportsman*
die Kunst	→ der Künst**ler** *artist*	die Wissenschaft	→ der Wissenschaft**ler**
der Profit	→ der Profit**ler** *profiteer*		*scientist*

In some instances -*er* is used rather than -*ler* to form nouns from other nouns:

die Eisenbahn	→ der Eisenbahn**er**	die Taktik	→ der Taktik**er** *tactician*
railway worker			

(iii) Some nouns in -*er* from verbs denote an instrument:

bohren → der Bohr**er** *drill*	empfangen → der Empfäng**er** *receiver*

The base is often a whole phrase, especially in technical language:

Staub saugen → der Staubsaug**er** *vacuum cleaner*

(iv) Nouns in -*er* from place names designate the inhabitants:

Frankfurt	→ der Frankfurt**er**	Österreich	→ der Österreich**er**
Hamburg	→ der Hamburg**er**	Wien	→ der Wiener

Some of these are rather irregular:

Hannover → der Hannover**aner**	Zürich → der Zürch**er**

(e) -*heit*, -*(ig)keit* **(feminine)**

These suffixes are used productively to form **abstract nouns** from adjectives denoting a quality:

bitter	→ die Bitter**keit** *bitterness*	heftig	→ die Heft**igkeit** *violence*
gleich	→ die Gleich**heit** *similarity*	geschwind	→ die Geschwind**igkeit** *speed*
eitel	→ die Eitel**keit** *vanity*	genau	→ die Genau**igkeit** *precision*

The distribution of the forms -*heit*, -*keit* and -*igkeit* is not wholly regular. -*heit* is the most common form; -*keit* is used with adjectives ending in -*bar*, -*ig*, -*lich* and -*sam* and with most in -*el* and -*er* (but not all, e.g. *die Dunkelheit*, *die Sicherheit*); -*igkeit* is used with adjectives ending in -*haft* and -*los* (e.g. *die Glaubhaftigkeit*) and a few others, especially those which end in -*e* (e.g. *müde* → *die Müdigkeit*).

(f) -*in* **(feminine)**

The productive suffix -*in* forms nouns denoting the **feminine** of persons and animals. The root vowel usually has *Umlaut*:

der Arzt	→ die **Ärztin** *woman doctor*
der Fuchs	→ die Füch**sin** *vixen*
der Präsident	→ die Präsident**in** *female president*
der Rocker	→ die Rocker**in** *female rock singer*

If the base word ends in *-erer*, e.g. *der Herausforderer* 'challenger', the final *-er* is dropped before adding the suffix *-in*, e.g. *die Herausforderin*.

NB: For the use of these feminine forms see 1.1.4a.

(g) *-ling* (masculine)

This productive suffix is used to form nouns from verbs or adjectives.

(i) Nouns in *-ling* from verbs denote persons who are the object of the action:

| prüfen | → der Prüf**ling** *examinee* | strafen | → der Sträf**ling** *prisoner* |

(ii) Nouns in *-ling* from adjectives designate persons possessing that quality:

| feige | → der Feig**ling** *coward* | fremd | → der Fremd**ling** *stranger* |

Similar formations denoting plants and animals are common, e.g. *der Grünling* 'greenfinch', but they are no longer productive.

(h) *-nis* (neuter or feminine)

Nouns in *-nis* are **abstract nouns** from verbs or adjectives. Those from verbs (which often have irregular forms or use the past participle as a base) often denote the result of the verbal action. The suffix is no longer productive:

erleben	→ das Erleb**nis** *experience*	finster	→ die Finster**nis** *darkness*
ersparen	→ das Erspar**nis** *savings*	geheim	→ das Geheim**nis** *secret*
gestehe	→ das Geständ**nis** *confession*	wild	→ die Wild**nis** *wilderness*

(i) *-schaft* (feminine)

The productive use of this suffix is to form nouns from other nouns designating a **collective** or a **state**:

| der Student | → die Studenten**schaft** *student body* |
| der Freund | → die Freund**schaft** *friendship* |

Other derivational patterns with *-schaft*, i.e. from adjectives (e.g. *die Schwangerschaft* 'pregnancy') or from participles (e.g. *die Errungenschaft* 'achievement'), are no longer productive.

(j) *-tum* (neuter)

-tum is used productively in modern German with nouns referring to persons to form nouns denoting **institutions**, **collectives** or **characteristic features**:

der Beamte	→ das Beamten**tum** *civil servants*	der König	→ das König**tum** *monarchy*
		der Papst	→ das Papst**tum** *papacy*
der Deutsche	→ das Deutsch**tum** *Germanness*	das Volk	→ das Volks**tum** *national traditions*

(k) *-ung* (feminine)

This very productive suffix is used to form nouns from verbs referring simply to the **action of the verb**:

bedeuten *mean* → die Bedeut**ung** *meaning*

landen *land* → die Land**ung** *landing*

bilden *form* → die Bild**ung** *formation*

töten *kill* → die Töt**ung** *killing*

22.2.2 Noun derivation by means of prefixes

All these prefixes except *Ge-* are stressed, see 23.1.6c. The gender of nouns with prefixes is the same as that of the root noun, with the exception of those in *Ge-*, which are mostly neuter, see 1.1.8c.

(a) *Erz-* = 'arch-', 'out and out'

der Bischof → der **Erz**bischof *archbishop*

der Gauner → der **Erz**gauner *out and out scoundrel*

(b) *Ge-*

Nouns in *Ge-* (often with the suffix *-e* in addition) can be formed from verbs or from other nouns:

(i) Nouns in *Ge-* from verbs denote a repeated or protracted activity. They often have a pejorative sense, like nouns in *-erei*, see 22.2.1c, to which those in *Ge-* are often an alternative:

laufen → das **Ge**laufe *running about, bustle* (esp. to no real purpose)

schwätzen → das **Ge**schwätz *idle talk, gossip*

(ii) Nouns in *Ge-* from other nouns are collectives. The root vowel has *Umlaut* if possible (and *-e-* changes to *-i-*):

der Ast → das **Ge**äst *branches*   der Berg → das **Ge**birge *mountain range*

(c) *Grund-* = 'basic', 'essential'

die Tendenz → die **Grund**tendenz *basic tendency*

(d) *Haupt-* = 'main'

der Bahnhof → der **Haupt**bahnhof *main station*

(e) *Miss-* designates an opposite or a negative

It sometimes has a pejorative sense:

der Brauch → der **Miss**brauch *misuse*

der Erfolg → der **Miss**erfolg *failure*

Fehl- is now at least as productive as *Miss-* to express an opposite or a negative, e.g.:

die Einschätzung → die **Fehl**einschätzung *false estimation*

(f) *Mit-* = co-, etc.

der Arbeiter → der **Mit**arbeiter *colleague, collaborator*

der Reisende → der **Mit**reisende *fellow traveller*

(g) *Nicht-* = non-

der Raucher → der **Nicht**raucher *non-smoker*

(h) *Riesen-* has an augmentative sense

der Erfolg → der **Riesen**erfolg *enormous success*

Riesen- is particularly common in speech, and colloquial German is rich in other augmentative prefixes, e.g.: *Superhit, Spitzenbelastung, Bombengeschäft, Heidenlärm, Höllendurst, Mordsapparat, Teufelskerl, Topmanager*, etc.

(i) *Rück-* occurs with many nouns related to verbs in *zurück-*

die Fahrt → die **Rück**fahrt *return journey* (cf.: *zurückfahren*)

The full form *Zurück-* is usually kept with nouns in *-ung* from verbs, e.g. *zurückhalten* → *die Zurückhaltung*.

(j) *Un-* = opposite, abnormal

der Mensch	→ der **Un**mensch *inhuman person*
die Ruhe	→ die **Un**ruhe *unrest*
die Summe	→ die **Un**summe *vast sum*
das Wetter	→ das **Un**wetter *bad weather*

(k) *Ur-* = 'original'

die Sprache → die **Ur**sprache *original language*

22.2.3 **Other methods of noun formation**

(a) Many nouns are formed from verb roots without a suffix

These are almost all masculine, see 1.1.5b. This means of derivation is no longer productive, although German still has many words which have been formed this way. It is most common with strong verbs (which may themselves be prefixed), and the root vowel is often changed:

ausgehen	→ der Ausgang *exit*	schließen	→ der Schluss *close*
brechen	→ der Bruch *break*	stechen	→ der Stich *stab, sting*
ersetzen	→ der Ersatz *replacement*	zurückfallen	→ der Rückfall *relapse*

(b) Verb infinitives can be used as nouns

e.g. *das Aufstehen* 'getting up', *das Reiten* 'riding'. These often correspond to English 'ing'-forms used as nouns and refer to the action as such. They are all neuter (see 1.1.3e) and further information about them is given in 13.4.

(c) Adjectives and participles can be used as nouns

e.g. *der/die Fremde* 'stranger', *der/die Vorsitzende* 'chair(person)' (see 6.4 for further examples). Such nouns from adjectives often co-exist with derived nouns:

fremd	→ der Fremde *and* der Fremdling
einbrechen	→ der Einbrechende *and* der Einbrecher

In these cases the noun derived by means of a suffix has a more developed sense than the adjective used as a noun. Both *der Fremde* and *der Fremdling* mean 'stranger', but the latter is rather pejorative. *der Einbrecher* means, specifically, 'burglar', but *der Einbrechende* simply means 'the person breaking in at present' (who may not necessarily be a criminal).

22.2.4 **Compound nouns**

The ease with which compound nouns can be formed is a feature of German, and the use of compounds has increased significantly in recent years. In particular, while two-part compounds like *Krankenhaus* and *Schreibtisch* have always been common, there has been an extension in the use of compounds with three or more elements over the last hundred years, especially in technical language, e.g. *Fahrpreisermäßigung, Autobahnraststätte, Roggenvollkornbrot*. Even so, compounds with more than four elements are (thankfully) still unusual.

NB: Compound nouns usually take the gender of the last part, see 1.1.9a.

(a) Types of noun compound

Almost any part of speech can combine with a noun to form a compound, e.g.:

(i)	**noun + noun:**	das Haar + die Bürste	→ die Haarbürste *hair brush*
(ii)	**adjective + noun:**	edel + der Stein	→ der Edelstein *gem*
(iii)	**numeral + noun:**	drei + das Rad	→ das Dreirad *tricycle*
(iv)	**verb + noun:**	hören + der Saal	→ der Hörsaal *lecture theatre*
(v)	**preposition + noun:**	unter + die Tasse	→ die Untertasse *saucer*
(vi)	**adverb + noun:**	jetzt + die Zeit	→ die Jetztzeit *the present day*

(b) A linking element is inserted in many noun + noun compounds

e.g.: *die Lieblingsfarbe, die Straßenecke*. These linking elements (called *Fugenelemente* in German) occur in about a third of all compounds, and they are notoriously unpredictable. A few words form some compounds with a link and some without one, e.g. *der Lobgesang* **but** *die Lobeshymne*. Other words form some compounds with one link and others with a different one, e.g. *das Tagebuch* **but** *die Tageszeitung*. Austrian and Swiss usage often differs from that in Germany, e.g. Austrian *der Zugsführer* for German *der Zugführer*. In practice, each compound needs to be learnt with its link. These linking elements depend on the **first** part of the compound, and the following are found:

(i) *-e-* occurs with a few nouns, especially those with a plural in *-e*. The root vowel often has *Umlaut* if the plural has *Umlaut*, e.g. *der Pferdestall, der Gänsebraten*.

(ii) *-(e)s-* (i.e. the ending of the genitive) occurs with many masculine and neuter nouns (and a few feminines), e.g. *die Windeseile, das Kalbsleder, der Liebesbrief*.

(iii) *-(e)n-* is used with many feminine nouns, with 'weak' masculine nouns (see 1.3.2) and with adjectives used as nouns, e.g. *der Scheibenwischer, die Heldentat*.

(iv) *-er-* is found with some nouns which have a plural in *-er*. *Umlaut* is usually present if possible, e.g. *die Männerstimme, die Rinderzucht*.

(c) Restrictions on the formation of compound nouns

It seems easy to make up compound words in German, but there are restrictions on their formation which are not fully understood, and it is not possible to give clear rules. A few hints are given here for guidance, but it is good practice to be cautious in forming compounds which one has not actually seen or heard used.

(i) In a German compound noun, the first element carries the main stress and usually defines the second. Thus, *Rathaus* is a type of *Haus* and *Tiefkühltruhe* is a kind of *Truhe*. A compound like *Blauhimmel* for 'blue sky', on the other hand, is not possible, because it is not a type of sky. We must say *der blaue Himmel*.

In particular, compounds like *Vatermitarbeiter* or *Ulmbesuch,* whose first element is an individual person or place, are odd because they are not 'types' of colleague or visit; a full phrase: *der Mitarbeiter meines Vaters* or *sein Besuch in Ulm is normally preferred*. However, under the influence of English, compounds like this have been becoming more widely used recently, although purists still consider them to be incorrect.

(ii) Adjective + noun compounds tend to be very restricted. In practice they always mean something rather different from when the relevant adjective is used as an epithet with the noun. Thus, *eine Großstadt* is more than *eine große Stadt*, and *ein Junggeselle* is not simply *ein junger Geselle*.

(d) Semi-compound suffixes

A few nouns are so widely used in modern German as the basis for compound nouns that they must be considered as suffixes rather than as distinct words in their own right. Words with these semi-suffixes are very typical of modern official German. The most frequent are:

(i) *-gut*
Nouns in *-gut* express the set of material used in a process, or the totality of things expressed in the first element:

> streuen *scatter, grit* (roads)   → das Streugut *material for gritting roads*
> der Gedanke *thought*   → das Gedankengut *whole body of thought*

(ii) *-werk*
Nouns in *-werk* from nouns (often plural, and often denoting plants or materials) are typically collective, indicating the whole of something:

> das Blatt *leaf*   → das Blätterwerk *foliage*
> der Zucker *sugar*   → das Zuckerwerk *sweets, candies*

(iii) *-wesen*
Nouns in *-wesen* express the whole systematic collectivity of people and institutions involved in the first element:

> die Gesundheit *health*   → das Gesundheitswesen *health sysyem*
> die Schule *school*   → das Schulwesen *school system*

(iv) *-zeug*
Nouns in *-zeug* express a set of things used in a particular activity:

> nähen *sew*   → das Nähzeug *sewing kit*
> schlagen *hit*   → das Schlagzeug *drum kit*

22.3 The formation of adjectives

22.3.1 Adjective derivation by means of suffixes

(a) *-bar*
This very productive suffix forms adjectives from verbs with the sense of English '-able', '-ible':

> brauchen   → brauch**bar** *usable*   essen   → ess**bar** *edible*

Adjectives in *-bar* are a frequent alternative to passive constructions, see 15.4.8.

(b) *-(e)n, -ern*
These suffixes are formed from nouns denoting a material, and the adjective indicates that the qualified noun is made from that material. The form *-ern* is normally associated with *Umlaut*:

> das Gold   → gold**en** *golden*   das Silber   → silbern *silver*
> das Holz   → hölz**ern** *wooden*   der Stahl   → stählern *steel*

NB: Note the difference between adjectives in *-(e)n* or *-ern* and those in *-ig* (see (d) below) from the same noun, e.g. *silbern* '(made of) silver', *silbrig* 'silvery' (i.e. like silver).

(c) -haft

Adjectives formed from nouns with the suffix -haft indicate a quality like the person or thing denoted by the noun, e.g.:

der Greis → greisen**haft** *senile* der Held → helden**haft** *heroic*

(d) -ig

-ig is a common and productive suffix, often associated with *Umlaut*. It is mainly used to form adjectives from nouns:

(i) with the idea of possessing what is denoted by the noun, e.g.:

das Haar → haar**ig** *hairy* der Staub → staub**ig** *dusty*

(ii) indicating a quality like the person or thing denoted by the noun:

die Milch → milch**ig** *milky* der Riese → ries**ig** *gigantic*

Adjectives in -ig can be formed from whole phrases. *blauäugig* 'blue-eyed', *heißblütig* 'hot-blooded'.

(iii) indicating duration (from time expressions):

zwei Stunden → zweistünd**ig** *lasting two hours*

Note the difference between these adjectives in -ig (which express duration) and those in -lich (which express frequency), e.g. *zweistündlich* 'every two hours', see (f) below.

(iv) -ig forms adjectives from adverbs, e.g.:

dort	→ dort**ig**	heute	→ heut**ig**
ehemals	→ ehemal**ig**	morgen	→ morg**ig**
hier	→ hies**ig**	sonst	→ sonst**ig**

(e) -isch

This is a productive suffix, often associated with *Umlaut*, used mainly to form adjectives from nouns:

(i) adjectives from proper names and geographical names:

England	→ engl**isch** *English*	Homer	→ homer**isch** *Homeric*
Europa	→ europä**isch** *European*	Sachsen	→ sächs**isch** *Saxon*

(ii) adjectives which indicate a quality like that of the person or thing denoted by the noun. They are often pejorative:

der Held	→ held**isch** *heroic*	das Kind	→ kind**isch** *puerile*
der Herr	→ herr**isch** *imperious*	der Wähler	→ wähler**isch** *fastidious*

Compare the pejorative *kindisch* with the neutral *kindlich* 'childlike'.

(iii) adjectives from nouns of foreign origin. These adjectives are always stressed on the penultimate syllable, see. 23.1.6d:

die Biologie	→ biolog**isch** *biological*	die Musik	→ musikal**isch** *musical*
die Mode	→ mod**isch** *fashionable*	der Nomade	→ nomad**isch** *nomadic*

(f) *-lich*

This is a common suffix with a wide range of functions. Adjectives formed with *-lich* often have *Umlaut*:

(i) Adjectives from nouns in *-lich* indicate a relationship to that person or thing, or indicate the possession of the quality denoted by it:

der Arzt	→ ärzt**lich** *medical*	der Preis	→ preis**lich** *in respect of price*
der Buchstabe	→ buchstäb**lich** *literal*	der Tod	→ töd**lich** *fatal, deadly*
der Fürst	→ fürst**lich** *princely*		

This is the only use of *-lich* which is still productive in modern German.

(ii) Adjectives in *-lich* from time expressions denote frequency:

zwei Stunden → zweistünd**lich** *every two hours*

NB: For the difference between adjectives in *-ig* and *-lich* from time expressions, see (d) above.

(iii) Adjectives in *-lich* from verbs indicate ability:

bestechen	→ bestech**lich** *corruptible*	verkaufen	→ verkäuf**lich** *saleable*

This use of *-lich* is no longer productive, having been replaced by *-bar*, see (a) above.

(iv) Adjectives in *-lich* from other adjectives usually indicate a lesser degree of the relevant quality:

arm	→ ärm**lich** *shabby; humble*	krank	→ kränk**lich** *sickly*
klein	→ klein**lich** *petty*	rot	→ röt**lich** *reddish*

(g) *-los*

-los is used to form adjectives from nouns and corresponds to English '-less':

die Hoffnung	→ hoffnungs**los** *hopeless*	die Wahl	→ wahl**los** *indiscriminate*

(h) *-mäßig*

This suffix is very productive in modern German, especially in formal registers, to derive adjectives from nouns:

(i) with the sense of 'in accordance with':

die Gewohnheit	→ gewohnheits**mäßig** *habitual*
der Plan	→ plan**mäßig** *according to plan*

-gemäß is an alternative to *-mäßig* in this sense, but it is less common, e.g. *plangemäß, ordnungsgemäß*.

(ii) with the sense of 'in respect of something', 'pertaining to':

der Instinkt	→ instinkt**mäßig** *instinctive*
der Verkehr	→ verkehrs**mäßig** *relating to traffic*

(iii) with the sense of 'like someone or something':

der Fürst	→ fürsten**mäßig** *princely*
das Lehrbuch	→ lehrbuch**mäßig** *like a textbook*

(i) *-sam*

This suffix is no longer productive in modern German. Adjectives in *-sam* have two main sources:

(i) from verbs (especially reflexive verbs), expressing a possibility or a tendency:

sich biegen   → bieg**sam** *flexible*   sparen   → spar**sam** *thrifty*

(ii) from nouns, indicating a quality

die Furcht   → furcht**sam** *timid*   die Gewalt   → gewalt**sam** *violent*

22.3.2 Adjective derivation by means of prefixes

These prefixes are usually stressed and form adjectives from other adjectives.

(a) *erz-*, *grund-*, *hoch-* **have intensifying meaning**

erz- is mainly used with a rather negative sense, whereas *grund-* and *hoch-* tend to be more positive. Both *erz-* and *grund-* are rather limited in use:

reaktionär   → **erz**reaktionär *very reactionary*
ehrlich   → **grund**ehrlich *thoroughly honest*
verschieden   → **grund**verschieden *totally different*
begabt   → **hoch**begabt *highly talented*
intelligent   → **hoch**intelligent *very intelligent*

(b) *un-* **negates and/or produces an opposite meaning**

It closely resembles English 'un-'. It is not always stressed, see 23.1.6c.

artig   → **un**artig *naughty*
vorsichtig   → **un**vorsichtig *incautious*
wahrscheinlich → **un**wahrscheinlich *improbable*

If an adjective already has a simple word as its opposite (e.g. *klug – dumm*), the form in *un-* gives a negative rather than an opposite. Thus, whilst *dumm* means 'stupid', *unklug* means 'unwise'. In general, only adjectives with a positive meaning can form an opposite with *un-*. Thus, whilst *unschön* (← *schön*) is fairly common, one does not find *unhässlich* from *hässlich*.

(c) *ur-* **with adjectives usually intensifies the sense**

alt   → **ur**alt *very old*
komisch   → **ur**komisch *very comical*

Sometimes, it gives the idea of 'original' or 'typical', e.g. *urdeutsch* 'typically German'.

22.3.3 Adjective compounding

In general, adjective compounding is similar to noun compounding, see 22.2.4.

(a) Types of adjective compounds

In practice only the following are at all common:

(i)	**noun + adjective:**	die Pflicht + treu	→ pflichttreu *dutiful*
(ii)	**verb + adjective:**	trinken + fest	→ trinkfest *able to hold one's drink*
(iii)	**adjective + adjective:**	klein + laut	→ kleinlaut *meek*

Adjective + adjective compounds are often 'additive', i.e. the qualities of both adjectives apply, e.g. *nasskalt* 'cold and wet'.

(b) Many noun + adjective compounds have a linking element

These are similar to those in noun + noun compounds, see 22.2.4b. *-s-* and *-n-* are the most common, e.g. *geisteskrank, gesundheitsschädlich, seitenverkehrt*.

(c) Some compound elements forming adjectives have now become suffixes

A number of adjectives are so widely used in modern German as the basis for compound adjectives that they can be considered as suffixes rather than as distinct words.

(i) with the sense of having or possessing something:

-haltig	→ koffein**haltig**
-reich	→ erlebnis**reich**
-stark	→ charakter**stark**
-(s)voll	→ rücksicht**svoll**

(ii) with the sense of lacking something:

-arm	→ nikotin**arm**
-frei	→ alkohol**frei**
-leer	→ gedanken**leer**

(iii) with the sense of being protected from something:

-dicht	→ schall**dicht**
-echt	→ kuss**echt**
-fest	→ hitze**fest**
-sicher	→ kugel**sicher**

(iv) with the sense of being similar to something:

-artig	→ kugel**artig**
-förmig	→ platten**förmig**
-gleich	→ masken**gleich**

(v) with the sense of being capable of something:

-fähig → strapazier**fähig**

(vi) with the sense of being worth(y of) something:

-wert	→ lesens**wert**
-würdig	→ nachahmens**würdig**

(vii) with the sense of needing something:

-bedürftig → korrektur**bedürftig**

22.4 The formation of verbs: inseparable prefixes

New verbs are formed in German primarily by means of prefixes – largely because all verbs have to have inflectional suffixes to show categories like tense, person and number. There are three main types of verb prefix in German:

(i) inseparable prefixes like *be-, emp-, ent-, er-, ge-, ver- and zer-*, e.g. *bestellen, erstehen, verbringen*. They are called inseparable prefixes because they always remain fixed to the root, and they are always unstressed, see 23.1.6c. Their past participle does not have the prefix *ge-*, (e.g. *bestellt*, *erstanden*, *verbracht*, see 12.2.1h). The formation of verbs with inseparable prefixes is treated in this section 22.4.

(ii) separable prefixes, of which there are a large number. The most typical are like prepositions, e.g. *ab-*, *an-*, *auf-*, etc., e.g. *abfahren*, *ankommen*, *aufmachen*, but they can also come from nouns, adverbs and other parts of speech, e.g. *teilnehmen*, *totschlagen*, *weglaufen*. They are called separable prefixes because they are separated from the root under certain conditions, e.g. *Sie **kamen** in München **an*** (see 12.2.1i), and they are always stressed, see 23.1.6c. The formation of verbs with separable prefixes is dealt with in section 22.5.

(iii) variable prefixes are separable in some cases and inseparable in others, usually with a difference in meaning, e.g. *Sie übersetzte den Brief* 'She translated the letter' – *Sie setzten zum anderen Ufer über* 'They crossed over to the other bank'. The prefixes *durch-*, *über-*, *um-* and *unter-* and one or two less common ones are variable in this way. They are explained in section 22.6.

Many patterns of forming verbs with inseparable prefixes are common or productive. They are dealt with in the remainder of this section, in alphabetical order of the individual prefixes.

22.4.1 *be-*

(a) *be-* makes intransitive verbs transitive

See 18.3.5b. If the simple intransitive verb is used with a dative object or a prepositional object, that becomes the accusative object of the prefixed verb with *be-*, e.g.:

> jdn. **be**dienen *serve sb.* (← jdm. dienen)
> eine Frage **be**antworten *answer a question* (← auf eine Frage antworten)

(b) With transitive verbs *be-* can change the action to a different object

> jdn. mit etwas **be**liefern *supply sb. with sth.* (← jdm. etwas liefern *deliver sth. to sb.*)

(c) *be-* forms verbs from nouns with the idea of providing something

With some verbs the suffix *-ig-* is added:

das Wasser	→ **be**wässern *irrigate*	die Nachricht	→ **be**nachrichtigen *notify*
der Reifen	→ **be**reifen *put tyres on*		

(d) *be-* makes verbs from adjectives with the sense of giving someone or something that quality

With some verbs the suffix *-ig-* is added:

feucht	→ **be**feuchten *moisten*	gerade	→ **be**gradigen *straighten*
frei	→ **be**freien *liberate*	ruhig	→ **be**ruhigen *calm*

22.4.2 *ent-*

NB: The prefix *emp-* is a variant of *ent-*, used before some roots beginning with *f*, e.g. *empfehlen*, *empfinden*.

(a) Verbs in *ent-* from verbs of motion have the idea of escaping or going away

What is being escaped from usually appears as a dative object with these verbs, see 18.4.1c, e.g.:

gleiten	→ jdm. **ent**gleiten *slip away from sb.* (e.g. glass from hand)
laufen	→ jdm./etwas **ent**laufen *run away/escape from sb./sth.*
reißen	→ jdm. etwas **ent**reißen *snatch sth. from sb.*

(b) Verbs in *ent-* from nouns, adjectives or other verbs can have the sense of removing something

In this sense, *ent-* often corresponds to the English prefixes 'de-' or 'dis-':

das Gift	→ **ent**giften *decontaminate*	scharf	→ **ent**schärfen *tone down*
der Mut	→ **ent**mutigen *discourage*	spannen	→ **ent**spannen *relax*

22.4.3 *er-*

(a) Verbs in *er-* from other verbs often express the achievement or conclusion of an action

bitten	→ **er**bitten *get (sth.) by asking for it*
schießen	→ **er**schießen *shoot (sb.) dead*

A productive use of *er-* is to form verbs from verbs or nouns with the idea of acquiring something by the action expressed by the simple verb or the noun. Compare *erbitten* above and the following:

arbeiten	→ Er hat etwas **er**arbeitet	*He got sth. by working for it*
die List	→ Er hat etwas **er**listet	*He got sth. through cunning*

This use of *er-* is so productive that it is widely used with new roots from English, e.g. *etwas erbloggen* 'get sth. by blogging', *etwas ersurfen* 'to get sth. by surfing'

A handful of verbs in *er-* from other verbs point to the start of an action, e.g. *erklingen* 'ring out', *erbeben* 'tremble'.

(b) Verbs in *er-* formed from adjectives express a change of state

i.e. either intransitive verbs with the idea of becoming something, or transitive verbs with the idea of making somebody or something have the quality expressed by the adjective. These verbs often have *Umlaut* of the root vowel, e.g.:

blind	→ **er**blinden *become blind*	frisch	→ **er**frischen *refresh*
rot	→ **er**röten *turn red, blush*	leichter	→ **er**leichtern *make easier*

22.4.4 *ver-*

This is the most widely used inseparable prefix, with a range of meanings. The following are the most frequent or productive:

(a) Many verbs in *ver-* from verbs express the idea of finishing or 'away'

blühen	→ **ver**blühen *fade* (flowers)	hungern	→ **ver**hungern *starve to death*
brauchen	→ **ver**brauchen *consume*	klingen	→ **ver**klingen *fade away* (sounds)

(b) Some verbs in *ver-* from other verbs convey the notion of 'wrongly' or 'to excess'

biegen	→ **ver**biegen *bend out of shape*
lernen	→ **ver**lernen *unlearn, forget*
salzen	→ **ver**salzen *put too much salt in sth.*

This use is very productive and used widely with new roots, e.g.: *Vergoogeln Sie keine Zeit!* 'Don't waste your time searching on google'.

Some reflexive verbs in *ver-* have the idea of making a mistake, e.g.:

fahren   → sich **ver**fahren *get lost, take a wrong turning*
wählen   → sich **ver**wählen *misdial*

A few verbs in *ver-* are opposites, e.g.:

achten   → **ver**achten *despise*   kaufen   → **ver**kaufen *sell*

(c) Verbs in *ver-* formed from adjectives often express a change of state

As with *er-*, these can be intransitive verbs with the idea of becoming something., or transitive verbs with the idea of making somebody or something have the quality expressed by the adjective:

arm   → **ver**armen *become poor*   länger   → **ver**längern *make longer*
einfach   → **ver**einfachen *simplify*   stumm   → **ver**stummen *become silent*

Some verbs in *ver-* from nouns have a similar meaning, e.g.:

das Unglück   → **ver**unglücken *have an accident*
der Sklave   → **ver**sklaven *enslave*

(d) Many verbs formed from nouns with *ver-* convey the idea of providing with something

das Glas   → **ver**glasen *glaze*   der Körper → **ver**körpern *embody*
das Gold   → **ver**golden *gild*   der Zauber → **ver**zaubern *enchant*

This use of *ver-* is very productive and now widely used with originally English roots, e.g. *Verlink deine Seite gegen Geld* 'Link up your website for cash'.

22.4.5 *zer-*

Verbs in *zer-*, which are usually formed from other verbs, always convey the notion of 'in pieces':

beißen   → **zer**beißen *bite into pieces*   fallen   → **zer**fallen *disintegrate*
brechen   → **zer**brechen *smash*   streuen → **zer**streuen *disperse*

22.5 The formation of verbs: separable prefixes

Separable prefixes are so called because they are separated from the root under certain conditions, e.g. *Sie kamen in München an* (see 12.2.1i). For the difference between them and inseparable prefixes, see 22.4. Most separable prefixes also exist as independent words, chiefly as adverbs, prepositions, nouns or adjectives. The forms of separable verbs, in particular the position of the prefix, are explained in 12.2.1i. Separable prefixes are always **stressed**.

22.5.1 Simple separable prefixes

The majority of these derive from prepositions or adverbs and their meanings are often transparent. The examples below illustrate some common and productive patterns of derivation.

NB: Prefixes from prepositions expressing direction (e.g. *ab-*, *an-*, *auf-*) often have a less transparent or figurative sense because direction can be indicated by using a prefix with *her-* or *hin-*, see 7.2.4d.

(a) *ab-*

(i) = 'away':

abfahren *depart, leave*   **ab**fliegen *take off*

(ii) = 'down':

absteigen *get down*

absetzen *put, set down*

(iii) completing an action:

abdrehen *switch off*

ablaufen *wear out* (i.e. shoes)

(b) *an-*
(i) with the idea of approaching:

ankommen *arrive*

ansprechen *address (sb.)*

(ii) indicating the start of an action, partially:

anmachen *switch on*

anbrennen *catch fire*

(c) *auf-*
(i) = 'up' or 'on':

aufbleiben *stay up*

aufsetzen *put on* (hat, water)

(ii) with the idea of a sudden start:

auflachen *burst out laughing*

aufleuchten *light up*

(d) *aus-* = 'out' often pointing to the completion of an action:

ausbrennen *burn out*

ausbloggen *finish a blog*

(e) *ein-* is related to the preposition *in*
It often conveys the idea of becoming used to something:

einfahren *run in* (i.e. new car)

sich **ein**leben *settle down*

(f) *los-* most often has the meaning of beginning something:

losgehen *set off, start*

losreißen *tear off, away*

(g) *mit-*
(i) accompanying or cooperating:

mitarbeiten *cooperate*

mitgehen *go with sb.*

(h) *vor-*
(i) going on or preceding:

vorgehen *go ahead; be fast* (clock)

vorstoßen *push forward*

(ii) demonstrating:

vorlesen *read aloud*

vormachen *show sb. how to do sth.*

(i) *weg-* = 'away'

wegbleiben *stay away*

weglaufen *run away*

fort- is a less common (and more formal) alternative to *weg-* with some verbs: *fortbleiben, fortlaufen*.

(j) *weiter-* = 'on', 'continue'

weiterfahren *drive on*   **weiter**machen *continue*

(k) Other simple prefixes are less frequent or no longer productive

bei-:	**bei**treten	*join* (e.g. club)	**bei**tragen	*contribute*
da-:	**da**bleiben	*stay on/behind*	**da**stehen	*stand there*
dar-:	**dar**stellen	*depict, represent*	**dar**legen	*explain, expound*
fehl-:	**fehl**gehen	*miss one's way*	**fehl**greifen	*miss one's hold*
inne-:	**inne**haben	*occupy* (position)	**inne**halten	*pause*
nach-:	**nach**ahmen	*imitate*	**nach**gehen	*follow*
nieder-:	**nieder**brennen	*burn down*	**nieder**lassen	*lower, let down*
zu-:	**zu**drehen	*turn off* (tap)	**zu**steigen	*get on, board* (train)

22.5.2 Compound separable prefixes

Some compound elements, mainly from adverbs, are widely used as separable prefixes

dabei-	(indicating proximity):	**dabei**stehen	*stand close by*
daneben-	(indicating missing sth.):	**daneben**schießen	*miss* (a shot)
davon-	('away'):	**davon**eilen	*hurry away*
dazu-	(indicating an addition):	**dazu**kommen	*be added*
empor-	('upwards'):	**empor**blicken	*look up*
entgegen-	('towards'):	**entgegen**nehmen	*receive, accept*
überein-	(indicating agreement):	**überein**kommen	*agree*
voraus-	(= 'in advance'):	**voraus**sagen	*foretell, predict*
vorbei-, vorüber-	(= 'past')	**vorbei**gehen	*pass*
zurück-	(= 'back')	**zurück**fahren	*drive back, return*
zusammen-	(= 'together' or 'up')	**zusammen**rücken	*move together*
		zusammenfalten	*fold up*

The compound directional adverbs in *hin-* and *her-*, see 7.2.4, are also commonly used as separable prefixes, e.g. *hinausgehen, herunterkommen*. Other compound elements, e.g. *drauf-, hintan-, vorweg-, zuvor-* are used with one or two verbs only, e.g. *vorwegnehmen* 'anticipate'.

22.5.3 Separable prefix or separate word?

In the old spelling, some nouns, verbs and adjectives were treated as separable prefixes and written together with the verb according to the same rules as for separable prefixes, e.g. *achtgeben* 'pay heed', *radfahren* 'cycle', *liebgewinnen* 'grow fond of', *offenlassen* 'leave open'. As there were no clear rules as to which combinations could be treated as separable verbs, there were many exceptions and anomalies, and the new spelling rules prescribe that most of these combinations should be spelled as separate words in all their forms, e.g. *Acht geben, Rad fahren, lieb gewinnen, offen lassen*.

The following rules now apply:

(a) Combinations of noun + verb are now normally spelled as separate words

Halt machen: ich mache Halt, sie machte Halt, sie haben Halt gemacht
Maß halten: ich halte Maß, sie hielt Maß, sie haben Maß gehalten
Ski laufen: ich laufe Ski, sie lief Ski, sie sind Ski gelaufen

An exception is made of the following nouns, which are taken to have lost their full meaning in combinations with a verb and are seen as separable prefixes:

heim-   irre-   preis-   stand-   statt-   teil-   wett-   wunder-

heimgehen	*go home*	stattfinden	*take place*
irreführen	*mislead*	teilnehmen	*participate*
preisgeben	*expose*	wettmachen	*make up for*
standhalten	*stand firm*	wundernehmen	*surprise*

leidtun is now treated like this again, following the most recent reform, and forms which do not exist as separate words are also treated as separable prefixes, e.g. *fehlschlagen, feilbieten, kopfstehen, kundgeben, weismachen*

(b) Combinations of adjective or adverb + verb are normally written together

aneinanderfügen	*join together*	kurztreten	*go easy*
anheimfallen	*fall victim to*	leichtmachen	*make sth. easy*
aufwärtsgehen	*do better*	nahelegen	*suggest*
durcheinanderbringen	*muddle up*	überhandnehmen	*get out of hand*
fernliegen	*be far from*	übrigbleiben	*be left over*

In particular adjectives and adverbs with a preposition and *-einander* are always written together with the verb. However, if the first element is a phrase (or derives from a phrase, e.g. *instand setzen*, it is always written separately from the verb (see also 23.3.1).

Similarly, adjectives and adverbs which cannot be used in the comparative in conjunction with the verb, or be modified by *sehr* or *ganz*, are seen to form fixed idiomatic combinations with the verb; they are considered to be separable prefixes and thus always written together:

bereithalten	*have ready*	gutschreiben	*credit*
bloßstellen	*show up*	schwarzarbeiten	*moonlight*
fernsehen	*watch TV*	totschlagen	*kill*
festsetzen	*fix*		

One can, for instance say *ich sehe fern*, but it is not possible to say **ich sehe ferner*, and *ich sehe sehr fern* can only have its literal meaning of 'I am looking a long way'.

However, if the adjective expresses a property which is the result of the action of the verb, the two parts can be written together or separately. The most frequent of these are:

kaltstellen/kalt stellen *exclude, put out of the way*
kaputtmachen/kaputt machen *break, smash*
kleinschneiden/klein schneiden *cut up small*

(c) Combinations of verb or participle + verb are generally written as separate words

gefangen nehmen	*take captive*	spazieren gehen	*go for a walk*
laufen lernen	*learn to walk*	verloren gehen	*be lost*

However, combinations with *bleiben* or *lassen*, and also the combination *kennen lernen* can be written together, especially if the combination is felt to have a distinct meaning. In practice this means that either possibility is allowed:

fallen lassen/fallenlassen *drop*
kennen lernen/kennenlernen *get to know*
stehen bleiben/stehenbleiben *stop*

(d) Combinations with the verb *sein* are always written as separate words

This applies even with forms which are normally taken as separable prefixes:

da sein	*be there*	vorbei sein	*be past*
inne sein	*be conscious of*	zufrieden sein	*be satisfied*
los sein	*be up*	zurück sein	*be back*

NB: Some verbs look as if they have prefixes, but they are formed from compound nouns and the first element does not separate, e.g. *frühstücken* 'breakfast': *Ich frühstücke, ich habe gefrühstückt*, etc. Similarly: *handhaben* 'manipulate', *langweilen* 'bore', *liebkosen* 'caress', *wetteifern* 'compete'.

(e) Defective compound verbs are always written as a single word

These are verbs which have a special meaning and are only used in the form of the infinitive and/ or the past participle. They are especially frequent in technical language.

(i) Some compounds only exist in the infinitive form:

brustschwimmen	*swim breast-stroke*	segelfliegen	*glide*
kettenrauchen	*chain-smoke*	wettlaufen	*race*

One can say, for instance *ich gehe morgen segelfliegen*, but not **ich segelfliege*

(ii) Some compounds are only used in the infinitive and the past participle:

seiltanzen	*walk the tightrope*
uraufführen	*perform for the first time*

With these, one can say, for example, *Das neue Stück wird morgen uraufgeführt*, but not **Morgen uraufführt man das neue Stück*.

(iii) There may be uncertainty in the formation of the past participle of such verbs. With a number, the first element can be treated as if it were a separable prefix, and the prefix *ge-* of the participle inserted between this and the root of the verb, e.g.:

notlanden *make an emergency landing* → genotlandet *or* notgelandet
schutzimpfen *innoculate* → geschutzimpft *or* schutzgeimpft

The same applies to some recent verbs loaned from or modelled on English with prepositions or adverbs as their first element, e.g.:

doppelklicken	→ gedoppelklickt *or* doppelgeklickt
downloaden	→ gedownloadet *or* downgeloadet
outsourcen	→ outgesourct *or* geoutsourct
upgraden	→ geupgradet *or* upgegradet

If such verbs have -ge- inserted in the past participle, the *zu* of the infinitive can also be incorporated in the verb, e.g. *doppelzuklicken, outzusourcen*.

22.6 The formation of verbs: variable prefixes

A small number of prefixes can form both separable and inseparable verbs (for the difference between these, see 22.4). **If the verb is separable, the prefix is stressed, if it is inseparable, the prefix is unstressed.**

22.6.1 *durch-*

durch- always expresses the idea of 'through', whether separable or inseparable.

(a) A few compounds with *durch-* are only inseparable

durch'denken	*think through*
durch'leben	*experience*
durch'löchern	*make holes in*

NB: Separable *'durchdenken* is also found with the identical meaning to *durch'denken*, but it is less common.

(b) Many compounds with *durch-* are only separable

'durchblicken	*look through*
'durchkommen	*get through, succeed*
'durchfallen	*fall through/fail*
'durchkriechen	*crawl through*
'durchführen	*carry out*
'durchrosten	*rust through*
'durchhalten	*hold out, survive*
'durchsehen	*look through*

(c) Some verbs form separable and inseparable compounds with *durch-*

The separable compounds always mean 'right the way through'. The inseparable verbs emphasise penetration without necessarily reaching the other side. However, the distinction may be fine, especially with verbs of motion. Compare:

Er **eilte** durch die Vorhalle **durch**	*He hurried through the vestibule*
Er **durcheilte** die Vorhalle	*He hurried across the vestibule*
Er **ritt** durch den Wald **durch**	*He crossed the forest on horseback*
Er **durchritt** den Wald	*He rode through the forest*

Similarly:

durchbrechen	*break through*
durchschauen	*see through*
durchdringen	*penetrate*
durchsetzen	*carry through*
durchfahren	*travel through*
durch'setzen	*infiltrate*
durchlaufen	*run through*
durchstoßen	*break through*
durchreisen	*travel through*
durchwachen	*stay awake*

With *durchkämmen* 'comb through' the distinction is clear. Separable *'durchkämmen* is only used in a literal sense, of hair, whereas inseparable *durch'kämmen* has the figurative meaning of 'search thoroughly in'.

22.6.2 *hinter-* normally forms inseparable compounds

hinter'gehen	*deceive*
hinter'fragen	*analyse*
hinter'lassen	*leave, bequeathe*

| hinter'legen | *deposit* |
| hinter'treiben | *foil, thwart* |

Separable compounds with *hinter-* are non-standard colloquial regionalisms, e.g. *'hinterbringen* 'take to the back', *'hintergehen* 'go to the back'.

22.6.3 *miss-* is generally inseparable

It has two main senses, i.e.:

(i) 'opposite':

missachten *despise, disdain*   **misstrauen** *distrust*

(ii) 'badly', 'wrongly':

missdeuten *misinterpret*   **misshandeln** *ill-treat*

With a few verbs *miss-* can be treated as separable in the past participle and the infinitive with *zu*, e.g. *missgeachtet, misszuachten*, see 13.1.4b. These forms are alternatives to the regular inseparable forms *missachtet, zu missachten* and are generally less frequent, with the exception of *missverstehen*, where the extended infinitive most commonly has the form *misszuverstehen*.

22.6.4 *ob-* is mainly inseparable

There are very few verbs with the prefix *ob-* in current use, e.g. *obliegen* 'to be incumbent', *obsiegen* 'to prevail', and they are limited to use in formal registers. They are most often inseparable, e.g. *Die Beweislast obliegt dem Ankläger* 'The burden of proof is on the prosecutor'. However, all can be used separably, e.g. *Das liegt dem Ankläger ob*, although this alternative is less frequent.

22.6.5 *über-*

(a) A few compounds with *über-* are only separable

They are all intransitive and have the literal meaning 'over', e.g.:

'überhängen	*overhang*
'überkippen	*keel over*
'überkochen	*boil over*

(b) A large number of compounds with *über-* are only inseparable

They are all transitive and have a variety of meanings, i.e.:

(i) repetition:

über'arbeiten *rework*   über'prüfen *check*

(ii) more than enough:

über'fordern *overtax*   über'treiben *exaggerate*

(iii) failing to notice:

über'hören *fail to hear*   über'sehen *overlook*

(iv) 'over':

über'denken *think over*	über'fallen *attack*

(c) Many verbs form both separable and inseparable compounds with *über-*

The separable compounds are mostly intransitive. They all have the literal meaning 'over'. The inseparable verbs are mostly transitive, with a more figurative meaning often similar to those given under (b) above:

	separable	inseparable
überfahren	*cross over*	*run over*
überführen	*transfer*	*convict*
übergehen	*turn into sth.*	*leave out*
überlaufen	*overflow; desert*	*overrun*
überlegen	*put sth. over sb./sth.*	*consider*
übersetzen	*ferry over*	*translate*
überspringen	*jump over*	*skip*
übertreten	*change over*	*infringe*
überziehen	*put on*	*cover*

NB: *übersiedeln* 'move (house)' can be used as a separable **or** inseparable verb with no distinction in meaning.

22.6.6 *um-*

(a) A large number of compounds in *um-* are only separable

Most express the idea of turning or changing a state:

'umblicken	*look round*
'umbringen	*kill*
'umdrehen	*turn round*
'umfallen	*fall over*
'umschalten	*switch*
'umsteigen	*change* (trains, etc.)

(b) Many compounds in *um-* are only inseparable

They all express encirclement or surrounding:

um'armen	*embrace*
um'fassen	*embrace, encircle*
um'geben	*surround*
um'ringen	*surround*
um'segeln	*sail round, circumnavigate*
um'zingeln	*surround, encircle*

(c) Many verbs form separable and inseparable compounds in *um-*

The difference in meaning corresponds to that given in (a) and (b) above:

	separable	inseparable
umbauen	*rebuild*	*enclose*
umbrechen	*break up*	*set* (i.e. type)
umfahren	*run over, knock down*	*travel round*
umgehen	*circulate*	*avoid*
umreißen	*tear down*	*outline*

umschreiben	*rewrite*	*paraphrase*
umstellen	*rearrange*	*surround*

22.6.7 *unter-*

(a) A large number of compounds in *unter-* are only separable

They generally have a literal meaning, i.e. 'under', e.g.:

'unterbringen *accommodate*
'untergehen *sink, decline*
'unterkommen *find accommodation*
'untersetzen *put underneath*

(b) Many compounds in *unter-* are only inseparable

They have a variety of meanings, i.e.:

(i) less than enough:

unter'bieten	*undercut*
unter'schätzen	*underestimate*
unter'schreiten	*fall short*
unter'steuern	*understeer*

(ii) 'under':

unter'drücken	*suppress, oppress*
unter'liegen	*be defeated*
unter'schreiben	*sign*
unter'stützen	*support*

(iii) other, miscellaneous meanings:

unter'bleiben	*cease*
unter'brechen	*interrupt*
unter'lassen	*refrain from*
unter'laufen	*occur*
unter'richten	*teach*
unter'sagen	*forbid, prohibit*
unter'suchen	*investigate*

(c) Many verbs form separable and inseparable compounds with *unter-*

The separable verbs are mostly intransitive and have the meaning 'under'. The inseparable compounds are all transitive, and most have a more figurative meaning:

	separable	**inseparable**
unterbinden	*tie underneath*	*prevent*
untergraben	*dig in*	*undermine*
unterhalten	*hold underneath*	*entertain*
unterlegen	*put underneath*	*underlay*
unterschieben	*foist*	*insinuate*
unterschlagen	*cross* (e.g. legs)	*embezzle*
unterstellen	*keep, store*	*assume*
unterziehen	*put on underneath*	*undergo*

22.6.8 *voll-*

(a) Many verbs form compounds with *voll-* which are only separable

They all have the meaning 'full', e.g.:

'vollbekommen	*manage to fill*
'vollstopfen	*cram full*
'vollschreiben	*fill with writing*
'volltanken	*fill up* (car with fuel)

(b) A few compounds with *voll-* are only inseparable

Most of these are words used in formal registers with the meaning 'complete', 'finish' or 'accomplish':

voll'bringen	*achieve, accomplish*
voll'enden	*complete*
voll'führen	*execute, perform*
voll'strecken	*execute, carry out*
voll'ziehen	*execute, carry out*

22.6.9 *wider-* usually forms inseparable verbs

wider'legen	*refute*
wider'stehen	*resist*

Only two verbs in *wider-* are separable, i.e.: *'widerhallen* 'echo, reverberate' and *'widerspiegeln* 'reflect'. *widerspiegeln* is sometimes, if less commonly, used inseparably.

22.6.10 *wieder-* usually forms separable verbs

'wiederkehren	*return*
'wiedersehen	*see again*

Only **one** verb prefixed with *wieder-* is inseparable: *wieder'holen* 'repeat'.

22.7 Verb formation by means other than prefixes

By far the most productive means of creating verbs is by means of prefixes, as has been explained in 22.4–22.6. Nevertheless, a few other patterns are frequent or productive.

22.7.1 Many verbs are formed simply from nouns or adjectives

The simplest way to convert a noun or an adjective to a verb is to add verbal endings (i.e. those indicating person, number, tense, etc.) to the root of the noun or the adjective. These have a variety of meanings, and some add *Umlaut*, especially the verbs from adjectives which have the sense of giving something a particular quality:

der Dampf	→ dampfen *steam*		falsch	→ fälschen *forge, falsify*
der Donner	→ donnern *thunder*		krank	→ kranken *suffer*
die Feder	→ federn *be springy*		kurz	→ kürzen *shorten*
der Fluch	→ fluchen *curse*		leer	→ leeren *empty*
das Fohlen	→ fohlen *foal (of mare)*		reif	→ reifen *ripen*

der Hammer	→ hämmern *hammer*	scharf	→ schärfen *sharpen*
die Kachel	→ kacheln *tile*	schwarz	→ schwärzen *blacken*
der Kellner	→ kellnern *work as a waiter*	trocken	→ trocknen *dry*
der Löffel	→ löffeln *spoon*	wach	→ wachen *be awake*
der Splitter	→ splittern *splinter*	welk	→ welken *wilt*

This means of verb formation is also widely employed with new roots from English, e.g. *bloggen* (from *das Blog*), *jetten* (from *der Jet*), *simsen* (from *die SMS* = 'short message service'), *tweeten* (from *die Tweet*).

22.7.2 Some verbs meaning 'cause to do' have been formed from strong verbs by means of a vowel change

This pattern is no longer productive, but its results are still common. In general, a transitive weak verb has been formed from an intransitive strong verb:

ertrinken *drown*	→ ertränken *drown*	sitzen *sit*	→ setzen *set*
(intr.)	(trans.)	springen *jump*	→ sprengen *blow up*
fallen *fall*	→ fällen *fell*		

22.7.3 Verbs in *-eln* express a weaker form of the action

They usually have *Umlaut*:

husten *cough*	→ hüsteln *cough slightly*	lachen *laugh*	→ lächeln *smile*
krank *ill, sick*	→ kränkeln *be sickly*	streichen *stroke*	→ streicheln *caress*

Some such verbs have a pejorative sense, e.g.: tanzen *dance* → tänzeln *prance*.

This formation is productive and can be based on nouns or adjectives as well as on other verbs:

fromm *pious*	→ frömmeln *affect piety*
der Schwabe *Swabian*	→ schwäbeln *talk like a Swabian*

22.7.4 The suffix *-ieren* is mainly used to form verbs from foreign words

The source of most verbs in *-ieren* (and its derivatives *-isieren* and *-ifizieren*) is French or Latin. Some have entered German directly from French verbs in *-er*, e.g. *arranger* → *arrangieren*. Others have been formed in German from the roots of words taken into German from these or other languages, e.g. *das Tabu* → *tabuisieren*. Only a very few are formed from German roots – *der Buchstabe* → *buchstabieren* is the most noteworthy exception.

23 Spelling, pronunciation and punctuation

GERMAN spelling and punctuation are relatively consistent, but some rules are quite different to those for English, and this chapter gives information on a selection of such problematic points. The rulings given are those accepted as authoritative throughout the German-speaking countries.

Uniform official spelling rules for all the German-speaking countries were first established in 1901/02. Towards the end of the 20th century it was felt that the rulings made then had left some unnecessary inconsistencies and anomalies which needed to be eliminated. For this reason, the countries where German is an official language agreed in 1994/95 on a set of reforms which began to be introduced in primary schools in 1996. For a transitional period the old and the new spellings were permitted, but from 2006 only the new spellings have been regarded as correct for official purposes, in particular in schools and other state institutions.

Although the changes were not far-reaching, this spelling reform gave rise to considerable controversy, and numerous steps were undertaken, even through the law-courts, to reverse the decision to introduce it. Although these were ultimately unsuccessful, and the waves of protest have subsided to a certain extent, they resulted in a succession of (relatively minor) changes to the reforms.

The authorities involved agreed a final version of the new rules in March 2006, and by 2010 most newspapers and books were using the reformed spellings. Nevertheless, some well-known authors, like Daniel Kehlmann, have insisted on keeping to the traditional rules. Many people who finished their schooling before the reform stick to the old rules for private use – or a mixture of old and new, because the successive modifications to the reform have created a widespread feeling of uncertainty about what is actually correct.

Thus learners are likely to be confronted with both sets of rules for some time, but they are recommended to adhere strictly to the new rules, as they are the only ones regarded as officially correct. For this reason the most recent version of the reformed spelling has been applied consistently, in this book, and the information given in this chapter relates exclusively to it. In particular, we deal with:

- **spelling** and **pronunciation** (section 23.1)
- the use of **capital letters** (section 23.2)
- whether to write **one word or two** (section 23.3)
- the use of *ß* **and** *ss* (section 23.4)
- other **miscellaneous points** of spelling (section 23.5)
- the use of the **comma** (section 23.6)
- the use of other **punctuation marks** (section 23.7)

23.1 **Spelling and pronunciation**

The relationship between letters and the sounds they represent is much more straightforward in German than in English and, in general, each sound of German corresponds to a single letter or group of letters. However, there are a few exceptions to this, and the main aim of this section is to give information on these cases. Where necessary, the symbols of the International Phonetic Alphabet (IPA) are used to make clear precisely what sounds are involved and, following normal conventions, they are given in square brackets. A table of the IPA symbols can be found on page xvi.

The accepted 'standard' pronunciation of German is based on the norms originally set down by a commission which met in 1898 to establish the best pronunciation for use on the stage. This is now usually referred to as *Hochlautung*, or often simply as *Hochdeutsch* (although this term strictly speaking covers standard grammar and vocabulary as well as pronunciation). This was originally a set of rather formal norms, but a modified form of them is now widely accepted as an ideal to aim for, especially for the foreign learners, and the information in this section is based on this. Although these norms are predominantly North German, they are generally regarded as reflecting the 'best' usage, and they are acceptable everywhere. There is, of course, much variation in actual usage within Germany and (especially) the other German-speaking countries, but a book such as this can only give information on the most important instances of such variation.

23.1.1 *b, d* and *g*

(a) At the end of a word or syllable, or before a consonant, *b, d* and *g* are pronounced as [p], [t] and [k]

Sieb	[ziːp]	abfahren	[apfaːʁən]	habt	[haːpt]
Rad	[ʁaːt]	kundgeben	[kʊntgeːbən]	sagt	[zaːkt]
Zug	[tsuːk]	wegfahren	[vɛkfaːʁən]		

Otherwise, i.e. at the beginning of a word or between vowels, *b, d* and *g* are pronounced [b], [d] and [g], as in English.

(b) There are two major exceptions to this rule in respect of *g*

(i) In the ending *-ig*, *g* is pronounced as *ch*, i.e. [ç]

König	[køːnɪç]	sandig	[zandɪç]	Außig	[aʊsɪç]

(ii) In North and central Germany, *g* is often pronounced like *ch* (i.e. as [ç] or [x]) in all other cases when it occurs at the end of a word or syllable, or before a consonant

Zug	[tsuːx]	wegfahren	[vɛçfaːʁən]	sagt	[zaːxt]

This pronunciation is not considered standard, but it is in practice almost universal usage by a majority of speakers across the northern two-thirds of Germany, i.e north of the river Main.

23.1.2 *ch*

(a) The pronunciation of *ch* differs depending on the preceding sound

(i) After low and back vowels, i.e. *a, o* and *u*, *ch* is pronounced [x]

Bach	[baːx]	Loch	[lɔx]	Buch	[buːx]	Bauch	[baʊx]

(ii) After front vowels, i.e. *i, e, ü* and *ö*, after *l* and *r*, and in the suffix *-chen, ch* is pronounced [ç]

mich	[mɪç]	echt	[ɛçt]	Bücher	[byçɐ]	Löcher	[lœçɐ]
Milch	[mɪlç]	Kirche	[kɪʁçə]	Veilchen	[faɪlçən]		

(b) The pronunciation of *ch* at the beginning of a word varies

(i) In most words it is always pronounced [k], e.g.:

Chamäleon, Chaos, Charakter, Chlor, Cholera, Chor, Christ, Chrom, Chronik

(ii) In words originally from French it is pronounced [ʃ], e.g.:

Champagner, Chance, Charme, Chauffeur, Chef, Chirurg

(iii) In a few words it is pronounced [ç] in the North (i.e. north of the Main), but in the South (including Austria and Switzerland) it is pronounced [k]. Either pronunciation is accepted as standard. The most important are: *Charisma, Chemie, Chile, China*.

(c) The combination *chs* is pronounced [ks]

wachsen	[vaksən]	Fuchs	[fʊks]	Achse	[aksə]

23.1.3 **Other consonants**

(a) *s* is pronounced [s] except in the following contexts

(i) At the beginning of a word before a vowel, and between vowels, *s* is pronounced [z]:

suchen	[zuːxən]	sandig	[zandɪç]	lesen	[leːzən]

(ii) At the beginning of a word before *p* and *t*, *s* is pronounced [ʃ]:

spielen	[ʃpiːlən]	Straße	[ʃtraːsə]

(b) *ng* is always pronounced [ŋ]

It is never pronounced [ŋg] as in some English words. Compare, for example, the difference between English *finger* [fɪŋgə] and German *Finger* [fɪŋɐ].

23.1.4 **Long and short vowels**

English-speaking learners need to pay considerable attention to the distinction between long and short vowels in German, as there are significant differences from English. In particular, German long vowels are consistently long. The task is not helped by the fact that this distinction is the area where German spelling is least systematic, and the difference between long and short vowels is not always clearly shown in the spelling. The main rules (and exceptions) are as follows:

(a) Vowels before double consonants are always short

This rule applies whether the double consonant is in the middle or at the end of the word.

bitte	[bɪtə]	fallen	[falən]	Klasse	[klasə]	Acker	[akɐ]
Butt	[bʊt]	Schiff	[ʃɪf]	knapp	[knap]	Pack	[pak]

NB: *k* is never doubled, and *ck* is used instead.

(b) Vowels before single consonants are usually long

This rule applies whether the consonant is in the middle or at the end of the word.

geben	[ge:bən]	lösen	[lø:zən]	Hefe	[he:fə]	üben	[y:bən]
gab	[ga:p]	Tag	[ta:k]	Chor	[ko:ʁ]	Mut	[mu:t]

Note that *ß* counts as a single consonant, and this is the main reason why it is used in contrast to *ss* (see also 23.4). Compare:

Fuß [fu:s] Fluss [flʊs] Maße [ma:sə] Masse [masə]

Some loan-words from English are an exception to this rule, as they end in a single consonant but have a short vowel, e.g. *Bus* [bʊs], *Jet* [dʒɛt]. When such words have an ending, the consonant is doubled: *Busse, jetten*.

(c) Vowels before clusters of consonants are usually short

Gang	[gaŋ]	Pflicht	[pflɪçt]	Mast	[mast]	Werk	[vɛʁk]
sitzen	[zɪtsən]	Sünde	[zʏndə]	schuften	[ʃʊftən]	Wespe	[vɛspə]

However, this rule is not consistent, and there are several common exceptions, e.g.:

Art	[a:ʁt]	atmen	[a:tmən]	Geburt	[gəbu:ʁt]	Jagd	[ja:kt]
Krebs	[kʁe:ps]	Mond	[mo:nt]	regnen	[ʁe:gnən]	trösten	[tʁø:stən]

Inflected forms of words or derived words keep a long vowel, even if the ending results in a consonant cluster:

lösen [lø:zən] → löste [lø:stə]   Tag [ta:k]   → Tags [ta:ks]
Hof [ho:f]   → höflich [hø:flɪç]   sagen [za:gən] → sagbar [za:kba:ʁ]

(d) Vowels before *ch* may be either long or short

In practice, each word needs to be learned separately:

Loch	[lɔx]	Hochzeit	[hɔxtsaɪt]	brechen	[brɛçən]
hoch	[ho:x]	fluchen	[flu:xən]	brach	[bra:x]

(e) Other ways of marking long vowels

(i) Especially before *m*, *n*, *l* and *r*, a long vowel can be shown by the silent letter *h*:

lahm [la:m] Bühne [by:nə] Höhle [hø:lə] fahren [fa:ʁən]

(ii) In a few words, a long vowel is shown by doubling the vowel letter:

Schnee [ʃne:] Saal [za:l] Heer [he:ʁ] Moos [mo:s]

(iii) Long [i:] is most commonly spelled *ie*, e.g.: *Lied* [li:t], *Sieg* [zi:k], *Miene* [mi:nə]

(iv) A single vowel at the end of a word is long, e.g.: *du* [du:], *wo* [vo:]

23.1.5 **The vowel *ä***

Short *ä* is always pronounced [ɛ], i.e. identically to *e*, e.g. *Kräfte* [kʁɛftə], *Gäste* [gɛstə]. Standard pronunciation prescribes that long *ä* should be pronounced [ɛ:], e.g.:

wäre	[vɛ:ʁə]	gäbe	[gɛ:bə]	Bär	[bɛ:ʁ]	Väter	[vɛ:tɐ]

However, this ruling is widely ignored, especially in North Germany, and many people usually pronounce long *ä* and long *e* identically, as [eː], e.g. *wäre* [veːʁə], *gäbe* [geːbə], etc. Indeed, the pronunciation [ɛː] can be considered affected. In practice it is most often used, if at all, in subjunctive forms like *gäbe*, in order to make the distinction from the indicative form *gebe* clear.

23.1.6 Word stress

Like in English, one syllable in all German words of more than one syllable is pronounced with rather more force than the others. This syllable is said to be stressed or bear the stress. However, there is no absolute hard and fast rule about **which** syllable in a German word is stressed, although there are certain clear regularities.

(a) In most native German words the stress falls on the first syllable of the word

'Monat   'Bruder   'gestern   'Glaube   'Arbeit   'Elend   'Segel

There are very few exceptions to this rule, the most common are:

Fo'relle   Ho'lunder   Hor'nisse   Kar'toffel   le'bendig   Wach'older

(b) The position of the stress is 'fixed' in German native words

i.e. it falls on the same syllable irrespective of any endings which might be added:

'Monate   'glauben   'glaubhaft   'Glaubhaftigkeit   'glaubwürdig

The only exception is that the suffix -*ei* is always stressed: *Bäcker'ei*, *Bücher'ei*

(c) Stress in words with prefixes

(i) A number of prefixes are always unstressed, whether on nouns, adjectives or verbs, i.e. *be-, emp-, ent-, er-, ge-, ver-, zer-*. With verbs these prefixes are inseparable, see 22.4.

emp'fangen   Emp'fang   emp'fänglich   Ge'schichte   ver'stehen   Ver'stand

(ii) Most other prefixes are stressed. With verbs, these prefixes are separable, see 22.5.

'abfahren   'Abfahrt   'abhängig   'einfallen   'Einfall   'einfältig

(iii) A few verb prefixes can be stressed or unstressed, usually with a difference in meaning, see 22.6. Nouns derived from these verbs normally keep the same stress as the original verb:

über'fahren *run over*   'überfahren *cross over*   'Überfahrt *crossing*
über'legen *consider*   'überlegen *put/lay over*   Über'legung *consideration*

The prefix *miss-* is variable with verbs, see 22.6.3, but with nouns in *miss-* the prefix is always stressed:

miss'brauchen *misuse*   'Missbrauch *misuse*

(iv) The prefix *un-* is usually stressed in nouns and adjectives if the form with *un-* is a straightforward negative of the form without *un-*, see 22.2.2j and 22.3.2b:

schuldig *guilty*   'unschuldig *innocent*   Wetter *weather*   'Unwetter *bad weather*

However, *un-* with some adjectives is not stressed. This is especially (but not universally) the case if there is no corresponding adjective without *un-*, or if there is some change of meaning other than simple negation, e.g.:

    unauf'**hör**lich *incessant*   uner'**hört** *outrageous*   un'**mög**lich *impossible*

In addition, *un-* is most often not stressed in adjectives with the prefix *un-* and the suffix *-bar*, or with the suffix *-lich* where it corresponds to English *-able* or *-ible*, cf. 22.3.1.

    unbe'**wohn**bar *uninhabitable*   unent'**behr**lich *indispensable*

(d) Stress in words of foreign origin

German words of French, Greek or Latin origin often have a different stress pattern to native words.

(i) They are characteristically stressed on the final syllable, e.g.:

ak'**tiv**	feu'**dal**	Phy'**sik**	Reper'**toire**
Al'**tar**	Konso'**nant**	Poli'**zist**	Ro'**man**
Biolo'**gie**	Kon'**trast**	Reforma**tion**	Stu'**dent**
Ele'**ganz**	Na'**tur**	Re'**gime**	Universi'**tät**

NB: A few words in *-ik* are stressed on the penultimate syllable, i.e. *Gram'matik*, *'Logik*.

(ii) Foreign words with some endings are characteristically stressed on the penultimate syllable. These often have the vowel [ə] in the final syllable, or the final syllable is *-as*, *-is*, *-os*, *-us* or *-um*, e.g.:

'**Album**	Fa'**milie**	manipu'**lieren**	Schoko'**lade**
'**Atlas**	'**Fiskus**	Pas'**sage**	Sozia'**lismus**
Bri'**gade**	'**Kosmos**	Prog'**nose**	Sozio'**loge**
Chi'**nese**	La'**vendel**	ren'**tabel**	Ta'**belle**

Note the different treatment of words spelled with final *-ie*. If it is pronounced [i:] it is stressed, e.g. *Biolo'gie*, but if it is pronounced [jə] the preceding syllable is stressed, e.g. *Fa'milie*.

(iii) Words in the suffixes *-on* and *-or* are usually stressed on the preceding syllable, e.g.:

'**Autor**	'**Dämon**	Di'**rektor**	'**Doktor**	Pro'**fessor**	'**Traktor**

In these words the stress shifts when the plural ending *-en* is added:

Au'**toren**	Dä'**monen**	Direk'**toren**	Dok'**toren**	Profes'**soren**	Trak'**toren**

NB: *Motor* can be stressed on either syllable, i.e. *'Motor* or *Mo'tor*. The plural is always *Mo'toren*.

(iv) Adjectives in *-isch* from foreign roots (see 22.3.1e) are stressed on the preceding syllable:

    bio'**logisch**   '**mo**disch   musi'**ka**lisch   no'**ma**disch

23.2 The use of capital letters

The basic rules are that initial capital letters are used:

(i) for the first word in a sentence (or a line of poetry)

(ii) for all nouns, e.g. *der Sack, die Schwierigkeit, das Bürgertum, die Pfirsiche*

(iii) for the 'polite' second person pronoun *Sie* and all its forms (e.g. *Ihnen, Ihr,* etc., see 3.3)

(iv) for proper names, e.g. *Frankfurt, Deutschland, das Schwarze Meer*

All other words begin with a small letter. Some provisos are necessary in respect of these basic rules, as explained below.

23.2.1 **The use of capital letters with nouns and proper names**

(a) Other parts of speech used as nouns are written with an initial capital letter

beim Lesen	das Für und Wider	das Ich	das Entweder-Oder
eine Drei	ein Drittel	der Vorsitzende	Bekanntes
alles Gute	nichts Schlechtes		

The exceptions to this rule under the previous spelling rules have been partly eliminated, and all nouns are now spelled with an initial capital letter, e.g. *im Allgemeinen* 'in general', *im Großen und Ganzen* 'in general', *alles Mögliche* 'everything possible', *aufs Neue* 'afresh'. However, small letters can still be used in some idiomatic expressions which do not include distinct nouns. In these cases, adjectives without an ending are always spelled with a small letter, but declined adjectives can be spelled with a small OR a capital letter, e.g.:

durch dick und dünn	*through thick and thin*
gegen bar	*for cash*
schwarz auf weiß	*in black and white*
über kurz oder lang	*sooner or later*
von klein auf	*from childhood*
von nah und fern	*from near and far*
binnen kurzem/Kurzem	*in a short time*
seit langem/Langem	*for a long time*
bei weitem/Weitem	*by far*
von weitem/Weitem	*from afar*
ohne weiteres/Weiteres	*without thinking*

(b) Adjectives are spelled with an initial small letter if a preceding (or following) noun is understood

Das rote Kleid hat mir nicht gepasst, ich musste das **blaue** nehmen
Es ist wohl das **schnellste** von diesen drei Autos

(c) The determiners *ander, beide* **and** *ein* **have small letters in most contexts**

This applies even in contexts where it would appear that they are being used as nouns, e.g. *etwas anderes, diese beiden, das eine und das andere.* However, *ander* can be used with an initial capital letter if it refers to something quite specific:

die Suche nach dem **Anderen** *the search for otherness*

(d) Usage with geographical and other proper names

(i) Adjectives forming part of geographical or other names referring to something or somebody unique have an initial capital letter:

das Schwarze Meer	*the Black Sea*
das Neue Testament	*the New Testament*
das Auswärtige Amt	*the Foreign Office*
der Eiserne Vorhang	*the Iron Curtain*
Karl der Erste	*Charles the First*
die Olympischen Spiele	*the Olympic Games*
die Französische Revolution	*the French Revolution*

However, the following, and others like them, are not names of unique things, and they are spelled with a small letter:

die goldene Hochzeit	*golden wedding*
der schwarze Markt	*the black market*

(ii) Indeclinable adjectives in *-er* from the names of towns and countries have an initial capital:

der Kölner Dom   die Berliner Straßen   das Wiener Rathaus

(iii) Adjectives formed from proper names with the suffix *-isch* (or *-sch*) normally have a small letter:

die goetheschen Gedichte   das elisabethanische Drama   das ohmsche Gesetz

However, these adjectives can be used with an apostrophe after the name to emphasise the person involved, in which case they are written with an initial capital, e.g. *die Grimm'schen Märchen*.

(e) Usage with *deutsch* and other adjectives of nationality

(i) Adjectives of nationality are written with a capital letter when used as a noun to refer to the language or the school subject (see 6.4.6a):

Er kann kein Wort Deutsch   Das ist (kein) gutes Deutsch   auf Deutsch *in German*
Wir haben Deutsch in der Schule   Ich habe eine Drei in Deutsch
Sie spricht, kann, lernt, liest (kein, gut) Deutsch, Russisch, Englisch
Das Buch ist in Deutsch und Englisch erschienen

As an adjective used as a noun *der/die Deutsche* 'German' is also always spelled with a capital letter.

(ii) When used as adjectives they have a small letter:

das deutsche Volk	ein deutsches Lied	die deutsche Bundesrepublik
italienische Weine	ein britisches Schiff	dieser französische Käse

This runs counter to English usage, which requires a capital letter ('the German people', 'Italian wines', etc.). Only in names is a capital used in German, e.g. *die Österreichischen Bundesbahnen*.

(iii) They have a small letter when used as the equivalent of an adverb:

Der Minister hat mit ihr deutsch gesprochen
Redet sie jetzt deutsch oder niederländisch?

(f) Capital and small letters with superlatives

(i) Superlatives with *am* (see 8.4.1) are spelled with a small letter, e.g.:

am besten, am schönsten

(ii) Superlative forms used with the definite article are written with a capital letter, e.g.

Es ist das Beste, wenn wir ihr alles sagen.

(iii) Superlatives with the preposition *aufs* (see 8.4.3) can be written with a capital or a small letter:

aufs Heftigste/heftigste

(g) Possessive pronouns with the form of an adjective after a definite article can be spelled with a small or a capital initial letter

(see 5.2.3b), e.g.:

(i) *der meinige/Meinige* 'mine', *der deinige/Deinige* 'yours', *der uns(e)rige/Uns(e)rige* 'ours', etc.

(ii) *der meine/Meine* 'mine', *der deine/Deine* 'yours', *der uns(e)re/Uns(e)re* 'ours', etc.

23.2.2 Nouns used as other parts of speech are written with a small letter

This applies in particular to:

(i) nouns used as prepositions, see 20.4, e.g.:

angesichts, kraft, mittels, statt, trotz

(ii) nouns used as adverbs, e.g.:

abends, anfangs, kreuz und quer, mitten, morgens, rechtens, rings, sonntags, teils, willens

NB: Capital letters are used for words denoting a part of the day used in conjunction with *heute, gestern* and *morgen*, e.g. *gestern Abend, heute Mittag* (see 11.6.2).

(iii) nouns used in indefinite expressions of number, e.g.:

ein bisschen	*a little*
ein paar	*a few* (see 5.5.6. Compare *ein Paar* 'a pair')

(iv) some nouns used as adjectives with the verbs *sein, bleiben* and *werden*: this applies to *Angst, Bange, Gram, Leid, Pleite, Schade* and *Schuld*

Mir ist/wird **angst**	*I am/am becoming afraid*
Er blieb ihr **gram**	*He bore her ill-will*
Die Firma ist **pleite**	*The firm is bankrupt*
Es ist **schade**	*It's a pity*
Sie war **schuld** daran	*It was her fault*

With other verbs, these words have an initial capital letter, e.g. *Ich habe Angst.*

(v) Nouns which have become idiomatic separable prefixes are spelled with a small letter, see 22.5.3a, e.g. stattfinden, teilnehmen.

23.2.3 Capitalisation of pronouns and related forms

All forms of the 'polite' second person pronoun *Sie* are spelled with a capital letter, see Table 3.1, e.g. *Sie, Ihnen, Ihre Frau*, etc.

No other pronouns have initial capital letters (except when they begin a sentence). The other second person pronouns *du, ihr* and their forms can be spelled with small initial letters or capitals in letter-writing, e.g. *Ich danke dir/Dir recht herzlich für deinen/Deinen Brief.*

23.3 One word or two?

The general rule is that **compounds are written as a single word if they are felt to be a single concept**. On the other hand, where the individual words are still felt to retain full meaning, they are written separately. The word stress often gives a clue to this, as a true compound only has one main stress, whereas separate words are still stressed independently. Compare:

'gut 'schreiben *write well*   'gutschreiben *credit*
'so 'weit *so far*   so 'weit *on the whole*

Some uncertainties in respect of the writing of compound words were eliminated in the revised spelling, but after subsequent revisions the 'old' and 'new' spellings are permitted in a number of cases. The main principles are explained with examples in the remainder of this section. However, the spelling of separable and compound verbs, e.g. *Rad fahren, kundgeben* is treated in detail in section 22.5.3.

23.3.1 Combinations of preposition + noun

These have the function of adverbs or prepositions and they are written separately if the individual words are still felt to retain independent meanings:

  mit Bezug auf, unter Bezug auf   zu Ende gehen   in/außer Kraft treten, sein

On the other hand, such adverbs or prepositions are written as single words if they are considered to be single entities, e.g. *anhand, beiseite, infolge, inmitten, vonnöten, vonstatten, vorderhand, zuhanden, zurzeit, zuzeiten.*

Alternative forms are permitted in some set phrases where it is debatable whether the words involved retain their separate meanings or not:

  außerstand/außer Stand setzen, sein
  imstande/im Stande sein
  infrage/in Frage stellen
  instand/in Stand setzen
  nachhause/nach Hause gehen
  zugrunde/zu Grunde gehen
  zuhause/zu Hause sein
  zuleide/zu Leide tun
  zumute/zu Mute sein
  zurande/zu Rande kommen
  zuschanden/zu Schanden machen, werden
  sich etwas zuschulden/zu Schulden kommen lassen
  zustande/zu Stande bringen
  zutage/zu Tage bringen, fördern
  zuwege/zu Wege bringen

Some prepositions from complex phrases also have alternative spellings, i.e. *aufgrund/auf Grund, zugunsten/zu Gunsten, mithilfe/mit Hilfe, anstelle/an Stelle.*

23.3.2 **Combinations of a noun or an adverb with a participle or an adjective**

Compounds which involve an underlying phrase are written together.

das bahnbrechende Werk	*the pioneering work*
(from: *sich eine Bahn brechend*)	
der angsterfüllte alte Mann	*the terrified old man*
(from: *von Angst erfüllt*)	
ein himmelschreiendes Unrecht	*an outrageous injustice*
(from: *zum Himmel schreiend*)	
die staubbedeckten Bücher	*the books covered with dust*
(from: *mit Staub bedeckt*)	

Other combinations of an adjective with a participle can always be written as separate words: *ein Aufsehen erregendes Ereignis, die Eisen verarbeitende Industrie*. However, it is permissible to write the words together if they are felt to express a single idea, e.g. *eine allein erziehende/alleinerziehende Mutter; ein klein geschnittenes/kleingeschnittenes Radieschen, selbst gebackene/selbstgebackene Kekse.*

If the combination is qualified by an adverb of degree (see 7.4), and the qualification relates to the whole combination, then it is written together, e.g. *ein äußerst kraftraubende Trainingsmethode.*

23.3.3 **Compound adverbs with *so-*, *wie-* and *wo-***

Note the difference between the following pairs (see 19.3.6 for details on the conjunctions in *so-*):

sobald *as soon as*	so bald *so soon*
solange *as long as*	so lange *so long*
sooft *as often as*	so oft *so often*
wieweit? *to what extent?*	wie weit? *how far, what distance?*
woanders *elsewhere* (see 7.1.5d)	wo anders? *where else?*
womöglich *possibly*	wo möglich *if possible*

NB: (i) *so dass* 'so that', see 19.5.2, may alternatively be spelled *sodass*.
   (ii) Most combinations with *viel* and *wenig* are spelled as separate words, e.g. *so viel, wie viel, zu wenig*, see 5.5.25e, but when used as a conjunction in the meaning 'as far as' *soviel* is written as a single word, see 19.7.4.

23.4 *ss* or *ß*?

The distinction between *ss* and *ß* (called *scharfes s* or *eszett*) is universally observed in Germany and Austria. In Switzerland, though, no distinction is made and *ss* is used in all cases. Foreign learners are strongly recommended to follow the majority practice.

(a) *-ss* is used if the preceding vowel is short

dass, der Fluss, die Flüsse, gewiss, lassen, er lässt, müssen, es muss, wissen, ich wusste, das Wasser

(b) *-ß* is used if the preceding vowel is long or a diphthong

beißen, die Buße, der Fuß, die Füße, groß, der Gruß, der Maß, die Maße, die Straße

The letter *ß* now fits consistently with the rule in German which stipulates that long vowels are followed by a single consonant in the spelling.

NB: (i) Some family names are spelled with a final *-ss*, e.g.: *Günther Grass, Theodor Heuss, Richard Strauss* (**but** *Johann Strauß*), *Carl Zeiss*.
   (ii) *ß* was originally only a small letter, but its use as a capital is now permitted, e.g. *BONNER STRAßE*. However, many people still always write *-SS-* in capitals: *STRASSE*.

23.5 Other points of spelling

23.5.1 The plural of nouns in -ee and -ie

These nouns do not add an extra -e in the spelling of the plural, even if the plural ending is pronounced as a distinct syllable, e.g.:

der See, die Seen [zeːən]   das Knie, die Knie [kniːə]
die Industrie, die Industrien [ɪndʊstriːən]

Similarly in verb forms, see 12.2.1d:

knien [kniːən] *kneel*   wir schrien [ʃriːən] *we cried*

23.5.2 Double vowels are simplified under *Umlaut*

(a) in plurals (see 1.2.2a):
der Saal *room* – die **Säle**

(b) in diminutives (see 22.2.1a):
das Paar *pair* – das **Pär**chen

23.5.3 Letters are not omitted in compounds

The former rule that sequences of three letters should be simplified no longer applies. Thus forms like *Brennnessel* 'stinging nettle', *Schifffahrt* 'travel by ship', *Schlussszene* 'closing scene' and *Schneeeule* 'snowy owl' are now standard.

23.6 The use of the comma

Unlike English, the comma in German is used to mark off grammatical units, **not** to signal a pause when speaking. Germans adhere to the rules for inserting commas quite strictly, regarding deviations from them as seriously as spelling mistakes.

This principle that commas are used to mark off larger syntactic units means that, unlike English, adverbs and adverbial phrases within the sentence are **never** separated by commas. Compare:

Er konnte ihr jedoch helfen   *He was, however, able to help her*
Bringen Sie mir bitte eine Zeitung   *Bring me a newspaper, please*

23.6.1 The use of commas with coordinated clauses and phrases

i.e. those linked by one of the coordinating conjunctions, like *aber*, *oder* and *und*.

(a) Clauses and phrases joined by *und* or *oder* do not need a comma
Die alte Dame öffnete ihm die Tür und er ging in den Garten
Christa rief an und er erzählte ihr, was passiert war
Ich gehe morgen ins Theater oder besuche ein Konzert

Parallel subordinate clauses linked by *und* or *oder* do not have a comma between them:

Er sagte, dass ich sofort kommen müsste und dass er mir etwas sehr Wichtiges zu berichten hätte
Sie wird nicht kommen, weil sie nicht kann oder weil sie einfach keine Lust hat

A comma can be used if the writer feels the need to make the sentence clearer or avoid ambiguity:

Sie begegnete ihrem Trainer, und dessen Mannschaft musste lange auf ihn warten

No comma is necessary before conjunctions with a similar meaning to *oder* and *und*, i.e. *beziehungsweise*, *sowie*, *weder . . . noch*, etc. (see 19.1.3 and 19.1.4).

(b) A comma is used before the conjunctions *aber, denn, doch, jedoch* **and** *sondern*

Er runzelte die Stirn, aber sie sagte nichts
Ich machte Licht, denn es war inzwischen dunkel geworden
Der Lohn ist karg, doch man genießt die abendlichen Stunden
Das Kleid war nicht grün, sondern hellblau

(c) A comma is used between parallel clauses and phrases which have no linking conjunction

Das Licht geht aus, der Vorhang hebt auf, das Spiel beginnt
Berlin, Paris, London, Madrid sind europäische Hauptstädte

23.6.2 **The use of commas with subordinate clauses**

In principle, all subordinate clauses are separated from the rest of the sentence by commas, whether they are introduced by a conjunction or not:

Er fragte, ob ich morgen nach Halberstadt fahren wollte
Weil ich morgen arbeiten muss, werde ich keine Zeit haben
Sie sagte, sie habe diesen Mann nie vorher gesehen
Unsere Lage wäre unmöglich gewesen, hätte er diesen Plan nicht ausgedacht

23.6.3 **The use of commas with participial clauses and infinitive clauses with** *zu*

(a) In general, such clauses do not need to be separated by commas from the rest of the sentence

Sie beschloss den Betrag möglichst bald zu überweisen
Ich hoffte in der nächsten Runde zu gewinnen
Diesen Vorgang wollen wir zu erklären versuchen
Ich brauche heute nicht ins Geschäft zu gehen
Aus vollem Halse lachend kam er auf mich zu
Er sank zu Tode getroffen zu Boden.

However, a comma can be used if the writer feels the need to make the sense clear or avoid ambiguities, as with the following example, where the comma shows which part of the sentence *heute* belongs to:

Das Kind versprach heute, nichts mehr von dem Kuchen zu essen
Das Kind versprach, heute nichts mehr von dem Kuchen zu essen

(b) However, a comma is used before an infinitive clause in the following cases

(i) if the infinitive clause is introduced by *(an)statt, außer, ohne* or *um* (see 13.2.7):

Ich konnte nichts tun, um ihn zu beruhigen
Er verließ das Haus, ohne gesehen zu werden

(ii) if the infinitive clause depends on a noun:

Umsonst machte er einen letzten Versuch, seine Frau zu retten
Ich habe nicht die geringste Absicht, ihr 1000 Euro zu leihen

(iii) if the infinitive clause depends on an anticipatory *es* (see 3.6.2e and 3.6.3), or a prepositional adverb (see 13.2.4e)

> Ich konnte es kaum ertragen, ihn so leiden zu sehen
> Sie hat ihn daran erinnert, Blumen für seine Mutter zu kaufen

23.6.4 Interjections, exclamations, explanatory phrases, phrases in apposition and parenthetical words and phrases

If these are seen as separate elements they are normally separated from the rest of the sentence by commas, e.g.:

> **Ach,** kannst du morgen wirklich nicht zu uns kommen?
> **Kurz und gut,** die Lage ist kritisch
> **Wissen Sie,** ich kann Ihnen da leider nicht mehr helfen
> Das macht, **grob gerechnet,** vierzig Prozent von unserem Absatz aus
> Ich habe jetzt, **wie gesagt,** keine Zeit dazu
> Wir wurden durch Herrn Meiring, **den Direktor des Instituts,** aufs Herzlichste empfangen

Comparative phrases introduced by *als* or *wie* are not normally separated by commas, e.g.:

> Sie ist jetzt wohl größer als ihre ältere Schwester
> Dieser Mann sah aus wie ein Schornsteinfeger

23.6.5 Two or more adjectives qualifying a noun are divided by commas if they are of equal importance

i.e. if they could be linked by *und*, e.g.:

> gute, billige Äpfel (*the apples are good* and *cheap*)

No comma is used if the second adjective forms a single idea with the noun:

> gute englische Äpfel (*i.e. English apples which are good*)

In practice, this rule is not always followed consistently (any more than the similar rule in English is), and many German writers use no commas in any series of adjectives.

23.7 Other punctuation marks

German usage differs from English in respect of the use of some other punctuation marks.

23.7.1 The semi-colon is little used in German

In principle, the semi-colon is used as in English. However, a comma or full stop, as appropriate, tends to be preferred in German. In particular, it is much more common in German than in English to have main clauses not linked by a conjunction, and these are commonly separated by commas:

> Geh in die Stadt und kaufe Mehl, unterdessen heize ich schon den Ofen an

23.7.2 **A colon, not a comma, is used when direct speech is introduced by a verb of saying**

Dann sagte sie: „Ich kann es nicht"

Similarly with reported phrases and the like:

Das Sprichwort heißt: Der Apfel fällt nicht weit vom Stamm

When a colon introduces a full sentence, it is usually followed by a capital letter, but a small letter is now permitted: *Das Sprichwort heißt: der Apfel fällt nicht weit vom Stamm.*

23.7.3 **The first of a set of inverted commas is placed on the line**

i.e. **not** above it as in English. This applies equally to single and double inverted commas:

Dann sagte sie: „Ich kann ihn überhaupt nicht verstehen".
Er fragte mich: „Kennen Sie Brechts Stück, ‚Mutter Courage und ihre Kinder'?"

23.7.4 **The exclamation mark**

(a) **The exclamation mark is used after interjections and exclamations**

Ach!   Donnerwetter!   Pfui Teufel!   Guten Tag!

(b) **Commands are followed by an exclamation mark:**

Komm sofort zurück!   Hören Sie sofort auf!
Seid doch vorsichtig, Kinder!   Einsteigen und die Türen schließen!

Standard usage traditionally required the use of the exclamation mark with commands in German, but this rule is not always followed nowadays. Many Germans prefer to use a full stop, especially if the command is not felt to be particularly forceful.

(c) **An exclamation mark can be used after the words of address at the beginning of a letter**

Sehr geehrter Herr Dr. Fleischmann!   Liebe Petra!

This traditional usage has now largely been replaced by the use of the comma, as in English. However, if a comma is used, a capital letter should not be used for the first word of the letter proper, as, strictly speaking, it is not the beginning of a sentence, e.g.:

Lieber Martin,
es hat uns sehr gefreut, wieder mal von dir zu hören . . .

List of sources

The examples illustrating points of grammar and usage have been drawn from a wide range of sources and registers, spoken as well as written. Many of the unattributed examples which are new to this revised edition have been simplified or amended from modern texts, from phrases and sentences heard in conversation or on radio and television, etc. and in large number from the computerised corpus of modern spoken and written German set up by the Institut für deutsche Sprache in Mannheim. Longer examples quoted verbatim or with minor simplifications have been attributed wherever possible. The following sources have provided such material:

Authors

A. Andersch
S. Andres
I. Bachmann
K. Bednarz
W. Bergengruen
T. Bernhard
P. Bichsel
B. Biehl
K.H. Borst
H. Böll
B. Brecht
S. Brinkmann
J. Bumke
M. Dönhoff
F. Dürrenmatt
H. Fallada
H. Fischer
M.L. Fleißer
M. Frisch

G. Gaiser
A. Goes
G. Grass
K.H. Großmann
M. von der Grün
B. Grzimek
S. Haffner
E.W. Heine
S. Hermlin
Th. Heuss
S. Heym
P. Heyse
W. Hildesheimer
M. Horbach
E.H. Jacob
W. Jens
U. Johnson
E. Jünger
G. Kapp

E. Kästner
D. Kehlmann
F.X. Kroetz
E. Langgässer
S. Lenz
K. Mann
Th. Mann
I. Morgner
R. Müller
R. Musil
R. Pörtner
E.M. Remarque
G. Reuter
H. von Rimscha
J. Roth
B. Schlink
H.G.F. Schneeweiß
P. Schneider
W. Schnurre

R. Schoof
A. Seghers
K. Sonnenberg
E. Strauß
E. Strittmatter
A. Surminski
P. Süßkind
Th. Valentin
M. Walse
P. Weiß
I. Wendt
C. Weyden
U. Wickert
E. Wiechert
G. Wohmann
C. Wolf
S. Zweig
G. Zwerenz

Newspapers

The following newspapers or periodicals have provided material. Some titles have been abbreviated as indicated:

BILD	*BILD-Zeitung*	MM	*Mannheimer Morgen*
BZ	*Berliner Zeitung*	ND	*Neues Deutschland*
FAZ	*Frankfurter Allgemeine Zeitung*	NZZ	*Neue Zürcher Zeitung*
FR	*Frankfurter Rundschau*	NUZ	*Nürnberger Zeitung*
HA	*Hamburger Abendblatt*	OH	*Odenwälder Heimatzeitung*
HMP	*Hamburger Morgenpost*		*(Die) Presse*
HAZ	*Hannoversche Allgemeine Zeitung*		*Quick*
	Horizont	SGT	*Sankt Galler Tagblatt*
	Kurier		*(Der) Spiegel*
LV	*Leipziger Volkszeitung*		*Stern*

SZ   *Süddeutsche Zeitung*
      (*Die*) *Welt*
      (*Die*) *Zeit*

In addition, the Baedeker series of travel guides, Knaur's encyclopedia, and Innsbruck university *Vorlesungsverzeichnis* provided examples, as did the following radio and television stations: ARD, NDR, SWF, WDR, ZDF.

Bibliography and references

This list gives a selection of the most important works which were consulted for this and previous revisions of *Hammer's Grammar*. Major dictionaries and general accounts of German and English grammar are given first, followed by a selection of works containing more extensive accounts of specific points of grammar and usage, arranged according to the individual chapters of this book.

In principle, the references are limited to major reference books on each topic; users requiring more detailed bibliographical information are referred to: Helmut Frosch, Roman Schneider, Bruno Strecker & Peter Eisenberg, *Bibliographie zur deutschen Grammatik 1994-2002*. Tübingen: Stauffenburg Verlag, 2003 and Helmut Frosch, Roman Schneider and Bruno Strecker, *Bibliographie zur deutschen Grammatik 2003-2007*. Tübingen: Stauffenburg Verlag, 2008 Details of these and more recent work is accessible through the *grammis* website of the *Institut für Deutsche Sprache* (http://hypermedia.ids-mannheim.de/pls/public/bib.ansicht)

Dictionaries

DUDEN, *Das große Wörterbuch der deutschen Sprache*. 3rd ed. 10 vols. Dudenverlag: Mannheim, 1999. Götz, D., Haensch, G. and Wellmann, H. (eds), *Langenscheidts Großwörterbuch Deutsch als Fremdsprache*. New ed. Langenscheidt: Berlin, etc., 2008.
Scholze-Stubenrecht, W. and Sykes, J.B. (eds), *The Oxford Duden German Dictionary*. 3rd ed. OUP: Oxford, 2005.
Terrell, P. et al. (eds), *Collins German–English English–German Dictionary*. 6th ed. HarperCollins: Glasgow, 2010.
Trask, R.L., *A Dictionary of Grammatical Terms in Linguistics*. Routledge: London and New York, 1993.
Wahrig, G., *Deutsches Wörterbuch*. 2nd rev. ed. dtv: München, 2009.

Works on German grammar and usage

Abraham, W., *Deutsche Syntax im Sprachvergleich: Grundlegung einer typologischen Syntax des Deutschen*. 2nd ed. Stauffenburg: Tübingen, 2005.
Buscha, J. et al., *Grammatik in Feldern. Ein Lehr- und Übungsbuch für Fortgeschrittene*. Hueber: Ismaning, 2002.
Davies, W. & Langer, N., *The Making of Bad Language*. Peter Lang: Frankfurt/Main et al., 2006
Dodd, W. *et al., Modern German Grammar. A Practical Guide*. 2nd ed. Routledge: London, New York, 2003.
Dovalil, V., *Sprachnormenwandel im geschriebenen Deutsch an der Schwelle zum 21. Jahrhundert*. Peter Lang: Frankfurt/Main et al., 2006
DUDEN, *Richtiges und gutes Deutsch. Wörterbuch der sprachlichen Zweifelsfälle*. 6th ed. by Peter Eisenberg. Dudenverlag: Mannheim, etc., 2007.
DUDEN, *Grammatik der deutschen Gegenwartssprache*. 8th ed. Dudenverlag: Mannheim, etc., 2009.
Eichhoff, J., *Wortatlas der deutschen Umgangssprachen*. Vols 1–2, Francke: Bern and Munich, 1977–78; Vols 3–4, Saur, Munich, 1998–2000.
Eisenberg, P., *Grundriß der deutschen Grammatik*. 2 vols. 3rd ed. Metzler: Stuttgart, Weimar, 2006.
Engel, U., *Deutsche Grammatik*. 2nd rev. ed. iudicium: München, 2009.
Engel, U., *Syntax der deutschen Gegenwartssprache*. 4th ed. Erich Schmidt: Berlin, 2009.
Eroms, H.-W., *Syntax der deutschen Sprache*. de Gruyter: Berlin and New York, 2000.
Flämig, W., *Grammatik des Deutschen. Einführung in Struktur- und Wirkungszusammenhänge erarbeitet auf der theoretischen Grundlage der 'Grundzüge einer deutschen Grammatik'*. Akademie: Berlin, 1991.
Fox, A., *The Structure of German*. 2nd ed. OUP: Oxford, 2005.
Freund, F. and Sundqvist, B., *Tysk grammatik*. Natur och Kultur: Stockholm, 1988.
Glück, H. and Sauer, W., *Gegenwartsdeutsch*. 2nd ed. Metzler: Stuttgart, 1997.

Götze, L. and Hess-Lüttich, E.W.B., *Grammatik der deutschen Sprache. Sprachsystem und Sprachgebrauch*. rev ed. Wissen-Media-Verlag: Gütersloh *et al.*, 2005.

Hawkins, J.A., *A Comparative Typology of English and German. Unifying the Contrasts*. Croom Helm: London, Sydney, 1986.

Heidolph, K.E., Flämig, W. and Motsch, W. (eds), *Grundzüge einer deutschen Grammatik*. Akademie: Berlin, 1981.

Helbig, G. & Buscha, J., *Deutsche Grammatik. Ein Handbuch für den Ausländerunterricht*. 15th ed. Langenscheidt: Berlin *et al.*, 2007.

Hentschel, E., *Deutsche Grammatik*. de Gruyter: Berlin & New York, 2010.

Lang, E. and Zifonun, G. (eds), *Deutsch typologisch*. de Gruyter: Berlin & New York, 1996

Lockwood, W.B., *German Today: The Advanced Learner's Guide*. Clarendon Press: Oxford, 1987.

Neuland, E. (ed.), *Variation im heutigen Deutsch. Perspektiven für den Sprachunterricht*. Peter Lang: Frankfurt/Main *et al.*, 2006.

Sanders, W., *Gutes Deutsch – Besseres Deutsch. Praktische Stillehre der deutschen Gegenwartssprache*. Wissenschaftliche Buchgesellschaft: Darmstadt, 1986.

Sanders, W., *Sprachkritikastereien und was der „Fachler" dazu sagt*. Wissenschaftliche Buchgesellschaft: Darmstadt, 1992.

Schanen, F. and Confais, J.-P., *Grammaire de l'allemand. Formes et fonctions*. Nathan: Paris, 2001.

Schlobinski, P. *Syntax des gesprochenen Deutsch*. Westdeutscher Verlag: Opladen, 1997.

Schulz, D. and Griesbach, H., *Grammatik der deutschen Sprache*. 11th ed. Hueber: Munich, 1981.

Schwitalla, J., *Gesprochenes Deutsch. Eine Einführung*. Erich Schmidt: Berlin, 3rd ed. 2006.

Sommerfeldt, K.-E. and Starke, G., *Einführung in die Grammatik der deutschen Gegenwartssprache*. 3rd ed. Niemeyer: Tübingen, 1998.

ten Cate, A.P. et al., *Deutsche Grammatik. Eine kontrastiv deutsch-niederländische Beschreibung für den Zweitspracherwerb*. Coutinho: Bussum.

Weinrich, H., *Textgrammatik der deutschen Sprache*. 4th ed. Olms: Hildesheim & New York, 2007.

Zifonun, G. et al., *Grammatik der deutschen Sprache*. de Gruyter: Berlin and New York, 1997.

Works on English grammar and usage

Graustein, G. et al. (eds), *English Grammar. A University Handbook*. 6th ed. Enzyklopädie: Leipzig, 1989.

Huddleston, R. & G. Pullum, *The Cambridge Grammar of the English Language*. CUP: Cambridge, 2002.

Lamprecht, A., *Grammatik der englischen Sprache*. 9th ed. Cornelsen: Berlin, 1977.

Quirk, R. et al., *A Comprehensive Grammar of the English Language*. Longman: London, 1995.

Swan, M., *Practical English Usage*. 3rd ed. OUP: Oxford, 2005.

1: Nouns

Corbett, G., *Gender*. CUP: Cambridge, 1991.

Doleschal, U., *Movierung im Deutschen. Eine Darstellung der Bildung und Verwendung weiblicher Personenbezeichnungen*. Lincom Europa: Unterschließheim/Munich, 1992.

Gregor, B., *Genuszuordnung. Das Genus englischer Lehnwörter im Deutschen*. Niemeyer: Tübingen, 1983.

Hoberg, U., *Das Genus des Substantivs*. IDS: Mannheim, 2004

Köpcke, K.-M., *Untersuchungen zum Genussystem der deutschen Gegenwartssprache*. Niemeyer: Tübingen, 1982.

Wegener, H., *Die Nominalflexion des Deutschen – verstanden als Lerngegenstand*. Niemeyer: Tübingen, 1995.

Wegera, K.-P., *Das Genus: Ein Beitrag zur Didaktik des Daf-Unterrichts*. iudicium: Munich, 1997.

2: Case

Blake, B.J., *Case*. 2nd ed. CUP: Cambridge, 2001.

Dürscheid, C., *Die verbalen Kasus des Deutschen. Untersuchungen zur Syntax, Semantik und Perspektive*. de Gruyter: Berlin and New York, 1999.

Wegener, H., *Der Dativ im heutigen Deutsch*. Narr: Tübingen, 1985.

3: Personal pronouns

Behr, I. *et al.* (eds.), *Der Ausdruck der Person im Deutschen*. Stauffenburg: Tübingen, 2007.
Besch, W., *Duzen, Siezen, Titullieren. Zur Anrede im Deutschen heute und gestern*. Vandenhoeck and Ruprecht: Göttingen, 1996.
Marx-Moyse, J., *Untersuchungen zur deutschen Satzsyntax. 'Es' als vorausweisendes Element eines Subjektsatzes*. Steiner: Wiesbaden, 1983.
Zifonun, G., *Das Pronomen. Teil I: Überblick und Personalpronomen*. IDS: Mannheim, 2001.

4: The articles

Bisle-Müller, H., *Artikelwörter im Deutschen. Semantische und pragmatische Aspekte ihrer Verwendung*. Niemeyer: Tübingen, 1991.
Grimm, H.-J., *Untersuchungen zum Artikelgebrauch im Deutschen*. Enzyklopädie: Leipzig, 1986.
Grimm, H.-J., *Lexikon zum Artikelgebrauch*. Enzyklopädie: Leipzig, 1987.

5: Other determiners and pronouns

Ahrenholz, B., *Verweise mit Demonstrativa im gesprochenen Deutsch. Grammatik, Zweitspracherwerb und Deutsch als Fremdsprache*. de Gruyter: Berlin & New York, 2007.
Bethke, I., *'der', 'die', 'das' als Pronomen*. iudicium: Munich, 1990.
Zifonun, G., *Das Pronomen. Teil IV: Indefinita im weiteren Sinne*. IDS: Mannheim, 2006.

6: Adjectives

Schmale, G., *Das Adjektiv im heutigen Deutsch*. Stauffenburg: Tübingen, 2011.
Sommerfeldt, K.-E. and Schreiber, H., *Wörterbuch zur Valenz und Distribution deutscher Adjektive*. 3rd ed. Bibliographisches Institut: Leipzig, 1983.

7: Adverbs

Renz, I., *Adverbiale im Deutschen*. Niemeyer: Tübingen, 1993.

10: Modal particles

Helbig, G. and Helbig, A., *Deutsche Partikeln – Richtig gebraucht?* 2nd ed. Langenscheidt/Enzyklopädie: Leipzig, etc., 2001.
Métrich, R. & E. Faucher, *Wörterbuch deutscher Partikeln. Unter Berücksichtigung ihrer französischen Äquivalente*. Walter de Gruyter: Berlin & New York, 2009.
Möllering, M., *The Acquisition of German Modal Particles. A Corpus-Based Approach*. Peter Lang: Bern *et al.*, 2004.
Weydt, H. *et al.*, *Kleine deutsche Partikellehre*. Klett: Stuttgart, 1989.

12: Verbs: conjugation

Jaeger, C., *Probleme der syntaktischen Kongruenz. Theorie und Normvergleich im Deutschen*. Niemeyer: Tübingen, 1992.

13: The infinitive and the participles

Bech, G., *Studien über das deutsche Verbum infinitum*. 2nd ed. Niemeyer: Tübingen, 1983.
Buscha, J. and Zoch, I., *Der Infinitiv*. 2nd ed. Enzyklopädie: Leipzig, 1992.
Marillier, J.-F. & C. Rozier (eds.), *Der Infinitiv im Deutschen*. Stauffenburg: Tübingen, 2005

14: Uses of the tenses

Comrie, B., *Tense*. CUP: Cambridge, 1985.

Dieling, K. and Kempter, F., *Die Tempora*. 2nd ed. Langenscheidt/Enzyklopädie: Leipzig *et al.*, 1989.

Latzel, S., *Die deutschen Tempora Perfekt und Präteritum. Eine Darstellung mit Bezug auf die Erfordernisse des Faches 'Deutsch als Fremdsprache'*. Hueber: Munich, 1977.

O. Leirbukt (ed.), *Tempus/Temporalität und Modus/Modalität im Sprachenvergleich*. Stauffenburg: Tübingen, 2004

Thieroff, R., *Das finite Verb im Deutschen. Tempus – Modus – Distanz*. Narr: Tübingen, 1992.

15: The passive

Fagan, S.M.B., *The Syntax and Semantics of Middle Constructions. A Study with Special Reference to German*. CUP: Cambridge, 1992.

Helbig, G. and Heinrich, G., *Das Vorgangspassiv*. 4th ed. Bibliographisches Institut: Leipzig, 1983.

16: Mood: the imperative and the subjunctive

Bausch, K.-H., *Modalität und Konjunktivgebrauch in der gesprochenen deutschen Standardssprache. Sprachsystem, Sprachvariation und Sprachwandel im heutigen Deutsch*. Hueber: Munich, 1979.

Buscha, J. and Zoch, I., *Der Konjunktiv*. 5th ed. Langenscheidt/Enzyklopädie: Leipzig, 1999.

Jäger, S., *Empfehlungen zum Gebrauch des Konjunktivs*. Schwann: Düsseldorf, 1970.

17: The modal auxiliaries

Diewald, G., *Die Modalverben im Deutschen. Grammatikalisierung und Polyfunktionalität*. Niemeyer: Tübingen, 1999.

Hansen, B. & F. de Haan (eds.), *Modals in the Langauges of Europe. A Reference Work*. Mouton de Gruyter: Berlin & New York, 2009..

Öhlschläger, G., *Zur Syntax und Semantik der Modalverben des Deutschen*. Niemeyer: Tübingen, 1989.

18: Verbs: valency

Ágel, V., *Valenztheorie*. Narr: Tübingen, 2000.

Engel, U. and Schuhmacher, H., *Kleines Valenzlexikon deutscher Verben*. 2nd ed. Narr: Tübingen, 1978.

Fischer, K. *et al.* (eds.), *Valenz und Deutsch als Fremdsprache*. Peter Lang: Frankfurt *et al.*, 2010.

Helbig, G. and Schenkel, W., *Wörterbuch zur Valenz und Distribution deutscher Verben*. 8th ed. Niemeyer: Tübingen, 1991.

Sonnenberg, B., *Korrelate im Deutschen. Beschreibung, Geschichte und Grammatiktheorie*. Niemeyer: Tübingen, 1992.

19: Conjunctions and subordination

Buscha, J., *Lexikon deutsche Konjunktionen*. 2nd ed. Langenscheidt: Leipzig, 1995.

20: Prepositions

Schmitz, W., *Der Gebrauch der deutschen Präpositionen*. 9th ed. Hueber: Ismaning, 1995.

Schröder, J., *Lexikon deutscher Präpositionen*. 2nd ed. Enzyklopädie: Leipzig, 1990.

21: Word order

Eroms, H.W., *Funktionale Satzperspektive*. Niemeyer: Tübingen, 1986.

Haftka, B., *Deutsche Wortstellung. Studienbibliographie*. Groos: Heidelberg, 2000.

Hoberg, U., *Die Wortstellung der geschriebenen deutschen Gegenwartssprache: Untersuchungen zur Elementenfolge im einfachen Verbalsatz*. Hueber: Munich, 1981.

22: Word formation

Donalies, E., *Wortbildung im Deutschen*. Narr: Tübingen, 2002.
Erben, J. *Einführung in die deutsche Wortbildungslehre*. 5th ed. Erich Schmidt: Berlin, etc., 2006.
Fleischer, W. and Barz, I., *Wortbildung der deutschen Gegenwartssprache*. 3rd. ed. Niemeyer: Tübingen, 2007.
Hentschel, Elke, & Vogel, P.M. (eds.), *Deutsche Morphologie*. de Gruyter: Berlin & New York, 2009.
Lohde, Michael (2006), *Wortbildung des modernen Deutschen. Ein Lehr- und Übungsbuch*. (narr studienbücher). Tübingen: Narr.

23: Spelling, pronunciation and punctuation

Deutsche Rechtschreibung. Regeln und Wörterverzeichnis. Entsprechend den Empfehlungen des Rats für deutsche Rechtschreibung. Überarbeitete Fassung des amtlichen Regelwerks 2004. München und Mannheim Februar 2006 (downloadable at: www.ids-mannheim.de/service/reform)
DUDEN, *die deutsche Rechtschreibung*. 25th. ed. Dudenverlag: Mannheim, etc., 2000.
Eroms, H.-W. and Munske, H.H. (eds), *Die Rechtschreibreform. Pro und Contra*. Erich Schmidt: Berlin, etc., 1997.
Hall, C., *Modern German Pronunciation. An Introduction for Speakers of English*. 2nd ed. Manchester University Press: Manchester & New York, 2003.
Johnson, S., *Spelling Trouble. Language, Ideology and the Reform of German Orthography*. Multilingual Matters: Clevedon *et al.*, 2005.

Glossary

The explanations include references to sections or chapters where more detail is given. Words in small capitals are themselves explained in the glossary.

accusative	a CASE (2.2) which indicates the DIRECT OBJECT of TRANSITIVE verbs (18.3): *Ich sehe **den Hund***. It is also used after some PREPOSITIONS (20.1, 20.3): *Ich gehe durch **den Wald***, as well as in some ADVERBIAL constructions (11.4.1): *Sie kommt **jeden Tag***.
accusative object	the DIRECT OBJECT of the verb, in the ACCUSATIVE case (18.3): *Der Wolf fraß **den Esel***.
adjective	a word which modifies, or describes a NOUN (Chapter 6). **Attributive** adjectives are used before a noun: *die **schöne** Stadt*; **predicative** adjectives are used after a COPULAR VERB: *die Stadt ist schön*.
adverb	a word which modifies a VERB, an ADJECTIVE or a whole CLAUSE, often giving extra information on **how**, **when**, **where** or **why** (Chapter 7): *Sie singt **gut**; Sie war **sehr** freundlich*.
adverbial	any part of a SENTENCE which has the **function** of an ADVERB (18.1.4). It can be a single word (an ADVERB), or a phrase, or a whole CLAUSE: *Sie sang **gut**; Sie sang **mit einer hellen Stimme**; Sie sang, **als sie ins Zimmer kam***.
agreement	copying a grammatical feature from one word to another, so that certain words have ENDINGS according to the words they are used with or refer to. In German, DETERMINERS and ADJECTIVES 'agree' with the NOUN (4.1, 6.1): *dieses Buch; mit **meinem neuen** Auto*, and VERBS 'agree' with their SUBJECT (12.1.4): *ich **singe**, du **singst***.
apposition	a phrase used to modify a NOUN PHRASE without a connecting PREPOSITION is **'in apposition'** to it (2.6): *Wilhelm, **der letzte deutsche Kaiser**, starb im Exil*.
article	the most important of the DETERMINERS (Chapter 4). German has a **definite article** *der*, *die*, *das*, etc. (= English *the*) and an **indefinite article** *ein*, *eine*, etc. (= English *a*).
auxiliary verb	a VERB used in combination with the INFINITIVE or PAST PARTICIPLE of another verb to form a COMPOUND TENSE or the PASSIVE (12.3–4): *Karin **hat** einen Hund **gekauft***, or, in the case of the MODAL AUXILIARIES (Chapter 17), to indicate the attitude of the speaker with regard to what is being said: *Sie **muss** sofort **kommen***.
bracket	the **'bracket' construction** is typical of German CLAUSES, with most words and phrases in a CLAUSE bracketed between two parts of the verb (21.1): *Wir [**kommen** um 17 Uhr in Innsbruck **an**]*.

cardinal number	the numerals used in counting (9.1): *eins, zwei, . . . hundert.*
case	indicates the function of a NOUN PHRASE in the CLAUSE (Chapter 2). German has four **cases**: NOMINATIVE *der Igel*; ACCUSATIVE *den Igel*; GENITIVE *des Igels* and DATIVE *dem Igel.*
clause	a part of a SENTENCE with a VERB and its COMPLEMENTS (18.1). A **main clause** can stand on its own: *Dein Vater kommt.* A **subordinate clause** (Chapter 19) is dependent on another clause in the sentence and is usually introduced by a CONJUNCTION: *Ich weiß, dass dein Vater kommt.*
comparative	the form of an ADJECTIVE or ADVERB used to express a comparison (Chapter 8): *schneller, höher, weiter.*
complement	an element in a CLAUSE which is closely linked to the VERB and completes its meaning (18.1). The most important complements of the verb are its SUBJECT and OBJECTS.
complement clause	a **subordinate** CLAUSE which has the same role as a verb COMPLEMENT (19.2): *Dass sie gekommen war, hat mich erstaunt* (the clause is the SUBJECT of the verb); *Ich wusste, dass sie gekommen war* (the clause is the DIRECT OBJECT of the verb).
compound tense	a TENSE formed by using an AUXILIARY VERB with the INFINITIVE or PAST PARTICIPLE of another **verb** (12.3), e.g. the PERFECT tense: *Sie hat geschlafen,* or the FUTURE tense: *Sie wird kommen.*
compound word	a word formed by joining two or more words (22.1): *Kindergarten, dunkelrot.*
conditional	a compound form of KONJUNKTIV II formed from the **past subjunctive** form of the AUXILIARY VERB *werden,* i.e. *würde,* and the INFINITIVE of another verb (12.5.2, 16.4–5): *Ich würde gehen.*
conditional sentence	a SENTENCE which expresses a condition, i.e. 'If X, then Y' (16.5). The SUBJUNCTIVE mood is often used in conditional sentences in German.
conjugation	the forms of a VERB, in particular the pattern of ENDINGS and/ or **vowel changes** which show AGREEMENT with the SUBJECT and indicate the various TENSES or the MOOD, etc., (Chapter 12): *ich komme, du kommst, wir kamen, wir kämen,* etc.
conjunction	a word used to link CLAUSES within a SENTENCE (Chapter 19). **Coordinating conjunctions** link main clauses (e.g. *und, aber*), and **subordinating conjunctions** introduce subordinate clauses (e.g. *dass, obwohl, weil, wenn*).
copular verb	a **linking** VERB, which typically links the SUBJECT with a PREDICATE COMPLEMENT, i.e. an ADJECTIVE or a NOUN PHRASE in the NOMINATIVE case (18.6). The most frequent **copular verbs** in German are *sein, werden* and *scheinen: Er ist ein guter Lehrer; Die alte Frau wurde blass.*

count noun	a NOUN referring to a thing or object which can be counted. Count nouns, unlike MASS NOUNS, can be used in the PLURAL and with the **indefinite** ARTICLE.
dative	a CASE (2.5) used to mark some OBJECTS of the VERB: *Sie hat **meiner Schwester** die CD gegeben, Ich helfe **meinem Bruder**.* It can also indicate **possession**: *Sie zog **dem Kind** die Jacke aus,* it is used after some ADJECTIVES (6.5): *Er sieht **meinem Vater** ähnlich,* and after many PREPOSITIONS (20.2–3): *Er hat mit **den Kindern** gespielt.*
dative object	a COMPLEMENT of the VERB in the DATIVE case (18.4). With some verbs it is the only object: *Sie wollte **dem kleinen Mädchen** helfen,* with verbs which also have an ACCUSATIVE (DIRECT) OBJECT, it is the INDIRECT OBJECT: *Sie hat **dem kleinen Mädchen** das Heft gegeben.*
declension	the pattern of ENDINGS on a NOUN (1.3), an ADJECTIVE (6.1–2), or a DETERMINER (4.1, Chapter 5) which show CASE, NUMBER and GENDER: *der gute Hund, des guten Hundes, den guten Hunden.*
demonstrative	a DETERMINER or PRONOUN (5.1) which points to something specific, e.g. *dieser, jener.*
derivation	forming words from other words, typically by using SUFFIXES and/or PREFIXES (Chapter 22): *beglaubigen* (< *Glaube*), *Gesundheit* (< *gesund*).
determiner	a function word used with NOUNS (Chapters 4 and 5). They include the ARTICLES (*der, ein*), the DEMONSTRATIVES (*dieser*, etc.), the POSSESSIVES, (*mein*, etc.) and INDEFINITES (*einige, viele*, etc.). They typically come **before** ADJECTIVES in the NOUN PHRASE.
direct object	a verb COMPLEMENT, typically a person or thing directly affected by the action (18.3). It is in the ACCUSATIVE case. *Der Löwe fraß **den Esel**; Die böse Frau schlug **den Hund**.*
direction complement	a COMPLEMENT used with verbs of **motion**, indicating **where** the SUBJECT is going or where the DIRECT OBJECT is being put (18.8): *Sie fuhr **nach Ulm**; Er stellt den Besen **in die Ecke**.*
ending	a SUFFIX which gives grammatical information, e.g. about CASE, NUMBER OR TENSE. All the **endings** of a NOUN, ADJECTIVE or DETERMINER make up its DECLENSION; all the endings of a VERB make up its CONJUGATION.
feminine	one of the three GENDERS into which nouns are classified (1.1).
finite verb	a form of the VERB which has an ENDING in agreement with the SUBJECT (12.1): *Ich **komme**; Wir **haben** geschlafen; Sie **wurden** betrogen; Ihr **könnt** gehen.*
future tense	a TENSE formed with the auxiliary VERB *werden* and an INFINITIVE (12.3), and used to refer to future time (14.4): *Ich **werde** das Buch nicht **lesen**.*
future perfect	a tense formed with the AUXILIARY VERB *werden* and a **compound** INFINITIVE (12.3), used to refer to an action or event which will

occur before another in the future: *Sie **wird** das Buch **gelesen haben*** (14.4).

gender	the division of nouns into three classes in German, called MASCULINE, FEMININE and NEUTER (1.1). The **gender** of a noun is shown by the ENDINGS of the DETERMINER or ADJECTIVE in the NOUN PHRASE: ***der** Mann, **diese** Frau, **klares** Wasser*.
genitive	a CASE which is mainly used to show possession or to link NOUNS together (2.3): *das Buch **meines Vaters**; die Geschichte **dieser Stadt***. A few verbs have a **genitive** OBJECT (18.7), and it is used after a few PREPOSITIONS (see 20.4): *trotz **des Wetters***.
imperative	a MOOD of the VERB used to give commands or instructions, or to make a request (16.2): ***Komm** hierher! **Seid** vorsichtig! **Steigen** Sie bitte **ein**!*
indefinite	an **indefinite** PRONOUN or DETERMINER is one which does not refer to a specific person or thing (5.5): ***etwas, jemand, irgendwelcher***.
indicative	the most usual MOOD of the VERB, used to make statements and ask questions (Chapter 16): *Sie **kam** gestern. **Siehst** du das Licht?*
indirect object	a verb COMPLEMENT, typically a person indirectly affected by the action expressed by the VERB, especially someone who is being given something or benefiting from the action (18.4.2). It is in the DATIVE case: *Sie gab **ihrem Vater** das Geld*.
indirect speech	a construction by which what was said is incorporated into a sentence rather than given in the speaker's original words (16.6). Compare **'direct speech'** *Er sagte: „Ich bin heute krank."* with the corresponding **'indirect speech'**: *Er sagte, dass er heute krank sei*.
infinitive	the basic form of a VERB, ending in *-en* or *-n* (12.1–2, 13.1–4): *kommen, betteln, tun*. It is the form of the **verb** given in dictionaries.
infinitive clause	a **subordinate** CLAUSE containing an INFINITIVE, typically with the particle *zu* (13.2): *Sie hat mir geraten **nach Hause zu gehen***.
inflection	changing the form of words, most often by ENDINGS, to indicate some grammatical idea, like CASE or TENSE. The **inflection** of NOUNS, ADJECTIVES and DETERMINERS is called DECLENSION, while the **inflection** of VERBS is called CONJUGATION.
inseparable verb	a **prefixed** VERB whose PREFIX is not stressed and always remains attached to the **verb** (12.2.1, 22.4): *besuchen, erwarten, verstehen*.
interrogative	**interrogative** DETERMINERS, ADVERBS or PRONOUNS (5.3, 7.5) are used to ask a question: ***Welches** Hemd kaufst du? **Warum** geht er nicht? **Wem** sagst du das?*
intransitive verb	a VERB is **intransitive** if it does not have an ACCUSATIVE (DIRECT) OBJECT (18.3): *Wir **schwimmen**; Dort **stand** er und **wartete** auf Luise; Meine Schwester **hilft** mir*.

irregular verb	a VERB with a CONJUGATION which does not follow the pattern of the WEAK VERBS or the STRONG VERBS (12.1.3, 12.2.2): *wissen – ich weiß – ich wusste – gewusst*.
Konjunktiv	The German term for the SUBJUNCTIVE **mood** (12.5, 16.3–7). There are two main forms: *Konjunktiv I*, used mainly in INDIRECT SPEECH (16.6): *Sie sagte, er **sei** nicht gekommen*, and *Konjunktiv II*, which indicates **unreal conditions** (16.5): *Ich **würde lachen**, wenn sie **käme***.
masculine	one of the three GENDERS into which NOUNS are divided (1.1).
mass noun	a NOUN referring to an indivisible entity, typically a substance or an abstract idea: ***das Gold, der Frieden***. Mass nouns, unlike COUNT NOUNS, are not normally used with the indefinite article or in the plural.
modal auxiliaries	the VERBS *dürfen, können, mögen, müssen, sollen* and *wollen*, which indicate the attitude of the speaker with regard to what is being said (Chapter 17). They are highly IRREGULAR (12.2.2), and as AUXILIARY VERBS they are normally only used with the INFINITIVE of another verb (13.3.1): *Sie **darf spielen**; Ich **musste gehen**; Du **sollst** das Fenster **aufmachen***.
modal particle	a small word which indicates the speaker's attitude to what is being said (Chapter 10): *Es gibt **ja** hier nur zwei gute Restaurants, Das Bier ist **aber** kalt!* (surprise).
mood	forms of the VERB which indicate the speaker's attitude (Chapter 16). German has three **moods**: INDICATIVE (neutral, factual): *Er **geht** nach Hause*; IMPERATIVE (commands, requests): ***Geh** nach Hause!* and SUBJUNCTIVE (possibly not factual): *Wenn er nach Hause **ginge**,. . .*
neuter	one of the three GENDERS into which German NOUNS are divided (1.1).
nominative	a CASE (2.1) which most often indicates the SUBJECT of a VERB (18.2): ***Du** lügst; **Der Hund** bellt*. It is also used in the PREDICATE COMPLEMENT of COPULAR VERBS (18.8): *Ich bin **der neue Lehrer***, or when a word occurs in isolation (i.e. not as part of a full SENTENCE).
non-finite	a form of the VERB which does not have an ENDING in AGREEMENT with the SUBJECT (12.1–2), i.e. the INFINITIVE and the PARTICIPLES.
noun	a type of word which typically refers to a person, a living being, a thing, a place or an idea and can normally be used with a **definite** ARTICLE: *der Tisch, die Idee, das Pferd*. German nouns are all classified into one of three GENDERS.
noun phrase	A set of words which consists of at least one NOUN or PRONOUN and any other words accompanying it, i.e. a DETERMINER and/or an ADJECTIVE: *Brot, weißes Brot, das weiße Brot*.
number	the grammatical distinction between SINGULAR and PLURAL.

object	certain complements of the verb are known as its **objects** (Chapter 18), i.e. the DIRECT OBJECT, the INDIRECT OBJECT and the prepositional OBJECT.
ordinal number	a form of a numeral used as an ADJECTIVE: *sein zwanzigster Geburtstag*. (9.2)
participle	NON-FINITE forms of the VERB (12.1–2, 13.5–7) which can be used as ADJECTIVES. German has two **participles**: the PRESENT PARTICIPLE, e.g. *spielend*, and the PAST PARTICIPLE, e.g. *gespielt*.
passive voice	a form of a VERB where the doer of the action is not necessarily mentioned and the SUBJECT is typically a person or thing to which something happens (12.4, Chapter 15): German has two **passive** constructions, using the AUXILIARY VERBS *werden* or *sein* and the PAST PARTICIPLE: *Die Schlange wurde (von dem Jäger) getötet*; *Die Stadt war zerstört*. The **passive voice** contrasts with the (more frequent) **active voice**: *Der Jäger tötet die Schlange*.
past tense	the **simple** (i.e. one-word) TENSE (12.2) used to relate an action, state or event in the **past** (14.3): *Ich kam an*; *Sie sah mich*.
past participle	a NON-FINITE form of the VERB, typically with the prefix *ge-* and the ENDING *-t* with WEAK VERBS or *-en* with STRONG VERBS (12.1–2): *gekauft*; *gekommen*. It is most often used to form COMPOUND TENSES (12.3), or as an ADJECTIVE (13.5).
perfect tense	a COMPOUND TENSE formed with the PRESENT TENSE of the AUXILIARY VERBS *haben* or *sein* and the PAST PARTICIPLE (12.3), used to relate an action, state or event in the **past** (14.3): *Ich habe sie gesehen*; *Sie sind gekommen*.
person	a grammatical category indicating the person speaking, i.e. the **'first'** person: *ich, wir*; the person addressed, i.e. the **'second'** person: *du, ihr, Sie*; or other persons or things, i.e. the **'third'** person: *er, sie, es* (3.1). The FINITE VERB has ENDINGS in AGREEMENT with the **person** and NUMBER of its SUBJECT (12.1).
personal pronoun	simple words standing for the various PERSONS or referring to a NOUN PHRASE (Chapter 3): *ich, mich, mir, du, sie*, etc.
place complement	a typical COMPLEMENT with verbs that indicate **position**, indicating **where** something is situated (18.8): *Die Flasche steht auf dem Tisch*; *Ich wohne in Berlin*.
pluperfect tense	a COMPOUND TENSE formed with the PAST TENSE forms of the AUXILIARY VERBS *haben* or *sein* and the PAST PARTICIPLE (12.3), and used to relate actions or events further back in the past than the context (14.5): *Ich hatte sie gesehen*; *Sie waren gekommen*.
plural	a grammatical term referring to **more than one** person or thing, whereas SINGULAR refers to just one. German nouns have special ENDINGS to show the **plural** (1.2).

possessive	a word used to indicate **possession** (5.2), either as a DETERMINER: *sein Fahrrad*, or as a PRONOUN: *das ist meines*.
predicate complement	the typical VERB COMPLEMENT with a COPULAR VERB, normally an ADJECTIVE or a NOUN PHRASE in the NOMINATIVE CASE which describes the SUBJECT (18.8): *Mein neuer BMW ist rot*; *Er wird bestimmt ein guter Tennisspieler*.
prefix	an element added to the beginning of a word to form another word (Chapter 22): *Urwald, unglücklich, verbessern, weggehen*.
preposition	a word used to introduce a NOUN PHRASE and typically indicating position, direction, time, etc. (Chapter 20): *an, auf, aus, neben, ohne*, etc. All German **prepositions** are followed by a NOUN PHRASE in a particular CASE: *Er kam ohne seinen Hund* (acc.); *Er kam mit seinem Hund* (dat.); *Er kam wegen seines Hundes* (gen.).
prepositional adverb	a compound of *da(r)-* with a PREPOSITION, typically used as a pronoun referring to things (3.5, 18.6.14): *darauf* 'on it', 'on them', *damit* 'with it', 'with them'.
prepositional object	a COMPLEMENT of the VERB introduced by a PREPOSITION (18.5). Typically, the **preposition** does not have its usual full meaning, and the choice of **preposition** depends on the individual **verb**: *Wir warten auf meine Mutter*; *Sie warnte mich vor dem großen Hund*.
prepositional phrase	the combination of a NOUN PHRASE with a PREPOSITION: *an diesem Tag, aus dem Haus, zwischen den Häusern*.
present participle	a NON-FINITE form of the VERB, formed by adding the suffix *-d* to the infinitive (12.1–2): *leidend, schlafend*. It is used most often as an ADJECTIVE (13.5): *das schlafende Kind*.
present tense	the simple TENSE (12.2) used to relate something going on at the moment of speaking, or which takes place regularly or repeatedly (14.2): *Jetzt kommt sie*; *In Irland regnet es viel*.
principal parts	the **three main forms** in the CONJUGATION of a VERB, i.e. the INFINITIVE, the PAST TENSE and the PAST PARTICIPLE (12.1–2): *machen – machte – gemacht* (WEAK VERB); *kommen – kam – kommen* (STRONG VERB). The other forms of most verbs are constructed on the basis of these three forms.
pronoun	typically a little word which stands for a whole NOUN PHRASE, e.g. PERSONAL PRONOUNS (Chapter 3), e.g. *ich, mich, sie*; DEMONSTRATIVE **pronouns** (5.1), e.g. *dieser*, POSSESSIVE **pronouns** (5.2), e.g. *meiner, seines*; INDEFINITE **pronouns** (5.5), e.g. *man, niemand*.
reflexive pronoun	a PRONOUN in the ACCUSATIVE or DATIVE CASE referring back to the SUBJECT of the VERB (3.2): *Sie wäscht sich*; *Ich habe es mir so vorgestellt*.
reflexive verb	a VERB used in combination with a REFLEXIVE PRONOUN (18.3.6): *sich erinnern* (remember), *sich weigern* (refuse).

register	differences of usage linked to different **situations** and **addressees**, typically associated with degrees of formality/informality, as found, for example, in differences between **spoken** and **written** language.
relative clause	a **subordinate** CLAUSE used in the function of an ADJECTIVE to describe a NOUN: *der Mann, **der** dort spielt*. **Relative clauses** are introduced by a RELATIVE PRONOUN (5.4).
relative pronoun	a PRONOUN which, like English 'who', 'which' or 'that', is used to introduce a RELATIVE CLAUSE: (5.4): *der Mann, **den** ich gegrüßt hatte, die Männer, **denen** ich helfen konnte*.
root	the base form of a word, without ENDINGS, PREFIXES or SUFFIXES: *wieder**komm**en, **arbeit**en, un**interessant***.
sentence	the longest unit of grammar, ending with a full stop in writing. It must have at least one **main** CLAUSE: *Else hat mir geantwortet*, and the main clause(s) can have one or more dependent **subordinate clauses**: *Else hat mir geantwortet, dass Sie nicht nach New York gehen wollte*.
sentence pattern	A limited number of combinations of COMPLEMENTS occur commonly with German verbs, since many verbs have the same VALENCY. Such combinations are known as **sentence patterns** (18.1.3).
separable verb	a verb with a **stressed** PREFIX which detaches from the FINITE VERB in MAIN CLAUSES and is placed at the **end** of the CLAUSE (12.2.1, 22.5), e.g. **an**kommen: *Wir **kommen** morgen um zwei Uhr in Dresden **an***.
singular	a grammatical term referring to **one** person or thing, whereas PLURAL refers to more than one. The PRONOUNS *ich, du, es* and the NOUNS *der kleine Hund* or *das Kind* are **singular**.
stress	Like in English, one syllable in all German words of more than one syllable is pronounced with rather more force than the others, and this syllable is said to be stressed or bear the **stress** (23.1.6)
strong adjective declension	a set of ENDINGS used with ADJECTIVES which are like the **endings** of the **definite** ARTICLE or *dieser* (6.1–2). They are used when there is no DETERMINER in the noun phrase, or when the **determiner** has no **ending** of its own: *stark**es** Bier, mein alt**er** Freund*.
strong verb	a VERB which changes its vowel in the PAST TENSE (and often in the PAST PARTICIPLE, too), and has the ENDING *-en* in the **past participle** (12.1.2, 12.2): *bitten – bat – gebeten*.
subject	the NOUN PHRASE in the NOMINATIVE CASE with which the FINITE VERB **agrees** for PERSON and NUMBER (12.1.4, 18.2): *Du kommst morgen; Die Leute beschwerten sich über die Preise*. Typically it is the person or thing carrying out the action expressed by the verb.
subjunctive mood	a MOOD of the VERB typically used to indicate that an action, event or state may not be factual (16.3–7). There are two forms of the

subjunctive in German (12.5): KONJUNKTIV I is used most often to mark INDIRECT SPEECH (16.6): *Sie sagte, er sei nicht gekommen* and KONJUNKTIV II indicates **unreal conditions** (16.5): *Ich würde lachen, wenn sie käme.*

suffix   an element added to the end of a word or root to form a new word by DERIVATION (Chapter 22): *freundlich, Freundlichkeit* or, as an INFLECTION in the form of an ENDING, to give grammatical information: *Kinder, machte.*

superlative   the form of an ADJECTIVE OR ADVERB which expresses the highest degree of comparison (Chapter 8): *der höchste Baum, das Auto fährt am schnellsten.*

tense   a form of the VERB which indicates the **time** of an action, event or state in relation to the moment of speaking (Chapter 14). German has **simple tenses**, of one word (12.2): PRESENT *ich warte*; PAST *ich wartete* and COMPOUND TENSES (12.3): FUTURE *ich werde warten*; PERFECT *ich habe gewartet*; PLUPERFECT *ich hatte gewartet*; FUTURE PERFECT *ich werde gewartet haben.*

topic   the **first element** in a **main** CLAUSE, before the FINITE VERB (21.2): *Max ist gestern nach Rom gefahren; Gestern ist Max nach Rom gefahren; Nach Rom ist Max gestern gefahren.* It is typically something we are emphasising because we want to say something about it.

transitive verb   a VERB is **transitive** if it can have a DIRECT OBJECT in the ACCUSATIVE CASE (18.3): *Sie sah mich; Ich grüsste meinen Freund; Meine Schwester kauft die Bücher.*

valency   the construction used with a particular VERB, i.e. the number and type of COMPLEMENTS which it requires to form a **fully grammatical** CLAUSE or SENTENCE (Chapter 18).

verb   a type of word which refers to an action, event, process or state: *schlagen, passieren, recyceln, schlafen.*

weak adjective declension   a set of ENDINGS used with adjectives when there is a DETERMINER with its own ENDING preceding it in the NOUN PHRASE (6.1–2): *das starke Bier, die jungen Frauen.*

weak masculine noun   one of a small set of MASCULINE NOUNS which have the ENDING **-(e)**n in the ACCUSATIVE, genitive and DATIVE CASES in the SINGULAR as well as in the PLURAL (1.3.2): *der Affe, den Affen, des Affen, dem Affen, die Affen,* etc.

weak verb   the mainly regular VERBS of German, which form their PAST TENSE with the ENDING **-te** and their PAST PARTICIPLE with the ending **-t** (12.1.2, 12.2): *machen – machte – gemacht.*

Index

The index lists all the German and English words and the grammatical topics about which specific information is given in this book. However, individual words in lists illustrating points of grammar are not included. To facilitate finding particular entries, German words are given in regular type, English words in *italics* and grammatical topics in SMALL CAPITALS (with any German terms *ITALICISED*)